Public Speaking

Public Speaking
AN AUDIENCE-CENTERED APPROACH

EDITION 7

Steven A. Beebe
Texas State University —San Marcos

Susan J. Beebe
Texas State University —San Marcos

PEARSON

and

Boston   New York   San Francisco
Mexico City   Montreal   Toronto   London   Madrid   Munich   Paris
Hong Kong   Singapore   Tokyo   Cape Town   Sydney

Editor-in-Chief: Karon Bowers
Development Editor: Jessica Carlisle
Associate Development Editor: Jen DeMambro
Series Editorial Assistant: Susan Brilling
Marketing Manager: Suzan Czjakowski
Production Supervisor: Beth Houston
Editorial Production Service: Lifland et al., Bookmakers
Composition Buyer: Linda Cox
Manufacturing Buyer: JoAnne Sweeney
Electronic Composition: Modern Graphics, Inc.
Interior Design: The Davis Group
Photo Research: Annie Pickert
Cover Administrator: Joel Gendron

For related titles and support materials, visit our online catalog at www.ablongman.com.

Between the time website information is gathered and then published, it is not unusual for some sites to have closed. Also, the transcription of URLs can result in typographical errors. The publisher would appreciate notification where these errors occur so that they may be corrected in subsequent editions.

Library of Congress Cataloging-in-Publication Data

Beebe, Steven A., 1950-
  Public speaking: an audience-centered approach / Steven A. Beebe, Susan J. Beebe. — 7th ed.
     p. cm.
  Includes bibliographical references and index.
  ISBN-13: 978-0-205-54301-4 (alk. paper)
  ISBN-10: 0-205-54301-4 (alk. paper)
1. Public speaking. 2. Oral communication.   I. Beebe, Susan J.   II. Title.
PN4129.15.B43 2009
808.5'1—dc22

                                                         2007051560

Printed in the United States of America

10 9 8 7 6 5 4 3 2 1   12 11 10 09 08

Dedicated to our parents,
Russell and Muriel Beebe
and Herb and Jane Dye

And to our sons,
Mark and Matthew Beebe

Why You Need This New Edition

The seventh edition of *Public Speaking: An Audience-Centered Approach* continues to emphasize the importance of analyzing and considering the audience at every point in the speechmaking process. Bringing theory, research, and practice together is a hallmark of the finished product and remains a goal for each revision, and the newest edition narrows the gap between the classroom and the textbook in several ways. Every chapter of the book boasts fresh examples and current research and develops a strong link between the rhetorical tradition of communication and skill development in public speaking. New end-of-chapter workshops provide students with strategies and suggestions to help them deliver successful speeches, and a new focus on the management of communication apprehension is developed through expanded chapter coverage and a new marginal feature that will help students find productive ways to connect more confidently to their audience. Pages xxviii–xxx of the Preface provide detailed chapter-by-chapter information on what is new to the seventh edition; a brief overview follows.

- Updated coverage of communication apprehension in Chapter 1 starts things off with a strong foundation that includes applications of the latest communication research coupled with concrete suggestions to help students better manage speaker anxiety.

- Each chapter includes a new feature, *Confidently Connecting with Your Audience*, that provides practical advice on controlling and overcoming public speaking apprehension.

- New art on the inside back cover offers a panoramic overview of specific ideas and research-based suggestions that give students the tools to manage apprehension at each stage of the speechmaking process.

- The *Great Speakers* feature has been renamed *Learning from Great Speakers* and now identifies specific lessons students can learn from the profiled speakers.

- Each chapter features a new end-of-chapter *Speech Workshop* that offers activities, strategies, and suggestions for helping students work through and deliver a successful speech.

- A new student example refreshes the popular *Developing Your Speech Step by Step* feature and continues to provide a practical and specific model for developing a speech.

- In each chapter, the *Speaker's Homepage* offers new and updated Web sites to help students use the Internet to improve their speech writing skills.

- New examples throughout update and refresh the text, including new references to contemporary technology such as iPods in Chapter 14.

- New speeches, such as Bill Gates's recent Harvard University commencement speech, fill out an already impressive sample speech Appendix that inspires and instructs students as they work with their own material.

Brief Contents

Contents

CHAPTER 2

Previewing the Audience-Centered Speechmaking Process   25

CHAPTER 3
Speaking Freely and Ethically

45

CHAPTER 4
Listening to Speeches

61

CHAPTER 5
Analyzing Your Audience

89

CHAPTER 6
Developing Your Speech

123

CHAPTER 8
Using Supporting Material

CHAPTER 9
Organizing Your Speech

CHAPTER 7
Gathering Supporting Material   147

CHAPTER 8
Using Supporting Material   173

CHAPTER 9
Organizing Your Speech   195

CHAPTER 10

Introducing and Concluding Your Speech   219

CHAPTER 11
Outlining and Editing Your Speech

239

CHAPTER 12
Using Words Well: Speaker Language and Style

257

CHAPTER 13

Delivering Your Speech   275

CHAPTER 16
Understanding Principles of Persuasive Speaking   355

APPENDIX C
Speeches for Analysis and Discussion

450

Preface

The goal of the seventh edition of *Public Speaking: An Audience-Centered Approach* remains the same as that of the previous six editions: to be a practical and user-friendly guide to help speakers connect their hearts and minds with those of their listeners. The distinguishing focus of the book is our audience-centered approach. Over 2,300 years ago, Aristotle said, "For of the three elements in speechmaking—speaker, subject, and person addressed—it is the last one, the hearer, that determines the speaker's end and object." We think Aristotle was right. Effective and ethical public speaking is anchored in considering the needs, values, and viewpoints of the audience. To do so is not simply to tell listeners only what they want to hear—that would be a manipulative, speaker-centered approach. Rather, the audience-centered speaker is ethically responsive to audience interests without abandoning the speaker's "end and object."

This book is written to be the primary text in a course intended to help students become better public speakers. We are delighted that since the first edition of the book was published almost two decades ago, educators and students of public speaking have found our book a distinctively useful resource to enhance public-speaking skill. We've worked to make our latest edition a preeminent resource for helping students enhance their speaking skills.

As in the development of the previous editions, we have listened to students and instructors to make the seventh edition an even more useful tool to help students improve their public-speaking abilities. Throughout every chapter of the book we've provided updated examples, added new research conclusions about the speaking and listening process, and provided a stronger link between the rhetorical tradition of communication instruction and public speaking skill development.

One of the biggest challenges many students have when learning how to speak in public is to overcome their apprehension of speaking to others. To address their need, we've updated our coverage of communication apprehension in Chapter 1, offered new margin tips throughout the book for confidently connecting to the audience, and summarized key tips and strategies for managing speech anxiety on the inside back cover of the book. We've retained our popular *Speaker's Homepage* feature, adding new Web links that point to the power of the Internet to help students learn communication principles and skills. We've expanded our *Great Speakers* feature, now called *Learning from Great Speakers*, to help students learn from the best and most well-known public speakers from both the past and the present. We've also revised and updated our distinctive feature called *Developing Your Speech Step by Step,* which walks a student through the public-speaking development and presentation process with clear examples. In addition, many new sample student speeches are now available on video on the Internet with the click of a mouse, through the powerful and innovative MySpeechLab resource. We have endeavored to keep what students and instructors liked best, while adding powerful new features and content to help students become skilled public speakers.

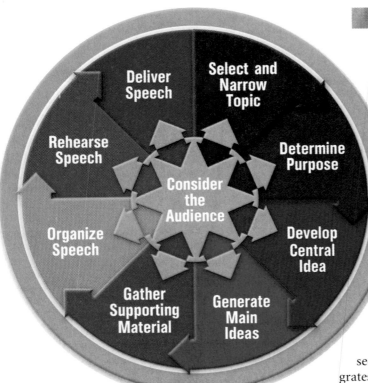

Our Audience-Centered Approach

A good speech centers on the needs, values, and hopes of the audience, who should be foremost in the speaker's mind during every step of the speech development and delivery process. Thus, in a very real sense, the audience writes the speech.

It is not unusual or distinctive for a public-speaking book to discuss audience analysis. What *is* unique about our audience-centered approach is that our discussion of audience analysis and adaptation is not confined to a single chapter; rather, we emphasize the importance of considering the audience throughout our entire discussion of the speech preparation and delivery process. From the opening overview of the public-speaking process until the final chapter, we illuminate the positive power of helping students relate to their audience by keeping their listeners foremost in mind.

Preparing and delivering a speech also involves a sequence of steps. Our audience-centered model integrates the step-by-step process of speech preparation and delivery with the ongoing process of considering the audience.

Our audience-centered model of public speaking, shown here and introduced in Chapter 2, reappears throughout the text to remind students of the steps involved in speech preparation and delivery, while simultaneously emphasizing the importance of considering the audience. Viewing the model as a clock, the speaker begins the process at the "12 o'clock" position with "Select and Narrow Topic" and moves around the model clockwise to "Deliver Speech." Each step of the speech preparation and delivery process touches the center portion of the model labeled "Consider the Audience." Arrows connecting the center with each step of the process illustrate how the audience influences each of the steps involved in designing and presenting a speech. Arrows pointing in both directions around the central process of "Consider the Audience" represent how a speaker may sometimes revise a previous step because of further information or thought about the audience. You may, for example, decide after you have gathered supporting material for the speech that you need to go back and revise your speech purpose. Visual learners will especially appreciate the illustration of the entire public-speaking process provided by the model. The colorful, easy-to-understand synopsis will also be appreciated by people who learn best by having an overview of the entire process before beginning the first step of speech preparation.

After introducing the model in Chapter 2, we continue to emphasize the centrality of considering the audience by providing a visual reminder in the form of a miniature version of the model, like the icon shown here in the margin. *When you see this icon, it will remind you that the material presented has special significance for considering your audience.*

Our Focus on Communication Apprehension

One of the biggest barriers that keeps a speaker, especially a novice public speaker, from connecting to his or her audience is apprehension. Fear of failure, forgetting, or fumbling words is a major distraction. New to this edition is an emphasis on helping students focus on their listeners rather than on their fear. We've expanded our discussion of communication apprehension in Chapter 1, adding the most contemporary research conclusions we can find to help students overcome the anxiety that many of them experience when speaking publicly. But rather than restrict this discussion to the beginning of the book, we remind students of powerful pointers for managing anxiety in every chapter in a new margin feature called *Confidently Connecting with Your Audience*. This feature provides timely tips for helping students integrate confidence-boosting strategies throughout their study of public speaking. To provide yet additional help for managing apprehension, we've distilled several seminal ideas keyed to our audience-centered model on the inside back cover. So, from Chapter 1 until the literal last page in the book, we help students manage their apprehension.

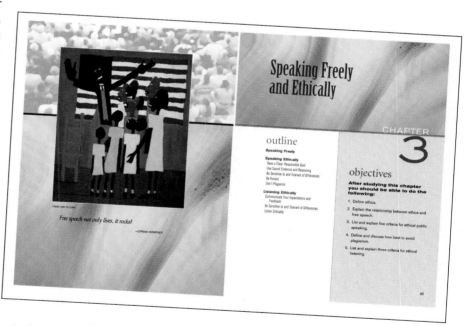

Our Focus on Ethics

Being audience-centered does not mean that a speaker tells an audience only what they want to hear; if you are not true to your own values, you will have become a manipulative, unethical communicator rather than an audience-centered one. Audience-centered speakers articulate truthful messages that give audience members free choice in responding to a message, while also using effective means of ensuring message clarity and credibility.

From the first chapter onward, we link being an audience-centered speaker with being an ethical speaker. Our principles and strategies for being rhetorically skilled are anchored in ethical principles that assist speakers in articulating a message that connects with their audience. We not only devote an entire chapter (Chapter 3) to being an ethical speaker, but we also offer reminders, tips, and strategies for making ethical speaking and listening an integral part of human communication. At the end of each chapter, students and instructors will find questions to spark discussion about and raise awareness of ethical issues in effective speechmaking.

Our Focus on Diversity

Just as the topic of audience analysis is covered in most public-speaking textbooks, so is diversity. Sometimes diversity is discussed in a separate chapter; sometimes it is presented in "diversity boxes" sprinkled throughout a book. We choose to address diversity not as an add-on to the main discussion but rather as integral to being an audience-centered speaker. To be audience-centered is to acknowledge the various ethnic and cultural backgrounds, attitudes, beliefs, values, and other differences present when people assemble to hear a speech. We suggest that inherent in the process of being audience-centered is a focus on the diverse nature of listeners in contemporary audiences. The topic of adapting to diverse audiences is therefore not a superficial, boxed afterthought, but integrated into every step of our audience-centered approach.

 # Our Focus on Skill Development

We are grateful for our ongoing collaboration with public-speaking teachers, many of whom have used our audience-centered approach for nearly two decades. We have retained those skill-development features of Previous editions that both teachers and students have applauded. What instructors tell us most often is, "You write like I teach" or, "Your book echoes the same kind of advice and skill development suggestions that I give my students." We are gratified by the continued popularity of *Public Speaking: An Audience-Centered Approach*.

CLEAR AND INTERESTING WRITING STYLE Readers have especially valued our polished prose, concise style, and engaging, lively voice. Students tell us that reading our book is like having a conversation with their instructor.

OUTSTANDING EXAMPLES Not only do students need to be *told* how to speak effectively, they need to be *shown* how to speak well. Our powerful and interesting examples, both classic and contemporary, drawn from both student speakers and famous orators, continue to resonate with student speakers.

BUILT-IN LEARNING RESOURCES We've retained the following built-in pedagogical features of previous editions:

- Recap boxes (periodic summaries of important material)
- Chapter outlines
- Learning objectives
- Crisply written narrative summaries

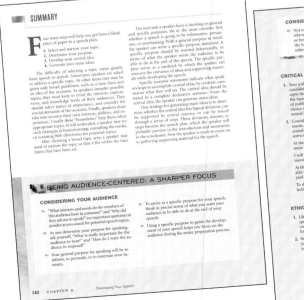

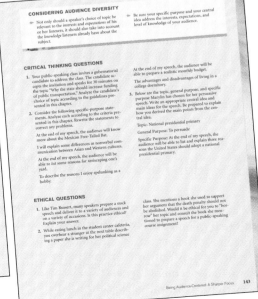

- Our *A Sharper Focus* feature that highlights material about both diversity and audience-centeredness
- Discussion-inducing chapter-end questions that develop critical thinking skills and invite a discussion of ethical issues

New to the Seventh Edition

We've not only retained what readers like best but refined and updated the book you are holding in your hands, to create a powerful and contemporary resource for helping speakers connect to their audience. We've added several new features and revised features that both instructors and students have praised.

NEW MARGIN FEATURE: CONFIDENTLY CONNECTING WITH YOUR AUDIENCE

As noted earlier, a new emphasis of the seventh edition is a comprehensive focus on helping students manage their anxiety and apprehension. A new margin feature provides tips and strategies for managing communication apprehension that are related to the chapter content. This new margin feature, new research and tips included in Chapter 1, plus the new inside back cover help students manage their number-one concern about taking a public-speaking course.

EXPANDED AND UPDATED FEATURE: LEARNING FROM GREAT SPEAKERS

An expansion of the popular feature first introduced in the previous edition (simply called *Great Speakers* in that edition), this feature identifies specific tips and lessons students can learn from great speakers. Students will enhance their rhetorical literacy as well as their rhetorical skill as they learn from great speakers of the past and present.

NEW CHAPTER-END FEATURE: SPEECH WORKSHOP

This new, practical feature provides a cornucopia of activities, worksheets, strategies, and suggestions for helping students develop their speeches and become effective audience-centered speakers. This feature will help students with what they are most concerned about: how to develop and deliver a speech with confidence.

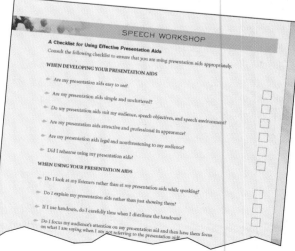

NEW INSIDE BACK COVER: TIPS FOR CONFIDENTLY CONNECTING WITH YOUR AUDIENCE

A summary of strategies for helping students manage communication apprehension, this feature is part of the new emphasis in this edition on helping students manage communication apprehension. Our audience-centered model of public speaking is annotated with specific ideas and research-based suggestions to give students a panoramic overview of specific ways to manage communication apprehension at each step of the public-speaking process.

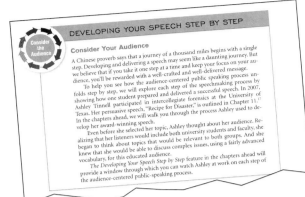

New Extended Example for the Developing Your Speech Step by Step Feature

A new student example gives students a practical "how to" lesson in developing a speech from start to finish.

Updated Speaker's Homepage

We've reviewed and updated the wealth of information to help students enhance their speaking skill by identifying the best Web sites we can find about public speaking.

New Speeches

We've added new annotated student speeches and speech examples throughout the book. In addition, we've added many new speeches in our revised Appendix C to provide positive models of effective speeches.

New Examples and Illustrations

New examples and illustrations integrated throughout the book in every chapter provide both classic and contemporary models to help students master the art of public speaking. As in previous editions, we draw on both student speeches and speeches delivered by well-known people.

New Material in Every Chapter

In addition to these new and expanded features, each chapter has been revised with new examples, illustrations, and references to the latest research conclusions. Here's a cogent summary of some of the changes and revisions we've made:

CHAPTER 1: SPEAKING WITH CONFIDENCE

- New chapter opening text
- New research that documents the importance of communication (Table 1.1)
- New strategies and new research identified for managing communication apprehension

CHAPTER 2: PREVIEWING THE AUDIENCE-CENTERED SPEECHMAKING PROCESS

- Revised and expanded discussion of how to analyze information about your audience
- New overview (Recap box) that previews how to design and deliver a speech, complete with chapter references

CHAPTER 3: SPEAKING FREELY AND ETHICALLY

- New chapter opening text
- Discussion of the universality of some ethical principles, the cultural and individual nature of others
- Updated history of free speech in the United States

CHAPTER 4: LISTENING TO SPEECHES

- Specific strategies for both listener and speaker to use to overcome listening barriers
- New information about how speakers can accurately interpret nonverbal messages of audience members

CHAPTER 5: ANALYZING YOUR AUDIENCE

- New strategies for establishing common ground with listeners
- New information about how to analyze and adapt to audiences of differing age levels
- New explicit description of how students can adapt to a culturally diverse audience
- New information about adapting to cultural differences in orientations to time

CHAPTER 6: DEVELOPING YOUR SPEECH

- New speech for *Developing Your Speech Step by Step* feature
- Updated list of potential speech topics

CHAPTER 7: GATHERING SUPPORTING MATERIAL

- Streamlined and updated discussion of the Internet
- Updated list of search engines
- Discussion of using vertical search engines to narrow a search
- Updated discussion and examples of online databases
- Discussion of Wikipedia and why it is unsuitable for academic research

CHAPTER 8: USING SUPPORTING MATERIAL

- Updated examples throughout the chapter
- Discussion of why illustrations are especially compelling supporting material

CHAPTER 9: ORGANIZING YOUR SPEECH

- More explicit connection of organizational strategies with the "natural divisions/reasons/steps" approach to generating main ideas
- Reordering of organizational strategies to acknowledge that the topical strategy is used for a majority of speeches
- Breakout of primacy, recency, and complexity as section headings
- Updated speech outlines on such topics as the iPod and YouTube

CHAPTER 10: INTRODUCING AND CONCLUDING YOUR SPEECH

- New chapter opening text
- Reorganized and revised discussion of purposes of introductions and conclusions
- Updated Web resources for anniversaries of historic events

CHAPTER 11: OUTLINING AND EDITING YOUR SPEECH

- New chapter opening text
- New sample outlines

CHAPTER 12: USING WORDS WELL: SPEAKER LANGUAGE AND STYLE

- Discussion of metaphor and simile revised for clarity and supported by new examples
- Reorganization of section on creating cadence, which now begins with "Repetition," followed by "Parallelism"; expanded discussion of how the two strategies differ

CHAPTER 13: DELIVERING YOUR SPEECH

- New information about how to prepare quickly for an impromptu speech
- Updated discussion of how to deliver a manuscript speech
- New information about how to respond to audience-member questions

CHAPTER 14: USING PRESENTATION AIDS

- New information about visual rhetoric
- New information and latest research about using PowerPoint™
- New information about using new technology such as MP3 players (iPods)

CHAPTER 15: SPEAKING TO INFORM

- New and expanded information about using analogies to inform listeners
- New information about how to use the unexpected, mystery, and suspense
- New and revised discussion about making messages brief and memorable

CHAPTER 16: UNDERSTANDING PRINCIPLES OF PERSUASIVE SPEAKING

- New and expanded discussion of how persuasion works, including an expanded discussion of ELM persuasion theory
- Updated discussion of Maslow's hierarchy
- New section on emphasizing benefits, not just features, when persuading listeners

CHAPTER 17: USING PERSUASIVE STRATEGIES

- New references to research about humor and credibility
- Reference to new research about culture and evidence
- New information about credibility and reluctant testimony

CHAPTER 18: SPEAKING FOR SPECIAL OCCASIONS AND PURPOSES

- Revised chapter opening text
- Integration of material on group presentations formerly found in Chapter 19

- Introduction of the rhetorical terms *kairos* and *epideictic* to the section on ceremonial speaking
- New section on humorous topics—i.e., when humor is appropriate
- Although Chapter 19 has been cut from the new edition to streamline the book, we have retained virtually all of the key content in an expanded discussion in Chapter 18 and a revised Appendix B

 # Our Partnership with Instructors and Students

Public speaking students rarely learn how to be articulate speakers only from reading a book. Students learn best in partnership with an experienced instructor who can guide them through the process of being an audience-centered speaker. For more information about all of our book- and course-specific supplements for public speaking, as well as to view samples, please visit www.mycoursetoolbox.com.

INSTRUCTOR SUPPLEMENTS

To enrich instructors' skill and knowledge in teaching public speaking, we offer a wealth of resources to supplement their advice, encouragement, and guidance.

PRINT RESOURCES

- **Classroom Kit, Volumes I and II**, by Joy Daggs, Columbia College; Steve Strickler, Southwestern Oklahoma State University; and Richard Falvo, El Paso Community College. Our unparalleled Classroom Kit includes every instruction aid a public-speaking professor needs to manage the classroom. We have made our resources even easier to use by placing all of our print supplements in two convenient volumes, and electronic copies of all of our resources on one CD-ROM, available separately. Organized by chapter, each volume contains materials from an Instructor's Manual and Test Bank, as well as slides from the PowerPoint™ Presentation Package that accompanies this text. Electronic versions of the Instructor's Manual, Test Bank, Power-Point™ Presentation Package, images from the text, and select video clips—all searchable by key terms—are made easily accessible to instructors on the separate Classroom Kit CD-ROM.

  The Instructor's Manual material has been completely updated and revised by Joy Daggs, Columbia College, and includes chapter at-a-glance overviews, chapter summaries, learning objectives, chapter outlines, discussion questions, activities, online teaching plans, and worksheets.

  The Test Bank, prepared by Steve Strickler, Southwestern Oklahoma State University, contains multiple choice, true/false, fill-in, short answer, and essay questions. Each question's difficulty is rated on a scale of 1 to 3, making question selection easy. Answers for each question are given, along with the page number where they can be found within the book.

- **Great Ideas for Teaching Speech (GIFTS), 3/e** by Raymond Zeuschner, California Polytechnic University–Pomona. This instructional booklet provides descriptions of and guidelines for assignments successfully used by experienced public-speaking instructors in their classrooms.

- **New Teacher's Guide to Public Speaking, 4/e.** This guide helps new teachers teach the public-speaking course effectively. It covers such topics as preparing for the term, planning and structuring your course, evaluating speeches, utilizing the textbook, integrating technology into the classroom, and much more.

● **Public Speaking Transparency Package, Version II.** One hundred full-color transparencies created with PowerPoint™ software provide visual support for classroom lectures and discussions.

ELECTRONIC RESOURCES

● **MySpeechLab** Where students learn to speak with confidence! MySpeechLab is an interactive and instructive online solution for introductory public speaking. Designed to be used as a supplement to a traditional lecture course or as a complete online course, MySpeechLab combines multimedia, video, speech preparation activities, research support, tests and quizzes to make teaching and learning fun! Students benefit from a wealth of video clips of student and professional speeches with running commentary, questions to consider, and helpful tips—all geared to help students learn to speak with confidence. Visit www.myspeechlab.com (access code required; please contact your Pearson representative for more information).

● **Classroom Kit CD-ROM,** by Joy Daggs, Columbia College; Steve Strickler, Southwestern Oklahoma State University; and Richard Falvo, El Paso Community College. This exciting new supplement for instructors will bring together electronic copies of the Instructor's Manual, the Test Bank, the PowerPoint™ Presentation Package, images from the text, and select video clips for easy instructor access. The CD-ROM is organized by chapter and is searchable by key term.

● **TestGen EQ: Computerized Test Bank.** The user-friendly interface enables instructors to view, edit, and add questions, transfer questions into tests, and print tests in a variety of fonts. Search and Sort features allow instructors to locate questions quickly and arrange them in preferred order. Available through our Instructor's Resource Center at www.pearsonhighered .com/irc (access code required).

● **PowerPoint™ Presentation Package,** by Richard Falvo, El Paso Community College. This text-specific package consists of a collection of lecture outlines and graphic images keyed to every chapter in the text. Available on the Web at www.pearsonhighered.com/irc (access code required)

● **Communication Digital Media Archive, Version 3.0.** The Digital Media Archive CD-ROM contains electronic images of charts, graphs, maps, tables, and figures, along with media elements such as video clips, audio clips, and related Web links. These media assets are fully customizable to use with our pre-formatted PowerPoint™ outlines or to import into an instructor's own lectures. Available in Windows and Mac formats.

● **Lecture Questions for Clickers** by William Keith, University of Wisconsin–Milwaukee. An assortment of questions and activities covering a multitude of topics in public speaking and speech delivery are presented in PowerPoint™. These slides will help liven up your lectures and can be used along with the Personal Response System to get students more involved in the material. Available on the Web at www.pearsonhighered.com/irc (access code required).

● **PowerPoint™ Presentation for Public-Speaking,** by Richard Falvo, El Paso Community College. This course-specific PowerPoint™ outline adds visual punch to public speaking lectures with colorful screen designs and clip art. Our expanded Public Speaking PowerPoint™ package now includes 125 slides and a brief User's Guide. Book-specific PowerPoint™ presentations also are available for many texts. Available on the Web at www .pearsonhighered.com/irc (access code required).

● **VideoWorkshop for Public Speaking Version 2.0** by Tasha Van Horn of Citrus College and Marilyn Reineck of Concordia University, St. Paul.

VideoWorkshop for Public Speaking is more than just video footage—it's a total learning system. Our complete program includes quality video footage on an easy-to-use dual-platform CD-ROM plus a Student Learning Guide. The result? A program that brings textbook concepts to life with ease and helps your students understand, analyze, and apply the objectives of the course.

VIDEO RESOURCES

- **A&B Contemporary Classic Speeches DVD.** This exciting supplement includes over 120 minutes of video footage in an easy-to-use DVD format. Each speech is accompanied by a biographical and historical summary that helps students understand the context and motivation behind each speech. Speakers featured include Martin Luther King Jr., John F. Kennedy, Barbara Jordan, the Dalai Lama, and Christopher Reeve.

- **A&B Public Speaking Video Library.** Allyn & Bacon's Public Speaking Video Library contains a range of different types of speeches delivered on a multitude of different topics, allowing you to choose the speeches best suited for your students. Please contact your Pearson representative for details and a complete list of videos and their contents to choose which would be most useful in your class. Some restrictions apply.

STUDENT SUPPLEMENTS

PRINT RESOURCES

- **Speech Preparation Workbook** by Jennifer Dreyer and Gregory H. Patton of San Diego State University. This workbook takes students through the stages of speech creation—from audience analysis to writing the speech—and includes guidelines, tips, and easy-to-fill-in pages.

- **The Speech Outline: Outlining to Plan, Organize, and Deliver a Speech: Activities and Exercises**, by Reeze L. Hanson and Sharon Condon of Haskell Indian Nations University. This brief workbook includes activities, exercises, and answers to help students develop and master the critical skill of outlining.

- **Study Card for Public Speaking.** Colorful, affordable, and packed with useful information, Allyn & Bacon's Study Cards make studying easier, more efficient, and more enjoyable. Course information is distilled down to the basics, helping students quickly master the fundamentals, review a subject for understanding, or prepare for an exam. Because they're laminated for durability, these Study Cards can be kept for years to come and students can pull them out whenever they need a quick review.

- **Multicultural Activities Workbook**, by Marlene C. Cohen and Susan L. Richardson, both of Prince George's Community College, Maryland. This workbook is filled with hands-on activities that help broaden the content of speech classes to reflect the diverse cultural backgrounds of the class and society. The book includes checklists, surveys, and writing assignments that all help students succeed in speech communication by offering experiences that address a variety of learning styles.

- **Public Speaking in the Multicultural Environment**, 2/e by Devorah Lieberman of Portland State University. This two-chapter essay focuses on speaking and listening to a culturally diverse audience and emphasizes preparation, delivery, and how speeches are perceived.

- **Preparing Visual Aids for Presentations**, 4/e by Dan Cavanaugh. This brief booklet provides a host of ideas for using today's multimedia tools to improve presentations, including suggestions for planning a presentation, guidelines for designing visual aids and storyboarding, and a walkthrough that shows how to prepare a visual display using PowerPoint™.

- ➤ **ResearchNavigator.com Guide: Speech Communication.** This updated booklet, by Steven L. Epstein of Suffolk County Community College, includes tips, resources, and URLs to aid students conducting research on Pearson Education's research Web site, www.researchnavigator.com. The guide contains a student access code for the Research Navigator™ database, offering students unlimited access to a collection of more than 25,000 discipline-specific articles from top-tier academic publications and peer-reviewed journals, as well as the *New York Times* and popular news publications. The guide introduces students to the basics of the Internet and the World Wide Web and includes tips for searching for articles on the site and a list of journals useful for research in their discipline. Also included are hundreds of Web resources for the discipline, as well as information on how to correctly cite research.

ELECTRONIC SUPPLEMENTS

- ➤ **MySpeechLab** Where students learn to speak with confidence! MySpeech-Lab is an interactive and instructive online solution for introductory public speaking. Designed to be used as a supplement to a traditional lecture course or as a complete online course, MySpeechLab combines multimedia, video, speech preparation activities, research support, tests and quizzes to make teaching and learning fun! Students benefit from a wealth of video clips of student and professional speeches with running commentary, questions to consider, and helpful tips— all geared to help students learn to speak with confidence. Visit www.myspeechlab.com (access code required).

- ➤ **Public Speaking Study Site.** This course-specific Web site features public speaking study materials for students, including flashcards and a complete set of practice tests for all major topics. Students also will find links to Web sites with speeches in text, audio, and video formats, as well as links to other valuable sites. Visit http://www.abpublicspeaking.com.

- ➤ **News Resources for Speech Communication Access Code Card.** News Resources for Speech Communication with Research Navigator™ is one-stop access to keep students abreast of the latest news events and for all of their research needs. Highlighted by an hourly feed of the latest news in the discipline from the *New York Times,* the resource helps students stay up-to-date throughout the semester. In addition, Pearson's Research Navigator™ is the easiest way for students to start a research assignment or research paper. Complete with extensive help on the research process and four exclusive databases of credible and reliable source material, including the EBSCO Academic Journal and Abstract Database, *New York Times* Search by Subject Archive, and *Financial Times* Article Archive and Company Financials, Research Navigator™ helps students quickly and efficiently make the most of their research time.

- ➤ **Speech Writer's Workshop CD-ROM, Version 2.0.** This speechwriting software includes a Speech Handbook with tips for researching and preparing speeches, a Speech Workshop that guides students step-by-step through the speechwriting process, a Topics Dictionary that gives students hundreds of ideas for speeches, and the Documentor citation database that helps them format bibliographic entries in either MLA or APA style.

- ➤ **VideoLab CD-ROM.** This interactive study tool for students can be used independently or in class. It provides digital video of student speeches that can be viewed in conjunction with corresponding outlines, manuscripts, notecards, and instructor critiques. A series of drills to help students analyze content and delivery follows each speech.

- **VideoWorkshop for Public Speaking Version 2.0** by Tasha Van Horn of Citrus College and Marilyn Reineck of Concordia University, St. Paul. *VideoWorkshop for Public Speaking* is more than just video footage—it's a total learning system. Our complete program includes quality video footage on an easy-to-use dual-platform CD-ROM plus a Student Learning Guide. The result? A program that brings textbook concepts to life with ease and helps students understand, analyze, and apply the objectives of the course.

Acknowledgments

Writing a book is a partnership not only with each other as co-authors, but with many people who have offered us the benefit of their experience and advice about how to make this the best possible teaching and learning resource. We appreciate all of the authors and speakers we have quoted or referenced; their words and wisdom have added resonance to our knowledge and richness to our advice. We are grateful for our students, colleagues, adopters, friends, and the skilled editorial team at Allyn and Bacon.

Many talented reviewers have helped us shape the content and features of this edition. These talented public-speaking teachers have supplemented our experience to help us make decisions about how to present and organize the content of this book. We express our sincere appreciation to the following reviewers who have shared their advice, wisdom, and expertise:

Reviewers of the seventh edition:
Richard I. Falvo, El Paso Community College
Patricia S. Hill, University of Akron
Marjorie Keeshan Nadler, Miami University
Renton Rathbun, Owens Community College
Argentina R. Wortham, Northeast Lakeview College

Reviewers of previous editions:
Melanie Anson, Citrus College
Richard Armstrong, Wichita State University
Nancy Arnett, Brevard Community College
David E. Axon, Johnson County Community College
Ernest W. Bartow, Bucks County Community College
John Bee, University of Akron
Jaima L. Bennett, Golden West College
Donald S. Birns, SUNY–Albany
Tim Borchers, Moorhead State University
Barry Brummett, University of Wisconsin, Milwaukee
John Buckley, University of Tennessee
Thomas R. Burkholder, University of Nevada–Las Vegas
Judy H. Carter, Amarillo College
Mark Chase, Slippery Rock University
Marilyn J. Cristiano, Paradise Valley Community College
Dan B. Curtis, Central Missouri State University
Ann L. Darling, University of Illinois, Urbana–Champaign
Conrad E. Davidson, Minot State University
Terrence Doyle, Northern Virginia Community College

David E. Walker, Middle Tennessee State University
Lynn Wells, Saddleback College
Nancy R. Wernm, Glenville State College
Charles N. Wise, El Paso Community College
Merle Ziegler, Liberty University

We are again grateful to our friend and colleague Tom Burkholder from the University of Nevada–Las Vegas, who wrote the excellent essay in Appendix B. It is the best distillation of the history of classical rhetoric that we have read. Kosta Tovstiadi is a good friend and trusted researcher who provided help in checking the Web sites for the *Speaker's Homepage* feature. Tori Forncrook, another former student and now good friend also helped assess the accuracy of the Web sites. We are grateful that Editor-in-Chief Karon Bowers continued to be a strong source of support and encouragement to us as we worked on this edition, as she was on previous editions. Our Development Editor, Jessica Carlisle, has done a brilliant job of offering skilled advice and creative suggestions to make this a better book.

We have enjoyed strong support and mentorship from a number of teachers, friends, and colleagues who have influenced our work over the years. Our colleagues at Texas State University–San Marcos continue to be supportive of our efforts. Tom Willett, retired professor from William Jewell College; Dan Curtis, emeritus professor at the University of Central Missouri; John Masterson at Texas Lutheran University; and Thompson Biggers at Mercer University are long-time friends and exemplary teachers who continue to influence our work and lives. Sue Hall, Department of Communication Studies senior administrative assistant at Texas State, again provided exceptional support and assistance to keep our work on schedule. Sondra Howe, also an administrative assistant at Texas State, helped us in innumerable ways.

We view our work as authors of a textbook as primarily a teaching process. Both of us have been blessed with gifted teachers whose dedication and mentorship continues to inspire and encourage us. Mary Harper, former speech, English, and drama teacher at Steve's high school alma mater, Grain Valley High School, Grain Valley, Missouri, and Sue's speech teacher, the late Margaret Dent, who taught at Hannibal High School, Hannibal, Missouri, provided initial instruction in public speaking that remains with us today. We also value the life lessons and friendship we receive from Erma Doty, also a former teacher at Grain Valley High, who continues to offer us encouragement and support not only with what she says but by how she lives her life in service for others. We appreciate the patience and encouragement we received from Robert Brewer, our first debate coach at the University of Central Missouri, where we met each other almost 40 years ago and the ideas for this book were first discussed. We both served as student teachers under the unforgettable energetic guidance of the late Louis Banker at Fort Osage High School, near Buckner, Missouri. Likewise, we have both benefited from the skilled instruction of Mary Jeanette Smythe of the University of Missouri–Columbia. We wish to express our appreciation to Loren Reid, Emeritus Professor also from the University of Missouri–Columbia; to us, he remains the quintessential speech teacher.

Finally, we value the patience, encouragement, proud support, and love of our sons, Mark and Matthew Beebe. They offer many lessons in overcoming life challenges and infusing life with music that inspire us. They continue to be our most important audience.

Steven A. Beebe
Susan J. Beebe
San Marcos, Texas

Albert Besnard (1849–1934). *The Paris First Night of the Opera Hernani (Ernani)* by Verdi, text after Victor Hugo's novel. 1850. Canvas. Erich Lessing/Art Resource, N.Y.

There are two kinds of speakers: those that are nervous and those that are liars.

—MARK TWAIN

Speaking with Confidence

CHAPTER

outline

objectives

After studying this chapter you should be able to do the following:

1. Explain why it is important to study public speaking.

2. Describe how public speaking differs from casual conversation.

3. Sketch and explain a model that illustrates the components and process of communication.

4. Discuss in brief the history of public speaking.

5. Explain how becoming an audience-centered public speaker can help you speak effectively to diverse audiences.

6. Describe why speakers sometimes feel nervous about speaking in public.

7. Use several techniques to become a more confident speaker.

Perhaps you think you have heard this speaker—or even taken a class from him:

> His eyes were buried in his script. His words in monotone emerged haltingly from behind his mustache, losing volume as they were sifted through hair. Audiences rushed to see and hear him, and after they had satisfied their eyes, they closed their ears. Ultimately, they turned to small talk among themselves while the great man droned on.[1]

The speaker described here in such an unflattering way is none other than Albert Einstein. Sadly, although the great physicist could attract an audience with his reputation, he could not sustain their attention and interest because he lacked public-speaking skills.

As you begin reading this book, chances are that you are also beginning a course in public speaking. You're in good company; nearly a half million college students each year take a public speaking class.[2] If you haven't had much previous experience speaking in public, you're also in good company. In a recent study, 66 percent of students beginning a public speaking course reported having little or no public speaking experience.[3]

The good news is that this book and this course will provide you with the knowledge and experience needed to become what Einstein was not: a competent public speaker. Right now, however, the experience may seem less like an opportunity and more like a daunting task. Why undertake it?

Why Study Public Speaking?

As you study public speaking, you will learn and practice strategies for effective delivery and critical listening. You will discover new applications for skills you may already have, such as focusing and organizing ideas and gathering information from print and electronic sources. In addition to learning and applying these fundamental skills, you will gain long-term advantages related to *empowerment* and *employment*.

EMPOWERMENT

You will undoubtedly be called on to speak in public at various times in your life: as a student participating in a seminar class; as a businessperson convincing your boss to let you undertake a new project; as a concerned citizen addressing the city council's zoning board. In each of these situations, the ability to speak with competence and confidence will provide **empowerment**. To be empowered is to have the resources, information, and attitudes that allow you to take action to achieve a desired goal. Being a skilled public speaker will give you an edge that other, less skilled communicators lack—even those who may have superior ideas, training, or experience. It will position you for greater things. Former presidential speechwriter James Humes, who labels public speaking "the language of leadership," says, "Every time you have to speak—whether it's in an auditorium, in a company conference room, or even at your own desk—you are auditioning for leadership."[4]

You feel truly empowered when you speak with confidence, knowing that your ideas are expressed with conviction and assurance. Yet if you're typical, you may ex-

empowerment
Having resources, information, and attitudes that lead to action to achieve a desired goal

Table 1.1 Top Skills Valued by Employers

Rank	Results of Survey of Personnel Directors[8]	Results of Survey of a College Career Services Department[9]	Results of Survey of Prospective Employers[10]	Survey Results from Several Research Studies[11]
1	Spoken communication skills	Communication and interpersonal skills	Communication skills	Communication skills
2	Written communication skills	Intelligence	Honesty and integrity	Analytical/research skills
3	Listening ability	Enthusiasm	Teamwork	Technical skills
4	Enthusiasm	Flexibility	Interpersonal skills	Flexibility/adaptability
5	Technical competence	Leadership	Motivation/initiative	Interpersonal skills

perience fear and anxiety about speaking in public. As you start your journey of becoming an effective public speaker, you may have questions about how to bolster your confidence and manage your apprehension. Before you finish this chapter, you'll have read about more than a dozen strategies to help you feel both more empowered and more confident. Being both a confident and an empowered public speaker is within your grasp. And being an empowered speaker can open up leadership and career opportunities for you.

EMPLOYMENT

It was industrialist Charles M. Schwab who said, "I'll pay more for a person's ability to speak and express himself than for any other quality he might possess."[5] If you can speak well, you possess a skill that others will value highly. Whether you're currently employed as an entry-level employee or aspire to the highest rung of the corporate leadership ladder, being able to communicate effectively with others is key to success in any line of work. The skills you learn in a public-speaking course, such as how to ethically adapt information to listeners, organize your ideas, persuade others, and hold listeners' attention, are among the skills most sought after by any employer. In a nationwide survey, prospective employers of college graduates said they seek candidates with "public-speaking and presentation ability."[6] Other surveys of personnel managers, both in the United States and internationally, have confirmed that they consider communication skills the top factor in helping graduating college students obtain employment (see Table 1.1).[7]

Public Speaking and Conversation

As you begin to study and practice public speaking, you will discover that it has much in common with conversation, a form of communication in which you engage every day. Like conversation, public speaking requires you to focus and verbalize your thoughts:

"Alicia, do you ever feel that people here are giving you trouble because you're Hispanic?" asks her roommate Sharon.

Alicia wrinkles her brow in thought, then replies, "I guess once in a while, but not for the reasons you'd expect. Like I notice the White kids getting all nervous when I stand close to them when we talk. And they don't like to look me in the eye for a long time."

Alicia could easily build a speech about differences between Hispanics and Whites on these two nonverbal behaviors.

When you have a conversation, you have to make decisions "on your feet." If your friends look puzzled or interrupt with questions, you re-explain the idea you have been talking about. If they look bored, you insert a funny story or talk more animatedly. As a public speaker, you will learn to make similar adaptations based on your knowledge of who your listeners are, their expectations for your speech, and their reactions to what you are saying. In fact, because we believe that the ability to adapt to your audience is so vital, this book focuses on public speaking as an audience-centered activity.

But if public speaking were exactly like conversation, Albert Einstein's lectures would have been more riveting, there would be no reason to take a public-speaking class, and there would be no need for this book. Let's take a look at some of the ways in which public speaking differs from conversation.

PUBLIC SPEAKING IS PLANNED

First, public speaking is more planned than conversation. Although there may be times when you are asked to speak on the spur of the moment, you will usually know in advance whether you will be expected to give a talk at a specific occasion. A public speaker may spend hours or even days planning and practicing his or her speech. Al Gore worked with speechwriters through 17 drafts of his August 2000 acceptance of the Democratic nomination for president. A few hours before he delivered the speech, an aide quipped, "It's in draft 625."[12] Gore's relentless revising reflects the forethought and planning typical of public speaking.

PUBLIC SPEAKING IS FORMAL

Public speaking is also more formal than conversation. The slang or casual language we often use in conversation is not appropriate for most public speaking. Audiences expect speakers to use standard English grammar and vocabulary. The nonverbal communication of public speakers is also more formal than nonverbal behavior in ordinary conversation. People engaged in conversation often sit or stand close together, gesture spontaneously, and move about restlessly. The physical distance between public speakers and their audiences is usually greater than that between people in conversation. And although public speakers may certainly use extemporaneous gestures while speaking, they also plan and rehearse some gestures and movement to emphasize especially important parts of their speeches.

THE ROLES OF PUBLIC SPEAKERS AND AUDIENCES ARE CLEARLY DEFINED

Finally, public speaking is less fluid and interactive than conversation. People in conversation may alternately talk and listen, and perhaps even interrupt one another, but in public speaking the roles of speaker and audience are more clearly defined and remain stable. Rarely do audience members interrupt or even talk to speakers, although some cultures and contexts invite more speaker–audience interaction than do others. Even under these circumstances, however, the roles of speaker and audience are still clearly defined and stable.

Speaking in public, then, requires you to sharpen existing communication skills and to learn and apply new ones. To better understand what is involved, let's look now at several models of communication that illustrate the public-speaking process and its components.

Public Speaking and Conversation

SIMILARITIES BETWEEN PUBLIC SPEAKING AND CONVERSATION

◆ Both public speaking and conversation involve vocalized thoughts; words are spoken and nonverbal behavior is expressed.

◆ Both public speaking and conversation involve adapting messages to listeners.

DIFFERENCES BETWEEN PUBLIC SPEAKING AND CONVERSATION

Public Speaking	Conversation
More likely to be planned	More likely to be spontaneous
Typically involves more formal language and nonverbal communication	Typically involves more casual language and nonverbal communication
The roles of speaker and listener are more clearly defined.	The roles of speaker and listener are fluid and less clearly delineated.

 ## The Communication Process

Even the earliest communication theorists recognized that communication is a process. The models they formulated were linear, suggesting a simple transfer of meaning from a sender to a receiver, as shown in Figure 1.1. More recently, theorists have tried to create models that better demonstrate the complexity of the communication process. Let's explore what some of those models can teach us about what happens when we communicate.

COMMUNICATION AS ACTION

Although they were simplistic, the earliest linear models of communication as action identified most of the elements of the communication process. We will explain each element as it relates to public speaking.

SOURCE A public speaker is a **source** of information and ideas for an audience. The job of the source or speaker is to **encode,** or translate, the ideas and images in his or her mind into verbal or nonverbal symbols (a **code**) that an audience can recognize. The speaker may encode into words (for example, "The fabric should be 2 inches square") or into gestures (showing the size with his or her hands).

source
The public speaker

encode
To translate ideas and images into verbal or nonverbal symbols

code
A verbal or nonverbal symbol for an idea or image

Figure 1.1 *A model of communication as action*

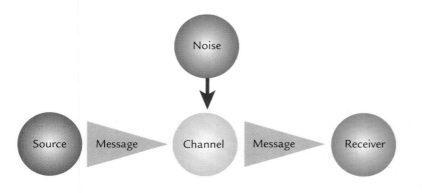

MESSAGE   The **message** in public speaking is the speech itself—both what is said and how it is said. If a speaker has trouble finding words to convey his or her ideas or sends contradictory nonverbal symbols, listeners may not be able to **decode** the speaker's verbal and nonverbal symbols back into a message.

CHANNELS   A message is usually transmitted from sender to receiver via two **channels**: *visual* and *auditory*. Audience members see the speaker and decode his or her nonverbal symbols—eye contact (or lack of it), facial expressions, posture, gestures, and dress. If the speaker uses any visual aids, such as graphs or models, these too are transmitted along the visual channel. The auditory channel opens as the speaker speaks. Then the audience members hear words and such vocal cues as inflection, rate, and voice quality.

RECEIVER   The **receiver** of the message is the individual audience member, whose decoding of the message will depend on his or her own particular blend of past experiences, attitudes, beliefs, and values. As already emphasized, an effective public speaker should be receiver- or audience-centered.

NOISE   Anything that interferes with the communication of a message is called *noise*. Noise may be physical and **external**. If your 8 A.M. public-speaking class is frequently interrupted by the roar of a lawn mower running back and forth under the window, it may be difficult to concentrate on what your instructor is saying. A noisy air-conditioner, a crying baby, or incessant coughing may make it difficult for audience members to hear or concentrate on a speech.

Noise may also be **internal**. It may stem from either *physiological* or *psychological* causes and may directly affect either the source or the receiver. A bad cold (physiological noise) may cloud a speaker's memory or subdue his or her delivery. An audience member worrying about an upcoming exam (psychological noise) is unlikely to remember much of what the speaker says. Regardless of whether it is internal or external, physiological or psychological, or whether it originates in the sender or the receiver, noise interferes with the transmission of a message.

COMMUNICATION AS INTERACTION

Realizing that linear models were overly simplistic, later communication theorists designed models that depicted communication as a more complex process (see Figure 1.2). These models were circular, or interactive, and added two important new elements: feedback and context.

FEEDBACK   As noted earlier, one way in which public speaking differs from casual conversation is that the public speaker does most or all of the talking. But public speaking is still interactive. Without an audience to hear and provide **feedback**, public speaking serves little purpose. Skillful public speakers are audience-centered. They depend on the nods, facial expressions, and murmurs of the audience to adjust their rate of speaking, volume, vocabulary, type and amount of supporting material, and other variables to communicate their message successfully.

CONTEXT   The **context** of a public-speaking experience is the environment or situation in which the speech occurs. It includes such elements as the time, the place, and the speaker's and audience's cultural traditions and expectations. To paraphrase John Donne, no *speech* is an island. No speech occurs in a vacuum. Rather, each speech is a blend of circumstances that can never be replicated exactly again.

The person whose job it is to deliver an identical message to a number of different audiences at different times and in different places can attest to the uniqueness of

message
The content of a speech and the mode of its delivery

decode
To translate verbal or nonverbal symbols into ideas and images

channel
The visual and auditory means by which a message is transmitted from sender to receiver

receiver
A listener or an audience member

external noise
Physical sounds that interfere with communication

internal noise
Physiological or psychological interference with communication

feedback
Verbal and nonverbal responses provided by an audience to a speaker

context
The environment or situation in which a speech occurs

each speaking context. If the room is hot, crowded, or poorly lit, these conditions affect both speaker and audience. The audience that hears a speaker at 10 A.M. is likely to be fresher and more receptive than a 4:30 P.M. audience. A speaker who fought rush-hour traffic for 90 minutes to arrive at his or her destination may find it difficult to muster much enthusiasm for delivering the speech.

Many of the skills that you will learn from this book relate not only to the preparation of effective speeches (messages), but also to the elements of feedback and context in the communication process. Our audience-centered approach focuses on "reading" your listeners' responses and adjusting to them as you speak.

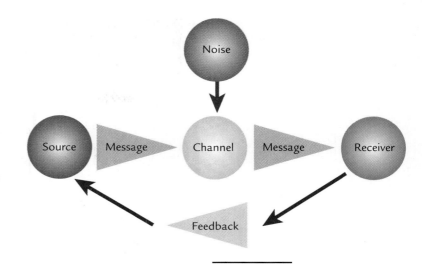

Figure 1.2 *An interactive model of communication*

COMMUNICATION AS TRANSACTION

The most recent communication models do not label individual components. Transactive models focus instead on communication as a simultaneous process. As the model in Figure 1.3 suggests, we send and receive messages concurrently. In a two-person communication transaction, both individuals are sending and receiving at the same time. When you are listening, you are simultaneously expressing your thoughts and feelings nonverbally.

An effective public speaker should not only be focused on the message he or she is expressing, but also be tuned in to how the audience is responding to the message. A good public speaker shouldn't wait until the speech is over to gauge the effectiveness of a speech but rather, because of the transactive nature of communication, should be scanning the audience during the speech for nonverbal clues to assess the audience's reaction.

Although communication models have been developed only recently, the elements of these models have long been recognized as the keys to successful public speaking. As you study public speaking, you will continue a tradition that goes back to the very beginnings of Western civilization.

Figure 1.3 *A transactive model of communication*

The Rich Heritage of Public Speaking

Long before many people could read, they listened to public speakers. As you'll read in Appendix B, the study of *rhetoric* is ancient. **Rhetoric** is another term for the use of words and symbols to achieve a goal. Although rhetoric is often defined as the art of speaking or writing aimed at persuading others (changing or reinforcing attitudes, beliefs, values, or behavior), whether you're informing, persuading, or even entertaining listeners, you are using rhetoric, because you are trying to achieve a goal.

The fourth century B.C. was a golden age for rhetoric in the Greek Republic, where the philosopher Aristotle formulated guidelines for speakers that we still

rhetoric
The use of words and symbols to achieve a goal

Martin Luther King Jr. (1920–1968)

Civil rights leader and human rights activist Dr. Martin Luther King Jr. delivered one of the great speeches of history as the keynote of the August 1963 civil rights march on Washington, D.C. Addressing an audience of some 200,000 people from the steps of the Lincoln Memorial, King used Biblical language, African American oral traditions, stirring examples, and the simple repetition of the line "I have a dream" to move both his audience and the United States Congress to action. Two months after King's speech, Congress passed a new civil rights bill.[13]

Dr. King was a master extemporaneous speaker. He planned his messages well in advance of his presentation, yet he was also skilled in observing and responding to his listeners during his speech. He used his clear objectives and well-prepared outline to create a powerful message, keenly focusing on the reactions of his audience to his prepared remarks. As you deliver your speeches, being aware of your listeners' responses to your message, especially their nonverbal responses, will help you decide what to emphasize or what to delete from your talk. You'll also find that by focusing more on connecting with your listeners than on any fear of speaking you may have, you'll give a better presentation.

[Photo: AP Images]

follow today. As politicians and poets attracted large followings in ancient Rome, Cicero and Quintilian sought to define the qualities of the "true" orator. On a lighter note, it is said that Roman orators invented the necktie. Fearing laryngitis, they wore "chin cloths" to protect their throats.[14]

In medieval Europe, the clergy were the most polished public speakers. People gathered eagerly to hear Martin Luther expound his Articles of Faith. In the eighteenth century, British subjects in the colonies listened to the town criers and impassioned patriots of what was to become the United States.

Vast nineteenth-century audiences heard speakers such as Henry Clay and Daniel Webster debate states' rights; they listened to Frederick Douglass, Angelina Grimke, and Sojourner Truth argue for the abolition of slavery, and to Lucretia Mott plead for women's suffrage; they gathered for an evening's entertainment to hear Mark Twain as he traveled the lecture circuits of the frontier.

Students of nineteenth-century public speaking spent very little time developing their own speeches. Instead, they practiced the art of **declamation**—the delivery of an already famous address. Favorite subjects for declamation included speeches by such Americans as Patrick Henry and William Jennings Bryan, and by the British orator Edmund Burke. Collections of speeches, such as Bryan's own ten-volume set of *The World's Famous Orations,* published in 1906, were extremely popular.

Hand in hand with declamation went the study and practice of **elocution**, the expression of emotion through posture, movement, gestures, facial expression, and voice. From the mid-nineteenth to the early twentieth century, elocution manuals, providing elaborate and specific prescriptions for effective delivery, were standard references not only in schools, but also in nearly every middle-class home in the United States.[15] Mark Twain was undoubtedly thinking back to the practitioners of

declamation
The delivery of an already famous speech

elocution
The expression of emotion through posture, movement, gestures, facial expression, and voice

declamation and elocution he had heard in his youth when he described the Reverend Mr. Sprague in *The Adventures of Tom Sawyer:*

> At church "sociables" he was always called upon to read poetry; and when he was through, the ladies would lift up their hands and let them fall helplessly in their laps, and "wall" their eyes, and shake their heads, as much as to say, "Words cannot express it; it is too beautiful, too beautiful for this mortal earth."[16]

In the first half of the twentieth century, radio made it possible for people around the world to hear Franklin Delano Roosevelt decry December 7, 1941, as "a date which will live in infamy." In the last half of the century, television provided the medium through which audiences saw and heard the most stirring speeches:

- Martin Luther King Jr. proclaiming, "I have a dream"
- Ronald Reagan beseeching Mikhail Gorbachev to "tear down this wall"
- Holocaust survivor Elie Wiesel looking beyond the end of one millennium toward the next with "profound fear and extraordinary hope"
- Six-year-old Bindi Irwin eulogizing her father, Australian "Crocodile Hunter" Steve Irwin, as "my hero—he was always there for me when I needed him. He listened to me and taught me so many things, but most of all he was fun."

With the twenty-first century dawned a new era of speechmaking. It was to be an era that would draw on age-old public-speaking traditions—an era in which the Declaration of Independence would be declaimed on July 4, 2001, at Philadelphia's Independence Hall by actors Michael Douglas, Morgan Freeman, Mel Gibson, Whoopi Goldberg, Kevin Spacey, and others. But it was also to be an era that would expand the parameters of public speaking—an era in which U.S. soldiers serving in Iraq would watch their children's commencement addresses live via streaming video. And it was to be an era that would summon public speakers to meet some of the most difficult challenges in history—an era in which a U.S. president would face a nation badly shocked by the events of September 11, 2001, and assure them that "Terrorist attacks can shake the foundations of our biggest buildings, but they cannot touch the foundation of America. These acts shattered steel, but they cannot dent the steel of American resolve."[17] Speakers of the future will continue to draw on a long and rich heritage, in addition to forging new frontiers in public speaking.

RECAP

The Rich Heritage of Public Speaking

TIME PERIOD	EVENT
Fourth century B.C.	Greek rhetoric flourishes—Age of Aristotle (see Appendix B).
Fifteenth century	European clergy are the primary practitioners of public speaking.
Eighteenth century	American patriots make impassioned public pleas for independence.
Nineteenth century	Abolitionists and suffragists speak out for change; frontier lecture circuits flourish.
Twentieth century	Electronic media make possible vast audiences.
Twenty-first century	A new era of speechmaking begins, using rapidly evolving technology and media, but drawing on a rich heritage of providing information, influencing thought and action, entertaining, and paying tribute via the spoken word.

Public Speaking and Diversity

Although the history of public speaking is as old as the history of civilization, only since the last half of the twentieth century has attention focused on the rhetorical implications of diversity. People are just beginning to understand that such factors as the gender, ethnicity, and culture of both speaker and audience are crucial components of the context of a speaking event.

Diverse audiences have different expectations for appropriate and effective speech topics, argument structure, language style, and delivery. For example, a speech that may be quite persuasive to Native Americans may not have the same effect on White Americans, who do not share the beliefs and values underlying the message.

Similarly, a presentation that seems perfectly sensible and acceptable to a U.S. businessperson who is accustomed to straightforward, problem-oriented logic may seem shockingly rude to a Chinese businessperson who expects more circuitous, less overtly purposeful rhetoric. And some African American audiences "come to participate in a speech event,"[18] expecting the speaker to generate audience response through rhythmic "call response formulas"[19] from the African American oral tradition.

To be effective, then, public speakers need to understand, affirm, and adapt to diverse audiences. And it is with this acknowledgment of the critical role of the audience that we come full circle. Aristotle declared the audience the most important component in the communication process—and he was right. It was true in the fifth century B.C., when students listened to the Greek rhetorician Gorgias. It was true in the nineteenth century, when parents of elocution students attended a school recital. And it was still true on May 26, 2007, when Doonesbury creator Garry Trudeau assured the graduating class of Goucher College, "Your day will come. My generation will fade away and you will take the stage and you will be spectacular."[20] It is the focus on audience that provides a coherent framework for the history of public speaking, from classical rhetoric to the contemporary rhetoric of diversity.

Adapting to diverse audiences also provides the unifying principle of this text. In Chapter 2 we present a model of speech preparation that emphasizes the importance of the audience. Then, throughout the text, we illustrate how this focus on and consideration of audience can guide a speaker effectively through each stage of speech preparation and delivery. In addition, at the end of each chapter we offer a feature entitled Being Audience-Centered: A Sharper Focus. This feature, which follows the chapter summary, synthesizes the chapter content that is specifically related to the concepts of audience and audience diversity.

Although our focus is on the audience, we also realize that as a student of public speaking, you have concerns and even fears about speaking in public. Focusing on your audience instead of on your anxiety is an audience-centered principle that can help you manage your apprehension. But you may need even more specific strategies and information to boost your confidence. Read on for some practical advice.

 ## Improving Your Confidence as a Speaker

As one anonymous sage observed, "The mind is a wonderful thing. It starts working the minute you're born and never stops . . . until you get up to speak in public." Perhaps public speaking is a required class for you, but, because of the anxiety you feel when you deliver a speech, you've put it off as long as possible.

The first bit of comfort we offer is this: *It's normal to be nervous.* In a survey seeking to identify people's phobias, public speaking ranked as the most anxiety-producing experience most people face. Forty-one percent of all respondents reported public speaking as their most significant fear; fear of death ranked only sixth![21] Based on these statistics, comedian Jerry Seinfeld suggests, "Given a choice, at a funeral most of us would rather be the one in the coffin than the one giving the eulogy." Other studies have found that more than 80 percent of the population feel anxious when they speak to an audience.[22] Some people find that public speaking is quite frightening; studies suggest that about 20 percent of all college students are highly apprehensive about speaking in front of others.[23]

You may find comfort in knowing you are not alone in experiencing speech anxiety. Even if your anxiety is not overwhelming, you can benefit from learning some positive approaches that allow your nervousness to work *for you.*[24] First, we will help you understand why you become nervous. Knowledge is power. Then we will offer specific strategies to help you speak with greater comfort and less anxiety.

UNDERSTAND YOUR NERVOUSNESS

What makes you feel nervous about speaking in public? Why do your hands sometimes shake, your knees quiver, your stomach flutter, and your voice seem to go up an octave? What is happening to you? Believe it or not, your brain is signaling your body to help you with a difficult task. Sometimes, however, because your brain offers more "help" than you need, this assistance is not useful.

Your view of the speaking assignment, your perception of your speaking skill, and your self-esteem interact to create anxiety.[25] You want to do well, but you're not sure that you can or will. Presented with this conflict, your body responds by increasing your breathing rate, pumping more adrenaline, and causing more blood to rush through your veins. In short, your body summons more energy to deal with the conflict you are facing. Your brain switches to its default fight-or-flight mode: You can either fight to respond to the challenge or flee to avoid the cause of the anxiety. To put it more technically, you are experiencing physiological changes because of your psychological state, which explains why you may have a more rapid heartbeat, shaking knees and hands, a quivering voice, and increased perspiration.[26] You may experience butterflies in your stomach because of changes in your digestive system. As a result of your physical discomfort, you may make less eye contact with your audience, use more vocalized pauses ("Um," "Ah," "You know"), and speak too rapidly. Although you see your physical responses as hindrances, your body is simply trying to help you with the task at hand.

What makes people feel nervous when speaking in public? A study by two communication researchers found that among the causes were fear of humiliation, concern about not being prepared, worry about one's looks, pressure to perform, personal insecurity, concern that the audience wouldn't be interested in oneself or the speech, lack of experience, fear of making mistakes, and an overall fear of failure.[27] Another study found that men are likely to experience more anxiety than women when speaking to people from a culture different from their own.[28] As you read the list, you'll probably find a reason that resonates with you—as we've mentioned, most people feel some nervousness when they speak before others. You're not alone if you are apprehensive about giving a speech.

Increasingly, researchers are concluding that communication apprehension may have a genetic or biological basis; some people may inherit a tendency to feel anxious about speaking in public.[29] You may wonder, "So if I have a biological tendency to feel nervous, is there anything I can do to help manage my fear?" The answer is yes. Even if you are predisposed to feel nervous because of your genetic makeup, there are strategies you can use to help manage your apprehension.[30] A better understanding of why you feel apprehensive is a good starting point on the journey to speaking with greater confidence.[31]

When are you most likely to feel nervous about giving a speech in your communication class? Research suggests that many people feel most nervous right before they give their speech. If you're typical, you'll feel the second-highest level of anxiety when your instructor explains the speech assignment. You'll probably feel the *least* anxiety when you're preparing your speech. One practical application of this research is that now you can understand when you'll need the most help managing your anxiety—right before you speak. It will also help to remember that as you begin speaking, anxiety begins to decrease—often dramatically. Another application of the research is to help you realize that you'll feel less anxious about your speech when you're doing something positive to prepare for it. Don't put off working on your speech; if you start preparing well in advance, you'll not only have a better speech, you'll also feel less anxious about presenting it.

To identify patterns in how people experience communication apprehension, one researcher measured speakers' heart rates when they were delivering speeches and also asked them several questions about their fear of speaking.[32] After studying the results, he identified four styles of communication apprehension: (1) average, (2) insensitive, (3) inflexible, and (4) confrontation.

You have an *average style* of communication apprehension if you have a generally positive approach to communicating in public; your overall heart rate when speaking publically is in the average range. Speakers with this style rated their own speaking performance the highest. The *insensitive style* is likely to be your style only if you have had previous experience in public speaking. Perhaps because of your experience, you tend to be less sensitive to apprehension when you speak; you have a lower heart rate when speaking and rate your performance as moderately successful. If you have the *inflexible style,* you have the highest heart rate when speaking publicly. Some people use this high and inflexible level of anxiety to enhance their performance: Their fear motivates them to prepare and be at their best. For others, the anxiety of the inflexible style creates so much tension that their speaking performance is diminished. You have a *confrontation style* if, like many people, you have a very high heart rate as you begin presenting a speech, and then your heart rate tapers off to more average levels. This style occurred in people who reported a strong emotional or affective response to speaking and was characteristic of more experienced speakers or people with at least some public-speaking background.

What difference does it make what style of communication apprehension you have? First, it may help to know that you are not alone in how you experience apprehension and that others likely share your feelings. Although each person is unique, there are nonetheless general styles of apprehension. Second, having a general idea of your own style may give you greater insight into how to better manage your apprehension. For example, if you know that your apprehension tends to spike upward at the very beginning of speaking to an audience (the confrontation style), you will need to draw on strategies to help manage your anxiety at the outset of your talk. Finally, the research on apprehension styles lends support to the theory that communication apprehension may be a genetic trait or tendency.[33] That doesn't mean that there's nothing you can do to manage your anxiety; but it does mean that, depending on your own tendencies, you may need more information to help you develop constructive ways of managing the apprehension you may feel.

What else can you do to understand and manage your fear and anxiety? Consider the following observations.

YOU ARE GOING TO FEEL MORE NERVOUS THAN YOU LOOK When she finished her speech, Carmen sank into her seat and muttered, "Ugh, was I shaky up there! Did you see how nervous I was?"

"Nervous? You were nervous?" asked Kosta, surprised. "You looked pretty calm to me."

Realize that your audience cannot see evidence of everything you feel. If you worry that you are going to appear nervous to others, you may, in fact, increase your anxiety. Your body will exhibit more physical changes to deal with your self-induced state of anxiety.

ALMOST EVERY SPEAKER EXPERIENCES SOME DEGREE OF NERVOUSNESS President Kennedy was noted for his superb public-speaking skills. When he spoke, he seemed perfectly at ease. Former British prime minister Winston Churchill was also hailed as one of the twentieth century's great orators. Amazingly, both Kennedy and Churchill were extremely fearful of speaking in public. The list of famous people who admit to feeling nervous before they speak may surprise you: Katie Couric, Conan O'Brien, Jay Leno, Carly Simon, and Oprah Winfrey have all reported feeling anxious and jittery before they speak in public.[34] Almost everyone experiences some anxiety when speaking. It is unrealistic to try to eliminate speech anxiety. Instead, your goal should be to manage your nervousness so that it does not create so much internal noise that it keeps you from speaking effectively.

ANXIETY CAN BE USEFUL Extra adrenaline, increased blood flow, pupil dilation, increased endorphins to block pain, increased heart rate, and other physical changes caused by anxiety improve your energy level and help you function better than you might otherwise. Your heightened state of readiness can actually help you speak better, especially if you view the public-speaking event positively instead of negatively. Speakers who label their increased feelings of physiological arousal as "nervousness" are more likely to feel anxious and fearful, but the same physiological feelings are experienced as enthusiasm or excitement by speakers who don't label the increased arousal as fear, anxiety, or nervousness. You are more likely

There are many things you can do to help build your confidence as you speak. Learn as much as you can about your audience in advance, begin preparing your speech as soon as you know about the speaking engagement, and practice your speech several times before you deliver it.

[Photo: © David Young-Wolff/PhotoEdit]

to gain the benefits of the extra help your brain is trying to give you if you think positively rather than negatively about speaking in public. Don't let your initial anxiety convince you that you cannot speak effectively.

BUILD YOUR CONFIDENCE

"Is there anything I can do to help manage my nervousness and anxiety when I give a speech?" you may wonder. Both contemporary research and centuries of experience from seasoned public speakers suggest some practical advice.

DON'T PROCRASTINATE IN PREPARING YOUR SPEECH One research study confirmed what you probably already know: Speakers who are more apprehensive about speaking put off working on their speeches, in contrast to speakers who are less anxious about public speaking.[35] The fear of speaking often means that speakers delay preparing their speeches until the last minute. The lack of thorough preparation often results in a poorer speech performance, reinforcing the speaker's perception that public speaking is difficult. Realize that if you fear that you'll be nervous when speaking, you'll tend to put off working on your speech. Take charge by tackling the speech assignment early, giving yourself every chance to be successful. Don't let your fear freeze you into inaction. Prepare early.

KNOW YOUR AUDIENCE Know to whom you will be speaking, and learn as much about your audience as you can. The more you can anticipate the kind of reaction your listeners will have to your speech, the more comfortable you will be in delivering your message. As you are preparing your speech, periodically visualize your listeners' response to your message. Consider their needs, goals, and hopes as you prepare your message. Be audience-centered rather than speaker-centered. Don't keep telling yourself how nervous you are going to be.[36] An audience-centered speaker focuses on connecting to listeners rather than focusing on fear. Chapter 5 provides a detailed approach to analyzing and adapting to your audience.

SELECT AN APPROPRIATE TOPIC You will feel less nervous if you talk about something you are familiar with or have some personal experience of. Your comfort with the subject of your speech will be reflected in your delivery. In the chapters ahead, we offer more detailed guidance about how to select a topic.

BE PREPARED One formula applies to most speaking situations you are likely to experience: The better prepared you are, the less anxiety you will experience. Being prepared means that you have researched your topic and practiced your speech several times before you deliver it. One research study found clear evidence that rehearsing your speech reduces your apprehension.[37] Being prepared also means that you have developed a logically coherent outline rather than one that is disorganized and difficult to follow. Transitional phrases and summaries can help you present a well-structured, easy-to-understand message.

DEVELOP AND DELIVER A WELL-ORGANIZED SPEECH One of the key skills you'll learn in *Public Speaking: An Audience-Centered Approach* is the value of developing a well-organized message. For most North American listeners, speeches should have a beginning, middle, and end and should follow a logical outline pattern. Communication researcher Melanie Booth-Butterfield suggests that speakers can better manage their apprehension if they rely on the rules and structures of a speaking assignment, including following a clear outline pattern, when preparing

and delivering a speech.[38] Anxiety about a speech assignment decreased and confidence increased when speakers closely followed the directions and rules for developing a speech. So, to help manage your apprehension about speaking, listen carefully to what the specific assignment is, ask for additional information if you're unclear about the task, and develop a well-organized message.

KNOW YOUR INTRODUCTION AND YOUR CONCLUSION You are likely to feel the most anxious during the opening moments of your speech. Therefore, it is a good idea to have a clear plan for how you will start your speech. We aren't suggesting memorizing your introduction word for word, but you should have it well in mind. Being familiar with your introduction will help you feel more comfortable about the entire speech.

If you know how you will end your speech, you will have a safe harbor in case you lose your place. If you need to end your speech prematurely, a well-delivered conclusion can permit you to make a graceful exit.

RE-CREATE THE SPEECH ENVIRONMENT WHEN YOU PRACTICE When you practice your speech, imagine that you are giving the speech to the audience you will actually address. Stand up. Imagine what the room looks like, or consider rehearsing in the room in which you will deliver your speech. What will you be wearing? Practice rising from your seat, walking to the front of the room, and beginning your speech. Practice aloud, rather than just saying the speech to yourself. A realistic rehearsal will increase your confidence when your moment to speak arrives.

USE DEEP-BREATHING TECHNIQUES One of the symptoms of nervousness is a change in your breathing and heart rates. Nervous speakers tend to take short, shallow breaths. To help break the anxiety-induced breathing pattern, consider taking a few slow deep breaths before you rise to speak. No one will be able to detect that you are taking deep breaths if you just slowly inhale and exhale before beginning your speech. Besides breathing deeply, try to relax your entire body. Deep breathing and visualizing yourself as successful will help you relax.

CHANNEL YOUR NERVOUS ENERGY One common symptom of being nervous is shaking hands and wobbly knees. As we noted earlier, what triggers this jiggling is the extra boost of adrenaline your body is giving you—and the resulting energy that has to go somewhere. Your muscles may move whether you intend them to or not. Take control by channeling that energy. One way to release tension is to take a leisurely walk before you arrive wherever you will be speaking. Taking a slow, relaxing walk can help calm you down and use up some of your excess energy. Once you are seated and waiting to speak, grab the edge of your chair (without calling attention to what you are doing) and gently squeeze the chair to release tension. No one needs to know you're doing this—just unobtrusively squeeze and relax, squeeze and relax. You can also purposely tense and then release your muscles in your legs and arms while you're seated. You don't need to look like you're going into convulsions; just imperceptibly tense and relax your muscles to burn energy. One more tip: You may want to keep both feet on the floor and gently wiggle your toes rather than sitting with your legs crossed. Crossing your legs can sometimes cause one leg or foot to go to sleep. Keeping your feet on the floor and slightly moving your toes can ensure that all of you will be wide awake and ready to go when it's your turn to speak.

As you are waiting to be introduced, focus on remaining calm. Act calm to feel calm. Give yourself a pep talk; tense and release your muscles to help you relax. Then, when your name is called, walk to the front of the room in a calm and collected manner. Before you present your opening, attention-catching sentence, take a moment to look for a friendly, supportive face. Think calm and act calm to feel calm.

VISUALIZE YOUR SUCCESS   Studies suggest that one of the best ways to control anxiety is to imagine a scene in which you exhibit skill and comfort as a public speaker.[39] As you imagine giving your speech, picture yourself walking confidently to the front and delivering your well-prepared opening remarks. Visualize yourself giving the entire speech as a controlled, confident speaker. Imagine yourself calm and in command. Positive visualization is effective because it boosts your confidence by helping you see yourself as a more confident, accomplished speaker.[40]

Research has found that it's even helpful to look at a picture of someone confidently and calmly delivering a speech while visualizing yourself giving the speech; such positive visualization helps manage your apprehension.[41] You could even make a simple drawing of someone speaking confidently.[42] As you look at the image, imagine that it's you confidently giving the speech. It's helpful if the visual image you're looking at is a person you can identify with—someone who looks like you or someone you believe is more like you than not.[43]

GIVE YOURSELF A MENTAL PEP TALK   You may think that people who talk to themselves are slightly loony. But silently giving yourself a pep talk can give you confidence and take your mind off your nervousness. There is some evidence that simply believing that a technique can reduce your apprehension may, in fact, help reduce your apprehension.[44] Giving yourself a positive message such as "I can do this" may be a productive way to manage your anxiety. Here's a sample mental speech you could deliver to yourself right before you speak: "I know this stuff better than anyone else. I've practiced it. My message is well organized. I know I can do it. I'll do a good job." Research provides evidence that people who entertain thoughts of worry and failure don't do themselves any favors.[45] When you feel yourself getting nervous, use positive messages to replace negative thoughts that may creep into your consciousness. Examples include the following:

Negative Thought	Positive Self-Talk
I'm going to forget what I'm supposed to say.	I've practiced this speech many times. I've got notes to prompt me. If I lose my place, no one will know I'm not following my outline.

So many people are looking at me.	I can do this! My listeners want me to do a good job. I'll seek out friendly faces when I feel nervous.
People will think I'm dull and boring.	I've got some good examples. I can talk to people one-on-one, and people seem to like me.
I just can't go through with this.	I have talked to people all my life. I've given presentations in classes for years. I can get through this because I've rehearsed and I'm prepared.

FOCUS ON YOUR MESSAGE RATHER THAN ON YOUR FEAR The more you think about being anxious about speaking, the more you will increase your level of anxiety. Instead, think about what you are going to say. In the few minutes before you address your listeners, mentally review your major ideas, your introduction, and your conclusion. Focus on your ideas rather than on your fear.

LOOK FOR POSITIVE LISTENER SUPPORT FOR YOUR MESSAGE Evidence suggests that if you think you see audience members looking critical of you or your message, you may feel more apprehensive and nervous when you speak.[46] Stated more positively, when you are aware of positive audience support, you will feel more confident and less nervous. To reiterate our previous advice: It is important to be audience-centered. Although you may face some audiences that won't respond positively to you or your message, the overwhelming majority of listeners will be positive. Looking for positive, reinforcing feedback and finding it can help you feel more confident as a speaker. This research finding has implications for you as a listener: When you're listening to speakers in your communication class, help them by being a positive, supportive listener: Provide eye contact and offer additional positive nonverbal support, such as nodding in agreement and maintaining a positive but sincere facial expression. You can help your fellow students feel more comfortable as speakers, and they can do the same for you; watch for their support.

SEEK SPEAKING OPPORTUNITIES The more experience you gain as a public speaker, the less nervous you will feel. Researchers have found that those speakers who were the most nervous at the beginning of a public-speaking class experienced the greatest decreases in nervousness by the end of the class.[47] Another research study found that students who took a basic public-speaking course reported having less apprehension and more satisfaction about speaking than students who had not had a such a course.[48] Consider joining organizations and clubs such as Toastmasters, an organization dedicated to improving public-speaking skills by providing a supportive group of people to help you polish your speaking and overcome your anxiety. As you develop a track record of successfully delivering speeches, you will have more confidence.[49] This course in public speaking will give you opportunities to enhance both your confidence and your skill through frequent practice.

AFTER YOUR SPEECH, FOCUS ON WHAT YOU HAVE ACCOMPLISHED RATHER THAN ON YOUR ANXIETY When you conclude your speech, you may be tempted to fixate on your fear. You might amplify in your own mind the nervousness you felt and think everyone could see how nervous you looked.

confidently connecting with your audience

Begin with the End in Mind

One of the habits cited by well-known author Stephen Covey in his book *The 7 Habits of Highly Successful People* is "Begin with the end in mind."[50] From the moment you begin thinking about preparing and presenting your speech, picture yourself being confident and successful. If you find your anxiety level rising at any point in the speech-preparation process, change your mental picture of yourself and imagine that you've completed your speech and the audience has given you a rousing round of applause. Begin imagining success rather than focusing on your fear. Using the principles, skills, and strategies we discuss in this book will help you develop the habit of speech success.

Resist that temptation. When you finish your speech, tell yourself something positive to celebrate your accomplishment. Say to yourself, "I did it! I spoke and people listened." Don't replay your mental image of yourself as nervous and fearful. Instead, mentally replay your success in communicating with your listeners.

Because managing communication apprehension is such an important skill for most public speakers, in each chapter of this book we'll remind you of tips to help you enhance your confidence. Look for techniques of *confidently connecting with your audience* in the margin.

RECAP

Tips for Building Confidence

WHAT TO DO BEFORE YOU SPEAK

- ◆ Don't procrastinate—give yourself plenty of time to work on your speech.
- ◆ Learn as much as possible about your audience.
- ◆ Select a topic you are interested in or know something about.
- ◆ Be prepared and well organized.
- ◆ Be familiar with how you will begin and end your speech.
- ◆ Rehearse aloud while standing, and try to re-create the speech environment.
- ◆ Use breathing techniques to help you relax.
- ◆ Channel nervous energy.
- ◆ Visualize being successful.
- ◆ Give yourself a mental pep talk.

WHAT TO DO AS YOU SPEAK

- ◆ Focus on connecting your message to your audience rather than on your fear.
- ◆ Look for and respond to positive listener support for you and your message.

WHAT TO DO AFTER YOU SPEAK

- ◆ Seek other speaking opportunities to gain experience and confidence.
- ◆ Focus on your accomplishments and success rather than only reviewing what you may have done wrong.

SUMMARY

As you are likely to be called on to speak in public at various times throughout your life, skill in public speaking can empower you. It can also help you secure employment or advance your career.

Although similar in some ways to conversation, public speaking is more planned and formal, and the roles of speaker and audience are more clearly defined. Like other forms of communication, public speaking is a process. As you develop the skills you need to participate effectively in that process, your study will be guided by experience and knowledge gained over centuries of making and studying speeches. Throughout history, speechmakers have acknowledged that the audience is the most important element in the communication process. Focusing on and considering the audience help a speaker understand, affirm, and adapt to even those audiences whose expectations for appropriate and effective speech topics, argument structure, language style, and delivery may differ from those of the speaker.

Some beginning public speakers feel nervous at even the thought of giving a speech. Don't be surprised if you feel more nervous than you look to others. Remember that almost every speaker experiences some nervousness, and that some anxiety can actually be useful. Specific suggestions to help you manage your apprehension include being prepared and knowing your audience, imagining the speech environment when you rehearse, and using relaxation techniques such as visualization, deep breathing, and focusing thoughts away from your fears.

BEING AUDIENCE-CENTERED: A SHARPER FOCUS

CONSIDERING YOUR AUDIENCE

- As a public speaker, you will learn to adapt to your audience based on who your listeners are, their expectations for your speech, and their reactions to what you are saying.

- The decoding of a speaker's message depends on the receiver's, or listener's, particular blend of past experiences, attitudes, beliefs, and values.

- An audience member experiencing either external or internal noise is unlikely to hear or remember much of what a speaker says.

- Skilled speakers depend on the nods, facial expressions, and murmurings of the audience to adjust their rate of speaking, volume, vocabulary, type and amount of supporting material, and other variables in order to communicate their message successfully.

- The audience is the most important component in the communication process.

- Focus on connecting your message to your audience rather than dwelling on your fear and anxiety about public speaking; being audience-centered can help you manage your apprehension.

CONSIDERING AUDIENCE DIVERSITY

- Although audience members rarely interrupt or talk to speakers, some cultures and contexts invite more speaker-audience interaction than do others.

- Diverse audiences have diverse expectations for appropriate and effective speech topics, argument structure, language style, and delivery.

CRITICAL THINKING QUESTIONS

1. How do you think this course in public speaking can help you with your career goals? With your personal life?

2. Give an example of internal noise that is affecting you as you read this question.

3. Explain how you think your culture influences your expectations of a public speaker.

4. Mike Roberts, president of his fraternity, is preparing to address the university academic council in an effort to persuade them to support establishment of a Greek housing zone on campus. This is his first major task as president, and he is understandably nervous about his responsibility. What advice would you give to help him manage his nervousness?

ETHICAL QUESTION

Declamation is defined in this chapter as "the delivery of an already-famous address." Is it ethical to deliver a speech written and/or delivered by someone else? Explain your answer.

Improving Your Confidence as a Public Speaker

The following list identifies behaviors that will make your nervousness *worse*. Place a 1 in front of the behavior that you do most often when preparing or presenting a speech. Continue to rank the behaviors by placing a 2 beside the practice you do the next most often, a 3 by the third most common behavior, and so on, until you've ranked the top five behaviors that *increase* your anxiety.

_____ 1. I usually procrastinate and often wait until the last minute to prepare my speech.

_____ 2. I typically don't learn much information about my audience or think about my audience.

_____ 3. I often select a topic that I don't know much about.

_____ 4. My outline of my speech is often poor or disorganized.

_____ 5. I often don't have a real clear notion of how I will begin my speech.

_____ 6. I often haven't carefully thought out how I will end my speech.

_____ 7. I don't rehearse aloud while standing up; I just think about my speech rather than practice it.

_____ 8. I usually don't use deep breathing techniques to help me relax.

_____ 9. I usually don't channel my nervous energy.

_____ 10. I rarely visualize myself confidently giving my speech before I present it.

_____ 11. I usually don't give myself a pep talk to boost my confidence.

_____ 12. When I get nervous, I often focus on my nervousness rather than thinking about connecting my message with my audience.

_____ 13. I usually don't try to find friendly faces in the audience while I'm speaking; I just focus on my notes and try to get through the speech.

_____ 14. I avoid every speaking opportunity that comes my way because I'm so nervous.

_____ 15. When I'm finished with a speech, I focus on what I did wrong rather than congratulating myself on what I did well.

After you've identified the top five things you usually do to make your nervousness worse, develop a specific plan to change your behavior. Based on information presented in this chapter, identify specific strategies you could implement to counteract the behaviors that increase your nervousness. Begin with the behavior that you ranked number one.

Make a point of practicing these new strategies as you prepare for and present your next speech. Even if you don't practice all of the strategies for every speech, pick a few to focus on to help boost your confidence.

Abul Hassan dn Manohar, *Jahagir in Darbar*. From a manuscript of the Jahangirnama. North India, Mughal Period. Mughal reign of Jahanir. c. 1620. Govacho on Paper. 13 ⁵/₈" x 7 ⁵/₈". Frances Bartlett Donation of 1912 and Picture Fund. Courtesy, Museum of Fine Arts, Boston. Reproduced with permission.

If all my talents and powers were to be taken from me by some inscrutable Providence, and I had my choice of keeping but one, I would unhesitatingly ask to be allowed to keep the Power of Speaking, for through it, I would quickly recover all the rest.

—DANIEL WEBSTER

Previewing the Audience-Centered Speechmaking Process

outline

An Audience-Centered Speechmaking Model

Consider Your Audience
Gather and Analyze Information about Your Audience
Consider the Culturally Diverse Backgrounds of Your Audience

Select and Narrow Your Topic
Who Is the Audience?
What Are My Interests, Talents, and Experiences?
What Is the Occasion?

Determine Your Purpose
Determine Your General Purpose
Determine Your Specific Purpose

Develop Your Central Idea

Generate the Main Ideas
Does the Central Idea Have Logical Divisions?
Can You Think of Several Reasons the Central Idea Is True?
Can You Support the Central Idea with a Series of Steps?

Gather Supporting Material
Gather Interesting Supporting Material
Gather Visual Supporting Material

Organize Your Speech

Rehearse Your Speech

Deliver Your Speech

objectives

After studying this chapter you should be able to do the following:

1. Explain why it is important to be audience-centered during each step of the speechmaking process.
2. Select and narrow an appropriate topic for a speech.
3. Differentiate between a general speech purpose and a specific speech purpose.
4. Develop a sentence that captures the central idea of a speech.
5. Identify three strategies for generating the main ideas for a speech.
6. Describe several types of supporting material that could be used to support speech ideas.
7. Develop a speech with three main organizational parts—an introduction, a body, and a conclusion.
8. Identify successful strategies for rehearsing a speech.
9. Describe the essential elements of effective speech delivery.

nless you have some prior experience in higher mathematics, you may not have the foggiest notion of what calculus is when you first take a class in that subject. But when you tell people that you are taking a public-speaking class, most at least have some idea of what a public speaker does. A public speaker talks while others listen. You hear speeches almost every day. Each evening, when you turn on the news, you get a "sound bite" of some politician delivering a speech. Each day when you attend class, an instructor lectures. But even after hearing countless speeches, you may still have questions about how a speaker prepares and presents a speech.

In Chapter 1, we discussed the importance of learning to speak publicly and described the components of effective communication. We also presented tips and strategies for becoming a confident speaker. In this chapter, we will preview the preparation and presentation skills that you will learn in this course. Undoubtedly, you will be given a speech assignment early in your public-speaking course. Although it would be ideal to read *Public Speaking: An Audience-Centered Approach* from cover to cover before tackling your first speech, that would be impractical. To help you begin, we present this chapter, a step-by-step overview designed to serve as the scaffolding on which to build your skill in public speaking.

An Audience-Centered Speechmaking Model

You've been speaking to others since you were 2 years old. Talking to people has seemed such a natural part of your life that you may never have stopped to analyze the process. But as you think about preparing your first speech for your speech class, you may wonder, "What do I do first?" Your assignment may be to introduce yourself to the class. Or your first assignment may be a brief informative talk—to describe something to your audience. Regardless of the specific assignment, however, you need some idea of how to begin.

As we noted earlier, you don't need to read this book cover to cover before you give your first speech. But it is useful to have an overview of the various steps and skills involved in giving a speech. To help you see this overview, Figure 2.1 diagrams the various tasks involved in the speechmaking process, emphasizing the audience as the central concern at every step of the process. We'll refer to this audience-centered model of public speaking throughout the text. *To emphasize the importance of being audience-centered, we have placed a smaller version of this model in the margins throughout the text to draw your attention to information that discusses the importance of always being mindful of your audience.* (See the icon in the margin.) When you see the icon, it means we're discussing the central theme of this book: Always make choices in designing and delivering your speech with your audience in mind.

We will preview our discussion of the speechmaking process with the central element: considering your audience. We will then discuss each step of the process, starting with selecting and narrowing a topic, and moving clockwise around the model, examining each interrelated step.

Consider Your Audience

Why should the central focus of public speaking be the audience? Why is it not topic selection, outlining, or research? The simple truth is, your audience influences the topic you choose and every later step of the speechmaking process. Your selection of topic, purpose, and even major ideas should be based on a thorough understanding of your listeners. In a very real sense, your audience "writes" the speech.[1]

GATHER AND ANALYZE INFORMATION ABOUT YOUR AUDIENCE

Being audience-centered means keeping your audience in mind at every step of the speechmaking process. To do that, you need to first identify and then analyze information about your listeners. For example, just by looking at your audience in your speech class, you will be able to determine such basic information as approximately how old they are and the percentage of men and women in your audience; you also know that they are all students in a public-speaking class. To determine other, less obvious information, you may need to ask them questions or design a short questionnaire.

Audience analysis is not something you do only at the beginning of preparing your speech. It is an ongoing activity. The needs, attitudes, beliefs, values, and other characteristics of your audience influence the choices you make about your speech at every step of the speech-preparation process. That's why, in the audience-centered speech model, arrows connect the center of the diagram with each stage of designing and delivering your speech. At any point during the preparation and delivery of your message, you may need to revise your thinking or your material if you learn new information about your audience. So the model has arrows pointing both ways across the boundary between the central element and each step in the process. Chapter 5 includes a comprehensive discussion of the principles and strategies involved in analyzing your audience.

Being audience-centered involves making decisions about the content and delivery of your speech *before* you speak, based on knowledge of your audience's values, beliefs, and knowledge. It also means being aware of your audience's responses *during* the speech so that you can make appropriate adjustments.

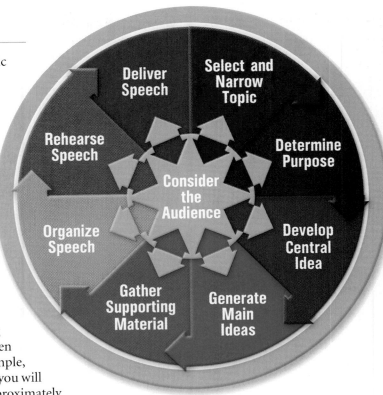

Figure 2.1 *This model of the speechmaking process emphasizes the importance of considering your audience as you work on each task involved in designing and presenting a speech. As we discuss each task in depth throughout the book, we also use a smaller image of this model to flag information and advice that remind you to consider your audience.*

CONSIDER THE CULTURALLY DIVERSE BACKGROUNDS OF YOUR AUDIENCE

You need not give speeches in foreign countries to recognize the importance of adapting to different cultural expectations of individual audience members. People in the United States are highly diverse in terms of their culture, age, ethnicity, and religious tradition. Consider the various cultural backgrounds of your classmates. How many different cultural and ethnic traditions do they represent? Several years ago, the typical college student was likely to be a recent high-school graduate between the ages of 18 and 21. Today your classmates probably reflect a much wider range of ages, backgrounds, and experiences. You will want to adjust not only your delivery style but also your topic, pattern of organization, and the examples you use, according to who your audience members are and what subject or subjects they are interested in.

Different cultures have radically different expectations about public speaking. In Russia, for example, speakers have a "no frills" approach that emphasizes content over delivery. When one of this book's authors taught public speaking for several semesters in the Bahamas, however, he shocked students by suggesting that they should achieve a conversational, informal delivery style. Bahamian audiences, he quickly discovered, expect formal oratory from their speakers, very much as U.S. audiences in the nineteenth century preferred the grandiloquence of Stephen A. Douglas to the quieter, homespun style of Abraham Lincoln. So your author had to embellish his own style when he taught the Bahamian class.

Being sensitive to your audience and adapting your message accordingly will serve you well not only when addressing listeners with different cultural backgrounds from your own, but in all types of situations. If you learn to analyze your audience and adapt to their expectations, you can apply these skills in numerous settings: at a job interview, during a business presentation or a city council election campaign—even while proposing marriage.

Select and Narrow Your Topic

While keeping your audience foremost in mind, your next task is to determine what you will talk about and to limit your topic to fit the constraints of your speaking assignment. Pay special attention to the guidelines your instructor gives you for your assignment.

If your first speech assignment is to introduce yourself to the class, your **speech topic** has been selected for you—*you* are the topic. It is not uncommon to be asked to speak on a specific subject. Often, though, you will be asked to speak but not given a topic. The task of selecting and narrowing a topic will be yours. Choosing or finding a topic on which to speak can be frustrating. "What should I talk about?" can become a haunting question.

Although there is no single answer to the question of what you should talk about, you may discover a topic by asking three standard questions: "Who is the audience?" "What are my interests, talents, and experiences?" and "What is the occasion?"

It's a good idea to give yourself plenty of time to select and narrow your topic. Don't wait until the last minute to ponder what you might talk about. One of the most important things you can do to be an effective speaker is to start preparing your speech well in advance of your speaking date. One research study identified some very practical advice: The amount of time you spend preparing for your speech is one of the best predictors of a good grade on your speech.[2]

WHO IS THE AUDIENCE?

Your topic may grow from basic knowledge of your audience. For example, if you know that your audience members are primarily between the ages of 25 and 40, this information should help you select a topic of interest to people who are probably working and either seeking partners or raising families. An older audience may lead you to other concerns or issues: "Will Social Security be there when I need it?" or "The advantages of belonging to the American Association of Retired Persons."

WHAT ARE MY INTERESTS, TALENTS, AND EXPERIENCES?

Rather than racking your brain for exotic topics and outlandish ideas, examine your own background. Your choice of major in college, your hobbies, and your ancestry

speech topic
The key focus of the content of a speech

Abraham Lincoln (1809–1865)

Abraham Lincoln's experience in law and politics gave him both motivation and opportunity to develop public-speaking skills. Lincoln's law partner, William Herndon, described Lincoln's speechmaking process:

Mr. Lincoln thought his speeches on his feet walking in the streets: he penned them in small scraps—sentences and paragraphs, depositing them in his hat for safety. When fully finished, he would recopy, and could always repeat easily by heart. . . .[3]

But Lincoln's success as a speaker came primarily from his being centered on the audience. A contemporary newspaper account of one Lincoln speech notes, "Mr. Lincoln spoke nearly two hours and we believe he would have held his audience had he spoken all night."[4]

Fortunately, you don't have to speak for two hours in most public-speaking situations. But like Lincoln, good ideas for your speech may come to you while you are doing something else. Give yourself plenty of time to prepare for a speech. Find ways of making notes or capturing your ideas even when you are not sitting at your computer or specifically working on your speech, so that you can incorporate your thoughts and creative ideas into your message.

[Photo: AP Images]

are sources for topic ideas. What issues do you feel strongly about? Reflect on jobs you've held, news stories that catch your interest, events in your hometown, your career goals, or interesting people you have met. Chapter 6 contains a discussion of specific strategies for finding topics.

Once you have chosen your topic, narrow it to fit the time limits for your talk. If you've been asked to deliver a ten-minute speech, the topic "how to find counseling help on campus" would be more manageable than the topic "how to make the most of your college experience." As our model suggests, your audience should be foremost in your mind when you work on your topic.

WHAT IS THE OCCASION?

Besides your audience, you should consider the occasion for the speech when choosing a topic. A commencement address calls for a different topic, for example, than does a speech to a model railroad club. Another aspect of the occasion you'll want to consider is the physical setting of your speech. Will you be speaking to people seated in chairs arranged in a circle, or will you be standing in front of rows of people? The physical surroundings as well as the occasion affect the degree of formality your audience expects in your choice of topics.

Determine Your Purpose

You might think that once you have your topic, you are ready to start the research process. Before you do that, however, you need to decide on both a general and a specific purpose.

DETERMINE YOUR GENERAL PURPOSE

Your **general purpose** is the overarching goal of your speech. There are three types of general purposes for speeches: to *inform*, to *persuade*, and to *entertain*.

When you inform, you teach, define, illustrate, clarify, or elaborate on a topic. The primary objective of class lectures, seminars, and workshops is to inform. Chapter 15 will show you how to construct an effective speech with an informative purpose.

A speech to persuade seeks to change or reinforce listeners' attitudes, beliefs, values, or behavior. Ads on TV, radio, and the Internet; sermons; political speeches; and sales presentations are examples of messages designed to persuade. To be a skilled persuader, you need to be sensitive to your audience's attitudes toward you and your topic. Chapters 16 and 17 will discuss principles and strategies for preparing persuasive speeches.

To entertain listeners is the third general purpose of a speech. After-dinner speeches and comic monologues are mainly intended as entertainment. Often the key to an effective entertaining speech lies in your choice of stories, examples, and illustrations, as well as in your delivery. Appendix C includes examples of speeches designed to inform, persuade, and entertain.

DETERMINE YOUR SPECIFIC PURPOSE

general purpose
The overarching goal of a speech—to inform, persuade, or entertain

specific purpose
A concise statement of the desired audience response, indicating what you want your listeners to remember, feel, or do when you finish speaking

Your **specific purpose** is a concise statement indicating what you want your listeners to be able to do, remember, or feel when your finish your speech. A specific purpose statement identifies the precise audience response you desire. Here again, we emphasize the importance of focusing on the audience as you develop your specific purpose. Perhaps you have had the experience of listening to a speaker and wondering, "What's the point? I know he's talking about education, but I'm not sure where he's going with this subject." You may have understood the speaker's general purpose, but the specific one wasn't clear. If you can't figure out what the specific purpose is, it is probably because the speaker does not know either.

RECAP — Determine Your Purpose

DEVELOP YOUR GENERAL PURPOSE

To inform	To share information by teaching, defining, illustrating, describing, or explaining
To persuade	To change or reinforce an attitude, belief, value, or behavior
To entertain	To amuse with humor, stories, or illustrations

DEVELOP YOUR SPECIFIC PURPOSE

What do you want your audience to remember, do, or feel when you finish your speech?

General Purpose	Specific Purpose
To inform	At the end of my speech, the audience will be able to identify three counseling facilities on campus and describe the best way to get help at each one.
To persuade	At the end of my speech, the audience will visit the counseling facilities on campus.
To entertain	At the end of my speech, the audience will be amused by the series of misunderstandings I created when I began making inquiries about career advisors on campus.

Deciding on a specific purpose is not difficult once you have narrowed your topic: "At the end of my speech, the class will be able to identify three counseling facilities on campus and describe the best way to get help at each one." Notice that this purpose is phrased in terms of what you would like the audience to be able to *do* by the end of the speech. Your specific purpose should be a fine-tuned, audience-centered goal. For an informative speech, you may simply want your audience to restate an idea, define new words, or identify, describe, or illustrate something. In a persuasive speech, you may try to rouse your listeners to take a class, buy something, or vote for someone.

Once you have formulated your specific purpose, write it down on a piece of paper or note card and keep it before you as you read and gather ideas for your talk. Your specific purpose should guide your research and help you choose supporting materials that are related to your audience. As you continue to work on your speech, you may even decide to modify your purpose. But if you have an objective in mind at all times as you move through the preparation stage, you will stay on track.

Develop Your Central Idea

You should now be able to write the **central idea** of your speech. Whereas your statement of a specific purpose indicates what you want your audience to do when you have finished your speech, your central idea identifies the essence of your message. Think of it as a one-sentence summary of your speech. Here's an example:

TOPIC:	The South Beach diet
GENERAL PURPOSE:	To inform
SPECIFIC PURPOSE:	At the end of my speech, the audience will be able to identify the three key elements in the South Beach diet.
CENTRAL IDEA:	The South Beach diet is based on reducing the amount of carbohydrates you eat, drinking more water, and increasing the amount of exercise you get.

Generate the Main Ideas

In the words of columnist H. V. Prochnow, "A good many people can make a speech, but saying something is more difficult." Effective speakers are good thinkers; they say something. They know how to play with words and thoughts to develop their **main ideas**. The ancient Romans called this skill **invention**— the ability to develop or discover ideas that result in new insights or new approaches to old problems. The Roman orator Cicero called this aspect of speaking the process of "finding out what [a speaker] should say."

Once you have an appropriate topic, a specific purpose, and a well-worded central idea down on paper, the next task is to identify the major divisions of your speech, or key points that you wish to develop. To determine how to subdivide your central idea into key points, ask these three questions:

1. Does the central idea have logical divisions?
2. Can you think of several reasons the central idea is true?
3. Can you support the central idea with a series of steps?

Let's look at each of these questions along with examples of how to apply them.

central idea
A one-sentence summary of the speech content

main ideas
The key points of a speech

invention
The development or discovery of ideas and insights

DOES THE CENTRAL IDEA HAVE LOGICAL DIVISIONS?

If the central idea is "There are three ways to interpret the stock-market page of your local newspaper," your speech can be organized into three parts. You will simply identify the three ways to interpret the stock-market page and use each as a major point. A speech about the art of applying theatrical makeup could also be organized into three parts: eye makeup, face makeup, and hair coloring. Looking for logical divisions in your speech topic is the simplest way to determine key points.

CAN YOU THINK OF SEVERAL REASONS THE CENTRAL IDEA IS TRUE?

If your central idea is "Medicare should be expanded to include additional coverage for individuals of all ages," each major point of your speech could be a reason you think Medicare should be expanded. For example, Medicare should be expanded because (1) not enough people are being served by the present system, (2) the people currently being served receive inadequate medical attention, and (3) the elderly cannot afford to pay what Medicare does not now cover. If your central idea is a statement that something is good or bad, you should focus on the reasons your central idea is true. Use these reasons as the main ideas of the speech.

CAN YOU SUPPORT THE CENTRAL IDEA WITH A SERIES OF STEPS?

Suppose your central idea is "Running for a campus office is easy to do." Your speech could be developed around a series of steps, telling your listeners what to do first, second, and third to get elected. Speeches describing a personal experience or explaining how to build or make something can usually be organized in a step-by-step progression.

Your time limit, topic, and the information gleaned from your research will determine how many major ideas will be in your speech. A three- to five-minute speech might have only two major ideas. In a very short speech, you may develop only one major idea with examples, illustrations, and other forms of support. Don't spend time trying to divide a topic that does not need dividing. In Chapters 6 and 9, we will discuss how to generate major ideas and organize them.

 ## Gather Supporting Material

With your main idea or ideas in mind, your next job is to gather material to support them—facts, examples, definitions, and quotations from others that illustrate, amplify, clarify, and provide evidence. Here, as always when preparing your speech, the importance of being an audience-centered speaker can't be overemphasized. There's an old saying that an ounce of illustration is worth a ton of talk. If a speech is boring, it is usually because the speaker has not chosen supporting material that is relevant or interesting to the audience. Don't just give people data; connect facts to their lives. As one sage quipped, "Data is not information any more than 50 tons of cement is a skyscraper."[5]

GATHER INTERESTING SUPPORTING MATERIAL

Supporting material should be personal and concrete, and it should appeal to your listeners' senses. Tell stories based on your own experiences and provide vivid descriptions of things that are tangible so that your audience can visualize what you are talking about. Besides sight, supporting material can appeal to touch, hearing, smell, and taste. The more senses you trigger with words, the more interesting your talk will be. Descriptions such as "the rough, splintery surface of weather-beaten wood" or "the sweet, cool, refreshing flavor of cherry Jell-O" evoke sensory images. In addition, relating abstract statistics to something tangible can help communicate your ideas more clearly. For example, if you say Frito-Lay sells 2.6 billion pounds of snack food each year, your listeners will have a hazy idea that 2.6 billion pounds is a lot of Fritos and potato chips; but if you add that 2.6 billion pounds is triple the weight of the Empire State Building, you've made your point more memorably.[6] We will discuss in Chapter 8 the variety of supporting material available to you.

Good research skills are essential to the speechmaking process.

[Photo: Creatas/Jupiter/Alamy]

How does a public speaker find interesting and relevant supporting material? By developing good research skills. President Woodrow Wilson once admitted, "I use not only all the brains I have, but all that I can borrow." Although it is important to have good ideas, it is equally important to know how to build on existing knowledge. You can probably think of a topic or two about which you consider yourself an expert. Chances are that if you gave a short speech about a sport that you had practiced for years or about a recent trip that you took, you would not need to gather much additional information. But sooner or later, you will need to do some research on a topic in order to speak on it intelligently to an audience. If your college classes up to this point have required only brief forays into the library or onto the Internet, that experience is about to change! By the time you have given several speeches in this course, you will have learned to use a number of resources: your library's computerized card catalog, the *Social Sciences Index*, the *Directory of American Scholars*, *Bartlett's Familiar Quotations*, government document holdings, your library's periodical indexes, and an assortment of Internet indexes. You would also be wise to spend some time learning to use electronic search engines such as Google and Yahoo! Throughout this book we identify useful Web sites in our Speaker's Homepage feature. These Web sites will help you both design and deliver your speeches.

In addition to becoming a skilled user of library and electronic resources, you will also learn to be on the lookout as you read, watch TV, and listen to the radio for ideas, examples, illustrations, and quotations that could be used in a speech. Finally, you will learn how to gather information through interviews and written requests for information on various topics. Chapter 7 will explain more thoroughly how to use all these resources.

GATHER VISUAL SUPPORTING MATERIAL

For many people, seeing is believing. Besides searching for verbal forms of supporting material, you can also seek visual supporting material. Almost any presentation can be enhanced by reinforcing key ideas with visual aids. Often the most effective visual aids are the simplest: an object, a chart, a graph, a poster, a model, a map, or a person—perhaps you—to demonstrate a process or skill. Today there are many technologies for displaying visual aids. One of the most basic is an overhead projector that displays $8\frac{1}{2}$- by 11-inch acetate transparencies. Most classrooms now have video players, so you can show brief video segments to introduce or reinforce a point. The latest graphics packages for personal computers can help you generate colorful graphs, charts, signs, and banners. And with today's technology you can project stunning video images with the proper equipment. Of course, using this high-tech equipment requires skill and often extra rehearsal time.

In Chapter 14 we discuss some basic advice about using presentation aids: Make your visual images large enough to be seen and allow plenty of time to prepare them; look at your audience, not at your presentation aid; control your audience's attention by timing your visual displays; and keep your presentation aids simple. Always concentrate on communicating effectively with your audience, not on dazzling your listeners with glitzy presentation displays.

 ## Organize Your Speech

A wise person once said, "If effort is organized, accomplishment follows." A clearly and logically structured speech helps your audience remember what you say. A logical structure also helps you feel more in control of your speech, and greater control helps you feel more comfortable while delivering your message.

Classical rhetoricians—early students of speech—called the process of developing an orderly speech **disposition**. Speakers need to present ideas, information, examples, illustrations, stories, and statistics in an orderly sequence so that listeners can easily follow what they are saying.

Every well-prepared speech has three major divisions: the introduction, the body, and the conclusion. The introduction helps capture attention, serves as an overview of the speech, and provides your audience with reasons to listen to you. The body

disposition
The organization and arrangement of ideas and illustrations

SAMPLE OUTLINE

TOPIC:

How to invest money

➤ Your instructor may assign a topic, or you may select it.

GENERAL PURPOSE:

To inform

➤ To inform, persuade, or entertain. Your instructor will probably specify your general purpose.

SPECIFIC PURPOSE:

At the end of my speech, the audience should be able to identify two principles that will help them better invest their money.

➤ A clear statement indicating what your audience should be able to do after hearing your speech

CENTRAL IDEA:

Knowing the source of money, how to invest it, and how money grows can lead to increased income from wise investments.

➤ A one-sentence summary of your talk

INTRODUCTION:

Imagine for a moment that it is the year 2050. You are 65 years old. You've just picked up your mail and opened an envelope that contains a check for $100,000! No, you didn't win the lottery. You smile as you realize your own modest investment strategy over the last fifty years has paid off handsomely.

➤ Attention-catching opening line

Today I'd like to answer three questions that can help you become a better money manager: First, where does money come from? Second, where do you invest it? And third, how does a little money grow into a lot of money?

➤ Preview major ideas.

presents the main content of your speech. The conclusion summarizes your key ideas. You may have heard this advice on how to organize a speech: "Tell them what you're going to tell them (the introduction), tell them (the body of the speech), and tell them what you told them (the conclusion)."

As a student of public speaking, you will study and learn to apply variations of this basic pattern of organization (chronological, topical, cause–effect, problem–solution) that will help your audience understand your meaning. You will learn about previewing and summarizing—methods of oral organization that will help your audience retain your main ideas. In the outline of a sample speech, notice how the introduction catches the listener's attention, the body of the speech identifies the main ideas, and the conclusion summarizes the key ideas.

Because your introduction previews your speech and your conclusion summarizes it, most public-speaking teachers recommend that you prepare your introduction and conclusion *after* you have carefully organized the body of your talk. If you have already generated your major ideas by divisions, reasons, or steps, you are well on your way to developing an outline. Indicate your major ideas by Roman numerals. Use capital letters for your supporting points. Use Arabic numerals if you need to subdivide your ideas further. Do *not* write your speech word for word. If you do, you will sound stilted and unnatural. It may be useful, however, to use brief notes—written cues on note cards—instead of a complete manuscript.

You may want to look in Chapters 9 and 11 for approaches to organizing a message and sample outlines. Chapter 10 provides more detailed suggestions for beginning and ending your speech. Some public-speaking teachers may require a

Knowing the answers to these three questions can literally pay big dividends for you. With only modest investments and a well-disciplined attitude, you could easily have an annual income of $100,000 or more.

➤ Tell your audience why they should listen to you.

BODY:

I. There are two sources of money.
   A. You already have some money.
   B. You will earn money in the future.

II. You can do three things with a dollar.
   A. You can spend your money.
   B. You can lend your money to others.
   C. You can invest your money.

III. Two principles can help make you rich.
   A. The "magic" of compound interest can transform pennies into millions.
   B. Finding the best rate of return on your money can pay big dividends.

➤ I. Major Idea
➤ A. Supporting idea
➤ B. Supporting idea

➤ II. Major Idea
➤ A. Supporting idea
➤ B. Supporting idea
➤ C. Supporting idea

➤ III. Major Idea
➤ A. Supporting idea
➤ B. Supporting idea

CONCLUSION:

Today I've identified three key aspects of effective money management: (1) sources of money, (2) what you can do with money, and (3) money-management principles that can make you rich. Now, let's go "back to the future"! Remember the good feeling you had when you received your check for $100,000? Recall that feeling again when you are depositing your first paycheck. Remember this simple secret for accumulating wealth: Part of all I earn is mine to keep. It is within your power to "go for the gold."

➤ Summarize main ideas and restate central idea.

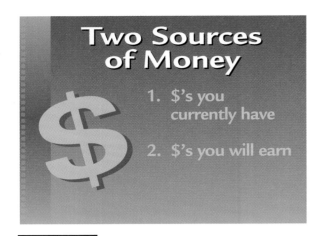

Figure 2.2 *Presentation graphic for the first major idea in your speech*

Figure 2.3 *Presentation graphic for the second major idea in your speech*

Figure 2.4 *Presentation graphic for the third major idea in your speech*

slightly different outline format. For example, your teacher may want you to outline your speech introduction using a Roman numeral I for the introduction, a II for the body, and a III for your conclusion. Make sure you follow the precise guidelines your instructor provides for outlining your speech. For your first speech, you may want to adapt the sample outline format shown on pages 34–35.[7] Your instructor may want you to add more detailed information about your supporting material in outlines you submit in class.

In addition to developing a written outline to use as you speak, consider using presentation aids to add structure and clarity to your major ideas. Developing simple visual reinforcers of your key ideas can help your audience retain essential points.

In Chapter 14 we offer tips for designing computer graphics using software such as PowerPoint. For example, the first major idea in the outline presented earlier could be summarized in a visual aid such as the one in Figure 2.2. The second major idea in our speech example could be emphasized with a visual like the one in Figure 2.3. The third major idea could be reinforced with a visual such as the one in Figure 2.4.

For all the steps we have discussed so far, your success as a speaker will ultimately be determined by your audience. That is why throughout the text we refer you to the audience-centered speechmaking model presented in this chapter.

Once you are comfortable with the structure of your talk and you have developed your visual aids, you are ready to rehearse.

Rehearse Your Speech

Remember this joke? One man asks another, "How do you get to Carnegie Hall?" The answer: "Practice, practice, practice." The joke may be older than Carnegie Hall itself, but it is still good advice to all beginners, including novice speakers. A speech is a performance. As with any stage performance, be it music, dance, or theater, you need to rehearse. Experienced carpenters know to "measure twice, saw once." Rehearsing your speech is a way to measure your message so that you get it right when you present it to your audience.

The best way to practice is to rehearse your speech aloud, standing just as you will when you deliver it to your audience. As you rehearse, try to find a comfortable way to phrase your ideas, but don't try to memorize your talk. In fact, if you have rehearsed your speech so many times that you are using exactly the same words every time, you have rehearsed long enough. Rehearse just enough so that you can discuss your ideas and supporting material without leaving out major parts of your speech. It is all right to use notes, but most public-speaking instructors limit the number of notes you may use.

As you rehearse, practice making eye contact with your imaginary audience as often as you can. Also, be certain to speak loudly enough for all in the room to hear. If you are not sure what to do with your hands when you rehearse, just keep them at your side. Focus on your message, rather than worrying about how to gesture. Avoid jingling change with your hand in your pocket or using

other gestures that could distract your audience. If you practice your speech as if you were actually delivering it, you will be a more effective speaker when you talk to the audience. And there is evidence that, like preparing early for your speech, spending time rehearsing your delivery will enhance the overall quality of your speech.[8]

Besides rehearsing your physical delivery, you also will make decisions about the style of your speech. "Style," said novelist Jonathan Swift, "is proper words in proper places." The words you choose and your arrangement of those words make up the style of your speech. As we have said, some audiences respond to a style that is simple and informal. Others prefer a grand and highly poetic style. To be a good speaker, you must become familiar with the language your listeners are used to hearing and must know how to select the right word or phrase to communicate an idea. Work to develop an ear for how words will sound to your audience.

 ## Deliver Your Speech

The time has come, and you're ready to present your speech to your audience. Delivery is the final step in the preparation process. Before you walk to the front of the room, look at your listeners to see if the audience assembled is what you were expecting. Are the people out there of the age, race, and gender that you had predicted? Or do you need to make last-minute changes in your message to adjust to a different mix of audience members?

When you are introduced, walk calmly and confidently to the front of the room, establish eye contact with your audience, smile naturally, and deliver your attention-catching opening sentence. Concentrate on your message and your audience. Deliver your speech in a conversational style, and try to establish rapport with your

confidently connecting with your audience

Use Your Communication Apprehension to Enhance Your Performance

Realize that virtually *everyone* experiences some nervousness about giving a speech. Rather than letting the anxiety become a barrier to success by dwelling on your fear, use it to help you enhance your performance. How? Remember that anxiety is your body's way of trying to give you more energy to help you improve your performance. Use the skill of reframing to get yourself to think positively rather than negatively about speaking in public. Don't dwell on the anxiety you feel; reframe your nervousness as your brain's way of increasing your mental powers. Knowing that some apprehension can enhance your mental alertness can help you deliver a well-presented speech.

PUBLIC SPEAKING STEP	WHAT TO DO	WHERE TO FIND MORE INFORMATION IN THIS BOOK
1. Consider the Audience	Gather information about your audience. Analyze the information to help you make choices about every aspect of preparing and presenting your speech.	Chapter 5: "Analyzing Your Audience"
2. Select and Narrow Your Topic	To select a good speech topic, consider ◆ Your audience ◆ Your own interests ◆ The specific occasion when you will be speaking	Chapter 6: "Developing Your Speech"
3. Determine Your Purpose	Determine whether your general purpose is to inform, to persuade or to entertain. Decide on your specific purpose—a statement of what you want your audience to be able to do when you finish your speech.	Chapter 6: "Developing Your Speech" Chapter 15: "Speaking to Inform" Chapter 16: "Understanding Principles of Persuasion" Chapter 17: "Using Persuasive Strategies" Chapter 18: "Speaking for Special Occasions and Purposes"
4. Develop Your Central Idea	Develop a one-sentence summary of your speech.	Chapter 6: "Developing Your Speech"
5. Generate Your Main Ideas	Identify your major ideas by determining whether your central idea has logical divisions, reasons why it is true, or steps.	Chapter 6: "Developing Your Speech"
6. Gather Supporting Material	Conduct research to identify useful and interesting stories, descriptions, definitions, statistics, analogies, and opinions that support your major ideas.	Chapter 7: "Gathering Supporting Material" Chapter 8: "Integrating Supporting Material"
7. Organize Your Speech	Develop your introduction, body, and conclusion. Use signposts and transitions to clarify your organization.	Chapter 9: "Organizing Your Speech" Chapter 10: "Introducing and Concluding Your Speech" Chapter 11: "Outlining and Editing Your Speech"
8. Rehearse Your Speech	Prepare your speaking notes and practice using them well in advance of your speaking date. Practice your speech out loud, standing as you would stand while delivering your speech. Develop appropriate and useful presentation aids.	Chapter 12: "Using Words Well: Speaker Language and Style" Chapter 13: "Delivering Your Speech" Chapter 14: "Using Presentation Aids"
9. Deliver Your Speech	Present your speech using ◆ Good eye contact ◆ Appropriate gestures and posture ◆ Appropriate vocal volume and variation	Chapter 13: "Delivering Your Speech"

OUR IMMIGRATION STORY

by Pao Yang Lee

Each one of us has our own story, a history of our lives that helps explain who we are and what motivates us to be the best we can be. My story starts with my parents. Most of our parents worked hard to raise us and get us an education. Today, I'm going to share with you a part of my story. I will tell you about my parents' struggle to leave Laos, a refugee camp in Thailand, and about our new life in America.

I will start my story with my parents' struggle to leave Laos to make their way to Thailand. As most of you know, many Hmong people had escaped Laos because they were being persecuted by the Communists and had to escape for their lives and freedom. My parents, who hadn't met yet, each took their journey across the Mekong River on a bamboo raft. My parents were lucky. They made it across to Thailand. According to my Dad, about 1000 Hmong people died making that exact journey. My parents' story merged at a refugee camp in Thailand. In Thailand, although they had escaped with their lives, their lives did not improve much because the camp that the Hmong people were put in when they came to Thailand was in very poor condition. My parents met at the refugee camp in Bon Vinai a couple months later when they arrived in Thailand. My Dad asked for my Mom's hand in marriage. At that time, my parents were very young. They didn't have any support from anybody. I was born in the refugee camp in Bon Vinai, February 18, 1980. Six months after I was born, we were sponsored by an American family, which allowed us to come to the United States.

The next chapter in our story continues in America, where each of us has our own challenge. My Dad had the most responsibility when it came to supporting our family. He knew it was important to get an education, so he started attending college. However, shortly after our arrival, my sisters were born. To make ends meet, my Dad had to drop out of college and work full time to support us all. My Mom also struggled with all the new aspects of her life. For example, in Laos, where she used to live, there wasn't any machine that would wash your clothes. However, in the United States, there are machines that will wash clothes for you. Another thing that she struggled with was using other appliances as well. Being able to operate the machine and use it properly was the hardest thing for my Mom because she wasn't able to read the directions. Probably the biggest struggle for my Mom was learning how to speak English and understand the language. It is interesting that when people can't understand you, they think you're stupid. But we are the people who speak the second language.

Like my Mother and Father, I had my own challenge. I had to live in both cultures at the same time. At school, I was trying to fit in by learning the rules about how to act. While at home, I was trying to be respectful to the Hmong custom and language. This is a very difficult thing to do. It was also difficult for me to be a translator for my parents. I was just a little kid and was expected to translate an adult conversation. I was also expected to be there for my parents whenever they needed me.

Now I'm able to see my life as a part of a bigger picture—a bigger story. I have learned that you have to work hard to succeed in life. Coming from a first-generation family in the United States, I have lived through and seen the struggle that my parents went through to raise my siblings and me.

Well, today I told you a little bit about my story, a part of my ancestry that has helped make me who I am. It is a story that has been repeated by 90,000 Hmong people in the United States. As you have taken the journey with my parents from Laos, to Thailand, and to America, I hope you will be able to think of your own stories and how they have brought us to this present place and time, to learn and grow together.

Pao captures his listeners' attention by telling them about his parents' struggle to leave Laos.

He sets the scene and provides a preview of what will be presented; audience members know that more details about the journey will be forthcoming, so they tune in to listen.

The speech is organized chronologically. Pao uses a step-by-step arrangement to describe the events that occurred.

Note how Pao signals a new idea by using the transition phrase "The next chapter in our story . . . ."

Revealing personal details and information adds interest to a story and holds listeners' attention.

As Pao concludes his speech, he summarizes by noting the "bigger story," or the implications of what he has learned. Speeches based on personal experiences are enhanced if the speaker can draw some concluding point or idea from the story.

The speech ends with a concise summary of the major idea of the speech. Pao also invites the audience to relate his story to their own lives.

Preparing carefully and keeping the audience always in mind will help you speak confidently on whatever topic you have chosen.

[Photo: Michael Newman/PhotoEdit]

listeners. Deliver your speech just as you rehearsed it before your imaginary audience: Maintain eye contact, speak loudly enough to be heard, and use some natural variation in pitch. Finally, remember the advice of columnist Ann Landers: "Be sincere, be brief, and be seated." The speech on page 39, by public-speaking student Pao Yang Lee, models many of the attributes of a well-crafted message that we have discussed.[9]

SUMMARY

To prepare for your first speaking assignment, you can follow the steps we have outlined for preparing and presenting a speech, showing how the audience is the central focus at each step. Our audience-centered model of public speaking suggests that throughout the speech-crafting and delivery process, the choices you make about the design and presentation of your message should be guided by your knowledge of your audience. Based on information about your listeners, you select and narrow your topic, determine your purpose, develop your central idea, and generate the main ideas. These speech-preparation steps are followed by gathering and organizing your supporting material, including visual aids. With a draft of your speech outline in hand, you are then ready to rehearse and deliver your speech.

BEING AUDIENCE-CENTERED: A SHARPER FOCUS

CONSIDERING YOUR AUDIENCE

- Being audience-centered means considering the background and interests of your listeners at each step in developing and presenting your speech.

- Adapt your language and choice of words to the education level of your listeners; be mindful of your listeners' backgrounds so that you neither speak "over their heads" nor use such simplistic words and phrases that you insult their intelligence.

CONSIDERING AUDIENCE DIVERSITY

- The cultural background of your audience will have a major effect on your listeners' expectations as to how you should organize, support, and present your speech.

- Because of the wide cultural variety in most communities and on most college campuses in the United States, you need not travel to an international destination to speak to people with differing cultural backgrounds.

CRITICAL THINKING QUESTIONS

1. Jason Reed has just received his assignment for his first speech in his public-speaking class. What key skills does he need to master to become a competent public speaker?

2. Shara Yobonski is preparing to address the city council in an effort to tell them about the Food for Friendship program she has organized in her neighborhood. What steps should she follow to prepare and deliver an effective speech?

ETHICAL QUESTIONS

1. One of your friends took a public-speaking course last year and still has a file of speech outlines. Since you will give the speech yourself, is it ethical to use one of her outlines as a basis for your speech? Explain.

2. Your first assignment is to give a speech about something interesting that has happened to you. You have decided to talk about the joys and hassles of a train trip you took last year. Your sister recently returned from a cross-country train trip and had several interesting tales to tell. Would it be ethical to tell one of her experiences as if it had happened to you? Why or why not?

3. You read an article in *Reader's Digest* that could serve as the basis for a great speech about the ravages of AIDS. Would it be ethical to paraphrase the article, using most of the same examples and the overall outline as the basis for your speech, if you *told* your listeners that your speech was based on the article?

How to Develop a Speech of Self-Introduction

A typical early assignment in a public-speaking class is to give a brief speech introducing yourself to your classmates. Here are some tips to help you develop a speech of self-introduction.

1. **Consider your audience.** Ask yourself these questions:
   - What would my classmates find interesting about me?
   - What is an experience, event I've attended, or something about my hobbies or background that my listeners would find interesting and memorable?

2. **Select and narrow your topic:**
   - Jot down notes about one or two interesting experiences that could become focal points for your speech.
   - Identify one or two stories you've heard, experiences you've had, or personal interests that would be of interest to your audience.

3. **Determine your purpose:**
   - Develop your specific purpose. Here's an example: "At the end of my speech, listeners should be able to identify three things about me that make me unique." On a separate sheet of paper, write a statement of your specific purpose: "At the end of my speech, listeners should be able to . . . ."

4. **Develop your central idea:**
   - On a separate sheet of paper, write a one-sentence summary of your speech. Here's an example: "The three things that make me unique are (1) my interest in playing the cello, (2) my collection of books about C. S. Lewis, and (3) my passion for travel."

5. **Generate your main ideas:**
   - Determine if your main ideas are a series of steps, reasons the central idea is true, or logical divisions. On a separate sheet of paper, identify your main ideas.

6. **Gather supporting material:**
   - Think about specific, brief stories or anecdotes that you could share with your listeners to illustrate each of the main points of your speech that support your central idea.

7. **Organize your ideas:**
   - Develop your outline, working first on the body of your speech. Use Roman numerals to identify each major idea.
     - Main idea I:
     - Main idea II:
     - Main idea III:
   - Develop a conclusion to your speech that summarizes the key points and ends with a final interesting story, question, quotation, or illustration.
   - Develop the beginning of your speech by thinking of an attention-catching opening sentence or example, providing a preview of your major ideas, and noting why your speech will be of interest to your listeners.

William H. Johnson (1901–1970) *Lift Up Thy Voice and Sing*. c. 1942–44. Oil on paperboard, 64.9 x 54.0 cm. Smithsonian American Art Museum, Washington, DC/Art Resource, N.Y.

Free speech not only lives, it rocks!

—OPRAH WINFREY

Speaking Freely and Ethically

outline

Speaking Freely

Speaking Ethically
Have a Clear, Responsible Goal
Use Sound Evidence and Reasoning
Be Sensitive to and Tolerant of Differences
Be Honest
Don't Plagiarize

Listening Ethically
Communicate Your Expectations and
    Feedback
Be Sensitive to and Tolerant of Differences
Listen Critically

objectives

After studying this chapter you should be able to do the following:

1. Define ethics.

2. Explain the relationship between ethics and free speech.

3. List and explain five criteria for ethical public speaking.

4. Define and discuss how best to avoid plagiarism.

5. List and explain three criteria for ethical listening.

I n April 2007, CBS Radio fired controversial talk radio host Don Imus for derogatory comments he had made on the air about members of the Rutgers University women's basketball team. In a commencement address at Queen's College two months later, author Susan Isaacs questioned the firing. "He is pretty much a pig," Isaacs agreed. "But the demands for his ouster were wrong."[1] She went on to explain that

> if you get rid of one talk show host, next to go is an offensive comedy show such as *South Park*, shock jock Howard Stern and conservative host Rush Limbaugh. "Then it's your turn (to be quieted)," the author warned.

While critical of Imus's *ethics*, Isaacs nevertheless defended his right to *free speech*.

In the United States, the right to speak freely goes hand in hand with the responsibility to speak ethically. **Ethics** are the beliefs, values, and moral principles by which we determine what is right or wrong. Some ethical values appear to be universal, or nearly so. For example, the major world religions share a remarkably similar moral code for how people should treat others.[2] For Christians, the Golden Rule—"Do unto others as you would have others do unto you"—is a fundamental value. Buddhism teaches a similar value: "One should seek for others the happiness one desires for oneself." Hinduism asks adherents to live by the precept "Do nothing to others which would cause pain if done to you." Judaism teaches, "What is hateful to you, do not do to others." And Islam declares, "No one of you is a believer until he desires for his brother that which he desires for himself."

Although the underlying ethic of how to treat others is fundamental to the world's religions, other ethical principles may reflect cultural norms, professional standards, or individual beliefs or values. Ethics serve as criteria for many of the decisions we make in our personal and professional lives, and also for our judgments of others' behavior. The student who refuses to cheat on a test, the employee who will not call in sick to gain an extra day of vacation, and the property owner who does not claim more storm damage than she actually suffered have all made choices based on ethics. We read and hear about ethical issues every day in the media. Cloning, stem-cell research, and drug testing have engendered heated ethical debates among medical professionals. Advertising by some attorneys has incensed those who believe that the overall increase in frivolous litigation is tarnishing the profession. And in the political arena, debates about reforms of social programs, fiscal responsibility, and the regulation of business and industry all hinge on ethical issues.

Although you are undoubtedly familiar with many of these ethical issues, you may have given less thought to ethics in public speaking. These center around one main concern: In a country in which **free speech** is protected by law, the right to speak freely must be balanced by the responsibility to speak ethically. In 1999, the National Communication Association developed a Credo for Communication Ethics, which emphasizes the fundamental nature and far-reaching impact of ethical communication:

ethics
The beliefs, values, and moral principles by which people determine what is right or wrong

free speech
Legally protected speech or speech acts

Ethical communication is fundamental to responsible thinking, decision making, and the development of relationships and communities within and across contexts, cultures, channels, and media. Moreover, ethical communication enhances human worth and dignity by fostering truthfulness, fairness, responsibility, personal integrity, and respect for self and others.[3]

Ethical considerations should guide every step of the public-speaking process we discussed in Chapter 2. As you determine the goal of your speech, outline your arguments, and select your evidence, think about the beliefs, values, and moral principles of your audience, as well as your own. Ethical public speaking is inherently audience-centered, always taking into account the needs and rights of the listeners.

The First Amendment protects the rights of protest speakers to speak out about controversial issues.

[Photo: A. Ramey/PhotoEdit]

In our discussion of speaking freely and ethically, we will turn first to free speech—both its protection and its restriction by law and public policy. Then we will discuss the ethical practice of free speech by speakers and listeners, providing guidelines to help you balance your right to free speech with your responsibilities as an audience-centered speaker and as a critical listener. Within this framework, we will define and discuss plagiarism, one of the most troublesome violations of public-speaking ethics.

Speaking Freely

I n 1791, the **First Amendment** to the U.S. Constitution was written to guarantee that "Congress shall make no law . . . abridging the freedom of speech." In the more than 200 years since then, entities as varied as state legislatures, colleges and universities, the American Civil Liberties Union, and the federal courts have sought to define through both law and public policy the phrase "freedom of speech."

Only a few years after the ratification of the First Amendment, Congress passed the Sedition Act, providing punishment for those who spoke out against the government. When both Thomas Jefferson and James Madison declared this act unconstitutional, however, it was allowed to lapse. During World War I, the U.S. Supreme Court ruled that it was lawful to restrict speech that presented "a clear and present danger" to the nation. This decision led to the founding, in 1920, of the American Civil Liberties Union, the first organization formed to protect free speech. In 1940, Congress declared it illegal to urge the violent overthrow of the federal government. However, even as they heard the hate speech employed by Hitler and the Nazis, U.S. courts and lawmakers argued that only by *protecting* free speech could the United States protect the rights of minorities and the disenfranchised. For most of the last half of the twentieth century, the U.S. Supreme Court continued to protect rather than to limit free speech, upholding it as "the core aspect of democracy."[4]

In 1964, the Supreme Court narrowed the definition of slander, or false speech that harms someone. The Court ruled that before a public official can recover damages for slander, he or she must prove that the slanderous statement was made

First Amendment
The amendment to the U.S. Constitution that guarantees free speech; the first of the ten amendments to the U.S. Constitution known collectively as the Bill of Rights

with "actual malice."[5] Another 1964 boost for free speech occurred not in the courts, but on a university campus. In December of that year, more than 1,000 students at the University of California in Berkeley took over three floors of Sproul Hall to protest the recent arrest of outspoken student activists. The Berkeley Free Speech Movement that arose from the incident permanently changed the political climate of U.S. college campuses. In a written statement on the 30-year anniversary of the protest, Berkeley's vice chancellor Carol Christ wrote, "Today it is difficult to imagine life in a university where there are serious restrictions on the rights of political advocacy."[6]

Free speech gained protection in the last two decades of the twentieth century, during which the Supreme Court found "virtually all attempts to restrain speech in advance . . . unconstitutional," regardless of how hateful or disgusting the speech may seem to some.[7] In 1989, the Supreme Court defended the burning of the U.S. flag as a "**speech act**" protected by the First Amendment. In 1997, the Court struck down the highly controversial federal Communications Decency Act of 1996, which had imposed penalties for creating, transmitting, or receiving obscene material on the Internet. The Court ruled that "the interest in encouraging freedom of expression in a democratic society outweighs any theoretical but unproven benefit of censorship."[8]

Perhaps no test of free speech received more publicity than the sensational 1998 lawsuit brought by four Texas cattlemen against popular talk-show host Oprah Winfrey. In a show on "mad cow disease," Winfrey had declared that she would never eat another hamburger. Charging that her statement caused cattle prices to plummet, the cattlemen sued for damages; however, Winfrey's attorneys successfully argued that the case was an important test of free speech. Emerging from the courtroom after the verdict in her favor, Winfrey shouted, "My reaction is that free speech not only lives, it rocks!"[9]

One month after the September 11, 2001, terrorist attacks on the United States, the pendulum again swung toward restriction of free speech, with the passage of the Patriot Act, which broadened the investigative powers of government agencies. Not surprisingly, the Patriot Act has been roundly criticized by various civil-rights, free-speech, and publishing groups. One coalition of such groups describes the Patriot Act as "the latest in a long line of abuses of rights in times of conflict."[10]

speech act

A behavior, such as flag burning, that is viewed by law as nonverbal communication and is subject to the same protections and limitations as verbal speech

RECAP

History of Free Speech in the United States

1791	First Amendment guarantees that "Congress shall make no law . . . abridging the freedom of speech"
1798	Sedition Act is passed
1919	U.S. Supreme Court suggests that speech presenting a "clear and present danger" may be restricted
1920	American Civil Liberties Union is formed
1940	Congress declares it illegal to urge the violent overthrow of the federal government
1964	U.S. Supreme Court restricts definition of slander; Berkeley Free Speech Movement is born
1989	U.S. Supreme Court defends the burning of the U.S. flag as a "speech act"
1997	U.S. Supreme Court strikes down Communications Decency Act of 1996, in defense of free speech on the Internet
1998	Oprah Winfrey successfully defends her right to speak freely on television
2001	September 11 terrorist attacks spark passage of the Patriot Act and new debate over the balance between national security and free speech
2006	State of Montana pardons those convicted under the Montana Sedition Act of 1918

It is ironic that even as Americans debate the restrictions imposed by the Patriot Act, they recognize and offer restitution for historical infringement on free speech. In May 2006, Montana Governor Brian Schweitzer formally pardoned 78 late citizens of Montana who had been imprisoned or fined under the Montana Sedition Act of 1918, convictions that "violated basic American rights of speech. . . ."[11] There can be little doubt that in the months and years to come, the United States will continue to debate "the balance among national security, free speech, and patriotism."[12]

Speaking Ethically

As the boundaries of free speech expand, the importance of **ethical speech** increases. Although there is no definitive ethical creed for a public speaker, teachers and practitioners of public speaking generally agree that an ethical speaker is one who has a clear, responsible goal; uses sound evidence and reasoning; is sensitive to and tolerant of differences; is honest; and avoids plagiarism. In the discussion that follows, we offer suggestions for observing these ethical guidelines.

HAVE A CLEAR, RESPONSIBLE GOAL

The goal of a public speech should be clear to the audience. For example, if you are trying to convince the audience that your beliefs on abortion are more correct than those of others, you should say so at some point in your speech. If you keep your true agenda hidden, you violate your listeners' rights. In addition, an ethical goal should be socially responsible. A socially responsible goal is one that gives the listener choices, whereas an irresponsible, unethical goal is psychologically coercive. Adolf Hitler's speeches, which incited the German people to hatred and genocide, were coercive, as were those of Chinese leader Deng Xiaoping, who tried to intimidate Chinese citizens into revealing the whereabouts of leaders of the unsuccessful 1989 student uprising in Tiananmen Square.

If your overall objective is to inform or persuade, it is probably ethical; if your goal is to coerce or manipulate, it is unethical. But lawyers and ethicists do not always agree on this distinction. As we have pointed out, Congress and the U.S. Supreme Court have at times limited speech that incites sedition, violence, and riot, but they have also protected free speech rights "for both the ideas that people cherish and the thoughts they hate."[13] Even those who defend a broad legal right to free speech recognize that they are defending the right to unethical, as well as ethical, speech. For example, faculty, administrators, and regents of the University of Colorado have for years debated the case of ethnic studies professor Ward Churchill, who, immediately following the 2001 terrorist attacks, compared some of those who died at the World Trade Center to Holocaust architect Adolf Eichmann. Even as the university's president and the governor of Colorado recommended Churchill's dismissal, others staunchly defended his right to speak freely.[14]

USE SOUND EVIDENCE AND REASONING

Ethical speakers use critical-thinking skills such as analysis and evaluation to draw conclusions and formulate arguments. Unethical speakers substitute false claims and manipulation of emotion for evidence and logical arguments.

In the early 1950s, Wisconsin senator Joseph McCarthy incited national panic by charging that Communists were infiltrating every avenue of American life. Thousands of people came under suspicion, many losing jobs and careers because of the false accusations. Never able to substantiate his claims, McCarthy nevertheless succeeded in his witch-hunt by exaggerating and distorting the truth. One United Press

ethical speech
Speech that is responsible, honest, and tolerant

reporter noted, "The man just talked in circles. Everything was by inference, allusion, never a concrete statement of fact. Most of it didn't make sense."[15] Although today we recognize the flimsiness of McCarthy's accusations, in his time he wielded incredible power. Like Hitler, McCarthy knew how to manipulate emotions and fears to produce the results he wanted. It is sometimes tempting to resort to false claims to gain power over others, but it is always unethical to do so.

Some speakers bypass sound evidence and reasoning in order to make their conclusions more provocative. One contemporary rhetoric scholar offers the following example of such short-circuited reasoning:

> Let's say two people are observing who speaks in college classrooms and they come up with
> 1. Women are not as good at public speaking as men.
> 2. In college classes on coed campuses where most professors are male, women tend to talk less in class than men.[16]

The first conclusion, based on insufficient evidence, reinforces sexist stereotypes with an inflammatory overgeneralization. The second, more qualified conclusion is more ethical.

One last, but important, requirement for the ethical use of evidence and reasoning is to share with an audience all information that might help them reach a sound decision, including information that may be potentially damaging to your case. Even if you proceed to refute the opposing evidence and arguments, you have fulfilled your ethical responsibility by presenting the perspective of the other side. And you can actually make your own arguments more convincing by anticipating and answering counter-arguments and evidence.

BE SENSITIVE TO AND TOLERANT OF DIFFERENCES

> The filmmaker who ate nothing but McDonald's meals for his Oscar-nominated movie Super Size Me apologized for a profanity-laced, politically incorrect speech at a suburban Philadelphia school.
> Among other things, Morgan Spurlock joked about the intelligence of McDonald's employees and teachers smoking pot while he was speaking at Hatboro-Horsham High School. . . .
> Spurlock, 35, told The Philadelphia Inquirer in a telephone interview that he "didn't think of the audience" and could have chosen his words better.[17]

As we noted in Chapter 2, being audience-centered requires that you become as aware as possible of others' feelings, needs, interests, and backgrounds. Spurlock clearly violated this ethical principle in his remarks.

Sometimes called **accommodation**, sensitivity to differences does not mean that speakers must abandon their own convictions for those of their audience members. It does mean that speakers should demonstrate a willingness to listen to opposing viewpoints and learn about different beliefs and values. Such willingness not only communicates respect; it can also help a speaker to select a topic, formulate a purpose, and design strategies to motivate an audience.

Your authors are currently involved in an informal educational exchange with a professor from the St. Petersburg Cultural Institute in Russia, and we recently had a chance to visit the professor and her family in St. Petersburg. In talking with the professor's talented teenage daughter, we inquired about her plans after she finished her university education. Smiling at us in both amusement and amazement, she replied, "Americans are always planning what they are going to do several years in the future. In Russia, we do not plan beyond two or three weeks. Life is too uncertain here." Having gained this insight into Russian life, we know now that it would raise false hopes to attempt to motivate Russian audiences with promises of benefits far in the future.

accommodation
Sensitivity to the feelings, needs, interests, and backgrounds of other people

Our new understanding not only helps us see that speaking of immediate, deliverable rewards is a more realistic and ethical approach to communication with our Russian friends, but it has broader implications as well. DePaul University Communication Professor Kathy Fitzpatrick notes,

> *Our success in public diplomacy will turn on our ability to speak in ways that recognize and appreciate how [our audiences] will interpret our messages.*[18]

A speaker who is sensitive to differences also avoids language that might be interpreted as in any way biased or offensive. Although it may seem fairly simple and a matter of common sense to avoid overtly abusive language, it is not so easy to avoid language that discriminates more subtly. In Chapter 12, we look at some specific words and phrases that can be unintentionally offensive and that ethical speakers should avoid.

BE HONEST

Knowingly offering false or misleading information to an audience is an ethical violation. In 2003, President George W. Bush and members of his staff accepted responsibility for having told the public that Iraq was getting nuclear fuel from Africa, even after intelligence reports several months earlier had discredited the claim. In 1999, Toronto Blue Jays manager Tim Johnson was fired after it was revealed that the stories he had told to his team about his combat experiences in Vietnam were false. During the war, it turned out, he actually played ball while serving with the Reserves in California.[19] Perhaps most famously, in January 1998, then-President Bill Clinton's finger-wagging declaration that "I did not have sexual relations with that woman—Miss Lewinsky" was a serious breach of ethics that came back to haunt him. Many Americans were willing to forgive the inappropriate relationship; fewer could forgive the dishonesty.

A seeming exception to the dictum to avoid false information is the use of hypothetical illustrations—illustrations that never actually occurred but that might happen. Many speakers rely on such illustrations to clarify or enhance their speeches. As

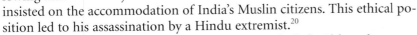

LEARNING FROM GREAT SPEAKERS

Mohandas Gandhi (1869–1948)

The great Indian spiritual and political leader Mohandas Gandhi guided the twentieth-century campaign for Indian independence from Britain. Even as Gandhi practiced free speech in the form of nonviolent protest, he accepted the responsibilities of ethical speech. His goal was clear; he accepted the consequences of his actions by allowing himself to be jailed several times; and he insisted on the accommodation of India's Muslin citizens. This ethical position led to his assassination by a Hindu extremist.[20]

An ethical speaker is true to his or her own beliefs. Although we encourage you to adapt your message to your audience, we don't recommend that you change your fundamental ethical principles just to avoid controversy. An effective and ethical audience-centered speaker maintains his or her core ethical beliefs while also considering the best strategies to make the message clear to his or her listeners.

[Photo: AP Images]

long as a speaker makes clear to the audience that the illustration is indeed hypothetical—for example, prefacing the illustration with a phrase such as "Imagine that . . ."—such use is ethical.

Honesty also requires that speakers give credit for ideas and information that are not their own. The *Publication Manual of the American Psychological Association* states that "an author does not present the work of another as if it were his or her own work. This can extend to ideas as well as written words."[21] Presenting the words and ideas of others without crediting them is called *plagiarism*. This ethical violation is both serious enough and widespread enough to warrant a separate discussion.

DON'T PLAGIARIZE

Most people are taught from earliest childhood that it is wrong to steal. Yet even those who would never think of stealing money or shoplifting may be tempted to **plagiarize**—to steal ideas. Perhaps you can remember copying a grade-school report directly from the encyclopedia, or maybe you've even purchased or "borrowed" a paper to submit for an assignment in high school or college. These are obvious forms of plagiarism. A less obvious form is **plagiaphrasing**—lacing a speech with compelling phrases you find in a source that you do not credit. Whether your lapse is intentional or due merely to careless or hasty note taking, it is a serious offense. Yet the Center for Academic Integrity reports that 75 percent of college students admit to having cheated at least once.[22] The Educational Testing Service has found that one Web site offering free term papers gets some 80,000 hits per day. And communication researcher Todd Holm reports that more than 50 percent of 300 students surveyed reported cheating in some way in a public speaking class.[23]

Most colleges impose stiff penalties on students who plagiarize. Plagiarists almost always fail the assignment in question, frequently fail the course, and are sometimes put on academic probation or even expelled. Penalties for plagiarism outside the classroom are severe as well, costing one U.S. senator his bid for the Democratic nomination for president. In August 1987, Delaware Senator Joseph Biden plagiarized the words of former British Labor Party Leader Neil Kinnock, in a speech in Des Moines, Iowa. When the plagiarism was exposed, along with evidence of a previous plagiarism from a speech by Robert Kennedy, Biden was forced to withdraw from the presidential race. The transgression would continue to shadow Biden during his bid for the 2008 presidential nomination. Even while praising Biden's performance in an early debate among the candidates, one political analyst noted, "You can see a glimpse of what made him such a star 20 years ago . . . before he got in trouble."[24] Publicized evidence of plagiarism also haunted Hamilton College (New York) President Eugene Tobin, who in September 2002 delivered to the college's freshman class a convocation speech that was later discovered to have been plagiarized from Amazon.com. And more recently, a New Jersey school superintendent found her job on the line after she addressed National Honor Society inductees with a speech taken from a Web site on how to speak in public. Biden, Tobin, and the superintendent violated their ethical responsibilities and paid the price for that violation with their reputations and careers.

DO YOUR OWN WORK The most flagrant cases of plagiarism result from not doing your own work. For example, while you are poking around the library for ideas to use in a speech assignment, you may discover an entire speech or perhaps an article that could easily be made into a speech. However tempting it may be to use this material, and however certain you are that no audience member could possibly have seen it, resist the urge to plagiarize. First, you will be doing yourself a disservice if you do not learn how to compose a speech on your own. After all, you are in college to acquire new skills. In addition, the risk may be much greater than you suspect.

A few years ago, one of your authors heard an excellent student speech on the importance of detecting cancer early. The only problem was, she heard the same speech again in the following class period! On finding the "speech"—actually a *Reader's Digest* article that was several years old—both students were certain that they had discovered a surefire shortcut to an A. Instead, they failed the assignment, ruined their

plagiarize
To present someone else's words or ideas as though they were one's own

plagiaphrasing
Failing to give credit for compelling phrases taken from another source

course grades, and lost your author's trust. The consequences of academic plagiarism can be even more dire, including expulsion in many schools.

Another way speakers sometimes attempt to shortcut the speech preparation task is to ask another person to edit a speech so extensively that it becomes more that other person's work than their own. This is another form of plagiarism, as well as another way of cheating themselves out of the skills they need to develop.

ACKNOWLEDGE YOUR SOURCES Our admonition to do your own work in no way suggests that you should not research your speeches and then share the results with audience members. In fact, as we have said, an ethical speaker is responsible for doing just that. Furthermore, some information is so widely known that you do not have to acknowledge a source for it. For example, you need not credit a source if you say that a person must be infected with the HIV virus in order to develop AIDS, or that the Treaty of Versailles was signed on June 28, 1919. This information is widely available in a variety of reference sources. However, if you decide to use any of the following in your speech, you must give credit to the source:

- Direct quotations, even if they are only brief phrases
- Opinions, assertions, or ideas of others, even if you paraphrase them rather than quote them verbatim
- Statistics
- Any nonoriginal visual materials, including graphs, tables, and pictures

To be able to acknowledge your sources, you must first practice careful and systematic note-taking. Indicate with quotation marks any phrases or sentences that you photocopy or copy by hand verbatim from a source, and be sure to record the author, title, publisher or Web site, publication date, and page numbers for all sources from which you take quotations, ideas, statistics, or visual materials. Additional suggestions for systematic note-taking are offered in Chapter 7.

In addition to keeping careful records of your sources, you must also know how to cite sources for your audience, both orally and in writing. Perhaps you have heard a speaker say, "Quote," while holding up both hands with index and middle fingers curved to indicate quotation marks. This is an artificial and distracting way to cite a source; an **oral citation** can be integrated more smoothly into a speech.

For example, you might use the approach illustrated in the sample oral citation below. The publication date and author of a source are usually sufficient information for an oral citation. In the example, the speaker also mentions the type of resource (online article) and the title of the fact sheet ("Compendium of Animal Rabies Prevention and Control, 2007"). Follow your instructor's preferences for the level of detail to include in your oral citations. Note that when you include an oral citation in a speech, the beginning and end of the quoted passage are indicated by pauses. The sample preparation outline in Chapter 11 gives additional examples of oral citations.

You can also provide a **written citation** for a source. In fact, your public-speaking instructor may ask you to provide a bibliography of sources along with the outline or other written materials he or she requires for each speech. Instructors who require a bibliography will usually specify the format in which they want the citations; if they do not, you can use a style guide such as that published by the MLA (Modern Language Association) or the APA (American Psychological Association), both of which are available online as well as in traditional print format. Here is an example of a written citation in MLA format for the source cited orally in the earlier example. Notice that the citation provides two dates: the date the material was posted online and the date it was accessed by the researcher. If you are unable to find the date the material was posted—or any other single element of information—proceed directly to the next item in the citation.

National Association of State Public Health Veterinarians. 27 December 2006. "Compendium of Animal Rabies Prevention and Control, 2007." 28 November 2007 <www.nasphv.org/Documents/RabiesCompendium.pdf>.

oral citation
The oral presentation of such information about a source as the author, title, and year of publication

written citation
The written presentation of such information about a source as the author, title, and year of publication, usually formatted according to a conventional style guide

In a December 2006 online article entitled "Compendium of Animal Rabies Prevention and Control, 2007," the National Association of State Public Health Veterinarians describes rabies as

"a fatal viral zoonosis and a serious public health problem. The disease is an acute progressive encephalitis caused by a lyssavirus."

◀ Provide the date.
◀ Specify the type of resource.
◀ Give the title.

◀ Provide the author or source.

◀ Pause briefly to signal that you are about to begin quoting.
◀ Quote the source.

◀ Pause again to indicate that you are ending the quoted passage.

Additional information about citing sources and preparing a bibliography can be found in Chapter 7.

Perhaps now you are thinking, "What about those 'gray areas,' those times when I am not certain whether information or ideas I am presenting are common knowledge?" A good rule is this: When in doubt, document. You will never be guilty of plagiarism if you document something you didn't need to, but you could be committing plagiarism if you do not document something you really should have.

Listening Ethically

Until now, we have been focusing primarily on the ethical exercise of free speech by the speaker. But audience members also share responsibility for ethical communication. In the fourth century B.C., Aristotle warned, "Let men be on their guard against those who flatter and mislead the multitude." And contemporary rhetorician Harold Barrett has said that the audience is the "necessary source of correction" for the behavior of a speaker.[25] The following guidelines for ethical listening incorporate what Barrett calls "attributes of the good audience."

RECAP  Speaker Ethics

THE ETHICAL PUBLIC SPEAKER . . .

Has a clear, responsible goal

Uses sound evidence and reasoning

Is sensitive to and tolerant of differences

Is honest

Doesn't plagiarize

Communicate Your Expectations and Feedback

As an audience member, you have the right—even the responsibility—to enter a communication situation with expectations about both the message and how the speaker will deliver it. Know what information and ideas you want to get out of the communication transaction. Expect a coherent, organized, and competently delivered presentation. Communicate your objectives and react to the speaker's message and delivery through appropriate nonverbal and verbal feedback. For example, maintain eye contact with the speaker. Nod in agreement when you support something the speaker says; look puzzled if you do not understand the speaker's point. Turn your head to one side and tilt it slightly forward to communicate that you are having trouble hearing. If a question-and-answer period follows the speech, ask questions you may still have about the speaker's topic or point of view.

Perhaps no public-speaking situation better illustrates the effectiveness of audience feedback than the traditional African American sermon, during which the congregation's willingness to "finish the preacher's sentence, shout encouragement or warn the preacher that he's wandered off the point . . . lets a preacher know whether he is misfiring or connecting from the pulpit."[26] Although such outspokenness is not appropriate to many public-speaking settings, the African American congregation's enthusiastic involvement is a good example of how listener feedback can affect the communication process.

Be Sensitive to and Tolerant of Differences

We have already discussed the importance of being a sensitive and tolerant speaker. But it is equally important for you to exercise social and cultural awareness and tolerance as a member of the audience. For example, suppose you were to attend a high-school baccalaureate ceremony at which the speaker was a dynamic African American minister used to the duet-style preaching described in the preceding section. If you were to dismiss the minister's delivery as too flamboyant, you might miss out on a powerful message.

Listeners share speakers' responsibility for maintaining high ethical standards for public speech. If a speaker is spewing messages filled with hatred and bias—or simply hiding or distorting information—don't hesitate to communicate your disapproval by frowning, looking away, or even walking out.

[Photo: David Butow/SABA/Corbis]

Understanding diverse cultural norms can sometimes pose quite a complex ethical-listening challenge. For example, Jesse Jackson has in the past been accused of making dishonest claims in some of his speeches about his background and behavior. He has said that he left the University of Illinois because of racism on the football team, which caused him to be passed over for starting quarterback—yet former teammates insist that he did not become starting quarterback simply because he was not the strongest player. Jackson has also overstated the poverty he experienced as a child, when in fact he grew up in a fairly comfortable middle-class home. Although many have criticized such exaggeration, at least one communication researcher has defended Jackson, arguing that although his "tall tales" are not necessarily "the truth" in a strictly objective sense, they are part of a valid African American oral tradition that focuses on the "symbolic import of the story" and in which speakers traditionally exaggerate to enhance the impact of their illustrations.[27]

Be attentive and courteous. Consider diverse cultural norms and audience expectations as part of the context within which you listen to and evaluate the speaker. Making an effort to understand the needs, goals, and interests of both the speaker and other audience members can help you judge how to react appropriately and ethically as a listener.

LISTEN CRITICALLY

Courtesy and tolerance are not the same as approval or agreement. In fact, the necessary check on free speech is the listener who recognizes and refuses to license abusive or dangerous ideas or plans. As University of Chicago professor and ethicist Richard M. Weaver explains, "It is the principle of our society that we can listen to propaganda

RECAP

Listener Ethics

THE ETHICAL LISTENER . . .

Communicates expectations and feedback

Is sensitive to and tolerant of differences

Listens critically

from all the special interests . . . and do a pretty fair job of sifting the true claims from the false."[28] In other words, it is the audience members' job to listen critically.

To listen critically is to hold a speaker to his or her ethical responsibilities. Is the speaker presenting both sides of the issue? Is the speaker disclosing all the information to which he or she has access, or is the speaker trying to hide something? Is the speaker being honest about the purpose of the speech? As already noted, you can communicate to the speaker through nonverbal feedback during a speech. Frowning, shaking your head, or looking away can signal to the speaker that you do not approve of his or her message. If there is a chance that you may have misunderstood the speaker, take advantage of opportunities after the speech to question him or her. Read more about the topic for yourself, to check the speaker's facts. And if you conclude that the speaker's message or motives are indeed unethical, discuss your opinion with others, and seek out or create a forum through which you can express your dissent. Although you can and should refuse to sanction unethical messages and tactics, seek ways to question and refute ideas and arguments without being discourteous or resorting to unethical tactics yourself. In Chapter 4 we provide further discussion of strategies for skillful listening.

confidently connecting with your audience

Remember That You Will Look More Confident Than You May Feel

As you listen to other people presenting speeches, note that most speakers don't appear to be nervous. This means that when you deliver your presentation, your listeners will not know that *you* may feel nervous. So don't think that people will be focusing on your anxiety when you speak. You may feel some apprehension, but unless you tell your audience that you're nervous, it's unlikely that they will know it.

SUMMARY

Ethical speaking and listening are very important in a society that protects free speech. Although Congress and the courts have occasionally limited free speech by law and policy, more often they have protected and broadened its application. The right to free speech has also been upheld by such organizations as the American Civil Liberties Union and by colleges and universities.

Speakers who exercise their right to free speech are responsible for tempering what they say by applying ethics, or moral principles and values. Although there is no definitive standard of ethics, most people agree that public speakers must be responsible, honest, and tolerant in order to be ethical.

Plagiarism is one of the most common violations of speech ethics. You can usually avoid plagiarizing by understanding what it is, doing your own work, and acknowledging the sources for any quotations, ideas, statistics, or visual materials you use in a speech.

Ethical listeners should provide feedback; be sensitive to and tolerant of differences; and listen critically, refusing to sanction unethical messages and tactics.

BEING AUDIENCE-CENTERED: A SHARPER FOCUS

CONSIDERING YOUR AUDIENCE

- Ethical public speaking is inherently audience-centered, always taking into account the needs and rights of the listeners.

- The goal of a speech should be clear to the audience. If you keep your true agenda hidden, you violate your listeners' rights.

- A socially responsible goal for a speech is one that gives the listener choices, whereas an irresponsible, unethical goal is psychologically coercive.

- An important requirement for the ethical use of evidence and reasoning is to share with an audience all information that might help them reach a sound decision, including information that may be potentially damaging to your case.

- Cite your sources for your audience, either orally or in writing, or both.

CONSIDERING AUDIENCE DIVERSITY

◆ Accommodation, or sensitivity to differences, leads speakers to demonstrate a willingness to listen to opposing viewpoints and learn about different beliefs and values.

◆ A speaker who is sensitive to differences avoids language that might be interpreted as in any way biased or offensive.

◆ The African American congregation's enthusiastic involvement in a sermon is a good example of how listener feedback can affect the communication process.

CRITICAL THINKING QUESTIONS

1. Explain how ethical behavior serves as a balance to free speech.

2. Why do you think the U.S. Supreme Court has historically considered flag burning and pornography to be "free speech acts"?

3. The following passage comes from a book entitled *Abraham Lincoln, Public Speaker*, by Waldo W. Braden:

    The Second Inaugural Address, sometimes called Lincoln's Sermon on the Mount, was a concise, tightly constructed composition that did not waste words on ceremonial niceties or superficial sentiment. The shortest Presidential inaugural address up to that time, it was only 700 words long, compared to 3,700 words for the First, and required from 5 to 7 minutes to deliver.[29]

    Which of the following statements should be credited to Braden if you were to use them in a speech?

    "Lincoln's second inaugural address is sometimes called Lincoln's Sermon on the Mount."

    "Because he was elected and sworn in for two terms as president, Abraham Lincoln prepared and delivered two inaugural addresses."

    "Lincoln's second inaugural address was 700 words and 5 to 7 minutes long."

ETHICAL QUESTIONS

1. From at least the time of Franklin Delano Roosevelt, speechwriters have written many of the best speeches made by U.S. presidents, including Ronald Reagan's eulogy for the astronauts of the space shuttle *Challenger* in 1986 and George W. Bush's speech to Congress and the nation following the September 11 terrorist attacks. Is such use of speechwriters ethical? Is it ethical to give credit to the presidents for memorable lines from speeches written by professional speechwriters?

2. In the fall of 2006, CBS News introduced an evening news feature entitled "Free Speech." On October 2, 2006, the day when five Amish children were murdered in a schoolhouse in Lancaster County, Pennsylvania, the father of a student killed seven years earlier at Columbine High School spoke during the "Free Speech" feature, blaming the Pennsylvania tragedy on the teaching of evolution and on abortion. Criticizing the controversial segment, one correspondent noted, "There's a difference between free speech and responsible speech."[30] Which should have taken precedence: the father's freedom of speech or CBS's ethical responsibility to its viewers?

Avoiding Plagiarism

After you have developed your speech outline and are preparing your speaking notes, use the following questions to make certain that you are properly and ethically giving credit for the ideas, opinions, images, and words of others.

1. Am I using ideas and sources that are not my own? Specifically, am I using
   - a direct quotation?
   - someone else's idea or opinion, even if I'm paraphrasing the idea or opinion rather than directly quoting the information?
   - a statistic?
   - a nonoriginal visual aid, graph, table, or picture?

2. Have I provided the appropriate oral citation of ideas, images, and words that are not my own? A proper oral citation includes the following:
   - date of the source
   - type of source (for example, a book, an article, a Web site)
   - title of the source
   - author of the source

3. When quoting material from a source, am I clearly indicating with my delivery when the quotation begins and ends?
   - Pause briefly before you begin quoting.
   - Read the quotation.
   - Pause briefly at the end of the quote.

Sir Joshua Reynolds (1723–1792). *Self-Portrait as a Deaf Man*, 1775. Tate London/Art Resource, N.Y.

Learn how to listen and you will prosper—even from those who talk badly.

—PLUTARCH

Listening to Speeches

outline

objectives

After studying this chapter you should be able to do the following:

1. Identify the stages in the listening process.

2. List and describe five barriers to effective listening.

3. Discuss strategies for becoming a better listener.

4. Identify strategies for improving your note-taking skills.

5. Discuss the relationship between listening and critical thinking.

6. Use criteria for evaluating speeches.

A re you a good listener? Considerable evidence suggests that your listening skills could be improved. Within twenty-four hours after listening to a lecture or speech, you will recall only about 50 percent of the message. Forty-eight hours later, you are above average if you remember more than 25 percent of the message.

A psychology professor had dedicated his life to teaching and worked hard to prepare interesting lectures, yet he found his students sitting through his talks with glassy-eyed expressions.[1] To learn what was wrong, and also find out what was on his students' minds if they were not focusing on psychology, he would, without warning, fire a blank from a gun and then ask his students to record their thoughts at the instant they heard the shot. Here is what he found:

20 percent were pursuing erotic thoughts or sexual fantasies.

20 percent were reminiscing about something (they weren't sure what they were thinking about).

20 percent were worrying about something or thinking about lunch.

8 percent were pursuing religious thoughts.

20 percent were reportedly listening.

12 percent were able to recall what the professor was talking about when the gun fired.

You hear more than one billion words each year. Yet how much information do you retain? In this chapter, we are going to focus on improving your listening skills. If you apply the principles and suggestions we offer, we believe you will become not only a better listener but also a better public speaker. In addition, improving your listening skills will strengthen your ability to think critically and evaluate what you hear and enhance your listening in one-on-one interpersonal interactions. In this chapter, we will discuss how people listen and identify barriers and pitfalls that keep both speakers and audiences from listening effectively. We will also make some suggestions for improving your listening and note-taking skills. Finally, we will discuss how you can enhance your ability to listen critically and evaluate speeches.

Barriers to Effective Listening

L istening barriers are created when we fail to select, attend to, or understand a message, or remember what was said. To **select** a sound is to single out a message from several competing messages. A listener has many competing messages to sort through, including personal thoughts. Your job as a public speaker is to develop a message that motivates your listeners to focus on *your* message.

The sequel to selecting is attending. To **attend** to a sound is to focus on it. Most people's average attention span while listening to someone talk is about 8 seconds.[2]

select
To single out a message from several competing messages

attend
To focus on incoming information for further processing

Listening to Speeches

One of your key challenges as a public speaker is to capture and hold the attention of your audience. Your choice of supporting material is often the key to gaining and maintaining attention; we'll talk much more about strategies for gathering and using supporting material in the chapters ahead.

Boiled down to its essence, *communication* is the process of making sense out of the world and sharing that sense with others.[3] *Understanding* is the process of making sense out of our experiences. To **understand** something, people assign meaning to the information that comes their way. Although no single theory explains how people make sense of words, we do know that you understand what you hear by relating it to something you have already seen or heard. As a speaker, your job is to facilitate listener understanding by making sure you clearly explain your ideas in terms and images to which your listeners can relate. Again, the challenge of being understood comes back to a focus on the audience.

The final stage in the listening process is *remembering*. To **remember** is to recall ideas and information. Most listening experts believe that the main way to determine if audience members have been listening is to determine what they remember. Your geography professor determines how well you understand geography by testing you on the content of his or her lecture. But intentionally or not, the professor is testing your listening skill as well as your knowledge of geography.

Your goal as a public speaker is to develop and deliver a speech that audience members will listen and respond to. The more you know about potential obstacles that keep your listeners from listening, the better able you will be to develop messages that hold their interest. Let's look at specific barriers that keep listeners from selecting, attending to, understanding, and remembering a message; we'll also suggest how you can overcome these barriers, both as a speaker and as an audience member.

INFORMATION OVERLOAD

We all spend a large part of each day listening. That's good news and bad news. The good news is that because we listen a lot, we have the potential to become very effective listeners. The bad news is that instead of getting better at it, we often "tune out," because we hear so much information that we get tired of listening.

There are things you can do to help manage the barrier of information overload, both as a public speaker—to help your audience listen to your message—and as a listener.

What you can do as a speaker. You can keep your audience from tuning out by making sure your speech has a good balance between new information and supporting material, such as stories and examples. A speech that is too dense—chock-full of facts, new definitions, and undeveloped ideas—can make listening a tedious process. On the other hand, listeners don't want to listen to a bare-bones outline of ideas: They need ideas that are fleshed out with illustrations. Pace the flow of new ideas and information. Communication expert Frank E. X. Dance recommends a 30/70 balance: 30 percent of your speaking time should be spent presenting new ideas and information, and 70 percent of your time should be spent supporting the ideas with vivid examples and interesting stories.[4]

Another way to combat information overload as a speaker is to build redundancy into your message. If listeners miss the idea the first time you present it, perhaps they will catch it during your concluding summary. Repeating key ideas can be part of that 70 percent of your message that extends the new information you present.

What you can do as a listener. If you find yourself tuning a speaker out because you're just tired of listening to someone talk, make a special effort to concentrate on the information you're hearing. The key to being a good listener is to recognize when you're *not* being a good listener and then adjust to how you are listening. Making sure that you are looking at the speaker, sitting up straight, and remaining focused on the message can help perk up your listening power.

understand
To assign meaning to the information to which you attend

remember
To recall ideas and information

PERSONAL CONCERNS

You are sitting in your African history class on a Friday afternoon. It's a beautiful day. You slump into your seat, open your notebook, and prepare to take notes on the lecture. As the professor talks about an upcoming assignment, you begin to think about how you are going to spend your Saturday. One thought leads to another as you mentally plan your weekend. Suddenly you hear your professor say, "For Monday's test, you will be expected to know the principles I've just reviewed." What principles? What test? You were present in class, and you did *hear* the professor's lecture, but you're not sure what was said.

Your own thoughts are among the biggest competitors for your attention when you are a member of an audience. Most of us would rather listen to our own inner speech than to the message of a public speaker. As the psychology professor with the gun found, sex, lunch, worries, and daydreams are major distractions for the majority of listeners.

What you can do as a speaker. To counteract the problem of listeners focusing on their personal concerns instead of your message, consciously work to maintain your audience's attention by using occasional "wake-up" messages such as "Now listen carefully because this will affect your future grade (or family, or employment)." Delivering your message effectively by using good eye contact, speaking with appropriate volume and vocal variation, and using appropriate gestures for emphasis can also help keep listeners listening.

What you can do as a listener. To stay focused, it's important that you stop the mental conversation you're having with yourself about ideas unrelated to the speaker's message. Be aware of thoughts, worries, and daydreams that are competing for your attention. Then, once you are aware that you are off task, return your attention to what the speaker is saying.

OUTSIDE DISTRACTIONS

While sitting in class, you notice that a fluorescent light is flickering overhead. Two classmates behind you are swapping stories about their favorite soap opera plots. Out the window you see a varsity football hero struggling to break into his car to retrieve the keys he left in the ignition. As your history professor drones on about the Bay of Pigs invasion, you find it difficult to focus on his lecture. Most of us don't listen well when physical distractions are competing with the speaker.

What you can do as a speaker. To minimize distractions, be aware of anything that might sidetrack your listeners' attention. For example, look at the way the room is arranged. Are the chairs arranged to allow listeners a clear view of you and any presentation aids you might be using? Is there distracting or irrelevant information written on a chalkboard or whiteboard? Try to empathize with listeners by imagining what they will be looking at when you speak. Check out the room ahead of time, sit where your audience will be seated, and look for possible distractions. Then reduce or eliminate distractions (such as by closing windows or lowering shades to limit visual and auditory distractions or turning off blinking fluorescent lights, if you can). Also, tactfully discourage whispering in the audience.

What you can do as a listener. When listening, you too can help manage the speaking and listening environment by being on the lookout for distractions or potential distractions. If you must, move to another seat if people near you are talking or a rude cell phone user continues a phone conversation. If the speaker has failed to monitor the listening environment, you may need to close the blinds, turn up the heat, turn off the lights, close the door, or do whatever is necessary to minimize distractions.

PREJUDICE

Your buddy is a staunch Democrat. He rarely credits a Republican with any useful ideas. So it's not surprising that when the Republican governor of your state makes a major televised speech outlining suggestions for improving the state's sagging economy, your friend finds the presentation ludicrous. As the speech is broadcast, your buddy constantly argues against each suggestion, mumbling comments about Republicans, business interests, and robbing the poor. The next day he is surprised to see editorials in the press praising the governor's speech. "Did they hear the same speech I did?" your friend wonders. Yes, they heard the same speech, but they listened differently. When you prejudge a message, your ability to understand it decreases.

A speaker facing a hostile audience should use arguments and evidence that will show that he or she is credible.

[Photo: Marilu Lopez-Fretts/Syracuse Newspapers/ The Image Works]

Another way to prejudge a speech is to decide that the topic has little value for you before you even hear the message. Most of us at one time or another have not given our full attention to a speech because we decided beforehand that it was going to bore us.

Sometimes we make snap judgments about a speaker based on his or her appearance and then fail to listen because we dismissed his or her ideas in advance as inconsequential or irrelevant. Female speakers often complain that males in the audience do not listen to them as attentively as they would to another male; members of ethnic and racial minorities may feel slighted in a similar way.

On the flip side, some people too readily accept what someone says just because they like the way the person looks, sounds, or dresses. For example, Tex believes that anyone with a Texas drawl must be an honest person. Such positive prejudices can also inhibit your ability to listen accurately to a message.

What you can do as a speaker. To keep your listeners from making inaccurate snap judgments based on **prejudice**, do your best to get your audience's attention at the beginning of your message. Make sure you're not using examples, words, or phrases that could be misinterpreted. Keep your message focused on your listeners' interests, needs, hopes, and wishes.

When addressing an audience that may be critical of or hostile toward your message, use detailed arguments and credible evidence. If you think audience members are likely to disagree with you, strong emotional appeals will be less successful than careful language, sound reasoning, and convincing evidence.

What you can do as a listener. One of the major problems with being prejudiced is being unaware of one's preconceived notions. Guard against becoming so critical of a message that you don't listen to it or so impressed that you decide too quickly that the speaker is trustworthy without carefully examining the evidence the speaker is using. As best you can, keep your focus on the message rather than on the messenger.

DIFFERENCES BETWEEN SPEECH RATE AND THOUGHT RATE

Ralph Nichols, a pioneer in listening research and training, has identified a listening problem that centers on the way you process the words you hear.[5] Most people talk at a rate of 125 words a minute. But you have the ability to listen to up to 700 words a minute; some studies suggest that you may be able to listen to 1,200 words a minute! Regardless of the exact numbers, you have the ability to process words much faster than you generally need to. The problem is that the difference gives you time to ignore a speaker periodically. Eventually, you stop listening. Your "extra" time allows you to daydream and drift from the message.

Nichols suggests that the different rates of speech and thought need not be a listening liability. Instead of drifting away from the speech, you can enhance your

prejudice
Preconceived opinions, attitudes, and beliefs about a person, place, thing, or message

listening effectiveness by mentally summarizing from time to time what the speaker is saying.

What you can do as a speaker. Be aware of your listeners' tendency to stop paying attention. If they can process your message much faster than you can say it, you need to build in message redundancy, use clear transitions, be well organized, and make your major ideas clear. Just talking faster won't do much good. Even if you could speak as fast as 200 words a minute, your listeners would still want to go about four times faster than that. So develop a well-structured message that uses appropriate internal summaries to help your listeners catch your message even if they've tuned out for a bit here and there.

What you can do as a listener. Because you have the ability to think much faster than people speak, you can use that dazzling mental power to stay focused on the message. Here's a powerful technique: Periodically making a mental summary of what a speaker is saying can dramatically increase your ability to remember the information. The difference in speech rate and thought rate gives you time to sprinkle in several mental summaries when listening to a message.

RECEIVER APPREHENSION

You already know about speaker apprehension, or the fear of speaking to others, but did you know that some people may be fearful of *listening* to information? Re-

RECAP

Barriers to Effective Listening

BARRIER	LISTENER'S TASKS	SPEAKER'S TASKS
Information overload	Concentrate harder on the message; identify the most important parts of the message.	Develop a message that is clear and easy to understand. Use interesting supporting material. Build in redundancy.
Personal concerns	Focus on the speaker's message rather than on your own self-talk.	Use attention-holding strategies and "wake-up" messages.
Outside distractions	Assertively attempt to control the listening environment.	Monitor the physical arrangements before you begin your speech. Take action by doing such things as closing the shades if there are distractions outside, or turning up the air-conditioner if it's too warm.
Prejudice	Focus on the message, not on the messenger.	Use strong opening statements that focus on listeners' interests.
Differences between speech rate and thought rate	Mentally summarize the speaker's message while you listen.	Build in redundancy. Be well organized and use strategies to maintain your listeners' attention throughout your speech.
Receiver apprehension	Make an audio recording of the speaker, mentally summarize the message, and take well-organized notes.	Provide a clear preview statement of your major ideas, use appropriate internal summaries, summarize major ideas at the end of your message, and use appropriate reinforcing presentation aids during your talk.

searchers have discovered a listening barrier called receiver apprehension. **Receiver apprehension** is fear of misunderstanding or misinterpreting, or of not being able to adjust psychologically to, messages spoken by others.[6] Some people are just uncomfortable or nervous about hearing new information; their major worry is that they won't be able to understand the message. If you are one of those people, you may have difficulty understanding all you hear because your anxiety about listening creates "noise" that may interfere with how much information you comprehend.

What you can do as a speaker. Be mindful that some listeners may be anxious about understanding your message. You can help people with receiver apprehension by being more redundant. Offer clear preview statements that give an overview of your main ideas. Include appropriate summaries while you're making transitions from one point to the next. Summarize major ideas at the end of your talk.[7] Using presentation aids to summarize key ideas visually—such as by listing major points on an overhead transparency, PowerPoint slide, chalkboard, or flipchart—can also help increase comprehension and decrease receiver apprehension.

What you can do as a listener. If you experience receiver apprehension, you will have to work harder to comprehend the information presented by others. Using a tape recorder to record a lecture may help you feel more comfortable and less anxious about trying to remember each point made by the speaker.[8] Another strategy to overcome this barrier is to summarize mentally what you hear a speaker saying during a speech. Taking accurate notes is an active strategy that can also help you feel more comfortable about being a listener.

How to Become a Better Listener

ow that we have examined barriers to effective listening and suggested a few strategies to overcome those barriers and be both a better speaker and a better listener, we offer a basketful of additional strategies for improving your listening skill. Specifically, we'll help you listen with your eyes. We'll help you be a mindful listener. And finally, we will note specific behaviors that can help you listen skillfully.

LISTEN WITH YOUR EYES AS WELL AS YOUR EARS

To listen with your eyes is to be attuned to the unspoken cues of a speaker. Nonverbal cues play a major role in communicating a message. One expert has estimated that as much as 93 percent of the emotional content of a speech is conveyed by nonverbal cues.[9] Even though this statistic does not apply in every situation, emotion is primarily communicated by unspoken messages. To "listen with your eyes," you need to accurately interpret what you see while ensuring that you don't allow yourself to be distracted by it, even if a speaker has poor delivery.

ACCURATELY INTERPRET NONVERBAL MESSAGES Because the nonverbal message plays such a powerful role in affecting how you respond to a speaker, it's important to accurately interpret what a speaker is expressing nonverbally. A speaker's facial expressions will help you identify the emotions being communicated; a speaker's posture and gestures often reinforce the intensity of the specific emotion expressed.[10] If you have trouble understanding a speaker because he or she speaks too softly or speaks in an unfamiliar dialect, get close enough so that you can see the speaker's mouth. A good view can increase your level of attention and improve your understanding.

To increase your skill in accurately interpreting nonverbal messages, consider the following suggestions:

receiver apprehension
The fear of misunderstanding or misinterpreting the spoken messages of others

- *Consider nonverbal cues in context.* Don't just focus on one nonverbal cue, consider the situation you and the speaker are in when interpreting an unspoken message.
- *Look for clusters of cues.* Instead of focusing on just one bit of behavior, look for several nonverbal cues to increase the accuracy of your interpretation of a speaker's message.
- *Look for cues that communicate liking, power, and responsiveness.* A nonverbal cue (eye contact, facial expression, body orientation) can often express whether someone likes us. We note people's degree of power or influence over us by the way they dress, how much space they have around them, or whether they are relaxed or tense. (People who perceive themselves as having more power than those around them are usually more relaxed.) Or we can observe whether someone is interested or focused on us by eye contact, head nods, facial expressions, and tone of voice.

ADAPT TO THE SPEAKER'S DELIVERY Good listeners focus on a speaker's message, not on his or her delivery style. To be a good listener, you must adapt to the particular idiosyncrasies some speakers have. You may have to ignore or overlook a speaker's tendency to mumble, speak in a monotone, or fail to make eye contact. Perhaps more difficult still, you may even have to forgive a speaker's lack of clarity or coherence. Rather than mentally criticizing an unpolished speaker, you may need to be sympathetic and try harder to concentrate on the message. Good listeners focus on the message, not the messenger.

Poor speakers are not the only challenge to good listening. You also need to guard against glib, well-polished speakers. Just because a speaker has an attractive style of delivery does not necessarily mean that his or her message is credible. Don't let a smooth-talking salesperson convince you to buy something without carefully considering the content of his or her message.

Listen Mindfully

To be a mindful listener is to be aware of what you are doing when listening to others. The unmindful listener is not conscious of whether he or she is paying attention or daydreaming. Skilled listeners are mentally focused on the listening task. How do you do that? Here are some specific strategies to help you be a mindful listener.

MONITOR YOUR EMOTIONAL REACTION TO A MESSAGE Heightened emotions can affect your ability to understand a message. If you become angry at a word or phrase a speaker uses, your listening comprehension decreases. Depending on their cultural backgrounds, religious convictions, and political views, listeners may become emotionally aroused by certain words. For most listeners, words that connote negative opinions about their ethnic origin, nationality, or religious views can trigger strong emotions. Cursing and obscene language are red flags for other listeners.

Yin Ping is an Asian American who has distinguished himself as a champion debater on the college debate team. One sly member of an opposing team sought to distract him by quoting a bigoted statement that disparaged Asian Americans for "taking over the country." It was tempting for Yin Ping to respond emotionally to the insult, but he kept his wits, refuted the argument, and went on to win the debate. When someone uses a word or phrase you find offensive, it's important to overcome your repugnance and continue to listen. Don't let a speaker's language close down your mind.

How can you keep your emotions in check when you hear something that sets you off? First, recognize when your emotional state is affecting your rational thoughts. Second, use the skill of self-talk to calm yourself down. Say to yourself, "I'm not going to let this anger get in the way of listening and understanding." You can also focus on your breathing for a moment to calm down.

AVOID JUMPING TO CONCLUSIONS "Not another speech about religion," you groan to yourself as your classmate, Frank Fuller, a divinity student, gets up to speak. "He's always preaching to us." As Fuller begins his PowerPoint lecture, you slump down in your seat, prepared to be bored and bothered. Sure enough, his opening line is "The Bible: It's not what you think!" But about halfway through the speech, you start listening to Fuller and realize that he is presenting some fascinating historical evidence connected with Noah's Ark. He's not trying to convert you; he's just describing some of the archaeological evidence related to one of the stories in the Bible. At the end of the speech, your classmates give him a hearty round of applause. Now you're sorry you missed the first part of the speech.

Don't jump to conclusions prematurely. Give a speaker time to develop and support his or her main point before you decide whether you agree or disagree or whether the message has any value. As we've already noted, if you mentally criticize a speaker's style or message, your listening efficiency will decline.

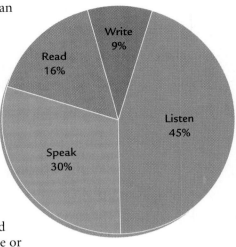

Figure 4.1 *What you do with your communication time*

BE A SELFISH LISTENER Although it may sound like a crass suggestion, being a selfish listener can help you maintain your powers of concentration. If you find your attention waning, ask yourself questions such as "What's in it for me?" and "How can I use information from this talk?" Granted, you will find more useful information in some presentations than in others—but be alert to the possibility in all speeches. Find ways to benefit from the information you are listening to, and try to connect it with your own experiences and needs.

LISTEN SKILLFULLY

Besides being aware of nonverbal messages and being mindful listeners, good listeners enact certain behaviors that help them stay focused and remember what they've heard. They identify their listening goal, listen for major ideas, practice good listening methods, adapt their listening style as necessary, and are active listeners.

IDENTIFY YOUR LISTENING GOAL If you are a typical student, you spend over 80 percent of your day involved in communication-related activities.[11] You spend about 9 percent of your communication time writing, 16 percent reading, 30 percent speaking, and at least 45 percent listening (see Figure 4.1). You listen a lot. Your challenge is to stay on course and keep your listening focused.

One way to stay focused is to determine your listening purpose. There are at least four major listening goals: listening for pleasure, to empathize, to evaluate, and to gain information. Being conscious of your listening goal can help you listen more effectively. If, for example, your listening goal is simply to enjoy what you hear, you need not listen with the same intensity as when you are trying to remember what you are hearing.

Listening for Pleasure You listen to some things just for the fun of it. You might watch TV, listen to music, go to a movie, or chitchat with a friend. You won't be tested on *Friends* reruns. Nor will you be asked to remember every joke in David Letterman's monologue. So, when listening for pleasure, just enjoy what you hear. You can, however, observe how effective speakers or entertainers gain and maintain your attention and keep you interested in their messages.

Listening to Empathize To have empathy means to make an attempt to feel what the speaker is feeling. Usually, empathic listening occurs in one-on-one listening situations with a good friend. Sometimes, in your job, you may need to listen empathically to a client, customer, or coworker. Listening to empathize requires these essential steps:

1. **Stop.** Stop what you are doing and give your complete attention to the speaker.
2. **Look.** Make eye contact and pay attention to nonverbal cues that reveal emotions.
3. **Listen.** Pay attention to both the details of the message and the major ideas.
4. **Imagine.** Visualize how you would feel if you had experienced what the speaker experienced.
5. **Check.** Check your understanding of the message by asking questions to clarify what you heard and by summarizing what you think you heard.

Listening to Evaluate When you evaluate a message, you are making a judgment about its content. You are interested in whether the information is reliable, true, or useful. When evaluating what you hear, the challenge is to not become so critical of the message that you miss a key point the speaker is making. That is, when listening, you must be able to juggle two very difficult tasks: You must make judgments as well as understand and recall the information you are hearing. Our point is this: When you are listening to a message and also evaluating it, you have to work harder than at other times to understand the speaker's message. Your biases and judgments act as noise, sometimes causing you to misunderstand the intended meaning of the message.

Listening for Information Since elementary school, you have been in listening situations in which someone wanted you to learn something. Keys to listening for information are listening for the details of a message and making certain you link the details to major ideas. Poor listeners either listen only for facts and pieces of a message or are only interested in "the bottom line." By concentrating on both facts and major ideas, while also mentally summarizing the information you hear, you can dramatically increase your ability to remember messages. Also, remember to compare unfamiliar information to ideas and concepts with which you are familiar.

Knowing your listening goal can help you develop an appropriate listening strategy. Be conscious of what you are seeking from a message.

LISTEN FOR MAJOR IDEAS In a classic study, Ralph Nichols asked both good and poor listeners what their listening strategies were.[12] The poor listeners indicated that they listened for facts, such as names and dates. The good listeners reported that they listened for major ideas and principles. Facts are useful only when you can connect them to a principle or concept. In speeches, facts as well as examples are used primarily to support major ideas. Try to mentally summarize the major ideas that the specific facts support.

If you had been present on that brisk March morning in 1933 to hear Franklin Delano Roosevelt deliver his first inaugural address, you would have heard him introduce his key idea in the fourth sentence of the speech: "This great Nation will endure as it has endured, will revive and will prosper. So, first of all, let me assert my firm belief that the only thing we have to fear is fear itself." A good listener would recognize this immediately as the core of the speech.

How can you tell what the major ideas in a speech are? A speaker who is well organized or familiar with good speaking techniques will offer a preview of the major ideas early in the speech. If no preview is provided, listen for the speaker to enumerate major points: "My first point is that the history of Jackson County is evident in its various styles of architecture." Transitional phrases and a speaker's internal summaries are other clues that can help you identify the major points. If your speaker provides few overt indicators, you may have to discover them on your own. In that event, mentally summarize the ideas that are most useful to you. As suggested earlier, be a selfish listener. Treat a disorganized speech as a river with gold in the sands. Take your mental mining pan and search for the meaningful nuggets.

PRACTICE LISTENING Because we've noted that you spend at least 45 percent of your day listening, you may wonder why we suggest that you practice listening. The reason is that listening skills do not develop automatically. You learn to swim by getting proper instruction; you're unlikely to develop good aquatic skills by just jumping in the water and flailing around. Similarly, you will learn to listen by practicing the methods we recommend. Researchers believe that poor listeners avoid challenge. For example, they listen to and watch TV situation comedies rather than documentaries or other informative programs. Skill develops as you practice listening to speeches, music, and programs with demanding content.

UNDERSTAND YOUR LISTENING STYLE New research suggests that not everyone listens to information the same way. There are at least four different **listening styles**—preferred ways of making sense out of spoken messages. Listening researchers Kitty Watson, Larry Barker, and James Weaver discovered that listeners tend to be either people-oriented, action-oriented, content-oriented, or time-oriented.[13] Understanding your listening style can help you become a better and more flexible listener.[14]

People-Oriented Listeners You're a **people-oriented listener** if you are comfortable listening to people express feelings and emotions. It's likely that you are highly empathic and that you seek common ground with the person you are listening to. You are easily moved by poignant illustrations and anecdotes.

Action-Oriented Listeners If you like information that is well organized, brief, and accurate, but don't like long stories or digressions from the main ideas, you're likely an **action-oriented listener**. The action-oriented listener wants people to get to the point and listens for actions that need to be taken. Action-oriented listeners also seem to be more skeptical than people who use other listening styles. They prefer being given evidence to support the recommendations for action.

Content-Oriented Listeners **Content-oriented listeners** prefer to listen to complex information that is laced with facts and details. You're a content-oriented listener if you reject messages because they don't have adequate support. Content-oriented listeners make good judges or lawyers, because they enjoy listening to debates and hearing arguments for and against ideas.[15]

Time-Oriented Listeners You're a **time-oriented listener** if you like your messages delivered succinctly. Time is important to you; you want the information you hear to be presented briefly because you are busy. Time-oriented listeners don't like rambling, long-winded messages with lots of filler. Like action-oriented listeners, they want the speaker to get to the point, but they are even more interested in saving time and getting the essential ideas in brief sound bites.

Knowing your listening style can help you better adapt to speakers who are not speaking in your preferred style. For example, if you are a time-oriented listener, and a speaker is spending more time than you'd like telling stories and meandering through the material, you'll have to tell yourself to concentrate harder on the message. If you are a people-oriented listener, and you're listening to a message that's primarily facts, principles, and ideas, you can be a better listener if you are conscious of why the message may not be holding your attention and work to focus on the

listening styles
Preferred ways of making sense out of spoken messages

people-oriented listener
Someone who is comfortable listening to others express feelings and emotions

action-oriented listener
Someone who prefers information that is well organized, brief, and accurate

content-oriented listener
Someone who prefers messages that are supported with facts and details

time-oriented listener
Someone who likes succinct messages

How to Enhance Your Listening Skills

	THE GOOD LISTENER . . .	THE POOR LISTENER . . .
Listen with Your Eyes As Well as Your Ears	Looks for nonverbal cues to enhance understanding	Focuses only on the words
	Adapts to the speaker's delivery	Is easily distracted by the delivery of the speech
Listen Mindfully	Controls emotions	Erupts emotionally when listening
	Listens before making a judgment about the value of the content	Jumps to conclusions about the value of the message
	Mentally asks, "What's in it for me?"	Does not attempt to relate to the information personally
Listen Skillfully	Identifies the listening goal	Does not have a listening goal in mind
	Listens for major ideas	Listens for isolated facts
	Seeks opportunities to practice listening skills	Avoids listening to difficult information
	Understands and adapts his or her listening style to the speaker	Is not aware of how to capitalize on his or her listening style
	Listens actively by re-sorting, rephrasing, and repeating what is heard	Listens passively by making no effort to engage with the information heard

message. We've emphasized the importance of being an audience-centered speaker but the opposite is true as well: As a listener you can increase your concentration if you adjust and adapt your listening style to the speakers you hear. As we note in Chapter 3, the key, whether you are speaker or listener, is to ethically adapt and adjust to enhance the quality of communication.

BECOME AN ACTIVE LISTENER An active listener is one who remains alert and mentally re-sorts, rephrases, and repeats key information when listening to a speech. As we noted, you can listen to words much faster than a speaker can speak them. Therefore, it's natural for your mind to wander. But you can use the extra time to focus on interpreting what the speaker says.

    1. Re-sort. Use your listening time to re-sort disorganized or disjointed ideas. If the speaker is rambling, seek ways to rearrange his or her ideas into a new, more logical pattern. For example, re-sort the ideas into a chronological pattern: What happened first, second, and so on? Or, even if the speaker hasn't chunked the ideas into a logical framework, see if you can find a structure to help you reorganize the information. Yes, it would be useful if the speaker had done that. But if the speaker isn't organized, you'll benefit if you can turn a jumbled mass of information into a structure that makes sense to you.

    2. Rephrase. Mentally summarize key points or information that you want to remember. Listen for the main ideas and then paraphrase those key ideas in your own

Active Listening

STEPS	DEFINITION	EXAMPLE
Re-sort	Reorganize jumbled or disorganized information.	What the speaker said: "There are several key dates to remember: 1776, 1492, and 1861." You re-sort: 1492, 1776, 1861.
Rephrase	Paraphrase the speaker's ideas, rather than trying to remember his or her exact words.	What the speaker said: "If we don't stop the destructive overspending of the defense budget, our nation will very quickly find itself much deeper in debt and unable to meet the many needs of its citizens." You rephrase: "We should spend less on defense, or we will have more problems."
Repeat	Periodically, mentally restate key ideas you want to remember.	Repeat your paraphrase five minutes further into the speech.

words. You are more likely to remember your mental paraphrase of the information than the exact words of the speaker. If you can, try to mentally summarize what the speaker is saying in a phrase that might fit on a bumper sticker. Listening for "information handles" provided by the speaker in the form of previews, transitions, signposts, and summary statements can also help you remain actively involved as a listener.

LEARNING FROM GREAT SPEAKERS

Cesar Chavez (1927–1993)

As a young man, American labor leader Cesar Chavez experienced the hard work and harsh working conditions of the migrant farm worker. Listening both to his fellow farm workers and to representatives of a self-help group called the Community Service Organization, Chavez became acutely aware of the way the workers were exploited. He became a part-time organizer for the Community Service Organization, registering farm workers to vote. By the early 1950s Chavez assumed a leadership role in informing field workers of their rights. One source notes,

He worried because he felt he wasn't a good speaker. So at first, he did more listening than speaking. In time, he grew more confident and found that people listened to him and liked his message.[16]

Cesar Chavez found that listening to others helped him learn to motivate others to listen to him. The union he founded, the United Farm Workers of America, continues to listen to the concerns of field workers.

Effective speakers not only listen to audience-member ideas before giving a presentation but also are sensitive to listener messages, both spoken ones and especially unspoken ones, while giving a speech. Skilled speakers also listen to audience reactions after the speech is presented, because those reactions will help them in preparing for the next speech.

[Photo: Adele Starr/AP Images]

3. Repeat. Finally, do more than just rephrase the information as you listen to it. Periodically, *repeat* key points you want to remember. Go back to essential ideas and restate them to yourself. If you follow these steps for active listening, you will find yourself feeling stimulated and engaged instead of tired and bored as you listen to even the dullest of speakers.

 ## Improving Your Note-Taking Skills

"What's everyone taking notes for?" wondered Carolyne, scanning the lecture hall during her U.S. history class. "Can't they remember the key points without trying to scribble them in their notebooks?" At the end of the lecture, however, Carolyne found that she was getting confused about the dates and events her professor had mentioned, and she ended up having to borrow some notes from one of her classmates.

So far in this chapter, we have suggested ways to improve your listening skills. But we also recognize that you will not remember everything you listen to. It is difficult to recall the details of a lengthy speech unless you have taken notes. Coupling improved listening skills with better skill in taking notes can greatly enhance your ability to retrieve information. Try the following suggestions to improve your note-taking skills.

PREPARE Come prepared to take notes, even if you're not sure you need to. Bring a pencil or pen and paper to every class, lecture, or meeting.

DETERMINE WHETHER YOU NEED TO TAKE NOTES After the presentation has started, decide whether you need to take notes. If you receive a handout that summarizes the content of the message, it may be best to pay attention, concentrate on the message, and take very few notes.

DECIDE ON THE TYPE OF NOTES YOU NEED TO TAKE If notes seem necessary, decide whether you need to outline the speech, identify facts and principles, jot down key words, or just record major ideas. Some speakers do not follow organized outline patterns, in which case it is tricky to outline the message. If you are going to take an objective test on the material, you may need to note only facts and principles. Noting key words may be enough to help you recall what was said if you are going to prepare a report for someone else to read. Or you may want to write down just major ideas. The type of notes you take will depend on how you intend to use the information you get from the speech.

MAKE YOUR NOTES MEANINGFUL Beware of taking too many notes; the goal is to remember the message, not to transcribe it. Instead, use the re-sorting and rephrasing techniques we discussed earlier and write down only what will be meaningful to you later.

Leave a blank area in your notes to use as a recall column.[17] A recall column is a blank margin about 2 or 3 inches wide that you leave to one side of your notes (see Figure 4.2).

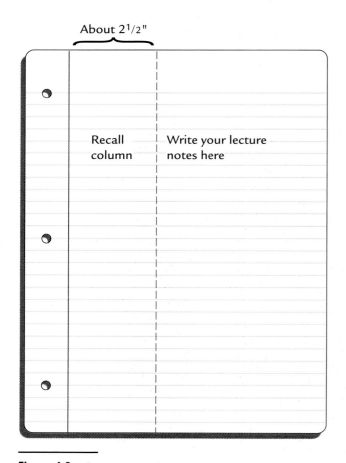

About 2 1/2"

Recall column

Write your lecture notes here

Figure 4.2 *Sample page for note-taking*

RECAP

Improving Your Note-Taking Skills

1. Prepare.
2. Determine whether you need to take notes.
3. Decide on the type of notes you need to take.
4. Make your notes meaningful.

Don't fill this column in while you are taking notes. Use it when reviewing your notes to sift through the ideas you have written down and pull out the key material you want to remember. After you have heard the entire message, you may have a better idea of the most significant content you want to recall later.

Listening and Critical Thinking

Effective listening also requires the ability to listen critically. Listening critically and thinking critically both involve a variety of skills we return to throughout this text. **Critical listening** is the process of listening to evaluate the quality, appropriateness, value, or importance of the information you hear. Related to being a critical listener is being a critical thinker. **Critical thinking** is a mental process of making judgments about the conclusions presented in what you see, hear, and read. The goal of a critical listener or a critical thinker is to evaluate information to make a choice. Whether you are listening to a political candidate giving a persuasive presentation to get your vote, a radio announcer extolling the virtues of a new herbal weight-loss pill, or someone asking you to invest in a new technology company, the goal of a critical listener is to assess the quality of the information and validity of the conclusions presented.

We should emphasize that being a critical listener does not mean you're only looking for what the speaker says that is wrong; we're not suggesting that you listen to a speaker only to pounce on the message and the messenger at the conclusion of the speech. Listen to identify what the speaker does that is effective, as well as to identify which conclusions don't hold up. Specifically, what does a critical listener do? Consider the following skills.

SEPARATE FACTS FROM INFERENCES

The ability to separate facts from inferences is one of the most basic critical-thinking and listening skills. **Facts** are based on something that has been proven true by direct observation. For example, it has been directly observed that water boils at 212 degrees Fahrenheit, that the direction of the magnetic north pole can be found by consulting a compass, and that U.S. presidents have been inaugurated on January 20 every four years for several decades. An **inference** is a conclusion based on partial information, or an evaluation that has not been directly observed. You infer that your favorite sports team will win the championship or that it will rain tomorrow. You can also infer, if more Republicans than Democrats are elected to Congress, that the next president might be a Republican. But you can only know this for a *fact* after

critical listening
Evaluating the quality of information, ideas, and arguments presented by a speaker

critical thinking
Making judgments about the conclusions presented in what you see, hear, and read

fact
Something that has been proven to be true by direct observation

inference
A conclusion based on partial information, or an evaluation that has not been directly observed

Critical listening is important whether you are a member of a small audience or a large one.

[Photo: Jim Craigmyle/Corbis]

the presidential election. Facts are in the realm of certainty; inferences are in the realm of probability and opinion—where most arguments advanced by public speakers reside. A critical listener knows that when a politician running for office claims, "It's a fact that my opponent is not qualified to be elected," this statement is *not* a fact, but an inference.

EVALUATE THE QUALITY OF EVIDENCE

Evidence consists of the facts, examples, opinions, and statistics that a speaker uses to support a conclusion. Researchers have documented that the key element in swaying a jury is the quality and quantity of the evidence presented to support a case.[18] Without credible supporting evidence, it would not be wise to agree with a speaker's conclusion.

What should you listen for when trying to decide if evidence is credible? When, for example, a radio announcer says, "It's a fact that this herbal weight-loss pill helps people lose weight," your job as a listener is to determine if that statement is, in fact, a fact. As we've just discussed, a fact is something that has been proven by direct observation to be true. The speaker has an obligation to provide evidence to support the statement asserted.

Some speakers support a conclusion with examples. But if the examples aren't typical, or only one or two examples are offered, or other known examples differ from the one the speaker is using, then you should question the conclusion.

Another form of evidence a speaker might use to convince you is an opinion. Simply stated, an opinion is a quoted comment from someone. The best opinions come from reliable, credible sources. What makes a source credible? A credible source is someone who has the credentials, experience, and skill to make an observation about the topic at hand. Listen for whom a speaker cites when quoting an expert on a subject.

A fourth kind of evidence often used, especially with a skeptical listener, is statistics. A statistic is a number that summarizes a collection of examples. Some of the same kinds of questions that should be raised about other forms of evidence should be raised about statistics: Are the statistics reliable, unbiased, recent, representative, and valid?

evidence

The facts, examples, opinions, and statistics that a speaker uses to support a conclusion

Here we've introduced you to the importance of *listening for* good evidence. Because evidence is an important element of public speaking, we'll provide more detailed information about how to *use* evidence when we discuss using supporting material, in Chapter 8, and using evidence to persuade, in Chapter 17.

EVALUATE THE UNDERLYING LOGIC AND REASONING

An effective critical listener listens not only for evidence, but also for the overall structure of the logic, or argument, the speaker uses to reach a conclusion. **Logic** is a formal system of rules applied to reach a conclusion. A speaker is logical if he or she offers appropriate evidence to reach a valid, well-reasoned conclusion. For example, Angela was trying to convince her listeners to take Slimlean as a weight-loss herb by pointing out that many stores sell this diet product, but that is not a strong logical framework for her conclusion. Just because Slimlean is readily available does not mean that it's effective and safe.

Reasoning is the process of drawing a conclusion from evidence within the logical framework of the arguments. Can we reasonably conclude that anyone can lose weight by taking Slimlean, simply because it's available in many stores? The evidence very likely does not support this conclusion. When a speaker is seeking to change your behavior, listen especially carefully to the logic or structure of the arguments presented. Is the speaker trying to convince you to do something by offering one or two specific examples? Or is the speaker reaching a conclusion based on a fundamental principle such as "All herbal diet supplements will cause you to lose weight"? The critical listener appropriately reviews the logic and reasoning used to reach a conclusion. When we discuss reasoning fallacies in Chapter 17, we will elaborate on different types of reasoning and we'll identify several ways speakers misuse logic, reasoning, and evidence.

You might reasonably suspect that a primary goal of a public-speaking class would be to enhance your speaking skill, and you'd be right. But in addition to becoming a better speaker, a study of communication principles and skills should also help you become a better *consumer* of messages. Becoming a critical listener and thinker is an important benefit you will enjoy by learning about how messages are constructed. Researchers have found that a student who has completed any communication course, such as debate, argumentation, or public speaking, is likely to show improved critical-thinking ability. The introduction to critical listening and thinking skills presented here is reinforced throughout the rest of the book by discussions of how to become an audience-centered public speaker.

 ## Analyzing and Evaluating Speeches

Your critical thinking and listening skills will help you evaluate not only the speeches of others, but also your own speeches. When you evaluate something, you judge its value and appropriateness. To make a judgment about the value of something, it's important to use criteria for what is and is not effective or appropriate. **Rhetorical criticism** is the process of using a method or standards to evaluate the effectiveness and appropriateness of messages.

To better understand the concept of rhetorical criticism, it's important to understand the meaning of the words *rhetoric* and *criticism*. The term *rhetoric* is both classical and contemporary.[19] The ancient Greek scholar Aristotle defined rhetoric as the faculty of discovering in any given case the available means of persuasion.[20] Another ancient Greek scholar, Isocrates, believed that effective rhetoric should have the

 logic
A formal system of rules used to reach a conclusion

reasoning
The process of drawing a conclusion from evidence

rhetorical criticism
The process of using a method or standards to evaluate the effectiveness and appropriateness of messages

"qualities of fitness for the occasion, propriety of style and originality of treatment."[21] A more contemporary rhetorical scholar, Kenneth Burke, said that rhetoric is a "symbolic means of inducing cooperation."[22] In summary, **rhetoric** is the process of using symbols to create meaning to achieve a goal. As public speaker you are a rhetorician in that you're using symbols (words, images, nonverbal cues) to create meaning in the minds of your listeners and achieve a goal (to inform, to persuade, to entertain).

To be a rhetorical critic is to evaluate the effectiveness and appropriateness of the message and delivery of a presentation. Rhetorical critics often point to educator and philosopher John Dewey's description of criticism:

> Criticism . . . is not fault-finding. It is not pointing out evils to be reformed. It is judgment engaged in discriminating among values. It is talking through as to what is better and worse . . . with some consciousness of why the worse is worse.[23]

A critic not only evaluates a message but also helps *illuminate* it.[24] To illuminate is to shine a metaphorical light on the message to help others make better sense of the message.

One important goal of studying public speaking is to help you be a better rhetorical critic of the many messages you hear every day. In our discussion of how to analyze and evaluate speeches, we'll first suggest criteria for evaluating messages and then offer specific strategies for sharing your evaluations with others.

UNDERSTANDING CRITERIA FOR EVALUATING SPEECHES

What makes a speech good? For more than 2,000 years, rhetorical scholars have been debating this question. Our purpose here is not to take you through the centuries of dialogue and debate about this issue but to offer some practical ways to help you evaluate your own messages as well as the messages of others.

Your public-speaking teacher will probably have you use an evaluation form that lists the precise criteria for evaluating your speeches. Figure 4.3 lists key questions to use in evaluating any speech. The questions reflect the audience-centered model of public speaking that we presented in Chapter 2.

Underlying any list of what a good speaker should do are two fundamental goals: *Any speech should be both effective and ethical.* The mission of the National Communication Association mirrors these same two goals—to promote effective and ethical communication. These two requirements can translate into general criteria for evaluating speeches you give as well as those you hear.

THE MESSAGE SHOULD BE EFFECTIVE To be effective, the message of a speech should be understandable to listeners and should achieve its intended purpose.[25] Public speaking is sometimes called *public communication*. A goal of any communication effort is to create a common understanding of the message on the part of both the sender and the receiver. The words *common* and *communication* resemble each other. If listeners fail to comprehend the speaker's ideas, the speech fails. Even more difficult than saying something is saying something a listener understands. In this course you'll learn an array of principles and strategies to help you develop a common understanding between you and your audience. The process of communicating to be understood is anchored first and foremost in considering the needs of your listeners. As you listen to speeches, a fundamental criterion for determining whether the message is a good one or not is whether you understand the message.

Another way to evaluate the effectiveness of a message is to assess whether it achieved its intended goal. When you communicate with an audience, you want to achieve a goal or accomplish something. Typical general goals of public speaking are to inform, to persuade, and to entertain. The challenge in using this criterion in

rhetoric
The use of symbols to create meaning to achieve a goal

Audience Orientation

- Did the speaker make a specific effort to adapt to the audience?

Topic Selection

- Was the topic appropriate for the audience, the occasion, and the speaker?
- Was the speech narrowed to fit the time limits?

Purpose

- Was the general purpose clear?
- Was the specific purpose appropriate for the audience?
- Was the purpose achieved?

Central Idea

- Was the central idea clear enough to be summarized in one sentence?

Main Ideas

- Were the main ideas clearly identified in the introduction of the speech, developed in the body of the speech, and summarized in the conclusion of the speech?

Supporting Material

- Did the speaker use varied and interesting supporting material?
- Did the speaker use effective and appropriate evidence to support conclusions?
- Did the speaker use credible supporting material?

Organization

- Did the speech have a clear introduction that caught attention, provided a preview of the speech, and established the speaker's credibility?
- Did the speaker organize the body of the speech in a logical way?
- Did the speaker use transitions, summaries, and signposts to clarify the organization?
- Did the speaker appropriately summarize the major ideas and provide closure to the speech during the conclusion?

Rehearse Speech

- Did the speech sound as though it was well rehearsed?
- Did the speaker seem familiar with the speech content?

Speech Delivery

- Did the speaker make appropriate eye contact with the audience?
- Did the speaker use appropriate volume and vocal variation?
- Did the speaker use gestures and posture appropriately?
- Did the speaker use presentation aids that were easy to see and handled effectively?
- Did the speaker use presentation aids that were of high quality?

Figure 4.3 *A checklist of effective public-speaking characteristics*

evaluating speeches is that you may not always know the speaker's true intent. Often the best you can do is try to determine the purpose by being a careful listener.

THE MESSAGE SHOULD BE ETHICAL As we discussed in Chapter 3, a good speaker is an ethical speaker. Ethics are the beliefs, values, and moral principles by which people determine what is right or wrong. An ethical public speaker tells the truth, gives credit for ideas and words where credit is due, and doesn't plagiarize. If a speaker's message is clearly understood by the audience and also gets the reaction the speaker desired, but the speaker has used unethical means to achieve the goal, the message may be an *effective* message, but it is not an *appropriate* message.

You will probably speak to audiences with a wide array of cultural backgrounds. Regardless of their cultural tradition, your listeners hold an underlying ethical code. As we noted in Chapter 3, although not every culture has the same ethical rules, many cultures adhere to precepts that in essence state the value of being audience-centered by considering how others would like to be treated. An ethical public speaker focuses not only on achieving the goal of the message but on doing so while being sensitive and responsive to listeners.

IDENTIFYING AND ANALYZING RHETORICAL STRATEGIES

As we noted in Chapter 1, *rhetoric* is the use of symbols to achieve goals. **Symbols** are words, images (a flag, a cross, a six-pointed star), and behaviors that create meaning for others. Whether you use them in an interview to convince an employer to hire you for a job or hear them in a TV commercial to persuade you to vote for a presidential candidate, words and images that symbolically inform and persuade are all around you. Public speakers, too, are rhetoricians who use symbols to achieve their goals. The study of rhetoric is centuries old. Appendix B provides a brief history of the classical origins of rhetorical study.

As we've pointed out, studying public speaking not only can make you a better speaker but can help you be a better consumer of the speeches you hear. One way to enhance your listening skill and become more mindfully aware of how messages influence your behavior is to analyze the rhetorical strategies a speaker is using. **Rhetorical strategies** are methods and techniques that speakers employ to achieve their speaking goals. It's especially important to be aware of how some speakers may use rhetorical techniques to deceive or manipulate you. Speakers sometimes use unethical strategies to achieve their goals, such as misusing evidence, relying too heavily on emotion to persuade, or fabricating information.

Rhetorician Robert Rowland offers a simple but comprehensive framework for describing and analyzing rhetorical messages:[26] Be conscious of the goal of the message, its organization, the speaker's role, the overall tone of the message, the intended audience, and the techniques the speaker uses to achieve the goal.[27] By considering the questions in Table 4.1, you can begin to understand how any speaker is using rhetorical strategies to achieve his or her goal. Using these questions will help you figure out what any speaker is really saying and better understand the techniques he or she is using. Whether it's a speaker in your public-speaking class, the president delivering a State of the Union address, a member of the clergy delivering a sermon, or a parent addressing the school board, each speaker is using rhetorical strategies to achieve a goal. The more clearly you can identify and analyze the speaker's methods, the more effectively you can assess whether the message and the messenger are worthy of your support. Although this particular chapter focuses on being a better listener or consumer of rhetoric, the entire book is designed to help you be a more discerning rhetorical critic of the messages you hear.

symbols
Words, images, and behaviors that create meaning

rhetorical strategies
Methods and techniques that speakers use to achieve their speaking goals

Table 4.1   Evaluating a Speaker's Rhetorical Strategies

Speech Goal	What is the overall goal of the message?
	What are the main points or themes of the message?
	What is the speaker asking the audience to do?
Speech Organization	What is the overall organizational structure of the message?
	How does the introduction set the tone for the message?
	How does the conclusion summarize the message and point listeners to what the speaker wants to happen next?
	How does the body of the speech support the primary objective of the speech?
Speaker Role	What is the role of the speaker?
	Is the speaker assuming either an explicit or an implied role, such as an authority figure or expert on the topic addressed?
	What kind of relationship has the speaker established with the audience?
Speaker Tone	What is the overall tone, or "feel," of the message?
	How does the speaker use language to establish a tone?
	How does the speaker use stories and other illustrations to establish a tone?
	How does the speaker deliver the message to establish a tone?
Speaker Techniques	What strategies or techniques does the speaker use to achieve the speech goals?
	➤ Does the speaker use rational, logical arguments? Stories? Artistic language?
	➤ Does the speaker appeal to the needs and values of the listeners?
	➤ Does the speaker develop high credibility?
	➤ Does the speaker attempt to move listeners by confronting them?
Audience	Who is the intended audience of the message?
	Who is present to hear the message?
	Is the message aimed at others who are not present?

GIVING FEEDBACK TO OTHERS

As you enhance your skills of listening to messages and identifying the rhetorical strategies a speaker uses, you may be asked to evaluate the speeches of others and provide feedback to them. Both the checklist of speech evaluation criteria in Figure 4.3 and the framework of questions to use in analyzing rhetorical strategies in Table 4.1

Developing Your Rhetorical Listening Skills

Rhetorical listening is the ability to critically evaluate the ideas and arguments you hear. One of the best ways to improve your rhetorical listening skills is to practice them. Go to one of the Web sites below to find speeches on which you can practice the listening and analysis skills we've emphasized in this chapter. Many of the speeches on these Web sites are polished political messages. Use the questions for evaluating rhetoric presented in Table 4.1 to describe and analyze what you hear.

To hear the speeches on these Web sites, you will need software such as RealAudio, which can be downloaded from www.real.com/.

◆ CLASSIC SPEECHES FROM THE HISTORY CHANNEL ARCHIVES
www.history.com/media.do

◆ AMERICAN RHETORIC
www.americanrhetoric.com

can serve you well as you evaluate others' messages. Your instructor may provide you with a speech evaluation form that will also help you focus on and evaluate essential elements of public speechmaking.

When you're invited to critique your classmates, your feedback will be more effective if you keep some general principles in mind. The word *criticism* comes from a Greek word meaning "to judge or discuss." Therefore, as noted earlier, to criticize a speech is to discuss the speech—identifying both strengths and aspects that could be improved. Effective criticism stems from developing a genuine interest in the speaker rather than from seeking to find fault. When given the opportunity to critique your classmates, supplement the evaluations you provide on your evaluation form with the following kinds of feedback.

1. Be Descriptive. In a neutral way, describe what you saw the speaker doing. Act as a mirror for the speaker to help him or her become aware of gestures and other nonverbal signals of which he or she may not be aware. (If you are watching a videotape of the speech together, you can help point out behaviors.) Avoid providing a list of only your likes and dislikes; describe what you observe.

Effective:	Stan, I noticed that about 50 percent of the time you had direct eye contact with your listeners.
Less Effective:	Your eye contact was lousy.

2. Be Specific. When you describe what you see a speaker doing, make sure your descriptions are precise enough to give the speaker a clear image of your perceptions. Saying that a speaker had "poor delivery" doesn't give him or her much information—it's only a general evaluative comment. Be as specific and thoughtful as you can.

Effective:	Dawn, your use of color on your overhead transparency helped to keep my attention.
Less Effective:	I liked your visuals.

3. Be Positive. Begin and end your feedback with positive comments. Beginning with negative comments immediately puts the speaker on the defensive and can create so much internal noise that he or she stops listening. Starting and ending with positive comments engenders less defensiveness. Some teachers call this approach the "feedback sandwich." First, tell the speaker something he or she did well. This will let the speaker know you're not an enemy who's trying to shoot holes in his or her performance. Then share a suggestion or two that may help the speaker improve the presentation. End your evaluation with another positive comment or restate what you liked best about the presentation.

Effective:	Gabe, I thought your opening statistic was very effective in catching my attention. You also maintained direct eye contact when you delivered it. Your overall organizational pattern would have been clearer to me if you had used more signposts and transition statements. Or perhaps you could use a visual aid to summarize the main points. You did a good job of summarizing your three points in your conclusion. I also liked the way you ended your speech by making a reference to your opening statistics.
Less Effective:	I got lost when you were in the body of your speech. I couldn't figure out what your major ideas were. I also didn't know when you made the transition between the introduction and the body of your speech. Your intro and conclusion were good, but the organization of the speech was weak.

4. Be Constructive. Give the speaker some suggestions or alternatives for improvement. It's not especially helpful to rattle off a list of things you don't like, without providing some suggestions for improvement. As a student of public speaking, your comments should reflect your growing skill and sophistication in the speech-making process.

Effective:	Jerry, I thought your speech had several good statistics and examples that suggest you spent a lot of time in the library researching your topic. I think you could add credibility to your message if you shared your sources with the listener. Your vocal quality was effective, and you had considerable variation in your pitch and tone, but at times the speech rate was a little fast for me. A slower rate would help me catch some of the details of your message.
Less Effective:	You spoke too fast. I had no idea whom you were quoting.

5. Be Sensitive. "Own" your feedback by using I-statements rather than you-statements. An *I-statement* is a way of phrasing your feedback so that it is clear that your comments reflect your personal point of view. "I found my attention drifting during the body of your speech" is an example of an I-statement. A *you-statement* is a less sensitive way of describing someone's behavior by implying that the other person did something wrong. "You didn't summarize very well in your conclusion" is an example of a you-statement. A better way to make the same point is to say, "I wasn't sure I understood the key ideas you mentioned in your conclusion." Here's another example:

Effective:	Mark, I found myself so distracted by your gestures that I had trouble focusing on the message.
Less Effective:	Your gestures were distracting and awkward.

6. Be Realistic. Provide usable information. Provide feedback about aspects of the presentation that the speaker can improve rather than about things he or she cannot control. Maybe you have heard this advice: "Never try to teach a pig to sing. It wastes your time. It doesn't sound pretty. And it annoys the pig." Saying "You're too short to be seen over the lectern," "Your lisp doesn't lend itself to public speaking," or "You looked nervous" is not constructive—comments like these will just annoy or frustrate the speaker, because they refer to things the speaker can't do much to change. Concentrate on behaviors over which the speaker has control.

Effective:	Taka, I thought your closing quote was effective in summarizing your key ideas, but it didn't end your speech on an uplifting note. Another quote from Khalil Gibran that I'll share

confidently connecting with your audience

Look for Positive Listener Support

Audience members want you to do well. In fact, many if not most listeners will express their support for your ideas with eye contact, nods of the head, and supportive facial expressions. Make a point to look for these reinforcing nonverbal cues as you deliver your message. (But don't forget to maintain eye contact with all members of the audience.) Let these signs of positive support from your listeners remind you that listeners want you to succeed.

with you after class would also summarize your key points and provide a positive affirmation of your message. You may want to try it if you give this speech again.

Less Effective: Your voice isn't well suited to public speaking.

As you provide feedback, whether in your public-speaking class or to a friend who asks you for a reaction to his or her speech, remember that the goal of feedback is to offer descriptive and specific information that helps a speaker build confidence and skill.

GIVING FEEDBACK TO YOURSELF

While you are collecting feedback from your instructor, classmates, family, and friends, keep in mind that *you* are the most important critic of your speeches. The ultimate goal of public-speaking instruction is to learn principles and skills that enable you to be your own best critic. As you rehearse your speech, use self-talk to comment about the choices you make as a speaker. After your speech, take time to reflect on both the speech's virtues and areas for improvement in your speechmaking skill. As an audience-centered speaker, you must learn to recognize when to make changes on your feet, in the middle of a speech. For example, if you notice that your audience just isn't interested in the facts and statistics you are sharing, you may decide to support your points with a couple of stories instead. We encourage you to consider the following principles to enhance your own self-critiquing skills.

LOOK FOR AND REINFORCE YOUR SKILLS AND SPEAKING ABILITIES Try to recognize your strengths and skills as a public speaker. Note how your audience analysis, organization, and delivery were effective in achieving your objectives. Such positive reflection can reinforce the many skills you are learning in this course. Resist the temptation to be too harsh or critical of your speaking skill.

EVALUATE YOUR EFFECTIVENESS BASED ON YOUR SPECIFIC SPEAKING SITUATION AND AUDIENCE Throughout the book we offer many suggestions and tips for improving your speaking skill. We also stress, however, that these prescriptions should be considered in light of your specific audience. Don't be a slave to rules. If you are giving a pep talk to the Little League team you are coaching, you might not have to construct an attention-getting opening statement. Be flexible. Public speaking is an art as well as a science. Give yourself permission to adapt principles and practices to specific speech situations.

IDENTIFY ONE OR TWO AREAS FOR IMPROVEMENT After each speaking opportunity, identify what you did right, and then give yourself a suggestion or two for ways to improve. You may be tempted to overwhelm yourself with a long list of things you need to do as a speaker. Rather than trying to work on a dozen goals, concentrate on two or three, or maybe even just one key skill you would like to develop. To help you decide which skill to focus on, keep in mind the audience-centered model of public speaking we introduced in Chapter 2.

Ultimately, the goal of this course is to teach you how to listen to your own commentary and become your own expert in shaping and polishing your speaking style.

SUMMARY

Listening is a process that involves selecting, attending to, understanding, and remembering. Some of the barriers that keep people from listening at peak efficiency include information overload, personal concerns, outside distractions, and prejudice. There are a number of ways to overcome these barriers and improve your listening skill:

Listen with Your Eyes as Well as Your Ears
    Accurately interpret nonverbal messages
    Adapt to the speaker's delivery

Listen Mindfully
    Monitor your emotional reaction to a message
    Avoid jumping to conclusions
    Be a selfish listener

Listen Skillfully
    Identify your listening goal
    Listen for major ideas
    Practice listening
    Understand your listening style
    Become an active listener

Effective notes can help you retain information that you hear. Learn the criteria for good speeches, and learn to give and receive evaluative feedback on speeches and exchanges with your peers and instructors.

BEING AUDIENCE-CENTERED: A SHARPER FOCUS

CONSIDERING YOUR AUDIENCE

➤ When speaking to an audience that may be hostile to or critical of your message, take care to use credible arguments and evidence rather than rely on emotional appeals.

➤ Find out what your listeners' objectives are; do your best to adjust and adapt to achieve your listeners' goals.

➤ An effective speech should be understood by the audience and should achieve the intended goal. A good speech is also ethical.

➤ Feedback you give to a speaker should provide information and suggestions the speaker can use.

CONSIDERING AUDIENCE DIVERSITY

➤ The cultural background of your audience will affect how they listen to your message; people from some cultures prefer stories and narratives rather than a message chock-full of statistics and data.

➤ Some people are more apprehensive than others about listening to a message. By using clear preview statements, adequate internal summaries, and appropriate visual aids, you can help anxious listeners feel more comfortable when listening to your message.

CRITICAL THINKING QUESTIONS

1. You are heading for your least favorite class: British Literature of the 1800s. You know you are in for another boring lecture delivered by a professor who does nothing but read in a monotone from yellowed notes. What are some strategies you can use to increase your listening effectiveness in this challenging situation?

2. For some reason, when Alberto hears the president speak, he just tunes out. What are some of the barriers that may keep Alberto from focusing on the message he is hearing?

3. Jackie aspires to be a broadcast journalist, following in the footsteps of well-known announcers such as Jane Pauley and Diane Sawyer. Although she is a pretty good listener, she often has difficulty taking accurate notes on what she hears. What strategies do effective note takers use to capture messages accurately?

ETHICAL QUESTIONS

1. Margo discovered that one of her classmates who had taken world history the previous semester was selling her lecture notes. Margo bought the notes and found that they allowed her to pass the exams without attending class. Is this kind of "listening" behavior ethical? Why or why not?

2. Chester was planning to attend a charity event at which a congressional candidate would be speaking. Chester decided he would bring a book to read during the speech, because the speaker was from a political party different from Chester's. Was Chester being fair to the speaker?

3. Janice was assigned the task of critiquing one of her classmate's speeches. Although she thought the speech was pretty good, she gave the speaker low marks because she strongly disagreed with what the speaker was saying. Was this an appropriate evaluation? Why or why not?

Evaluating a Speaker's Rhetorical Effectiveness

When listening to a speech, either a classmate's presentation or a speech you hear on TV or find on the Web, consider the following questions to help you evaluate the rhetorical effectiveness and appropriateness of the speaker and the message.

1. **Speech Goal:** What is the goal of the speech? What does the speaker want the listener to do?

2. **Speech Organization:** What is the overall organizational structure of the message?

3. **Speaker's Role:** What kind of relationship has the speaker established with the audience? Does he or she speak from a position of power? As an equal? How does the role established by the speaker influence the speech's effectiveness?

4. **Speaker's Tone:** What is the overall tone, or "feel," of the message? How does the speaker use supporting material and delivery cues to establish an overall tone of the speech?

5. **Speaker's Techniques:** What does the speaker do to establish credibility? Does the speaker use logical arguments, tell effective and interesting stories, use emotional appeals, and use interesting and precise language?

6. **Audience:** Who is the intended audience? How effectively and appropriately does the speaker connect to the interests, needs and background of the audience? How does the speaker make the connection with the audience?

Pierre Bonnard (1867–1947) *The Loge (Mme. Bernheim le Jeune at the Opera)*, 1908. Eric Lessing/Art Resource, N.Y.

For of the three elements in speechmaking—speaker, subject, and person addressed—it is the last one, the hearer, that determines the speech's end and object.

—ARISTOTLE

Analyzing Your Audience

outline

objectives

After studying this chapter you should be able to do the following:

1. Discuss the importance of audience analysis.

2. Describe informal and formal methods of analyzing your audience.

3. Explain how to gather demographic, psychological, and situational information about your audience and the speaking occasion.

4. Identify methods of assessing and adapting to your audience's reactions to your speech while it is in progress.

5. Identify methods of assessing audience reactions after you have concluded your speech.

t seemed harmless enough. Charles Williams was asked to speak to the Cub Scout pack about his experience as a young cowboy in Texas. The boys were learning to tie knots, and Williams, a retired rancher, could tell them how to make a lariat and how to make and use other knots.

His speech started out well. He seemed to be adapting to his young audience. However, for some reason, Williams thought the boys might also enjoy learning how to exterminate the screwworm, a pesky parasite of cattle. In the middle of his talk about roping cattle, he launched into a presentation about the techniques for sterilizing male screwworms. The parents in the audience fidgeted in their seats. The 7- and 8-year-olds didn't have the foggiest idea what a screwworm was, what sterilization was, or how male and female screwworms mate.

It got worse; his audience analysis skills deteriorated even more. Williams next talked about castrating cattle. Twenty-five minutes later he finally finished the screwworm–castration speech. The parents were relieved. Fortunately, the boys hadn't understood it.

Williams's downfall resulted from his failure to analyze his audience. He may have had a clear objective in mind, but he hadn't considered the background or knowledge of his listeners. Audience analysis is essential for any successful speech.

Becoming an Audience-Centered Speaker

Chapter 1 identified the key elements in communication: source, receiver, message, channel. All four elements are important, but perhaps the most important is the receiver. In public speaking, the receiver is the audience, and the audience is the reason for a speech.

In Chapter 2, we presented a model that provides an overview of the entire process of speech preparation and delivery; the model is shown again in Figure 5.1. We stressed in Chapter 2 and reemphasize here the concept of public speaking as an audience-centered activity. At each stage in crafting your speech, you must be mindful of your audience. The audience-analysis skills and techniques that we present in this chapter will help you throughout the public-speaking process. Consciousness of your audience will be important as you select a topic, determine the purpose of your speech, develop your central idea, generate main ideas, gather supporting material, firm up your organization, and rehearse and deliver your speech.

When you think of your audience, don't think of some undifferentiated mass of people waiting to hear your message. Instead, think of individuals. Public speaking is the process of speaking to a group of individuals, each with a unique point of view. Your challenge as an audience-centered public speaker is to find out as much as you can about these individuals. From your knowledge of the individuals, you can then develop a general profile of your listeners.

How do you become an audience-centered speaker? There are three steps. First, gather information about your audience. You can gather some information informally just by observing your listeners or asking general questions about them. Or you can take a more formal approach and administer a survey to obtain more specific information about them.

Second, analyze the information you have gathered. To analyze information is to categorize and evaluate what you have gathered to determine your listeners' psychological profile, as well as to consider the occasion at which you are speaking.

Finally, once you have gathered and analyzed information about your audience, use the information to ethically adapt to your listeners. As our audience-centered model illustrates, each decision you make when designing and delivering your message should consider the needs and backgrounds of your audience. We'll talk about these three steps in more detail and discuss the process of analyzing your audience before, during, and after you speak.

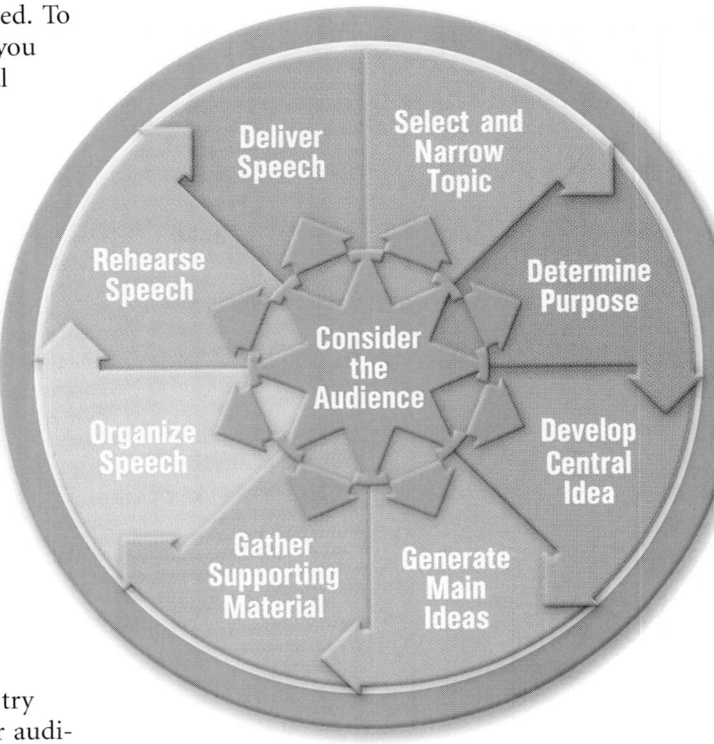

Gather Information about Your Audience

As an audience-centered speaker, you should try to find out as much as you can about your audience before planning your speech. You may wonder, "How do I go about gathering information about my audience?" There are two approaches you can take: an informal one and a formal one.

Figure 5.1 *Audience analysis is central to the speechmaking process.*

GATHERING INFORMATION INFORMALLY The simplest way to gather information about your audience informally is just to observe them and ask questions before you speak. Informal observations can be especially important in helping you assess obvious demographic characteristics. **Demographics** are statistical information on population characteristics such as age, race, gender, sexual orientation, educational level, and ideological or religious views of an audience. For example, you can observe how many members of your audience are male or female, and you can also make some inferences from their appearance about their education level, ethnic or cultural traits, and approximate age.

If, for example, you were going to address your local PTA meeting about a new store you were opening to help students and parents develop science projects, you could attend a meeting before your speaking date. You might note the general percentage of men and women in the audience and the ages of the parents who attended. You could also ask whether most parents who show up for PTA meetings are parents of elementary, middle-school, or high-school students. Knowing these key pieces of information would help you tailor your speech to address your listeners' interests.

Also, talk with people who know something about the audience you will be addressing. If you are invited to speak to a group you have not spoken to before, ask the person who invited you some general questions about the audience members: What is their average age? What are their political affiliations? What are their religious beliefs? What are their attitudes toward your topic? Try to get as much information as possible about your audience before you give your speech.

GATHERING INFORMATION FORMALLY Rather than relying only on inferences drawn from casual observation and conversations with others, you may, if time and

demographics
Statistical information about the age, race, gender, sexual orientation, educational level, and religious views of an audience

Figure 5.2 *Demographic audience-analysis questionnaire*

Demographic Audience-Analysis Questionnaire

1. Name (optional): _____

2. Sex: Male ☐ Female ☐

3. Occupation: _____

4. Religious affiliation: _____

5. Marital status: Married ☐ Single ☐ Divorced ☐

6. Major in school: _____

7. Years of schooling beyond high school: _____

8. Annual income: _____

9. Age: _____

10. Ethnic background: _____

11. Hometown and state: _____

12. Political affiliation: Republican ☐ Democrat ☐ Other ☐ None ☐

13. Membership in professional or fraternal organizations: _____

---

resources permit, want to conduct a more formal survey of your listeners. A survey allows you to gather both demographic information and information about what audience members like or dislike, believe to be true or false, or think is good or bad about the topic or issues you are discussing. To gather information formally requires developing a well-written survey or questionnaire.

How do you develop a formal survey? First, decide what you want to know about your audience that you don't already know. Let your topic and the speaking occasion help you determine the kinds of questions you should pose. Once you have an idea of what you would like to know, you can ask your potential audience straightforward questions about such demographic information as age, sex, occupation, and memberships in professional organizations. Figure 5.2 shows a sample questionnaire.

You can modify the questionnaire in Figure 5.2 according to your audience and topic. If your topic is the best approach to finding a rental apartment and you are speaking in a suburban area, find out how many members of your audience own a home and how many are presently living in an apartment. You may also want to ask how they found their current apartment, how many are now searching for an apartment, and how many anticipate searching for one. Answers to these questions can give you useful information about your audience and may also provide examples to use in your presentation.

Although knowing your audience's demographics can be helpful, again we caution you that inferences based on generalized information may lead to faulty conclusions. For example, it might seem reasonable to infer that if your audience consists mainly of 18- to 22-year-olds, they will not be deeply interested in retirement programs. But unless you have talked to them specifically about these topics, your inference may be incorrect. Whenever possible, ask specific questions about audience members' attitudes.

To gather useful information about audience members' attitudes, beliefs, and values, you can ask two basic types of questions. **Open-ended questions** allow for unrestricted answers, without limiting answers to choices or alternatives. Use open-ended questions when you want more detailed information from your audience. Essay questions, for example, are open-ended. **Closed-ended questions** offer several alternatives from which to choose. Multiple-choice, true/false, and agree/disagree questions are examples of closed-ended questions.

open-ended questions
Questions that allow for unrestricted answers by not limiting answers to choices or alternatives

closed-ended questions
Questions that offer alternatives from which to choose, such as true/false, agree/disagree, or multiple-choice questions

Figure 5.3 *Sample questions*

Open-Ended Questions

1. What are your feelings about having high-school health clinics dispense birth-control pills?
2. What are your reactions to the current rate of teenage pregnancy?
3. What would you do if you discovered your daughter was receiving birth-control pills from her high-school health clinic?

Closed-Ended Questions

1. Are you in favor of school-based health clinics dispensing birth-control pills to high-school students?

    Yes ☐   No ☐
2. Birth-control pills should be given to high-school students who ask for them in school-based health clinics. (Circle the statement that best describes your feeling.)

    Agree strongly   Agree   Undecided   Disagree   Disagree strongly
3. Check the statement that most closely reflects your feelings about school-based health clinics and birth-control pills.

    ☐ Students should receive birth-control pills in school-based health clinics whenever they want them, without their parents' knowledge.

    ☐ Students should receive birth-control pills in school-based health clinics whenever they want them, as long as they have their parents' permission.

    ☐ I am not certain whether students should receive birth-control pills in school-based health clinics.

    ☐ Students should not receive birth-control pills in school-based health clinics.
4. Rank the following statements from most desirable (1) to least desirable (5).

    ☐ Birth-control pills should be available to all high-school students in school-based health clinics, whenever students want them, and even if their parents are not aware that their daughters are taking the pills.

    ☐ Birth-control pills should be available to all high-school students in school-based health clinics, but only if their parents have given their permission.

    ☐ Birth-control pills should be available to high-school students without their parents' knowledge, but not in school-based health clinics.

    ☐ Birth-control pills should be available to high-school students, but not in school-based health clinics, and only with their parents' permission.

    ☐ Birth-control pills should not be available to high-school students.

After you develop the questions, it is wise to test them on a small group of people to make sure they are clear and will encourage meaningful answers. Suppose you plan to address an audience about in-school health clinics that dispense birth-control pills to high-school students. The sample questions in Figure 5.3 illustrate various open and closed questions that might yield useful audience information.

Analyze Information about Your Audience

Audience analysis is the process of examining information about the listeners who will hear your speech. That analysis helps you adapt your message so that your listeners will respond as you wish. You analyze audiences every day as you speak to others or join in group conversations. For example, most of us do not deliberately make offensive comments to family members or friends. Rather, we analyze our audience (often very quickly), and then we adapt our messages to the individuals with whom we are speaking. Public speaking involves the same sort of process.

audience analysis

The process of examining information about those who are expected to listen to a speech

Precisely what do you look for when analyzing the information that you have gathered about your audience? Consider answering the following questions:

1. How are audience members similar to one another?
2. How are audience members different from one another?
3. Based on their similarities and differences, how can I establish common ground with the audience?

ESTABLISH COMMON GROUND WITH YOUR AUDIENCE

When you know what your audience members have in common as well as how they differ, both in terms of demographic information (such as age or education level) and in terms of attitudes and beliefs they may have about you or your topic, then you can seek to establish common ground with your audience. To establish **common ground** with your audience is to identify ways in which you and your listeners are alike. The more your listeners identify with you and the goals of your message, the more likely they are to respond positively. Keep in mind that although each audience member is unique, with his or her own characteristics and preferences, when you analyze your audience, you are looking for general ways in which they are alike or different. Sometimes the only common ground you may find is that both you and your listeners believe that the issue you are addressing is a serious problem; you may have different views about the best solution. If, for example, you were addressing a group of people who were mostly against increasing taxes to pay teachers higher salaries, but you were in favor of a tax increase, you could establish common ground by noting that both you and your listeners value education and want high-quality teachers in the classroom.

When you meet someone for the first time, you may spend time identifying people that you both know or places you've both visited; you begin to establish a relationship with this person. A **relationship** is an ongoing connection you have with another person. A public speaker seeks to establish a relationship with his or her audience by identifying what the speaker has in common with the listeners. Use the information from your audience analysis to establish a relationship with your listeners; build bridges between you and your audience.

LOOK FOR AUDIENCE MEMBER SIMILARITIES

Knowing what several members of your audience have in common can help you craft a message that resonates with them. For example, if your audience members are approximately the same age, then you have some basis for selecting examples and illustrations that your listeners will understand.

When looking for similarities, consider the following questions. What ethnic and cultural characteristics do audience members have in common? Are they all from the same geographic region? Do they (or did they) attend the same college or university? Do they have similar levels of education? Do they all like the same kinds of things? Answering these and other questions will help you develop your own ideas and relate your message to your listeners.

LOOK FOR AUDIENCE MEMBER DIFFERENCES

Besides noting similarities, you can also note differences among your audience members. It is unlikely that audience members for the speeches you give in class will have similar backgrounds. The range of cultural backgrounds, ethnic ties, and religious traditions among students at most colleges and universities is rapidly expanding. You can also note a range of differences in age and gender, as well as perspectives about your topic.

common ground
Similarities between a speaker and audience members in attitudes, values, beliefs, or behaviors

relationship
An ongoing connection you have with another person

Winston Churchill (1874–1965)

The great British Prime Minister Winston Churchill was noted for his ability to connect with his listeners. He spoke to audiences as diverse as groups of schoolchildren; the citizens of Britain; academics at Westminster College in Fulton, Missouri, who first heard Churchhill use the phrase "iron curtain"; and the United States Congress. When awarding Churchill the Nobel Prize in Literature in 1953, the Nobel Committee praised his "brilliant oratory in defending exalted human values."[1]

Because Churchill was a master of empathizing with his audience's emotions, he knew how to motivate them to endure and persevere in the face of adversity. Like Churchill, be mindful of audience members' attitudes, beliefs, values, backgrounds, and emotions. An audience-centered speaker is skilled at speaking both to listeners' minds and to listeners' hearts.

[Photo: AP Images]

Adapt to Your Audience

Audience adaptation is the process of ethically using information you've gathered when analyzing your audience to help your audience clearly understand your message and to achieve your speaking objective. To adapt is to modify your message to enhance the clarity of your message and to enhance the likelihood that you will ethically achieve your goal. If you only analyze your audience but don't use the information to customize your message, the information you've gathered will be of little value. Using your skill both to learn about your listeners and then to adapt to them can help you maintain your listeners' attention and make them more receptive to your ideas.

Here's an example of how analyzing and adapting to others works: Mike spent a glorious spring break at Daytona Beach. He and three friends piled in a car and headed for a week of adventure. When he returned from the beach, sunburned and fatigued from merrymaking, people asked how his break had been. He described his escapades to his best friend, his mother, and his communication professor.

To his best friend, he bragged, "We partied all night and slept on the beach all day. It was great!" He informed his mother, "It was good to relax after the hectic pace of college." And he told his professor, "It was mentally invigorating to have time to think things out." It was the same vacation—but how different the messages were! Mike adapted his message to the people he addressed; he had analyzed his audiences.

When you are speaking in public, you should use the same process. The principle is simple, yet powerful: An effective public speaker is audience-centered. Several key questions can help you formulate an effective approach to your audience:

Consider Your Audience

- To whom am I speaking?
- What topic would be most suitable for my audience?

audience adaptation
The process of ethically using information about an audience in order to adapt one's message so that it is clear and achieves the speaking objective

Consider Your Speech Goal
- ➤ What is my objective?

Consider Your Speech Content
- ➤ What kind of information should I share with my audience
- ➤ How should I present the information to them?
- ➤ How can I gain and hold their attention?
- ➤ What kind of examples would work best?
- ➤ What method of organizing information will be most effective?

Consider Your Delivery
- ➤ What language differences and expectations do audience members have?
- ➤ What style of delivery will my audience members expect?

Being audience-centered does not mean you should tell your listeners only what they want to hear, or that you should fabricate information simply to please your audience or achieve your goal. If you adapt to your audience by abandoning your own values and sense of truth, then you will become an unethical speaker rather than an audience-centered one. It was President Truman who pondered, "I wonder how far Moses would have gone if he'd taken a poll in Egypt?"[2] The audience-centered speaker adjusts his or her topic, purpose, central idea, main ideas, supporting material, organization, and even delivery of the speech so as to encourage the audience to listen to his or her ideas. The goal is to make the audience come away from the speaking situation, if not persuaded, then at least feeling thoughtful rather than offended or hostile.

In this overview of how to become an audience-centered speaker, we've pointed out the importance of gathering information, analyzing it to establish common ground, and then using the information to ethically adapt to your listeners. Now we'll discuss these ideas in more detail. You'll want to gather and analyze information and use it to adapt to your listeners at three stages of the speechmaking process: before you speak, as you speak, and after you speak.

Analyzing Your Audience before You Speak

Learning about your audience members' backgrounds and attitudes can help you select a topic, define a purpose, develop an outline, and carry out virtually all other speech-related activities. You can gather and analyze three primary types of information:

1. Demographic
2. Psychological
3. Situational

DEMOGRAPHIC AUDIENCE ANALYSIS

As we noted earlier, *demographics* are statistics about such audience characteristics as age, gender, sexual orientation, race and culture, group membership, and socioeconomic status. Let's consider in more detail how demographic information, or **demographic audience analysis**, can help you better understand and adapt to your audience.

demographic audience analysis
Analyzing an audience by examining demographic information so as to develop a clear and effective message

AGE Although you must use caution in generalizing from only one factor such as age, that information can suggest the kinds of examples, humor, illustrations, and other types of supporting material to use in your speech. For example, many students in your public-speaking class will probably be in their late teens or early twenties. Some, however, may be older. The younger students may know the latest rap performers or musicians, for example, but the older ones may not be familiar with 50 Cent, UGK, or OutKast. If you are going to give a talk on rap music, you will have to explain who the performers are and describe or demonstrate their style if you want all the members of your class to understand what you are talking about.

For centuries, adults have lamented that younger generations don't seem to share the values of the older generation. Two researchers who have studied generational differences have found that different generations do have distinctive values and hold differing assumptions about work, duty, and certain values. Table 5.1 summarizes the values and generational characteristics of four generations—matures, baby boomers, generation X, and millennials.[3]

What do these generational differences have to do with public speaking? Over 2000 years ago, Aristotle noted that a good speaker knows how to adapt to audiences of different age levels. Your credibility as a speaker—how positively you are perceived by your audience—is dependent on your sensitivity to the values and assumptions of your listeners. Of course, the broad generalizations that we've summarized here don't apply across the board, but it's wise to consider how generational differences may affect how your message is interpreted.

Table 5.1   **Summary of Generational Characteristics**

Generation Name	Birth Years	Typical Values and Characteristics
Matures	1925–1942	Hard work Duty Sacrifice A sense of what is right Work fast
Baby Boomers	1943–1960	Personal fulfillment and optimism Crusading causes Buy now/pay later Everybody's rights Work efficiently
Generation X	1961–1981	Live with uncertainty Balance is important Live for today Save Every job is a contract
Millennials	1982–2002	Close to parents Feel "special" Goal-oriented Team-oriented A focus on achievement

GENDER Josh began his speech by thanking his predominantly female audience for taking time from their busy schedules to attend his presentation on managing personal finances. Not a bad way to begin a talk. He continued, however, by noting that their job of raising children, keeping their homes clean, and feeding their families was among the most important jobs there were. Josh thought he was paying his audience a compliment. He did not consider that today, most women work outside the home as well as in it. Many of his listeners were insulted. Many of his listeners stopped listening.

A key question to ask when considering your audience is, "What is the ratio of males to females?" No matter what the mix, avoid making sweeping judgments based on gender stereotypes. A person's **sex** is determined by biology, as reflected in his or her anatomy and reproductive system; someone is born either male or female. **Gender** is the culturally constructed and psychologically based perception of one's self as feminine or masculine. One's gender-role identity, which falls somewhere on the continuum from masculine to feminine, is learned or socially reinforced by others as well as by one's own personality and life experiences; genetics also plays a part in shaping gender-role identity. Try to ensure that your remarks reflect sensitivity to diversity in your listeners' points of view.

One goal of an audience-centered speaker is to avoid sexist language or remarks. A sexist perspective stereotypes or prejudges how someone will react based on his or her sex. Take time to educate yourself about what words, phrases, or perspectives are likely to offend or create psychological noise for your listeners. Think carefully about the implications of words or phrases you take for granted. For example, many people still use the words *ladies* or *matrons* without thinking about their connotations in U.S. culture. Be especially wary about jokes. Many are derogatory to one sex or the other. Avoid stereotypes in your stories and examples as well.

In addition, make your language and your message as inclusive as possible. If you are speaking to a mixed audience, make sure your speech relates to all your listeners, not just to one gender. If, for example, you decided to discuss breast cancer, you could note that men, too, can be victims of breast cancer and that the lives of husbands, fathers, and brothers of female victims are affected by the disease.

Finally, be cautious about assuming that men and women will respond differently to your message. Early social science research found some evidence that females were more susceptible to efforts to persuade them than were males.[4] For many years textbooks and communication teachers presented this conclusion to students. More contemporary research, however, suggests there may be no major differences between men and women in susceptibility to persuasive messages.[5]

Moreover, although some research suggests women are socialized to be more emotional and empathic than men, other evidence suggests men can be equally sensitive.[6] It is clear there are learned sex differences in language usage and nonverbal behavior, but we caution against making sweeping gender-based assumptions about your audience.

SEXUAL ORIENTATION An audience-centered speaker is sensitive to issues and attitudes about sexual orientation in contemporary society. The audience-centered speaker's goal is to enhance understanding rather than create noise that may distract an audience from becoming listeners, regardless of the attitudes or beliefs audience members may hold about sexual orientation. Stories, illustrations, and humor whose point or punch line rely on ridiculing a person because of his or her sexual orientation may lower perceptions of your credibility not only among gay and lesbian members of your audience, but also among audience members who disdain bias against gays and lesbians.

People evaluate credibility by behavior, not by intentions. Sometimes we unintentionally offend someone through more subtle misuse of language. For example, gays and lesbians typically prefer to be referred to as "gay" or "lesbian" rather than as "homosexual." Further, it is not appropriate to single out gays and lesbians as separate categories of people who are assumed to hold political, ideological, or religious

sex
A person's biological status as male or female, as reflected in his or her anatomy and reproductive system

gender
The culturally constructed and psychologically based perception of one's self as feminine or masculine

views consistently different from those of straight people. Monitor your language choice and use of illustrations and humor so you don't alienate members of your audience.[7]

CULTURE, ETHNICITY, AND RACE **Culture** is a learned system of knowledge, behavior, attitudes, beliefs, values, and norms shared by a group of people. **Ethnicity** is that portion of a person's cultural background that relates to a national or religious heritage. A person's **race** is his or her biological heritage—for example, Caucasian or Hispanic. The cultural, ethnic, or racial background of your audience influences the way they perceive your message. An effective speaker adapts to differences in culture, race, and ethnicity.

As you approach any public-speaking situation, avoid an ethnocentric mindset. **Ethnocentrism** is an assumption that your own cultural approaches are superior to those of other cultures. The audience-centered speaker is sensitive to cultural differences and avoids saying things that would disparage the cultural background of the audience.

You need not have international students in your class to have a culturally diverse audience. Unique ethnic and cultural traditions thrive among people who have lived in the United States all their lives. Students from a Polish family in Chicago, a German family in Texas, or a Haitian family in Brooklyn may be native U.S. citizens with cultural traditions different from your own. Effective public speakers seek to learn as much as possible about the cultural values and knowledge of their audience so that they can understand the best way to deliver their message.

Researchers classify or describe cultural differences along several lines.[8] Understanding these classifications may provide clues to help you adapt your message when you speak before diverse audiences.

confidently connecting with your audience

Learn as Much as You Can about Your Audience

By learning about your audience's interests, attitudes, and beliefs as well as demographic details about them, you'll be better able to customize a message for your listeners. The more you tailor your message directly to your audience, the more you'll be able to confidently connect to them. Because you have customized your message, they will want to hear it, and you'll be speaking directly to their interests and needs. Also, by focusing on your audience instead of on your nervousness about speaking, you can enhance your confidence. Because you're not dwelling on your own anxieties, you'll be focused on communicating your audience-centered message to others.

> **Individualistic and Collectivistic Cultures.** Some cultures place greater emphasis on individual achievement, whereas others place more value on group or collective achievement. Among the countries that tend to value individual accomplishment are Australia, Great Britain, the United States, Canada, Belgium, and Denmark. By contrast, Japan, Thailand, Colombia, Taiwan, and Venezuela are among countries that have more collectivistic cultures.

Adapting to listeners from individualistic and collectivistic cultures. Audience members from individualistic cultures, such as the majority of people from the United States, value and respond positively to appeals that encourage personal accomplishment and single out individual achievement. People from individualistic cultures are expected to speak up to champion individual rights.

Audience members from collectivistic cultures, such as people who were raised in an Asian culture, may be more likely to value group or team rewards. Community is an important value for those from collectivistic cultures. They also don't like to be singled out for individual accomplishments. And they value making sure that others are perceived in a positive way; it's important for them and others to save face—to be perceived as valued by others.

> **High-Context and Low-Context Cultures.** The terms *high-context* and *low-context* refer to the importance of unspoken or nonverbal messages. In high-context cultures, people place considerable importance on such contextual factors as tone of voice, gestures, facial expression, movement, and other nonverbal aspects of communication. People from low-context traditions are just the opposite. They place greater emphasis on the words themselves; the surrounding context has a relatively low impact on the meaning of the message. The Arab culture is a high-context culture, as are those of Japan, Asia, and southern Europe. Low-context

culture
A learned system of knowledge, behavior, attitudes, beliefs, values, and norms that is shared by a group of people

ethnicity
That portion of a person's cultural background that relates to a national or religious heritage

race
A person's biological heritage

ethnocentrism
The assumption that one's own cultural perspectives and methods are superior to those of other cultures

cultures, which place a high value on words, include those of Switzerland, Germany, the United States, and Australia.

Adapting to listeners from high-context and low-context cultures. Listeners from low-context cultures will need and expect more detailed and explicit information from you as a speaker. Subtle and indirect messages are less likely to be effective.

People from high-context cultures will pay particular attention to your delivery and to the communication environment when they try to interpret your meaning. These people will be less impressed by a speaker who boasts about his or her own accomplishments; such an audience will expect and value more indirect ways of establishing credibility. A listener from a high-context culture will also expect a less dramatic and dynamic style of delivery.

> **Tolerance of Uncertainty and Need for Certainty.** Some cultures are more comfortable with ambiguity and uncertainty than others. Those cultures in which people need to have details "nailed down" tend to develop very specific regulations and rules. People from cultures with a greater tolerance of uncertainty are more comfortable with vagueness and are not upset when all the details aren't spelled out. Cultures with a high need for certainty include those of Russia, Japan, France, and Costa Rica. Cultures that have a higher tolerance for uncertainty include those of Great Britain and Indonesia.

Adapting to listeners from cultures that tolerate or avoid uncertainty. If you are speaking to an audience of people who have a high need for certainty, make sure you provide concrete details when you present your message; they also want and expect to know what action steps they can take. People who value certainty will respond well if you provide a clear and explicit preview of your message in your introduction; they also seem to prefer a clear, logical, and linear step-by-step organizational pattern.

People from cultures that are more comfortable with uncertainty do not necessarily need to have the explicit purpose of the message spelled out for them. In addition, they are generally less likely to need specific prescriptions to solve problems compared to listeners who want to avoid uncertainty.

> **High-Power and Low-Power Cultures.** Power is the ability to influence or control others. Some cultures prefer clearly defined lines of authority and responsibility; these are said to be high-power cultures. People in low-power cultures are more comfortable with blurred lines of authority and less formal titles. Austria, Israel, Denmark, Norway, Switzerland, and Great Britain typically have an equitable approach to power distribution. Cultures that are high on the power dimension include those of the Philippines, Mexico, Venezuela, India, Brazil, and France.

Adapting to listeners from high-power and low-power cultures. People from high-power cultures are more likely to perceive people in leadership roles—including speakers—as credible. They also will be more comfortable with solutions that identify or acknowledge differences in social class.

Those from low-power cultures often favor more shared approaches to leadership and governance. They will expect a more democratic approach to solving problems and will value the extra time it may take for many people to be consulted to reach consensus on an issue.

> **Long-Term and Short-Term Orientation to Time.** Some cultures take the view that it simply may take a long time to accomplish certain goals. People from Asian cultures, for example, and some from South American cultures such as that of Brazil often value patience, persistence, and deferred gratification more than people from cultures with a short-term orientation to time. People with a short-term time orientation, which is often a characteristic of industrialized Western cultures such as those of Canada and the United States, are very attuned to time and time management. Short-term cultures also value quick responses to problems.

CULTURAL VALUE	CULTURAL CHARACTERISTIC	HOW TO ADAPT TO CULTURAL CHARACTERISTIC
Individualistic Culture	Individual achievement is emphasized more than group achievement.	➤ Stress the importance of individual rewards and recognition. ➤ Identify how audience members will benefit from your ideas or proposal.
Collectivistic Culture	Group or team achievement is emphasized more than individual achievement.	➤ Stress the importance of community values. ➤ Help audience members save face and be perceived in a positive way.
High-Context Culture	The context of a message—including nonverbal cues, tone of voice, posture, and facial expression—is often emphasized more than the words.	➤ Don't boast about your specific accomplishments. ➤ Use more subtle, less dramatic delivery style.
Low-Context Cultures	The words in a message are emphasized more than the surrounding context.	➤ Be sure to make your ideas and recommendations explicit. ➤ Although delivery cues are important, listeners will expect your message to be clear.
Tolerance for Uncertainty	People can accept ambiguity and are not bothered if they do not know all of the details.	➤ It is not as important to develop a specific solution to a problem you may present in your speech. ➤ The purpose of the speech need not be clearly explicated.
Need for Certainty	People want specifics and dislike ambiguity.	➤ Provide an explicit overview of what you will present in your speech. ➤ Create a logical and clear organizational pattern for your speech.
High-Power Culture	Status and power differences are emphasized; roles and chains of command are clearly defined.	➤ Remember that listeners perceive people in leadership positions as powerful and credible. ➤ Develop messages that acknowledge differences in status among people.
Low-Power Cultures	Status and power differences receive less emphasis; people strive for equality rather than exalting those in positions of leadership.	➤ Discuss shared approaches to governance and leadership. ➤ Develop solutions that involve others in reaching consensus.
Long-Term Time Orientation	Time is abundant, and accomplishing goals may take considerable time.	➤ Appeal to listeners' persistence, patience, and delayed gratification. ➤ Emphasize how ideas and suggestions will benefit future generations.
Short-Term Time Orientation	Time is an important resource.	➤ Identify how ideas and proposals you discuss will have an immediate impact on listeners. ➤ Note how actions will have a direct impact on achieving results.

Adapting to listeners from cultures with long-term and short-term time orientations. When speaking to people who take a long-term orientation to time, it is important to stress how issues and problems affect not only the present but also the future, especially future generations. It's not that people with a long-term orientation don't value efficiency and effectiveness; they simply accept that things don't always happen quickly.

People with a short-term orientation to time will want to know what immediate action steps can be taken to solve a problem. They also are results-oriented and expect that individual or group effort should result in a some specific positive outcome.

GROUP MEMBERSHIP It's said we are each members of a gang—it's just that some gangs are more socially acceptable than others. We are social creatures; we congregate in groups to gain an identity, to help accomplish projects we support, and to have fun. So it's reasonable to assume that many of your listeners belong to groups, clubs, or organizations. Knowing what groups your listeners belong to can help you make inferences about their likes, dislikes, beliefs, and values.

- **Religious Groups.** Marsha is a follower of Scientology, and she believes that the philosophy outlined in *Dianetics* (the book that is the basis of Scientology) is as important as the religious precepts in the Bible. Planning to speak before a Bible-belt college audience, many of whose members view Scientology as a cult, Marsha would be wise to consider how her listeners will respond to her message. This is not to suggest that she should refuse the speaking invitation. She should, however, be aware of her audience's religious beliefs as she prepares and presents her speech.

  When touching on religious beliefs or an audience's values, use great care in what you say and how you say it. Remind yourself that some members of your audience will undoubtedly not share your beliefs, and that few beliefs are held as intensely as religious ones. If you do not wish to offend your listeners, plan and deliver your speech with much thought and sensitivity.

- **Political Groups.** Are members of your audience active in politics? Knowing whether your listeners are active in such groups as Young Republicans or Young Democrats can help you address political topics. Members of environmental groups may also hold strong political opinions on various topics and political candidates.

- **Work Groups.** Most professions give rise to professional organizations or associations to which people can belong. If you are speaking to an audience of professionals, it's important to be aware of professional organizations they may belong to (there may be several) and to know, for example, if such organizations have taken formal stands that may influence audience members' views on certain issues. Work groups also may use abbreviations or acronyms that may be useful to know. Your communication instructor, for example, may be a member of the National Communication Association (NCA) and may belong to a specific division of the NCA, such as the IDD (Instructional Development Division).

- **Social Groups.** Some groups exist just so that people can get together and enjoy a common activity. Book clubs, film clubs, cycling clubs, cooking groups, dancing groups, and bowling teams exist to bring people with similar ideas of fun together to enjoy the activity. Knowing whether members of your audience belong to such groups may help you adapt your topic to them or, if you are involved in similar groups, establish common ground with them.

Service Groups. Many people are actively involved in groups that emphasize community service as their primary mission. If you are speaking to a service group such as the Lions Club or the Kiwanis Club, you can reasonably assume that your listeners value community service and will be interested in how to make their community a better place.

SOCIOECONOMIC STATUS Socioeconomic status is a person's perceived importance and influence based on such factors as income, occupation, and education level. In Europe, Asia, the Middle East, and other parts of the world, centuries-old traditions of acknowledging status differences still exist today. Status differences exist in the United States but are often more subtle. Having an idea about audience members' incomes, occupations, and education levels can be helpful as you develop a message that connects with listeners.

Income. Having some general idea of the income level of your listeners can be of great value to you as a speaker. For example, if you know that most audience members are struggling to meet weekly expenses, it is unwise to talk about how to see the cultural riches of Europe by traveling first class. But talking about how to get paid to travel to Europe by serving as a courier may hold considerable interest.

Occupation. Knowing what people do for a living can give you useful information about how to adapt your message to them. Speaking to teachers gives you an opportunity to use different examples and illustrations than if you were speaking to lawyers, ministers, or automobile assembly-line workers. Many college-age students may hold jobs, but don't yet hold the jobs they aspire to after they graduate from college. Knowing their future career plans can help you adjust your topic and supporting material to your listeners' professional goals.

Education. About one-third of U.S. high-school graduates obtain a college diploma. Less than 10 percent of the population earn graduate degrees. The educational background of your listeners is yet another component of socioeconomic status that can help you plan your message. For example, you have a good idea that your classmates in your college-level public-speaking class value education, because they are striving, often at great sacrifice, to advance their education. Knowing the educational background of your audience can help you make decisions about your choice of vocabulary, your language style, and your use of examples and illustrations.

ADAPTING TO DIVERSE LISTENERS The most recent U.S. Census figures document what you already know from your own life experiences: We all live in an age of diversity. For example,

- Two-thirds of immigrants worldwide come to the United States.[9]

- It is estimated that more than 40 million U.S. residents speak something other than English as their first language, including 18 million people whose first language is Spanish.[10]

- Whites are the minority ethnic group in nearly half of the largest cities in the United States.[11]

- People who have traditionally been called minorities are now in the majority in four states: Hawaii (75 percent), New Mexico (57 percent), California (57 percent), and Texas (52 percent).[12]

socioeconomic status
A person's perceived importance and influence based on income, occupation, and education level

Having someone sign your words as you speak is a way of adapting to audience members who may be deaf or hard of hearing.

[Photo: Jeff Greenberg/Alamy]

Virtually every state in the United States has experienced a dramatic increase in foreign-born residents. If trends continue as they have during the past quarter-century, cultural and ethnic diversity will continue to grow during your lifetime. This swell of immigrants translates to increased diversity in all aspects of society, including in most audiences you'll face—whether in business, at school-board meetings, or in your college or university classes.

Audience diversity, however, involves more factors than just ethnic and cultural differences. Central to our point about considering your audience is examining the full spectrum of audience diversity, not just cultural differences. Each topic we've reviewed when discussing demographic and psychological aspects of an audience contributes to overall audience diversity. Diversity simply means differences. Audience members are diverse. The question and challenge for a public speaker is, "How do I adapt to listeners with such different backgrounds and experiences?" We offer several general strategies. You could decide to focus on a target audience, consciously use a variety of methods of adapting to listeners, seek common ground, or consider using powerful visual images to present your key points.

➤ **Focus on a Target Audience.** A **target audience** is a specific segment of your audience that you most want to address or influence. You've undoubtedly been a target of skilled communicators and may not have been aware that messages had been tailored just for you. For example, most colleges and universities spend a considerable amount of time and money encouraging students to apply for admission. You probably received some of this recruitment literature in the mail during your high-school years. But not every student in the United States receives brochures from the same college. Colleges and universities targeted you based on your test scores, your interests, where you live, and your involvement in school-sponsored or extracurricular activities. Likewise, as a public speaker, you may want to think about the portion of your audience you most want to understand your message or be convinced.

target audience
A specific segment of an audience that you most want to influence

The challenge when consciously focusing on a target audience is not to lose or alienate the rest of your listeners—to keep the entire audience in mind while simultaneously making a specific attempt to hit your target segment. For example, Sasha was trying to convince his listeners to invest in the stock market instead of relying on the Social Security system. He wisely decided to focus on the younger listeners; those approaching retirement age have already made their major investment decisions. Although he focused on the younger members of his audience, however, Sasha didn't forget the mature listeners. He suggested that older listeners encourage their children or grandchildren to consider his proposal. He focused on a target audience, but didn't ignore others.

➤ **Use Diverse Strategies for a Diverse Audience.** Another approach you can adopt, either separately or in combination with a target audience focus, is to use a variety of strategies to reflect the diversity of your audience. Based on your efforts to gather information about your audience, you should know the various constituencies that will likely be present for your talk. Consider using several methods of reaching the different listeners in your audience. For example, review the following strategies:

- Use a variety of different types of supporting materials (illustrations, examples, statistics, opinions).

- Remember the power of stories. People from most cultures appreciate a good story. And some people, such as those from Asian and Middle Eastern cultures, prefer hearing stories and parables used to make a point or support an argument, rather than facts and statistics.

- If you're very uncertain about cultural preferences, use a balance of both logical support (statistics, facts, specific examples) and emotional support (stories and illustrations).

- Consider showing the audience an outline of your key ideas using an overhead transparency or computer-generated graphic. If there is a language barrier between you and your audience, being able to read portions of your speech as they hear you speaking may improve audience members' comprehension. If an interpreter is translating your message, an outline can also help ensure that your interpreter will communicate your message accurately.

➤ **Identify Common Values.** People have debated for a long time whether there are universal human values. Several scholars have made strong arguments that common human values do exist. Communication researcher David Kale suggests that all people can identify with the individual struggle to enhance one's own dignity and worth, although different cultures express that in different ways.[13] A second common value is the search for a world at peace. Underlying that quest is a fundamental desire for equilibrium, balance, and stability. Although there may always be a small but corrosive minority of people whose actions do not support the universal value of peace, the prevailing human values in most cultures ultimately do support peace.

Cultural anthropologists specialize in the study of behavior that is common to all humans. Cultural anthropologist Donald Brown has compiled a list of hundreds of "surface" universals of beliefs, emotions, or behavior. According to Brown, people in all cultures[14]

- Have beliefs about death

- Have a childhood fear of strangers

- Have a division of labor by sex

- Experience certain emotions and feelings, such as envy, pain, jealousy, shame, and pride

- Use facial expressions to express emotions

- Have rules for etiquette
- Experience empathy
- Value some degree of collaboration or cooperation
- Experience conflict and seek to manage or mediate conflict

Of course, not all cultures have the same beliefs about death or the same way of dividing up labor—but people in all cultures address these issues.

Intercultural communication scholars Larry Samovar and Richard Porter suggest other commonalities that people from all cultures share. They propose that all humans seek physical pleasure as well as emotional and psychological pleasure and confirmation and seek to avoid personal harm.[15] Although each culture defines what constitutes pleasure and pain, it may be useful to interpret human behavior with these general assumptions in mind. People also realize that their biological lives will end, that to some degree each person is isolated from all other human beings, that we each make choices, and that each person seeks to give life meaning. These similarities offer some basis for developing common messages with universal meaning.

Identifying common cultural issues and similarities can help you establish common ground with your audience. If you are speaking about an issue on which you and your audience have widely different views, identifying a larger common value that is relevant to your topic (such as the importance of peace, prosperity, or family) can help you find a foothold so that your listeners will at least listen to your ideas.

- **Rely on Visual Materials That Transcend Language Differences**. Pictures and images can communicate universal messages—especially emotional ones. Although there is no universal language, most listeners, regardless of culture and language, can comprehend visible expressions of pain, joy, sorrow, and happiness. An image of a mother holding the frail, malnourished body of her dying child communicates the ravages of famine without elaborate verbal explanations. The more varied your listeners' cultural experiences, the more effective it can be to use visual materials to illustrate your ideas.

PSYCHOLOGICAL AUDIENCE ANALYSIS

Demographic information lets you make some useful inferences about your audience and to predict likely responses. Learning how the members of your audience feel about your topic and purpose may provide specific clues about possible reactions. A **psychological audience analysis** explores an audience's attitudes toward a topic, purpose, and speaker, while probing the underlying beliefs and values that might affect these attitudes.

It is important for a speaker to distinguish among *attitudes*, *beliefs*, and *values*. The attitudes, beliefs, and values of an audience may greatly influence a speaker's selection of a topic and specific purpose, as well as various other aspects of speech preparation and delivery.

An **attitude** reflects likes or dislikes. Do you like health food? Are you for or against capital punishment? Should movies be censored? What are your views on nuclear energy? Your answers to these widely varied questions reflect your attitudes.

A **belief** is what you hold to be true or false. If you think the sun will rise in the east in the morning, you hold a belief about the sun based on what you perceive to be true or false.

A **value** is an enduring concept of good and bad, right and wrong. More deeply ingrained than either attitudes or beliefs, values are therefore more resistant to change. Values support both attitudes and beliefs. For example, you like health food because you believe that natural products are more healthful. And you *value* good

---

psychological audience analysis
Analyzing the attitudes, beliefs, values, and other psychological information about an audience in order to develop a clear and effective message

attitude
An individual's likes or dislikes

belief
An individual's perception of what is true or false

value
Enduring concept of good and bad, right and wrong

RECAP

- ➤ Focus on a target audience without losing or alienating the rest of your listeners.
- ➤ Use diverse supporting materials that reflect a balance of logical and emotional support.
- ➤ Use visual aids.
- ➤ Appeal to such common values as peace, prosperity, and family.

health. You are against capital punishment because you believe that it is wrong to kill people. You *value* human life. As with beliefs, a speaker who has some understanding of an audience's values is better able to adapt a speech to them.

ANALYZING ATTITUDES TOWARD THE TOPIC The topic of a speech provides one focus for an audience's attitudes, beliefs, and values. It is useful to know how members of an audience feel about your topic. Are they interested or apathetic? How much do they already know about the topic? If the topic is controversial, are they for or against it? Knowing the answers to these questions from the outset lets you adjust your message accordingly. For example, if you plan to talk about increasing taxes to improve education in your state, you probably want to know how your listeners feel about taxes and education.

When you are analyzing your audience, it may help to categorize the group along three dimensions: interested–uninterested, favorable–unfavorable, and captive–voluntary. With an *interested* audience, your task is simply to hold and amplify interest throughout the speech. If your audience is *uninterested*, you need to find ways to "hook" the members. In Chapter 16, we describe ways to motivate an audience by addressing issues related to their needs and interests. Given our visually oriented culture, consider using visual aids to gain and maintain the attention of apathetic listeners.

You may also want to gauge how *favorable* or *unfavorable* your audience may feel toward you and your message before you begin to speak. Some audiences, of course, are neutral, apathetic, or simply uninformed about what you plan to say. We provide explicit suggestions for approaching favorable, neutral, and unfavorable audiences in Chapter 17 when we discuss persuasive speaking. But even if your objective is simply to inform, it is useful to know whether your audience is predisposed to respond positively or negatively toward you or your message. Giving an informative talk about classical music would be quite challenging, for example, if you were addressing an audience full of die-hard punk-rock fans. You might decide to show the connections between classical music and punk, to arouse their interest.

YOUR SPEECH CLASS AS AUDIENCE You may think that your public-speaking class is not a typical audience because class members are required to attend. Your speech class is a *captive* audience rather than a *voluntary* one. A captive audience has externally imposed reasons for being there (such as a requirement to attend class). Because class members must show up to earn credit for class, you need not worry that they will get up and leave during your speech. However, your classroom speeches are still *real* speeches. Your class members are certainly real people with likes, dislikes, beliefs, and values.

Your classroom speeches should connect with your listeners so that they forget they are required to be in the audience. Class members will listen if your message gives them new, useful information; touches them emotionally; or persuades them to change their opinion or behavior in support of your position.

Adapting Your Message to Different Types of Audiences

TYPE OF AUDIENCE	EXAMPLE	HOW TO BE AUDIENCE-CENTERED
Interested	Mayors who attend a talk by the governor about increasing security and reducing the threat of terrorism	Acknowledge audience interest early in your speech; use the interest they have in you and your topic to gain and maintain their attention.
Uninterested	Junior high students attending a lecture about retirement benefits	Make it a high priority to tell your listeners why your message should be of interest to them. Remind your listeners throughout your speech how your message relates to their lives.
Favorable	A religious group that meets to hear a group leader talk about the importance of their beliefs	Use audience interest to move them closer to your speaking goal; you may be more explicit in telling them in your speech conclusion what you would like them to do.
Unfavorable	Students who attend a lecture by the university president explaining why tuition and fees will increase 15 percent next year	Be realistic in what you expect to accomplish; acknowledge their opposing point of view; consider using facts to refute misperceptions they may hold.
Voluntary	Parents attending a lecture by the new principal at their children's school	Anticipate why they are coming to hear you, and speak about the issues they want you to address.
Captive	Students in a public-speaking class	Find out who will be in your audience, and use this knowledge to adapt your message to them.

You will undoubtedly give other speeches to other captive audiences. Audiences at work or at professional meetings are often captive in the sense that they may be required to attend lectures or presentations to receive continuing-education credit or as part of their job duties. Your goal with a captive audience is the same as with other types of audiences. You should make your speech just as interesting and effective as one designed for a voluntary audience. You still have an obligation to address your listeners' needs and interests and to keep them engaged in what you have to say. A captive audience gives you an opportunity to polish your speaking skills.

ANALYZING ATTITUDES TOWARD YOU, THE SPEAKER Audience members' attitudes toward you in your role as speaker is another factor that can influence their reaction to your speech. Regardless of how they feel about your topic or purpose, if members of an audience regard you as credible, they will be much more likely to be interested in, and supportive of, what you have to say.

Your credibility—others' perception of you as trustworthy, knowledgeable, and interesting—is one of the main factors that will shape your audience's attitude toward you. If you establish your credibility before you begin to discuss your topic, your listeners will be more likely to believe what you say and to think that you are knowledgeable, interesting, and dynamic.

For example, when a high-school health teacher asks a former drug addict to speak to a class about the dangers of cocaine addiction, the teacher recognizes that the speaker's experiences make him credible and that his message will be far more convincing than if the teacher just lectured on the perils of cocaine use.

An audience's positive attitude toward a speaker can overcome negative or apathetic attitudes they may have toward the speaker's topic or purpose. If your analysis reveals that your audience does not recognize you as an authority on your subject, you will need to build your credibility into the speech. If you have had personal experience with your topic, be sure to let the audience know. You will gain credibility instantly. We will provide additional strategies for enhancing your credibility in Chapter 17.

SITUATIONAL AUDIENCE ANALYSIS

So far we have concentrated on the people who will be your listeners, as the primary focus of being an audience-centered speaker. You should also consider your speaking situation. **Situational audience analysis** includes an examination of the time and place of your speech, the size of your audience, and the speaking occasion. Although these elements are not technically characteristics of the *audience*, they can have a major effect on how your listeners respond to you.

Successful speakers analyze the situation in order to be sure to meet the specific needs of their particular audience.

[Photo: Cleve Bryant/PhotoEdit]

TIME You may have no control over when you will be speaking, but when designing and delivering a talk, a skilled public speaker considers the time of day as well as audience expectations about the speech length. If you are speaking to a group of exhausted parents during a midweek evening meeting of the band-boosters club, you can bet they will appreciate a direct, to-the-point presentation more than a long oration. If you are on a program with other speakers, speaking first or last on the program carries a slight edge, because people tend to remember what comes first or last. Speaking early in the morning when people may not be quite awake, after lunch when they may feel a bit drowsy, or late in the afternoon when they are tired may mean you'll have to strive consciously for a more energetic delivery to keep your listeners' attention.

Another aspect of time: Be mindful of your time limits. If your audience expects you to speak for 20 minutes, it is usually better to end either right at 20 minutes or even a little earlier; most North Americans don't appreciate being kept overtime for a speech. In your public-speaking class you will be given time limits, and you may wonder whether such strict time-limit expectations occur outside of public-speaking class. The answer is a most definite yes. Whether it's a business presentation or a speech to the city council or school board, time limits are often strictly enforced.

SIZE OF AUDIENCE The size of your audience directly affects speaking style and audience expectations about delivery. As a general rule, the larger the audience, the more likely they are to expect a more formal style. With an audience of ten or fewer, you can punctuate a very conversational style by taking questions from your listeners. If you and your listeners are so few that you can be seated around a table, they may expect you to stay seated for your presentation. Many business "speeches" are given around a conference table.

A group of between 20 to 30 people—the size of most public-speaking classes—will expect more formality than the audience of a dozen or less. Your speaking style can still be conversational in quality, but your speech should be appropriately structured and well organized; your delivery may include more expansive gestures than you display during a one-on-one chat with a friend or colleague.

situational audience analysis
An examination of the time and place of a speech, the audience size, and the speaking occasion in order to develop a clear and effective message

Audiences that fill a lecture hall will still appreciate a direct, conversational style, but your gestures may increase in size, and, if your voice will be unamplified, you will be expected to speak with enough volume and intensity so that people in the last row can hear you.

LOCATION In your speech class, you have the advantage of knowing what the room looks like, but in a new speaking situation, you may not have that advantage. If at all possible, visit the place where you will speak to examine the physical setting and find out, for example, how far the audience will be from the lectern. Physical conditions such as room temperature and lighting can affect your performance, audience response, and the overall success of the speech.

Room arrangement and decor may affect the way an audience responds. Be aware of the arrangement and appearance of the room in which you will speak. If your speaking environment is less than ideal, you may need to work especially hard to hold your audience's attention. Although you probably would not be able to make major changes in the speaking environment, it is ultimately up to you to obtain the best speaking environment you can. The arrangement of chairs, placement of audiovisual materials, and opening or closing of drapes should all be in your control.

OCCASION Another important way to gain clues about your listeners is to consider the reason this audience is here. What occasion brings this audience together? The mindset of people gathered for a funeral will obviously be different from that of people who've asked you to say a few words after a banquet. Knowing the occasion helps you predict both demographic characteristics of the audience and the members' state of mind.

If you're presenting a speech at an annual or monthly meeting, you have the advantage of being able to ask those who've attended previous presentations what kind of audience typically gathers for the occasion. Your best source of information may be either the person who invited you to speak or someone who has attended similar events. Knowing when you will speak on the program or whether a meal will be served before or after you talk will help you gauge what your audience expects from you.

In preparing for a speaking assignment, ask the following questions, and keep the answers in mind:

1. How many people are expected to attend the speech?
2. How will the audience seating be arranged?
3. How close will I be to the audience?
4. Will I speak from a lectern?
5. Will I be expected to use a microphone?
6. What time of day will I be speaking?
7. What is the room lighting like? Will the audience seating area be darkened beyond a lighted stage?
8. Will I have adequate equipment for my visual aids?
9. Where will I appear on the program?
10. Will there be noise or distractions outside the room?

Advance preparation will help you avoid last-minute surprises about the speaking environment and the physical arrangements for your speech. A well-prepared speaker adapts his or her message not only to the audience but also to the speaking environment.

Also keep in mind that when you arrive to give your speech, you can make changes in the previous speaker's room arrangements. For example, the purpose of the speaker immediately before Yue Hong was to generate interest in a memorial for

DEMOGRAPHIC CHARACTERISTICS

Age

Gender

Sexual orientation

Cultural, ethnic, or racial background

Group membership

Socioeconomic status

PSYCHOLOGICAL CHARACTERISTICS

Attitudes: Likes and dislikes

Beliefs: What is perceived to be true or false

Values: What is perceived to be good or bad

SITUATIONAL CHARACTERISTICS

Time

Audience size

Location

Occasion

ANALYZING AND ADAPTING TO THE SPEAKING SITUATION

Questions to Ask	Adaptation Strategies
Time	
What time of the day will I be speaking?	If your audience may be tired or not yet awake, consider increasing the energy level of your delivery.
Where will I appear on the program?	Audiences are more likely to get the strongest impressions from those who speak first or last.
What are the time limits for the speech?	Most listeners do not appreciate speakers who exceed their time limit. Unless you are a spellbinding speaker, don't speak longer than your listeners expect you to.
Size	
How many people will be in the audience?	Smaller audiences usually expect a more conversational, informal delivery quality; larger audiences usually expect a more formal presentation.
Will the audience be so large I'll need a microphone?	Make sure you understand the mechanics of the microphone system before you rise to speak.
Location	
How will the room be arranged?	If you want a more informal speaking atmosphere, consider arranging the chairs in a circle. In a large room, consider inviting people in the back of the room to move closer to the front, if necessary.
What is the room lighting like?	If the audience will be in the dark, it's more difficult to gauge their nonverbal responses. If you need to use presentation aids, make sure the room lighting is easy to adjust so people can see your images clearly.
Will there be noise or distractions outside the room?	Before the speech begins, consider strategies to minimize outside noise such as closing windows and doors, adjusting window blinds or shades, or politely asking that people in other nearby rooms be mindful of your presentation.
Occasion	
What occasion brings the audience together?	Make sure you understand what your listeners expect, and strive to meet those expectations.
Is the speech an annual or monthly event? Has a similar speaking occasion occurred with this audience before?	Learn how other speakers have adapted to the audience. Ask for examples of what successful speakers have done to succeed with this audience. Or ask whether certain issues or topics may offend your audience.

Asian Americans who fought in Vietnam. Because the previous speaker wanted to make sure the audience felt free to ask questions, the chairs were arranged in a semicircle and the lights were turned on. But Yue Hong was giving a more formal presentation on the future of the Vietnamese population, which included a brief slide show. So when the preceding speaker had finished, Yue Hong rearranged the chairs and darkened the room.

 ## Adapting to Your Audience as You Speak

So far, we have focused on discovering as much as possible about an audience before the speaking event. Prespeech analyses help with each step of the public-speaking process: selecting a topic, formulating a specific purpose, gathering supporting material, identifying major ideas, organizing the speech, and planning its delivery. Each of these components depends on understanding your audience. But audience analysis and adaptation do not end when you have crafted your speech. They continue as you deliver your speech.

Generally, a public speaker does not have an exchange with the audience unless the speech is part of a question-and-answer or discussion format. Once the speech is in progress, the speaker must rely on nonverbal clues from the audience to judge how people are responding to the message.

Once, when speaking in India, Mark Twain was denied eye contact with his listeners by a curtain separating him from his audience. Mark Twain's daughter, Clara, recalled this experience:

> One of Father's first lectures was before a Purdah audience; in other words, the women all sat behind a curtain through which they could peek at Mark Twain without being seen by him . . . a deadly affair for the poor humorist, who had not even the pleasure of scanning the faces of his mute audience.[16]

Mark Twain missed learning how well his speech was being received as he was speaking. You could experience the same disadvantage if you fail to look at your listeners while you're speaking.

IDENTIFYING NONVERBAL AUDIENCE CUES

Many beginning public speakers may find it challenging at first not only to have the responsibility of presenting a speech they have rehearsed but also to have to change or modify the speech on the spot. We assure you that with experience you can develop the sensitivity to adapt to your listeners, much as a jazz musician adapts to the other musicians in the ensemble, but it will take practice. Although it's not possible to read your listeners' minds, it is important to analyze and adapt to cues that can enhance the effectiveness of your message. The first step in developing this skill is to be aware of the often unspoken clues that let you know whether your audience either is hanging on every word or is bored. After learning to "read" your audience, you then need to consider developing a repertoire of behaviors to help you connect with your listeners.

Consider Your Audience

A Chinese proverb says that a journey of a thousand miles begins with a single step. Developing and delivering a speech may seem like a daunting journey. But we believe that if you take it one step at a time and keep your focus on your audience, you'll be rewarded with a well-crafted and well-delivered message.

To help you see how the audience-centered public speaking process unfolds step by step, we will explore each step of the speechmaking process by showing how one student prepared and delivered a successful speech. In 2007, Ashley Tinnell participated in intercollegiate forensics at the University of Texas. Her persuasive speech, "Recipe for Disaster," is outlined in Chapter 11.[17] In the chapters ahead, we will walk you through the process Ashley used to develop her award-winning speech.

Even before she selected her topic, Ashley thought about her audience. Realizing that her listeners would include both university students and faculty, she began to think about topics that would be relevant to both groups. And she knew that she would be able to discuss complex issues, using a fairly advanced vocabulary, for this educated audience.

The Developing Your Speech Step by Step feature in the chapters ahead will provide a window through which you can watch Ashley at work on each step of the audience-centered public-speaking process.

SPEAKER'S HOMEPAGE

Gathering Information about Your Audience

The following Web sites provide information that may help you better understand your listeners' backgrounds and interests.

➤ U.S. BUREAU OF LABOR STATISTICS
   This is a great source for socioeconomic data.
   www.bls.gov

➤ GALLUP POLL
   Provides selected results from the vast resources of the Gallup polling organization.
   www.gallup.com

➤ U.S. CENSUS BUREAU
   This is a valuable source that includes reports on demographics.
   www.census.gov/

EYE CONTACT Perhaps the best way to determine whether your listeners are maintaining interest in your speech is to note the amount of eye contact they have with you. The more contact they have, the more likely it is that they are listening to your message. If you find them repeatedly looking at their watches, looking down at the program (or, worse yet, closing their eyes), you can reasonably guess that they have lost interest in what you're talking about.

FACIAL EXPRESSION Another clue to whether an audience is "with you" is facial expression. Members of an attentive audience not only make direct eye contact but also have attentive facial expressions. Beware of a frozen, unresponsive face. We call this sort of expression the "in-a-stupor" look. The classic in-a-stupor expression consists of a slightly tilted head, a faint, frozen smile, and often, a hand holding up the chin. This expression may give the appearance of interest, but it more often means that the person is daydreaming or thinking of something other than your topic.

MOVEMENT An attentive audience doesn't move much. An early sign of inattentiveness is fidgeting fingers, which may escalate to pencil wagging, leg jiggling, and arm wiggling. Seat squirming, feet shuffling, and general body movement often indicate that members of the audience have lost interest in your message.

NONVERBAL RESPONSIVENESS Interested audience members respond verbally and nonverbally when encouraged or invited by the speaker. When you ask for a show of hands and audience members sheepishly look at one another and eventually raise a finger or two, you can reasonably infer lack of interest and enthusiasm. Frequent applause and nods of agreement with your message are indicators of interest and support.

VERBAL RESPONSIVENESS Not only will audiences indicate agreement nonverbally, some will also indicate their interests verbally. Audience members may shout out a response or more quietly express agreement or disagreement to people seated next to them. A sensitive public speaker is constantly listening for verbal reinforcement or disagreement.

RESPONDING TO NONVERBAL CUES

The value in recognizing nonverbal clues from your listeners is that you can respond to them appropriately. If your audience seems interested, supportive, and attentive, your prespeech analysis has clearly guided you to make proper choices in preparing and delivering your speech.

If your audience becomes inattentive, however, you may need to make some changes while delivering your message. If you think audience members are drifting off into their own thoughts or disagreeing with what you say, or if you suspect that they don't understand what you are saying, then a few spontaneous changes may help. It takes experience and skill to make on-the-spot changes in your speech. Consider the following tips from seasoned public speakers for adapting to your listeners.[18]

If Your Audience Seems Inattentive or Bored

- Tell a story.
- Use an example to which the audience can relate.
- Use a personal example.
- Remind your listeners why your message should be of interest to them.
- Eliminate some abstract facts and statistics.
- Use appropriate humor.
- Make direct references to the audience, using members' names or mentioning something about them.

- Ask the audience to participate by asking questions or asking them for an example.
- Ask for a direct response, such as a show of hands, to see whether they agree or disagree with you.
- Pick up the pace of your delivery.
- Pause for dramatic effect.

If Your Audience Seems Confused or Doesn't Seem to Understand Your Point

- Be more redundant.
- Try phrasing your information in another way, or think of an example you can use to illustrate your point.
- Use a visual aid such as a chalkboard or flip chart to clarify your point.
- If you have been speaking rapidly, slow your speaking rate.
- Clarify the overall organization of your message to your listeners.
- Ask for feedback from an audience member to help you discover what is unclear.
- Ask someone in the audience to summarize the key point you are making.

If Your Audience Seems to Be Disagreeing with Your Message

- Provide additional data and evidence to support your point.
- Remind your listeners of your credibility, credentials, or background.
- Rely less on anecdotes and more on facts to present your case.
- Write facts and data on a chalkboard, overhead transparency, or flip chart if one is handy.
- If you don't have the answers and data you need, tell listeners you will provide more information by mail, telephone, or e-mail (and make sure you get back in touch with them).

Remember, it is not enough to note your listeners' characteristics and attitudes. You must also *respond* to the information you gather by adapting your speech to retain their interest and attention. Moreover, you have a responsibility to ensure that your audience understands your message. If your approach to the content of your speech is not working, alter it and note whether your audience's responses change. If all else fails, you may need to abandon a formal speaker-listener relationship with your audience and open up your topic for discussion. Of course, in your speech class, your instructor may expect you to keep going, to fulfill the requirements for your assignment. With other audiences, however, you may want to consider switching to a more interactive question-and-answer session to ensure that you are communicating clearly. Later chapters on supporting material, speech organization, and speech delivery will discuss other techniques for adjusting your style while delivering your message.

STRATEGIES FOR CUSTOMIZING YOUR MESSAGE TO YOUR AUDIENCE

Many people value having something prepared especially for them. Perhaps you've bought a computer that you ordered to your exact specifications. In a restaurant you order food prepared to your specific taste. Audiences, too, prefer messages that are adapted just to them; they don't like hearing a "canned" message. As a speaker, you may have worked hard to adapt your message to your audience, but your audience won't give you credit for adapting your message to them unless you let them know

Analyzing and Adapting to Your Audience as You Speak

SIGNS THAT YOU ARE CONNECTING TO YOUR AUDIENCE	SIGNS THAT YOU ARE NOT CONNECTING TO YOUR AUDIENCE	STRATEGIES FOR ADAPTING TO AN UNSUPPORTIVE AUDIENCE
Audience members make eye contact; most audience members look you in the eye while you are speaking.	Audience members don't make eye contact with you.	◆ Tell a story. ◆ Use more personal examples or illustrations. ◆ Consider making direct references to your listeners by mentioning some people by name.
Listeners have sincere smiles or pleasant facial expressions.	Listeners frown or display blank or unresponsive facial expressions.	◆ Ask the audience members whether they understand your message. ◆ Increase your speaking energy. ◆ Remind your listeners why your message is important to them. ◆ Consider clarifying your message by using a chalkboard or other visual aid.
Audience members are quiet.	Audience members are talking to other audience members.	◆ Pause to gain listeners' attention. ◆ Ask the audience either a rhetorical question (one you don't expect them to actually answer) or a question to which you do expect a response.
Audience members are sitting quietly; there is little audience movement.	Audience members are restless; their hands and feet are moving.	◆ Pick up the pace of your delivery. ◆ Use appropriate humor. ◆ Use more concrete examples.
Audience members respond to your requests for information or your questions by raising their hands when you ask.	Audience members do not respond to your questions or do not show interest in your message.	◆ Ask audience members if they understand the question you've asked. ◆ Repeat your question, and make it clear that you'd like their response and participation.
Audience members make appropriate verbal responses; they laugh when you use humor.	Audience members don't respond to your questions; they don't laugh at your humor.	◆ If listeners are not responsive to your humor, rely less on jokes and use more stories or personal illustrations.

that you've done so. What are some ways to communicate to your listeners that your message is designed specifically for them? Here are a few suggestions:

◆ **Appropriately Use Audience Members' Names.** Consider using audience members' names in your talk to relate specific information to individual people. Obviously, you don't want to embarrass people by using them in an example that would make them feel uncomfortable. But you can selectively mention people you know who are in the audience. It's become a standard technique in many State of the Union speeches for the president to have someone sitting in the balcony who can be mentioned in his talk. That person becomes a living "visual aid" to provide focus on an idea or point made in the address. If you are uncertain whether you should mention someone by name, before you speak, ask the person for permission to use his or her name in your talk.

◆ **Refer to the Town, City, or Community.** Make a specific reference to the place where you are speaking. If you are speaking to a college audience, relate your message and illustrations to the school where you are speaking. Many politicians use this technique: They have a standard stump speech to tout their credentials but adapt the opening part of their message to the specific city or community in which they are speaking.

◆ **Refer to a Significant Event That Happened on the Date of Your Speech.** Most libraries have books (such as the *Speaker's Lifetime Library*) that identify significant events in world or national history.[19] An even easier way to find out what happened on any given day in history is to go to www.history.com and click on the link called "This Day in History." Type in any date and you'll quickly discover any number of events that occurred on that day. For example, on the day this paragraph was written, Julius Caesar was assassinated in 44 B.C. It's also known as the Ides of March—a day Caesar was warned about in Shakespeare's famous play. If you were giving a speech on this day, a reference to the Ides of March might be especially apropos if your goal was to encourage your audience to beware of whatever issue or topic you were discussing.

Many local papers keep records of local historical events and list what happened 10, 25, or 50 years ago on a certain date. Relating your talk to a historical event that occurred on the same date as your talk can give your message a feeling of immediacy. It tells your audience that you have thought about this specific speaking event.

◆ **Refer to a Recent News Event.** Always read the local paper to see whether there is a local news story that you can connect to the central idea of your talk. Or, perhaps you can use a headline from your university newspaper or a recent story that appeared on your university Web site. If there is a newspaper headline that connects with your talk, consider holding up the paper as you refer to it—not so that people will be able to read the headline, but to emphasize the immediacy of your message.

◆ **Refer to a Group or Organization.** If you're speaking to an audience of service, religious, political, or work group members, by all means make specific positive references to the group. But be honest—don't offer false praise; audiences can sniff out phony flattery. A sincere compliment about the group will be appreciated, especially if you can link the goals of the group to the goal of your talk.

◆ **Relate Information Directly to Your Listeners.** Find ways to apply facts, statistics, and examples to the people in your audience. If, for example, you know that four out of ten women are likely to experience gender discrimination, customize that statistic by saying, "Forty percent of women listening to me now are likely to experience gender discrimination. That means of the twenty women in this audience, eight of you are likely to be discriminated against." Or, if you live in a city of 50,000 people, you can cite the statistic that 50,000 people on our nation's highways become victims of drunk driving each year, and then point out that that number is equivalent to killing every man, woman, and child in your city. Relating abstract statistics and examples to your listeners communicates that you have them in mind as you develop your message.

Analyzing Your Audience after You Speak

fter you have given your speech, you're not finished analyzing your audience. It is important to evaluate your audience's positive or negative response to your message. Why? Because this evaluation can help you prepare your next speech. Postspeech analysis helps you polish your speaking skill, regardless of whether you will face the same audience again. From that analysis you can learn whether your examples were clear and your message was accepted by your listeners. Let's look at some specific methods for assessing your audience's response to your speech.

NONVERBAL RESPONSES

The most obvious nonverbal response is applause. Is the audience simply clapping politely, or is the applause robust and enthusiastic, indicating pleasure and acceptance? Responsive facial expressions, smiles, and nods are other nonverbal signs that the speech has been well received.

Realize, however, that audience members from different cultures respond to speeches in different ways. Japanese audience members, for example, are likely to be restrained in their response to a speech and to show little expression. Some Eastern European listeners may not maintain eye contact with you; they may look down at the floor when listening. In some contexts, African American listeners may enthusiastically voice their agreement or disagreement with something you say during your presentation.[20]

Nonverbal responses at the end of the speech may convey some general feeling of the audience, but they are not much help in identifying which strategies were the most effective. Also consider what the members of the audience say, both to you and to others, after your speech.

VERBAL RESPONSES

What might members of the audience say to you about your speech? General comments, such as "I enjoyed your talk" or "Great speech," are good for the ego—which is important—but are not of much analytic help. Specific comments can indicate where you succeeded and where you failed. If you have the chance, try to ask audience members how they responded to the speech in general as well as to points you are particularly interested in.

SURVEY RESPONSES

You are already aware of the value of conducting audience surveys before speaking publicly. You may also want to survey your audience after you speak. You can then assess how well you accomplished your objective. Use the same survey techniques discussed earlier. Develop survey questions that will help you determine the general reactions to you and your speech, as well as specific responses to your ideas and supporting materials. Professional speakers and public officials often conduct such surveys. Postspeech surveys are especially useful when you are trying to persuade an audience. Comparing prespeech and postspeech attitudes can give you a clear idea of your effectiveness. A significant portion of most political campaign budgets goes toward evaluating how a candidate is received by his or her constituents. Politicians want to know what portions of their messages are acceptable to their audiences so they can use this information in the future.

If your objective was to teach your audience about some new idea, a posttest can assess whether you expressed your ideas clearly. In fact, classroom exams are posttests that determine whether your instructor presented information clearly.

BEHAVIORAL RESPONSES

If the purpose of your speech was to persuade your listeners to do something, you will want to learn whether they ultimately behave as you intended. If you wanted them to vote in an upcoming election, you might survey your listeners to find out how many did vote. If you wanted to win support for a particular cause or organization, you might ask them to sign a petition after your speech. The number of signatures would be a clear measure of your speech's success. Some religious speakers judge the success of their ministry by the amount of contributions they receive. Your listeners' actions are the best indicators of your speaking success.

SUMMARY

It is important to become an audience-centered speaker. To be an effective speaker, learn as much as you can about your listeners before, during, and after your speech. Before your speech, you can perform three kinds of analysis: demographic, psychological, and situational. You can use informal and formal approaches to gather information about your listeners for your analyses.

While speaking, look for feedback from your listeners. Audience eye contact, facial expression, move-

ment, and general verbal and nonverbal responsiveness provide clues to how well you are doing. Finally, evaluate audience reaction after your speech. Again, nonverbal clues as well as verbal ones will help you judge your speaking skill. The best indicator of your speaking success is whether your audience is actually able or willing to follow your advice or remembers what you have told them.

BEING AUDIENCE-CENTERED: A SHARPER FOCUS

CONSIDERING YOUR AUDIENCE

- Becoming an audience-centered speaker involves two steps. First, analyze your audience to assess who your listeners are. Second, ethically adapt your message to meet their needs and achieve your speaking goals.

- Gather such demographic information about your listeners as their age, race, gender, socio-economic status, and religious views.

- Psychological audience analysis helps you gauge the interests, attitudes, beliefs, and values of listeners.

- Situational audience analysis includes examining the time and place of your speech, the size of your audience, and the speaking occasion.

- Observe the nonverbal cues of your listeners to determine whether you need to change or adapt your message to maintain interest and achieve your speaking objective.

CONSIDERING AUDIENCE DIVERSITY

- Consider the proportion of males and females in your audience to help you appropriately adapt your message to them; avoid sexist language and make sure your message addresses the needs and interests of both men and women in your audience.

- Strategies for adapting to a diverse audience include focusing on a target audience, using diverse strategies for a diverse audience, using common audience perspectives, and relying on visual materials that transcend language differences.

CRITICAL THINKING QUESTIONS

1. Dr. Cassandra Ruiz has been invited by a women's group to speak on birth control. She thought her audience would be women of child-bearing age. After writing her speech, however, she found out that all the women to whom she will be speaking are at least twenty years older than she expected. What changes, if any, should she make?

2. Phil Owens is running for a seat on the school board. He has agreed to speak to the chamber of commerce about his views, but he wants to know what his audience believes about a number of issues. How can he gather this information?

3. You are in the middle of your presentation, trying to persuade a group of investors to build a new shopping mall in your community. You notice a few of the audience members losing eye contact with you, shifting in their seats, and looking at their watches. What do you do to regain their attention?

ETHICAL QUESTIONS

1. Maria strongly believes the drinking age in her state should be increased to 22. Yet when she surveyed her classmates, the overwhelming majority thought the drinking age should be lowered to 18. Should Maria change her speech topic and her purpose to avoid facing a hostile audience? Why or why not?

2. Dan knows that most of the women in his audience will be startled and probably offended if he begins his speech by saying, "Most of you broads in this audience are too sensitive about sexist language." This is how Dan really feels. Should he alter his language just to appease his audience? Explain.

3. Do most politicians place too much emphasis on the results of political-opinion polls to shape their stands on political issues? Explain your position.

4. Has political correctness gotten out of hand on college campuses today? Are we becoming too sensitive to cultural, ethnic, and gender issues in our public dialogue? Or are we not sensitive enough? Explain.

Developing Communication Strategies to Adapt to Your Audience

Use the following worksheet to help you analyze your audience and adapt a message to them.

Audience Characteristics	What strategies will you use to adapt your message to your audience?
Demographic Characteristics	
Age range:	
Average age:	
Percentage of women:	
Percentage of men:	
Predominant ethnicity:	
Educational backgrounds:	
Group memberships:	
Socioeconomic status:	
Psychological Characteristics	
Attitudes toward my topic:	
Beliefs about my topic:	
Common audience values:	
Situational Analysis	
Time speech will be delivered:	
Size of audience:	
Location of speech:	
Occasion or reason for speech:	

Jacob Lawrence (1917–2000) © ARS, NY *Builders in the City*, 1993. Gouache on paper, 19 × 28 ¹/₂". Courtesy of SBC Communications, Inc. The Jacob and Gwendolyn Lawrence Foundation/Art Resource, N.Y.

In all matters, before beginning, a diligent preparation should be made.

—CICERO

Developing Your Speech

outline

objectives

After studying this chapter you should be able to do the following:

1. Select a topic for a classroom speech that is appropriate to the audience, the occasion, and yourself.

2. Narrow a topic so that it can be thoroughly discussed within the time limits allotted for a specific assignment.

3. Write an audience-centered specific-purpose statement for an assigned topic.

4. Explain three ways of generating main ideas from a central idea.

5. Develop a blueprint for a speech by combining the central idea and a preview of the main ideas.

6. Apply to a speaking assignment the four steps for getting from a blank sheet of paper to a plan for the speech.

123

Ed Garcia has arranged the books and papers on his desk into neat, even piles. He has sharpened his pencils and laid them out parallel to one another. He has even dusted his desktop and cleaned the computer monitor's screen. Ed can think of no other way to delay writing his speech. He opens a new word-processing document, carefully centers the words "Informative Speech" at the top of the first page, and then slouches in his chair, staring glumly at the blank expanse that threatens his well-being. Finally, he types the words "College Football" under the words "Informative Speech." Another long pause. Hesitantly, he begins his first sentence: "Today I want to talk to you about college football." Rereading his first ten words, Ed decides that they sound moronic. He deletes the sentence and tries again. This time the screen looks even blanker than before. He writes—deletes—writes—deletes. Half an hour later, Ed is exhausted and still mocked by a blank screen. And he is frantic—this speech *has* to be ready by 9 in the morning.

Getting from a blank screen or sheet of paper to a speech outline is often the biggest hurdle you will face as a public speaker. Fortunately, however, it is one that you can learn to clear. If your earlier efforts at speech writing have been like Ed Garcia's, take heart. Just as you learned to read, do long division, drive a car, and get through college registration, so too can you learn to prepare a speech.

The first steps in preparing a speech are as follows:

1. Select and narrow your topic.
2. Determine your purpose.
3. Develop your central idea.
4. Generate your main ideas.

At the end of step 4, you will have a plan for the speech and will be ready to develop and polish your main ideas further. For most brief classroom speeches (under 10 minutes), you should allow at least one week between selecting a topic and delivering your speech. A week gives you enough time to develop and research your speech. Many habitual procrastinators like Ed Garcia, who grudgingly decide to begin an assignment a week in advance, learn to their surprise that the whole process is far easier than it would be if they put off working until the night before they are supposed to deliver their speech.

As we observed in Chapter 5, audience-centered speakers consider the needs, interests, and expectations of their audience during the entire speech-preparation process—needs, interests, and expectations that will be as diverse as audiences themselves. As you move from topic selection to speech plan, remember that you are preparing a message for your listeners. Always keep the audience as your central focus.

Select and Narrow Your Topic

Your first task, as illustrated in Figure 6.1, is to choose a topic on which to speak. You will need to narrow this topic to fit your time limit. Sometimes you can eliminate one or both of these steps because the topic has been chosen and properly defined for you. For example, knowing that you visited England's Lake District on your tour of Great Britain last summer, your English literature teacher asks you to speak about the mountains and lakes of that region before your class studies the poetry of Wordsworth and Coleridge. Or, knowing that you chair the local drug-abuse task force, the Lions Club asks you to speak at its weekly meeting about the work of your group. In both cases, your topic and its scope have been decided for you.

In other instances, the choice of topic may be left entirely to you. In your public-speaking class, your instructor may provide such guidelines as a time limit and type of speech (informative, persuasive, or entertaining) but allow you to choose your topic. In this event, you should realize that the success of your speech may rest on this decision. But how do you go about choosing an appropriate, interesting topic?

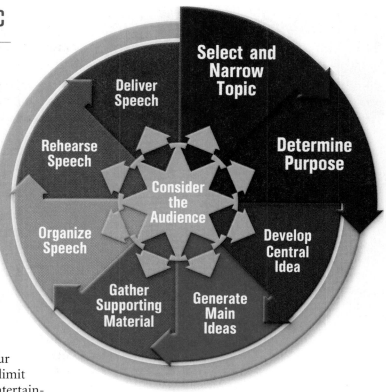

Figure 6.1 *Selecting and narrowing the topic and determining the general and specific purpose of the speech are early speech-making tasks.*

GUIDELINES FOR SELECTING A TOPIC

NBC political analyst and author Tim Russert, a popular speaker on college campuses, had delivered much the same speech more than once. Finally, during a presentation at Harvard, students called his bluff:

> *Equipped with cards listing pat phrases from past speeches, set out in a bingo-like format, they ticked off the passages as Mr. Russert spoke and then, having completed a row, shouted out "Bingo!"*[1]

CONSIDER THE AUDIENCE Russert's mistake was to rely on a standard spiel, rather than tailor his speeches to each specific audience. In Chapter 5 we discussed the reasons and methods for finding out about your audience. "What interests and needs do the members of this audience have in common?" and "Why did they ask me to speak?" are important questions to ask yourself as you search for potential speech topics. Keep in mind each audience's interests and expectations. For example, a university president invited to speak to a civic organization should talk about some new university program or recent accomplishment; a police officer speaking to an elementary school's PTA should address the audience's concern for the safety of young children.

Not only should a speaker's choice of topic be relevant to the *interests* and *expectations* of his or her listeners, it should also take into account the *knowledge* listeners already have about the subject. For example, the need for a campuswide office of disability services would not be a good topic to discuss in a speech to a group of students with disabilities, who would already be well aware of such a need. The speech would offer them no new information.

confidently connecting with your audience

Select an Interesting Topic

The more confident you are about the topic you have selected, the more confident you will be in speaking to your listeners. Your own interest in and passion about a topic can replace some of the anxiety you may feel about speaking to others. Instead of focusing on your fear, you will more naturally express your interest to your audience, who in turn will find your topic more interesting because you do. Selecting an interesting topic will help you speak with confidence.

Finally, speakers should choose topics that are *important*—topics that matter to their listeners, as well as to themselves. Student speaker Roger Fringer explains the stakes for students in a public-speaking class:

> *We work hard for our tuition, so we should spend it wisely. Spending it wisely means . . . we don't waste our classmates' time who have to listen to our speeches.*[2]

Several years ago communication scholar and then-president of the National Communication Association Bruce Gronbeck reminded an audience of communication instructors that students should be giving "the important kinds of . . . speeches that show . . . people how to confront the issues that divide them. . . ."[3] Table 6.1 offers examples of topics appropriate for the interests, expectations, knowledge, and concerns of given audiences.

CONSIDER THE OCCASION On December 17, 1877, Mark Twain was invited to be one of the after-dinner speakers for American poet John Greenleaf Whittier's seventieth-birthday celebration.[4] The guest list included such dignitaries as Oliver Wendell Holmes, Ralph Waldo Emerson, William Dean Howells, and Henry Wadsworth Longfellow.

When it was Twain's turn to speak, he began with a burlesque in the style of *Saturday Night Live*, featuring Longfellow, Emerson, and Holmes as drunken card-playing travelers in Nevada. Used to laughter and applause from his audiences, Twain was stunned by the silence that descended and seemed to grow as he continued.

What had gone wrong? Was Mark Twain's topic of *interest* to his listeners? Undoubtedly. Did they *expect* to hear someone talk about the distinguished guests? Yes. Could Twain *add to their knowledge* of the subject? Probably. Was his topic *appropriate to the occasion*? Definitely not!

Although after-dinner speeches are usually humorous, Twain's irreverence was inappropriate to the dignity of the birthday observance. Even though he had considered his audience, he had not considered carefully enough the demands of the occasion. Twain's irreverent talk aroused quite a commotion at the time and is said to have embarrassed him for years afterward. To be successful, a topic must be appropriate to both audience and occasion.

CONSIDER YOURSELF What do you talk about with good friends? You probably discuss school, mutual friends, political or social issues, hobbies or leisure activities, or whatever other topics are of interest and importance to you. Like most people's, your

Table 6.1 **Sample Audience-Centered Topics**

Audience	Topic
Retirees	Preserving Social Security benefits
Civic organization	The Special Olympics
Church members	Starting a community food bank
First graders	What to do in case of a fire at home
Teachers	Building children's self-esteem
College fraternity	Campus service opportunities

liveliest, most animated conversations revolve around topics of personal concern that arouse your deepest convictions.

The best public-speaking topics are also those that reflect your personal experience or especially interest you. Where have you lived? Where have you traveled? Describe your family or your ancestors. Have you held any part-time jobs? Describe your first days at college. What are your favorite classes? What are your hobbies or interests? What is your favorite sport? What social issues especially concern you? Here is one list of topics that was generated by such questions:

Blues music

"Yankee, go home": the American tourist in France

Why most diets fail

Behind the counter at McDonald's

My first day at college

Maintaining family ties while living a long distance from home

Getting involved in political campaigns

An alternative to selecting a topic with which you are already familiar is to select one you would like to know more about. Your interest will motivate both your research and your eventual delivery of the speech.

Think about your own experiences and the things you like to do as you are searching for a topic to speak about.

[Photo: Jeff Greenberg/PhotoEdit]

STRATEGIES FOR SELECTING A TOPIC

All successful topics reflect audience, occasion, and speaker. But just contemplating those guidelines does not automatically produce a good topic. Sooner or later, we all find ourselves unable to think of a good speech topic, whether it is for the first speech of the semester, for that all-important final speech, or for a speaking engagement long after our school years are over. Nothing is so frustrating to a public speaker as floundering for something to talk about!

Fortunately, there are several strategies that can help generate speech topics. They are somewhat more artificial than considering audience, occasion, and yourself to produce a "natural" topic choice. Nevertheless, they can yield good topics.

BRAINSTORMING A problem-solving technique widely used in such diverse fields as business, advertising, writing, and science, **brainstorming** can easily be used to generate ideas for speech topics as well.[5] To brainstorm a list of potential topics, get a sheet of paper and a pencil or pen. Set a minimum time limit of, say, 3 to 5 minutes. Write down the first topic that comes to mind. Do not allow yourself to evaluate it. Just write it down in a word or a phrase, whether it is a vague idea or a well-focused one. Now jot down a second idea—again, anything that comes to mind. The first topic may remind you of a second possibility. Such "piggybacking" of ideas is perfectly okay. Continue without any restraints until your time is up. At this stage, anything goes. Your goal is quantity—as long a list as you can think up in the time you have.

The following list of 21 possible topics came from a brainstorming session of about 3 minutes:

brainstorming
A creative problem-solving technique used to generate many ideas

Music	Censorship of music
Reggae	Movie themes
Bob Marley	Oscar-winning movies of the 1990s
Sound-recording technology	Great epic movies
Retro music	*Titanic* (the movie)
Buddy Holly	Salvaging the *Titanic* (the ship)
The Beatles	Treasure hunting
John Lennon	Key West, Florida
Alternative music	Ernest Hemingway
Popular rock bands	Cats
MTV	

If your brainstorming yields several good topics, so much the better. Set aside a page or two in your class notebook for topic ideas, and list the topics you don't end up choosing. You can reconsider them when you get your next assignment.

LISTENING AND READING FOR TOPIC IDEAS Very often something you see, hear, or read triggers an idea for a speech. A story on the evening news or in your local paper may suggest a topic. The following list of topics was brought to mind by recent headline stories in a large daily newspaper:

Long-term detention of suspected terrorists

Autism and vaccines

Corruption in Iraqi police forces

Canine genetic research

Alternative energy sources

Mortgage counseling

African films

In addition to discovering topics in news stories, you might find them in an interesting segment of *20/20, Dateline*, or even *Oprah*. Chances are that a topic covered in one medium has been covered in another as well, allowing extended research on the topic. For example, Oprah's interview of the parents of a child suffering from a genetic disease may be paralleled by *Newsweek*'s report on stem-cell research.

You may also find speech topics in one of your other classes. A lecture in an economics or political-science class may arouse your interest and provide a good topic

RECAP

How to Brainstorm for a Topic

◆ Start with a blank sheet of paper.

◆ Set a time limit for brainstorming.

◆ Begin writing as many possible topics for a speech as you can.

◆ Do not stop to evaluate your topics; just write them down.

◆ Let one idea lead to another—free-associate; piggyback off your own ideas.

◆ Keep writing until your time is up.

for your next speech. The instructor of that class could probably suggest additional references on the subject.

Sometimes even a subject you discuss casually with friends can be developed into a good speech topic. You have probably talked with classmates about such campus issues as dormitory regulations, inadequate parking, or your frustration with registration and advisers. Campuswide concerns would be relevant to the student audience in your speech class, as would such matters as how to find a good summer job or the pros and cons of living on or off campus.

Just as you jotted down possible topics generated by brainstorming sessions, remember to write down topic ideas you get from media, class lectures, or informal conversations. If you rely on memory alone, what seems like a great topic today may be only a frustrating blank tomorrow.

SCANNING WEB DIRECTORIES By now, you probably have a list of topics from which to choose. But if all your efforts have failed to produce any ideas that satisfy you, try the following strategy.

Access a Web directory such as Yahoo! (www.yahoo.com). Select a category at random. Click on it, and look through the subcategories that come up. Click on one

SPEAKER'S HOMEPAGE

Using the Web to Prime Your Creative Pump for a Speech Topic

In addition to the strategies for using the Web noted in this chapter, here are some additional ways to use the Internet to find speech topic ideas.

➤ NEWSPAPER HEADLINES

An excellent site that has links to many media outlets, including most major news networks, is Total News.

www.totalnews.com

➤ INTERNET SITES

This online catalog of Internet sites uses the Library of Congress classification system.

www.public.iastate.edu/~CYBERSTACKS/

of them. Continue to follow the chain of categories until you see a topic that piques your interest—or until you reach a dead end, in which case you can return to the Yahoo! homepage and try again.

A recent random directory search yielded the following categories, listed from general to specific:

Technology

MP3 players

Using your iPod to DJ

This search took only a few minutes (as will yours, as long as you resist the temptation to begin surfing the Web) and yielded at least one possible topic: using your iPod to DJ. An additional advantage of this strategy is that you begin to develop your preliminary bibliography while you are searching for a topic. In Chapter 7, we talk in more detail about Web directories and about gathering supporting materials.

NARROWING THE TOPIC

After brainstorming, reading the newspaper, surfing the Web, and talking to friends, you have come up with a topic. For some students, the toughest part of the assignment is over at this point. But others soon experience additional frustration because their topic is so broad that they find themselves overwhelmed with information. How can you cover all aspects of a topic as large as "television" in 3 to 5 minutes? Even if you trained yourself to speak as rapidly as an auctioneer, it would take days to get it all in!

The solution is to narrow your topic so that it fits within the time limits set by your assignment. The challenge lies in *how* to do this. If you have a broad, unmanageable topic, you might first try narrowing it by constructing categories similar to those created by Web directories. Write your general topic at the top of a list, and make each succeeding word in the list a more specific or concrete topic. Megan uses categories to help her narrow her general topic, music. She writes "Music" at the top of a sheet of paper and constructs a categorical hierarchy:

Music

Folk music

Irish folk music

The popularity of Irish folk music in the United States

Megan soon discovers that her topic is still a bit too broad. She simply cannot cover all the forms of Irish folk music popular in the United States in a talk of no more than 5 minutes. So she chooses one form of music—dance—and decides to talk about the kind of Irish hard-shoe dance music featured in *Riverdance*.

Be careful not to narrow your topic so much that you cannot find enough information for even a 3-minute talk. If you do, just go back a step. In our example, Megan could return to the broader topic of the popularity of Irish folk music in the United States.

 ## Determine Your Purpose

Now that you have selected and narrowed your topic, you need to decide on a purpose (as shown in Figure 6.1). If you do not know what you want your speech to achieve, chances are your audience won't either. Ask yourself, "What is really important for the audience to hear?" and "How do I want the audience to respond?" Clarifying your objectives at this stage will ensure a more interesting speech and a more successful outcome.

Consider the Audience

Select and Narrow Your Topic

While watching *Good Morning America* one Wednesday morning, Ashley finds herself caught up in a report on the recent fatal *E. coli* contamination of U.S. produce. She is surprised by the opinions of several experts that more outbreaks like this one are likely. As the feature comes to an end, Ashley begins to think that perhaps the safety of the U.S. food supply would make a good topic for her speech.

As she thinks further and does some preliminary research, Ashley realizes that her topic is too broad. Discussing safety issues related to seafood, red meat, poultry, produce, and food additives in one speech would be overwhelming. So she narrows her topic to the issue that prompted her topic: produce safety.

GENERAL PURPOSE

The *general purpose* of virtually any speech is either to inform, to persuade, or to entertain. The speeches you give in class will generally be either informative or persuasive. It is important that you fully understand what constitutes each type of speech so you do not confuse them and fail to fulfill an assignment. You certainly do not want to deliver a first-rate persuasive speech when an informative one was assigned! Although Chapters 15 through 18 discuss the three general purposes at length, we summarize them here so that you can understand the basic principles of each.

SPEAKING TO INFORM An informative speaker is a teacher. Informative speakers give listeners information. They define, describe, or explain a thing, person, place, concept, process, or function. In this excerpt from a student's informative speech on anorexia nervosa, the student describes the disorder for her audience:

> *Anorexia nervosa is an eating disorder that affects 1 out of every 200 American women. It is a self-induced starvation that can waste its victims to the point that they resemble victims of Nazi concentration camps.*
>
> *Who gets anorexia nervosa? Ninety-five percent of its victims are females between the ages of 12 and 18. Men are only rarely afflicted with the disease. Anorexia nervosa patients are usually profiled as "good" or "model" children who have not caused their parents any undue concern or grief over other behavior problems. Anorexia nervosa is perhaps a desperate bid for attention by these young women.*[6]

Most lectures you hear in college are informative. The university president's annual "state of the university" speech is also informative, as is the colonial Williamsburg tour guide's talk. Such speakers are all trying to increase the knowledge of their listeners. Although they may use an occasional bit of humor in their presentations, their main objective is not to entertain. And although they may provoke an audience's interest in the topic, their main objective is not to persuade. Chapter 15 provides specific suggestions for preparing an informative speech.

SPEAKING TO PERSUADE Persuasive speakers may offer information, but they use the information to try to change or reinforce an audience's convictions and often to urge some sort of action. For example, Brian offered compelling statistics to help persuade his audience to take steps to prevent and alleviate chronic pain:

A hundred million Americans, nearly a third of the population, [suffer] from chronic pain due to everything from accidents to the simple daily stresses on our bodies.[7]

The representative from Mothers Against Drunk Driving (MADD) who spoke at your high-school assembly urged you not to drink and drive and urged you to help others realize the inherent dangers of the practice. The fraternity president talking to your group of rushees tried to convince you to join his fraternity. Appearing on television during the last election, the candidates for president of the United States asked for your vote. All these speakers gave you information, but they used that information to try to get you to believe or do something. Chapters 16 and 17 focus in more detail on persuasive speaking.

SPEAKING TO ENTERTAIN The entertaining speaker tries to get the members of an audience to relax, smile, perhaps laugh, and generally enjoy themselves. Storyteller Garrison Keillor spins tales of the town and residents of Lake Wobegon, Minnesota, to amuse his listeners. Comedian Spike Davis delivers comic patter to make his audience laugh. Most after-dinner speakers talk to entertain the banquet guests. Like persuasive speakers, entertaining speakers may inform their listeners, but providing knowledge is not their main goal. Rather, their objective is to produce at least a smile and at best a belly laugh.

Early on, you need to decide which of the three general purposes your speech is to have. This decision keeps you on track throughout the development of your speech. The way you organize, support, and deliver your speech depends, in part, on your general purpose.

SPECIFIC PURPOSE

Now that you have a topic and you know generally whether your speech should inform, persuade, or entertain, it is time you decided on its *specific purpose.* Unlike the general purpose, which can be assigned by your instructor, you alone must decide on the specific purpose of your speech, because it depends directly on the topic you choose.

To arrive at a specific purpose for your speech, you must think in precise terms of what you want your audience to be able to *do* at the end of your speech. This kind of goal or purpose is called a **behavioral objective**, because you specify the behavior you seek from the audience. For a speech on how television comedy represents the modern family, you might write, "At the end of my speech, the audience will be able

behavioral objective
Wording of a specific purpose in terms of desired audience behavior

The specific purpose of a speaker whose purpose is to entertain is often simply to help the audience have a good time. Entertainer Mississippi Slim (Walter Horn) also hopes these students will learn something about the blues tradition.

[Photo: Bill Johnson/*Delta Democrat Times*/AP Images]

RECAP

General Purposes for Speeches

To inform	To share information with listeners by defining, describing, or explaining a thing, person, place, concept, process, or function
To persuade	To change or reinforce a listener's attitude, belief, value, or behavior
To entertain	To help listeners have a good time by getting them to relax, smile, and laugh

to explain how comedy portrays American family life today." The specific-purpose statement for a how-to speech using visual aids might read, "At the end of my speech, the audience will be able to use an online periodical index." For a persuasive speech on universal health care, your specific-purpose statement could say, "At the end of my speech, the audience will be able to explain why the United States should adopt a plan of national health insurance." A speech to entertain has a specific purpose, too. A stand-up comic may have a simple specific purpose: "At the end of my speech, the audience will laugh and applaud." An after-dinner speaker whose entertaining message has more informative value than that of the stand-up comic may say, "At the end of my speech, the audience will list four characteristics that distinguish journalists from the rest of the human species."

FORMULATING THE SPECIFIC PURPOSE Note that almost all of the sample specific-purpose statements in the preceding paragraph begin with the same twelve words: "At the end of my speech, the audience will be able to . . . ." The next word should be a verb that names an observable, measurable action that the audience should be able to take by the end of the speech. Use verbs such as *list, explain, describe,* or *write.* Do not use words such as *know, understand,* or *believe.* You can discover what your listeners know, understand, or believe only by having them show their increased capability in some measurable way.

A statement of purpose does not say what you, the *speaker,* will do. The techniques of public speaking help you achieve your goals, but they are not themselves goals. To say, "In my speech, I will talk about the benefits of studying classical dance" emphasizes your performance as a speaker. The goal of the speech is centered on you, rather than on the audience. Other than restating your topic, this statement of purpose provides little direction for the speech. But to say, "At the end of my speech, the audience will be able to list three ways in which studying classical dance can benefit them" places the audience and their behavior at the center of your concern. This latter statement provides a tangible goal that can guide your preparation and by which you can measure the success of your speech.

The following guidelines will help you prepare your statement of purpose.

➤ **Use Words That Refer to Observable or Measurable Behavior.**

Not Observable: At the end of my speech, the audience will know some things about Hannibal, Missouri.

Observable: At the end of my speech, the audience will be able to list five points of interest in the town of Hannibal, Missouri.

➤ **Limit the Specific Purpose to a Single Idea.** If your statement of purpose has more than one idea, you will have trouble covering the extra ideas in your speech. You will also run the risk of having your speech "come apart at the seams." Both unity of ideas and coherence of expression will suffer.

Consider the Audience

DEVELOPING YOUR SPEECH STEP BY STEP

Determine Your Purpose

Because Ashley's assignment is to develop and present a persuasive speech, she knows that her general purpose is to persuade. She will have to try to change or reinforce her listeners' attitudes and beliefs about the safety of the U.S. produce supply and perhaps also get them to take some sort of action.

Ashley also knows that her specific purpose must begin with the phrase, "At the end of my speech, the audience will be able to . . . " So she jots down

> *At the end of my speech, the audience will be able to know how to make our produce supply safer.*

As Ashley thinks about this draft specific purpose, she sees some problems with it. What specifically does she want her audience to know? How will she determine whether they know it? She edits the statement to read,

> *At the end of my speech, the audience will be able to list ways to make our produce supply safer.*

This version is more measurable, but perhaps more appropriate for an informative speech than a persuasive one. Maybe a better persuasive purpose statement would be

> *At the end of my speech, the audience will take steps to ensure a safer produce supply.*

Ashley is pleased with her third version. It reflects a persuasive general purpose and includes a measurable behavioral objective. She is ready to move on to the next step of the process.

- **Make Sure Your Specific Purpose Reflects the Interests, Expectations, and Knowledge Level of Your Audience.** Also be sure that your specific purpose is important. Earlier in this chapter, we discussed these criteria as guidelines for selecting a speech topic. Consider them again as you word your specific-purpose statement.

Behavioral statements of purpose help remind you that the aim of public speaking is to win a response from the audience. In addition, using a specific purpose to guide the development of your speech helps you focus on the audience during the entire preparation process.

USING THE SPECIFIC PURPOSE Everything you do while preparing and delivering the speech should contribute to your specific purpose. The specific purpose can help you assess the information you are gathering for your speech. For example, you may find that an interesting statistic, although related to your topic, does not help achieve your specific purpose. In that case, you can substitute material that directly advances your purpose.

As soon as you have decided on it, write the specific purpose on a 3-by-5-inch note card. That way you can refer to it as often as necessary while developing your speech.

Develop Your Central Idea

Having stated the specific purpose of your speech, you are ready to develop your *central idea*, the first step highlighted in Figure 6.2. The central idea is a one-sentence summary of the speech. The central idea (sometimes called the *thesis*), like the purpose statement, restates the speech topic. But whereas a purpose statement focuses on audience behavior, the central idea focuses on the content of the speech.

Professional speech coach Judith Humphrey explains the importance of a central idea:

> Ask yourself before writing a speech . . . "What's my point?" Be able to state that message in a single clear sentence. Everything else you say will support that single argument.[8]

The following guidelines can help you put your central idea into words.

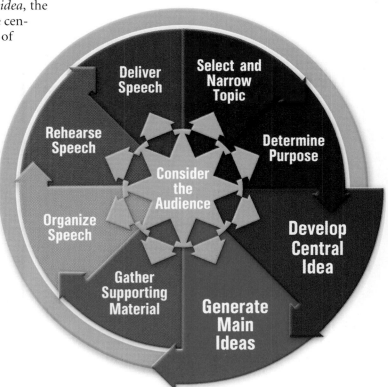

Figure 6.2 *State your central idea as a one-sentence summary of your speech, and then generate main ideas by looking for natural divisions, reasons, or steps to support your central idea.*

A COMPLETE DECLARATIVE SENTENCE

The central idea should be a complete declarative sentence— not a phrase or clause, and not a question.

Phrase:	Car maintenance
Question:	Is regular car maintenance important?
Complete Declarative Sentence:	Maintaining your car regularly can ensure that it provides reliable transportation.

Frederick Douglass (1817–1895)

Born a slave in Maryland in 1817, Frederick Douglass became the first African American to serve in a major government position (Ambassador to Haiti) and is widely credited with convincing Abraham Lincoln to sign the Emancipation Proclamation. But Douglass was perhaps best known by his contemporaries as a great orator. He felt passionate about his topics—abolition, the rights of all people—and discovered his main ideas in his own experiences. Charles W. Chestnutt would later write about Douglass's speeches that

One can easily imagine their effect upon a sympathetic or receptive audience, when delivered with flashing eye and deep-toned resonant voice by a man whose complexion and past history gave him the highest right to describe and denounce the iniquities of slavery and contend for the rights of a race.[9]

By speaking on topics about which he was passionate, Frederick Douglass was able to draw on strong personal convictions to persuade his listeners. As you select topics for speeches, consider issues and ideas about which you feel strongly. Speaking about such subjects will boost your energy and augment your power to share your ideas with your listeners.

[Photo: AP Images]

The phrase "car maintenance" is really a topic, not a central idea. It does not say anything about car maintenance. The question "Is regular car maintenance important?" is more complete but does not reveal whether the speaker is going to support the affirmative or the negative answer. By the time you word your central idea, you should be ready to summarize your stand on your topic in a complete declarative sentence.

DIRECT, SPECIFIC LANGUAGE

The central idea should use direct, specific language rather than qualifiers and vague generalities.

DEVELOPING YOUR SPEECH STEP BY STEP

Develop Your Central Idea

Ashley knows from reading Chapter 6 of *Public Speaking: An Audience-Centered Approach* that her central idea should be a complete declarative statement of a single audience-centered idea. She writes,

We must take action to sharpen the U.S. government's focus on produce safety.

Qualified Language:	In my opinion, censorship of school textbooks threatens the rights of schoolchildren.
Direct Language:	Censorship of school textbooks threatens the rights of schoolchildren.
Vague:	A May 2007 tornado affected Greensburg, Kansas.
Specific:	When an F5 tornado destroyed the town of Greensburg, Kansas, and killed 10 people on May 4, 2007, it changed forever the lives of the town's citizens.

A SINGLE IDEA

The central idea should be a single idea.

Two Ideas:	Deforestation by lumber interests and toxic-waste dumping are major environmental problems in the United States today.
One Idea:	Toxic-waste dumping is a major environmental problem in the United States today.

More than one central idea, like more than one idea in a purpose statement, only leads to confusion and lack of coherence in a speech.

AN AUDIENCE-CENTERED IDEA

The central idea should reflect consideration of the audience. You considered your audience when selecting and narrowing your topic and when composing your purpose statement. In the same way, you should consider your audience's needs, interests, expectations, and knowledge when stating your central idea. If you do not consider your listeners, you run the risk of losing their attention before you even begin developing the speech. If your audience consists mainly of college juniors and seniors, the second of the following central ideas would be better suited to your listeners than the first.

Inappropriate: Scholarships from a variety of sources are readily available to first-year college students.

Appropriate: Although you may think of scholarships as a source of money for freshmen, a number of scholarships are available only to students who have completed their first year of college.

Generate and Preview Your Main Ideas

Next to selecting a topic, probably the most common stumbling block in developing speeches is coming up with a speech plan. Trying to decide how to subdivide your central idea into two, three, or four *main ideas* can make you chew your pencil, scratch your head, and end up as you began, with a blank sheet of paper. The task will be much easier if you use the following strategy.

GENERATING YOUR MAIN IDEAS

Write the central idea at the top of a clean sheet of paper. Then ask these three questions:

- Does the central idea have *logical divisions*? (These may be indicated by such phrases as "three types" or "four means.")
- Can you think of several *reasons* the central idea is true?
- Can you support your central idea with a series of *steps* or a chronological progression?

You should be able to answer yes to one or more of these questions. With your answer in mind, write down the divisions, reasons, or steps you thought of. Let's see this technique at work with several central idea statements.

FINDING LOGICAL DIVISIONS Suppose your central idea is "A liberal arts education benefits the student in three ways." You now turn to the three questions. But for this example, you needn't go beyond the first one. Does the central idea have logical divisions? The phrase "three ways" indicates that it does. You can logically divide your speech into ways in which the student benefits:

1. Job opportunities
2. Appreciation of culture
3. Concern for humankind

A brief brainstorming session at this point could help you come up with more specific examples of ways in which a liberal arts education might benefit students. At this stage, you needn't worry about Roman numerals, parallel form, or even the order in which the main ideas are listed. We will discuss these and the other features of outlining in Chapter 11. Your goal now is simply to generate ideas. Moreover, just because you write them down, don't think that the ideas you come up with now are engraved in stone. They can—and probably will—change. After all, this is a *preliminary* plan. It may undergo many revisions before you actually deliver your speech. In our example, three points may well prove to be too many to develop in the brief time allowed for most classroom speeches. But because it is much easier to eliminate ideas than to invent them, list them all for now.

ESTABLISHING REASONS Suppose your central idea is "Upholstered furniture fires are a life-threatening hazard."[10] Asking yourself whether this idea has logical divisions is no help at all. There are no key phrases indicating logical divisions—no "ways," "means," "types," or "methods" appear in the wording. The second question, however, is more productive: Having done some initial reading on the topic, you can think of *reasons* this central idea is true. Asking yourself "Why?" after the statement yields three answers:

1. Standards to reduce fires caused by smoldering cigarettes have lulled furniture makers into a false sense of security.
2. Government officials refuse to force the furniture industry to reexamine its standards.
3. Consumers are largely ignorant of the risks.

Notice that these main ideas are expressed in complete sentences, whereas the ones in the preceding example were in phrases. At this stage, it doesn't matter. What does matter is getting your ideas down on paper. You can rewrite and reorganize them later.

TRACING SPECIFIC STEPS "NASA's space shuttle program has known both great achievement and tragic failure." You stare glumly at the central idea you so carefully formulated yesterday. Now what? You know a lot about the subject; your aerospace science professor has covered it thoroughly this semester. But how can you organize all the information you have? Again, you turn to the three-question method.

Does the main idea have logical divisions? You scan the sentence hopefully, but you can find no key phrases suggesting logical divisions.

Can you think of several reasons why the central idea is true? You read the central idea again and ask "Why?" at the end of it. Answering that question may indeed produce a plan for a speech, one in which you would talk about the reasons for the achievements and failures. But your purpose statement reads, "At the end of my speech, the audience will be able to trace the history of the space shuttle." Giving reasons for the space shuttle program's achievements and failures would not directly contribute to your purpose. So you turn to the third question.

Can you support your central idea with a series of steps? Almost any historical topic, or any topic requiring a chronological progression (for example, topics of how-to speeches), can be subdivided by answering the third question. You therefore decide that your main ideas will be a chronology of important space shuttle flights:[11]

1. April 1981: Test flight of the space shuttle.
2. January 1986: Shuttle *Challenger* explodes on launch.
3. April 1990: Deployment of the Hubble space telescope.
4. October–November 1998: Flight of John Glenn, age 77, who had been the first American in orbit in 1962.
5. May–June 1999: Shuttle *Discovery* docks with the International Space Station
6. February 2003: Shuttle *Columbia* disintegrates on re-entry.
7. June 2007: Shuttle *Atlantis* astronauts deliver materials to the International Space Station and perform four space walks.

You know that you can add to, eliminate, or reorganize these ideas later. But you have a start.

Notice that for this last example, you consulted your purpose statement as you generated your main ideas. If these main ideas do not help achieve your purpose, you need to rethink your speech. You may finally change either your purpose or your main ideas; but whichever you do, you need to synchronize them. Remember, it is much easier to make changes at this point than after you have done your research and produced a detailed outline.

RECAP

Generating Main Ideas

ASK WHETHER YOUR CENTRAL IDEA . . .

Has *logical divisions*

Is true for a number of *reasons*

Can be supported with *steps*

PREVIEWING YOUR MAIN IDEAS

Once you have generated your main ideas, you can add a preview of those main ideas to your central idea to produce a **blueprint** for your speech. Preview the ideas in the same order you plan to discuss them in the speech. In Chapter 9, we discuss in greater detail how to organize your speech.

Some speakers, like Nicole, integrate their central idea and preview into one blueprint sentence:

Obsolete computers are straining landfills because they contain hazardous materials and take a distinctively long time to decay.[12]

In this example, Nicole started with a central idea: "Obsolete computers are straining landfills." Asking herself "Why?" yielded two reasons, which became her two main points: "They contain hazardous materials" and "They take a distinctively long time to decay." Combining these reasons with her central idea produced a blueprint.

Other speakers, like Erin, state their blueprints in several sentences:

Today I would like to expose the myth that owning a gun guarantees your personal safety. First, I will discuss the fact that guns are rarely reached in time of need. Then I will address the risk of accidental shootings and how this is greatly increased by people's failure to receive proper gun-handling training. And finally, I will propose an alternative solution, self-defense.[13]

Erin also started with a central idea: "Owning a gun does not guarantee your personal safety." Like Nicole, she generated reasons for her central idea, which in this case were that "guns are rarely reached in time of need" and that "the risk of accidental shootings is increased." She decided also to discuss martial-arts self-defense as a solution to the problem. Thinking that a single sentence might become unwieldy, Erin decided to use four shorter sentences for her blueprint.

Meanwhile, Back at the Computer . . .

It's been a while since we abandoned Ed Garcia, the student in the opening paragraphs of this chapter who was struggling to write a speech on college football. Even though he has procrastinated, if he follows the steps we have discussed, he should still be able to plan a successful informative speech.

Ed has already chosen his topic. His audience is likely to be interested in his subject. Because Ed is a varsity defensive tackle, the audience will probably expect him to talk about college football. And he himself is passionately interested in and knowledgeable about the subject. It meets all the requirements of a successful topic.

But "college football" is too broad for a 3- to 5-minute talk. Ed needs to narrow his topic to a manageable size. He goes online to Yahoo! and clicks on the category

blueprint

The central idea of a speech plus a preview of main ideas

Sports. This search yields a fairly long list of subcategories. He is just about to select College and University when another category catches his eye: Medicine. Sports medicine? Hmmmm. . . . Ed has suffered several injuries and feels qualified to talk about this aspect of football. Ed doesn't need to go further. He has his topic: "Injuries in college football."

Now that he has narrowed the topic, Ed needs a purpose statement. He decides that his audience may know something about how players are injured, but they probably do not know how these injuries are treated. He types, "The audience will be able to explain how the three most common injuries suffered by college football players are treated."

A few minutes later, Ed derives his central idea from his purpose: "Sports medicine specialists have developed specific courses of treatment for the three most common kinds of injuries suffered by college football players."

Generating main ideas is also fairly easy now. Because his central idea mentions three kinds of injuries, he can plan his speech around those three ideas (logical divisions). Under the central idea, Ed lists three injuries:

1. Bruises
2. Broken bones
3. Ligament and cartilage damage

Now Ed has a plan and is well on his way to developing a successful 3- to 5-minute informative speech.

DEVELOPING YOUR SPEECH STEP BY STEP

Consider the Audience

Generate Your Main Ideas

With her central idea in hand, Ashley knows that she next needs to generate her main ideas. She asks three questions:

- Does my central idea have *logical divisions?*
- Can I establish several *reasons* my central idea is true?
- Can I support my central idea by tracing specific *steps?*

Ashley's central idea does not seem to have logical divisions, but she can certainly think of reasons it is true. She jots down her central idea and writes *because* at the end of it:

> *We must take action to sharpen the U.S. government's focus on produce safety* <u>because</u>

And she quickly adds,

1. Programs for government inspection of produce are not working.
2. The current system endangers everyone.

Now Ashley has two possible main ideas—a good start. But she looks back at her specific purpose statement and remembers that she also wants her listeners to take action to solve the problem. So she adds a third main idea:

3. We must take steps that include congressional legislation, a reallocation of funds, and personal action.

Now Ashley has main ideas that both support her central idea and fulfill her specific purpose.

SUMMARY

Four main steps will help you get from a blank piece of paper to a speech plan:

1. Select and narrow your topic.
2. Determine your purpose.
3. Develop your central idea.
4. Generate your main ideas.

The difficulty of selecting a topic varies greatly from speech to speech. Sometimes speakers are asked to address a specific topic. At other times they may be given only broad guidelines, such as a time limit and an idea of the occasion. As speakers consider possible topics, they must keep in mind the interests, expectations, and knowledge levels of their audiences. They should select topics of importance, and consider the special demands of the occasion. Finally, speakers must take into account their own interests, abilities, and experiences. Usually these "boundaries" help them select appropriate topics. If still undecided, a speaker may try such strategies as brainstorming, consulting the media, or scanning Web directories for potential topics.

After choosing a broad topic area, a speaker may need to narrow the topic so that it fits within the time limits that have been set.

The next task a speaker faces is deciding on general and specific purposes. He or she must consider first whether a speech is going to be informative, persuasive, or entertaining. With a general purpose in mind, the speaker can write a specific-purpose statement. A specific purpose should be worded behaviorally, in terms of what the speaker wants the audience to be able to do at the end of the speech. The specific purpose serves as a yardstick by which the speaker can measure the relevance of ideas and supporting materials while developing the speech.

Specific-purpose statements indicate what speakers hope to accomplish; central ideas, by contrast, summarize what they will say. The central idea should be stated in a complete declarative sentence. From the central idea, the speaker can generate main ideas.

One strategy for generating main ideas is to determine whether the central idea has logical divisions, can be supported by several reasons, or can be traced through a series of steps. These divisions, reasons, or steps become the speech plan, which the speaker will probably preview in the introduction and summarize in the conclusion. Now the speaker is ready to move on to gathering supporting material for the speech.

BEING AUDIENCE-CENTERED: A SHARPER FOCUS

CONSIDERING YOUR AUDIENCE

➤ "What interests and needs do the members of this audience have in common?" and "Why did they ask me to speak?" are important questions to ponder as you search for potential speech topics.

➤ As you determine your purpose for speaking, ask yourself, "What is really important for the audience to hear?" and "How do I want the audience to respond?"

➤ Your general purpose for speaking will be to inform, to persuade, or to entertain your listeners.

➤ To arrive at a specific purpose for your speech, think in precise terms of what you want your audience to be able to *do* at the end of your speech.

➤ Using a specific purpose to guide the development of your speech helps you focus on the audience during the entire preparation process.

CONSIDERING AUDIENCE DIVERSITY

➤ Not only should a speaker's choice of topic be relevant to the *interests* and *expectations* of his or her listeners, it should also take into account the *knowledge* listeners already have about the subject.

➤ Be sure your specific purpose and your central idea address the interests, expectations, and level of knowledge of your audience.

CRITICAL THINKING QUESTIONS

1. Your public-speaking class invites a gubernatorial candidate to address the class. The candidate accepts the invitation and speaks for 30 minutes on the topic "Why the state should increase funding of public transportation." Analyze the candidate's choice of topic according to the guidelines presented in this chapter.

2. Consider the following specific-purpose statements. Analyze each according to the criteria presented in this chapter. Rewrite the statements to correct any problems.

   At the end of my speech, the audience will know more about the Mexican Free-Tailed Bat.

   I will explain some differences in nonverbal communication between Asian and Western cultures.

   At the end of my speech, the audience will be able to list some reasons for xeriscaping one's yard.

   To describe the reasons I enjoy spelunking as a hobby.

   At the end of my speech, the audience will be able to prepare a realistic monthly budget.

   The advantages and disadvantages of living in a college dormitory.

3. Below are the topic, general purpose, and specific purpose Marylin has chosen for her persuasive speech. Write an appropriate central idea and main ideas for the speech. Be prepared to explain how you derived the main points from the central idea.

   Topic: National presidential primary

   General Purpose: To persuade

   Specific Purpose: At the end of my speech, the audience will be able to list and explain three reasons the United States should adopt a national presidential primary.

ETHICAL QUESTIONS

1. Like Tim Russert, many speakers prepare a stock speech and deliver it to a variety of audiences and on a variety of occasions. Is this practice ethical? Explain your answer.

2. While eating lunch in the student center cafeteria, you overhear a stranger at the next table describing a paper she is writing for her political science class. She mentions a book she used to support her argument that the death penalty should not be abolished. Would it be ethical for you to "borrow" her topic and consult the book she mentioned to prepare a speech for a public-speaking course assignment?

Strategies for Selecting a Speech Topic

Use the following questions to help you identify and narrow a topic for a speech.

Step One: Determine the purpose of your speech.

1. What is the general purpose of your speech (to inform, to persuade, or to entertain)?

2. What are the time limits for your speech?

Step Two: Determine your audience's interests.

3. What common interests or experiences have brought the members of your audience together?

4. What are the educational, career, or other goals of your audience?

5. What are the general demographic characteristics of your audience?

Step Three: Identify your own interests.

6. What do you like to do for fun?

7. Where have you traveled?

8. What social or political issues concern you?

9. What books, magazines, Web sites, or blogs to do you read?

10. What movies, TV programs, or videos do you like to watch?

11. What problems have you or someone close to you experienced that would be a good topic (e.g., serious illness or accident)?

12. What world, national, or local problems do you consider interesting and important?

13. What behaviors would you like people to do or not do (e.g., exercise more, eat more healthful foods)?

Step Four: Review newspapers, magazines, TV programs, and Web sites to identify stories and topics that are of interest to you and your audience.

Step Five: Brainstorm a list of topics that relate to your own interests. Then review the list to identify those topics that would also be of interest to your listeners.

Step Six: Narrow the topic to fit the time limits. Identify subdivisions or elements of your topic that could fit within the scope of your speech assignment.

Joseph Cornell (1903–1972) © VAGA NY. *Untitled (Paul and Virginia)*, c. 1946–48. Construction. 12 ½ × 9 ¹⁵/₁₆ × 4 ³/₈ in. Edward Owen/Art Resouce, N.Y.

Learn, compare, collect the facts! . . .
Always have the courage to say to yourself—
I am ignorant.

—IVAN PETROVICH PAVLOV

Gathering Supporting Material

outline

objectives

After studying this chapter you should be able to do the following:

1. List five potential sources of supporting material for a speech.

2. Discuss the variety of resources available on the World Wide Web.

3. Explain six criteria for evaluating Web sites.

4. List seven types of library resources.

5. Plan and conduct an effective interview.

6. Explain what items of information a researcher should record to document resources.

Apple pie is your specialty. Your family and friends relish your flaky crust, spicy filling, and crunchy crumb topping. Fortunately, not only do you have a never-fail recipe and technique, but you also know where to go for the best ingredients. Fette's Orchard has the tangiest pie apples in town. For your crust, you use only Premier shortening, which you buy at Meyer's Specialty Market. Your crumb topping requires both stone-ground whole-wheat flour and fresh creamery butter, available on Tuesdays at the farmer's market on the courthouse square.

Just as making your apple pie requires that you know where to find specific ingredients, creating a successful speech requires knowledge of both sources of and types of supporting material that speechmakers typically use. Chapters 7 and 8 together cover the speech-development step illustrated by Figure 7.1: Gather Supporting Material. In this chapter we identify various sources of information and discuss ways to access them. In Chapter 8, we focus on recognizing and effectively using various types of supporting material.

Personal Knowledge and Experience

Because you will probably give speeches on topics you are particularly interested in, you may find that *you* are your own best source. Your speech may be on a skill or hobby in which you are expert, such as keeping tropical fish, stenciling, or stamp collecting. Or you may talk on a subject with which you have had some personal experience, such as buying a used car, deciding whether to join a club, or seeking assisted living for an elderly relative. Don't automatically run to your computer or the library to find every piece of supporting material for every topic on which you speak. It is true that most well-researched speeches include some objective material gathered from outside sources. But you may also be able to provide an effective illustration, explanation, definition, or other type of support from your own knowledge and experience. As an audience-centered speaker, you should realize, too, that personal knowledge often has the additional advantage of heightening your credibility in the minds of your listeners. They will accord you more respect as an authority when they realize that you have firsthand knowledge of a topic.

The Internet

In the decades since its inception, the **Internet** has gone from a novel, last-resort resource to the first place most people turn when faced with a research task. More specifically, it is the **World Wide Web**, the most popular information-delivery system of the Internet, that is of primary interest when you are searching for supporting material for a speech. Understanding the World Wide Web, the tools for accessing it, and some of the amazing types of information available can help make research easier, more productive, and even more fun.

Internet
A vast collection of hundreds of thousands of computers accessible to millions of people all over the world

World Wide Web
The most popular information-delivery system of the Internet

DIRECTORIES AND SEARCH ENGINES

You have probably accessed material on the Web with Google or Yahoo!, both of which offer both directory and search engine capabilities. A **directory** allows you to click on subject categories that are in turn broken down into ever-more-specific subcategories; a **search engine** uses a subject or key word search.

Only a few years ago, students struggled to find enough information for speeches and papers. One of the ways in which the World Wide Web has changed research is that today, students are more likely to find themselves overwhelmed by too much material.

One tool that can help you narrow your search is a specialized **vertical search engine** such as Google Scholar, which indexes academic sources, or Indeed, which indexes job Web sites. One technical writer explains the difference between general-purpose and vertical search engines this way:

> Regular search— when you go to . . . any general-purpose search engine—is a "horizontal" search in that you are searching across a wide spectrum of material. Information from sports sites, news sites, medical sites, shopping sites—the entire horizontal spectrum of topics is represented.
>
> With vertical search, you slice down vertically through one topic area. You search only against the news sites or against the medical information, for example. This type of focus can make for more relevant results.[1]

Another strategy that can help you narrow your search is a **Boolean search**. A Boolean search lets you enclose phrases in quotation marks or parentheses so that a search yields only those sites on which all words of the phrase appear in that order, rather than sites that contain the words at random. Boolean searches also permit you to insert "AND" or "+" between words and phrases to indicate that you wish to see results that contain both phrases. Conversely, Boolean searches let you exclude certain words and phrases from your search. And they let you restrict the dates of your hits, so that you see only documents posted within a specified time frame. These relatively simple strategies can help you narrow a list of hits from, in some cases, millions of sites, to a more workable number.

Here is an example of how the advanced search capabilities of Google can help you limit a search for information for your speech on the Volkswagen Beetle:

1. Type the key word *beetle* in the search box, and click on Google Search. Google finds a staggering 20,700,000 sites.[2]

2. Click on the Advanced Search option. In the box labeled Find Results Without the Words, type in *insect* to communicate that you are interested only in sites on beetles that are not about the insect known as a beetle. Google Search yields 2,380,000 sites—still a huge number, but only about 10% of the original.

3. Clarify that you want only sites about the Volkswagen Beetle. Return to *Advanced Search*. This time, in the box labeled Find Results With the Exact Phrase, type in *Volkswagen Beetle*. Google Search finds 1,160,000 sites.

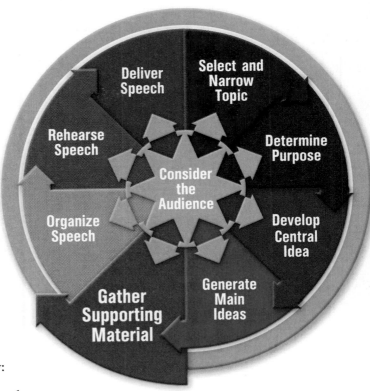

Figure 7.1 *Finding, identifying, and effectively using supporting material are activities essential to the speech-preparation process.*

directory

A site that works by offering the user ever-more-specific categories of information from which to select

search engine

A Web site that works much like a traditional card catalog or index, allowing access to the World Wide Web through a subject or key word search

vertical search engine

A Web site that indexes World Wide Web information in a specific field.

Boolean search

An advanced Web-searching technique that allows a user to narrow a subject or key word search by adding various requirements

4. Return once again to Advanced Search. Scroll down to Language, and select English. Under Date, select Past 3 Months. Under Occurrences, select Anywhere in the Page. And under Domain, type in .gov (see Figure 7.2). Now you are searching for government sites in English that have been posted or updated in the past three months and that contain the phrase "Volkswagen Beetle." Google Search yields six sites—a far more reasonable number with which to begin your research.

Different search engines use slightly different syntaxes for advanced searches. Most provide search tips that can help you format searches and interpret results.

EVALUATING WEB RESOURCES

Although the Web is a great victory for those who support free speech, the lack of legal, financial, or editorial restriction on what is published presents both a logistical and an ethical challenge to researchers.

As you begin to explore the sites you discover, you need to evaluate them according to a consistent standard. The following six criteria can serve as such a standard.[3]

ACCOUNTABILITY Find out what individual or organization is responsible for the Web site. In most cases, search engines will label those sites that have paid to be listed. In a Google search, you may find a light tan box with the phrase "Sponsored Links" in the upper right-hand corner of your results. A Yahoo! search may bring up a light blue box labeled "Sponsor Results." Any sites listed in these shaded boxes have paid to advertise.

If a page is not a paid advertisement, look to see whether it is signed. If you find the name of the author, but not his or her qualifications, you need to seek further information in order to be able to assess the author's expertise and authority. You may be able to get such information by following hyperlinks from the page you found to other documents. Another way to get information is to enter the author's name in a search engine. You may find either information about, or other pages by, this author.

Figure 7.2 *Parameters for an advanced search with Google*

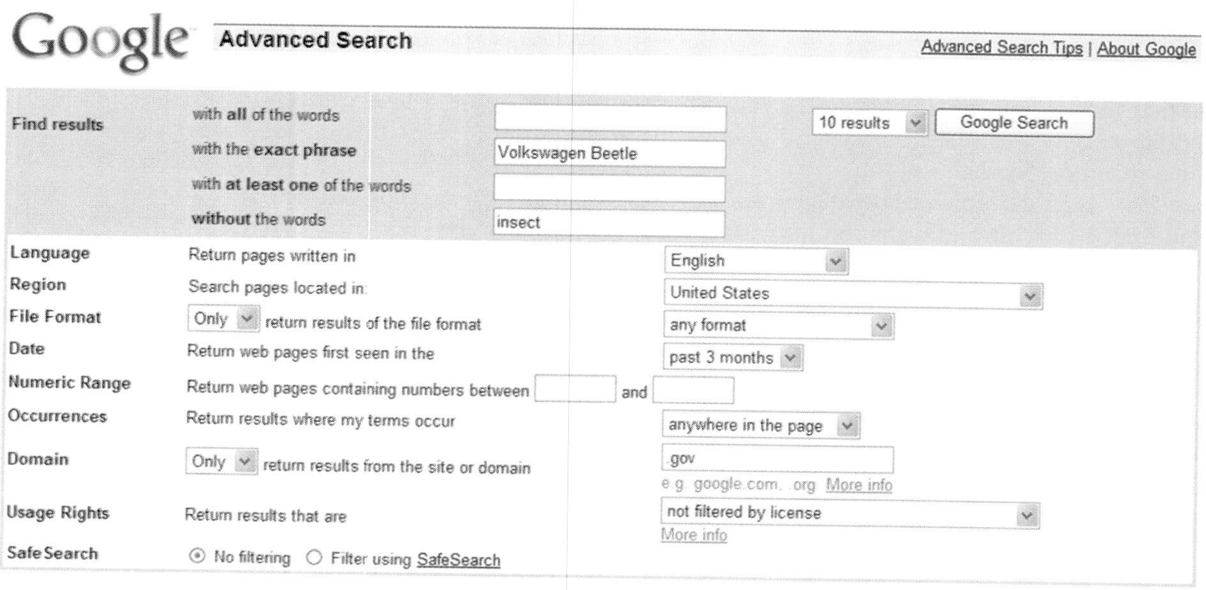

If the Web site is unsigned, you may still be able to find out what organization sponsors it. Look for a header or footer that indicates affiliation. Or you may be able to follow a hyperlink at the top or bottom of the page to the homepage of which this document is a part. If you can identify an organization, but still do not know anything about its reputation, the *domain*, indicated by the last three letters of a site's URL, can give you additional information. The following domains are used by the types of organizations indicated:[4]

.com or **.net**	commercial sites
.org	nonprofit groups
.edu	educational institutions
.gov	government agencies
.mil	military groups

You can also try entering the name of the organization, enclosed in quotation marks, in a search engine.

If you have tried these strategies and still cannot identify or verify the author or sponsor of a Web site, be extremely wary of the site. If no one is willing to be accountable for the information it contains, you cannot be accountable to your audience for using the information in a speech. Continue your search elsewhere.

ACCURACY Unless you are an expert in the area a particular Web site addresses, it may be difficult to determine whether the information it contains is accurate. However, two considerations can help you assess accuracy,

First, realize that accuracy is closely related to accountability. If the author or sponsoring organization of a Web site is a credible authority on the subject, the information posted on the site is more likely to be accurate than is information on an anonymous or less thoroughly documented site.

Second, assess the care with which the Web site has been written. References or hyperlinks should be provided for any information that comes from a secondary source. The site should also be relatively free of common errors in usage and mechanics. A site laden with such errors may contain content errors, as well.

If you find yourself still somewhat uncertain about the accuracy of information you find on a Web site, conduct further research. You may be able to verify or refute the information by consulting another site or a print resource.

OBJECTIVITY Like accuracy, objectivity is related to accountability. Once you know who is accountable for a site, consider the interests, philosophical or political biases, and source of financial support of that individual or organization. Are these interests or biases likely to slant the information presented? The more objective the author, the more credible the facts and information presented. Consider, too, any advertisements on the site that might influence its content.

DATE Look for evidence that the site was posted recently or is kept current. At the bottom of many sites you will find a statement of when the site was posted and when it was last updated. If you do not find a date there, click on the View menu at the top of your browser screen and go down to Page Info. When you click on Page Info, you will open a screen that includes a Last Modified date. Still another strategy is to search for the title of the Web site on a search engine. The information that comes up should include a date.

Once you know the date the site was posted or last updated, check to see whether the document includes the dates on which any factual or statistical information was gathered. In general, when you are concerned with factual data, the more recent, the better.

RECAP

Finding Supporting Material on the Web

1. Use a directory or search engine to find relevant sites.
2. Evaluate Web sites according to these six criteria: accountability, accuracy, objectivity, date, usability, and diversity.

USABILITY The layout and design of the site should facilitate its use. Frames, graphics, and multimedia resources can enhance a site but may also slow down the rate at which it loads or cause your computer to freeze. Some sites offer a "text-only" or "non-tables" option. Also consider whether there is a fee to gain access to any of the information on the site. Balance the graphics features and any possible cost against practical efficiency.

DIVERSITY A diversity-sensitive Web site will be free of material that communicates bias against either gender; against any ethnic, racial, or sexual-preference subgroup; or against people with disabilities.[5] Such a site may also offer divergent perspectives through hyperlinks or invite divergent perspectives through interactive forums. A site friendly to people with disabilities may offer a large-print option or an audio alternative to printed text.

U.S. government Web sites are required to comply with a set of standards that include such requirements as making sure hyperlinks can be detected by color-blind users and supplying written captions for audio and video clips for people with hearing impairment.[6]

The first four of the criteria just listed can serve as guides to evaluating any resource, regardless of whether it is a Web site, a print document, or even information you obtain in an interview. In Chapter 8, we provide additional criteria to help you make your final selection of supporting material from both electronic and print resources.

SPEAKER'S HOMEPAGE

Evaluating Web Sites

The following three sites provide criteria, resources, and tips for evaluating Web sites:

www.library.cornell.edu/olinuris/ref/research/webeval.html

www.lib.berkeley.edu/TeachingLib/Guides/Internet/Evalute.html

Lib.nmsu.edu/instruction/evalcrit.html

Library Resources

Despite the rapid development of the World Wide Web, the more traditional holdings of libraries remain rich sources of supporting material. Although your college or university library may seem a forbidding maze, all libraries, from the smallest village library to the huge Library of Congress, house the same sorts of material and are organized in a similar way.

Become familiar with your library's layout and services. Some libraries offer staff-guided tours; most others will at least have floor plans and location guides available. Before you have to do research under pressure, explore the library at a leisurely pace. Find out what electronic resources are available and where you can access them. In addition, find where and how to find the following resources and services:

Books

Periodicals

Full-text databases

Newspapers

Reference resources

Government documents

Special services

Despite the proliferation of Internet resources, a library is still a rich source of supporting material for a speech.

[Photo: Moodboard/Corbis]

BOOKS

When you think of libraries, you generally think of books. And with good reason: Most of the floor space of a library is devoted to books.

STACKS Libraries' collections of books are called the **stacks**. Stacks may be either open or closed, depending on library policy. In an open-stack library, collections are on open shelves and available to anyone who wishes to browse through them. Open stacks give researchers the chance to make lucky finds, because books on a particular subject are shelved next to one another. For example, if you are looking for a specific book on play therapy, you may, on the same shelf, find two or three other books on the same subject. The main drawback to open stacks is that they are vulnerable to both loss of materials and misplacement of books by careless users.

The closed-stack library is one in which only people granted certain privileges are allowed in the stacks—most generally, librarians, library aides, faculty, and graduate students. Undergraduates and others must consult the card catalog and copy onto a retrieval card or call slip the title, author, and call number of the book they want. This card or slip is then given to a librarian at the circulation desk, who sends it to the appropriate area of the stacks. A library worker there finds the desired book and sends it to circulation, where the borrower can either check it out or use it in the study area of the library.

The advantages of the closed-stack library are that users are saved some legwork and that stacks generally stay more orderly than in an open-stack system. The chief disadvantages are the length of time it can sometimes take to get materials and the impossibility of making a lucky find. Whatever the setup, you will have to adapt to the particular method your library uses.

stacks
The collection of books in a library

CARD CATALOG Just how do you find what you want from among those several floors in your college library? You probably have used a **card catalog** in a smaller public library or school library. College libraries are no different. Even though their holdings are much larger than those of the average public library, college libraries also contain card catalogs. Today even very small community and school libraries are likely to have computerized card catalogs. Instead of running around a huge number of filing cabinets, trying to find the drawers you need, you go to a computer and follow the directions given on the screen. Often you do not even have to go to the library to access the card catalog. Many libraries' card catalogs are available online, allowing researchers to build preliminary bibliographies of books and call numbers before they ever come to the library building. Figure 7.3 illustrates a sample entry from a computerized card catalog.

The books you find in your library will be important sources as you prepare your speeches. Books can provide in-depth coverage of topics, which is simply not possible in shorter publications. However, books are inherently outdated. Most books are written 2 or 3 years before they are published. If your speech addresses a current topic or if you want to use current examples, you will probably not find these in books. For up-to-date information, turn to periodicals and newspapers.

card catalog
A file of information about the books in a library; may be an index-card filing system or a computerized system

PERIODICALS

The term *periodicals* refers to both general-interest magazines, such as *Newsweek*, *Consumer Reports*, and *Sports Illustrated*, and trade and professional journals, such

Figure 7.3 *An entry from a computerized card catalog. The same entry appears on the screen regardless of whether the book is accessed using title, author, or subject.*

Author:	Krotoszynski, Ronald J., 1967-
Title:	The First Amendment in cross-cultural perspective : a comparative legal analysis of the freedom of speech / Ronald J. Krotoszynski, Jr.
Publication Info:	New York : New York University Press, c2006.
URL to This Record:	*http://catalog.library.txstate.edu:80/record=b1628870a*

Title
Author/Editor

Location	Call No.	Status
General Collection, Floor 6	K3254.K76 2006	AVAILABLE

[Display Related Subjects]

Description:	xvi, 301 p. ; 24 cm
Series:	Critical America
Bibliography:	Includes bibliographic references and index.
Contents:	Comparative law, free speech, and the "central meaning" of the First Amendment -- Freedom of speech in the United States -- Free speech in Canada : balancing free speech and a commitment to communitarian values -- Free speech in Germany : militant democracy and the primacy of dignity as a preferred constitutional value -- Freedom of speech in Japan : disentangling culture, community, and freedom of expression -- Freedom of expression in the United Kingdom : free speech and the limits of a written constitution -- Free speech and the culturally contingent nature of human rights : some concluding observations.
Subject:	Freedom of speech -- Cross-cultural studies. Freedom of speech -- United States. United States. Constitution 1st Amendment.
Local Subject:	0653F
ISBN:	0814747876 (cloth : alk. paper) 9780814747872 (cloth : alk. paper)

Subject

as *Communication Monographs*, the *Quarterly Journal of Economics*, and *American Psychologist*. Both types of periodicals are useful to researchers. As we just observed, periodicals are more timely than books. Current periodicals may be only a few days old. These days, many periodicals are available online, as well as in hard copy.

Just as you need a card catalog to help you find books, you need help to decide what periodicals might be useful. A large number of **periodical indexes** are published, covering a huge range of subject areas and listing most of the thousands of periodicals published on a regular basis. Many of these indexes are available both in print and in electronic formats that can be accessed from remote locations via your library's Web site. Some of the best-known indexes include the following:

- The *Reader's Guide to Periodical Literature* is the oldest and most frequently consulted periodical index. It lists both popular magazines and a few trade and professional journals. Articles are alphabetized according to both subject and author. The most convenient way to use the *Reader's Guide* is to search for subjects or key words, much as you would when using a Web search engine or a card catalog.

- The *Reader's Guide* is a cumulative index, published every 2 weeks. The indexes are combined into quarterly and annual volumes. Its cumulative structure allows the *Reader's Guide* to list very current material, as well as information from past years. Many libraries now subscribe to one of several available *Reader's Guide* electronic databases. Figure 7.4 illustrates a typical subject entry in the *Reader's Guide Full Text*.

- The *Social Sciences Index* and the *Humanities Index* list professional, trade, and specialty publications dealing with the social sciences and the humanities. Originally published as the *Reader's Guide Supplement*, the *Social Sciences Index* and the *Humanities Index* are organized and cumulated like the *Reader's Guide*. Like the *Reader's Guide*, these indexes are now available as full-text online databases.

- The *Education Index* lists articles not only about education but also on various subjects that are taught (think about the wide range of departments within a university, and you will have some idea of the scope). Its format is similar to that of the other periodical indexes.

periodical index
A listing of bibliographical data for articles published in a group of magazines and/or journals during a given time period

Figure 7.4 *A typical subject entry from the* Reader's Guide. *A key to abbreviations can be found in each volume.*

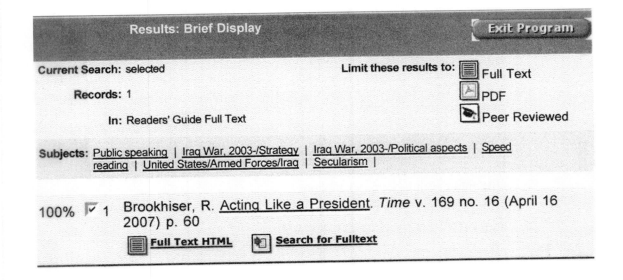

➤ The *Public Affairs Information Service (P.A.I.S.) Bulletin* indexes both periodicals and books in such fields as sociology, political science, and economics. Entries are listed alphabetically by subject, in much the same format as the other indexes. An electronic *P.A.I.S.* is also available.

Other specialized indexes may also prove valuable, depending on your topic and purpose. The *Business Periodicals Index*, the *Psychology Index*, the *Music Index*, the *Art Index*, and the *Applied Science and Technology Index* are a few of these specialized publications that you may wish to explore at one time or another.

ONLINE DATABASES

Instead of turning first to a single print index, many researchers today start researching periodicals by performing a key word or subject search of an **online database**. Periodicals are the most common type of resource indexed in this way, although newspapers, government documents, and even books are included in some databases. Full-text databases allow you to locate not only bibliographic information, but the full text of the resources themselves.

Among the rapidly increasing number of online databases that you may find useful is *Academic Search Complete*, the largest multidisciplinary database, which provides full text of more than 5,300 periodicals from virtually every academic field. Coverage is updated daily and currently dates as far back as 1865.

Other, more specialized full-text databases include *ABI/Inform*, which indexes more than 1,000 business and trade periodicals, and *ERIC*, which focuses on education. Your university library's Web page probably has a link to online databases. Use this link, or contact your library directly, to find out what full-text databases are available to you, as well as how to access them from remote (off-campus) sites.

NEWSPAPERS

Just as periodicals are more up-to-date than books, so newspapers are more current than periodicals. By reading the latest edition of a daily newspaper, you may be able to find information that is only hours old. Newspapers also offer more detailed coverage of events and special stories than do periodicals, simply because they are published more often. Finally, newspapers usually cover stories of local significance that most often would not appear in national news magazines.

Generally, libraries have only the latest newspapers in their racks. Back issues are quickly transferred to microfilm for more efficient and permanent storage. Don't let microfilm intimidate you. Microfilm readers are easy to use, and most librarians or aides working in the newspaper section will be glad to show you how to set up the reader with the film you need. In recent years, newspapers ranging in size and circulation from major national newspapers to local and college newspapers have also become available online.

As with any research, before you can consult a newspaper, you have to know where to look. To find relevant information on your subject, you need to consult a **newspaper index** or database. The database *Newspaper Source* provides not only citations but also full text of selected articles from 30 national and international newspapers and more than 200 regional U.S. newspapers, as well as transcripts of television and radio news shows. In addition, a number of medium-sized and large newspapers publish their own electronic indexes, and most newspapers that are available online include an index function.

REFERENCE RESOURCES

All major libraries contain reference resources. Reference resources are indexed in the card catalog with a *ref* prefix or suffix on their call numbers, to show that they are

online database
An electronic indexing resource that may include abstracts and/or the full texts of entries, in addition to bibliographic data.

newspaper index
A listing of bibliographical data for articles published in a newspaper (or group of newspapers) during a given period

housed in the reference section of the library. Reference resources include encyclopedias, dictionaries, directories, atlases, almanacs, yearbooks, books of quotations, and biographical dictionaries. All may, at one time or another, prove useful to a speaker. Let's examine a few of the most frequently consulted reference works, many of which today are available in electronic as well as print versions.

- **Encyclopedias.** The standard general encyclopedia has for many years been the *Encyclopaedia Britannica*. Nearly every library has a fairly recent set of *Britannica*, as well as several other general encyclopedias, such as the *Encyclopedia Americana*. Your library may provide access to online encyclopedias, in addition to having bound sets.

  In addition, there are a number of specialized encyclopedias. Art, philosophy, psychology, and music are just a few of the fields covered by specialty encyclopedias.

  No discussion of encyclopedias today would be complete without mentioning Wikipedia, the free online encyclopedia that often comes up as the first hit on a Web search. Created in 2001, Wikipedia has rapidly become one of the largest sites on the Web.[7] Wikipedia can be a useful general resource, especially for information on current events and new technology that may not find its way into print encyclopedias for years. But users need to keep in mind that anyone, regardless of expertise, can add an entry or change the content of any entry, making Wikipedia inherently unreliable and not generally suited for academic use.

- **Dictionaries.** The foremost dictionary of the English language is the *Oxford English Dictionary*, or *OED*. Published in twenty large volumes or available electronically, the *OED* provides definitions, pronunciations, etymologies, and usage histories for every word in the dictionary. No other dictionary is this comprehensive. Realistically, however, you will rarely need as much information about a word as the *OED* provides. A good desktop dictionary, such as *Webster's Collegiate Dictionary*, will serve most purposes.

  Specialty dictionaries also exist. *Black's Law Dictionary*, which provides legal definitions, is one example. Such diverse fields as geography, music, and economics also have their own special dictionaries.

- **Directories.** The *Encyclopedia of Associations*, the *National Directory of Nonprofit Organizations*, and other directories, including telephone directories, are usually available in the reference section.

- **Atlases.** An atlas is a geographical tool that provides maps, tables, pictures, and facts about the people and resources of various regions. Frequently used atlases include *Goode's World Atlas*, the *Rand McNally College World Atlas*, and the *Township Atlas of the United States*. There are also specialized atlases of history and politics.

- **Almanacs and Yearbooks.** Almanacs and yearbooks are compilations of facts. The *Statistical Abstract of the United States* is published annually by the Census Bureau and contains statistics on nearly every facet of life in the United States, including birth and mortality rates, income, education, and religion. An abridged version is available online at <www.census.gov/compendia/statab/>. The *World Almanac* contains factual information about almost every subject imaginable—anything from facts about monarchs of the eighteenth century to a list of every winner of the Kentucky Derby.

- **Books of Quotations.** These are compilations of quotes on almost every conceivable subject. Most of these books are arranged alphabetically by subject; a few are arranged according to author, with the subject entered in an index. The *Oxford Dictionary of Quotations* and *Bartlett's Familiar Quotations* are two widely consulted works. A searchable electronic version of *Bartlett's* is now available online at <www.bartleby.com/>.

- **Biographical Dictionaries.** These are reference works that contain biographical articles—some short, others not—on people who have achieved some recognition. Biographical dictionaries are usually organized alphabetically. Probably the best-known general works of this kind are the *Who's Who* series, which include brief biographies of international, national, and regional figures of note. The *Dictionary of National Biography* provides biographies of famous British citizens who are no longer living; the *Dictionary of American Biography* does the same for deceased Americans of note. The *Directory of American Scholars* provides information about American academicians. (You can probably find profiles of some of your current professors in this work.) And if none of the resources just mentioned has the biography you are seeking, you might try the *Biography Index*, a quarterly publication that lists current articles and books containing biographical sketches. One of these directories or indexes might be especially useful to the speaker who wants to quote a reputed expert but does not know anything about the expert's credentials.

Like periodicals, newspapers, and microfilms, print reference resources are usually available only for in-house research and cannot be checked out. That limitation may be overcome in part through an online reference library that includes encyclopedias, dictionaries, thesauruses, and books of quotations. One such online resource to which many public and university libraries subscribe is Credo Reference (www.credoreference.com).

One final note: Reference librarians are specialists in the field of information science. They are often able to suggest additional print or electronic resources that you might otherwise overlook. A suggestion: If you plan to use the reference section, visit the library during day-time working hours. A full-time reference librarian is more likely to be on hand and available to help you at that time than in the evenings or on weekends.

GOVERNMENT DOCUMENTS

Government agencies at all levels publish information on almost every conceivable subject, as well as keeping records of most official proceedings. Once a challenging complex collection of pamphlets, special reports, and texts of speeches and debates, government documents today are much more readily accessible online.

The most important index of government documents has long been the *Monthly Catalog of U.S. Government Publications*, available online in recent years. At present, several government agencies are working to develop a more comprehensive online *National Bibliography of U.S. Government Publications*.[8]

SPECIAL SERVICES

In addition to the resources just described, most libraries offer a number of special services. These include interlibrary loan and reciprocal borrowing privileges with other area libraries.

Interlibrary loan is one way to obtain resources that you have found indexed, but that your library does not own. You might, for example, discover in an article you are reading a reference to a book that you might also want to read. But your library does not have the book in its collection. Interlibrary loan can locate the book at another library and get it to you, usually within a few days. Some libraries charge a small fee for this service.

Many libraries also have reciprocal borrowing arrangements with libraries of neighboring colleges and universities. You may find that in addition to your own college library, two or three others within a fairly convenient radius are available for your use.

Interviews

If you don't know the answers to some of the important questions raised by your speech topic, but you can think of someone who might, consider interviewing that person to get material for your speech. For example, if you are preparing a speech on the quality of food in the dining hall, who better to ask about the subject than the director of food services? If you want to discuss the pros and cons of building a new prison in an urban area, you might interview an official of the correctional service, a representative of the city administration, and a resident of the area. Or if you want to explain why Al Gore lost the 2000 presidential election even though he won the popular vote, you might consult your professor of political science or American history.

Consider a word of caution, however, before you decide that an interview is necessary: Be sure that your questions cannot be answered easily by looking at a Web site or reading a newspaper article or a book. Do some preliminary reading on your subject before you decide to take up someone's valuable time in an interview. If you decide that only an interview can give you the material you need, you should prepare for it in advance.

PREPARING FOR THE INTERVIEW

DETERMINE YOUR PURPOSE The first step in preparing for an interview is to establish a purpose or objective for it. Specifically, what do you need to find out? Do you need hard facts that you cannot obtain from other sources? Do you need the interviewee's expert testimony on your subject? Does the person you are going to interview have a particularly significant personal experience that you wish to hear described firsthand? Or do you need an explanation of some of the information you have found in print sources? Decide now just what you want to have or know when the interview is over.

SCHEDULE THE INTERVIEW Once you have a specific purpose for the interview and have decided whom you need to speak with, arrange a meeting. Several days in advance, telephone the person you hope to interview, explain briefly who you are and why you are calling, and ask for an appointment. Most people are flattered to have their authority and knowledge recognized and willingly grant interviews to serious students if schedules permit.

If you are considering recording the interview on audio- or videotape, ask for the interviewee's okay during this initial contact. If the person does not grant permission, be prepared to gather your information without electronic assistance.

Eleanor Roosevelt (1884–1962)

First Lady of the United States, delegate to the United Nations, and social activist Eleanor Roosevelt found supporting material for her speeches in a variety of sources. She saw poverty and racism firsthand as she traveled across the nation. She interviewed such authorities as the presidents of historically Black colleges and universities. And she received thousands of letters detailing lives plagued by hardship and pleading for assistance. Eleanor Roosevelt used this material to support her tireless campaigns for civil rights, quality education, and world peace.[9]

As you seek supporting material for your speeches, draw on stories, examples, and illustrations from your own life. Anecdotes from your family, your travels, and even your everyday activities can help you support your ideas and add interest as well. In addition to your own experiences, consider interviewing others who are experts on your topic so that you can also personalize your message with comments from others.

[Photo: AP Images]

PLAN YOUR QUESTIONS Before your interview, find out as much as you can about both your subject and the person you are interviewing. Prepare questions that take full advantage of the interviewee's specific knowledge of your subject. You can do this only if *you* already know a good deal about your subject.

It is also helpful to think about how you should combine the two basic types of interview questions: closed-ended and open-ended.

As we discussed in Chapter 5, closed-ended questions call for a Yes or No answer or some brief statement of fact. "How many years have you served in the job?" and "Do you think that next month's tax referendum will pass?" are examples of closed-ended questions.

If you ask only closed-ended questions, however, you will limit and possibly frustrate your interviewee. You may also frustrate yourself. Open-ended questions allow the interviewee to express a personal point of view more fully. They interviewee may also give you more of the kind of information you probably want: expert testimony and personal experience. "Why do you think the asbestos should not be removed?" and "What, in your opinion, are the most serious potential consequences if it is removed?" are examples of open-ended questions. Open-ended questions often follow closed-ended questions. If the person you are interviewing answers a closed-ended question with a simple Yes or No, you may wish to follow up by asking "Why?"

CONDUCTING THE INTERVIEW

ON YOUR MARK . . . Dress appropriately for the interview. For most interviews, conservative, businesslike clothes show that you are serious about the interview and that you respect the norms of your interviewee's world.

Take paper and pen or pencil for note-taking. Even if you are planning to record the interview, you may want to turn the recorder off at some point during the interview, so you'll need an alternative. Or Murphy's Law may break your recorder. Ensure that the interview can continue, in spite of any mishaps.

GET SET . . . Arrive for the interview a few minutes ahead of the scheduled hour. Be prepared, however, to wait patiently, if necessary. Although the interview may be a high priority for you, the person you will interview has granted it as a courtesy and may need to complete something before speaking with you.

Once you are settled with the person you will interview, remind him or her of your purpose. If you are familiar with and admire the work the interviewee has done or published, don't hesitate to say so. Sincere flattery can help set a positive tone for the exchange. If you have decided to use a recorder, set it up. You may keep it out of sight once the interviewee has seen it, but never try to hide a recorder at the outset—such a ploy is unethical. If you are going to take written notes, get out your paper and pen. Now you are ready to begin asking your prepared questions.

GO! As you conduct the interview, use the questions you have prepared as a guide but not a rigid schedule. If the person you are interviewing mentions an interesting angle you haven't thought of, don't be afraid to pursue the point. Listen carefully to the person's answers, and ask for clarification of any ideas you don't understand.

Do not prolong the interview beyond the time limits of your appointment. The person you are interviewing is probably very busy and has been courteous enough to fit you into a tight schedule. Ending the interview on time is simply returning the courtesy. Thank your interviewee for his or her contribution, and leave.

If both parties are comfortable with it, the use of a tape recorder can free the interviewer and the interviewee from the need to concentrate on careful note taking.

[Photo: Bonnie Kamin/PhotoEdit]

FOLLOWING UP THE INTERVIEW

As soon as possible after the interview, read through your notes carefully and rewrite any portion that may be illegible. If you recorded the interview, label the recording with the date and the interviewee's name. You will soon want to transfer any significant facts, opinions, or anecdotes from either notes or recording to index cards or to a word-processing file. You will find a format for transcribing notes later in this chapter.

Resources from Special-Interest Groups and Organizations

Business and industrial groups, nonprofit organizations, and professional societies produce pamphlets, books, fact sheets, and other information about an extraordinarily wide variety of subjects. How do you find out about such resources? Those available online may be discovered through Web searches. Others may be found by consulting some of the reference works we have already discussed, such as the *Encyclopedia of Associations* and the *National Directory of Nonprofit Organizations*. Although these reference works do not indicate specific publications, they provide the names, addresses, and telephone numbers of businesses and organizations that may have a special interest in, and produce resources related to, your topic. Such resources may be available online or by mail at little or no cost.

confidently connecting with your audience

Prepare Early

Gathering useful and interesting supporting material for your speech takes time. So it's a good idea to give yourself plenty of time to gather examples, stories, statistics, opinions, quotations, and other supporting material. By starting your speech preparation early, you'll get a bonus: Research suggests that people who prepare early rather than waiting until the last minute experience less apprehension about speaking in public.[10] So preparing early will give you time to find interesting supporting material *and* help you manage your anxiety; you'll feel more confident if you prepare well in advance and have interesting ideas to share.

Remember that private companies and organizations set up Web sites and produce printed resources because they have a vested interest in the topic. You can expect resources produced by oil companies, for example, to minimize the harm oil spills can do to an environment. The criteria offered earlier in this chapter for evaluating Web sites should be applied to all kinds of resources obtained from special-interest groups and organizations.

Research Strategies

You have Internet access. You know the kinds of materials and services your library offers and how to use them. In short, you're ready to begin researching your speech. But unless you approach this next phase of speech preparation systematically, you may find yourself wasting a good deal of time and energy retracing steps to find bits of information you remember seeing but forgot to bookmark, print out, or write down the first time.

Well-organized research strategies can make your efforts easier and more efficient. You need to develop a preliminary bibliography, locate potential resources, evaluate their usefulness, take notes, and identify possible visual aids.

DEVELOP A PRELIMINARY BIBLIOGRAPHY

Creating a **preliminary bibliography**, or list of promising resources, should be your first research goal. The preliminary bibliography should include electronic resources as well as print materials. You will probably discover more resources than you actually look at or refer to in your speech; at this stage, the bibliography simply serves as a menu of possibilities.

You will need to develop a system for keeping track of your resources. Web browsers let you bookmark pages for future reference and ready access; your bookmarks can serve as one part of your preliminary bibliography. If you are searching an online database, you may be able to print out the references you discover. These printouts can be a second part of your preliminary bibliography. If you are using more traditional catalogs and indexes, you will need to copy down the necessary bibliographical information, a process we will discuss in more detail shortly. Using 3- by 5-inch note cards will give you the greatest flexibility. Later you can omit some of the cards, add others, write comments on them, or alphabetize them much more easily than if you had made a list on a sheet of paper.

The key to developing a useful bibliography is to establish a consistent format so that you can easily find and cite the page number, title, publisher, or some other vital fact about a publication. As noted in Chapter 3, the two most common formats, or documentation styles, are those developed by the MLA (Modern Language Association) and the APA (American Psychological Association). MLA style is usually used in the humanities; APA style in the natural and social sciences. Although we describe and use the MLA format here, check with your instructor about which format he or she prefers.

For a book, you should record the author's name, title of the book, publisher and date of publication, and the library's call number. Figure 7.5 illustrates how to trans-

preliminary bibliography

A list of potential resources to be used in the preparation of a speech

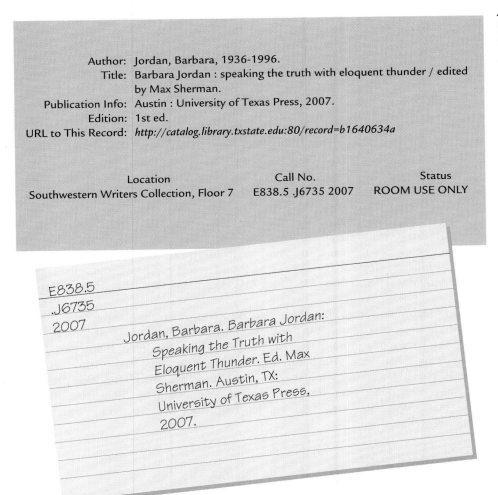

Figure 7.5 *Transferring information from an electronic catalog entry to a bibliography card*

fer information from an electronic catalog entry to a bibliography card. For an article in a periodical or newspaper, you should document the author's name, title of the article, title of the periodical, date of publication, and inclusive page numbers of the article. Figure 7.6 illustrates a bibliography entry in MLA style for an article in *Newsweek*.

For government publications, pamphlets, newsletters, fact sheets, or other specialized information formats, as long as you record the title, author, publisher, date, and page number, you will probably have at hand the information you need to locate any print material. For a government document, you will also need to record the Superintendent of Documents classification number, available in the *Catalog of U.S. Government Publications*.

Documentation formats for Web pages and other electronic resources are still evolving, although they are similar to the formats for other kinds of material. Following is the basic MLA format:

Author's name (last name first). "Title of article" (if any; enclosed in quotation marks). Title of Web site (underlined) or a description such as Homepage (not underlined). Date of Internet publication. Date of your access <URL>. (The URL should be enclosed in angle brackets, as illustrated here. Break a URL from one line to the next only after a slash.)

Figure 7.6 *A bibliography entry in MLA style for an article in* Newsweek

Henig, Samantha. "The End of Fake IDs?" <u>Newsweek</u> 11 June 2007: 14.

If you cannot find one element of this information (such as author, or date of Internet publication), simply skip it and go directly to the next item.

The most distinctive features of Web documentation are, of course, the address of the Web page and the date you accessed the page. Figure 7.7 illustrates an MLA bibliography entry for an online article in *The New York Times*.

If you have additional questions about how to format electronic resources, the Web itself can be your best ally. A number of sites provide instructions on how to cite electronic resources according to various style guides. For example, Purdue University's On-Line Writing Lab (OWL) can be found at owl.english.purdue.edu. This resource provides links to both MLA and APA documentation formats for electronic resources.

How many resources should you list in a preliminary bibliography for, say, a 10-minute speech? A reasonable number might be ten or twelve that look promising. If you have many more than that, you may feel overwhelmed. If you have fewer, you may have too little information. Out of a list of three books, three articles, three Web pages, and a pamphlet, you might find that two of the Web pages are not really very useful, your library does not have a couple of the articles, and one of the books is checked out. If you are left with three or four good resources, you are doing well.

LOCATE RESOURCES

You should have no trouble obtaining the actual texts of resources from the Web and online databases. But for all the other items in your preliminary bibliography, you will need to locate the resources yourself.

BOOKS Let's suppose that you decide to look first for the books you want. In a closed-stack library, you fill out a request card listing the books you're interested in. Take the card to the circulation desk and wait nearby for your books to arrive.

In an open-stack library, you look for books yourself. To find them, remember that books are shelved according to call numbers. The first character in a call number indicates the general type of book—literature, social science, religion, and so on. Letters or numbers following the initial designation indicate a subcategory. A location guide can tell you the floor or section of the stacks that houses books with the call numbers in which you are interested.

Figure 7.7 *A bibliography entry in MLA style for an article in* The New York Times *on the Web*

Abelson, Reed. "In Health Care, Cost Isn't Proof of High Quality." <u>The New York Times on the Web</u> 14 June 2007. 20 June 2007 <http://www.nytimes.com/2007/06/14/health/14insure.html_r=>.

Once you know where to find a book you want, go to that area and check the call-number guides on the ends of the bookcases to find exactly where on the shelves your book should be. Like dictionary guide words, the call-number guides indicate the call numbers of the first and last book in each bookcase. All books with call numbers between the two guide numbers are located in that bookcase.

If the title you want is not where it should be and you think it will be an important resource for your speech, you can go to the circulation desk and ask to place a hold on the book. Then when the book is returned by its current borrower, it will be reserved for you.

PERIODICALS Before searching for an article in a periodical, you need to determine whether your library subscribes to the periodical you need. You can find out by consulting a periodicals list or checking with a librarian. Once you know what periodicals are available, your library's location guide will tell you where they are housed. Some libraries devote a floor or section just to periodicals. All the bound periodicals will be arranged on shelves there, in alphabetical order. Current issues may be displayed on magazine racks, or they may be located in a reading room or other special area of the library.

Other libraries shelve their periodicals in the stacks. You look up the title of the periodical in the card catalog, copy the call number, and proceed as if you were looking for a book. As a rule, periodicals cannot be checked out, so you need to take notes at the library or photocopy the articles you want for further reference.

Microfilm or microfiche periodicals are probably stored in large filing cabinets with labeled drawers. Microfilm and microfiche readers are usually located near these cabinets. Don't hesitate to ask for help from a librarian if you are inexperienced with microfilm and microfiche.

NEWSPAPERS Newspapers are usually housed together in their own section of the library, although current newspapers, like current magazines, may be in a separate reading room. As mentioned earlier, older issues of newspapers are usually on microfilm, and many newspapers are now on the Web.

GOVERNMENT DOCUMENTS The Government Documents section of a library usually arranges material according to the Superintendent of Documents classification number, which can be found in the *Monthly Catalog of U.S. Government Publications*. Government Documents sections may have various ways of storing their material, including in vertical files. If you do not have much experience using government documents, the librarian in that section can be very helpful.

REFERENCE MATERIAL Reference material is usually housed in the Reference Section of the library and cannot be removed from that area. You must either take notes or make photocopies of the information you want.

EVALUATE THE USEFULNESS OF RESOURCES

It makes sense to gauge the potential usefulness of your resources before you begin to read more closely and take notes. Think critically about how the various resources you have found are likely to help you achieve your purpose and about how effective they are likely to be with your audience. Glance over the tables of contents of books, and flip quickly through the texts to note any charts, graphs, or other visual materials that might be used as visual aids. Skim a key chapter or two. Skim shorter articles, pamphlets, and fact sheets as well.

You may wish to devise a number or letter system to rank your resources according to their potential. You can write this code on your bibliography card or printout. If none of the resources looks particularly good, you may need to return to the bibliography-building stage to try to locate more potential resources.

Take Notes

Once you have located, previewed, and ranked your resources, you are ready to begin more careful reading and note-taking. Start with the resources that you think have the greatest potential. If you are looking at a Web page, an article, a pamphlet, an encyclopedia entry, or another kind of short document, you can read the whole text fairly quickly. But you probably do not have time to read entire books, so read only those chapters or sections that seem particularly relevant and potentially useful to your speech.

We discuss specific types of supporting material in Chapter 8. For now, it is sufficient to say that when you find an example, a statistic, an opinion, or other material that might be useful to your speech, write it down, photocopy it, download it into a computer file, or print it. Be sure to identify the source.

Don't create extra work for yourself by scribbling notes on scratch paper, the inside of a book cover, a checkbook, or a printout of the latest e-mail from Mom. Instead, have on hand a notebook, flash drive (if computers are available where you will be working), or note cards. Even if you plan to photocopy or enter most of your notes into a word-processing file, it is a good idea to carry a few note cards with you whenever you are working on a speech. You can use one to jot down an idea that comes to mind while you are sipping coffee or to record a fact you discover in a magazine article you read in a doctor's office or at a friend's house. Another advantage of using note cards is that you can later arrange them in the order of your speech outline, simplifying the integration of your ideas and supporting material into the speech.

What should you include in your notes? First, put only one item of supporting material or one idea on each card or each page of your speech notebook or word-processing file. If you are photocopying your sources or printing out Web pages, and you find a single page with several pieces of supporting material, you may want to "cut and paste"—literally cut the page apart and paste the separate items onto separate note cards. There is no rule as to how many note cards or pages you will have for each source. You may write only one note from one article you read, five from another, and twenty from a third. The amount of useful supporting material you find will vary widely from one source to another.

If you copy a phrase, sentence, or paragraph verbatim from a source, be sure to put quotation marks around it when you write it down or enter it. You may need to know later in the preparation process whether it was a direct quote or a paraphrase. This information will be obvious, of course, on printouts or photocopies.

DEVELOPING YOUR SPEECH STEP BY STEP

Gather Supporting Material

With her purpose statement, central idea, and main ideas in hand, Ashley begins to research produce safety. She decides to start online.

Seeking resources that meet the criteria of accountability, accuracy, objectivity, timeliness, usability, and diversity, Ashley goes to her university library's Web site. There she accesses the database *Newspaper Source*, where she discovers full texts of relevant recent articles from *The New York Times*, the *Chicago Daily Herald*, and the *Los Angeles Times*. She prints out several articles.

Ashley next checks out two online news sources: CNN and MSNBC. Both yield additional useful material. She bookmarks these sites.

With her resources in hand, Ashley begins to read and take notes. She puts quotation marks around any material copied verbatim from a source.

In addition to copying the information itself, you need to indicate its source. In Chapter 3, we discussed the ethical importance of crediting sources of ideas and information. If you consistently record your sources when you take notes, you will avoid the possibility of committing unintentional plagiarism later. You may wish to number the entries in your bibliography and then place the source number at the top of each note card or page of information or quotes from that source. Then you will need to add only the page number of each note. A somewhat more elaborate option is to use only the author's last name, title, and page number or Web address on the note card. Or you may wish to write a complete bibliographic reference on each card or page. This procedure takes more time but ensures that you will have vital reference information immediately at hand as you work on your speech later.

Finally, leave enough space at the top of each note card or page to summarize the idea expressed in the note. Such headings make it easier to find a particular bit of material quickly when you are ready to assemble the speech. Figure 7.8 illustrates two note cards—one with a paraphrased note and one with a direct quotation.

Paraphrased Note

Crossburning as Free Speech

Russomanno, Joseph. Speaking Our Minds: Conversations with the People Behind Landmark First Amendment Cases. Mahwah, NJ: Lawrence Erlbaum, 2002. 45.

R.A.V. v. city of St. Paul, MN, a case that involved a crossburning, resulted in a Supreme Court decision declaring unconstitutional a St. Paul ordinance limiting free speech acts.

Direct Quotation

Government Backlash against Internet Free Speech

Godwin, Mike. Cyber Rights: Defending Free Speech in the Digital Age. Cambridge, MA: MIT Press, 2003. 22.

"Here in the United States, the government has frequently used the fear of Net crimes and Net criminals as justification for imposing greater control on the Net as a whole."

Figure 7.8 *Sample note cards*

RECAP

Research Strategies

1. Develop a preliminary bibliography.
2. Locate sources.
3. Consider the potential usefulness of sources.
4. Take notes.
5. Identify possible presentation aids.

IDENTIFY POSSIBLE PRESENTATION AIDS

As we noted earlier in this chapter, in addition to discovering verbal supporting material in your sources, you may also find charts, graphs, photographs, or other potentially valuable visual material. You may think you will be able to remember what visuals were in which sources. But many speakers have experienced frustrating searches for that "perfect" presentation aid they remember seeing somewhere while they were taking notes for their speech. Even if you are not certain at this point that you will even use presentation aids in your speech, it can't hurt to print out, photocopy, or sketch on a note card any good possibilities, recording sources of information just as you did for your written materials. Then, when the time comes to consider if and where presentation aids might enhance the speech, you will have some readily at hand. In Chapter 14, we discuss types of presentation aids and provide guidelines for their use.

SUMMARY

Public speakers need to know where and how to find supporting material to use in their speeches. Five sources of supporting material are personal knowledge and experience; the Web; library resources; interviews; and resources from government agencies, special-interest groups, and organizations.

Most speakers can provide some illustrations, explanations, definitions, or other supporting material from their own knowledge and experience. Such material has the advantage of increasing the audience's respect for the speaker's authority.

The Web provides a vast collection of resources, easily accessible through directories and search engines. Because Web sites are not subject to any quality control or censorship, a speaker needs to evaluate who is accountable for the resources and whether they are accurate, objective, current, usable, and sensitive to diversity.

Even with access to the Web, most speakers also use library resources—books, periodicals, full-text databases, newspapers, reference resources, and government documents—as sources of supporting material. This chapter discussed how these resources are indexed and the general kinds of supporting material a speaker might expect to find in each. Libraries may also offer such special services as interlibrary loan and reciprocal borrowing privileges with area libraries.

Interviewing someone who is an expert on the subject of the speech or who has a unique point of view about the subject is a fourth way to gather supporting material. Interviewers may take written notes or tape their interviews; later, they can transcribe the information they have gathered onto note cards.

Finally, information about many topics is available from various special-interest groups and organizations. Because many such entities produce printed resources primarily to support their vested interests, a speaker should consider how accountable, accurate, objective, and current such resources are.

Once a speaker discovers possible resources, he or she should develop a preliminary bibliography of those resources, locate them, consider their potential usefulness, take notes, and identify possible presentation aids.

BEING AUDIENCE-CENTERED: A SHARPER FOCUS

CONSIDERING YOUR AUDIENCE

- Your audience will accord you more respect as an authority when they realize that you have firsthand knowledge of a topic.

- If no one is willing to be accountable for the content of a Web site, you cannot be account-able to your audience for using the information from that Web site in a speech.

- Think critically about whether the various resources you discover are likely to be effective with your audience.

CONSIDERING AUDIENCE DIVERSITY

- A diversity-sensitive Web site is free of material that communicates bias against any subgroup. Such a site may also offer or invite divergent perspectives and/or offer print, graphic, or audio alternatives for users with disabilities.

CRITICAL THINKING QUESTIONS

1. Imagine that you are preparing an informative speech on buying a new computer. Specifically, you want your audience to be able to make informed choices about platform, power, speed, and various available options. Explain how you might use each of the five key sources of supporting material in developing this speech.

2. For each of the following topics, list at least two library resources likely to yield relevant information:

   The Battle of San Jacinto
   The charter-school movement
   The Devil's Triangle
   Election reform
   El Niño
   How HMOs operate
   The trial of Julius and Ethel Rosenberg

3. In what reference works would you look first for the following information?

   A list of all the vice presidents of the United States
   Biographical information on Anne Brontë
   The history of opera
   The origin of the term *spoonerism*
   The ten most popular names for newborn boys in the United States in 2005
   The name of the person who said, "Democracy becomes a government of bullies tempered by editors."

ETHICAL QUESTIONS

1. As the Internet has become increasingly accessible, questions regarding copyright and fair use have become increasingly complex. A speaker can find graphs, pictures, and other potentially valuable visual aids simply by clicking a mouse. Under what conditions, if any, is it ethical to use such material in a speech?

2. While in the library gathering material for a speech on endangered species in your region, you find a wonderful, quotable magazine article from which you take copious notes. However, in your excitement, you neglect to record bibliographic information for this source on your note cards. You discover your omission as you begin composing your speech the night before you must deliver it; you have no time to return to the library. How can you solve your problem in an ethical way?

3. Both electronic and print indexes and databases sometimes include abstracts of books and articles, rather than full texts. If you have read only the abstract of a source, is it ethical to include that source on your speech bibliography?

Gathering Supporting Material for Your Speech

Before gathering supporting material, you must identify what needs supporting: the main ideas and subordinate ideas that form the outline of your message. Here's a worksheet to use as you gather supporting material for the key ideas in your speech.

1. Identify your specific purpose sentence: *At the end of my speech, the audience should be able to*

2. Identify your central idea (a one-sentence summary of your speech):

3. Generate the main ideas of your speech (based on steps, natural divisions, or reasons the central idea is true). You may have only one major idea, or you may have several. For a short classroom speech, you will probably not have more than three or four major ideas, and you may have fewer. Use Roman numerals when listing your main ideas.

    I.

    II.

    III.

    IV.

4. For each major idea, identify possible sources of information to support that idea. Here's a checklist of possible research sources or methods:

_____ Internet:

Consult a search engine such as Google or Yahoo! (see pages 149–150).

_____ Library:

Consult a librarian to help you locate sources.

Consult the card catalog for books (see page 154).

Consult a periodical index (e.g., *Reader's Guide to Periodical Literature*—see pages 155–156).

Consult an online database (e.g., *Academic Search Complete*—see page 156).

Consult a newspaper index or database (e.g., *Newspaper Source*—see page 156).

Consult reference resources (see pages 156–158).

Consult government documents (see page 158).

_____ Personal Interviews

_____ Resources from Special-Interest Groups and Organizations

Guido Reni (1575–1642). *Saints Peter and Paul.* Photo: Mauro Magliani, 1999. Alinari/Art Resource, N.Y.

I use not only all the brains I have, but all I can borrow.

—WOODROW WILSON

Using Supporting Material

outline

objectives

After studying this chapter you should be able to do the following:

1. Explain the importance of supporting material to a speech.

2. List the six main types of supporting material.

3. Explain at least one guideline for using each of the six types of supporting material.

4. List and explain six criteria for determining which supporting material to use in a speech.

Tobacco heir Patrick Reynolds speaks frequently at universities, corporate seminars, and political hearings around the country.[1] He has appeared on numerous major network and cable news and talk shows, including *Good Morning America* and *Larry King Live*. Reynolds's objective is not, as one might suppose, to defend the tobacco industry, but instead to campaign aggressively against it.

Citing information from the American Cancer Society, the American Lung Association, and the federal government, Reynolds points out that one out of every five deaths in the United States is caused by smoking, making it the leading killer in this country. He tells his audiences that 60 percent of all smokers start by age 14, with 90 percent becoming addicted by the age of 19. And then Reynolds adds his own personal, tragic, and ironic illustrations: His father, mother, aunt, and half-brother all died of smoking-related causes.

Patrick Reynolds has been described as a compelling speaker. Why? One listener explains,

> His ability to weave political perspective, impact of smoking on quality of life and health, emotional ramifications, psychology of marketing and advertising, and education considerations makes a huge and favorable impact on the audience.[2]

In other words, Reynolds is skilled at combining a variety of effective supporting material to capture and maintain his listeners' attention.

As you saw in the previous chapter, gathering appropriate supporting material is an essential step in the speech-preparation process. And once you have gathered a variety of material, you will need to make decisions about how to use your information to best advantage. You will need to look at your speech from your listeners' perspective and decide where an explanation might help them understand a point, where statistics might convince them of the significance of a problem, and where an illustration might stir their emotions. In this chapter, we will discuss these and other types of supporting material and present guidelines for using them effectively.

Illustrations

Novelist Michael Cunningham, acclaimed author of *The Hours*, often reads to standing-room-only crowds. He explains the appeal of such live readings in this way:

> *It's very much about storytelling. . . . you're all gathered around the campfire— "I'm going to tell you about these people, and what happened then."*[3]

illustration

A story or anecdote that provides an example of an idea, issue, or problem a speaker is discussing

Cunningham is right. A story or anecdote—an **illustration**—almost always guarantees audience interest by appealing to their emotions. "Stories get you out of your head and into your gut" is how one professional speech coach explains the universal appeal of illustrations.[4]

Let's look more closely at different kinds of illustrations and examine some guidelines for using them.

BRIEF ILLUSTRATIONS

A **brief illustration** is often no longer than a sentence or two. Arizona Senator John McCain offered three brief illustrations "to put faces on a few" of the 200 illegal immigrants who died in Arizona during a single recent year:

- Maria Hernandez Perez was No. 93. She was almost 2. She had thick brown hair and eyes the color of chocolate.
- Kelia Velazquez-Gonzales, 16, carried a Bible in her backpack. She was No. 109.
- John Doe, No. 143, died with a rosary encircling his neck. His eyes were wide open.[5]

Why use multiple brief illustrations? Sometimes a series of brief illustrations can have more impact than either a single brief illustration or a more detailed extended illustration. In addition, although an audience could dismiss a single illustration as an exception, two or more strongly suggest a trend or norm.

EXTENDED ILLUSTRATIONS

Longer and more detailed than the brief illustration, the **extended illustration** resembles a story. It is more vividly descriptive than a brief illustration, and it has a plot—an opening, complications, a climax, and a resolution.

Speechwriter Andrew Wilson told the story of one of the great lines in 20th century presidential speeches in the following extended illustration:

> A few weeks before [Ronald Reagan] was to speak at an event commemorating [Berlin's] 750th birthday, Peter Robinson, Reagan's speechwriter, went to Berlin to gather information and ideas.
>
> The first person he went to see was John Kornblum, the ranking U.S. diplomat in Berlin. Kornblum gave him this advice: "Be sophisticated. Don't let Reagan bash the Soviets. Don't mention the wall. Berliners have gotten used to it."
>
> Later Robinson joined a dozen or so West Berliners for dinner. He asked them, "Is it true, you've gotten used to the wall?"
>
> There was stunned silence. Then—pointing toward the wall—one man said, "My sister lives twenty miles in that direction, but I haven't seen her for two decades. Do you think that I can get used to that?"
>
> Then another man spoke of a soldier that he saw at a guard tower on his way to work every day: "He speaks the same language I speak. He shares the same history. But one of us is an animal, and the other is a zookeeper, and I am never quite certain which is which."
>
> Finally, an elegant-looking woman—who had been angered by the question— told the speechwriter: "If this man Gorbachev is serious with his talk of glasnost and perestroika, he can prove it. He can get rid of this wall."
>
> And there was the inspiration for one of the great lines in oratory. Reagan said, "Mr. Gorbachev, tear down this wall."[6]

To use an extended illustration takes more time than to cite a brief example, but longer stories can be more dramatic and emotionally compelling. As we discuss in Chapter 10, extended illustrations can work well as speech introductions. And Chapter 15 discusses the use of extended illustrations in informative speeches.

brief illustration
An unelaborated example, often only a sentence or two long

extended illustration
A detailed example

Hypothetical Illustrations

Hypothetical illustrations may be either brief or extended. They are different from the illustrations we have discussed so far, because they describe situations or events that have not actually occurred. Rather, they are scenarios that *might* happen. Any story set in the future is a hypothetical example, because the event cannot yet have happened. Plausible hypothetical illustrations enable your listeners to imagine themselves in a particular situation. The following hypothetical illustration comes from a speech on encouraging diversity:

> *Envision the year 2026. . . . Imagine, if you will, a world where economic justice is color-blind, gender-blind, and nationality-blind. Imagine a world that's never been more inter-connected, socially, culturally, and economically.*[7]

Notice the word *imagine* in this illustration. The purpose of a hypothetical illustration is not to trick your listeners into believing a bogus story. They should be aware from the beginning that the illustration is hypothetical.

Using Illustrations Effectively

Illustrations are almost guaranteed attention getters, as well as a way to support your statements. But even this excellent form of support can be ineffective if not used to its best advantage. The following suggestions can help you use illustrations more effectively in your speeches.

- **Be certain that your illustrations are directly relevant to the idea or point they are supposed to support.** As obvious as this principle seems, many student speakers, learning of the value of illustrations, go to great lengths to use as many of them as they can in their speeches. They are so eager, in fact, that some of their illustrations have little bearing on the specific point they are trying to make. Their listeners become confused. Never leave your audience in doubt as to why you used a certain illustration. Be sure that illustrations are obviously related to the idea they support.

- **Choose illustrations that represent a trend.** It is not ethical to find one or two isolated illustrations and use them as though they were typical. If your illustrations are rare instances, you owe it to your listeners to tell them so.

- **Make your illustrations vivid and specific.** You probably know people who cannot tell a joke. They just can't relate a story or deliver a punch line. Or they lack the sense of timing needed to make a joke funny. Unfortunately, some speakers bumble their best illustrations in a similar way. Some years ago, a speech professor was fascinated to discover that one of his students had been on the last voyage of the ill-fated Italian ship *Andrea Doria*. Early in the semester, he urged the young man to relate his experience as part of an informative speech on how humans respond to danger. The professor expected a speech with great dramatic impact. Instead, much to his surprise, the student's narrative went something like this: "Well, there was a loud noise and then the sirens went off and we all got in lifeboats and the ship sank."[8] Hardly the stuff great drama is made of! If you have chosen to tell a poignant story, give it enough detail to make it come alive in the minds of your listeners. Paint a mental picture of the people, places, and things involved.

- **Use illustrations with which your listeners can identify.** Just as you should use illustrations that are typical, so too should you use audience-centered illustrations—ones the members of your audience can relate to. The best illustrations are the ones that your listeners can imagine experiencing themselves. Other compelling stories, like the sinking of the *An-*

hypothetical illustration
An example that might happen but that has not actually occurred

Garrison Keillor (1942–)

Host of the syndicated weekly radio show *A Prairie Home Companion*, Garrison Keillor is perhaps best known for the stories he tells about his imaginary hometown, Lake Wobegon, Minnesota. Keillor's illustrations and anecdotes, told with vivid and concrete detail and humor, make listeners feel as though each week they are visiting the people of Lake Wobegon, gathered in the Chatterbox Café or attending a potluck at Our Lady of Perpetual Responsibility Church.

One of Keillor's storytelling gifts is his ability to visualize his characters and then make his mental picture come alive in the minds of his listeners. As you incorporate stories in your speeches, carefully develop the images of the people that appear in your story. Imagine what they are wearing, doing, seeing, experiencing, and feeling. Provide enough details so that your listeners can picture the people in your stories with their own "mind's eye," but not so many details that you smother the listeners' imagination.

[Photo: *The Daily Progress*/AP Images]

drea Doria, can illustrate such great human drama that everyone listening will be immediately interested and attentive. If you cannot find a plausible example, you may want to invent a hypothetical one, which you can gear specifically to your audience. You can then be sure of its pertinence to your listeners.

➤ **Remember that the best illustrations are personal ones.** Speakers gain conviction and enthusiasm when they talk about personal experiences. Patrick Reynolds, for example, introduced at the beginning of this chapter, is a compelling speaker in large part because he shares his own tragic personal experiences of the results of smoking. Of course, you will not have had personal experience with every topic on which you may speak. In a speech on the conflict between the legislative and executive branches of government, a good illustration might focus on the working relationship between the president and the speaker of the house. The best illustrations for a speech on American military strategy during the Revolutionary War might come from the letters of George Washington. But if you *have* had personal experience with the subject on which you are speaking, be sure to describe that experience to the audience.

Descriptions and Explanations

Probably the most commonly used forms of support are descriptions and explanations. A **description** provides the details that allow audience members to develop mental pictures of what a speaker is talking about. An **explanation** is a statement that makes clear how something is done or why it exists in its present form or existed in its past form.

description
A word picture of something

explanation
A statement that makes clear how something is done or why it exists in its present form or existed in its past form

DESCRIBING

Write for the eye, the ear, the nose, and all the senses. In other words, be as vivid as you possibly can.[9]

This advice from a professional speechwriter acknowledges that effective description creates images that allow listeners mentally to see, hear, smell, touch, or taste what you are describing. The more senses you appeal to with your word pictures, the better. Good descriptions are vivid, accurate, and specific; they make people, places, and events come alive for the audience. More specific instructions for constructing word pictures are given in Chapter 15.

Description may be used in a brief example, an extended illustration, a hypothetical instance, or by itself. In his speech commemorating the 60th anniversary of D-Day, President George W. Bush described the crossing of the English Channel by Allied Forces on June 6, 1944:

Only the ones who made that crossing can know what it was like. They tell of the pitching deck, the whistles of shells from the battleships behind them, the white jets of water from enemy fire around them, and then the sound of bullets hitting the steel ramp that was about to fall.[10]

EXPLAINING HOW

Edwin Pittock, president of the Society of Certified Senior Advisors, explained to a group of businesspeople how depression develops in the elderly:

Bad things happen, they layer, and you become more depressed as time goes along. You come to expect that bad things will happen to you, and your attitude becomes a self-fulfilling prophecy.[11]

Words can paint pictures that allow your listeners to envision and even experience vicariously your encounters with objects, people, and settings. What sensory details would you use to describe for an audience this colorful scene on a Colombian river?

[Photo: Jeremy Horner/Stone/Getty Images]

Speakers who discuss or demonstrate processes of any kind rely at least in part on explanations of how those processes work.

EXPLAINING WHY

Explaining why involves giving reasons for or consequences of a policy, principle, or event. NASA Deputy Administrator Shana Dale explained to an audience why lunar exploration continues to be an important element of America's space program:

> *The Moon is a foothold to further exploration, preparing us for future human and robotic missions to Mars and other destinations.*[12]

Often, having explained causes or reasons, a speaker can then tailor a solution to those specific causes. A student seeking to reverse a university policy forbidding freshmen to have cars on campus can first explain why that policy was adopted and then point out why it is no longer needed. In short, explaining why some condition or event exists provides an analysis that often leads to better solutions.

USING DESCRIPTIONS AND EXPLANATIONS EFFECTIVELY

Perhaps because they are the most commonly used forms of support, descriptions and explanations are also among the most frequently abused. When large sections of a speech contain long, nonspecific explanations, audience eyelids are apt to fall. The following suggestions can help you use descriptions and explanations effectively in your speeches.

- **Keep your descriptions and explanations brief.** An explanation should supply only as many details as necessary for an audience to understand how or why something works or exists. Too many details may make your listeners say your speech was "everything I *never* wanted to know about the subject."
- **Use language that is as specific and concrete as possible.** Vivid and specific language brings your descriptions and explanations alive. Liveliness helps you hold the audience's attention and paint in your listeners' minds the image you are trying to communicate. Chapter 12 provides more tips for making your language specific.
- **Avoid too much description and explanation.** You can hold your audience's attention more effectively if you alternate explanations and descriptions with other types of supporting material, such as brief examples or statistics.

Definitions

Steve thought and thought but couldn't come up with a good opening for his speech. In desperation, he turned to the dictionary. To introduce his speech on modern legal training in the United States, he decided to define *lawyer*. Much to Steve's disappointment, his introduction only succeeded in putting his 8 A.M. class soundly back to sleep. Steve's problem? He had misused a perfectly legitimate form of support. He did not need to define *lawyer* for a college class—or for any class beyond elementary school, for that matter. Steve had resorted to an unnecessary definition as a crutch, and it didn't hold up.

Definitions have two justifiable uses in speeches. First, a speaker should be sure to define any and all specialized, technical, or little-known terms in his or her speech. If Steve had discussed "tort reform," he would have needed to define that phrase early in his speech. Such definitions are usually achieved by *classification*, the kind of definition you would find in a dictionary. Alternately, a speaker may define a term by showing how it works or how it is applied in a specific instance—what is known as an *operational definition*. Let's look at examples of both types of definitions.

DEFINITIONS BY CLASSIFICATION

If you have to explain the meaning of a term, you may use a **definition by classification** from the *Oxford English Dictionary*, *Webster's*, or another reputable general dictionary, or you may turn to a specialized dictionary, such as *Black's Law Dictionary*. Any of these references defines words by classification—that is, by first placing a term in the general class, group, or family to which it belongs and then differentiating it from all the other members of that class. A dictionary definition also has authority. This can be an important advantage, especially when you are discussing a controversial subject. If you quote a reputable dictionary, the audience usually accepts without question the definition you are using.

In simpler or less controversial instances, it is also possible to define by classification in your own words, as Shannon did in her speech on the dangers of vaccines: "A vaccine is basically a dead viral cell that is injected into the patient's body."[13] Note how this definition fits our explanation of how to define by classification: Generally speaking, a vaccine fits into the class of "dead viral cell," but it differs from other dead viruses by being "injected into the patient's body."

OPERATIONAL DEFINITIONS

As noted earlier, sometimes a word or phrase may be familiar to an audience, but as a speaker you may be applying it in a unique or specific way that needs to be clarified. At other times, defining a word by classification may result only in an abstract notion that does not particularly clarify the word's meaning. In such cases, you would be better off providing a more concrete **operational definition**, explaining how something works or what it does.

Sidney Taurel, chairman and CEO of the pharmaceutical company Eli Lilly and Co., defined *RNA interference* operationally:

> *I won't drag you through the details, but basically this allows scientists to figure out what genes do by switching them on and off.*[14]

Operational definitions are usually original; they are not found in dictionaries. Although they may lack the credibility of dictionary definitions by classification, they can be specifically tailored to a speech.

USING DEFINITIONS EFFECTIVELY

The following suggestions can help you use definitions more effectively in your speeches.

➤ **Use a definition only when needed.** As we mentioned, novice speakers too often use a definition as an easy introduction or a time-filler. Resist the temptation to provide a definition unless you are using a relatively obscure term or one with several definitions. Unnecessary definitions are boring and, more serious still, insulting to the listeners' intelligence.

➤ **Be certain that your definition is understandable.** You probably have had the frustrating experience of looking up a word in the dictionary, only to

definition
A statement about what a term means or how it is applied in a specific instance

definition by classification
A "dictionary definition," constructed by first placing a term in the general class to which it belongs and then differentiating it from all other members of that class

operational definition
A statement that shows how something works or what it does

find that the full definition is as confusing as the word itself. The word *dogmatic*, for example, may be defined as "characterized by or given to the use of dogmatism." To find a more satisfactory definition, you can look down the column until you find *dogmatism*. Your listeners do not have that capability, so make certain you give them definitions that are immediately and easily understandable—or you will have wasted your time and perhaps even lost your audience.

- **Be certain that your definition and your use of a term are consistent throughout a speech.** Even seemingly simple words can create confusion if not defined and used consistently. For example, Roy opened his speech on the potential hazards of abusing nonprescription painkillers by defining *drugs* as nonprescription painkillers. A few minutes later, he confused his audience by using the word *drug* to refer to cocaine. Once he had defined the term, he should have used it only in that context throughout the speech.

Analogies

An **analogy** is a comparison. Like a definition, it increases understanding; unlike a definition, it deals with relationships and comparisons—between the new and the old, the unknown and the known, or any other pairs of ideas or things. In her speech to the 1990 graduating class of Wellesley College, Barbara Bush found the concept of color a unifying analogy for the speaker, the occasion, and school tradition:

> Now I know your first choice for today was Alice Walker, known for The Color Purple. Instead you got me—known for the color of my hair! Of course, Alice Walker's book has a special resonance here. At Wellesley, each class is known by a special color, and for four years the class of '90 has worn the color purple. Today you meet on Severance Green to say goodbye to all that, to begin a new and very personal journey, a search for your own true colors.[15]

Analogies can help your listeners understand unfamiliar ideas, things, and situations by showing how these matters are similar to something they already know.

There are two types of analogies. A *literal* analogy compares things that are actually similar (two sports, two cities, two events). A *figurative* analogy may take the form of a simile or a metaphor. It compares things that at first seem to have little in common (such as the West Wind and revolution in Percy Bysshe Shelley's poem "Ode to the West Wind") but share some vital feature (a fierce impetus for change).

LITERAL ANALOGIES

Attorney Stephen Dannhauser, speaking to the European Banking and Financial Forum in Prague, compared traveling across the United States and traveling across Western Europe, now that Western European countries all use a single currency:

> As an American accustomed to traveling 3,000 miles from coast to coast in the United States without having to concern myself with a diversity of currencies, enjoying a similar experience across much of Western Europe is welcome.[16]

Dannhauser's comparison of the two experiences is a **literal analogy**—a comparison between two similar things. If your listeners are from a culture or group other than your own or the one from which the speech derives, literal analogies that draw on the listeners' culture or group may help them understand more readily the less familiar places, things, and situations you are discussing. Literal analogies are often employed by people who want to influence public policy. For example, proponents of trade restrictions argue that because Japan maintains its trade balance through stringent

analogy
A comparison between two things

literal analogy
A comparison between two similar things

import controls, so should the United States. Or, if Columbia, Missouri, solved both ecological and financial woes by successfully instituting an aluminum can tax, why not try the same approach in Lawrence, Kansas? The more similarities a policymaker can show between the policies or situations being compared, the better his or her chances of being persuasive.

FIGURATIVE ANALOGIES

On a warm July afternoon in 1848, feminist Elizabeth Cady Stanton delivered the keynote address to the first women's rights convention in Seneca Falls, New York. Near the end of her speech, she offered this impassioned analogy:

> *Voices were the visitors and advisers of Joan of Arc. Do not "voices" come to us daily from the haunts of poverty, sorrow, degradation, and despair, already too long unheeded? Now is the time for the women of this country, if they would save our free institutions, to defend the right, to buckle on the armor that can best resist the keenest weapons of the enemy—contempt and ridicule.*[17]

A literal analogy might have compared the status of women in medieval France to that of women in nineteenth-century America. But the **figurative analogy** Stanton employed compared the voices that moved Joan of Arc to the social ills facing nineteenth-century women.

Because it relies not on facts or statistics, but rather on imaginative insights, the figurative analogy is not considered "hard" evidence. But because it is creative, it is inherently interesting and should help grab an audience's attention. In a speech entitled "Solid Connections in a Liquid World," Ralph W. Shrader, chairman and CEO of the management consulting firm Booz Allen Hamilton, used this figurative analogy:

> *The world is liquid. What do I mean by that? I mean that today's world is so fluid and changing that it is more akin to whitewater and riptides than a flat plateau.*[18]

USING ANALOGIES EFFECTIVELY

These suggestions can help you to use literal and figurative analogies more effectively.

- **Be sure that the two things you compare in a literal analogy are very similar.** If you base your speech on a literal analogy, it is vital that the two things you compare be very much alike. One reason socialized medicine has not been adopted in the United States is that critics of the idea have pointed out how dissimilar the United States is to most of the countries that have adopted such programs. What works in those nations would not work here, they argue. The more alike the two things being compared, the more likely it is that the analogy will stand up under attack.

- **Be sure that the essential similarity between the two objects of a figurative analogy is readily apparent.** When you use a figurative analogy, it is crucial to make clear the similarity on which the analogy is based. If you do not, your audience will end up wondering what in the world you are talking about. It may be a good idea to try out a figurative analogy on an honest friend before using it during a speech. Then you can be certain that your point is clear.

Statistics

figurative analogy
A comparison between two essentially dissimilar things that share some common feature on which the comparison depends

statistics
Numerical data that summarize facts or samples

Many of us live in awe of numbers, or **statistics**. Perhaps nowhere is our respect for statistics so evident—and so exploited—as in advertising. If three out of four doctors surveyed recommend Pain Away aspirin, it must be the best. If Sudsy Soap is 99.9 percent pure (whatever that means), surely it will help our complexions. And if nine out of ten people like Sloppy Catsup in the taste test, we will certainly buy some for this weekend's barbecue. How can the statistics be wrong?

The truth about statistics lies somewhere between such unconditional faith in numbers and the wry observation that "There are three kinds of lies: lies, damned lies, and statistics."

USING STATISTICS AS SUPPORT

Just as three or four brief examples may be more effective than just one, a statistic that represents hundreds or thousands of individuals may be more persuasive still.

Statistics can help a speaker express the magnitude or seriousness of a situation:

As a company with 360,000 employees, 88,000 vehicles, and 2,850 operating facilities worldwide, UPS has a significant impact on society, the global economy, and the environment.[19]

Or a statistic can be a percentage that expresses the relationship of a part to the whole:

The National Highway Traffic Safety Administration reports that a whopping 40 percent of car repair costs last year were either fraudulent or unnecessary.[20]

Whatever their purpose, statistics are considered by most people to be the ultimate "hard" evidence—firm, convincing fact.

USING STATISTICS EFFECTIVELY

The following discussion can help you analyze and use statistics effectively and correctly.

USE RELIABLE SOURCES It has been said that figures don't lie, but liars figure! And indeed, statistics can be produced to support almost any conclusion desired. Your goal is to cite *reputable*, *authoritative*, and *unbiased* sources.

- **Reputable.** The most reputable sources of statistics are usually government agencies, independent survey organizations, scholarly research reports, and such statistical reference works as the *World Almanac* and the *Statistical Abstract of the United States*. Private businesses may also be reputable, but you should view their statistics with a bit more caution. These organizations may use questionable data-collection methods, or their data may be biased by special interests.

- **Authoritative.** Statistical sources should also be authoritative. No source is an authority on everything and thus cannot be credible on all subjects. For example, we expect the U.S. Surgeon General's office to gather and release statistics on smokers' risks of developing lung cancer. But we would look askance at statistics from that same office that dealt with the numbers of hurricanes that have hit the coastal United States in the last 100 years. The most authoritative source is the **primary source**—the original collector and interpreter of the data. If you find an interesting statistic in a newspaper or magazine article, look closely to see whether a source is cited. If it is, try to find that source and the original reporting of the statistic. Do not just assume that the secondhand account, or **secondary source**, has reported the statistic accurately and fairly. As often as possible, go to the primary source.

- **Unbiased.** As well as being reputable and authoritative, sources should be as unbiased as possible. We usually extend to government research and various independent sources of statistics the courtesy of thinking them unbiased.

primary source
The original collector and interpreter of information or data

secondary source
An individual, organization, or publication that reports information or data gathered by another entity

Because they are, for the most part, supposed to be unaffiliated with any special interest, their statistics are presumed to be less biased than those coming from such organizations as the American Tobacco Institute, the AFL-CIO, or Microsoft. All three organizations have some special interest at stake, and data they gather are more likely to reflect their biases.

As you evaluate your sources, try to find out how the statistics were gathered. For example, if a statistic relies on a sample, how was the sample taken? A Thursday afternoon telephone poll of 20 registered voters in Brooklyn is not an adequate sample of New York City voters. The sample is too small and too geographically limited. In addition, it excludes anyone without a telephone or anyone unlikely to be at home when the survey was conducted. Sample sizes and survey methods do vary widely, but most legitimate polls involve samples of 500 to 2,000 people, selected at random from a larger population. Of course, finding out about the statistical methodology may be more difficult than discovering the source of the statistic, but if you can find it, the information will help you to analyze the value of the statistic.

INTERPRET STATISTICS ACCURATELY People are often swayed by statistics that sound good but have in fact been wrongly calculated or misinterpreted. In an interview for *The New York Times*, Joel Best, author of *Damned Lies and Statistics: Untangling Numbers from the Media, Politicians, and Activists*, offered his favorite "bad statistic":

> A student of mine quoted an article that contained the sentence, "Every year since 1950, the number of American children gunned down has doubled." This is [a] mutant statistic. If one child were gunned down in 1950, and two in 1951, then by 1995 . . . there would have been 35 trillion children gunned down, more than the total number of people who ever lived.[21]

A misinterpretation of statistics became a national issue with the appointment of former Houston, Texas, School Superintendent Rod Paige as Secretary of Education. It was later revealed that Houston's amazing gains on such education indicators as dropout rates had actually resulted, not from visionary leadership, but from

> classifying, or coding [dropouts] as leaving for acceptable reasons: transferring to another school or returning to their native country.[22]

Both as a user of statistics in your own speeches and as a consumer of statistics in articles, books, and speeches, be constantly alert to what the statistics actually mean.

MAKE YOUR STATISTICS UNDERSTANDABLE AND MEMORABLE You can make your statistics easier to understand and more memorable in several ways. First, you can *compact* a statistic, or express it in limits that are more meaningful or more easily understandable to your audience. A fairly common way to compact a statistic is to express a staggering amount of money in terms of cents on the dollar:

> By 2016, health costs are scheduled to exceed $4 trillion, or almost 20% of [Gross Domestic Product]. That means that within less than 10 years, 20 cents out of every dollar produced in America will be spent on health care.[23]

You might also make your statistics more memorable by *exploding* them. Exploded statistics are created by adding or multiplying related numbers—for example, cost per unit times number of units. Because it is larger, the exploded statistic seems more significant than the original figures from which it was derived. J. Edward Hill, former president of the American Medical Association, used the "exploding" strategy to drive home the significance of the number of Americans who died in the 1918 influenza pandemic:

Private Health Insurance Coverage in the United States by Age	
Age	Number insured (in thousands)
Under 18 years	48,686
18 to 24 years	16,733
25 to 34 years	25,751
35 to 44 years	31,903
45 to 54 years	33,114
55 to 64 years	23,543
65 years and over	21,437

Figure 8.1 *Example of a table of statistics*[24]

If the same percentage of Americans were to lose their lives today, in a similar time frame, one and a half million people would die from flu between [October] and New Year's Day.[25]

Finally, you can *compare* your statistic with another that heightens its impact. In his 2007 "state of the state" address, California Governor Arnold Schwarzenegger noted that

California's population is expected to increase by as much as 30 percent over the next 20 years. This is the equivalent of adding three new cities the size of Los Angeles.[26]

ROUND OFF NUMBERS It is much easier to grasp and remember "2 million" than 2,223,147. Percentages, too, are more easily remembered if they are rounded off. And most people seem to remember percentages even better if they are expressed as fractions. "About 30 percent" is a better way to express "31.69 percent," and "about one third" is even easier to understand and remember. However, do not round off a statistic unless you can do so without distorting or falsifying the statistic.

USE VISUAL AIDS TO PRESENT YOUR STATISTICS Most audience members have difficulty remembering a barrage of numbers thrown at them during a speech. But if the numbers are displayed in a table or graph in front of your listeners, they can more easily grasp the statistics. Figure 8.1 illustrates how a speaker could lay out a table of statistics on how private health insurance coverage in the United States is distributed among various age groups. Using such a table, you would still need to explain what the numbers mean, but you wouldn't have to recite them. We discuss visual aids in Chapter 14.

Opinions

Three types of **opinions** may be used as supporting material in speeches: the testimonies of expert authorities, the testimonies of ordinary (lay) people with firsthand or eyewitness experience, and quotations from literary works. If the person you quote is a recognized authority on your topic, citing his or her opinion may add credibility to your own arguments. Or the person you quote may have "said it in a nutshell"—phrased an argument or observation clearly, succinctly, and memorably. Let's look at the specific purposes and advantages of both expert testimonies and literary quotations.

opinion
A statement expressing an individual's attitudes, beliefs, or values

The opinion of an expert can provide very effective support for a speech.

[Photo: Jon Feingersh/Masterfile]

EXPERT TESTIMONY

Having already offered statistics on the number of cigars Americans consume annually, Dena emphasized the danger to both smokers and recipients of secondhand smoke by providing **expert testimony** from a National Cancer Institute adviser:

> *James Repace, an adviser to the National Cancer Institute, states, "If you have to breathe secondhand smoke, cigar smoke is a lot worse than cigarette smoke."*[27]

Whether your topic is controversial or not, the testimony of a recognized authority can add a great deal of weight to your arguments. Or, if your topic requires that you make predictions—statements that can be supported in only a marginal way by statistics or examples—the statements of expert authorities may prove to be your most convincing support. You may quote experts directly or paraphrase their words, as long as you are careful not to alter the intent of their remarks.

LAY TESTIMONY

You are watching the nightly news. Newscasters, reporting on the forest fires that continue to rage in California, explain how these fires started. They provide statistics on how many thousands of acres have burned and how many hundreds of homes have been destroyed. They describe the intense heat and smoke at the scene of one of the fires, and ask an expert—a veteran firefighter—to predict the likelihood that the fires will be brought under control soon. But the most poignant moment of this news story is an interview with a woman who has just been allowed to return to her home and has found it in smoldering ashes. She is a layperson—not a firefighter or an expert on forest fires, but someone who has experienced the tragedy firsthand.

Like illustrations, **lay testimony** can stir an audience's emotions. And, although neither as authoritative nor as unbiased as expert testimony, lay testimony is often more memorable.

LITERARY QUOTATIONS

Another way to make a point memorable is to include a **literary quotation** in your speech. Speaking on the complex issue of using race as a factor in college admissions,

expert testimony
An opinion offered by someone who is an authority on a subject

lay testimony
An opinion or description offered by a nonexpert who has firsthand experience

literary quotation
An opinion or description by a writer who speaks in a memorable and often poetic way

University of Hartford President Walter Harrison turned to writer F. Scott Fitzgerald:

> *The use of race as a factor in selective college admissions processes . . . is complex and emotionally charged. In 1935, the American novelist F. Scott Fitzgerald wrote, "The test of a first-rate intelligence is the ability to hold two opposed ideas in the mind at the same time, and still retain the ability to function."*[28]

Fitzgerald's words are especially appropriate because they appeal to the intelligence of the listeners. Note too that the quotation is short. Brief, pointed quotations usually have greater audience impact than longer, more rambling ones. As Shakespeare said, "Brevity is the soul of wit" (*Hamlet*, II:2).

Literary quotations have the additional advantage of being easily accessible. You'll find any number of quotation dictionaries on the Web and in the reference sections of most libraries. Arranged alphabetically by subject, these compilations are easy to use.

USING OPINIONS EFFECTIVELY

Here are a few suggestions for using opinions effectively in your speeches.

Be certain that any authority you cite is an expert on the subject you are discussing. Unless the authority you are calling on has expertise in the subject on which he or she is expressing an opinion, your quote will have little value. Quoting the opinions of an atomic scientist about works of art, for example, is to do little more than accept the opinions of the average person. Be sure, then, that the sources you quote are not merely recognized authorities but recognized in the particular subject area they are talking about. Advertisers, especially, ignore this rule when they have well-known athletes endorse such items as flashlight batteries, breakfast cereals, and cars. Athletes may indeed be experts on athletic shoes, tennis rackets, or stopwatches, but they lack any specific qualifications to talk about most of the products they endorse.

Identify your sources. Perhaps you chose an eminently qualified authority on your subject. Unless the audience, too, is aware of the qualifications of your authority, they may not grant him or her any credibility. If a student quotes the director of the Harry Ransom Humanities Research Center at the University of Texas but identifies that person only as Tom Staley, few listeners will recognize the name, let alone acknowledge his authority.

In Chapter 3, we discussed the importance of citing your sources orally. In the course of doing so, you can provide additional information about the qualifications of those sources. Note how the student speakers in the following examples use a variety of phrases and sentence structures to help them identify their sources for their audiences in a fluent way:

> *Military survivors facing a combination of misinformation and a lack of financial resources find it hard to cope. Regina Asaro, a military wife and psychiatric nurse, told the July 5, 2006, Richmond Times Dispatch, "You lose the safety and security of a predictable future."*[29]

> *Eugene Richardson, an Illinois police officer who inspects hundreds of car seats annually, told the August 24, 2006, Chicago Tribune, "One car seat may fit in your vehicle perfectly and not in your wife's vehicle at all."*[30]

Cite unbiased authorities. Just as the most reliable sources of statistics are unbiased, so too are the most reliable sources of opinion. The chairman of General Motors may offer an expert opinion that the Chevy Lumina is the best midsized car

on the market today. His expertise is unquestionable, but his bias is obvious and makes him a less-than-trustworthy source of opinion on the subject. A better source would be the *Consumer Reports* analyses of the reliability and repair records of midsized cars.

Cite opinions that are representative of prevailing opinion. Perhaps you have found a bona fide expert who supports your conclusions. Unless most of the experts in the field share his or her opinion, its value is limited. Citing such opinion only leaves your conclusions open to easy rebuttal.

Quote your sources accurately. If you quote or paraphrase either an expert or a layperson, be certain that your quote or paraphrase is accurate and within the context in which the remarks were originally made. Major misunderstandings may result from someone's being quoted inaccurately. "Letters to the Editor" columns in major newspapers or magazines often include letters from irate readers who have found themselves misquoted in recent articles.

Use literary quotations sparingly. Even though a relevant literary quote may be just right for a speech, use it with caution. Overuse of such quotations often

bores an audience and causes them to doubt your creativity and research ability and to view you as somewhat pretentious. It is sometimes better not to use any quotation than to use literary quotations out of desperation, just because you can't find anything better. Be sure that you have a valid reason for citing a literary quotation, and then use only one or two at most in a speech.

Selecting the Best Supporting Material

In Chapter 7, we discussed six criteria for evaluating Web sites: accountability, accuracy, objectivity, timeliness, usability, and diversity. Throughout this chapter, we have presented guidelines for using each of the six types of supporting material effectively. However, even after you have applied these criteria and guidelines, you may still have more supporting material than you can possibly use for a short speech. How do you decide what to use and what to eliminate? The following considerations can help you make that final cut.

Select Interesting Supporting Material

You'll feel more confident and relaxed if you know you've selected interesting supporting material and can share it with ease. What makes something interesting? It's interesting if the information relates to your *listeners* or if it contains concrete images that your listeners can visualize. What makes supporting material easy to share? You'll find that it's easier to share supporting material that *you* enjoy talking about. Sharing personal stories or a fascinating tidbit of information that you've found during your research can ease your apprehension. Using interesting supporting material will help you focus on your audience and your message rather than your fear.

- **Magnitude.** Bigger is better. The larger the numbers, the more convincing your statistics. The more experts who support your point of view, the more your expert testimony will command your audience's attention.

- **Proximity.** The best supporting material is whatever is the most relevant to your listeners, or "closest to home." If you can demonstrate how an incident could affect audience members themselves, that illustration will have far greater impact than a more remote one.

- **Concreteness.** By themselves, abstract assertions and explanations bore an audience. If you need to discuss principles and theories, explain them with concrete examples and specific statistics.

- **Variety.** Even if your supporting material meets the first four requirements, if it is all of the same type, your audience may lose interest or question your research. A mix of illustrations, opinions, definitions, and statistics is much more interesting and convincing than the exclusive use of any one type of supporting material.

- **Humor.** Audiences usually appreciate a touch of humor in an example or opinion. Only if your audience is unlikely to understand the humor or if your speech is on a *very* somber and serious topic is humor not appropriate.

- **Suitability.** Your final decision about whether to use a certain piece of supporting material will depend on its suitability to you, your speech, the occasion, and—as we continue to stress throughout the book—your audience. For example, you would probably use more statistics in a speech to a group of scientists than in an after-luncheon talk to the local Rotary Club.

SUMMARY

Interesting, convincing supporting material is essential to a successful speech. You can choose from various types of supporting material, including illustrations, descriptions and explanations, definitions, analogies, statistics, and opinions.

Once you find material to support your ideas, fol-low the suggestions presented in this chapter to gauge the validity and reliability of your evidence. Six additional criteria—magnitude, proximity, concreteness, variety, humor, and suitability—can help you choose the most effective support for your speech.

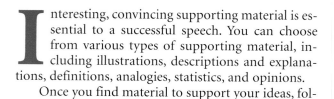

BEING AUDIENCE-CENTERED: A SHARPER FOCUS

CONSIDERING YOUR AUDIENCE

- An illustration almost always ensures audience interest.

- Vivid and specific language in a description or explanation helps you hold the audience's attention and paint in your listeners' minds the image you are trying to communicate.

- The best supporting material is whatever is the most relevant to your listeners, or "closest to home."

- Abstract assertions and explanations by themselves bore an audience. Use concrete examples and specific statistics.

- A mix of illustrations, opinions, definitions, and statistics is much more interesting and convincing than the exclusive use of any one type of supporting material.

CONSIDERING AUDIENCE DIVERSITY

- Once you have gathered a variety of supporting material, look at your speech from your audience's perspective and decide where an explanation might help listeners understand a point, where statistics might convince them of the significance of a problem, and where an illustration might stir their emotions.

- If your listeners are from a culture or group other than your own or the one from which

the speech derives, literal analogies that draw on the listeners' culture or group may help them understand more readily the less familiar places, things, and situations you are discussing.

- Your final decision about whether to use a certain piece of supporting material will depend on its suitability to your audience.

CRITICAL THINKING QUESTIONS

The following excerpts from student speeches contain various types of supporting material discussed in this chapter. Read each excerpt and then identify the type of supporting material it contains. (Some may contain more than one type. In that case, identify the *primary* type of supporting material contained in the excerpt.)

_____ 1. It was another beautiful day at the amusement park. Warm sunshine, the smell of cotton candy, the kids, and the rides. The roller coaster's whooshing 60-miles-per-hour speed was accompanied by the familiar screams of delight from kids of all ages. Another ride, the comet, was flying gracefully through the heavens when suddenly a chain broke, flinging one of the gondolas 75 feet into the air before it crashed, killing a man and seriously injuring his son.[31]

_____ 2. The problem of binge drinking and its effects points to a deeply ingrained culture of student drinking in America—a culture that spends $5.5 billion on alcohol each year, more than [it spends] on soft drinks, tea, milk, juice, coffee, and textbooks combined.[32]

_____ 3. "The bottom line," says former CPSC Chairwoman Nancy Steorts, "is that the American consumer has no way of knowing the level of safety on a particular ride at a particular location. In effect, we are forcing the consumer to play amusement ride roulette with his or her family's safety."[33]

_____ 4. Maryland has one of the best [amusement-park] safety records in the country, and it is essential that all states adopt and consistently enforce the same thorough regulations.[34]

_____ 5. Do you remember what the weather was like a few months ago? Recall when it was cold; when you would shiver getting out of bed, getting out of the shower, walking outside; when it was most wise to stay inside, wrap yourself in a warm blanket, and turn up the heat.[35]

_____ 6. Imagine you are poor, according to a wide variety of government standards. It is nearly impossible for you to pay your heating bills. So you would be eligible for a portion of the . . . [money] allocated for this program. . . .[36]

_____ 7. [Solar] storms cause the sun to throw off electrically charged ions that, combined with charged particles, enter the Earth's atmosphere from outer space.[37]

ETHICAL QUESTIONS

1. Go back through the chapter and reread each of the guidelines for each type of supporting material. Which of these guidelines for *effective* use of supporting material might also be considered a guideline for *ethical* use of supporting material? Explain your choices.

2. Is it ever ethical to invent supporting material if you have been unable to find what you need for your speech? Explain.

Identifying a Variety of Supporting Material for Your Speech

A good speech includes several different types of supporting material. As you prepare your speech, use this worksheet to categorize the different types of supporting material for your speech. If you are using only one or two types of supporting material you may need to use your research skills to search for additional types of support to enhance both the clarity and the interest of your message.

Illustration: A story that provides an example of an idea, issue, or problem. The illustration could be short or long, real or hypothetical (see pages 174–177).

1.

2.

3.

Description and Explanation: Words that clarify a person, place, thing, idea, or process (see pages 177–179).

1.

2.

3.

Definition: A statement about what a term means or how it is applied in a specific instance (see pages 179–181).

1.

2.

3.

Analogy: A comparison between two things. The analogy could compare two similar things (a literal analogy) or two dissimilar things that share some common feature (a figurative analogy) (see pages 181–182).

   1.

   2.

   3.

Statistics: Numerical data that summarize facts and examples (see pages 182–185).

   1.

   2.

   3.

Opinion: A statement expressing a person's attitudes, beliefs, or values (see pages 185–189).

   1.

   2.

   3.

Marc Chagall (1887–1985) *Grandfather Clock with Blue Wing.* 1949. Oil on canvas, 92 × 79 cm. Giraudon/Art Resource, N.Y.

Organized thought is the basis of organized action.

—ALFRED NORTH WHITEHEAD

Organizing Your Speech

outline

objectives

After studying this chapter you should be able to do the following:

1. List and describe five patterns for organizing the main ideas of a speech.

2. Explain how organizational strategies can vary according to culture.

3. List five patterns of organization applicable to subpoints.

4. Describe how to integrate supporting material into a speech.

5. List and explain four organizational strategies specifically adapted to supporting material.

6. List and define three types of verbal and nonverbal speech signposts.

7. Explain how visual aids can supplement signposts.

aria went into the lecture hall feeling exhilarated. After all, Dr. Anderson was a Nobel laureate in literature. He would be teaching and lecturing on campus for at least a year. What an opportunity! Maria took a seat in the middle of the fourth row, where she had a clear view of the podium. She opened the notebook she had bought just for this lecture series, took out one of the three pens she had brought with her, and waited impatiently for Dr. Anderson's appearance. She didn't have to wait long. Dr. Anderson was greeted by thunderous applause when he walked out onto the stage. Maria was aware of an almost electric sense of expectation among the audience members. Pen poised, she awaited his first words.

Five minutes later, Maria still had her pen poised. He had gotten off to a slow start. Ten minutes later, she laid her pen down and decided to concentrate just on listening. Twenty minutes later, she still had no idea what point Dr. Anderson was trying to make. And by the time the lecture was over, Maria was practically asleep. Disappointed, she gathered her pens and her notebook (which now contained one page of lazy doodles) and promised herself she would skip the remaining lectures in the series.

Dr. Anderson was not a dynamic speaker. But his motivated audience of young would-be authors and admirers might have forgiven that shortcoming. What they were unable to do was to unravel his hour's worth of seemingly pointless rambling—to get some sense of direction or some pattern of ideas from his talk. Dr. Anderson had simply failed to organize his thoughts.

The scenario described above actually happened. Dr. Anderson (not his real name) disappointed many who had looked forward to his lectures. His inability to organize his ideas made him an ineffectual speaker. You, too, may have had an experience with a teacher who possessed awesome knowledge and ability in his or her field but could not organize his or her thoughts well enough to lecture effectively. No matter how knowledgeable speakers may be, they must organize their ideas in logical patterns to ensure that their audience can follow, understand, and remember what is said. Our model of audience-centered communication emphasizes that speeches are organized *for* audiences, with decisions about organization being based in large part on an analysis of the audience.

In the first eight chapters of this book, you learned how to plan and research a speech based on audience needs, interests, and expectations. The planning and research process has taken you through five stages of speech preparation:

- Selecting and narrowing a topic
- Determining your purpose
- Developing your central idea
- Generating main ideas
- Gathering supporting material

As the arrows on the model in Figure 9.1 suggest, you may have moved *recursively* through these first five stages, returning at times to earlier stages to make changes and revisions based on your consideration of the audience. Now, with the results of your audience-centered planning and research in hand, it is time to begin to put the speech together—in other words, to organize your ideas and information. The next stage in the audience-centered public-speaking process is simply that:

➤ Organize your speech

In this chapter, we will discuss the patterns of organization commonly used to arrange the main ideas of a speech. Then we will discuss how to organize subpoints and supporting materials. Finally, we will talk about transitions, previews, and summaries. Chapter 10 discusses introductions and conclusions, and Chapter 11 deals with outlining, the final two components of the organizational stage of the preparation process.

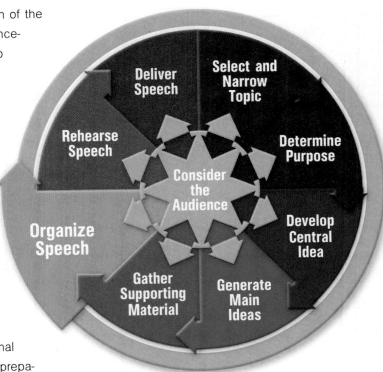

Figure 9.1 *Organize your speech to help your audience remember your key ideas and to give your speech clarity and structure.*

Organizing Your Main Ideas

In Chapter 6, we discussed how to generate a preliminary plan for your speech by determining whether your central idea had logical divisions, could be supported by several reasons, or could be explained by identifying specific steps. These divisions, reasons, or steps became the main ideas of the body of your speech and the basis for the organization task highlighted in Figure 9.1.

Now you are ready to decide which of your main ideas to discuss first, which one second, and so on. You can choose from among five organizational patterns: (1) topical, (2) chronological, (3) spatial, (4) causal, and (5) problem–solution. Or you can combine several of these patterns. One additional variation of the problem–solution pattern is the motivated sequence. Because it is used almost exclusively in persuasive speeches, the motivated sequence is discussed in Chapter 17.

ORGANIZING IDEAS TOPICALLY

If your central idea has natural divisions, you can often organize your speech topically. Speeches on such diverse topics as factors to consider when selecting a mountain bike, types of infertility treatments, and the various classes of ham-radio licenses all could reflect **topical organization.**

Natural divisions are often essentially equal in importance. It may not matter which point you discuss first, second, or third. You can simply arrange your main ideas as a matter of personal preference. At other times, you may organize your main points based on one of three principles: primacy, recency, or complexity.

topical organization

Organization of the natural divisions in a central idea according to recency, primacy, complexity, or the speaker's discretion

confidently connecting with your audience

Organize Your Message

Taking the time to plan a well-organized message can boost your confidence. A jumble of ideas and information without a logical structure is more difficult to remember and present than a well-organized speech. Researchers have discovered that the less organized you are, the more apprehensive you may feel.[1] A logically organized speech can help you feel more confident about the content you're presenting.

PRIMACY The principle of **primacy** suggests that you discuss your most important or convincing point *first* in your speech. The beginning of your speech can be the most important position if your listeners are either unfamiliar with your topic or hostile toward your central idea.

If your listeners are uninformed, your first point must introduce them to the topic and define unfamiliar terms integral to its discussion. What you say early in your speech will affect your listeners' understanding of the rest of your speech. If your listeners are likely to be hostile toward your central idea, putting your most important or convincing point first will lessen the possibility that you might lose or alienate them before you reach the end of your speech. In addition, your strongest idea may so influence your listeners' attitudes that they will be more receptive to your central idea.

Recognizing the controversial nature of stem-cell research, the speaker in the following example arranges the three main points of the speech according to primacy, advancing the most persuasive argument first.

PURPOSE STATEMENT: At the end of my speech, the audience will be able to explain the applications of stem-cell research.

CENTRAL IDEA: Stem-cell research has three important applications.

MAIN IDEAS:
I. At the most fundamental level, understanding stem cells can help us to understand better the process of human development.
II. Stem-cell research could streamline the way we develop and test drugs.
III. Stem-cell research can generate cells and tissue that could be used for "cell therapies."[2]

RECENCY According to the principle of **recency**, the point discussed *last* is the one audiences will remember best. If your audience is at least somewhat knowledgeable about and generally favorable toward your topic and central idea, you should probably organize your main points according to recency.

For example, if your speech is on the various living arrangements available to college students, you may decide to discuss living at home, rooming in a dorm, joining a fraternity or sorority, and renting an apartment. If you want your audience of fellow students to consider living at home because of the savings involved, you would probably discuss that possibility as the fourth and last option. Your speech might have the following structure:

PURPOSE STATEMENT: At the end of my speech, the audience will be able to discuss the pros and cons of four living arrangements for college students.

CENTRAL IDEA: College students have at least four living arrangements available to them.

MAIN IDEAS:
I. Living in a dormitory
II. Renting an apartment
III. Joining a fraternity or sorority
IV. Living at home

COMPLEXITY One other set of circumstances may dictate a particular order of the main ideas in your speech. If your main ideas range from simple to complicated, it makes sense to arrange them in order of **complexity**, progressing from the simple to the more complex. If, for example, you were to explain to your audience how to

primacy
Arrangement of ideas from the most to the least important

recency
Arrangement of ideas from least to most important

complexity
Arrangement of ideas from the simple to the more complex

compile a family health profile and history, you might begin with the most easily accessible source and proceed to the more involved.

PURPOSE STATEMENT:	At the end of my speech, the audience will be able to compile a family health profile and history.
CENTRAL IDEA:	Compiling a family health profile and history can be accomplished with the help of three sources.
MAIN IDEA:	I. Elderly relatives
	II. Old hospital records and death certificates
	III. National health registries[3]

Teachers, from those in the very early elementary grades on up, use order of complexity to organize their courses and lessons. The kindergartner is taught to trace circles before learning to print a lowercase *a*. The young piano student practices scales and arpeggios before playing Beethoven sonatas. The college freshman practices writing 500-word essays before attempting a major research paper. You have learned most of your skills in order of complexity.

ORDERING IDEAS CHRONOLOGICALLY

If you decide that your central idea could be explained best by a number of steps, you will probably organize those steps chronologically. **Chronological organization** is organization by time or sequence; that is, your steps are ordered according to when each step occurred or should occur. Historical speeches and how-to speeches are the two kinds of speeches usually organized chronologically.

Examples of topics for historical speeches might include the history of the women's movement in the United States, the sequence of events that led to the 1974 resignation of President Richard Nixon, or the development of the modern Olympic Games. You can choose to organize your main points either from earliest to most recent (forward in time) or from recent events back into history (backward in time). The progression you choose depends on your personal preference and on whether you want to emphasize the beginning or the end of the sequence. As we observed earlier, according to the principle of recency, audiences tend to remember best what they hear last.

In the following outline for a speech on the development of the Apple iPod, the speaker moves forward in time, making his last point the one that remains fresh in the minds of his audience at the end of his speech.

PURPOSE STATEMENT:	At the end of my speech, the audience will be able to trace the major events in the development of the iPod.
CENTRAL IDEA:	Introduced to the American public in 2001, the Apple iPod has evolved rapidly into one of the decade's most popular technological devices.
MAIN IDEAS:	I. October 2001: iPod introduced
	II. June 2003: One millionth iPod sold
	III. January 2005: iPod Shuffle launched
	IV. June 2007: iPhone debuted[4]

How-to explanations are also likely to follow a sequence or series of steps arranged from beginning to end, from the first step to the last—forward in time. A speech explaining how to strip painted furniture might be organized as follows:

PURPOSE STATEMENT:	At the end of my speech, the audience will be able to list the four steps involved in stripping old paint from furniture.
CENTRAL IDEA:	Stripping old paint from furniture requires four steps.
MAIN IDEAS:	I. Prepare work area and gather materials.

chronological organization
Organization by time or sequence

II. Apply chemical stripper.

III. Remove stripper with scrapers and steel wool.

IV. Clean and sand stripped surfaces.

In another chronologically organized speech, this one discussing the development of *YouTube*, the speaker wants to emphasize the inauspicious origins of the popular video site. Thus, she organizes the speech backward in time:

PURPOSE STATEMENT: At the end of my speech, the audience will be able to describe *YouTube*'s rapid rise from humble beginnings.

CENTRAL IDEA: The popular video site *YouTube* grew rapidly from humble beginnings.

MAIN IDEAS:
I. November 2006: *YouTube* acquired by Google
II. December 2005: *YouTube* site publicly launched
III. February 2005: *YouTube* founded in a garage in Menlo Park, California[5]

Chronological organization, then, involves either forward or backward progression, depending on which end of a set of events the speaker intends to emphasize. The element common to both organization schemes is that dates and events are discussed in sequence rather than in random order.

ARRANGING IDEAS SPATIALLY

When you say, "As you enter the room, the table is to your right, the easy chair to your left, and the kitchen door straight ahead," you are using **spatial organization**: arranging ideas—usually natural divisions of the central idea—according to their location and direction. It does not usually matter whether you progress up or down, east or west, forward or back, as long as you follow a logical progression. If you skip up, down, over, and back, you will only confuse your listeners, rather than painting a distinct word picture.

Speeches on such diverse subjects as the National Museum of the American Indian, the travels of Robert Louis Stevenson, and the structure of an atom can all be organized spatially. Here is a sample outline for the first of those topics:

PURPOSE STATEMENT: At the end of my speech, the audience will be able to list and describe the four habitats recreated on the grounds of the National Museum of the American Indian in Washington, D.C.

CENTRAL IDEA: The grounds of the National Museum of the American Indian in Washington, D.C., are divided into four traditional American Indian habitats.

MAIN IDEAS:
I. Upland hardwood forest
II. Lowland freshwater wetlands
III. Eastern meadowlands
IV. Traditional croplands[6]

The organization of this outline is spatial, progressing through the grounds of the museum.

ORGANIZING IDEAS TO SHOW CAUSE AND EFFECT

If your central idea can be developed by discussing either steps or reasons, you might consider organizing your main ideas by **cause and effect**. A speech organized to show cause and effect may first identify a situation and then discuss the effects that result from it (cause→effect). Or the speech may present a situation and then seek its causes (effect→cause). As the recency principle would suggest, the cause–effect pattern emphasizes the effects; the effect–cause pattern emphasizes the causes.

spatial organization
Organization based on location or position

cause-and-effect organization
Organization that focuses on a situation and its causes or a situation and its effects

In the following example, Vonda organizes her speech according to cause–effect, discussing the cause (widespread adult illiteracy) as her first main idea, and its effects (poverty and social costs) as her second and third main ideas:

PURPOSE STATEMENT: At the end of my speech, the audience will be able to identify two effects of adult illiteracy.

CENTRAL IDEA: Adult illiteracy affects everyone.

MAIN IDEAS:
  I. (*Cause*): Adult illiteracy is widespread in America today.
  II. (*Effect*): Adult illiterates often live in poverty.
  III. (*Effect*): Adult illiteracy is costly to society.[7]

In contrast, Laurel organizes her speech on writing wills according to an effect–cause pattern, discussing the effect (people not writing wills) as her first main idea, and its causes (having to face mortality and being ignorant of how to prepare a will) as her second and third main ideas:

PURPOSE STATEMENT: At the end of my speech, the audience will be able to explain and counter the reasons people don't write wills.

CENTRAL IDEA: People fail to prepare wills for several reasons.

MAIN IDEAS:
  I. (*Effect*): People are hesitant to write wills.
  II. (*Cause*): Writing a will brings people face to face with their own mortality.
  III. (*Cause*): Many people don't know how to prepare a will.[8]

In both of the preceding examples, the speakers may decide in what order they will discuss their points II and III by considering the principles of recency, primacy, or complexity discussed earlier in this chapter.

ORGANIZING IDEAS BY PROBLEM AND SOLUTION

If you want to discuss why a problem exists or what its effects are, you will probably organize your speech according to cause and effect, as discussed in the previous section. However, if you want to emphasize how best to *solve* the problem, you will probably use a **problem-and-solution** pattern of organization.

Like causes and effects, problems and solutions can be discussed in either order. If you speak to an audience that is already fairly aware of a problem but uncertain how to solve it, you will probably discuss the problem first and then the solution(s), as in this example:

PURPOSE STATEMENT: At the end of my speech, the audience will be able to list and explain three ways in which crime on university campuses can be reduced.

CENTRAL IDEA: Crimes on university campuses can be reduced by implementing three safety measures.

MAIN IDEAS:
  I. (*Problem*): Crimes against both persons and property have increased dramatically on college campuses over the last few years.
  II. (*Solution*): Crimes could be reduced by stricter enforcement of the Student Right to Know and Campus Security Acts.
  III. (*Solution*): Crimes could be reduced by assigning student identification numbers that are different from students' Social Security numbers.
  IV. (*Solution*): Crimes could be reduced by converting campus buildings to an integrated security system requiring key cards for admittance.[9]

problem-and-solution organization
Organization focused on a problem and then various solutions or a solution and the problems it would solve

If your audience knows about an action or program that has been implemented but does not know the reasons for its implementation, you might select instead a solution–problem pattern of organization. In the following example, the speaker knows that her listeners are already aware of a new business–school partnership program in their community but believes that they may be unclear about why it has been established:

PURPOSE STATEMENT: At the end of my speech, the audience will be able to explain how business–school partnership programs can help solve two of the major problems facing our public schools today.

CENTRAL IDEA: Business–school partnership programs can help alleviate at least two of the problems faced by public schools today.

MAIN IDEAS:
I. (*Solution*): In a business–school partnership, local businesses provide volunteers, financial support, and in-kind contributions to public schools.
II. (*Problem*): Many public schools can no longer afford special programs and fine-arts programs.
III. (*Problem*): Many public schools have no resources to fund enrichment materials and opportunities.

Note that in both of the preceding examples, the main ideas are natural divisions of the central idea.

ACKNOWLEDGING CULTURAL DIFFERENCES IN ORGANIZATION

Although the five patterns just discussed are typical of the way speakers in the United States are expected to organize and process information, they are not necessarily typical of all cultures.[10] In fact, each culture teaches its members patterns of thought and organization that are considered appropriate for various occasions and audiences. On the whole, U.S. speakers tend to be more linear and direct than speakers from Semitic, Asian, Romance, or Russian cultures. Semitic speakers support their main points by pursuing tangents that might seem "off topic" to many U.S. speakers. Asians may only allude to a main point through a circuitous route of illustration and parable. And speakers from Romance and Russian cultures tend to begin with a basic principle and then move to facts and illustrations that they only gradually connect to a main point. The models in Figure 9.2 illustrate these culturally diverse patterns of organization.

Figure 9.2 *Organizational patterns by culture*

(*Source*: D. A. Lieberman, *Public Speaking in the Multicultural Environment.* Copyright © 2000. All rights reserved. Reprinted by permission of Allyn and Bacon.)

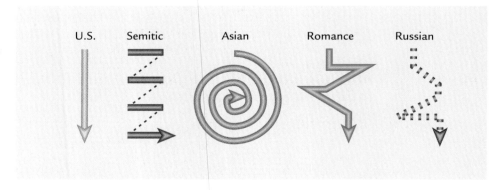

Desmond Tutu (1931–)

When Archbishop Desmond Tutu won the Nobel Peace Prize in 1984 for his leadership in the struggle against apartheid policies in South Africa, he delivered an impassioned Nobel lecture. In that speech, Tutu combined cause-and-effect and problem-and-solution patterns of organization. He first described a cause—apartheid—and its effects: hunger, the dissolution of families, a segregated education system, legal injustice, and violence. He went on to offer a solution to the problem of apartheid: the guarantee of human rights for all.[11] Tutu continues to be a widely sought-after speaker, relaying his message of peace and equality to audiences throughout the world.

Tutu's messages have a clear, logical structure. He also masterfully uses illustrations to support his major ideas. As you organize your message, plan the structure so that it will be clear to your listeners. Then integrate the illustrations, statistics, and other forms of support you have chosen to illustrate your points. Placing interesting and well-told stories and illustrations on a solid organizational scaffolding will help make your speech both easy to follow and interesting to hear.

[Photo: Alan Mothner/PhotoEdit]

Of course, these are very broad generalizations. But as an audience member, recognizing the existence of cultural differences when you are listening to a speech can help you appreciate and understand the organization of a speaker from a culture other than your own. He or she may not be disorganized, but simply using organizational strategies different from the ones presented earlier in this chapter.

RECAP

Organizing Your Main Points

PATTERN	DESCRIPTION
Topical	Organization according to primacy, recency, or complexity
Chronological	Organization by time or sequence
Spatial	Organization based on location or position
Cause-and-effect	Organization that focuses on a situation and its causes or a situation and its effects
Problem-and-solution	Organization that focuses on a problem and then various solutions or a solution and then the problems it would solve

Subdividing Your Main Ideas

After you have decided how to organize your main ideas, you may need to subdivide at least some of them. For example, if you give a how-to speech on dog grooming, your first main idea may be

I. Gather your supplies.

"Supplies" indicates that you need more than one piece of equipment, so you add subpoints that describe the specific supplies needed:

I. Gather your supplies.

    A. Soft brush

    B. Firm brush

    C. Wide-toothed comb

    D. Fine-toothed comb

    E. Scissors

    F. Spray-on detangler

Note that you can arrange your main ideas according to one pattern and your subpoints according to another. For example, the organization of the main ideas of this speech on dog grooming is chronological, but the subpoints of the first main idea are arranged topically. Any of the five organizational patterns that apply to main ideas can apply to subpoints as well.

Right now, don't worry about such outlining details as Roman numerals, letters, and margins. We cover them in Chapter 11. Your goal at this point is to get your ideas and information on paper. Keep in mind, too, that until you've delivered your speech, none of your decisions is etched in stone. You may add, regroup, or eliminate main ideas or subpoints at any stage in the preparation process, as you consider the needs, interests, and expectations of your audience. Multiple drafts indicate that you are working and reworking ideas to improve your product and make it the best you can. They do *not* mean that you are a poor writer or speaker.

SPEAKER'S HOMEPAGE

Internet Resources to Help You Organize Your Speech

◆ ALLYN AND BACON PUBLIC SPEAKING WEBSITE
Following is the address of a page that can give you additional suggestions for organizing your speech. In addition to explaining various organizational patterns, the page provides links to both audio and text copies of speeches that apply the patterns discussed.
http://wps.ablongman.com/
    ab_public_speaking_2/
    0,9651,1593275-,00.html

◆ ADVANCED PUBLIC SPEAKING INSTITUTE
This Web site provides a wealth of information about speech preparation, including tips on developing and organizing ideas:
http://www.public-speaking.org/
    public-speaking-articles.htm

Integrating Your Supporting Material

Once you have organized your main ideas and subpoints, you are ready to flesh out the speech with your supporting material. If you have entered your supporting material into a word-processing file, you may want to print out a hard copy of your supporting material so that you can have it in front of you while you work on your speech plan. When you determine where in the speech you need supporting material, find what you need on the hard copy and then go back into the word-processing file to cut and paste that supporting material electronically into your speech plan.

If you have written or pasted supporting material on note cards, write each main idea and subpoint on a separate note card of the same size as the ones on which you recorded your supporting material. Arrange these note cards in the order in which you have organized your speech. Then go through your supporting-material note cards, one by one, and decide where in the speech you will use each one. The headings you wrote at the top of each card should help in this process. Place each supporting-material card behind the appropriate main-idea or subpoint card. You now have a complete plan for your speech on note cards.

If most of your supporting material is photocopied, search these copies for what you need and then write or type this supporting material into your speech plan. Regardless of which strategy you use to integrate your supporting material, take care not to lose track of the source of the supporting material.

Once your supporting material is logically placed into your plan, your next goal is to incorporate it smoothly into your speech so as not to interrupt the flow of ideas. Notice how skillfully this goal is met by a speaker delivering a speech on the danger of using a cell phone while driving:

SAMPLE INTEGRATION OF SUPPORTING MATERIAL

Using a cell phone while driving can have devastating consequences. According to *The Olympian* of June 19, 2007, text messaging while behind the wheel caused an Idaho driver to lose control of her car and seriously injure herself and a passenger.[12] With their expanded capabilities to serve as cameras, computers, and mp3 players, cell phones also expand the ways in which they can distract a driver.

➤ State the point. The statement should be concise and clear, as it is here.

➤ Cite the source of the supporting material. As noted in the discussion of oral citations in Chapter 3, you should provide the author's name (if available) and the title and date of the publication.

➤ Present the supporting material. In this example, the supporting material is a brief illustration.

➤ Explain how the supporting material substantiates or develops the point. Do not assume that audience members will automatically make the connection.

Your listeners may not remember many specific facts and statistics after a speech, but they should remember the important points. Connecting ideas and supporting material make it more likely that they will.

Organizing Your Supporting Material

Suppose you have decided what supporting material to use and identified the ideas in your speech that require support. Now you realize that in support of your second main idea you have an illustration, two statistics, and an opinion. In what order should you present these items?

You can sometimes use the five standard organizational patterns to arrange your supporting material, as well as your main ideas and subpoints. Illustrations, for instance, may be organized chronologically. In the following excerpt from a speech on childhood obesity, the speaker arranges several brief examples in a chronological sequence:

> *I can think of at least three moments in the past half century that dramatically shifted the course of America's medical and scientific history.*
>
> *The first time came [on] March 26, 1953—when Jonas Salk called a press conference to announce the discovery of a polio vaccine.*
>
> *The second time, amazingly, came just four weeks later, when Watson and Crick published their discovery of the double helix structure of DNA.*
>
> *The third time was in 1964, when U.S. Surgeon General Luther Terry courageously reported that cigarette smoking does cause cancer and other deadly diseases. . . .*
>
> *On March 9, 2004, the CDC Director declared that obesity is overtaking smoking and tobacco use as the number-one cause of preventable death in America.*[13]

At other times, however, none of the five patterns may seem suited to the supporting materials you have. In those instances, you may need to turn to an organizational strategy more specifically adapted to your supporting materials. These strategies include (1) primacy or recency, (2) specificity, (3) complexity, and (4) "soft" to "hard" evidence.

PRIMACY OR RECENCY

We have already discussed how the principles of primacy and recency can determine whether you put material at the beginning or the end of your speech. These patterns are used so frequently to arrange supporting materials that we mention them again here. Suppose that you have several statistics to support a main point. All are relevant and significant, but one is especially gripping. In a recent speech, American Cancer Society CEO John Seffrin showed images of and described the following brief examples of international tobacco advertising:

> *The effort to build brand loyalty begins early. Here is an example of that in Africa—a young man wearing a hat with a cigarette brand logo. . . .*
>
> *Look at this innocent baby wearing a giant Marlboro logo on his shirt. . . .*
>
> *Notice how this ad links smoking to American values that are attractive to third-world kids—wealth, sophistication, and urbanity. It also shows African Americans living the American Dream. If you're a poor kid in Africa, this image can be very powerful.*
>
> *And finally, this one from Bucharest, Romania, which is my favorite. When the Berlin Wall came down, no one rushed into Eastern Europe faster than the tobacco industry. Here you can see the Camel logo etched in the street lights. In my opinion, this is one of the most disturbing examples of the public sector partnering with private industry to the detriment of its citizens.*[14]

Organize Your Speech

As she begins to integrate supporting material into her speech on produce safety, Ashley finds that she has both an explanation and an illustration to support her point that produce contamination puts consumers' health at risk.

Knowing that the illustration will have the greatest impact on her listeners, Ashley decides to order these two items of supporting material according to the principle of *recency*—so that the item she discusses last is the one her listeners will remember best:

1. *ABC Nightline* reveals that food-borne pathogens can cause abdominal cramps, dangerously high fever, seizure disorders, and diabetes.
2. Seventy-six-year-old William Barkay knows the dangers of contaminated foods all too well. According to the *Omaha World-Herald* of February 23, 2007, after consuming salmonella-contaminated peanut butter, William and his wife, Roberta, were hospitalized. William barely recovered, but Roberta died on January 30, 2007.

It is evident that Seffrin applied the principle of recency to his examples, as he identifies the final one as "my favorite" and "one of the most disturbing." The principle of primacy or recency can also be applied to groups of statistics, opinions, or any combination of supporting material.

SPECIFICITY

Sometimes your supporting material will range from very specific examples to more general overviews of a situation. You may either offer your specific information first and end with your general statement, or make the general statement first and support it with specific evidence.

Another application of specificity might be to compact or explode statistics, as discussed in Chapter 8. In her speech on unnecessary prescription drugs, Kristin begins with a sweeping statistic and then compacts it:

Thirty percent of Americans have asked their doctor about a medicine they saw advertised on TV. And of those, . . . 44 percent received the prescription. That translates into one in eight Americans seeing a drug on TV and later picking it up at their local pharmacy.[15]

COMPLEXITY

We have already discussed organizing subtopics by moving from the simple to the complex. The same method of organization may also determine how you order your supporting material. In many situations, it makes sense to start with the simplest ideas that are easy to understand and work up to more complex ones. In her speech on solar radiation, Nichole first explains the most obvious effects of solar peaks—electrical blackouts and disruptions in radio broadcasts—and then goes on to the more complex effect, cosmic radiation:

The sun produces storms on its surface in eleven-year cycles. During solar maximum, these storms will make their presence known to the land-bound public through electrical blackouts and disruptions in radio broadcasts. These storms cause the sun to

throw off electrically charged ions that, combined with charged particles, enter the Earth's atmosphere from outer space. This is known collectively as cosmic radiation.[16]

FROM SOFT TO HARD EVIDENCE

Supporting material can also be arranged from "soft" to "hard." **Soft evidence** rests on opinion or inference. Hypothetical illustrations, descriptions, explanations, definitions, analogies, and opinions are usually considered soft. **Hard evidence** includes factual examples and statistics. Actually, it is more accurate to think of soft and hard as two ends of a continuum, with various supporting material falling somewhere between. The U.S. Surgeon General's analysis of the AIDS crisis, for example, would be placed nearer the hard end of the continuum than would someone's experience of seeing the NAMES Project AIDS Memorial Quilt, even though both would be classified as opinions. The Surgeon General is a more credible speaker whose analysis is the result of his or her extensive knowledge of and research into the subject.

Soft-to-hard organization of supporting material relies chiefly on the principle of recency—that the last statement is remembered best. Note how Beth moves from an illustration to expert testimony (both soft evidence) to a statistic (hard evidence) in her speech on the danger of sand holes:

Illustration (soft evidence)

An article in the Corpus Christi Caller Times *of June 21, 2007, describes how a hidden sand hole on a beach proved fatal to 17-year-old Matthew Gauruder. Playing football on a Rhode Island beach with friends, Matthew jumped to catch a pass and came down into an 8-foot-deep hole that someone had dug on the beach earlier in the day. Almost instantly, the sand caved in around him, burying and suffocating him before rescuers could reach him.*

Expert testimony (soft evidence)

Dr. Bradley Maron of Harvard Medical School explains that "the walls of the hole unexpectedly collapsed, leaving virtually no evidence of the hole or location of the victim."

Statistic (hard evidence)

Although people worry more about shark attacks, according to University of Florida statistics, 16 deaths occurred in sand holes or tunnels between 1990 and 2006, compared with 12 fatal shark attacks for that same period.[17]

soft evidence
Supporting material based mainly on opinion or inference; includes hypothetical illustrations, descriptions, explanations, definitions, and analogies

hard evidence
Factual examples and statistics

The speaker has arranged her supporting material from soft to hard.

Organizing Your Supporting Material

STRATEGY	DESCRIPTION
Primacy	Most important material first
Recency	Most important material last
Specificity	From specific information to general overview or from general overview to specific information
Complexity	From simple to more complex material
Soft to hard	From opinion or hypothetical illustration to fact or statistic

Developing Signposts

Once you have organized your note cards, you have a logically ordered, fairly complete plan for your speech. But if you tried to deliver the speech at this point, you would find yourself frequently groping for some way to get from one point to the next. Your audience might become frustrated or even confused by your hesitations and awkwardness. Your next organizational task is to develop **signposts**—words and gestures that allow you to move smoothly from one idea to the next throughout your speech, showing relationships between ideas and emphasizing important points. Three types of signposts can serve as glue to hold your speech together: transitions, previews, and summaries.

TRANSITIONS

Transitions indicate that a speaker has finished discussing one idea and is moving to another. Transitions may be either verbal or nonverbal. Let's consider some examples of each type.

VERBAL TRANSITIONS A speaker can sometimes make a verbal transition simply by repeating a key word from an earlier statement or by using a synonym or a pronoun that refers to an earlier key word or idea. This type of transition is often used to make one sentence flow smoothly into the next. The previous sentence itself is an example: "This type of transition" refers to the sentence that precedes it. Other verbal transitions are words or phrases that show relationships between ideas. Note the italicized transitional phrases in the following examples:

- *In addition to* transitions, previews and summaries are *also* considered to be signposts.
- *Not only* does plastic packaging use up our scarce resources, it contaminates them *as well*.
- *In other words*, as women's roles have changed, they have *also* contributed to this effect.
- *In summary*, Fanny Brice is probably the best remembered star of Ziegfeld's Follies.
- *Therefore*, I recommend that you sign the grievance petition.

Simple enumeration (*first, second, third*) can also point up relationships between ideas and provide transitions.

signpost
A verbal or nonverbal signal that a speaker is moving from one idea to the next

One type of transitional signpost that can occasionally backfire and do more harm than good is one that signals the end of a speech. *Finally* and *in conclusion* give the audience implicit permission to stop listening, and they often do. If the speech has been too long or has otherwise not gone well, the audience may even audibly express relief. Better strategies for moving into a conclusion include repeating a key word or phrase, using a synonym or pronoun that refers to a previous idea, offering a final summary, or referring to the introduction of the speech. We will discuss the final summary in more detail later in this chapter. Both of the last two strategies are also covered in Chapter 10.

Internal previews and summaries, which we will discuss shortly, are yet another way to provide a verbal transition from one point to the next in your speech. They have the additional advantage of repeating your main ideas, thereby enabling audience members to understand and remember them.

Repetition of key words or ideas, the use of transitional words or phrases, enumeration, and internal previews and summaries all provide verbal transitions from one idea to the next. You may need to experiment with several alternatives before you find the smooth transition you seek in a given instance. If none of these alternatives seems to work well, consider a nonverbal transition.

NONVERBAL TRANSITIONS Nonverbal transitions can occur in several ways, sometimes alone and sometimes in combination with verbal transitions. A change in facial expression, a pause, an altered vocal pitch or speaking rate, or a movement all may indicate a transition.

For example, a speaker talking about the value of cardiopulmonary resuscitation began his speech with a powerful anecdote of a man suffering a heart attack at a party. No one knew how to help, and the man died. The speaker then looked up from his notes and paused, while maintaining eye contact with his audience. His next words were "The real tragedy of Bill Jorgen's death was that it should not have happened." His pause, as well as the words that followed, indicated a transition into the body of the speech.

Like this speaker, most good speakers use a combination of verbal and nonverbal transitions to move from one point to another through their speeches. You will study more about nonverbal communication in Chapter 13.

RECAP

Verbal Transitions

STRATEGY	EXAMPLE
Repeating a key word, or using a synonym or pronoun that refers to a key word	"*These problems* cannot be allowed to continue."
Using a transitional word or phrase	"*In addition* to the facts that I've mentioned, we need to consider one more problem."
Enumerating	"*Second*, there has been a rapid increase in the number of accidents reported."
Using internal summaries and previews	"*Now that we have discussed the problems* caused by illiteracy, *let's look at some of the possible solutions.*"

PREVIEWS

In Chapter 12, we discuss the differences between writing and speaking styles. One significant difference is that public speaking is more repetitive. Audience-centered speakers need to remember that the members of their audiences, unlike readers, cannot go back to review a missed point. As its name indicates, a *preview* is a statement of what is to come. Previews help to ensure that audience members will first anticipate and later remember the important points of a speech. Like transitions, previews also help to provide coherence.

Two types of previews are usually used in speeches: the preview statement or initial preview, and the internal preview. We discussed the preview statement in Chapter 6. It is a statement of what the main ideas of the speech will be and is usually presented in conjunction with the central idea as a blueprint for the speech at or near the end of the introduction. Speaking on illiteracy among athletes, Melody offers the following blueprint at the end of her introduction:

> *Illiteracy among athletes must be stopped. In order to fully grasp the significance of this problem, we will look at the root of it, and then move to [its] effects, and finally, we will look at the solution.*[18]

In this blueprint, Melody clearly previews her main ideas and introduces them in the order in which she will discuss them in the body of the speech.

Sometimes speakers enumerate their main ideas to identify them even more clearly:

> *To solve this issue, we must first examine the problem itself. Second, we'll analyze the causes of the problem, and finally we'll turn to a number of solutions to the problem of children in the diet culture.*[19]

Notice that both of the preceding examples consist of two sentences. As we noted in Chapter 6, a preview statement need not necessarily be one long, rambling sentence.

In addition to using previews near the beginning of their speeches, speakers also use them at various points throughout. These **internal previews** introduce and outline ideas that will be developed as the speech progresses. As noted, internal previews also serve as transitions. The following speaker, for example, has just discussed the dangers associated with organic farming. She then provides this transitional preview into her next point:

> *Having seen the dangers of our anti-pesticide attitude, we can now look to some solutions to stop the trend toward organic foods.*[20]

Having heard this preview, her listeners expect her next to discuss solutions to the problems associated with organic farming. Their anticipation increases the likelihood that they will later remember the information.

Sometimes speakers couch internal previews in the form of questions they plan to answer. Note how the question in this example provides an internal preview:

> *Now that we know about the problem of hotel security and some of its causes and impacts, the question remains, what can we do, as potential travelers and potential victims, to protect ourselves?*[21]

internal preview
A statement in the body of a speech that introduces and outlines ideas that will be developed as the speech progresses

Just as anticipating an idea helps audience members remember it, so mentally answering a question helps them plant the answer firmly in their minds.

SUMMARIES

Like previews, summaries provide additional exposure to a speaker's ideas and can help ensure that audience members will grasp and remember them. Most speakers use two types of summaries: the final summary and the internal summary.

A final summary occurs just before the end of a speech, often doing double duty as a transition between the body and the conclusion.

The final summary is the opposite of the preview statement. The preview statement gives an audience their first exposure to a speaker's main ideas; the final summary gives them their *last* exposure to those ideas. Here is an example of a final summary from a speech on U.S. Customs:

> *Today, we have focused on the failing U.S. Customs Service. We have asked several important questions, such as "Why is Customs having such a hard time doing its job?" and "What can we do to remedy this situation?" When the cause of a serious problem is unknown, the continuation of the dilemma is understandable. However, the cause for the failure of the U.S. Customs Service is known: a lack of personnel. Given that fact and our understanding that Customs is vital to America's interests, it would be foolish not to rectify this situation.*[22]

This final summary leaves no doubt as to the important points of the speech. We discuss the use of final summaries in more detail in Chapter 10.

Internal summaries, as their name suggests, occur within and throughout a speech. They are often used after two or three points have been discussed, to keep those points fresh in the minds of the audience as the speech progresses. Susan uses this internal summary in her speech on the teacher shortage:

> *So let's review for just a moment. One, we are endeavoring to implement educational reforms; but two, we are in the first years of a dramatic increase in enrollment; and three, fewer quality students are opting for education; while four, many good teachers want out of teaching; plus five, large numbers will soon be retiring.*[23]

Like internal previews, internal summaries can help provide transitions. In fact, internal summaries are often used in combination with internal previews to form transitions between major points and ideas. Each of the following examples makes clear what has just been discussed in the speech as well as what will be discussed next:

> *Now that we've seen how radon can get into our homes, let's take a look at some of the effects that it can have on our health once it begins to build.*[24]

> *So now [that] we are aware of the severity of the disease and unique reasons for college students to be concerned, we will look at some steps we need to take to combat bacterial meningitis.*[25]

internal summary
A restatement in the body of a speech of ideas that have been developed so far

> *It seems as though everyone is saying that something should be done about Nutra-Sweet. It should be retested. Well, now that it is here on the market, what can we do to see that it does get investigated further?*[26]

RECAP

Types of Signposts

Verbal transitions

Nonverbal transitions

Preview statements

Internal previews

Final summaries

Internal summaries

Supplementing Signposts with Presentation Aids

Transitions, summaries, and previews are the "glue" that holds a speech together. Such signposts can help you achieve a coherent flow of ideas and help your audience remember those ideas. Unfortunately, however, you cannot guarantee that your audience will be attentive to your signposts. In Chapter 1 we discussed the concept of noise as it affects the public-speaking process. It is possible for your listeners to be so distracted by internal or external noise that they fail to hear or process even your most carefully planned verbal signposts.

One way you can increase the likelihood of your listeners' attending to your signposting is to prepare and use presentation aids to supplement your signposts. For example, you could display on an overhead transparency a bulleted or numbered outline of your main ideas as you initially preview them in your introduction, and again as you summarize them in your conclusion. Some speakers like to use one transparency or PowerPoint slide for each main point. Transitions between points are emphasized as the speaker displays the next transparency or slide. In Chapter 14, we discuss guidelines for developing and using such presentation aids. Especially if your speech is long or its organization complex, you can help your audience remember your organization if you provide visual support for your signposts.

SUMMARY

The process of organization is by nature audience-centered. Speeches are organized for audiences, with the speaker keeping in mind at all times the unique needs, interests, and expectations of the particular audience. Organize your speech in a logical way so that audience members can follow, understand, and remember your ideas.

First, consider how best to organize your main ideas. Five common patterns of organization include topical, chronological, spatial, cause–effect, and problem and solution. These patterns are sometimes combined, and yet other organizational patterns may be dictated by culture.

Main ideas are often subdivided. Organize subpoints so that audience members can readily grasp, understand, and remember them. The five patterns for organizing main ideas can apply to subpoints as well.

With points and subpoints organized, your next task is to integrate your supporting material into a speech. It may help to begin by putting all main points, subpoints, and supporting material on note cards and then arranging those cards in order. Once you have placed supporting material where it belongs in your plan, incorporate the supporting material smoothly into your speech by (1) stating the point, (2) citing the source, (3) presenting the supporting material, and (4) explaining how the supporting material substantiates or develops the point.

When you have more than one piece of supporting material for a main idea or subpoint, you can organize the supporting material according to one of the five common patterns, or according to such strategies as primacy, recency, specificity, complexity, or soft-to-hard.

Finally, various types of signposts can help you communicate your organization to your audience. Signposts include verbal and nonverbal transitions, previews, and summaries. Presentation aids increase the likelihood that your listeners will attend to your signposting.

Chapters 10 and 11 cover the two remaining parts of the organizational task: preparing your introduction and conclusion, and outlining your speech.

CONSIDERING YOUR AUDIENCE

- Organize your ideas in logical patterns to en-sure that audiences can follow, understand, and remember what you say.

- If your topic is controversial and you know or suspect that your audience will be skeptical of or hostile to your ideas, you may want to or-ganize your main ideas according to the princi-ple of primacy, putting the most important or convincing idea first.

- You may add, regroup, or eliminate main ideas or subpoints at any stage in the preparation process, as you consider the needs, interests, and expectations of your audience.

- Your listeners may not remember many spe-cific facts and statistics after a speech, but they should remember the important points. Con-necting ideas and supporting material make it more likely that they will.

- Audience-centered speakers need to remember that the members of their audiences, unlike readers, cannot go back to review a missed point. Previews and summaries help to ensure that audience members will first anticipate and later remember the important points of a speech.

CONSIDERING AUDIENCE DIVERSITY

- Each culture teaches its members patterns of thought and organization that are considered appropriate for various occasions and audi-ences. For example, most North Americans prefer a direct, linear organizational pattern. Semitic, Asian, Romance, and Russian speakers are more likely to prefer a less direct, less linear organizational pattern. Romance and Russian cultures tend to begin with a basic principle and then use facts and illustrations to support the main idea.

CRITICAL THINKING QUESTIONS

Here are some examples of central ideas and main ideas. Identify the organizational pattern used in each group of main ideas. If the pattern is topical, do you think the speaker also considered primacy, recency, or complexity? If so, identify which one.

1. PURPOSE STATEMENT: At the end of my speech, the audience will be able to list and explain the three factors to consider in buying or renting a home.

   CENTRAL IDEA: The prospective home buyer or renter should consider three factors in select-ing a home.

   MAIN IDEAS:
   I. Interior decorating
   II. Layout
   III. Location

2. PURPOSE STATEMENT: At the end of my speech, the audience will be able to explain three theories about what happened to the dinosaurs.

CENTRAL IDEA: There are at least three distinct theories about what happened to the dinosaurs.

MAIN IDEAS:
  I. A large asteroid hit Earth.
  II. A gradual climate shift occurred.
  III. The level of oxygen in the atmosphere gradually changed.

3. PURPOSE STATEMENT: At the end of my speech, the audience will be able to explain why provision for the mentally ill is inadequate in the United States.

CENTRAL IDEA: The process of caring for the mentally ill has broken down in the United States.

MAIN IDEAS:
  I. Fewer than half of the needed number of community-based "halfway houses" exist.
  II. Funding is inadequate.
  III. Involuntary commitment is rare.[27]

4. PURPOSE STATEMENT: At the end of my speech, the audience will be able to describe the layout and features of the new university multipurpose sports center.

CENTRAL IDEA: The new university multipurpose sports center will serve the activity needs of the students.

MAIN IDEAS:
  I. The south wing will house an Olympic-size pool.
  II. The center of the building will be a large coliseum.
  III. The north wing will include handball and indoor tennis facilities as well as rooms for weight lifting and aerobic workouts.

ETHICAL QUESTIONS

1. On page 53, we suggested that a speaker should provide the credentials of the authors of supporting material used in a speech. If a speaker is unable to discover an author's credentials, could the speaker omit the author's name altogether? If no, why not? If so, under what circumstances?

2. The principles of primacy and recency are referred to several times in this chapter. If a speaker has a statistic that offers overwhelming evidence of the severity of a given problem, is it ethical for the speaker to save that statistic for last, or should the speaker reveal immediately to the audience how severe the problem really is? In other words, is there an ethical distinction between primacy and recency? Discuss your answer.

Organizing Your Ideas

Use the following worksheet to help you identify the overall organizational strategy for your speech.

GENERAL PURPOSE:

_____ To inform   _____ To persuade   _____ To entertain

SPECIFIC PURPOSE:

At the end of my speech the audience will be able to

CENTRAL IDEA (one sentence summary of your speech):

MAIN IDEAS:

Ask yourself the following three questions to help you identify the organizational structure of your speech:

1. Does the central idea have logical divisions?

If the answer is yes, your speech may be organized *topically* (by natural divisions), *spatially* (by physical arrangement), by *cause and effect*, or by *problem and solution*.

2. Are there reasons that the central idea sentence is true?

If the answer is yes, then your speech is probably persuasive, and you are trying to convince the audience that your central idea sentence is true. Your reasons may be organized by *primacy* (most important reason first), *recency* (most important reason last), *complexity* (simplest reason first and most complex reason last), or *cause and effect*.

3. Does your central idea involve a series of steps?

If the answer is yes, then your speech can be organized *chronologically*. Identify the major steps involved in the process you are describing; those major steps become your main points. Although you should have only a few main ideas, you may have several subdivisions of each one.

Thinker of Images (*Le Penseur d'Images*), 1980. Jean Plichart (20th C. French). Copper engraving. Jean Plichart/SuperStock

The average man thinks about what he has said; the
above average man about what he is going to say.

—ANONYMOUS

Introducing and Concluding Your Speech

outline

objectives

After studying this chapter you should be able to do the following:

1. Discuss why introductions and conclusions are important to the overall success of a speech.

2. Explain the five purposes of the introduction to a speech.

3. List and describe ten ways to introduce a speech.

4. Explain the two purposes of the conclusion to a speech.

5. List and describe four ways to conclude a speech.

Like all teachers, public speaking instructors have pet peeves when it comes to their students' work. Of pet peeves identified by public speaking teachers in a recent study, more than 25 percent relate to introductions and conclusions. They include the following:

- Beginning a speech with "OK, ah . . ."
- Apologizing or making excuses at the beginning of the speech for not being prepared
- Beginning a speech with "Hello, my speech is on . . ."
- Saying "In conclusion"
- Ending a speech with "Thank you"
- Ending a speech with "Are there any questions?"[1]

Of course, not every public speaking instructor considers all of the above to be pet peeves or even necessarily tactics to be avoided. But the fact that they appear on this list at all suggests that you will probably want to consider alternatives. After all, your introduction and conclusion provide your listeners with important first and final impressions of both you and your speech.

Like many speakers, you may think the first task in preparing a speech is to start drafting your introduction. Actually, the introduction is more often the last part of the speech you develop. A key purpose of your introduction is to provide an overview of your message. How can you do that until you know what the message is going to be? In Chapter 9, we discussed patterns and strategies for organizing the body of your speech, and we explained how to use appropriate transitions, previews, and summaries. Organizing the body of your speech should precede the crafting of both the introduction and the conclusion. In this chapter we will further explore organization by discussing introductions and conclusions.

Purposes of Introductions

Within a few seconds of meeting a person, you form a first impression that is often quite lasting. So, too, do you form a first impression of a speaker and his or her message within the opening seconds of a speech. The introduction may convince you to listen carefully because this is a credible speaker presenting a well-prepared speech, or it may send the message that the speaker is ill-prepared and the message not worth your time. In a ten-minute speech, the introduction will probably last no more than a minute and a half. To say that the introduction needs to be well planned is an understatement, considering how important and yet how brief this portion of any speech is.

As a speaker, your task is to ensure that your introduction convinces your audience to listen to you. Specifically, a good introduction must perform five important functions:

- Get the audience's attention.
- Give the audience a reason to listen.
- Introduce the subject.
- Establish your credibility.
- Preview your main ideas.

Let's examine each of these five functions in more detail.

GET THE AUDIENCE'S ATTENTION

A key purpose of the introduction is to gain favorable attention for your speech. Because listeners form their first impressions of the speech quickly, if the introduction does not capture their attention and cast the speech in a favorable light, the rest of the speech may be wasted on them. The speaker who walks to the podium and drones, "Today I am going to talk to you about . . ." has probably lost most of the audience in those first few boring words. Some specific ways to gain the attention of audiences will be discussed later in this chapter.

We emphasize *favorable* attention for a very good reason. It is possible to gain an audience's attention but in so doing to alienate them or disgust them so that they become irritated instead of interested in what you have to say. For example, a student began a pro-life speech with a graphic description of the abortion process. She caught her audience's attention but made them so uncomfortable that they could hardly concentrate on the rest of her speech.

Another student gave a speech on the importance of donating blood. Without a word, he began by savagely slashing his wrists in front of his stunned audience. As blood spurted, audience members screamed, and one fainted. The blood was real blood, but it wasn't his. The speaker worked at a blood bank, and he was using the bank's blood. He had placed a device under each arm that allowed him to pump out the blood as if from his wrists. He certainly captured his audience's attention! But they never heard his message. The shock and disgust of seeing such a display made that impossible. He did not gain favorable attention.

The moral of our two tales: By all means, be creative in your speech introductions. But also use common sense in deciding how best to gain the favorable attention of your audience. Alienating them is even worse than boring them.

GIVE THE AUDIENCE A REASON TO LISTEN

Even after you have captured your listeners' attention, you have to give them some reason to want to listen to the rest of your speech. An unmotivated listener quickly tunes out. You can help establish listening motivation by showing the members of your audience how the topic affects them directly.

In Chapter 8 we presented seven criteria for determining the effectiveness of your supporting material. One of those criteria was *proximity*, the degree to which the information affects your listeners directly. Just as proximity is important to supporting materials, it is also important to speech introductions. "This concerns me" is a powerful reason to listen. Notice how Chandra involves her audience members with the Hepatitis C risk inherent in tattooing:

> *If you're one of the millions wanting to show your patriotism by getting a star-spangled banner tattooed across your back, ask questions regarding its potential risks.*[2]

Sheena also uses proximity to motivate her audience to empathize with people who suffer from exposure to toxic mold:

Headaches, fatigue, dizziness, and memory impairment seem like ailments that each person in this room has had at one point, right? You stay up late cramming for an exam. The next day, you are fatigued, dizzy, and cannot remember the answers.[3]

It does not matter so much *how* or *when* you demonstrate proximity. But it is essential that like Chandra and Sheena, you *do* at some point establish that your topic is of vital personal concern to your listeners.

INTRODUCE THE SUBJECT

Perhaps the most obvious purpose of an introduction is to introduce the subject of a speech. Within a few seconds after you begin your speech, the audience should have a pretty good idea what you are going to talk about. Do not get so carried away with jokes or illustrations that you forget this basic purpose. Few things will frustrate your audience more than having to wait until halfway through your speech to figure out what you are talking about! The best way to ensure that your introduction does indeed introduce the subject of your speech is to include a statement of your central idea in the introduction. For example, in introducing his speech on the needs of the aged, this speaker immediately established his subject and central idea:

If you take away just one thing from what I have to say, I hope you'll come to understand in the next few minutes that the exploding population of seniors demands a conscious, considered, and collaborative response to plan for the health, financial, and social implications of an older population.[4]

ESTABLISH YOUR CREDIBILITY

Credibility is a speaker's believability. A credible speaker is one whom the audience judges to be a believable authority and a competent speaker. A credible speaker is also someone the audience believe they can trust. Although we discuss credibility in greater detail in Chapter 17, we stress here that as you begin your speech, you should be mindful of your listeners' attitudes toward you. When thinking of your listeners, ask yourself, "Why should they listen to me? What is my background with respect to the topic? Am I personally committed to the issues I am going to speak about?"

Many people have so much admiration for a political or religious figure, an athlete, or an entertainer that they sacrifice time, energy, and money to hear these celebrities speak. When Pope Benedict XVI travels abroad, people travel great distances and stand for hours in extreme heat or cold to celebrate Mass with him. But ordinary people cannot take their own credibility for granted when they speak. If you can establish your credibility early in a speech, it will help motivate your audience to listen. One way to build credibility in the introduction is to be well prepared and to appear confident. Speaking fluently while maintaining eye contact does much to convey a sense of confidence. If you seem to have confidence in yourself, your audience will have confidence in you.

A second way to establish credibility is to tell the audience of your personal experience with your topic. Instead of considering you boastful, most audience members will listen to you with respect. In a speech to a group of women executives, the president of the St. Louis, Missouri, Board of Education offered this insight into her experience:

If any of you have ever had the blessing of serving on a school board—and that's what I consider it to be, a blessing—you know how difficult it is. There are always too many needs to meet, never enough money to meet those needs, and a multitude

credibility
An audience's perception of a speaker as competent, trustworthy, knowledgeable, and dynamic

of competing stakeholders who know exactly how you should allocate scarce resources: on the one thing that matters most to them, which is always different than what's important to the person standing next to them. And that's when times are good and things are going well.[5]

PREVIEW YOUR MAIN IDEAS

A final purpose of the introduction is to preview the main ideas of your speech. As you saw in Chapter 9, the preview statement usually comes near the end of the introduction, included in or immediately following a statement of the central idea. The preview statement allows your listeners to anticipate the main ideas of your speech, which in turn helps ensure that they will remember those ideas after the speech.

As also noted in Chapter 9, a preview statement is an organizational strategy called a *signpost*. Just as signs posted along a highway tell you what is coming up, a signpost in your speech tells the listeners what to expect by enumerating the ideas or points that you plan to present. If, for example, you were giving a speech about racial profiling, you might say,

> *To end these crimes against color, we must first paint an accurate picture of the problem, then explore the causes, and finally establish solutions that will erase the practice of racial profiling.*[6]

Identifying your main ideas helps organize the message and enhances listeners' learning.

The introduction to your speech, then, should get your audience's attention, give the audience a reason to listen, introduce the subject, establish your credibility, and preview your main ideas. All this—and brevity too—may seem impossible to achieve. But it isn't!

A well-known speaker like Lance Armstrong does not have to work as hard as an unknown speaker to establish his credibility, because the audience already knows and respects him.

[Photo: Bob Daemmrich/The Image Works]

RECAP

Purposes of Your Introduction

PURPOSE	METHOD
Get the audience's attention.	Use an illustration, a startling fact or statistic, a quotation, humor, a question, a reference to a historical event or to a recent event, a personal reference, a reference to the occasion, or a reference to a preceding speech.
Give the audience a reason to listen.	Tell your listeners how the topic directly affects them.
Introduce the subject.	Present your central idea to your audience.
Establish your credibility.	Offer your credentials. Tell your listeners about your commitment to your topic.
Preview your main ideas.	Tell your audience what you are going to tell them.

Effective Introductions

With a little practice, you will be able to write satisfactory central ideas and preview statements. It may be more difficult to gain your audience's attention and give them a reason to listen to you. Fortunately, there are several effective methods for developing speech introductions. Not every method is appropriate for every speech, but chances are that you can discover among these alternatives at least one type of introduction to fit the topic and purpose of your speech, whatever they might be.

Specifically, we will discuss ten ways of introducing a speech:

- Illustrations or anecdotes
- Startling facts or statistics
- Quotations
- Humor
- Questions
- References to historical events
- References to recent events
- Personal references
- References to the occasion
- References to preceding speeches

ILLUSTRATIONS OR ANECDOTES

Not surprisingly, because it is the most inherently interesting type of supporting material, an illustration or **anecdote** can provide the basis for an effective speech introduction. In fact, if you have an especially compelling illustration that you had planned to use in the body of the speech, you might do well to use it in your introduction instead. A relevant and interesting anecdote will introduce your subject and almost invariably gain an audience's attention. Barack Obama opened a speech on shortcomings of the U.S. health care industry with this extended illustration:

> *A few hours north of here, Amy and Lane run a small business that offers Internet service to their community. They were the very first company to provide broadband access in their remote corner of northeastern Iowa, and every day, hundreds of people count on the services they provide to do their jobs and live their lives.*
>
> *But today they are on the brink of bankruptcy—a bankruptcy that has nothing to do with any poor business decision they made or slump in the economy they weren't prepared for.*
>
> *Lane was diagnosed with cancer when he was twenty-one years old. He lost a lung, a leg bone, and part of a hip. Seventeen years later, he is cancer-free, but the cost of health insurance for him, his wife, and his three kids is now over $1,000 per month. Their family's premiums keep rising hundreds of dollars every year, and as hard as they look, they simply cannot find another provider that will insure them.*
>
> *Amy and Lane are now paying forty percent of their annual income in health care premiums. They have no retirement plan and nothing saved. They can no longer afford to buy new clothes or fill up their cars with gas, they have racked up more credit card debt then they know what to do with, and Amy wrote to us and said that the day she heard the loan officer say the word "bankruptcy" was one of the worst in her life.[7]*

anecdote
An illustration or brief story

Obama's story effectively captured the attention of his audience and introduced the subject of his speech.

STARTLING FACTS OR STATISTICS

A second method of introducing a speech is to use a startling fact or statistic. Startling an audience with the extent of a situation or problem invariably catches its members' attention and motivates them to listen further as well as helping them remember afterward what you had to say. Kristin's audience must have come to attention quickly when they heard these opening words:

> Frances Dodd is a 67-year-old grandmother. But it's not her two grandkids that make her special. Rather, what sets Frances Dodd apart is that she is a drug smuggler.[8]

Kristin went on to explain that the drugs in question are in fact prescription medications, for which Frances Dodd pays in Canada only a fraction of what they would cost her in the United States.

QUOTATIONS

Using an appropriate quotation to introduce a speech is a common practice. Often a past writer or speaker has expressed an opinion on your topic that is more authoritative, comprehensive, or memorable than what you can say. Terrika opened her speech on the importance of community with a quotation from poet Johari Kungufu:

> Sisters, Men
> What are we doin?
> What about the babies, our children?
> When we was real we never had orphans or children in joints.
> Come spirits
> drive out the nonsense from our minds and the crap from our dreams
> make us remember what we need, that children are the next life.
> bring us back to the real
> bring us back to the real

> "The Real." Johari Kungufu, in her poem, specifically alludes to a time in African history when children were not confused about who they were.[9]

A different kind of quotation, this one from an expert, was chosen by another speaker to introduce the topic of the disappearance of childhood in America:

> "As a distinctive childhood culture wastes away, we watch with fascination and dismay." This insight of Neil Postman, author of Disappearance of Childhood, raised a poignant point. Childhood in America is vanishing.[10]

Because the expert was not widely recognized, the speaker included a brief statement of his qualifications. This authority "said it in a nutshell"—he expressed in concise language the central idea of the speech.

Although a quote can effectively introduce a speech, do not fall into the lazy habit of turning to a collection of quotations every time you need an introduction. There are so many other interesting, and sometimes better, ways to introduce a speech that quotes should be used only if they are extremely interesting, compelling, or very much to the point.

Like the methods of organization discussed in Chapter 9, the methods of introduction are not mutually exclusive. Very often, two or three are effectively combined in a single introduction. For example, Thad combined a quotation and an illustration for this effective introduction to a speech on the funeral industry:

> "Dying is a very dull, dreary affair. And my advice to you is to have nothing whatsoever to do with it." These lingering words by British playwright Somerset

Maugham were meant to draw a laugh. Yet the ironic truth to the statement has come to epitomize the grief of many, including Jan Berman of Martha's Vineyard. In a recent interview with National Public Radio, we learn that Ms. Berman desired to have a home funeral for her mother. She possessed a burial permit and was legally within her rights. But when a local funeral director found out, he lied to her, telling her that what she was doing was illegal.[11]

HUMOR

Humor, handled well, can be a wonderful attention-getter. It can help relax your audience and win their goodwill for the rest of the speech. University of Texas Professor of Journalism Marvin Olasky told this humorous story to open a speech on disaster response:

Let me begin with a Texas story about how officials do offer help. It starts with a mom on a farm looking out the window. She sees the family cow munching on grass and her daughter talking with a strange man. The mom furiously yells out the window, "Didn't I tell you not to talk to strangers? You come in this house right now." The girl offers a protest: "But mama, this man says he's a United States senator." The wise mother replies, "In that case, come in this house right now, and bring the cow in with you."

Let's talk about responses to disaster.[12]

Another speaker used humor to express appreciation for being invited to speak to a group by beginning his speech with this story:

Three corporate executives were trying to define the word fame.

One said, "Fame is getting invited to the White House to see the President."

The second one said, "Fame is being invited to the White House and while you are visiting, the phone rings and he doesn't answer it."

The third executive said, "You're both wrong. Fame is being invited to the White House to visit with the President when his Hot Line rings. He answers it, listens a minute, and then says, 'Here, it's for you!' "

Being asked to speak today is like being in the White House and the call's for me.[13]

Humor need not always be the slapstick comedy of the Three Stooges. It does not even have to be a joke. It may take more subtle forms, such as irony or incredulity. When General Douglas MacArthur, an honor graduate of the U.S. Military Academy at West Point, returned to West Point in 1962, he delivered his now-famous "Farewell to the Cadets." He opened that speech with this humorous illustration:

As I was leaving the hotel this morning, a doorman asked me, "Where are you bound for, General?" And when I replied, "West Point," he remarked, "Beautiful place. Have you ever been there before?"[14]

MacArthur's brief illustration caught the audience's attention and made them laugh—in short, it was an effective way to open the speech.

If your audience is linguistically diverse or composed primarily of listeners whose first language is not English, you may want to choose an introduction strategy other than humor. Because much humor is created by verbal plays on words, people who do not speak English as their native language may not perceive the humor in an anecdote or quip that you intended to be funny. And humor rarely translates well. Former President Jimmy Carter recalls speaking at a university near Kyoto, Japan, and being startled by unexpectedly hearty laughter in response to a short humorous anecdote he related. When he later asked his interpreter how he had translated the story so successfully, the interpreter finally admitted sheepishly, "I told them, 'President Carter has just told a funny story. Everyone laugh.'"[15]

Just as certain audiences may preclude your use of a humorous introduction, so may certain subjects—for example, Sudden Infant Death Syndrome or rape. Used with discretion, however, humor can provide a lively, interesting, and appropriate introduction for many speeches.

QUESTIONS

Remember the pet peeves listed at the beginning of this chapter? Another pet peeve for some is beginning a speech with a question ("How many of you . . . ?"). The problem is not so much the strategy itself, but the lack of mindfulness in the "How many of you?" phrasing. A thoughtful **rhetorical question**, on the other hand, can prompt your listeners' mental participation in your introduction, getting their attention and giving them a reason to listen.

Lisa opened her speech on geographic illiteracy with a series of questions:

Can you name the states that border the Pacific Ocean? What country lies between Panama and Nicaragua? Can you name the Great Lakes?[16]

And Richard opened his speech on teenage suicide with this simple question:

Have you ever been alone in the dark?[17]

To turn questions into an effective introduction, the speaker must do more than just think of good questions to ask. He or she must also deliver the questions effectively. Effective delivery includes pausing briefly after each question, so that audience members have time to try to formulate a mental answer. After all, the main advantage of questions as an introductory technique is to "hook" the audience by getting them to engage in a mental dialogue with you. The speaker who delivers questions most effectively is also one who may look down at notes while he or she asks the question, but who then reestablishes eye contact with listeners. As we discuss in more detail in Chapter 13, eye contact signals that the communication channel is open. Establishing eye contact with your audience following a question provides additional motivation for them to think of an answer.

Although it does not happen frequently, an audience member may blurt out a vocal response to a question intended to be rhetorical. If you plan to open a speech with a rhetorical question, be aware of this remote possibility, and plan possible appropriate reactions. If the topic is light, a Jay Leno–style return quip may win over the audience and turn the interruption into an asset. If the topic is more serious or the interruption is inappropriate or contrary to what you expected, you might reply with something like "Perhaps most of the rest of you were thinking . . . ," or you might answer the question yourself.

Questions are commonly combined with another method of introduction. For example, Beth opened her speech on the inadequacies of the current U.S. driver's license renewal system with three brief startling facts followed by a question:

In 31 states, a blind man can be licensed to drive. In 5 states, just send in your check and they will send back your renewed license, no questions asked.

In 1916 my grandfather got his license for the first time. No exam was required; no exam has been required since. Ever wonder why our highways seem a bit unsafe today?[18]

Either by themselves or in tandem with another method of introduction, questions can provide effective openings for speeches. Like quotations, however, questions can also be "crutches" for speakers who have not taken the time to explore other op-

rhetorical question
A question intended to provoke thought, rather than elicit an answer

tions. Unless you can think of a truly engaging question, work to develop one of the other introduction strategies.

REFERENCES TO HISTORICAL EVENTS

What American is not familiar with the opening line of Lincoln's classic Gettysburg Address: "Four score and seven years ago, our fathers brought forth on this continent a new nation, conceived in liberty, and dedicated to the proposition that all men are created equal"? Note that Lincoln's famous opening sentence refers to the historical context of the speech. You, too, may find a way to begin a speech by making a reference to a historic event.

Every day is the anniversary of something. Perhaps you could begin a speech by drawing a relationship between a historic event that happened on this day and your speech objective. How do you discover anniversaries of historic events? You could consult "This Day in History" (www.history.com/tdih.do), a Web page from The History Channel's site, or "On This Day" (news.bbc.co.uk/onthisday), sponsored by the BBC. Many local newspapers also have a feature that identifies key events that occurred on "this day in history." If, for example, you know you are going to be speaking on April 6, you could consult a copy of a newspaper from April 6 of last year to discover the key commemorative events for that day.

We are not recommending that you arbitrarily flip through one of these sources to crank up your speech; your historical reference should be linked clearly to the purpose of your speech. Note how Vice President Dick Cheney opened his remarks at a 2006 Pentagon observance of the anniversary of September 11th:

> Five years ago, September 11th forever ceased to be an ordinary date on the calendar. So we gather, once again, to recall events that still have the power to move us, and always will. And we honor the men, women, and children whose lives were taken, so suddenly and so coldly, here at the Pentagon, at the World Trade Center, and on a field in Pennsylvania. We remember all that we saw, and heard, and felt on that Tuesday morning, and also how much the world changed on the 11th of September, 2001.[19]

REFERENCES TO RECENT EVENTS

If your topic is timely, a reference to a recent event can be a good way to open your speech. An opening taken from a recent news story can take the form of an illustration, a startling statistic, or even a quotation, gaining the additional advantages discussed under each of those methods of introduction. Moreover, referring to a recent event increases your credibility by showing that you are knowledgeable about current affairs.

"Recent" does not necessarily mean a story that broke just last week or even last month. An event that occurred within the past year or so can be considered recent. Even a particularly significant event that is slightly older can qualify. The key, says one speaker,

> is to avoid being your grandfather. No more stories about walking up hill both ways to school with a musket on your back and seventeen Redcoats chasing you. Be in the now, and connect with your audience.[20]

PERSONAL REFERENCES

A reference to yourself can take several forms. You might express appreciation or pleasure at having been asked to speak, as did this speaker:

> I would like, if I may, to start on a brief personal note. It is a great pleasure for me to be speaking in Cleveland, Ohio. This is where I grew up. Since then, I have traveled all over the world, but I have never stopped missing Ohio.[21]

Senator Edward Kennedy speaks at the dedication of Boston's Rose Fitzgerald Kennedy Greenway, named in honor of his mother. An effective introduction to such a speech would undoubtedly include a reference to the special occasion or the significance of the day.

[Photo: Chitose Suzuki/AP/Wide World Photos]

Or you might share a personal experience, as did philanthropist Glenn Schaffer at the beginning of his speech at the dedication of the University of Iowa Writers' Workshop library:

> The celebrated Workshop spans 70 years, and has produced illustrious alumni whose pedigrees in the literary field are unrivaled. By another extra stroke of good fortune, I happened to be enrolled there in the middle 1970s alongside a cohort of ambitious, greatly talented writers, many of whom have since earned an honored place in the nation's literary pantheon: T. C. Boyle, Alan Gurganus, Jane Smiley, and Jorie Graham, to cite a few. In my own small way, I suspect, I served to hold down the Workshop's otherwise high achievement average.[22]

Although personal references take a variety of forms, what they do best, in all circumstances, is to establish a bond between you and your audience.

REFERENCES TO THE OCCASION

References to the occasion are often made at weddings, birthday parties, dedication ceremonies, and other such events. For example, when First Lady Laura Bush spoke at a White House Salute to America's Authors, she opened her remarks this way:

> Good afternoon. Welcome to the "White House Salute to America's Authors." This program, the second in a series on American authors, celebrates one of the richest literary periods in American history, the Harlem Renaissance, and the authors whose genius brought it to life.[23]

The reference to the occasion can also be combined with other methods of introduction, such as an illustration or a rhetorical question.

REFERENCES TO PRECEDING SPEECHES

If your speech is one of several being presented on the same occasion, such as in a speech class, at a symposium, or as part of a lecture series, you will usually not know until shortly before your own speech what other speakers will say. Few experiences will make your stomach sink faster than hearing a speaker just ahead of you speak on

your topic. Worse still, that speaker may even use some of the same supporting materials you had planned to use. When this happens, you must decide on the spot whether referring to one of these previous speeches will be better than using the introduction you originally prepared. It may be wise to refer to a preceding speech when another speaker has spoken on a topic so related to your own that you can draw an analogy. In a sense, your introduction becomes a transition from that earlier speech to yours. Here is an example of an introduction delivered by a fast-thinking student speaker under those circumstances:

> *When Juli talked to us about her experiences as a lifeguard, she stressed that the job was not as glamorous as many of us imagine. Today I want to tell you about another job that appears to be more glamorous than it is—a job that I have held for two years. I am a bartender at the Rathskeller.*[24]

In summary, as you plan your introduction, remember that any combination of the methods just discussed is possible. With a little practice, you will become confident at choosing from several good possibilities as you prepare your introduction.

 ## Purposes of Conclusions

Your introduction creates an important first impression; your conclusion leaves an equally important final impression. Long after you finish speaking, your audience is likely to remember the effect, if not the content, of your closing remarks.

Unfortunately, many speakers pay less attention to their conclusions than to any other part of their speeches. They believe that if they can get through the first 90 percent of a speech, they can think of some way to conclude it. Perhaps you have had the experience of listening to a speaker who failed to plan a conclusion. Awkward final seconds of stumbling for words may be followed by hesitant applause from an audience that is not even sure the speech is over. It is hardly the best way to leave people who came to listen to you.

An effective conclusion will serve two purposes. It will summarize the speech and provide closure.

Just as you learned ways to introduce a speech, you can learn how to conclude one. We will begin by considering the purposes of conclusions and will go on to explore methods to help you achieve those purposes.

SUMMARIZE THE SPEECH

A conclusion is a speaker's last chance to review his or her central idea and main ideas for the audience.

REEMPHASIZE THE CENTRAL IDEA IN A MEMORABLE WAY The conclusions of many famous speeches rephrase the central idea in a memorable way. For example, General Douglas MacArthur's farewell to the nation at the end of his career concluded with these memorable words:

> *"Old soldiers never die; they just fade away." And like the old soldier of that ballad, I now close my military career and just fade away—an old soldier who tried to do his duty as God gave him the light to see that duty. Good-bye.*[25]

Likewise, when on July 4, 1939, New York Yankees legend Lou Gehrig addressed his fans in an emotional farewell to a baseball career cut short by a diagnosis of ALS (Amyotrophic Lateral Sclerosis), he concluded with the memorable line,

> *I may have had a tough break, but I have an awful lot to live for.*[26]

But memorable endings are not the exclusive property of famous speakers. With practice, most people can prepare similarly effective conclusions. Chapter 12 offers ideas for using language to make your statements more memorable. As a preliminary example of the memorable use of language, here is how Noelle concluded her speech on phony academic institutions on the Internet:

> *What we have learned from all this is that we, and only we, have the power to stop [fraudulent learning institutions]. So we don't get www.conned.*[27]

This speaker's clever play on "dot.com" helped her audience remember her topic and central idea.

The end of your speech is your last chance to impress the central idea on your audience. Do it in such a way that they cannot help but remember it.

RESTATE THE MAIN IDEAS In addition to reemphasizing the central idea of the speech, the conclusion is also likely to restate the main ideas. Note how John effectively summarized the main ideas of his speech on emissions tampering, casting the summary as an expression of his fears about the problem and the actions that could ease those fears:

> *I'm frightened. Frightened that nothing I could say would encourage the 25 percent of emissions-tampering Americans to change their ways and correct the factors that cause their autos to pollute disproportionately. Frightened that the American public will not respond to a crucial issue unless the harms are both immediate and observable. Frightened that the EPA will once again prove very sympathetic to industry. Three simple steps will alleviate my fear: inspection, reduction in lead content, and, most importantly, awareness.*[28]

Most speakers summarize their main ideas in the first part of the conclusion or perhaps even as the transition between the body of the speech and its conclusion.

PROVIDE CLOSURE

Probably the most obvious purpose of a conclusion is to provide **closure**—to cue the audience that the speech is coming to an end by making it "sound finished."

USE VERBAL OR NONVERBAL CUES TO SIGNAL THE END OF THE SPEECH You can attain closure both verbally and nonverbally. Verbal techniques include using such transitions as "finally," "for my last point," and perhaps even "in conclusion."

You may remember that "in conclusion" appears on the list of instructors' pet peeves at the beginning of the chapter. Like opening your speech by asking a rhetorical question, signaling your closing by saying "in conclusion" is not inherently wrong. It is a pet peeve of some instructors because of the carelessness with which student speakers often use it. Such a cue gives listeners unspoken permission to tune out. (Notice what students do when their professor signals the end of class. Books and notebooks slam shut, pens are stowed away, and the class generally stops listening.) A concluding transition needs to be followed quickly by the final statement of the speech.

You can also signal closure with nonverbal cues. You may want to pause between the body of your speech and its conclusion, slow your speaking rate, move out from behind a podium to make a final impassioned plea to your audience, or signal with falling vocal inflection that you are making your final statement.

MOTIVATE THE AUDIENCE TO RESPOND Another way to provide closure to your speech is to motivate your audience to respond in some way. If your speech is informative, you may want your audience to take some sort of appropriate action—write a letter, buy a product, make a telephone call, or get involved in a cause. In fact, an *action* step is essential to the persuasive organizational strategy called the motivated sequence, which we discuss in detail in Chapter 17.

At the close of her speech on negligent landlords, Melanie included a simple audience response as part of her action step:

> By a show of hands, how many people in this room rely on rental housing? Look around. It's a problem that affects us all, if not directly, then through a majority of our friends. . . .[29]

Another speaker ended a speech to an audience of travel agents by recommending these specific action steps:

- Continuously develop and improve your professional and business skills.
- Embrace and utilize the new technologies. You are either riding on the new technology highway, or you are standing in the dust, left behind.
- Continuously build and strengthen your top industry organizations locally and nationally so their brands, endorsement, and influence can work powerfully on your behalf.
- Develop a passion for this business and inspire the same in your employees and co-workers.[30]

In both of the preceding examples, the speakers draw on the principle of proximity, discussed earlier in this chapter, to motivate their audiences. If audience members feel that they are or could be personally involved or affected, they are more likely to respond to your message.

closure
The quality of a conclusion that makes a speech "sound finished"

Introducing and Concluding Your Speech

RECAP

Purposes of Your Speech Conclusion

PURPOSE	TECHNIQUE
Summarize the speech	Reemphasize the central idea in a memorable way.
	Restate the main ideas.
Provide closure	Use verbal or nonverbal cues to signal the end of the speech.
	Motivate the audience to respond.

Effective Conclusions

Effective conclusions may employ illustrations, quotations, personal references, or any of the other methods of introduction we have already discussed. In addition, there are at least two other distinct ways of concluding a speech: with references to the introduction and with inspirational appeals or challenges.

METHODS ALSO USED FOR INTRODUCTIONS

Any of the methods of introduction discussed earlier can also help you conclude your speech. Quotations, for example, are frequently used in conclusions, as in this speech on long-term care:

> Winston Churchill said, "Americans finally do the right thing, but only after they have exhausted all other possibilities." I think we've pretty much exhausted all the wrong possibilities regarding long-term care. Let's work together and bring about, once and for all, independence and dignity for all Americans as we grow old.[31]

REFERENCES TO THE INTRODUCTION

In our discussion of closure, we mentioned referring to the introduction as a way to end a speech. Finishing a story, answering a rhetorical question, or reminding the audience of the startling fact or statistic you presented in the introduction are excellent ways to provide closure. Like bookends at either side of a group of books on your desk, a related introduction and conclusion provide unified support for the ideas in the middle.

Sonja's topic dealt with the health problems caused by the reprocessing of medical devices. She had opened her speech with an illustration of a 7-year-old Cub Scout named Timothy Anderson, who was killed when his heart was sliced by a reprocessed heart catheter. Her conclusion was this:

> Because while we all want our health care to be affordable, we need to resist the push to do so at the expense of our health. After all, Timothy Anderson will never build the model '57 Chevy he was to receive on his eighth birthday.[32]

John had begun his speech on the need for catastrophic health insurance by quoting Robert Browning:

confidently connecting with your audience

Be Familiar with Your Introduction and Conclusion

You may feel the most nervous just as you begin your speech. But if you have a well-prepared and well-rehearsed introduction you'll be able to start with confidence. Rehearse your opening sentences enough times that you can present them while maintaining direct eye contact with your listeners. Being familiar with your conclusion can give you a safe harbor to head for as you end your message. A thoughtfully planned and well-rehearsed introduction and conclusion can help you start and end your speech with poise and assurance.

> *Grow old along with me!*
> *The best is yet to be,*
> *The last of life, for which the first was made.*[33]

He concluded his speech by referring to that Browning quotation:

> *Robert Browning tells us the last of life is as precious as the first. While the future will always hold uncertainty, with catastrophic health insurance we can more fully prepare for whatever is yet to be.*[34]

Benjamin had introduced his speech by talking about the downfalls inevitably suffered by the heroes of Greek mythology. He drew an analogy between the risks they faced and the risks inherent in the use of antibiotics—the dangers of overuse. Here is how Benjamin ended his speech:

> *The demise of Medusa carries with it one final message. With her death, Perseus received two drops of blood. One drop had the power to kill and spread evil; the other, to heal and restore well-being. Similarly, antibiotics offer us two opposite paths. As we painfully take stock in our hubris, in assuming that we can control the transformation of nature, we may ponder these two paths. We can either let antibiotics do the work of our immune systems and proper farm management, which may return us to the times when deathly plagues spread across the world, or we can save these miracle drugs for the times when miracles are truly needed.*[35]

Each of the three examples just given is quite different. In the first, the speech opened and closed with an illustration; in the second, both introduction and conclusion centered on a quotation; and in the third, beginning and ending relied on an analogy between mythology and modern medicine. In all three speeches, the conclusion alluded to the introduction to make the speech memorable, to motivate the audience to respond, and to provide closure.

Inspirational Appeals or Challenges

Another way to end your speech is to issue an inspirational appeal or challenge to your listeners, rousing them to a high emotional pitch at the conclusion of the speech. The conclusion becomes the climax. Speechwriter and communication consultant James W. Robinson explains why such conclusions can work well:

> *It's almost as if, for a few brief moments [the audience] escape from the stressful demands of our high-pressure world and welcome your gifts: insightful vision, persuasive rhetoric, a touch of philosophy, a little emotion, and yes, even a hint of corniness.*[36]

One famous example of a concluding inspiration appeal comes from Martin Luther King Jr.'s "I Have a Dream" speech:

> *From every mountainside, let freedom ring, and when this happens . . . when we allow freedom to ring, when we let it ring from every village and every hamlet, from every state and every city, we will be able to speed up that day when all of God's children, black men and white men, Jews and Gentiles, Protestants and Catholics, will be able to join hands and sing in the words of the old Negro spiritual, "Free at last! Thank God Almighty, we are free at last!"*[37]

That King's conclusion was both inspiring and memorable has been affirmed by the growing fame of that passage through the years since he delivered the speech.

In the conclusion of his investiture speech, Jake Schrum, president of Southwestern University in Georgetown, Texas, issued this unique and effective inspirational challenge to his listeners:

> *Before I end my remarks, I invite all Southwestern alumni and all Southwestern students to stand and to remain standing for my final words.*
>
> *Years ago, I knew a woman named Audry Dillow who had been a school teacher all of her adult life. In her eighties when I met her, we often reflected on the*

Patrick Henry (1736–1799)

Lawyer, supporter of American independence, Governor of Virginia, and staunch advocate of the Bill of Rights, Patrick Henry is today best remembered for a single line—the conclusion of a speech he delivered to the Virginia Convention on March 23, 1775. In one of the most famous inspirational appeals in history, Henry declared,

I know not what the course other may take; but as for me, give me liberty or give me death!

As you prepare your speech introduction, consider using a powerful quotation from a great speaker to grab your listeners' attention. Or, as you conclude your talk, use a quotation to reemphasize your central idea in a memorable way.

[Photo: The Granger Collection]

attributes and beliefs of college students. Frankly, she was not as positive about the goodness of students as I was.

One day, she asked me, "Jake, are there students today who truly care about someone other than themselves, who really care about the world, who are genuinely good at heart?" I said, "Yes." She said, "Who?" I said, "What do you mean, 'Who?'" She said, "Who—who are they? Give me their names."

I said, "You want me to give you the actual names of people who will basically fight the world's fight?" She said, "Yes, I want names."

If she were here today to ask me the same question, may I give her your name? The world is waiting for your reply.

Your answer will change the world.[38]

King's and Shrum's inspiring conclusions reemphasized their central ideas in a memorable way, provided closure to their speeches, and inspired their listeners.

SUMMARY

It is important to begin and end your speech in a way that is memorable and that also provides the repetition audiences need. A good introduction gets the audience's attention, gives the audience a reason to listen, introduces your subject, establishes your credibility, and previews your main ideas.

Introducing your subject and previewing the body of your speech can be accomplished by including your central idea and preview statement in the introduction. You can gain favorable attention and provide a motivation for listening by using any of the following, alone or in combinations: illustrations, startling facts or statistics, quotations, humor, questions, references to historical events, references to recent events, personal references, references to the occasion, or references to preceding speeches, if there are any.

Concluding your speech is just as important as introducing it, for it is the conclusion that leaves the final impression. Specifically, a conclusion should summarize your speech and provide closure.

Conclusions may take any one of the forms used for introductions. In addition, you can refer to the introduction or make inspirational appeals or challenges.

Once you have planned the introduction and the conclusion, you have completed the final organizational step of the speech-preparation process.

CONSIDERING YOUR AUDIENCE

- Introductions and conclusions provide audiences with important first and final impressions of speaker and speech.

- As a speaker, your task is to ensure that your introduction convinces your audience to listen to you.

- A credible speaker is one whom the audience judges to be a believable authority and a competent speaker. Establishing your credibility early in a speech helps motivate your audience to listen.

- A speech conclusion leaves an important final impression. Long after you finish speaking, your audience is likely to remember the effect, if not the content, of your closing remarks.

- Your speech conclusion is your last chance to repeat your main ideas for your listeners.

CONSIDERING AUDIENCE DIVERSITY

- To demonstrate proximity, you must acknowledge the diverse experiences and involvement of your listeners with your topic.

- If your audience is linguistically diverse or composed primarily of listeners whose first language is not English, it may be preferable not to use humor in your introduction. Because much humor is created verbally, it may not be readily understood and rarely translates well.

CRITICAL THINKING QUESTIONS

1. Nakai is planning to give his informative speech on Native American music, displaying and demonstrating the use of such instruments as the flute, the Taos drum, and the Yaqui rain stick. He asks you to suggest a good introduction for the speech. How do you think he might best introduce his speech?

2. Knowing that you have recently visited the Vietnam Veterans Memorial, your American history professor asks you to make a brief presentation to the class about the Wall: its history; its symbolic meaning; and its impact on the families, comrades, and friends of those memorialized there. Write both an introduction and a conclusion for this speech.

3. How could you establish a motivation for your classroom audience to listen to you on each of the following topics?

   Cholesterol
   Elvis Presley
   The history of greeting cards
   Ozone depletion
   Text messaging
   Speed traps

ETHICAL QUESTION

Marty and Shanna, who are in the same section of a public-speaking class, are discussing their upcoming speeches. Marty has discovered an illustration that she thinks will make an effective introduction. When she tells Shanna about it, Shanna is genuinely enthusiastic. In fact, she thinks it would make a great introduction for her own speech, which is on a different topic. When the students are given schedules for their speeches, Shanna realizes that she will speak before Marty. She badly wants to use the introductory illustration that Marty has discovered. Can she ethically do so, if she cites in her speech the original source of the illustration?

Developing the Introduction and Conclusion to Your Speech

Use this worksheet as you develop your speech introduction.

Catch attention using one of the following:

- Illustration
- Interesting fact or statistic
- Appropriate humor
- A quotation
- A rhetorical question
- A reference to the occasion
- A reference to an event in history

Give the audience a reason to listen (tell your listeners how your topic affects them).

Introduce the subject (state your central idea).

Establish your credibility by answering one or more of the following questions:

- What are your credentials—why should audience members listen to you speak about this topic?
- What experience have you had with this topic?
- Why are you talking to this audience about this topic?

Preview your main ideas.

Summarize your speech.

- Reemphasize the central idea in a memorable way.
- Restate your main idea.

Provide closure.

- Plan verbal or nonverbal cues to signal the end of your speech.
- Motivate your audience to respond, especially if your message is persuasive.

End with a quotation, a reference to your introduction, an answer to your opening rhetorical question, a final story or illustration, or an inspirational appeal or challenge.

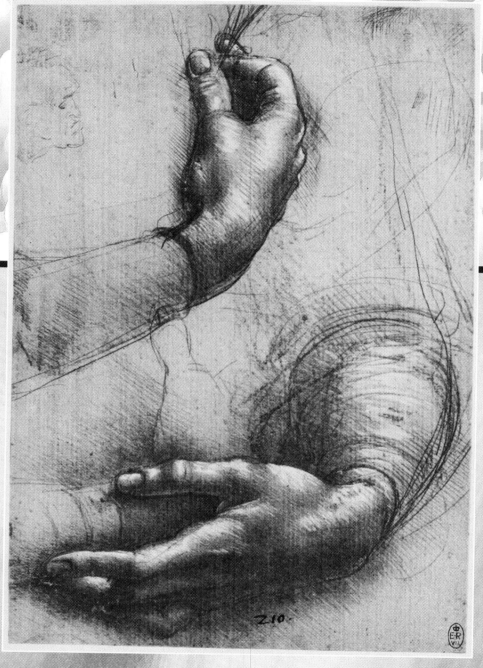

Leonardo da Vinci (1452–1519). *Study of female hands*. Drawing. Alinari/Art Resource, N.Y.

Every discourse ought to be a living creature, having a body of its own and head and feet; there should be a middle, a beginning, and end, adapted to one another and to the whole.

—PLATO

Outlining and Editing Your Speech

outline

objectives

After studying this chapter you should be able to do the following:

1. Describe the purposes of a preparation outline and a delivery outline.

2. Identify and explain guidelines for preparing a preparation outline and a delivery outline.

3. Demonstrate standard outline form.

4. Prepare a preparation outline and a delivery outline for a speech you are working on.

5. Edit a speech.

6. Deliver a speech from speaking notes.

How much time do you spend preparing the speeches you give? And what percentage of your preparation time do you spend on the various individual tasks involved in the speechmaking process?

Communication researchers recently tried to determine the answers to these and related questions with a group of nearly 100 college students.[1] Students kept journals throughout the semester in their public-speaking class, using the first few minutes of each class meeting to describe in writing what they had done since the last class to prepare for their next speech and to estimate how much time they had spent on each reported activity. When the researchers examined the students' journals, they discovered that on average, students reported spending nearly half of their total preparation time outlining and editing their speeches.

If you are typical of the students in the study, then this chapter will be critical to your success as a speaker. Specifically, we will examine the purposes and requirements of three important tasks: (1) developing your preparation outline; (2) editing your speech; and (3) developing your delivery outline and speaking notes.

Developing Your Preparation Outline

Although few speeches are written in paragraph form, most speakers develop a detailed **preparation outline** that includes main ideas, subpoints, and supporting material. It may also include the specific purpose, introduction, blueprint, conclusion, and signposts. One CEO notes,

Unless you sit down and write out your thoughts and put them in a cogent order, you can't deliver a cogent speech. Maybe some people have mastered that art. But I have seen too many people give speeches that they really haven't thought out.[2]

THE PREPARATION OUTLINE

To begin your outlining task, you might try a technique known as **mapping**, or clustering. Write on a sheet of paper all the main ideas, subpoints, and supporting material for the speech. Then use geometric shapes and arrows to indicate the logical relationships among them, as shown in Figure 11.1.

Nationwide Insurance speechwriter Charles Parnell favors yet another technique for beginning an outline:

I often start by jotting down a few ideas on the [computer] screen, then move them around as necessary to build some sort of coherent pattern. I then fill in the details as they occur to me.

What that means is that you can really start anywhere and eventually come up with an entire speech, just as you can start with any piece of a puzzle and eventually put it together.[3]

Whatever technique you choose to begin your outline, your ultimate goal is to produce a plan that lets you judge the unity and coherence of your speech, to see how well the parts fit together and how smoothly the speech flows. Your finished prepara-

preparation outline
A detailed outline of a speech that includes main ideas, subpoints, and supporting material, and that may also include specific purpose, introduction, blueprint, internal previews and summaries, transitions, and conclusion

mapping
Using geometric shapes to sketch how all the main ideas, subpoints, and supporting material of a speech relate to the central idea and to one another

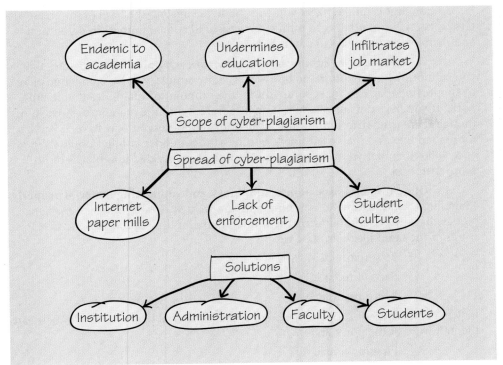

Figure 11.1 *A map that shows the relationships among each of Valerie's three main ideas and their subpoints. Main ideas are enclosed by rectangles; subpoints, by ovals. Supporting material could be indicated by another shape and connected to the appropriate subpoints.*

tion outline will help you make sure that all main ideas and subpoints are clearly and logically related and adequately supported.

The following suggestions will help you complete your preparation outline. However, keep in mind that different instructors may have different expectations for both outline content and outline format. Be sure to understand and follow your own instructor's guidelines.

➤ **Write your preparation outline in complete sentences, like those you will use when delivering your speech.** Unless you write complete sentences, you will have trouble judging the coherence of the speech. Moreover, complete sentences will help during your early rehearsals. If you write cryptic phrases, you may not remember what they mean.

➤ **Use standard outline form.** Although you did not have to use standard outline form when you began to outline your ideas, you need to do so now. **Standard outline form** lets you see at a glance the exact relationships among various main ideas, subpoints, and supporting material in your speech. It is an important tool for evaluating your speech, as well as a requirement in many public-speaking courses. An instructor who requires speech outlines will generally expect standard outline form. To produce a correct outline, follow the instructions given here.

➤ **Use standard outline numbering.** Logical and fairly easy to learn, outline numbering follows this sequence:

 I. First main idea
  A. First subpoint of I
  B. Second subpoint of I
    1. First subpoint of B
    2. Second subpoint of B
      a. First subpoint of 2
      b. Second subpoint of 2
 II. Second main idea

standard outline form
Numbered and lettered headings and subheadings arranged hierarchically to indicate the relationships among parts of a speech

Although it is unlikely that you will subdivide beyond the level of lowercase letters (a, b, etc.) in most speech outlines, next would come numbers in parentheses and then lowercase letters in parentheses.

➤ **Use at least two subdivisions, if any, for each point.** Logic dictates that you cannot divide anything into one part. If, for example, you have only one piece of supporting material, incorporate it into the subpoint or main idea that it supports. If you have only one subpoint, incorporate it into the main idea above it. Although there is no firm limit to the number of subpoints you may have, if you have more than five, you may want to place some of them under another point. An audience will remember your ideas more easily if they are divided into blocks of no more than five.

➤ **Indent main ideas, points, subpoints, and supporting material properly.** Main ideas, indicated by Roman numerals, are written closest to the left margin. Notice that the *periods* following the Roman numerals line up, so that the first *words* of the main ideas also line up.

    I. First main idea

   II. Second main idea

  III. Third main idea

Letters or numbers of subpoints and supporting material begin directly underneath the first *word* of the point above.

    I. First main idea

       A. First subpoint of I

If a main idea or subpoint takes up more than one line, the second line begins under the first *word* of the preceding line:

    I. Every speech has three parts.

       A. The first part, both in our discussion and in actual delivery, is the introduction.

The same rules of indentation apply at all levels of the outline.

➤ **Write and label your specific purpose at the top of your preparation outline.** Unless your instructor directs you to do otherwise, do not work the specific purpose into the outline itself. Instead, label it and place it at the top of the outline. Your specific purpose can serve as a yardstick by which to measure the relevance of each main idea, subpoint, and piece of supporting material. Everything in the speech should contribute to your purpose.

➤ **Add the blueprint, key signposts, and an introduction and conclusion to your outline.** Place the introduction after the specific purpose, the blueprint immediately following the introduction, the conclusion after the outline of the body of the speech, and other signposts within the outline. Follow your instructor's guidelines for incorporating these elements into your numbering system.

Note that if you are using a word-processing program, you may find it easier to format your outline with the Autoformat feature turned off. The program's attempt to "help" you may be more frustrating than helpful and may cause you to make more errors in your outline than you would if you formatted it yourself.

SAMPLE PREPARATION OUTLINE

The sample outline that follows is for a ten-minute persuasive speech by student speaker Ashley Tinnell, whose speech preparation process we have been following since Chapter 5.[4] Notice that in this example, the purpose, introduction, blueprint, signposts, and conclusion are separated from the numbered points in the body of the speech. Be sure to learn and follow your own instructor's specific requirements for incorporating these elements.

Once you have completed your preparation outline, you can use it to help analyze and possibly revise the speech. The following questions can help you in this critical thinking task.

- **Does the speech as outlined fulfill the purpose you have specified?** If not, you need to revise the specific purpose or change the direction and content of the speech itself.
- **Are the main ideas logical extensions (natural divisions, reasons, or steps) of the central idea?** If not, revise either the central idea or the main ideas. Like the first question, this one relates to the unity of the speech and is critical to making certain the speech "fits together" as a whole.
- **Do the signposts enhance the comfortable flow of each idea into the next?** If not, change or add previews, summaries, or transitions. If signposts are not adequate, the speech will lack coherence.
- **Does each subpoint provide support for the point under which it falls?** If not, then either move or delete the subpoint.
- **Is your outline form correct?** For a quick reference, check the earlier Recap box, Summary of Correct Outline Form.

Having considered these five questions, you are ready to rehearse your speech, using the preparation outline as your first set of notes. See Chapter 13 for additional tips on effective rehearsal.

RECAP

Summary of Correct Outline Form

RULE

1. Use standard outline numbers and letters.

2. Use at least two subpoints, if any, for each main idea.

3. Properly indent main ideas, subpoints, and supporting material.

EXAMPLE

I.
  A.
    1.
      a.
        (1)
          (a)

I.
  A.
  B.

I. First main idea
  A. First subpoint of I
    1. First subpoint of A
    2. Second subpoint of A
  B. Second subpoint of I
II. Second main idea

PURPOSE

At the end of my speech, the audience will take steps to ensure a safer produce supply.

INTRODUCTION

Graduate student Jillian Kohl took pride in her health. As a marathoner, eating well and staying fit were her top priorities. However, after experiencing unexplained muscle aches, fever, and stomach cramps, she knew something was seriously wrong. *ABC Nightline* of October 5, 2006, notes that after two weeks in the hospital, Jillian was sent home with only 10 percent of her normal kidney function and was forced to give up running.

According to a January 12, 2007, article from the *Gannett News Service*, Jillian was one of over two hundred reported illnesses and three deaths that were all caused by one outbreak of *E. coli* contaminated spinach. Even though our attention on food dangers has historically focused on the meat industry, *CNN* of March 7, 2007, reveals that contaminated produce is responsible for more food-borne illnesses than fish, poultry, beef, and seafood combined.

CENTRAL IDEA

We must take action to sharpen the U.S. government's focus on produce safety.

PREVIEW

We will first explore why produce inspection cuts have been made; next, understand the damaging effects; and finally, discover some solutions to make us safer.

BODY

I. Programs for government inspection of produce are severely fractured and suffer from under-funding.

    A. Because there are so many agencies responsible for regulating our food supply, there is little organization or oversight.

        1. The *Congressional Quarterly* of February 8, 2007, notes that fifteen different agencies are responsible for regulating the safety of our food, including the FDA and Centers for Disease Control and Prevention.

        2. *The New York Times* of March 13, 2007, adds that revised rules to prevent food-borne illness in fresh-cut produce announced on March 12th are "unenforceable" and only recommendations.

    B. There are insufficient funds to inspect our food supply.

        1. The *Chicago Daily Herald* of March 1, 2007, explains that the federal government has failed to allot the required funds to meet new regulations.

        2. According to the *Los Angles Times* of December 25, 2006, the FDA would need an additional $176 million to perform the same level of protection it did four years ago.

        3. An even smaller portion of imported produce is inspected. *MSNBC* of February 23, 2007, explains that last year, FDA inspectors were only able to physically inspect 1.3 percent of imported foods.

        4. More disturbingly, the FDA doesn't even have the funds to efficiently trace contaminated produce back to the source. For example, it took two weeks for the FDA to trace the contaminated spinach back to California, during which time Americans remained exposed to the deadly pathogen.

Writing the purpose statement at the top of the outline helps the speaker keep it in mind. But always follow your instructor's specific requirements for formatting your preparation outline.

Ashley catches her listeners' attention by opening her presentation with an illustration. Other strategies for effectively getting audience attention were discussed in Chapter 10.

Ashley writes out and labels her central idea and preview, which together form the blueprint of her speech. Again, follow your instructor's requirements for what to include in, and how to label, the various components of your preparation outline.

The first main point of the speech, which explores causes of the problem, is indicated by the Roman numeral I. It previews the two subpoints, indicated by A and B.

Subpoints 1 and 2 provide supporting material, with appropriate oral citations, for A.

Subpoints 1, 2, 3, and 4 provide supporting material, with appropriate oral citations, for B.

Signpost: The lack of organization or oversight of regulatory agencies and the lack of funding to inspect our produce supply jeopardize our health, damage our economy, and leave us vulnerable to terrorist attacks on our food supply.

II. This deeply flawed system endangers us all.

    A. Produce contamination puts our health at risk.

        1. *ABC Nightline* reveals that food-borne pathogens can cause abdominal cramps, dangerously high fever, seizure disorders, and diabetes.

        2. 76-year-old William Barkay knows the dangers of contaminated foods all too well. According to the *Omaha World-Herald* of February 23, 2007, after consuming salmonella-contaminated peanut butter, William and his wife, Roberta, were hospitalized. William barely recovered, but Roberta did not. She died on January 30th this year because of a food safety system that is ineffective and unreliable.

    B. While the illnesses and deaths caused by our government's negligence are appalling, economic effects are devastating as well.

        1. According to a January 2007 edition of *Progressive Grocer Magazine*, after an outbreak, people become much more cautious about what produce they buy, catastrophically affecting fruit and vegetable producers.

        2. A March 12, 2007, online article from *thecalifornian.com* explains that following the spinach recall six months ago, the leafy greens industry has lost over $100 million dollars, costs that producers are forced to pass on to us.

        3. Additionally, *Time Magazine* of February 27, 2007, notes that imported foods pose the largest threat to our food safety. The fact that our government only bothers to inspect a miniscule portion of imported food leaves us susceptible to terrorist attacks and sabotage. As the previously cited *Chicago Daily Herald* adds, this is "terrible for us to think about at the dinner table, but quite appetizing for the terrorists seeking to do us harm."

Signpost: The collapse of our produce safety system requires immediate action.

III. To prevent an even graver epidemic, we must take steps that include congressional legislation, a reallocation of funds, and personal action.

    A. Congress must consolidate the fractured structure of the system.

    B. The federal government must appropriately allocate funds among all food safety agencies.

    C. Visit the Web site of the nonprofit organization STOP—Safe Tables Our Priority—at safetables.org, and use its resources, such as tips about how to properly wash and cook your fruits and vegetables, as well as advice about growing your own.

CONCLUSION

Although Jillian was forced to leave graduate school and move back in with her parents, she feels lucky to be alive. Unfortunately, her doctors don't think she will ever fully recover.

    After looking at the causes, effects, and solutions associated with produce safety, it is clear we need to take action to stop future illnesses and deaths. With our current system, *CNN* of March 7, 2007, explains that it is certain we will continue to see food-borne pathogens in our fruits and vegetables. Unless we make a concerted effort to do something about it, the safety of our produce will continue to be a recipe for disaster.

The signpost summarizes Ashley's first main idea—that government produce-inspection programs are fractured and under-funded—and previews her second main idea—effects of the problem.

Ashley places in quotation marks exact words she wants to quote from the *Chicago Daily Herald* article.

Having established causes and effects, Ashley turns to solutions.

While the first two solutions (A & B) must be implemented on the federal government level, the third (C) talks about what audience members can do as individuals.

In her conclusion, Ashley first returns to her opening illustration.

Then she summarizes her main ideas and restates her central idea.

Ashley closes her speech with a memorable play on the word *recipe.*

Editing Your Speech

Audiences will forgive a speaker many speaking errors, but one of the hardest for audiences to forgive is speaking for too long. Although you want an appreciative audience, you don't want your listeners to break into applause out of relief that you have finally finished speaking. Often when you rehearse using your preparation outline, you discover you've got too much information. You have to cut your speech. Here are a few tips to help you edit a speech that is too long.[5]

Review your specific purpose. Many speeches are too long because you are trying to accomplish too much. With your audience in mind, take a hard look at your specific purpose statement. If, for example, you want your audience to be able to list and describe five advantages of staying on standard time rather than switching to daylight savings time, you may have to decide on a less ambitious purpose and describe only three advantages—pick your best three.

Consider your audience. You may be weary of this advice, but it is critical to consider your audience. What do audience members really need to hear? Go back over your speech outline and take a hard look at it. Which parts of your message will be most and least interesting to your listeners? Cut those portions that are of least potential interest.

Simply say it. You can cut some time from your speech if you just get to the point. Consider these suggestions.

Eliminate phrases that add no meaning to your message. When political correspondent and author William Saletan criticized Senator John Kerry's use of "pointless embellishments," Saletan demonstrated how Kerry could have deleted unnecessary words and phrases from this statement:[6]

> Let me just ~~very quickly~~ say that the ~~horrifying~~ abuse of Iraqi prisoners ~~which the world has now seen~~ is ~~absolutely~~ unacceptable ~~and inexcusable~~. And the response of the administration— ~~certainly the Pentagon~~—has been slow ~~and inappropriate~~.

A speaker can keep the audience interested by cutting portions of a speech that have the least potential to stimulate interest.

[Photo: Jim Bourg/Corbis]

Here are some additional phrases you could eliminate from your speech outline:

In my opinion (just state the opinion)

And all that (meaningless)

When all is said and done (just say it)

As a matter of fact (just state the fact)

Before I begin, I'd like to say (you've already begun—just say it)

Avoid narrating your speaking technique. There's no need to say, "Here's an interesting story that I think you will like." Just tell the story. Or why say, "I'd like to now offer several facts about this matter"? Just state the facts. Yes, it's useful to provide signposts and internal summaries throughout your message—redundancy is needed in oral messages—but be careful of providing cluttering narration about the techniques you're using.

Avoid long phrases when a short one will do. Say things as succinctly as possible. Here are some examples:

Instead of saying . . .	*Say . . .*
So, for that reason	So
But at the same time	But
In today's society	Today
Due to the fact	Because
In the course of	During
In the final analysis	Finally

 Keep only the best supporting material. Your stories, illustrations, quotations, and other supporting material may be soaking up your time. Of course, stories and other types of supporting material help you make your point and maintain interest. So you don't want to reduce your speech to a bare bones outline. But do you need two stories to make your point, or will one do? Is there a shorter, more pithy quotation that will add punch and power to your prose? Scan your speech for supporting material that can be cut.

Ask a listener to help you cut. It's often easier to have someone else help you cut material. Ask a friend or roommate to listen to your speech and help you note parts that are less powerful, clear, or convincing.

Look at your introduction and conclusion. Your introduction should generally be about 10 percent of your speaking time; the same 10 percent estimate applies to your conclusion. If either your introduction or your conclusion exceeds this guideline, see if you can shorten an illustration or summarize with greater brevity.

Developing Your Delivery Outline and Speaking Notes

As you rehearse your speech, you will find that you need your preparation outline less and less. Both the structure and the content of your speech will become set in your mind. At this point, you are ready to prepare a **delivery outline**.

delivery outline

Condensed and abbreviated outline from which speaking notes are developed

THE DELIVERY OUTLINE

A delivery outline, as the name implies, is meant to give you all you will need to present your speech in the way you have planned and rehearsed. However, it should not be so detailed that it encourages you to read it rather than speak to your audience. Here are a few tips:

- **Make the outline as brief as possible, and use single words or short phrases rather than complete sentences.** That said, make certain the information is not so abbreviated that it becomes unclear. NASA actually blamed the loss of the Space Shuttle *Columbia* in part on the fact that an outline on possible wing damage was "so crammed with nested bullet points and irregular short forms that it was nearly impossible to untangle."[7]

- **Include the introduction and conclusion in much shortened form.** As we noted in Chapter 10, you may feel more comfortable if you have the first and last sentences written in full in front of you. Writing out the first sentence eliminates any fear of a mental block at the outset of your speech. And writing a complete last sentence ensures a smooth ending to your speech and a good final impression.

- **Include supporting material and signposts.** Write out statistics, direct quotations, and key signposts. Writing key signposts in full ensures that you will not grope awkwardly for a way to move from one point to the next. In the sample delivery outline that follows, notice the statistics and sources written out in the introduction, and the transitions written out at key junctures—between IB and II and between IIB and III. After you have rehearsed the speech several times, you will know where you are most likely to falter and can add or omit written transitions as needed.

- **Do not include your purpose statement in your delivery outline.**

- **Use standard outline form.** This will allow you to easily find the exact point or piece of supporting material you are seeking when you glance down at your notes.

SAMPLE DELIVERY OUTLINE

Note that the following delivery outline for Ashley's speech on produce safety does not include a statement of the purpose and that the introduction and conclusion appear in shortened and bulleted form.

As you rehearse your speech, you will probably continue to edit the delivery outline. You may decide to cut further or revise signposts. Your outline should provide

RECAP

Two Types of Speech Outlines

TYPE	PURPOSE
Preparation outline	Allows speaker to examine speech for completeness, unity, coherence, and overall effectiveness. Serves as first rehearsal outline.
Delivery outline	Serves as basis for speaking notes.

just enough information to ensure smooth delivery. It should not burden you with unnecessary notes or compel you to look down too often during the speech.

SPEAKING NOTES

Many speakers find paper difficult to handle quietly, so they transfer their delivery outlines to note cards. Note cards are small enough to hold in one hand, if necessary, and stiff enough not to rustle. Two or three note cards will give you enough space for a delivery outline; the exact number of cards you use will depend on the length of your speech. Type or print your outline neatly on one side, making sure that the letters and words are large enough to read easily. You may find it helpful to plan your note cards according to logical blocks of material, using one note card for the introduction, one or two for the body, and one for the conclusion. At any rate, plan so that you do not have to shuffle note cards in midsentence. Number the note cards to prevent a fiasco if your notes get out of order.

Instead of using an outline, you might use an alternative format for your speaking notes. For example, you could use a map, like the one in Figure 11.1. Or you could use a combination of words, pictures, and symbols, as in the notes reproduced in Figure 11.2. Whatever form your notes take, they should make sense to *you*.

A final addition to your speaking notes will be delivery cues and reminders, such as "Louder," "Pause," or "Move in front of podium." (See Figure 11.3.) You could write your delivery cues in the margins by hand, or if the entire outline is hand-written, in ink of a different color. President Gerald Ford once accidentally read the delivery cue "Look into the right camera" during an address. Clearly differentiating delivery cues from speech content will help prevent such mistakes.

confidently connecting with your audience

Use Your Well-Prepared Speaking Notes When You Rehearse

Resist the temptation to write your speech out word for word. Reading your speech will diminish your connection with your audience and may raise your anxiety. However, do use enough notes to remind you of key ideas and supporting material as you speak. And when you rehearse your speech, use the same speaking notes that you will use when you deliver your speech. Rehearsing and delivering your speech from the same notes will help enhance your confidence.

SAMPLE DELIVERY OUTLINE

INTRODUCTION

- Jillian Kohl, marathoner: eating well & staying fit
- Unexplained muscle aches, fever, & stomach cramps = something seriously wrong.
- *ABC Nightline*, October 5, 2006—after 2 weeks in hospital, Jillian sent home w/ <10% normal kidney function; ~~running~~.
- *Gannett News Service*, January 12, 2007—Jillian 1/ >200 reported illnesses, 3 deaths caused by E. coli contaminated spinach.
- *CNN* of March 7, 2007—contaminated produce responsible for > food-borne illnesses than fish, poultry, beef, & seafood combined.

For the delivery outline, Ashley does not need to write out her purpose statement, as she will not actually say it in her speech.

Ashley formats her introduction as a bullet list so that she will be able to see each part at a glance.

CENTRAL IDEA

We must take action to sharpen the U.S. govn.'s focus on produce safety.

PREVIEW

1. Why inspection cuts
2. Damaging effects
3. Solutions to make us safer

Ashley includes and labels her initial preview and signposts throughout the outline so that she can find them quickly when she glances down while speaking.

BODY

I. Programs for govn. inspection of produce =
- Severely fractured
- Under-funded

   A. Many agencies = little organization or oversight.

   1. *Congressional Quarterly*, February 8, 2007—15 different agencies responsible for regulating food safety, incl.
      - FDA
      - Centers for Disease Control & Prevention

   2. *The New York Times*, March 13, 2007—revised rules of March 12th are "unenforceable" & only recs.

   B. Insufficient $.

   1. *Chicago Daily Herald*, March 1, 2007—federal govn. failed to allot required $

   2. *Los Angles Times*, December 25, 2006—FDA would need addl. $176 million to perform protection of 4 years ago.

   3. *MSNBC*, February 23, 2007—FDA inspectors only able to inspect 1.3% imported foods.

   4. FDA lacks $ to trace contam. produce back to source—2 weeks to trace contam. spinach back to CA.

Signpost: The lack of organization or oversight of regulatory agencies & the lack of funding to inspect our produce supply jeopardize our health, damage our economy, & leave us vulnerable to terrorist attacks on our food supply.

II. System endangers all.

   A. Health @ risk.

   1. *ABC Nightline*—food-borne pathogens can cause abdominal cramps, dangerously high fever, seizure disorders, & diabetes.

Although both main ideas and subpoints are shorter than in the preparation outline, source citations are still provided in full.

The shorthand Ashley uses in her delivery outline includes both abbreviations (such as "govn." and "incl.") and symbols such as > or < for "more than" or "less than"; @ for "at"; $ to indicate a price or cost; and w/ for "with."

2. 76-year-old William Barkay
  - *Omaha World-Herald*, February 23, 2007—after consuming salmonella-contaminated peanut butter, William & Roberta hospitalized.
  - William barely recovered.
  - Roberta died 1/30/07 b/c of ineffective & unreliable food safety system.

B. Economic effects devastating.

1. ~~*Progressive Grocer Magazine*, January 2007—after outbreak, caution catastrophically affects fruit & vegetable producers.~~

1. *thecalifornian.com*, March 12, 2007—following spinach recall, leafy greens industry lost > $100 million dollars, passed on to us.

2. *Time Magazine*, February 27, 2007—imported foods = largest threat to food safety yet
  - Govn. only inspects miniscule portion of imported food = terrorist attacks & sabotage.
  - *Chicago Daily Herald*—"terrible for us to think about @ the dinner table, but quite appetizing for the terrorists seeking to do us harm."

Signpost: The collapse of our food safety system requires immediate action.

III. Steps
  - Congressional legislation
  - Re-allocation of funds
  - Personal action

A. Congress must consolidate fractured structure of system.

B. Fed. govn. must appropriately allocate funds among all agencies.

C. Visit the Web site of STOP—Safe Tables Our Priority—@ safetables.org, & use its resources:

  - Tips about how to properly wash & cook fruits & veg.

  - Advice about growing your own.

CONCLUSION

  - Jillian forced to leave grad. school & move back in w/her parents.
  - Lucky to be alive.
  - Drs. don't think she will ever fully recover.
  - After looking @ causes, effects, & solutions ass. w/ produce safety, it is clear we need to take action to stop future illnesses & deaths.
  - *CNN*, March 7, 2007—we will continue to see food-borne pathogens in our fruits & vegetables. Unless we make a concerted effort to do something about it, the safety of our produce will continue to be a recipe for disaster.

- In her editing process, Ashley cut the reference to *Progressive Grocer Magazine*, so she cuts it from her delivery outline as well. Her speaking notes will eliminate the reference altogether.

- To ensure that she quotes the *Chicago Daily Herald* accurately, Ashley writes out the quoted passage in full.

- Ashley writes out her final sentence to ensure that she can end her presentation fluently.

Figure 11.2 *Speaking notes used by Mark Twain for a lecture entitled* Roughing It, *delivered in Liverpool, England, in 1874.*

Source: Milton Meltzer, *Mark Twain Himself* (New York: Wings Books, 1960) 121.

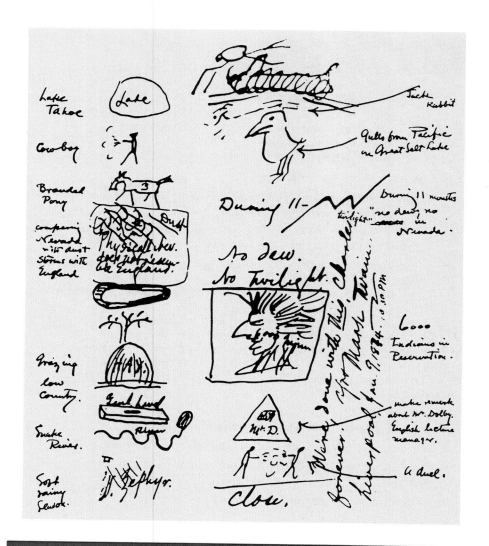

LEARNING FROM GREAT SPEAKERS

Mark Twain (1835–1910)

American humorist Mark Twain was perhaps best known in his own time as a speaker. Years on the Redpath lecture circuit and international speaking tours, as well as innumerable after-dinner speeches, provided him with the opportunity to hone his speaking skills. Some of Twain's speaking notes survive. They combine words, pictures, and symbols in a way that may seem quite strange to most of us. What is important, though, is that they made sense to *him*.

As you prepare your speaking outline and notes, don't try to cram in so much information that it is difficult to see at a glance the word or phrase you need to jog your memory. Make your speaking notes thorough enough that you feel secure knowing you have at hand the information you need to present your well-rehearsed talk, but not so comprehensive that you focus more on your notes than on your audience.

[Photo: North Wind Picture Archives]

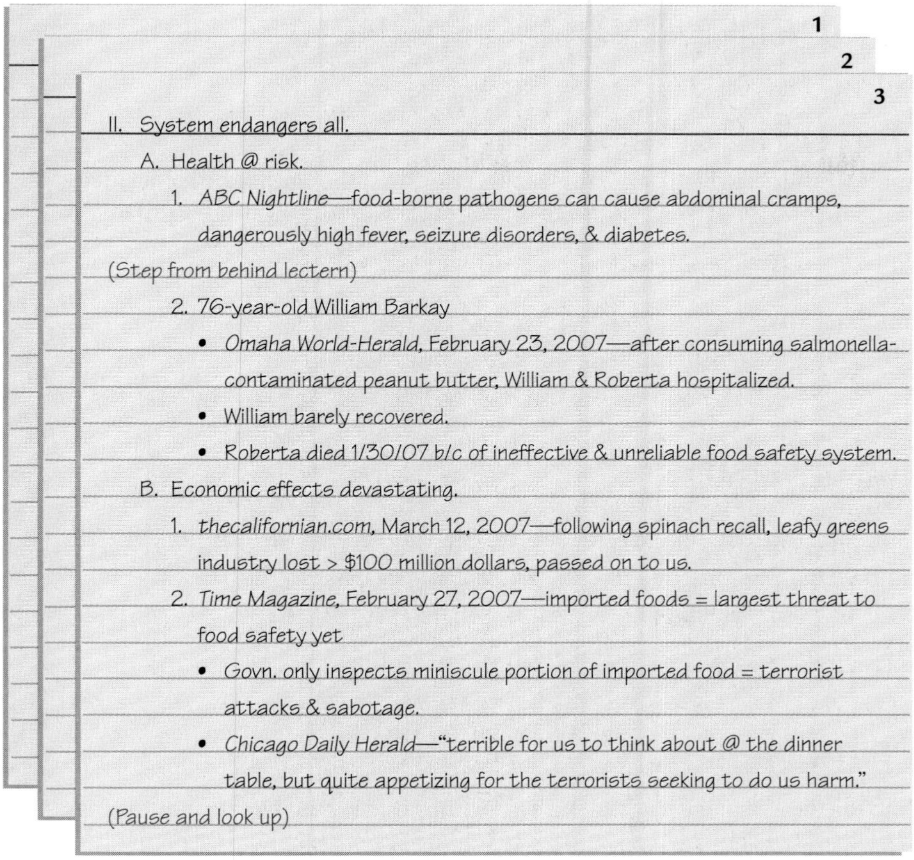

Figure 11.3 *Your speaking notes can include delivery cues and reminders.*

II. System endangers all.

  A. Health @ risk.

    1. *ABC Nightline*—food-borne pathogens can cause abdominal cramps, dangerously high fever, seizure disorders, & diabetes.

(Step from behind lectern)

    2. 76-year-old William Barkay

      • *Omaha World-Herald*, February 23, 2007—after consuming salmonella-contaminated peanut butter, William & Roberta hospitalized.

      • William barely recovered.

      • Roberta died 1/30/07 b/c of ineffective & unreliable food safety system.

  B. Economic effects devastating.

    1. *thecalifornian.com*, March 12, 2007—following spinach recall, leafy greens industry lost > $100 million dollars, passed on to us.

    2. *Time Magazine*, February 27, 2007—imported foods = largest threat to food safety yet

      • Govn. only inspects miniscule portion of imported food = terrorist attacks & sabotage.

      • *Chicago Daily Herald*—"terrible for us to think about @ the dinner table, but quite appetizing for the terrorists seeking to do us harm."

(Pause and look up)

SUMMARY

Most public speakers proceed through three stages during the speech outlining process: (1) developing a preparation outline; (2) editing the speech; and (3) developing a delivery outline and speaking notes.

A preparation outline includes your carefully organized main ideas, subpoints, and supporting material; it may also include your specific purpose, introduction, blueprint, internal previews and summaries, transitions, and conclusion. Write each of these elements in complete sentences and standard outline form. Use the preparation outline to begin rehearsing your speech.

As you rehearse, consider whether your speech falls within the time limits allotted to you. If not, you may need to edit your speech. Strategies for editing a speech that is too long include reviewing your specific purpose, considering your audience, simply saying it, keeping only the best supporting material, asking a listener to help you cut, and looking again at your introduction and conclusion.

After you have rehearsed several times from the preparation outline and edited your speech if necessary, prepare a delivery outline. This, with slight adjustments, becomes your final speaking notes. You need not include the purpose statement or central idea. Note all other ideas and materials in only as much detail as you will need when delivering the speech. You may eventually transfer the delivery outline to note cards and add delivery cues.

CONSIDERING YOUR AUDIENCE

- An instructor who requires speech outlines will generally expect standard outline form.

- An audience will remember your ideas more easily if they are divided into blocks of no more than five. If you have more than five subpoints at any level of an outline, you may want to place some of them under another point.

- Your delivery outline should not be so detailed that it encourages you to read it rather than speak to your audience.

CONSIDERING AUDIENCE DIVERSITY

- Different instructors may have different expectations for outline content and format. Be sure to understand and follow your own instructor's guidelines.

CRITICAL THINKING QUESTIONS

1. The following delivery outline for the body of a speech contains a number of errors in standard outline form. Find five of those errors.

   Title: "The College Work-Study Program"

   I. Program Eligibility

      A. Four initial requirements for work-study students

         1. Have need for employment

         2. Good grades

         3. Be a full-time student

         4. Be a citizen or permanent resident of the United States

      B. Application

         1. Submit financial-aid form to Central State

   II. Job Assignments

      A. Jobs related to your major field of study

      B. Jobs using your special interests and skills

2. Myorka thinks it is silly to worry about using correct outline form for either her preparation outline or her delivery outline. Do you agree with her? Give at least two reasons for your answer.

3. Geoff plans to deliver his speech using some hastily scrawled notes on a sheet of paper torn from his notebook. What advice would you offer him for preparing more effective and efficient speaking notes?

ETHICAL QUESTION

Can a speaker legitimately claim that a speech is extemporaneous if he or she has constructed a detailed preparation outline? Explain your answer.

Outlining Your Speech

Use this worksheet to help you prepare a delivery outline for your speech. Depending on the length of your talk, you may need more or fewer main points and subpoints. Review the sample delivery outline on pages 250–251 as a model.

Introduction

Blueprint

Central idea

Preview

Body

I.
  A.

  B.

Transition to next main idea

II.
  A.

  B.

Transition to next main idea

III.
  A.

  B.

Transition to conclusion

Conclusion

Paul Gauguin (1848–1903), *The Vision after the Sermon (Jacob Wrestling with the Angel)*, 1888. Art Resource, N.Y.

A speech is poetry: cadence, rhythm, imagery, sweep!
A speech reminds us that words, like children, have the
power to make dance the dullest beanbag of a heart.

—PEGGY NOONAN

Using Words Well: Speaker Language and Style

outline

objectives

After studying this chapter you should be able to do the following:

1. Describe three differences between oral and written language styles.

2. List and explain three ways to use words effectively.

3. Explain how to adapt your language style to diverse listeners.

4. List and define three common figures of speech.

5. List and explain seven techniques for creating drama and cadence.

6. Offer tips for using language effectively in public speeches.

People lazily scanning the classified ads and headlines of their local newspapers must have rubbed their eyes in disbelief when they read the following:[1]

FORECLOSURE LISTINGS
Entire state of NJ available. Deal directly
with owners. 5–8 months before auction.
Call 201-286-1156.

BABYSITTER
Looking for infant
to babysit in my home.
Excellent references.

NEED Plain Clothes Security. Must have
shoplifting experience. Apply between
8 A.M.–3 P.M. Mon.–Fri., at suite 207.

Unemployment Not Working, Critics Say

FAMILY CATCHES FIRE JUST IN TIME, CHIEF SAYS . . .

STORE CLERK BETTER AFTER BEING SHOT

The Richard Harder family Sunday returned
home from church just in time, Lindsey Fire
Chief Tom Overmyer said. The family . . . got
back from church about 11:15 A.M. to find
their kitchen table on fire and . . .

These ads and headlines from the "Headlines" files of comedian Jay Leno are, as he notes, funny "because they were never intended to be funny in the first place. That they're checked and rechecked by a proofreader makes them funnier still." Certainly they illustrate that using language accurately, clearly, and effectively can be a challenge, even for professional wordsmiths!

For public speakers, the task is doubly challenging. One must speak clearly and communicate ideas accurately. At the same time, it is important to present those ideas in such a way that your audience will listen to, remember, and perhaps act on what you have to say.

In this chapter we will focus on the power of language. We will suggest ways to communicate your ideas and feelings to others accurately and effectively. We will also discuss how the choice of words and word structures can help give your message a distinctive style.

 ## Oral versus Written Language Style

Your instructor has probably told you not to write your speech out word for word. The professor has said this because of the differences between speaking and writing. There are at least three major differences between oral and written language styles.

ORAL STYLE IS MORE PERSONAL THAN WRITTEN STYLE

When speaking, you can look your listeners in the eye and talk to them directly. If you see that they don't like or don't understand what you are saying, you can adjust your statements and explanations to gain greater acceptance. In other words, you and your audience can interact, something a writer and a reader cannot do. This interaction provides you, the public speaker, with personal contact and the potential to experience the warm response of your audience, an experience not available to the writer working in seclusion.

That warmth and personal contact affect your speech and your verbal style. As a speaker, you are likely to use more pronouns (*I, you*) than you would in writing. You are also more likely to address specific audience members by name.

ORAL STYLE IS LESS FORMAL THAN WRITTEN STYLE

Written communication often uses a rather formal language and structure. It should be noted that memorized speeches usually sound as if they were written because the words and phrases are longer, more complex, and more formal than those used by most speakers. Spoken communication, by contrast, is usually less formal, characterized by shorter words and phrases and less complex sentence structures. Speakers generally use many more contractions and colloquialisms than writers. Oral language is also much less varied than written language, with only fifty words accounting for almost 50 percent of what we say. Finally, spoken language is often less precise than written language. Speakers are more likely than writers to use somewhat vague quantifying terms, such as *many, much*, and *a lot*. The use of such terms may, in fact, be an asset to a speaker who wants to be thought of by his audience as "personal" and "connected." You may remember hearing President George W. Bush append the phrase "a heck of a" to such diverse people and places as Condoleezza Rice ("a heck of a secretary of state"), First Lady Laura Bush ("a heck of a person"), and post-Katrina New Orleans ("a heck of a place to bring your family"). Rutgers Professor and political-language specialist Montague Kern explains Bush's use of the phrase:

> *It's a way to be a common person, and it may be who he is.*[2]

However, there are great variations within both oral and written styles. One speech may be quite personal and informal, whereas another may have characteristics more often associated with written style. For example, George W. Bush used these simple words and short sentences in his December 13, 2000, election-victory speech:

> *Republicans want the best for our nation. And so do Democrats. Our votes may differ, but not our hopes.*[3]

Compare Bush's straightforward language and sentence structure with the more formal language and more complex sentence structures used by Al Gore to express a similar thought in his concession speech on that same evening:

> *While we yet hold and do not yield our opposing beliefs, there is a higher duty than the one we owe to political party. This is America, and we put country before party.*[4]

Regardless of whether the communication is written or oral, the personality of the speaker or writer, the subject of the discourse, the audience, and the occasion all affect the style of the language used.

Using understandable, appropriate language is essential if a speaker is to communicate effectively and meet the specific needs of an audience, such as this roomful of anxious citizens who may be forced to evacuate their town.

[Photo: Lacy Atkins/San Francisco Chronicle/Corbis]

ORAL STYLE IS MORE REPETITIVE THAN WRITTEN STYLE

When you don't understand something you are reading in a book or an article, you can stop and reread a passage, look up unfamiliar words in the dictionary, or ask someone for help. When you're listening to a speech, those opportunities usually aren't available. For this reason, an oral style is and should be more repetitive.

When you study how to organize a speech, you learn to preview main ideas in your introduction, develop your ideas in the body of the speech, and summarize these same ideas in the conclusion. You build in repetition to make sure that your listener will grasp your message. Even during the process of developing an idea, it is sometimes necessary to state it first, restate it in a different way, provide an example, and finally, summarize it.

RECAP

Oral versus Written Style

Written style	Less personal, with no immediate interaction between writer and reader
	More formal
	Less repetitive
Oral style	More personal, facilitating interaction between speaker and audience
	Less formal
	More repetitive

 ## Using Words Effectively

 As a speaker, your challenge is to use words well so that you can communicate your intended message. Ideally, language should be specific and concrete, simple, and correct. We'll discuss each of these factors.

USE SPECIFIC, CONCRETE WORDS

If you were to describe your pet snake to an audience, you would need to do more than say it is a serpent. Instead, you would want to use the most specific term possible, describing your snake as a ball python or, if you were speaking to an audience of scientists, perhaps as a *Python regius*. Specific words or terms such as *ball python* refer to individual members of a class of more general things such as *serpent* or *snake*.

Specific words are often concrete words, which appeal to one of our five senses, whereas general words are often abstract words, which refer to ideas or qualities. A linguistic theory known as *general semantics* holds that the more concrete your words, the clearer your communication. Semanticists use a "ladder of abstraction" to illustrate how something can be described in either concrete or abstract language. Figure 12.1 shows an example. The words are most abstract at the top of the ladder and become more concrete as you move down the ladder.

Specific, concrete nouns create memorable images, as in this speech delivered by a Wake Forest University student:

> *Sometimes when I sleep, I can still hear the voices of my life—night crickets, lions' mating calls, my father's advice, my friend's laughter; I can still hear the voices of Africa.*[5]

Specific, concrete verbs can be especially effective. The late Representative Barbara Jordan of Texas, whose language skills one speechwriter describes as "legendary," recognized the power of concrete verbs.[6] For example, the first draft of a passage in her 1992 Democratic National Convention keynote stated,

> *The American dream is not dead. It is injured, it is sick, but it is not dead.*

Jordan revised the line to read,

> *The American dream is not dead. It is gasping for breath, but it is not dead.*

The concrete verb phrase "gasping for breath" brings alive the image Jordan intended to create.

At the opposite end of the language spectrum from specific, concrete words is the **cliché**, the overused expression that may make listeners "start tuning out and completely miss the message."[7] A poll of 5,000 people from some 70 countries found that in one recent year the most annoying cliché was *at the end of the day*, followed by *at this moment in time*. Also on the list are *24/7, absolutely, awesome, ballpark figure*, and *I hear what you're saying*. Like most clichés, these phrases were at one time original and interesting, but their overuse has doomed them. Substitute specific, concrete words for clichés.

When searching for a specific, concrete word, you may want to consult a **thesaurus**. But in searching for an alternative word, do not feel that you have to choose the most obscure or unusual term to vary your description. Simple language can often evoke a vivid image for your listeners.

USE SIMPLE WORDS

The best language is often the simplest. Your words should be immediately understandable to your listeners. Don't try to impress them with jargon and pompous language. Instead, as linguist Paul Roberts advises,

> *Decide what you want to say and say it as vigorously as possible . . . and in plain words.*[8]

In his classic essay "Politics and the English Language," George Orwell lists rules for clear writing, including this prescription for simplicity:

Figure 12.1 *A "ladder of abstraction" is used by semanticists to show how a concept, idea, or thing can be described in either concrete or abstract terms.*

cliché
An overused expression

thesaurus
An alphabetical list of words and their synonyms

RECAP

Using Words Effectively

To hold your audience's attention, keep your language specific and concrete.

To keep your language simple, avoid a long word when a short one will do.

To use your language correctly, consider connotative as well as denotative meanings.

Never use a long word where a short one will do. If it is possible to cut a word out, always cut it out. Never use a foreign phrase, a scientific word, or a jargon word if you can think of an everyday English equivalent.[9]

Record your practice sessions. As you review the recording, listen for chances to express yourself with simpler and fewer words. Used wisely, simple words communicate with great power and precision.

USE WORDS CORRECTLY

I was listening to the car radio one day when a woman reading the news referred to someone as a suede-o-intellectual. I pondered through three traffic lights until I realized she wasn't talking about shoes, but a pseudointellectual.[10]

A public speech is not the place to demonstrate your lack of familiarity with English vocabulary and grammar. In fact, your effectiveness with your audience depends in part on your ability to use the English language correctly. If you are unsure of the way to apply a grammatical rule, seek assistance from a good English usage handbook. If you are unsure of a word's pronunciation or meaning, use a dictionary.

Perhaps the greatest challenge to using words correctly is remaining aware of connotations as well as denotations. Language operates on two levels. The **denotation** of a word is its literal meaning, the definition you find in a dictionary. For example, the denotation of the word *notorious* is "famous." The **connotation** of a word is not usually found in a dictionary, but consists of the meaning we associate with the word, based on our past experiences. *Notorious* connotes fame for some dire deed. *Notorious* and *famous* are not really interchangeable. It is just as important to consider the connotations of the words you use as it is to consider the denotations.

During times of war, politicians and members of the military consider the connotations of words carefully and deliberately. Wartime language

must . . . enable combatants and noncombatants alike to see the other side as killable, to overcome the innate queasiness over the taking of human life.[11]

For example, soldiers use the word *enemy* instead of *person*, because *enemy* has "a fear-inducing connotation."

Sometimes connotations are private. For example, the word *table* is defined denotatively as a piece of furniture consisting of a smooth, flat slab affixed on legs. But when you think of the word *table*, you may think of the old oak *table* your grandparents used to have; *table* may evoke for you an image of playing checkers with your grandmother. This is a private connotation of the word, a unique meaning based on your own past experiences. Private meanings are difficult to predict, but as a public speaker you should be aware of the possibility of triggering audience members' private connotations. This awareness is particularly important when you are discussing highly emotional or controversial topics.

denotation
The literal meaning of a word

connotation
The meaning listeners associate with a word, based on past experience

And finally, if your audience includes people whose first language is not English, to whom the nuances of connotation may not be readily apparent, it may be necessary to explain your intentions in more detail, rather than relying on word associations.

Adapt your language so that you and your listeners are on linguistic "common ground."

[Photo: Terry Ashe/AP Images]

Adapting Your Language Style to Diverse Listeners

To communicate successfully with the diverse group of listeners who comprise your audience, make sure your language is understandable, appropriate, and unbiased.

USE LANGUAGE THAT YOUR AUDIENCE CAN UNDERSTAND

Even if you and all your public-speaking classmates speak English, you probably speak many varieties of the language. Perhaps some of your classmates speak in an **ethnic vernacular**, such as "Spanglish," the combination of English and Spanish often heard near the United States–Mexico border; Cajun, with its influx of French words, frequently spoken in Louisiana; or the African American language variety sometimes known as "Ebonics." Some of you may reflect where you grew up by your **regionalisms**, words or phrases specific to one part of the country but rarely used in quite the same way in other places. Others of you may frequently use **jargon**, the specialized language of your profession or hobby.

If you give a speech to others who share your ethnic, regional, or professional background, you can communicate successfully with them using these specialized varieties of English. However, if you give a speech to an audience as diverse as the members of your public-speaking class, where do you find a linguistic "common ground"? Not only public-speaking students struggle with this question. An analysis of former President Herbert Hoover's speeches reveals that Hoover's high vocabulary level and technical jargon were "not well suited for ordinary audiences."[12]

The answer is to use standard U.S. English. **Standard U.S. English** is the language taught by schools and used in the media, business, and the government in the United States. "Standard" does not imply that standard U.S. English is inherently right and all other forms are wrong, only that it conforms to a standard that most speakers of U.S. English will readily understand—even though they may represent a variety of ethnic, regional, and professional backgrounds.

USE APPROPRIATE LANGUAGE

Shortly after the September 11, 2001, terrorist attacks, U.S. Vice President Dick Cheney made remarks in which he referred to Pakistanis as "Paks." Although he was speaking admiringly of the Pakistani people, he was chided for his use of the term. The variation *Paki* is considered a slur, and *Pak* is only slightly less offensive. Columnist William Safire remarked, "Cheney probably picked up *Paks* in his Pentagon days, but innocent intent is an excuse only once; now he is sensitized, as are we all."[13]

A speaker whose language defames any subgroup—people of particular ethnic, racial, and religious backgrounds or sexual orientations; women; people with

ethnic vernacular
A variety of English that includes words and phrases used by a specific ethnic group

regionalism
A word or phrase used uniquely by speakers in one part of a country

jargon
The specialized language of a profession

standard U.S. English
The English taught by schools and used in the media, business, and government in the United States

disabilities—or whose language might be otherwise considered offensive or risqué runs a great risk of antagonizing audience members. In fact, one study suggests that derogatory language used to describe people with disabilities adversely affects an audience's perceptions of the speaker's persuasiveness, competence, trustworthiness, and sociability.[14]

USE UNBIASED LANGUAGE

Even speakers who would never dream of using overtly offensive language may find it difficult to avoid language that more subtly stereotypes or discriminates. Sexist language falls largely into this second category.

For example, not many years ago, a singular masculine pronoun (*he, him, his*) was the accepted way to refer to a person of unspecified sex:

Everyone should bring his *book to class tomorrow.*

This usage is now considered sexist and unacceptable. Instead, you may include both a masculine and a feminine pronoun:

Everyone should bring his or her *book to class tomorrow.*

Or you may reword the sentence so that it is plural and thus gender neutral:

All students should bring their *books to class tomorrow.*

Also now considered sexist is the use of a masculine noun to refer generically to all people. The editors of *The American Heritage Dictionary of the English Language*, Fourth Edition, consulted a usage panel of 200 writers and scholars on such questions as whether the word *man* was acceptable as meaning "human" in some instances.[15] Only 58 percent of the women on the panel found such usage appropriate. To put it another way: If you were speaking to an audience of these distinguished women, you would offend 42 percent of them by using a phrase such as *modern man*. Although the word *man* is the primary offender, you should also monitor your use of such masculine nouns as *waiter, chairman, fireman,* and *Congressman*. Instead choose such gender-neutral alternatives as *server, chair, firefighter,* and *member of Congress*.

In addition to avoiding masculine nouns and pronouns to refer to all people, avoid sexist language that patronizes or stereotypes people:

Sexist	Unbiased
Barbara Bush, daughter of President George W. Bush and Laura, graduated from Yale University.	Barbara Bush, daughter of President and Mrs. Bush, graduated from Yale University.
	or
	Barbara Bush, daughter of George W. and Laura Bush, graduated from Yale University.
The policeman is an underpaid professional who risks his life daily.	Police are underpaid professionals who risk their lives daily.
The male nurse took good care of his patients. (*Note:* The phrase "male nurse" implies that nursing is a typically female profession. The pronoun *his* clarifies the sex of the nurse.)	The nurse took good care of his patients.

As noted earlier, it is not always easy to avoid biased language. Even with good intentions and deliberate forethought, you can find yourself at times caught in a dou-

To communicate successfully with diverse listeners, use language your audience can understand.

To avoid offending your audience, use appropriate language.

To communicate sensitivity to diverse subgroups, use unbiased language.

ble bind. For example, suppose that Dr. Pierce is a young black female M.D. If you don't mention her age, race, and gender when you refer to her, you may reinforce your listeners' stereotypical image of a physician as middle-aged, white, and male. But if you *do* mention these factors, you may be suspected of implying that Dr. Pierce's achievement is unusual. There is no easy answer to this dilemma or others like it. You will have to consider your audience, purpose, and the occasion in deciding how best to identify Dr. Pierce.

As women and members of racial, ethnic, and other minorities have become increasingly visible in such professions as medicine, law, engineering, and politics, the public has grown to expect unbiased, inclusive language from news commentators, teachers, textbooks, and magazines—and from public speakers. Language that does not reflect these changes will disrupt your ability to communicate your message to your audience, which may well include members of the minority group to which you are referring.

confidently
connecting
with your
audience

Use Words to Manage Your Anxiety

Even as you work on polishing your language for your listeners, give yourself an affirming mental pep talk. If you find your anxiety level increasing, remind yourself that you are knowledgeable and prepared to connect with your audience. Think positively, and translate that positive thinking into words of affirmation for yourself.

Crafting Memorable Word Structures

The President of the United States is scheduled to make an important speech in your hometown. You attend the speech and find his thirty-minute presentation both interesting and informative. In the evening, you turn on the news to see how the networks cover his address. All three major networks excerpt the same ten-second portion of his speech. Why? What makes certain portions of a speech quotable or memorable? Former presidential speechwriter Peggy Noonan has said,

> *Great speeches have always had great soundbites. . . . They sum up a point, or make a point in language that is pithy or profound.*[16]

In other words, memorable speeches are stylistically distinctive. They create arresting images. And they have what a marketing-communication specialist has termed "ear appeal":

> *"Ear appeal" phrases can be like the haunting songs of a musical that the members of the audience find themselves humming on the way home. Even if people want to forget them, they can't.*[17]

Earlier in this chapter, we discussed the importance of using words that are concrete, unbiased, vivid, simple, and correct. In this section, we turn our attention to groups of words—phrases and sentences—that create the drama, figurative images, and cadences needed to make a speech memorable by giving it both "eye and ear appeal."[18]

CREATING FIGURATIVE IMAGES

One way to make your message memorable is to use figures of speech to create arresting images. A **figure of speech** deviates from the ordinary, expected meanings of words, to make a description or comparison unique, vivid, and memorable. Common figures of speech include metaphors, similes, and personification.

METAPHORS AND SIMILES A **metaphor** is an implied comparison of two things that are similar in some vital way. Speaking at the July 2, 2005, Live 8 Concert, anti-apartheid Nobel laureate Nelson Mandela used a prison metaphor to describe the plight of people living in poverty:

> Millions of people in the world's poorest countries remain imprisoned, enslaved, and in chains. They are trapped in the prison of poverty.[19]

This metaphor was particularly appropriate and poignant for Mandela, himself a political prisoner for 27 years.

In a March 2007 speech commemorating the Selma, Alabama, voting rights march of 1965, Barack Obama metaphorically compared the marchers to giants:

> We're in the presence today of giants whose shoulders we stand on, people who battled, not just on behalf of African Americans but on behalf of all America. . . .[20]

And Obama followed his metaphor with a simile:

> Like Moses, they challenged Pharaoh. . . .

Whereas a metaphor is an implied comparison, a **simile** is a more direct comparison that includes the word *like* or *as*.

Speakers often turn to metaphor and simile in times that are especially momentous or overwhelming—times when, as one speaker has said, "the ordinary diction of our lives finds itself unequal to a challenge."[21] In the hours and days after the September 11, 2001, terrorist attacks on the United States, various speakers used such metaphorical phrases as "one more circle of Dante's hell"; "nuclear winter"; and "the crater of a volcano" to describe the site of the destroyed World Trade Centers in New York.[22] Such language is often categorized as **crisis rhetoric**.

PERSONIFICATION **Personification** is the attribution of human qualities to inanimate things or ideas. Franklin Roosevelt personified nature as a generous living provider in this line from his first inaugural address:

> Nature still offers her bounty and human efforts have multiplied it. Plenty is at our doorstep.[23]

CREATING DRAMA

Another way to make phrases and sentences memorable is to use the potential of such structures to create drama in your speech—to keep the audience in suspense or to catch them slightly off guard by saying something in a way that differs from the way they expected you to say it.

➤ **Use a short sentence to express a vitally important thought.** We have already talked about the value of using short, simple words. Short, simple sentences can have much the same power. Columnist George F. Will pointed out that the most eloquent sentence in Lincoln's memorable second inaugural address is just four words long:[24]

> And the war came.

figure of speech
Language that deviates from the ordinary, expected meaning of words to make a description or comparison unique, vivid, and memorable

metaphor
An implied comparison between two things or concepts

simile
A comparison between two things that uses the word *like* or *as*

crisis rhetoric
Language used by speakers during momentous or overwhelming times

personification
The attribution of human qualities to inanimate things or ideas

Other strategies for achieving drama in your speech include three stylistic devices: omission, inversion, and suspension.

➤ **Use omission: Leave out a word or phrase that the audience expects to hear.** When telegrams were a more common means of communication, senders tried to use as few words as possible because they were charged by the word, and the more they could leave out, the cheaper the telegram was. But, of course, the words you leave out must be understood by your listeners or readers. For example, a captain of a World War II Navy destroyer used **omission** to inform headquarters of his successful efforts at sighting and sinking an enemy submarine. He spared all details when he cabled back to headquarters: "Sighted sub—sank same." Using as few words as possible, he communicated his message in a memorable way. About 2,000 years earlier, another military commander informed his superiors in Rome of his conquest of Gaul with the economical message: "I came, I saw, I conquered." That commander was Julius Caesar.

➤ **Use inversion: Reverse the normal word order of a phrase or sentence.** John F. Kennedy used **inversion** when he changed the usual subject-verb-object sentence pattern to object-subject-verb in this brief declaration from his inaugural speech:

This much we pledge. . . .[25]

More recently, George W. Bush inverted the last two words of this statement in his 2003 eulogy for the seven astronauts of the Space Shuttle *Columbia*:

To leave behind Earth and air and gravity . . . was a dream fulfilled.[26]

➤ **Use suspension: Place a key word or phrase at the end of a sentence, rather than at the beginning.** When you read a mystery novel, you are held in suspense until you reach the end and learn "who done it." The stylistic technique of verbal **suspension** does something similar. In his first speech as leader of Britain's Labor Party, Gordon Brown employed suspension to emphasize the key phrase "challenge of change":

For families wanting their sons and daughters to get the chance of college or university, we will meet the challenge of change.[27]

Advertisers use the technique of suspension frequently. A few years ago, the Coca-Cola Company used suspension as the cornerstone of its worldwide advertising campaign. Rather than saying, "Coke goes better with everything," the copywriter decided to stylize the message by making *Coke* the last word in the sentence. The slogan became "Things go better with Coke." Again, the stylized version was more memorable because it used language in an unexpected way.

CREATING CADENCE

Even very small children can memorize nursery rhymes and commercial jingles with relative ease. As we grow older, we may make up rhythms and rhymes to help us remember such facts as "Thirty days hath September/April, June, and November" and "Red sky at night/A sailor's delight." Why? Rhythms are memorable. The public speaker can take advantage of language rhythms, not by speaking in singsong patterns, but by using such stylistic devices as repetition, parallelism, antithesis, and alliteration.

REPETITION **Repetition** of a key word or phrase gives rhythm and power to your message and makes it memorable. In a speech honoring the Tuskegee Airmen and addressing issues of race in the modern U.S. military, former Deputy Secretary of Defense Rudy de Leon claimed that recruitment of minorities is only one part of the task facing the military:

omission
Leaving out a word or phrase the listener expects to hear

inversion
Reversing the normal word order of a phrase or sentence

suspension
Withholding a key word or phrase until the end of a sentence

repetition
Use of a key word or phrase more than once for emphasis

In her brief convocation address to a grieving Virginia Tech community in April 2007, poet and Virginia Tech Professor Nikki Giovanni repeated no less than five times the ringing affirmation, "We are Virginia Tech." [29]

[Photo: Steve Helber/AP Images]

parallelism
Use of the same grammatical pattern for two or more phrases, clauses, or sentences

antithesis
Opposition, such as that used in two-part sentences in which the second part contrasts in meaning with the first

Our job is not finished if we fail to recognize that each generation has its own unique problems and perceptions when it comes to race and ethnicity.

We can ensure our rules and regulations are clear and fair.

But our job is not finished if people believe that those rules and regulations are not being enforced fairly.

Our job is not finished if the rules and regulations work for those in uniform, but they do not reach people in our civilian workforce. [emphasis added] [28]

The repeated mantra, "our job is not finished," rings in one's mind long after hearing or reading the passage.

PARALLELISM Whereas *repetition* refers to using identical words, **parallelism** refers to using different words but identical grammatical patterns. When he delivered the Phi Beta Kappa oration at Harvard in 1837, Ralph Waldo Emerson cast these simple expressions in parallel structures:

> *We will walk on our own feet; we will work with our own hands; we will speak our own minds.* [30]

The clauses "we will walk," "we will work," and "we will speak" include different words but follow the same grammatical pattern of *pronoun + future tense verb.*

George W. Bush employed parallel sentences to describe America's strength in the months and years following September 11, 2001:

> *In grief, we have found the grace to go on. In challenge, we rediscovered the courage and daring of a free people. In victory, we have shown the noble aims and good heart of America.* [31]

Bush's three parallel *prepositional phrase + subject + verb + object* structures add memorable cadence to his statement.

ANTITHESIS The word *antithesis* means "opposition." In language style, a sentence that uses **antithesis** has two parts with parallel structures, but contrasting meanings.

Speakers have long realized the dramatic potential of antithesis. In his first inaugural address, Franklin Roosevelt declared,

Our true destiny is not to be ministered unto but to minister to ourselves and to our fellow men.[32]

Both in meaning and in structure, Roosevelt's words foreshadowed the more famous remark of John F. Kennedy nearly thirty years later:

Ask not what your country can do for you; ask what you can do for your country.[33]

We will examine Kennedy's statement in greater detail later in this chapter.

Antithesis is not restricted to politicians. When William Faulkner accepted the Nobel Prize for literature in 1950, he spoke the now famous antithetical phrase,

I believe that man will not merely endure: he will prevail.[34]

An antithetical statement is a good way to end a speech. The cadence it creates will make the statement memorable.

ALLITERATION **Alliteration** is the repetition of a consonant sound (usually an initial consonant) several times in a phrase, clause, or sentence. Alliteration adds cadence to a thought. Consider these examples:

Alliterative Phrase	Speaker	Occasion
discipline and direction	Franklin Roosevelt	first inaugural address[35]
confidence and courage	Franklin Roosevelt	first fireside chat[36]
disaster and disappointment	Winston Churchill	speech urging British resistance[37]
virility, valour, and civic virtue	Winston Churchill	speech to U.S. Congress[38]
conviction, not calculation	Dick Cheney	campaign speech[39]

Used sparingly, alliteration can add cadence to your rhetoric.

LEARNING FROM GREAT SPEAKERS

John F. Kennedy (1917–1963)

The inaugural address of John F. Kennedy, the 35th president of the United States, is one of the great speeches of history, in large part because of its memorable style. Kennedy had told his speechwriter Ted Sorenson to study Lincoln's Gettysburg Address and discover the secrets of its success.[40] Sorenson discovered that Lincoln had relied heavily on short words; as a result, 71 percent of Kennedy's speech was composed of monosyllabic words. Kennedy also copied some of the sentence patterns Lincoln had used. The most famous stylistic device of Kennedy's speech, however, the antithetical "Ask not," was Kennedy's own.

You don't need a professional speechwriter to make your speeches memorable. To polish your prose, consider using short sentences or the techniques of omission, inversion or suspension. Use such devices as repetition, parallelism, antithesis, and alliteration to create a memorable cadence. You need not overdo it. Just one or two well-polished phrases in your talk can be like just the right notes in a song.

[Photo: AP Images]

alliteration
The repetition of a consonant sound (usually the first consonant) several times in a phrase, clause, or sentence

RECAP

Crafting Memorable Word Structures

WORD STRUCTURES WITH FIGURATIVE IMAGERY

Metaphor	Makes an implied comparison.
Simile	Compares by using the word *like* or *as*.
Personification	Attributes human qualities to inanimate things or ideas.

WORD STRUCTURES WITH DRAMA

Short sentence	Emphasizes an important idea by stating it in a short sentence.
Omission	Boils an idea down to its essence by leaving out understood words.
Inversion	Reverses the expected order of words and phrases.
Suspension	Places a key word at the end of a phrase or sentence.

WORD STRUCTURES WITH CADENCE

Repetition	Repeats a key word or phrase several times for emphasis.
Parallelism	Uses the same grammatical pattern.
Antithesis	Uses parallel structures but opposing meanings in two parts of a sentence.
Alliteration	Uses the same consonant sound several times in a phrase.

ANALYZING AN EXAMPLE OF MEMORABLE WORD STRUCTURE

We'd like to illustrate all techniques for creating drama and cadence with one final example.[41] If you asked almost anyone for the most quoted line from John F. Kennedy's speeches, that quote would probably be "Ask not what your country can do for you; ask what you can do for your country," from his inaugural address. Besides expressing a noble thought, a prime reason this line is so quotable is that it uses all stylistic techniques.

"Ask not . . ." is an example of omission. The subject, *you*, is not stated. "Ask not" is also an example of inversion. In casual everyday conversation, we would usually say "do not ask" rather than "ask not." The inversion makes the opening powerful and attention-grabbing.

The sentence also employs the technique of suspension. The key message of the phrase "ask what you can do for your country," is suspended, or delayed, until the end of the sentence. If the sentence structure had been reversed, the impact would not have been as dramatic. Consider: "Ask what you can do for your country rather than what your country can do for you."

Kennedy uses parallelism and antithesis. The sentence is made up of two clauses with parallel construction, one in opposition to the other.

He also uses the technique of repetition. He uses a form of the word *you* four times in a sentence of seventeen words. In fact, he uses only eight different words in his seventeen-word sentence. Just one word in the entire sentence, *not*, occurs only once.

Finally, Kennedy adds alliteration to the sentence with the words *ask, can,* and *country*. The alliterative *k* sound is repeated at more or less even intervals.

Although the passage we have analyzed does not include any figurative images, the speech from which it comes does have some memorable figurative language, most notably metaphors such as "chains of poverty," "beachhead of cooperation," and "jungle of suspicion." Kennedy used figurative imagery, drama, and cadence to give his inaugural address "eye and ear appeal" and make it memorable—not just to those who heard it initially, but also to those of us who hear, read, and study it more than 45 years later.

Tips for Using Language Effectively

Having reviewed ways to add style and interest to the language of your speech, we must now consider how best to put those techniques into practice.

- **Use distinctive stylistic devices sparingly.** Even though we have made great claims for the value of style, do not overdo it. Including too much highly stylized language can put the focus on your language rather than on your content.

- **Use stylistic devices at specific points in your speech.** Save your use of stylistic devices for times during your speech when you want your audience to remember your key ideas or when you wish to capture their attention. Some kitchen mixers have a "burst of power" switch to help churn through difficult mixing chores with extra force. Think of the stylistic devices we have reviewed as opportunities to provide a burst of power to your ideas. Use them in your opening sentences, statements of key ideas, and conclusion.

- **Short words are more forceful than long ones.** Think of those monosyllabic commands—Sit! March! Stop! When a technical term is unusual or cumbersome, find a way to describe the concept with another word, or use a simile or a metaphor. To talk about the process of *floccinaucinihilipilification* (the action or habit of estimating something as worthless) may make an interesting speech, but your audience will probably not remember the word itself.

- **Use stylistic devices to economize.** When sentences become too long or complex, see if you can recast them with antithesis or suspension. Also remember the possibility of omission.

SUMMARY

Carefully select and use words to give your ideas maximum impact. First, understand the differences between the way people talk and the way they write. In general, oral style is more personal, less formal, and more repetitive than written style.

Words should be specific and concrete, simple, and used correctly. Understand the connotations of words as well as their denotations.

It is also important to adapt your language style to diverse listeners. Use language your listeners can understand, use appropriate language to avoid offending them, and use unbiased language to communicate in a sensitive way to subgroups.

You can create arresting images through such figures of speech as metaphors, similes, and personification. You can create drama and cadence with word structures such as short sentences, omission, inversion, suspension, repetition, parallelism, antithesis, and alliteration.

Effective speakers take great care in wording their speeches. Well-chosen words and sentence structures can help you gain and maintain the attention of your audience, and can help your audience understand your message and remember what you say.

CONSIDERING YOUR AUDIENCE

- Specific, concrete, simple language can evoke clear images for listeners.

- Your effectiveness with your audience depends in part on your ability to use the English language correctly.

- As a public speaker you should be aware of the possibility of triggering audience members' private connotations.

- Carefully crafted phrases and sentences can create the drama, figurative images, and cadences needed to give a speech "eye and ear appeal" to an audience.

- Save your use of stylistic devices for times during your speech when you want your audience to remember your key ideas or when you wish to capture listeners' attention.

CONSIDERING AUDIENCE DIVERSITY

- If your audience includes people who speak English as a second language, to whom the nuances of connotation may not be readily apparent, it may be necessary to explain your intentions in more detail, rather than relying on word associations.

- To communicate successfully with diverse listeners, use language your audience can understand.

- To avoid offending your diverse audience, use appropriate language.

CRITICAL THINKING QUESTIONS

1. Toni practices her speech for you and asks for advice on polishing the speech, including polishing the style of her language. Offer Toni at least three general suggestions for using language effectively.

2. Not long ago, a reader wrote in a letter to "Dear Abby":

   . . . a woman does not have a maiden name until she takes a married name. What she has is a surname. "Maiden" refers to a former name that was given up in favor of her husband's name. Women who retain their own names (or their surnames) after marriage do not have a maiden name.

   This may sound picky to some, but for women (and their husbands) who choose this option, the term maiden name *is offensive.*[42]

   Analyze the reader's point in light of the discussion of sexist language in this chapter. Do you agree or disagree that the term *maiden name* is sexist? Why or why not?

3. The following are memorable metaphors from historical speeches:[43]

   I have but one lamp by which my feet are guided, and that is the lamp of experience.

   an iron curtain

   snake pit of racial hatred

   Speak softly and carry a big stick.

   First, explain what each metaphor means. Now express the same idea in ordinary language. What is gained or lost by doing so?

ETHICAL QUESTION

A high school salutatorian, who had been raped when she was a 14-year-old sophomore, wanted to mention the experience in her salutatory speech, thanking the people who had helped her, and assuring her classmates that they could overcome even the most devastating experiences in life.[44] The principal, however, edited her speech, changing the word *rape* to the phrase "a terrible thing." The student claimed she needed to use the concrete word to emphasize confronting such experiences head-on. The principal said he was simply suggesting ways to make the language of the speech more appropriate. Discuss the ethical implications of this debate over language style. Did the student have the right to call the attack "rape"? Or was the principal correct in censoring the term, out of consideration for the occasion and audience?

Conducting a "Language Style Audit" of Your Speech

To help make your speech interesting and memorable, do a "language style audit." Using either your preparation outline or your speaking notes, try to find one or more passages that you can edit by applying specific stylistic techniques to add vividness and interest. Use the following checklist to help you revise your words.

USE WORDS EFFECTIVELY

- Are you using **concrete** words? (See pages 260–261 for tips on making your words concrete.)
- Are you using **simple** words? (Be on the lookout for unnecessarily long or complex words; find shorter, simpler words. (See pages 261–262 for recommendations for making your words simple.)
- Are you using **correct** words? Double-check your grammar and word usage. (See pages 262–263 for reminders about using words correctly.)

USE WORDS TO ADD INTEREST

- Can you find a place to use an appropriate **metaphor** or **simile**? (See page 266 for tips on using metaphors and similes.)
- Can you find a way to make a long, complex sentence brief and to the point? (See pages 266–267 for examples of short sentences and **omission**.)
- Can you find a way to use **inversion** or **suspension**? (See page 267 for examples and tips on using these stylistic techniques.)
- Can you **repeat** key words or phrases, or cast them as **parallel** grammatical structures? (See pages 267–268.)
- Can you find a place in your speech to use **antithesis**? (See pages 268–269.)
- Can you find a passage in which you might use **alliteration**? (Use this technique sparingly. See page 269.)

Thinker with a Rose, 1999. Jeremy Hauser (20th-Century American). Oil on canvas. Private collection. © Jeremy Hauser/SuperStock

Speak the speech, I pray you, as I pronounced it to you, trippingly on the tongue.

—WILLIAM SHAKESPEARE

Delivering Your Speech

outline

objectives

After studying this chapter you should be able to do the following:

1. Identify three reasons delivery is important to a public speaker.

2. Identify and describe four types of delivery.

3. Identify and illustrate physical characteristics of effective delivery.

4. Describe the steps to follow when you rehearse your speech.

5. List four suggestions for enhancing the final delivery of your speech.

hat's more important: what you say or how you say it? Delivery has long been considered an important part of public speaking. But is the delivery of your speech more important than the content of your message? Since ancient Greece, people have argued about the role delivery plays in public speaking.

More than 2,300 years ago, some thinkers held that delivery was not an "elevated" topic of study. In his classic treatise *The Rhetoric,* written in 333 B.C., Aristotle claimed that "the battle should be fought out on the facts of the case alone; and therefore everything outside the direct proof is really superfluous." Writing in the first century, Quintilian, Roman rhetorician and author of the first book on speech training, acknowledged the importance of delivery when he said that the beginning speaker should strive for an "extempore," or conversational, delivery style. His countryman, the great orator Cicero, claimed that without effective delivery, "a speaker of the highest mental capacity can be held in no esteem, whereas one of moderate abilities, with this qualification, may surpass even those of the highest talent." Sixteen centuries later, the elocution movement carried the emphasis on delivery to an extreme. For elocutionists, speech training consisted largely of techniques and exercises for improving posture, movement, and vocal quality.[1]

Today, communication teachers believe that both content and delivery contribute to speaking effectiveness. One survey suggested that "developing effective delivery" is a primary goal of most speech teachers.[2] Considerable research supports the claim that delivery plays an important role in influencing how audiences react to a speaker and his or her message. It is your audience who will determine whether you are successful. Delivery counts.

Although some courses on public speaking are offered in various countries throughout the world, most of the formal instruction on how to deliver a speech is offered in the United States. Our advice about speech delivery, therefore, is closely related to the discipline of communication here in the United States. It's not possible for us to provide a comprehensive compendium of each cultural expectation you may face as you give speeches in a variety of educational and professional settings, but throughout this chapter we will try to sample conventions and preferences of other cultures as we discuss speech delivery.

The Power of Speech Delivery

The way you hold your notes, your gestures and stance, and your impatient adjustment of your glasses all contribute to the overall effect of your speech. **Nonverbal communication** is communication other than through written or spoken language that creates meaning for someone. Nonverbal factors such as your eye contact, posture, vocal quality, and facial expression play a major role in the communication process. As much as 65 percent of the social meaning of messages is based on nonverbal expression.[3] Why does your delivery hold such power to affect how your audience will receive your message? One reason is that lis-

nonverbal communication
Communication other than written or spoken language that creates meaning

teners expect a good speaker to provide good delivery. Your unspoken message is also how you express your feelings and emotions to an audience. And ultimately, an audience believes what it *sees* more than what you *say*.

LISTENERS EXPECT EFFECTIVE DELIVERY

In a public-speaking situation, nonverbal elements have an important influence on the audience's perceptions about a speaker's effectiveness. Communication researcher Judee Burgoon and her colleagues have developed a theory called **nonverbal expectancy theory**. The essence of the theory is this: People have certain expectations as to how you should communicate.[4] If you don't behave as people think you should, your listeners will feel that you have violated their expectations. The theory predicts that if a listener expects you to have effective delivery, and your delivery is poor, you will lose credibility. There is evidence that although many speakers do not deliver speeches effectively, audiences nevertheless expect a good speech to be well-delivered.

As we have also emphasized, audience members with different cultural backgrounds will hold different assumptions about how a speech should be presented. In our discussion of delivery, we note how the cultural and ethnic background of your audience affects the delivery style your listeners prefer.

More than 100 years ago, speakers were taught to deliver orations using a more formal style of speaking than most people prefer today. In old newsreels of speakers during the early part of the twentieth century, their gestures and movement look stilted and unnatural, because they were taught to use dramatic, planned gestures. What do most people consider effective delivery today? Effective speech delivery for most North American listeners has been described as "platform conversation." Effective delivery today includes having good eye contact with your listeners. It includes using appropriate gestures, just as you do in your interpersonal conversations with your friends (but, of course, avoiding distracting mannerisms such as jingling change in your pockets or unconsciously playing with your hair). Effective delivery also means your voice has a natural, conversational tone, varied inflection (rather than a droning monotone), and an intensity that communicates that you're interested in your listeners.

Of course, different audiences prefer different styles of delivery; there is not one "ideal" style of delivery or set of prescribed gestures that is appropriate for all audiences. If you are speaking to an audience of a thousand people, using a microphone to reach the back of the auditorium, your listeners may expect a more formal delivery style. But your public-speaking class members would probably find it odd if you spoke to them using a formal oratorical style that resembles the way a politician would have addressed a political rally in 1910.

LISTENERS MAKE EMOTIONAL CONNECTIONS WITH YOU THROUGH DELIVERY

Nonverbal behavior is particularly important in communicating feelings, emotions, attitudes, likes, and dislikes to an audience. One researcher found that we communicate as little as 7 percent of the emotional impact of a message by the words we use.[5] About 38 percent hinges on such qualities of voice as inflection, intensity, or loudness, and 55 percent hinges on our facial expressions. Generalizing from these findings, we may say that we communicate approximately 93 percent of emotional meaning nonverbally. Although some scholars question whether these findings can be applied to all communication settings, the research does suggest that the manner of delivery provides important information about a speaker's feelings and emotions.[6] Being aware of your audience's expectations can help you determine the amount of emotional expression you exhibit to your listeners.

nonverbal expectancy theory
A communication theory that suggests that if listeners' expectations about how communication should be expressed are violated, listeners will feel less favorable toward the communicator of the message

Audience members respond to a speaker's nonverbal behavior as strongly as they do to the verbal message. A good speaker uses facial expression and body language to connect with the audience emotionally.

[Photo: SuperStock]

Another reason to pay attention to how you communicate emotions when delivering a speech is that emotions are "contagious." **Emotional contagion theory** suggests that people tend to "catch" the emotions of others.[7] If you want your listeners to feel a certain emotion, then it's important for you to express that emotion yourself. Have you ever noticed that when you watch a movie in a crowded movie theatre where others are laughing, you're more likely to laugh too? Producers of TV situation comedies use a laugh track or record the laughter of a live audience to enhance the emotional reactions of home viewers; these producers know that emotions are contagious.

Your delivery enhances the overall feelings that listeners have toward you and your speech. One study found that when a speaker's delivery was effective, the audience felt greater pleasure and had a more positive emotional response than when the same speaker had poor delivery.[8] In addition to these stronger emotional responses, listeners seemed to understand speakers better and to believe them more when their delivery was good. Clearly, if you want your audience to respond positively to both you and your message, it pays to polish your delivery.

LISTENERS BELIEVE WHAT THEY SEE

"I'm very glad to speak with you tonight," drones the speaker in a monotone, eyes glued to his notes. His audience probably does not believe him. When our nonverbal delivery contradicts what we say, people generally believe the nonverbal message. In this case, the speaker is communicating that he's *not* glad to be talking to this audience.

We usually believe nonverbal messages because they are more difficult to fake. Although we can monitor certain parts of our nonverbal behavior, it is difficult to control all of it consciously. Research suggests that a person trying to deceive someone may speak with a higher vocal pitch, at a slower rate, and with more pronunciation mistakes than normal.[9] Blushing, sweating, and changed breathing patterns also often belie our stated meaning. As the saying goes, "What you do speaks so loud, I can't hear what you say."

 Methods of Delivery

The style of delivery you choose will influence your nonverbal behaviors. There are four basic methods of delivery from which a speaker can choose: manuscript speaking, memorized speaking, impromptu speaking, and extemporaneous speaking. Let's consider each in some detail.

MANUSCRIPT SPEAKING

You have a speech to present and are afraid you will forget what you have prepared to say. So you write your speech and then read it to your audience.

Speech teachers frown on this approach, particularly for public-speaking students. Reading is usually a poor way to deliver a speech. Although it may provide some insurance against forgetting the speech, **manuscript speaking** is rarely done

emotional contagion theory
A theory suggesting that people tend to "catch" the emotions of others

manuscript speaking
Reading a speech from a written text

well enough to be interesting. You have probably attended a lecture that was read and wondered, "Why doesn't he just make a copy of the speech for everyone in the audience rather than reading it to us?"

However, some speeches should be read. One advantage of reading from a manuscript is that you can choose words very carefully when dealing with a sensitive and critical issue. The president of the United States, for example, often finds it useful to have his remarks carefully scripted. There are times, however, when it is impossible to have a manuscript speech at hand.

When possible, during times of crisis, statements to the press by government, education, or business leaders should be carefully crafted rather than tossed off casually. An inaccurate or misspoken statement could have serious consequences.

On those occasions when you do need to use a manuscript, here are several tips to help you deliver your message effectively:[10]

- Type your speech in short, easy-to scan phrases.
- Use only the upper two-thirds of the paper for your manuscript.
- Establish eye contact with listeners; don't look over their heads.
- Make eye contact at the ends of sentences.
- Use your normal, natural speed of delivery.
- If you're afraid you'll lose your place, unobtrusively use your index finger to keep your place in the manuscript.
- Speak with natural vocal variation; vary your pitch, inflection, and rhythm so that you don't sound like you're reading.
- Practice with your manuscript.
- Use appropriate and natural gestures and movement.

MEMORIZED SPEAKING

"All right," you think, "since reading a speech is hard to pull off, I'll write my speech out word for word and then memorize it." You're pretty sure that no one will be able to tell, because you won't be using notes. **Memorized speaking** also has the advantage of allowing you to have maximum eye contact with the audience. But the key differences between speaking and writing are evident in a memorized speech, just as they can be heard in a manuscript speech. Most memorized speeches *sound* stiff, stilted, and overrehearsed. You also run the risk of forgetting parts of your speech and awkwardly searching for words in front of your audience. And you won't be able to make on-the-spot adaptations to your listeners if your speech is memorized. For these reasons, speech teachers do not encourage their students to memorize speeches for class presentation.

If you are accepting an award, introducing a speaker, making announcements, or delivering other brief remarks, however, a memorized delivery style is sometimes acceptable. But as with manuscript speaking, you must take care to make your presentation sound lively and interesting.

IMPROMPTU SPEAKING

You have undoubtedly already delivered many impromptu presentations. Your response to a question posed by a teacher in class, and an unrehearsed rebuttal to a comment made by a colleague during a meeting, are examples of impromptu presentations. The impromptu method is often described as "thinking on your feet" or "speaking off the cuff." The advantage of **impromptu speaking** is that you can speak informally, maintaining direct eye contact with the audience. But unless a speaker is extremely talented or has learned and practiced the techniques of

memorized speaking
Delivering a speech word for word from memory without using notes

impromptu speaking
Delivering a speech without advance preparation

impromptu speaking, the speech itself will be unimpressive. An impromptu speech usually lacks logical organization and thorough research. There are times, of course, when you may be called on to speak without advance warning or to improvise when something goes awry in your efforts to deliver your planned message. This was the case when former President Clinton was delivering his first State of the Union address in 1993 and the teleprompter scrolled the wrong text of his speech for seven minutes. What did he do as millions of people watched on television? He kept going. Drawing on his years of speaking experience, he continued to speak; no one watching knew about the error until afterward.

If you know you will be giving a speech, prepare and rehearse it. Don't just make mental notes or assume that you will find the words when you need it. It was Mark Twain who said, "A good impromptu speech takes about three weeks to prepare."

Reverend Jesse Jackson is known for his skill as an impromptu speaker. It's been reported that he got a *D* in his preaching class because he refused to write his sermons out word for word as his professor requested. He was able to deliver impromptu orations that skillfully and powerfully moved listeners to respond to his message. Once, knowing he was to speak next, after one of Jackson's charismatically delivered speeches, Martin Luther King Jr. allegedly developed a sudden case of laryngitis.[11] The Reverend Jackson certainly has speaking talent, but he also uses principles and skills that you can use to enhance your impromptu speaking ability. When you are called on to deliver an improvised or impromptu speech, the following guidelines can help ease you through it.

- **Consider your audience.** Just as you have learned to do in other speaking situations, when you are called on for impromptu remarks, think first of your audience. Who are the members of your audience? What are their common characteristics and interests? What do they know about your topic? What do they expect you to say? What is the occasion of your speech? A quick mental review of these questions will help ensure that even impromptu remarks are audience-centered.

- **Be brief.** When you are asked to deliver an off-the-cuff speech, your audience knows the circumstances and will not expect or even want a lengthy discourse. One to three minutes is a realistic time frame for most impromptu situations. Some spur-of-the-moment remarks, such as press statements, may be even shorter.

- **Organize!** Even off-the-cuff remarks need not falter or ramble. Effective impromptu speakers still organize their ideas into an introduction, body, and conclusion. Consider organizing your points using a simple organizational strategy such as chronological order or a topical pattern. A variation on the chronological pattern is the past, present, future model of addressing an issue. This pattern is well known to students who compete in impromptu speaking contests. The speaker organizes the impromptu speech by discussing (1) what has happened in the past, (2) what is happening now, and (3) what may happen in the future.

- **Speak honestly, but with reserve, from personal experience and knowledge.** Because there is no opportunity to conduct any kind of research before delivering an impromptu speech, you will have to speak from your own experience and knowledge. Remember, audiences almost always respond favorably to personal illustrations, so use any appropriate and relevant ones that come to mind. Of course, the more knowledge you have about the subject to be discussed, the easier it will be to speak about it off the cuff. But do *not* make up information or provide facts or figures you're not certain about. An honest "I don't know" or a very brief statement is more appropriate.

- **Be cautious.** No matter how much knowledge you have, if your subject is at all sensitive or your information is classified, be careful when discussing it

RECAP

Methods of Delivery

DELIVERY METHOD	DESCRIPTION	DISADVANTAGES	ADVANTAGES
Manuscript speaking	Reading your speech from a prepared text	➤ Your speech is likely to sound as if it is being read. ➤ It takes considerable skill and practice to make the message sound interesting.	➤ You can craft the message carefully, which is especially important if it is being presented to the media. ➤ The language can be beautifully refined, polished, and stylized.
Memorized speaking	Giving a speech from memory without using notes	➤ You may forget your speech. ➤ You may sound over-rehearsed and mechanical.	➤ You can have direct eye contact with the audience. ➤ You can move around freely or use gestures while speaking, since you don't need notes.
Impromptu speaking	Delivering a speech without preparing in advance	➤ Your speech is likely to be less well organized and smoothly delivered. ➤ Your lack of advance preparation and research makes it more difficult to cite evidence and supporting material for the message.	➤ You can more easily adapt to how your audience is reacting to you and your message during the speech. ➤ The audience sees and hears an authentic speech that is spontaneously delivered without notes.
Extemporaneous speaking	Knowing the major ideas, which have been outlined, but not memorizing the exact wording	➤ It takes time to prepare an extemporaneous speech. ➤ It takes skill to deliver the speech well.	➤ It is well organized and well researched. ➤ Your speech sounds spontaneous and yet appropriately polished.

during your impromptu speech. If asked about a controversial topic, give an honest but noncommittal answer. You can always elaborate later, but you can never take back something rash you have already said. It is better to be cautious than sorry!

EXTEMPORANEOUS SPEAKING

If you are not reading from a manuscript, reciting from memory, or speaking impromptu, what's left? **Extemporaneous speaking** is the approach most communication teachers recommend for most situations. When delivering a speech extemporaneously, you speak from a written or memorized general outline, but you do not have the exact wording in front of you or in memory. You have rehearsed the speech so that you know key ideas and their organization, but not to the degree that the speech sounds memorized. An extemporaneous style is conversational; it gives your audience the impression that the speech is being created as they listen to it, and to some extent it is. Martin Luther King Jr. was an expert in speaking extemporaneously; he typically did not use a manuscript when he spoke. He had notes, but he often drew

extemporaneous speaking
Speaking from a written or memorized speech outline without having memorized the exact wording of the speech

on the energy of his audience as well as his own natural speaking talents to make his oratory come alive.[12] You can use the same extemporaneous techniques he used to draw on your audience's energy and make your speech a living message rather than a canned presentation.

Audiences prefer to hear something live rather than something canned. Even though you can't tell the difference between a taped or live performance when it is broadcast on TV, you would probably prefer seeing it live. Seeing something happening now provides added interest and excitement. An extemporaneous speech sounds live rather than as though it were prepared yesterday or weeks ago. The extemporaneous method reflects the advantages of a well-organized speech delivered in an interesting and vivid manner.

How do you develop an extemporaneous delivery style? Here are tips for what to do at three stages in your rehearsal:

- Early rehearsal: When you first rehearse your speech, use as many notes as you need to help you remember your ideas; but each time you rehearse, rely less and less on your notes.

- Later rehearsal: When you find yourself starting to use exactly the same words each time you rehearse, you're memorizing your speech; either stop rehearsing or consider other ways of expressing your ideas.

- Final rehearsal: Revise your speaking notes so that you need only brief notes or only notes for lengthy quotations.

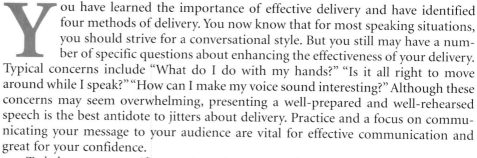

Characteristics of Effective Delivery

You have learned the importance of effective delivery and have identified four methods of delivery. You now know that for most speaking situations, you should strive for a conversational style. But you still may have a number of specific questions about enhancing the effectiveness of your delivery. Typical concerns include "What do I do with my hands?" "Is it all right to move around while I speak?" "How can I make my voice sound interesting?" Although these concerns may seem overwhelming, presenting a well-prepared and well-rehearsed speech is the best antidote to jitters about delivery. Practice and a focus on communicating your message to your audience are vital for effective communication and great for your confidence.

To help answer specific questions about presenting a speech, we consider seven major categories of nonverbal behavior that affect delivery. Specifically, we will help you improve your eye contact, use appropriate gestures, move meaningfully, maintain an appropriate posture, use facial expressions to communicate emotion, use your voice both to be understood and to maintain interest, and ensure that your personal appearance is appropriate. The ancient Roman orator Cicero, author of *De Oratore*, called these behaviors the "language of the body."[13]

EYE CONTACT

Of all the aspects of delivery discussed in this chapter, the most important one in a public-speaking situation for North Americans is eye contact. Eye contact with your audience opens communication, makes you more believable, and keeps your audience interested. Each of these functions contributes to the success of your delivery. Eye contact also provides you with feedback about how your speech is coming across.

Making eye contact with your listeners clearly shows that you are ready to talk to them. Most people start a conversation by looking at the person they are going to talk to. The same process occurs in public speaking.

Once you've started talking, continued eye contact lets you know how your audience is responding to your speech. You don't need to look at your listeners continuously. As the need arises, you should certainly look at your notes, but also look at your listeners frequently, just to see what they're doing.

Most listeners will think you are capable and trustworthy if you look them in the eye. Several studies document a relationship between eye contact and increased speaker credibility.[14] Speakers with less than 50 percent eye contact are considered unfriendly, uninformed, inexperienced, and even dishonest by their listeners.

Another study showed that those audience members who had more than 50 percent eye contact with their speaker performed better in postspeech tests than did those who had less than 50 percent eye contact.[15] However, not all people from all cultures prefer the same amount of direct eye contact when listening to someone talk. In interpersonal contexts, people from Asian cultures, for example, expect less direct eye contact when communicating with others than do North Americans.

Most audiences in the United States prefer that you establish eye contact with them even before you begin your speech with your attention-catching introduction. When it's your time to speak, walk to the lectern or to the front of the audience, pause briefly, and look at your audience before you say anything. Eye contact nonverbally sends the message, "I am interested in you; tune me in; I have something I want to share with you." You should have your opening sentence well enough in mind that you can deliver it without looking at your notes or away from your listeners.

Establish eye contact with the entire audience, not just with those in the front row or only one or two people. Look to the back as well as the front and from one side of your audience to the other, selecting an individual to focus on and then moving on to someone else. You need not rhythmically move your head back and forth like a lighthouse beacon; it's best not to establish a predictable pattern for your eye contact. Look at individuals, establishing person-to-person contact with them—not so long that it will make a listener feel uncomfortable, but long enough to establish the feeling that you are talking directly to that individual. *Don't* look over your listeners' heads; establish eye-to-eye contact.

GESTURES

The next time you have a conversation with someone, notice how both of you use your hands and bodies to communicate. Important points are emphasized with gestures. You also gesture to indicate places, to enumerate items, and to describe objects. Gestures have the same functions for public speakers. Yet many people who gesture easily and appropriately in the course of everyday conversations aren't sure what to do with their hands when they find themselves in front of an audience.

There is evidence that gestures vary from culture to culture. When he was mayor of New York City during the 1930s and 1940s, Fiorello La Guardia, fluent in Yiddish

RECAP

Techniques for Effective Eye Contact

➤ Establish eye contact with the *entire* audience, not just a few people in the front or the middle of your audience.

➤ Use your eye contact to connect to individuals; look at an individual for at least 2 to 3 seconds, if not longer.

➤ Remember that eye contact involves looking people in the eye—not looking over listeners' heads.

➤ Move your glance from person to person naturally rather than mechanically and predictably moving your head from side to side.

and Italian as well as in English, would speak the language appropriate for each audience. One researcher studied old newsreels of the mayor and discovered that with the sound turned off, viewers could still identify the language the mayor was speaking. How? When speaking English, he used minimal gestures. When speaking Italian, he used broad, sweeping gestures. And when speaking Yiddish, he used short and choppy hand movements.

Cultural expectations can help you make decisions about your approach to using gestures. Listeners from Japan and China, for example, prefer a quieter, less flamboyant use of gestures. One Web site that offers tips for people conducting business in India suggests "When you wish to point, use your chin or your full hand, but never just a single finger, as this gesture is used only with inferiors. The chin is not used to signal to superiors. The best way to point is with the full hand."[16] When one of your authors spoke in England, several listeners noted the use of "typical American gestures and movement." British listeners seem to prefer that the speaker stay behind a lectern and use relatively few gestures. Other Europeans agree they can spot an American speaker because Americans typically are more animated in their use of gestures, movement, and facial expressions than are European speakers.

Public-speaking teachers often observe several unusual, inappropriate, and unnatural gestures among their students. One common problem is keeping your hands behind your back in a "parade rest" pose. We are not suggesting that you never put your hands behind your back, only that standing at parade rest during an entire speech looks awkward and unnatural and may distract your audience.

Another common position is standing with one hand on the hip in a "broken wing" pose. Worse than the "broken wing" is both hands resting on the hips in a "double broken wing." The speaker looks as though he or she might burst into a rendition of "I'm a Little Teapot." Again, we are not suggesting that you should never place your hands on your hips, only that to hold that one pose throughout a speech looks unnatural and will keep you from using other gestures.

Few poses are more awkward-looking than when a speaker clutches one arm, as if grazed by a bullet. The audience half expects the speaker to call out reassuringly, "Don't worry, Ma; it's only a flesh wound." Similarly, keeping your hands in your pockets can make you look as if you were afraid to let go of your change or your keys.

Some students clasp their hands and let them drop in front of them in a distracting "fig leaf clutch." Gestures can distract your audience in various other ways as well. Grasping the lectern until your knuckles turn white or just letting your hands flop around without purpose or control does little to help you communicate your message.

FUNCTIONS OF GESTURES If you don't know what to do with your hands, think about the message you want to communicate. As in ordinary conversation, your hands should simply help emphasize or reinforce your verbal message. Specifically, your gestures can lend strength to or detract from what you have to say by (1) repeating, (2) contradicting, (3) substituting, (4) complementing, (5) emphasizing, and (6) regulating.

- **Repeating.** Gestures can help you repeat your verbal message. For example, you can say, "I have three major points to talk about today," while holding up three fingers. Or you can describe an object as 12 inches long while holding your hands about a foot apart. Repeating what you say through nonverbal means can reinforce your message.

- **Contradicting.** Because your audience will believe what you communicate nonverbally sooner than what you communicate verbally, monitor your gestures to make sure that you are not contradicting what you say. It is difficult to convey an image of control and confidence while using flailing gestures and awkward poses.

- **Substituting.** Not only can your behavior reinforce or contradict what you say, but your gestures can also substitute for your message. Without uttering a word, you can hold up the palm of your hand to calm a noisy crowd. Flashing two fingers to form a *V* for "victory" or raising a clenched fist are other common examples of gestures that substitute for a verbal message.

- **Complementing.** Gestures can also add further meaning to your verbal message. A politician who declines to comment on a reporter's question while holding up her hands to augment her verbal refusal is relying on the gesture to complement or provide further meaning to her verbal message.

- **Emphasizing.** You can give emphasis to what you say by using an appropriate gesture. A shaking fist or a slicing gesture with one or both hands helps emphasize a message. So does pounding your fist into the palm of your hand. Other gestures can be less dramatic but still lend emphasis to what you say. You should try to allow your gestures to arise from the content of your speech and your emotions.

- **Regulating.** Gestures can also regulate the exchange between you and your audience. If you want the audience to respond to a question, you can extend both palms to invite a response. During a question-and-answer session, your gestures can signal when you want to talk and when you want to invite others to do so.

USING GESTURES EFFECTIVELY One hundred years ago, elocutionists taught their students how to gesture to communicate specific emotions or messages. Today teachers of speech have a different approach. Rather than prescribe gestures for specific situations, they feel it is more useful to offer suitable criteria (standards) by which to judge effective gestures, regardless of what is being said. Here are some guidelines to consider when working on your delivery.

- **Stay natural.** Gestures should be *relaxed*, not tense or rigid. Your gestures should flow with your message. Avoid sawing or slashing through the air with your hands unless you are trying to emphasize a particularly dramatic point.

- **Be definite.** Gestures should appear *definite* rather than as accidental brief jerks of your hands or arms. If you want to gesture, go ahead and gesture. Avoid minor hand movements that will be masked by the lectern.

- **Use gestures that are consistent with your message.** Gestures should be *appropriate* for the verbal content of your speech. If you are excited, gesture more vigorously. But remember that prerehearsed gestures that do not arise naturally from what you are trying to say are likely to appear awkward and stilted.

- **Vary your gestures.** Strive for *variety* and versatility in your use of gesture. Try not to use just one hand or one all-purpose gesture. Gestures can be used for a variety of purposes, such as enumerating, pointing, describing, and symbolizing an idea or concept (such as clasping your hands together to suggest agreement or coming together).

- **Don't overdo it.** Gestures should be *unobtrusive*; your audience should focus not on the beauty or appropriateness of your gestures but on your message. Your purpose is to communicate a message to your audience, not to perform for your listeners to the extent that your delivery receives more attention than your message.

- **Coordinate gestures with what you say.** Gestures should be *well timed* to coincide with your verbal message. When you announce that you have three major points, your gesture of enumeration should occur simultaneously with your utterance of the word *three*. It would be poor timing to announce that you have three points, pause for a second or two, and then hold up three fingers.

➤ **Make your gestures appropriate to your audience and situation.** Gestures must be adapted to the audience. In more formal speaking situations, particularly when speaking to a large audience, bolder, more sweeping, and more dramatic gestures are appropriate. A small audience in a less formal setting calls for less formal gestures.

In summary, keep one important principle in mind: Use gestures that work best for you. Don't try to be someone you are not. Barak Obama's style may work for him, but you are not Barak Obama. Your gestures should fit your personality. It may be better to use no gestures—to just put your hands comfortably at your side—than to use awkward, distracting gestures or to try to counterfeit someone else's gestures. Your nonverbal delivery should flow from *your* message.

MOVEMENT

Should you walk around during your speech, or should you stay in one place? If there is a lectern, should you stand behind it, or would it be acceptable to stand in front of it or to the side? Is it all right to sit down while you speak? Can you move among the audience, as Oprah Winfrey does on her TV show? You may well find yourself pondering one or more of these questions while preparing for your speeches. The following discussion may help you answer them.

You may want to move purposefully about while delivering your speech, but take care that your movement does not detract from your message. If the audience focuses on your movement rather than on what you are saying, it is better to stand still. An absence of movement is better than distracting movement. In short, your movement should be consistent with the verbal content of your message. It should make sense rather than appear as aimless wandering.

Robert Frost said, "Good fences make good neighbors." Professional speech coach Brent Filson says, however, "For my money, good fences make lousy speeches."[17] He recommends, as do we, that you eliminate physical barriers between you and the audience. For more formal occasions you will be expected to stand behind a lectern to deliver your message. But even on those occasions, it can be appropriate to move from behind the lectern to make a point, signal a change in mood, or move to another idea.

Your movement and other nonverbal cues can help you establish immediacy with your listeners. According to psychologist Albert Mehrabian, **immediacy** is "the

immediacy
The degree of perceived physical or psychological closeness between people

RECAP

Characteristics of Effective Gestures

THE MOST EFFECTIVE GESTURES ARE . . .

➤ Natural: Your gestures should be a natural fit with both your message and your personality.

➤ Definite: Make your gestures look purposeful rather than accidental.

➤ Consistent with your words: Monitor your gestures to make sure they reinforce your verbal message.

➤ Varied: Use different types of gestures rather than only one.

➤ Unobtrusive: Your gestures should not call attention to themselves.

➤ Appropriate: Gestures should be adapted to your audience and the occasion.

degree of physical or psychological closeness between people."[18] **Immediacy behaviors** are those that literally or psychologically make your audience feel closer to you; because they create this perception of closeness, immediacy behaviors enhance the quality of the relationship between you and your audience.[19] Immediacy behaviors include

- Standing or moving closer to your listeners
- Coming out from behind a lectern
- Using appropriate levels of eye contact
- Smiling while talking, and more specifically, smiling at individual audience members
- Using appropriate gestures
- Having an appropriately relaxed posture
- Moving purposefully

Over three decades of research on the immediacy cues used by teachers in North American classrooms clearly establishes that teachers who are more immediate enhance student learning, increase student motivation to learn, and have higher teacher evaluations.[20] It seems logical to suggest that public speakers who increase immediacy will have similar positive results. One cautionary note: Listeners—not the speaker—determine the appropriate amount of immediacy. Be vigilantly audience-centered as you seek the appropriate level of immediacy between you and your listeners.

In addition to fostering immediacy, movement can signal the beginning of a new idea or major point in your speech. As you make a transition statement or change from a serious subject to a more humorous one, movement can be a good way to signal that your approach to the speaking situation is changing.

Your use of movement during your speech should make sense to your listeners. Avoid random pacing and overly dramatic gestures. Temper our advice about proximity and other delivery variables by adapting to the cultural expectations of your audience.

Although it may be acceptable to sit with your feet up when talking informally with someone, a good speaker makes sure his or her posture is appropriate for the speaking context.

[Photo: Eye Wire/Photodisc/Getty Images]

POSTURE

Although there have been few formal studies of posture in relation to public speaking, there is evidence that the way you carry your body communicates significant information. One study even suggests that your stance can reflect on your credibility as a speaker.[21] Slouching over the lectern, for example, does not project an image of vitality and interest in your audience.

Whereas your face and voice play the major role in communicating a specific emotion, your posture communicates the *intensity* of that emotion. If you are happy, your face and voice reflect your happiness; your posture communicates the intensity of your joy.[22]

Since the days of the elocutionists, few speech teachers or public-speaking texts have advocated specific postures for public speakers. Today, we believe that the specific stance you adopt should come about naturally, as a result of what you have to say, the environment, and the formality or informality of the occasion. For example, during a very informal presentation, it may be perfectly appropriate as well as comfortable and natural to sit on the edge of a desk. Most speech teachers, however, do not encourage students to sit while delivering classroom speeches. In general, avoid

immediacy behaviors

Behaviors such as making eye contact, making appropriate gestures, and adjusting physical distance that enhance the quality of the relationship between speaker and listeners

slouched shoulders, shifting from foot to foot, or drooping your head. Your posture should not call attention to itself. Instead, it should reflect your interest in the speaking event and your attention to the task at hand.

To help you stand tall when delivering a speech, here are two tips to keep in mind. First, stand up straight while pulling your shoulder blades back just a bit. In addition, imagine that your head is being held up by a string so that you have direct eye contact with your listeners while standing tall. You don't need to stay frozen in this position. But when you find yourself starting to slump or slouch, pulling your shoulders back and tugging on the imaginary string will give your posture an immediate positive boost.

FACIAL EXPRESSION

Media experts today doubt that Abraham Lincoln would have survived as a politician in our appearance-conscious age of telegenic politicians. His facial expression, according to those who saw him, seemed wooden and unvaried.

Your face plays a key role in expressing your thoughts, and especially your emotions and attitudes.[23] Your audience sees your face before they hear what you are going to say. Thus, you have an opportunity to set the emotional tone for your message before you start speaking. We are not advocating that you adopt a phony smile that looks insincere and plastered on your face, but a pleasant facial expression helps establish a positive emotional climate. Your facial expression should naturally vary to be consistent with your message. Present somber news with a more serious expression. To communicate interest in your listeners, keep your expression alert and friendly.

Although humans are physically capable of producing thousands of different facial expressions, we most often express only six primary emotions: happiness, anger, surprise, sadness, disgust, and fear. But when we speak to others, our faces are a blend of expressions rather than communicators of a single emotion. According to cross-cultural studies by social psychologist Paul Ekman, the facial expressions of these emotions are virtually universal, so even a culturally diverse audience will usually be able to read your emotional expressions clearly.[24] When you rehearse your speech, consider standing in front of a mirror—or, better yet, videotape yourself practicing your speech. Note whether you are allowing your face to help communicate the emotional tone of your thoughts.

VOCAL DELIVERY

Have you ever listened to a radio announcer and imagined what he or she looked like, only later to see a picture and have your image of the announcer drastically altered? Vocal clues play an important part in creating the impression we have of a speaker. Based on vocal clues alone, you make inferences about a person's age, status, occupation, ethnic origin, income, and a variety of other matters. As a public speaker, your voice is one of your most important delivery tools in conveying your ideas to your audience. Your credibility as a speaker and your ability to communicate your ideas clearly to your listeners will in large part depend on your vocal delivery.

Vocal delivery includes pitch, speech rate, volume, pronunciation, articulation, pauses, and general variation of the voice. A speaker has at least two key vocal obligations to an audience: Speak to be understood, and speak with vocal variety to maintain interest.

SPEAKING TO BE UNDERSTOOD To be understood, you need to consider four aspects of vocal delivery: volume, articulation, dialect, and pronunciation.

volume
The softness or loudness of a speaker's voice

➤ **Volume.** The fundamental purpose of your vocal delivery is to speak loudly enough that your audience can hear you. The **volume** of your speech is determined by the amount of air you project through your larynx, or voice box. More

Marcus Tullius Cicero (106–43 B.C.)

Although the ancient Greeks contributed much to the study and practice of public speaking, they focused very little on delivery. Marcus Tullius Cicero, a Roman, was one of the first to emphasize the importance of delivery, especially gestures and voice. In addition to writing about effective speaking, most notably in his three-volume *De Oratore*, Cicero himself was a great speaker. He became especially well known for his effective delivery, which he developed by studying the technique of actors and by rehearsing.

You, too, can benefit from the same techniques that Cicero used to enhance the effectiveness of your delivery, by practicing good eye contact and appropriate gestures and vocal variation, practicing speaking while standing, and imagining that you are presenting your speech to your audience. Spending time rehearsing your speech will not only help you feel more comfortable presenting your message, it will also enhance your ability to connect with your listeners.

[Photo: Araldo de Luca/Bettmann/Corbis]

air equals more volume of sound. In fact, the way you breathe has more impact on the sound of your voice than almost anything else. To ancient orators, a person's breath was the source of spiritual power. To breathe is to be literally filled with a positive, powerful source of energy.

In order to breathe properly, you need to understand how to use your breathing muscles. Your diaphragm, a muscle that lies between your lungs and abdomen, helps control sound volume by increasing air flow from your lungs through your voice box. If you put your hands on the hollow in the center of your rib cage and say, "Ho-ho-ho," you will feel your muscles contracting and the air being forced out of your lungs. Breathing from your diaphragm—that is, consciously expanding and contracting your abdomen as you breathe in and out, rather than merely expanding your chest as air flows into your lungs—can increase the volume of sound as well as enhance the quality of your voice.

◆ **Articulation.** The process of producing speech sounds clearly and distinctly is **articulation**. In addition to speaking loudly enough, say your words so that your audience can understand them. Without distinct enunciation, or articulation of the sounds that make up words, your listeners may not understand you or may fault you for simply not knowing how to speak clearly and fluently. Here are some commonly misarticulated words.[25]

Dint instead of *didn't*	*Soun* instead of *sound*
Lemme instead of *let me*	*Wanna* instead of *want to*
Mornin instead of *morning*	*Wep* instead of *wept*
Seeya instead of *see you*	*Whadayado* instead of *what do you do*

Many errors in articulation result from simple laziness. It takes effort to articulate speech sounds clearly. Sometimes we are in a hurry to express our ideas, but more often we simply get into the habit of mumbling, slurring, and abbreviating. Such speech flaws may not keep your audience from understanding you, but poor enunciation does reflect on your credibility as a speaker.

articulation
The production of clear and distinct speech sounds

The best way to improve your articulation of sounds is first to identify words or phrases that you have a tendency to slur or chop. Once you have identified them, practice saying the words correctly. Make sure you can hear the difference between the improper and proper pronunciation. A speech teacher can help you check your articulation.

Dialect. Most newscasters in North America use what is called standard American pronunciation and do not typically have a strong dialect. A **dialect** is a consistent style of pronouncing words that is common to an ethnic group or a geographic region such as the South, New England, or the upper Midwest. In the southern part of the United States, people prolong some vowel sounds when they speak. And in the northern Midwest, the word *about* sometimes sounds a bit like "aboat." It took a bit of adjustment for many Americans to get used to President John Kennedy's Bostonian pronunciation of Cuba as "Cuber" and Harvard as "Hahvahd." Lyndon Johnson's Texas twang was a sharp contrast to Kennedy's New England sound. And George W. Bush's Texas lilt also contrasts with the slight southern drawl of his predecessor, Bill Clinton.

Are dialects detrimental to effective communication with an audience? Although a speaker's dialect may pigeonhole that person as being from a certain part of the country, it won't necessarily affect the audience's comprehension of the information unless the dialect is so pronounced that the listeners can't understand the speaker's words. Research does suggest, however, that listeners tend to prefer a dialect similar to their own pronunciation style.[26] Many well-known and effective speakers have a distinct dialect; Jesse Jackson, Bill Clinton, George W. Bush, John Edwards, and Garrison Keillor all have some degree of a regional dialect. We don't recommend that you eliminate a mild dialect; but if your word pronunciation is significantly distracting to your listeners, consider modifying your dialect.

The four elements of a dialect include intonation pattern, vowel production, consonant production, and speaking rate. A typical North American intonation pattern is predominantly a rising and falling pattern. The pattern looks something like this:

"Good ^{morn}ing. How ^{are} you?"

Intonation patterns of other languages, such as Hindi, may remain on almost the exact same pitch level; native North American ears find the monotone pitch distracting.

A second element in any dialect is the way vowel sounds are produced. Many people who speak English as a second language often clip, or shorten, the vowel sounds, which can make comprehension more challenging. Stretching or elongating vowels within words can be a useful skill for such speakers to develop. If this is a vocal skill you need to cultivate, consider recording your speech and then comparing it with the standard American pronunciation you hear on TV or radio.

Consonant production, the third element in vocal dialects, varies depending on which language you are speaking. It is sometimes difficult to produce clear consonants that are not overdone. Consonants that are so soft as to be almost unheard may produce a long blur of unintelligible sound rather than a crisply articulated sound.

A fourth and final element in vocal dialect is speaking rate. People whose first language is not English sometimes speak too fast, in the hope this will create the impression of being very familiar with English. Slowing the rate just a bit often enhances comprehension for native English speakers listening to someone less familiar with English pronunciation. A rate that is too fast also

dialect
A consistent style of pronouncing words that is common to an ethnic group or geographic region

contributes to problems with clipped vowels, soft or absent consonants, and an intonation pattern that is on one pitch level rather than comfortably varied.

➤ **Pronunciation.** Whereas articulation relates to the clarity of sounds, **pronunciation** concerns the degree to which sounds conform to those assigned to words in standard English. Mispronouncing words can detract from a speaker's credibility.[27] Often, however, we are not aware that we are not using standard pronunciation unless someone points it out.

Some speakers reverse speech sounds, saying "aks" instead of "ask," for example. Some allow an *r* sound to intrude into some words, saying "warsh" instead of "wash," or leave out sounds in the middle of a word by saying "actchally" instead of "actually" or "Febuary" instead of "February." Some speakers also accent syllables in nonstandard ways; they say "po´lice" instead of "po lice´" or "um´brella" rather than "um brel´la."

If English is not your native language, you may have to spend extra time working on your pronunciation and articulation. Here are two useful tips to help you. First, make an effort to prolong vowel sounds. Speeeeak tooooo prooooolooooong eeeeeeach voooooowel soooooound yooooooooou maaaaaaaake. Second, to reduce choppy-sounding word pronunciation, blend the end of one word into the beginning of the next. Make your speech flow from one word to the next, instead of separating it into individual chunks of sound.[28]

SPEAKING WITH VARIETY To speak with variety is to vary your pitch, rate, and pauses. It is primarily through the quality of our voices, as well as our facial expressions, that we communicate whether we are happy, sad, bored, or excited. If your vocal clues suggest that you are bored with your topic, your audience will probably be bored also. Appropriate variation in vocal pitch and rate as well as appropriate use of pauses can add zest to your speech and help maintain audience attention.

➤ **Pitch.** Vocal **pitch** is how high or low your voice sounds. You can sing because you can change the pitch of your voice to produce a melody. Lack of variation in pitch has been consistently identified as one of the most distracting characteristics of ineffective speakers. A monotone is boring.

Everyone has a habitual pitch. This is the range of your voice during normal conversation. Some people have a habitually high pitch, whereas others have a low pitch. The pitch of your voice is determined by how fast the folds in your vocal cords vibrate. The faster the vibration, the higher the pitch. Male vocal folds open and close approximately 100 to 150 times each second; female vocal folds vibrate about 200 times per second, thus giving them a higher vocal pitch.

Your voice has **inflection** when you raise or lower the pitch as you pronounce words or sounds. Your inflection helps determine the meaning of your utterances. A surprised "ah!" sounds different from a disappointed "ah" or "ah?" Your vocal inflection is thus an important indicator of your emotions and gives clues as to how to interpret your speech.

In some cultures, vocal inflection plays a major role in helping people interpret the meaning of words. For example, Thai, Vietnamese, and Mandarin Chinese languages purposely use such inflections as monotone, low, falling, high, and rising.[29] If you are a native speaker of a language in which pitch influences meaning, be mindful that listeners do not expect this in many Western languages, although all languages rely on inflection to provide nuances of meaning.

The best public speakers appropriately vary their inflection. We're not suggesting that you need to imitate a top-forty radio disk jockey when you speak. But variation in your vocal inflection and overall pitch helps you communicate the subtlety of your ideas.

pronunciation
The use of sounds to form words clearly and accurately

pitch
How high or low your voice sounds

inflection
The variation in the pitch of the voice

Record your speech as you rehearse, and evaluate your use of pitch and inflection critically. If you are not satisfied with your inflection, consider practicing your speech with exaggerated variations in vocal pitch. Although you would not deliver your speech this way, it may help you explore the expressive options available to you.

Rate. How fast do you talk? Most speakers average between 120 and 180 words per minute. There is no "best" speaking rate. The skill of great speakers does not depend on a standard rate of speech. Daniel Webster purportedly spoke at about 90 words per minute, Franklin Roosevelt at 110, President Kennedy at a quick-paced 180. Martin Luther King Jr. started his "I Have a Dream" speech at 92 words a minute and was speaking at 145 words per minute during his conclusion.[30] The best rate depends on two factors: your speaking style and the content of your message.

A common fault of many beginning speakers is to deliver a speech too quickly. One symptom of speech anxiety is that you tend to rush through your speech to get it over with. Feedback from others can help you determine whether your rate is too rapid. Recording your message and listening critically to your speaking rate can also help you assess whether you are speaking at the proper speed. Fewer speakers have the problem of speaking too slowly, but a turtle-paced speech will almost certainly make it more difficult for your audience to maintain interest. Remember, your listeners can grasp information much faster than you can speak it.

You need not deliver your entire speech at the same pace. It is normal to speak more rapidly when talking about something that excites you. You slow your speaking rate to emphasize key points or ideas. Speaking rate is another tool you can use to add variety and interest to your vocal delivery. The pace of your delivery, however, should make sense in terms of the ideas you are sharing with your listeners.

Pauses. It was Mark Twain who said, "The right word may be effective, but no word was ever as effective as a rightly timed pause." An appropriate pause can often do more to accent your message than any other vocal characteristic. President Kennedy's famous line, "Ask not what your country can do for you; ask what you can do for your country," was effective not only because of its language but also because it was delivered with a pause dividing the two thoughts. Try delivering that line without the pause; it just doesn't have the same power without it.

Effective use of pauses, also known as *effective timing*, can greatly enhance the impact of your message. Whether you are trying to tell a joke, a serious tale, or a dramatic story, your use of a pause can determine the effectiveness of your anecdote. Jay Leno, David Letterman, Conan O'Brian, and Ellen Degeneres are masters at timing a punch line. Radio commentator Paul Harvey is known for his flair for vocal delivery. His dramatic pauses serve as meaningful punctuation in his talks.

Beware, however, of the vocalized pause. Many beginning public speakers are uncomfortable with silence and so, rather than pausing where it seems natural and normal, they vocalize sounds such as "umm," "er," "you know," and "ah." We think you will agree that "Ask not, ah, what your, er, country can do, ah, for you; ask, you know, what you, umm, can do, er, for your, uh, country" just doesn't have the same impact as the unadorned original statement.

One research study counted how frequently certain people use "uhs."[31] Science professors in this study said "uh" about 1.4 times a minute; humanities professors timed in at 4.8 times a minute—almost 3.5 times more. Another psychologist counted the "ums" per minute of well-known speakers. *Wheel of Fortune* host Pat Sajak won the count with almost 10 "ums" per minute; and, although he sometimes pokes fun at well-known politicians who use vocalized pauses, David Letterman was a close second with 8.1. Former President Bill Clinton had only .79 vocalized pause per minute. Former Vice President Dan Quayle had only .1. As a public speaker, you don't want to be the "winner" of this contest by having the most "uhs" and "ums" when you speak. Vocalized pauses will annoy your audience and detract from your credibility; eliminate them.

Silence can be an effective tool in emphasizing a particular word or sentence. A well-timed pause coupled with eye contact can powerfully accent your thought. Asking a rhetorical question of your audience such as "How many of you would like to improve your communication skills?" will be more effective if you pause after asking the question rather than rushing into the next thought. Silence is a way of saying to your audience, "Think about this for a moment." Pianist Arthur Schnabel said this about silence and music: "The notes I handle not better than many pianists. But the pauses between the notes, ah, that is where the art resides.[32] In speech, too, an effective use of a pause can add emphasis and interest.

USING A MICROPHONE "Testing. Testing. One . . . two . . . three. Is this on?" These are not effective, attention-catching opening remarks. Yet countless public speakers have found themselves trying to begin their speech, only to be upstaged by an uncooperative public address system. No matter how polished your gestures or well-intoned your vocal cues, if you are inaudible or use a microphone awkwardly, your speech will not have the desired effect.

There are three kinds of microphones, only one of which demands much technique. The **lavaliere microphone** is the clip-on type often used by newspeople and interviewees. Worn on the front of a shirt or dress, it requires no particular care other than not thumping it or accidentally knocking it off. The **boom microphone** is used by makers of movies and TV shows. It hangs over the heads of the speakers and is remote-controlled, so the speaker need not be particularly concerned with it. The third kind of microphone, and the most common, is the **stationary microphone**. This is the type that is most often attached to a lectern, sitting on a desk, or standing on the floor. Generally, the stationary microphones used today are multidirectional. You do not have to remain frozen in front of a stationary mike while delivering your speech. However, you do need to take some other precautions when using one.

First, if you have a fully stationary microphone, rather than one that converts to a hand mike, you will have to remain behind the microphone, with your mouth about the same distance from the mike at all times to avoid distracting fluctuations in the volume of sound. You can turn your head from side to side and use gestures, but you will have to limit other movements.

Second, microphones amplify sloppy habits of pronunciation and enunciation. Therefore, you need to speak clearly and crisply when using a mike. Be especially careful when articulating such "explosive" sounding consonants as *B* and *P*; they can be overamplified by the microphone and produce a slight popping sound. Similarly, a microphone can intensify the sibilance of the *S* sound at the beginning or ending of words (such as in *hiss, sometime,* or *specials*). You may have to articulate these sounds with slightly less intensity to avoid creating overamplified, distracting noises.

Third, if you must test a microphone, count or ask the audience whether they can hear you. Blowing on a microphone produces an irritating noise! Do not tap, pound, or shuffle anything near the microphone. These noises, too, will be heard by the audience loudly and clearly. If you are using note cards, quietly slide them aside as you progress through your speech.

Finally, when you are delivering your speech, speak directly into the microphone to make sure that your words are appropriately amplified. Some speakers lower their volume and become inaudible when they have a microphone in front of them.

Under ideal circumstances, you will be able to practice with the type of microphone you will use before you speak. If you have the chance, figure out where to stand

lavaliere microphone

A microphone that can be clipped to an article of clothing or worn on a cord around your neck

boom microphone

A microphone that is suspended from a bar and moved to follow the speaker; often used in movies and TV

stationary microphone

A microphone attached to a lectern, sitting on a desk, or standing on the floor

RECAP

Characteristics of Good Vocal Delivery

GOOD SPEAKERS	POOR SPEAKERS
Have adequate volume	Speak too softly to be heard
Articulate speech sounds clearly and distinctly	Slur speech sounds
Pronounce words accurately	Mispronounce words
Have varied pitch	Have a monotonous pitch
Vary their speaking rate	Consistently speak too fast or too slowly
Pause to emphasize ideas	Rarely pause or pause too long

for the best sound quality and how sensitive the mike is to extraneous noise. Practice will accustom you to any voice distortion or echo that might occur so that these sound qualities do not surprise you during your speech.

PERSONAL APPEARANCE

Most people have certain expectations about the way a speaker should look. One of your audience analysis tasks is to identify what those audience expectations are. This can be trickier than it might at first seem. John T. Molloy has written two books, *Dress for Success* and *Dress for Success for Women*, in an effort to identify what the well-dressed businessperson should wear. But as some of his own research points out, appropriate wardrobe varies, depending on climate, custom, culture, and audience expectations. For example, most CEOs who speak to their stockholders at the annual stockholders meeting typically wear a suit and tie—but not Steve Jobs, head of Apple. To communicate his casual and contemporary approach to business, he often wears jeans and a sweater.

SPEAKER'S HOMEPAGE

Evaluating Speaker Delivery

It's one thing to read about speech delivery, but it's quite another to actually see and hear speakers deliver a message. If you have the proper software (such as RealAudio, which you can download from the Internet at www.real.com/ or RealVideo, which you can access through Timecast at www.timecast.com/sites/index.html), you can hear and sometimes see former and current presidents present political speeches. At some sites you can watch well-known individuals give a presentation; other sites just permit you to listen to a speech.

➤ HISTORY CHANNEL ARCHIVE OF SPEECHES
Each day a famous speech is presented. There is also a Real Audio archive of famous speeches.
www.history.com/media.do

➤ MSU VINCENT VOICE LIBRARY
This site will permit you to hear recordings of U.S. presidents and other historical figures.
http:vvl.lib.msu.edu/index.cfm

➤ THE CMU PRONOUNCING DICTIONARY
This Web site, which can help you with your pronunciation, was developed at Carnegie Mellon University. It uses phonetic markings to indicate the proper pronunciations of words.
www.speech.cs.cmu.edu/cgi-bin/cmudict/

There is considerable evidence that your personal appearance affects how your audience responds to you and your message, particularly during the opening moments of your presentation. If you violate their expectations about appearance, you will be less successful in achieving your purpose. One study found, for example, that men who have a nose ring are less likely to be hired during a job interview.[33] Yet even this research conclusion, published in 2003, is based on a specific situation and time; years from now, a nose ring may not have any impact, either positive or negative, on a person's credibility. Our point: It's the audience and the cultural expectations of audience members that determine whether a speaker's personal appearance is appropriate or not, not some fashion guru or magazine editor.

Speaking to a racially diverse audience at an outdoor event may require a speaker to use a different style of delivery than he or she would use in another context.

[Photo: Kayte Deioma/PhotoEdit]

Audience Diversity and Delivery

Most of the suggestions we have offered in this chapter assume that your listeners will be expecting a typical North American approach to delivery. However, these assumptions are based on research responses from U.S. college students, who are predominantly White and in their late teens or early twenties, so our suggestions are not applicable to every audience. As we have stressed throughout the book, you need to adapt your presentation to the expectations of your listeners, especially those from different cultural backgrounds. Consider the following suggestions to help you develop strategies for adapting both your verbal and your nonverbal messages for a culturally diverse audience.

➤ **Avoid an ethnocentric mind-set.** As you learned in Chapter 5, *ethnocentrism* is the assumption that your own cultural approaches are superior to those of other cultures. When considering how to adapt your delivery style to your audience, try to view different approaches and preferences not as right or wrong but merely as different from your own.

➤ **Consider using a less dramatic style for predominantly high-context listeners.** As you recall from Chapter 5, a high-context culture places considerable emphasis on unspoken messages. Therefore, for a high-context audience, you need not be overly expressive. For example, for many Japanese people, a delivery style that included exuberant gestures, overly dramatic facial expressions, and frequent movements might seem overdone. A more subtle, less demonstrative approach would create less "noise" and be more effective.

➤ **Consult with other speakers who have presented to your audience.** Talk with people you may know who are familiar with the cultural expectations of the audience you will address. Ask specific questions. For example, when speaking in Poland, one of the authors expected the speech to start promptly at 11 A.M., as announced in the program and on posters. By 11:10 it was clear the speech would not begin on time. In Poland, it turns out, all students know about the "academic quarter." This means that most lectures and speeches begin at least 15 minutes, or a quarter hour, after the announced starting time. If the author had asked another professor about the audience's expectations, he would have known this custom in advance. As you observe or talk with speakers who have addressed your target audience, ask the following questions:

What are audience expectations about where I should stand while speaking?

Do listeners like direct eye contact?

When will the audience expect me to start and end my talk?

Will listeners find movement and gestures distracting or welcome?

➤ **Monitor your level of immediacy with your audience.** As we noted earlier, speaker immediacy involves how close you are to your listeners, the amount of eye contact you display, and whether you speak from behind or in front of a lectern. North Americans seem to prefer immediacy behaviors from speakers. Some cultures may expect less immediacy; the key is not to violate what listeners expect.[34] For example, we've been told that Japanese audiences don't expect speakers to move from behind a lectern and stand very close to listeners. Even in small seminars, Japanese speakers and teachers typically stay behind the lectern.

➤ **Monitor your expression of emotion.** Not all cultures interpret and express emotions the same way. People from the Middle East and the Mediterranean are typically more expressive and animated in their conversation than are Europeans.[35] As we noted in Chapter 5, people from a high-context culture—a culture in which nonverbal messages are exceptionally important (such as Japanese or Chinese culture)—place greater emphasis on your delivery of a message than do people from a low-context culture (such as North Americans).[36] Remember, however, that even though you may be speaking to an audience from a low-context culture—a culture that places a high value on verbal messages—you do not have license to ignore how you deliver a message. Delivery is *always* important. But audience members from a high-context culture will rely heavily on your unspoken message to help them interpret what you are saying.

➤ **Know the code.** Communication occurs when both speaker and listener share the same code system—both verbal and nonverbal. One of your authors embarrassed himself with a Caribbean audience because he used a circled thumb and finger gesture to signal "okay" to compliment a student. Later he discovered that this was an obscene gesture—like extending a middle finger to a North American audience. Even subtle nonverbal messages communicate feelings, attitudes, and cues about the nature of the relationship between you and your audience, so it is important to avoid gestures or expressions that would offend your listeners.

Although we cannot provide a comprehensive description of each cultural expectation you may face in every educational and professional setting, we can remind you to keep cultural expectations in mind when you rehearse and deliver a speech. We are not suggesting that you totally abandon your own cultural expectations about speech delivery. Rather, we urge you to become sensitive and responsive to cultural differences. There is no universal dictionary of nonverbal meaning, so spend some time asking people who are from the same culture as your prospective audience about what gestures and expressions your audience will appreciate.

Rehearsing Your Speech: Some Final Tips

Just knowing some of the characteristics of effective speech delivery will not make you a better speaker unless you can put these principles into practice. Effective public speaking is a skill that takes practice. Practicing takes the form of rehearsing. As indicated in Figure 13.1, rehearsing your speech helps you prepare to deliver your speech to an audience.

Do you want to make a good grade on your next speech? Research suggests that one of the best predictors of the effectiveness of a speech is the amount of time you spend preparing and rehearsing it; instructors gave higher grades to students who spent more time rehearsing their speeches and lower grades to students who spent less time preparing and rehearsing.[37] The following suggestions can help you make the most of your rehearsal time.

- ➤ **Finish drafting your speech outline at least two days before your speech performance.** The more time you have to work on putting it all together, the better.

- ➤ **Before you prepare the speaking notes to use in front of your audience, rehearse your speech aloud.** This will help you determine where you will need notes to prompt yourself.

- ➤ **Time your speech.** Revise your speech as necessary to keep it within the time limits set by your instructor or whoever invited you to speak.

- ➤ **Prepare your speaking notes.** Use whatever system works best for you. Some speakers use pictorial symbols to remind themselves of a story or an idea. Others use complete sentences or just words or phrases in an outline pattern to prompt them. Most teachers advocate using note cards for speaking notes.

- ➤ **Rehearse your speech standing up.** This will help you get a feel for your use of gestures as well as your vocal delivery. Do not try to memorize your speech or choreograph specific gestures. As you rehearse, you may want to modify your speaking notes to reflect appropriate changes.

- ➤ **If you can, present your speech to someone else so that you can practice establishing eye contact.** Seek feedback from your captive audience about both your delivery and your speech content.

- ➤ **If possible, record or videotape your speech during the rehearsal stage.** This will allow you to observe your vocal and physical mannerisms and make necessary changes. If you don't have a video camera, you may find it

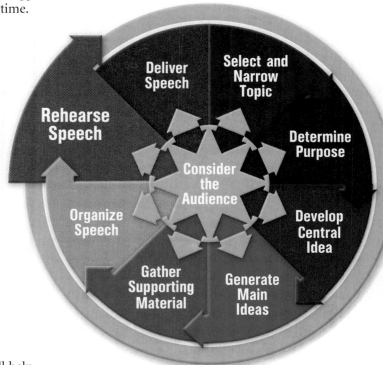

Figure 13.1 *Rehearsing your speech delivery will help you present your speech with confidence.*

DEVELOPING YOUR SPEECH STEP BY STEP

Rehearse Your Speech

Ashley begins to rehearse her speech. From the beginning, she stands and speaks aloud, practicing gestures and movements that seem appropriate to her message.

At first, Ashley uses her preparation outline (pp. 244–245) as speaking notes. These early rehearsals go pretty well, but the speech is running just slightly long. She needs to edit a bit.

Ashley considers her listeners again. What part of her speech might be least effective with them? The *Progressive Grocer Magazine* material is rather general in nature and doesn't really add much substance to her argument. She can even imagine a fellow student or two snickering at the publication's title. So she decides to cut that material before she prepares her speaking notes and continues rehearsing.

useful to practice before a mirror so that you can observe your body language—it's low-tech, but it still works.

- **Rehearse using all your presentation aids.** As we discuss in the next chapter, don't wait until the last minute to plan, prepare, and rehearse with flipcharts, slides, overhead transparencies, or other aids that you will need to manipulate as you speak.

- **Your final rehearsals should re-create, as much as possible, the speaking situation you will face.** If you will be speaking in a large classroom, find a large classroom in which to rehearse your speech. If your audience will be seated informally in a semicircle, then this should be the context in which you rehearse your speech. The more realistic the rehearsal, the more confidence you will gain.

- **Practice good delivery skills while rehearsing.** Remember this maxim: Practice *makes* perfect if practice *is* perfect.

Delivering Your Speech

The day of your speech arrives, and you are ready. Using information about your audience as an anchor, you have developed a speech on an interesting topic and with a fine-tuned purpose. Your central idea is clearly identified. You have gathered interesting and relevant supporting material and organized it well. Your speech has an appropriate introduction, a logically arranged body, and a clear conclusion that nicely summarizes your key theme. You have rehearsed your speech several times; it is not memorized, but you are comfortable with the way you express the major ideas. Your last task is calmly and confidently to communicate with your audience. You are ready to deliver your speech.

As the time for presenting your speech to your audience approaches, consider the following suggestions to help you prepare for a successful performance (see Figure 13.2).

- **At the risk of sounding like your mother, we suggest that you get plenty of rest before your speech.** Last-minute, late-night final preparations can take the edge off your performance. Many professional public speakers also advocate that you watch what you eat before you speak; a heavy meal or too much caffeine can have a negative effect on your performance.

- **Review the suggestions in Chapter 1 for becoming a confident speaker.** It is normal to have prespeech jitters. But if you have developed a well-organized, audience-centered message on a topic of genuine interest to you, you're doing all the right things to make your speech a success. Remember some of the other tips for developing confidence. Re-create the speech environment when you rehearse. Use deep breathing techniques to help you relax. Also, make sure you are especially familiar with your introduction and conclusion. Act calm to feel calm.

- **Arrive early for your speaking engagement.** If the room is in an unfamiliar location, give yourself plenty of time to find it. As we suggested in Chapter 5, you may want to rearrange the furniture or make other changes in the speaking environment. If you are using audiovisual equipment, check to see that it is working properly and set up your support material carefully. You might even project a slide or two to make sure they are in the tray right side up. Budget your time so you do not spend your moments before you speak hurriedly looking for a parking place or frantically trying to attend to last-minute details.

- **Visualize success.** Picture yourself delivering your speech in an effective way. Also, remind yourself of the effort you have spent preparing for your speech. A final mental rehearsal can boost your confidence and help ensure success.

Even though we have identified many time-tested methods for enhancing your speech delivery, keep in mind that speech delivery is an art rather than a science. The manner of your delivery should reflect your personality and individual style.

Adapting Your Speech Delivery for Television

You may not plan to be a newscaster or a politician whose messages are routinely broadcast on local or national radio or TV, but you may have an opportunity to be interviewed for a news story or find that a speech you deliver is also going to be videotaped. And with the advent of satellite video teleconferences and the increasing use of video software on the Internet, it is becoming increasingly common for messages to be transmitted electronically to audiences that are not physically present. Should you use a different style of speaking when speaking to the media? When your message is telecast to others, use the principles and skills we've discussed already and keep the following additional specific guidelines in mind.

◆ **Consider toning down gestures.** Most newscasters use subtle head nods and facial expressions rather than pronounced gestures to help emphasize their points. Keep your hands still, and don't fidget with pens, hair, or clothing. Also, keep your hands away from your face. Of course, if your primary audience are those who are physically present when you present your speech, they are the audience to whom you adapt your style of speaking. But if the target audience is watching on monitors elsewhere, tone down the gestures a bit.

In January, 2004, Democratic presidential hopeful Howard Dean delivered a screeching, arm-waving outburst to supporters after he finished third in the Iowa Caucus. A few days later, Dean defended the speech as appropriate to the "3,500 kids waving American flags who'd worked their hearts out for us for three weeks."[38] Unfortunately, Dean's emotionalism did not come across well to the television audience that was also watching, and some people believe it cost Dean the nomination.

◆ **Dress for TV success.** White clothing sometimes creates a glare on TV. Men who do not plan to wear a jacket may want to wear a light blue rather than a white dress shirt, and women should consider nonwhite clothing. You may also want to avoid black or dark gray—these colors can look too somber. Also, avoid large patterns, jangling or shiny jewelry, and overly frilly or complicated necklines. Solid colors look best. The camera can add five to ten pounds to your appearance. No, you don't need to go on a crash diet before a TV appearance, but do wear clothes that make you look and feel your best.

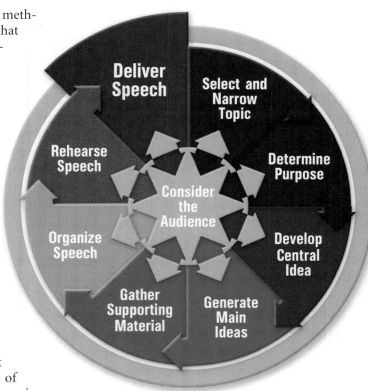

Figure 13.2 *You need to be audience-centered during the final step of the speechmaking process—delivering the speech.*

confidently connecting with your audience

Re-Create the Speech Environment When You Rehearse

As you rehearse delivering your speech, don't just sit at your desk and mentally review your message. Instead, stand up and imagine that you are in the very room in which you will deliver your speech. Or, if it is possible, rehearse your speech in the room in which you will present your speech. Even just by imagining the exact room and audience you will have when presenting your speech you are helping to manage your anxiety. When you actually give your speech, you will have less anxiety because you've had experience imagining or presenting your speech in the environment in which you will speak.

Deliver Your Speech

The long-awaited day of Ashley's speech has arrived at last. She slept well last night and ate a light breakfast before driving to campus.

Breathing deeply, Ashley visualizes herself delivering her speech calmly and confidently. When her name is called, she walks to the front of the room and establishes eye contact with her audience before she begins to speak.

During her speech, Ashley focuses on adapting her message to her listeners. She looks at individual members of her audience, uses purposeful and well-timed gestures, and speaks loudly and clearly.

Even before she hears the applause, Ashley knows that her speech has been a success.

◆ **Monitor your facial expressions.** Be aware that TV amplifies facial expressions. Your listeners are seeing your expression up close rather than from a distance, as they would in a live public-speaking context. Therefore, if you have a tendency to use exaggerated or exceptionally dramatic expressions, realize that the audience will see them from the camera's perspective. Smile appropriately, but make sure you're not smiling at inappropriate times. If you are asked a serious question but you have a big grin on your face when the camera cuts to you, it will appear that you are insensitive to the question.

◆ **Keep your target audience in mind.** If your message will be broadcast to many people, remind yourself whom you are trying to reach. If you're giving a persuasive presentation, realize that you do not necessarily want to persuade everyone in "TV land" who sees you.

◆ **Keep it short.** If you are giving a political speech or a presentation that you hope will be picked up by the media, realize that you will only be given a few seconds of air time for a news broadcast. Editors look for sound bites.

◆ **Choose your words with care and style.** The sound bites that often get quoted or broadcast are those phrases that are particularly attention catching or that communicate the essence of your message in a memorable way. Review the strategies for creating drama (omission, inversion, suspension) or creating cadence (parallelism, antithesis, repetition, alliteration) that we presented in Chapter 12. When we recently served as consultants to a political candidate, we were asked to review a draft of her speech declaring her candidacy for the U.S. House of Representatives. The speech was good but had no obvious attention-catching, stylized phrases that would lend themselves to good quotes for the media. We suggested she add some repetition, alliteration, and parallelism. Sure enough, the phrases quoted in the media were those she had taken special care to stylize.

◆ **Become familiar with the technology before you speak.** If you are being taped or broadcast in a studio, be sure to arrive in plenty of time so that you won't have to rush around making last-minute adjustments to your microphone.

Responding to Questions

I t's possible that a speech you deliver will be followed by a question-and-answer (Q & A) session. These sessions can be especially challenging, because although you may not know the questions in advance, you will still be expected to deliver your answers thoughtfully and smoothly. During a Q & A session, your delivery method changes to impromptu speaking. In addition to the suggestions for impromptu speaking we offered earlier, here are additional tips to make the Q & A period less challenging.[39]

Prepare. One of the best ways to prepare for a Q & A session is to anticipate what questions you may be asked. How do you anticipate questions? You analyze your audience. Think of possible questions those particular listeners might ask you, and then rehearse your answers. Prior to presidential debates, candidates have their staff members pepper them with questions so the candidates can practice responding. Perhaps your friends can ask you questions after you've rehearsed your speech for them.

Repeat or rephrase the question. Repeating a question helps in four ways. First, your paraphrase makes sure that everyone can hear the question. Second, paraphrasing ensures that you understand the question before you go charging off with your answer. Third, by paraphrasing, you can succinctly summarize rambling questions. And finally, repeating the question gives you just a bit of time to think about your answer.

Stay on message. Sometimes listeners may ask questions unrelated to your talk. If so, you'll want to find a way to gently guide your questioner back to the message you have prepared. Keep bringing the audience back to your central idea. Your answers, rather than the questions, are what are important. We're not suggesting that you dodge questions; you should address the question asked, but re-emphasize the key points you have made. Some seasoned speakers suggest that you save a bit of your speech to deliver during the Q & A session. It's called giving a "double-barreled" talk.[40] You present your speech, and then, during the Q & A period, you give your second, much briefer speech.

Respond to the audience, not just the person who asked the question. Although you can start your response by having eye contact with the person who asked you a question, make sure that you stay audience-centered. Look at the entire audience and keep in mind that your response should be relevant to them. If the questioner wants specific information that is only of interest to that person, you could speak with the questioner individually after your speech.

Ask yourself the first question. One way to prime the audience for the Q & A session is to ask yourself a challenging question first. For example, you might say, "As we move into Q & A, a number of you may be wondering . . . ." State the question and answer it. Doing this also gives you a comfortable way to make a transition between the speech and the Q & A period. Asking yourself a tough question tells the audience that you're open for serious questions, and it snaps them to attention as well.

Listen nonjudgmentally. Use the effective listening skills that we discussed in Chapter 4. Keep your eyes focused on the person asking the question, lean forward slightly, and give your full attention to the questioner. Audience members expect speakers to be polite and attentive. If you think the question is stupid, *don't* say so. Just listen and respond courteously. Audience members can judge for themselves whether a question was appropriate or not. Don't wince, grimace, or scowl at the questioner. You'll gain more credibility by keeping your cool than by losing your composure.

Neutralize hostile questions. Every hostile question gives you an opportunity to score points with your listeners. You'll have your listeners' attention; use that attention to your advantage. The following strategies can help.

Restate the question. If the question was a lengthy attack, focus on the essence of the issue. If the question is, "Your ideas are just wrong! I'm angry that you have no clue as to how to proceed. Your proposal has been a disaster in the past. Why are you still trying to make it work?" a paraphrase could be, "You're asking me why I'm still trying to implement a program that hasn't been successful. From your perspective, the program has failed."

Acknowledge emotions. For example, you could say, "I can understand why you are angry. I share your anger and frustration. It's because of my frustration that I want to give my proposal more time to work."

Don't make the issue personal. Even if the hostile questioner has made you the villain, don't attack the person who asked the question. Keep the conversation focused on issues, not on personalities.

Get to the heart of the issue. Respond directly to a hostile question. Consider restating the evidence you presented in your speech. Or provide new insights to support your position.

➤ **When you don't know, admit it.** If you've been asked a question to which you don't know the answer, just say so. You can promise to find out more information and then get back to the person later. (If you make such a promise, follow through on it. Ask for the person's business card or e-mail address at the end of the Q & A session.)

➤ **Be brief.** Even if you've anticipated questions and have a "double-barreled" talk, make it short and to the point.

➤ **Use organizational signposts.** Quickly organize your responses. If you have two responses to a question, let your listeners know it. Then use a verbal signpost (a statement that clues your audience in to how you're organizing your message) by saying, "I have two responses. First . . ." When you get to your second point, say, "My second point is . . . ." These signposts will both help you stay organized and impress your listeners with your clarity.

➤ **Indicate when the Q & A period is concluding.** Tell your audience, "I have time for two more questions." Let them know that the Q & A session will soon conclude. Even if you have someone helping you moderate the discussion, you should remain in charge of concluding the session.

SUMMARY

In this chapter, we discussed the importance of effective speech delivery and identified suggestions for enhancing your delivery. The way you deliver your speech is the primary way in which you communicate your thoughts and emotions to an audience. Audiences will believe what they see more readily than what they hear.

Of the four methods of delivery—manuscript, memorized, impromptu, and extemporaneous—the extemporaneous method is most desirable in most situations. Speak from an outline without memorizing the exact words.

We offered several suggestions for enhancing your delivery. Your gestures and movements should appear natural and relaxed, definite, consistent with your message, varied, unobtrusive, and coordinated with what you say. They should also be appropriate to your audience and situation. Eye contact is the single most important delivery variable: Looking at your audience helps control communication, establishes your credi-

bility, maintains audience interest, and provides feedback about how your speech is coming across. Your facial expressions and vocal cues are the primary ways in which you communicate your feelings and emotions to an audience. How loudly you speak, how clearly you articulate, and how correctly you pronounce the words you use determine how well your audience will understand your thoughts; your vocal pitch, rate of speaking, and use of pauses help provide variation to add interest to your talk.

The chapter concluded with several suggestions for rehearsing and delivering your speech, as well as for speaking on television and responding to questions. We suggested that you leave at least two days to focus on your speech delivery and develop your speaking notes. As much as possible, re-create the speech environment when you rehearse. You will be rewarded with a smoother delivery style and more confidence when you deliver your message.

CONSIDERING YOUR AUDIENCE

- Select your delivery style (manuscript, memorized, impromptu, or extemporaneous) to best connect with your audience, as well as to achieve your speaking goal.

- Your use of gestures can provide cues to your audience about whether you wish them to respond or ask questions about your message; an open-palm gesture, for example, often suggests you are open for questions or audience interaction.

- Speech gestures should not call attention to themselves; audience members should focus on your message rather than on the beauty of your gestures.

- Rehearse your speech while keeping your audience in mind; imagine that your speaking audience is in front of you as you practice presenting your message.

- When presenting a message that will be televised or broadcast, consider who constitutes your target audience—the people you most want to influence.

CONSIDERING AUDIENCE DIVERSITY

- Use of gestures while speaking varies from culture to culture; for example, listeners from Japan and China usually prefer calmer, less flamboyant gestures.

- If English is not your native language, you may have to spend extra time working on your pronunciation and articulation. Two helpful tips to consider: Prolong your vowel sounds and reduce choppy word pronunciation by blending the end of one word into the beginning of the next word.

- If you know that you will be speaking to a group of people from a cultural background different from your own, try to consult with other speakers who have presented to that audience.

- Monitor your expression of emotion; not all cultures interpret and express emotion in the same way. People from high-context cultures will likely place greater emphasis on your delivery of a message than will people from low-context cultures (such as North Americans).

CRITICAL THINKING QUESTIONS

1. Roger was so nervous about his first speech on the evolution of the television sitcom that he practiced it again and again. He could have given the speech in his sleep. He had some great examples, and his instructor had praised his outline. But as he gave his speech, he saw his classmates tuning out. What might he have done wrong, and how could he have rescued his speech?

2. Monique has difficulty knowing what to do with her hands when she speaks. Because she is self-conscious about her gestures, she often just puts her hands behind her back. What advice would you give Monique to help her use gestures more effectively?

3. Professor Murray speaks slowly and in a monotone; consequently, many of her students do not like to listen to her music history lectures. What can she do to give her voice some variety?

ETHICAL QUESTIONS

1. Most politicians at the state or national level hire image consultants to help them project the most positive impression of their skills and abilities. Is it ethical to use such consultants, especially if the sole objective is to manipulate constituents into thinking the speaker is more credible than he or she really is?

2. What can listeners do to be less distracted by the delivery and emotional elements of a speaker's message and focus more on the substance or content of the message?

Improving Your Speech Delivery

Make a video of your speech as you rehearse it. Before presenting your speech to your audience, use the following questions to evaluate your delivery.

Delivery Style

Did I use an extemporaneous delivery style?

Did I use appropriate notes, but not read or memorize my speech?

Eye Contact

Did I establish eye contact with my audience before I began my speech?

Did I maintain eye contact during my speech?

Physical Delivery

Did I use gestures in a natural way?

Did I have an appropriate posture?

Facial Expression

Did I have an appropriate facial expression?

Did I vary my facial expression?

Vocal Delivery

Did I speak loudly enough to be heard clearly?

Did I speak with vocal variety?

Marc Chagall (1887–1985), *Self-Portrait with Seven Fingers*. 1912–13. Oil on canvas. 132 × 93 cm. Banque d'Images, ADAGP/Art Resource, N.Y.

The soul never thinks without a picture.

—ARISTOTLE

Using Presentation Aids

outline

objectives

After studying this chapter you should be able to do the following:

1. Discuss five ways in which presentation aids help communicate ideas to an audience.

2. Describe the use of three-dimensional presentation aids.

3. Identify ways of producing and using two-dimensional presentation aids.

4. Discuss the uses of audiovisual aids.

5. Identify guidelines for developing presentation aids.

6. Identify guidelines for using presentation aids.

P erhaps it's happened to you. A professor flashes one PowerPoint slide after another while droning on about British history or some other topic. As you sit there, bored out of your socks, you think, "Why doesn't she just hand out the PowerPoint slides or simply put them online and let us go? I don't need someone to read their notes to me." Following such a mind-numbing experience, you can understand the phrase "Death by PowerPoint."

PowerPoint and the multitude of other presentation aids that speakers may use—especially visual aids—are powerful tools: They can help communicate your ideas with greater clarity and impact than can words alone. But they can also overwhelm your speech or be so redundant that your audience tunes you out. This chapter will help you avoid being a PowerPoint "executioner" and ensure that your presentation aids add life to your speech rather than kill your message.

A **presentation aid** is any object that reinforces your point visually so that your audience can understand it. Charts, photographs, posters, drawings, graphs, slides, movies, and videos are just some of the types of presentation aids that we will discuss. Some of these, such as movies and videos, call on sound as well as sight to help you make your point.

When you are first required to give a speech using presentation aids, you may scratch your head, wondering, "How can I use presentation aids in an informative or persuasive speech? Those kinds of speeches don't lend themselves to visual images." As it happens, almost any speech can benefit from presentation aids. A speech for which you are required to use presentation aids is not as different from other types of speeches as you might at first think. Your general objective is still to inform, persuade, or entertain. The key difference is that you will use supporting material that can be seen, rather than only heard, by an audience.

In this chapter, we look at presentation aids as an important communication tool and also examine several kinds. Toward the end of the chapter, we suggest guidelines for using presentation aids in your speeches.

The Value of Presentation Aids

P resentation aids are invaluable to an audience-centered speaker. They help your audience *understand* and *remember* your message and help you communicate the *organization* of ideas, gain and maintain *attention*, and illustrate a *sequence* of events or procedures.[1]

 Presentation aids enhance understanding. Of your five senses, you learn more from sight than from all the others combined. In fact, it has been estimated that more than 80 percent of all information comes to you through sight.[2] To many people, seeing is believing. We are a visually oriented society. For example, most of us learn the news by seeing it presented on TV. Because your audience is accustomed to visual reinforcement, it is wise to consider how you can increase their understanding of your speech by using presentation aids.

Presentation aids enhance memory. Your audience will not only have an improved understanding of your speech, but they will also better remember what

presentation aid
Anything tangible (drawings, charts, graphs, video images, photographs, sounds) that helps communicate an idea to an audience

you say as a result of visual reinforcement.[3] There is evidence that high-tech presentation aids enhance learning.[4] Researchers estimate that you remember 10 percent of what you read, 20 percent of what you hear, 30 percent of what you see, and 50 percent of what you simultaneously hear and see. For example, in your speech about the languages spoken in Africa, your audience is more likely to remember words in Arabic, Swahili, and Hausa if you display the words visually, rather than just say them.

➤ **Presentation aids help listeners organize ideas.** Most listeners need help understanding the structure of a speech. Even if you clearly lay out your major points, use effective internal summaries, and make clear transition statements, your listeners will welcome additional help. Listing major ideas on a chart, a poster, or an overhead transparency can add clarity to your talk and help your audience grasp your main ideas. Visually presenting your major ideas during your introduction, for example, can help your audience follow them as you bring them into the body of your speech. You can display key ideas during your conclusion to help summarize your message succinctly.

➤ **Presentation aids help gain and maintain attention.** Keshia began her speech about poverty in the United States by showing a photo of the face of an undernourished child. She immediately had the attention of her audience. Chuck began his speech with the flash of his camera to introduce his photography lecture. He certainly alerted his audience at that point. Midway through her speech about the lyrics in rap music, Tomoko not only spoke the words but also displayed a giant poster of the song lyrics so that her audience could read the words and sing along. Presentation aids not only grab the attention of your listeners but also keep their interest when words alone might not.

➤ **Presentation aids help illustrate a sequence of events or procedures.** If your purpose is to inform an audience about a process—how to do something or how something functions—you can do this best through actual demonstrations or with a series of visuals. Whether your objective is instructing people on how to

LEARNING FROM GREAT SPEAKERS

Ronald Reagan (1911–2004)

The 40th president of the United States, Ronald Reagan, has often been called "The Great Communicator." His early experience in radio and film served him well, as he spoke not only to the audience assembled in front of him, but to those listening and watching via television as well. Reagan's inaugural address in 1981 was the first to be delivered from a podium on the west side of the U.S. Capitol building. From this site, the television cameras could broadcast sweeping views of national monuments, fitting presentation aids for Reagan's patriotic address.[5]

Reagan was a master of using visual support to reinforce his rhetorical point. When you present your speeches, consider how well-selected presentation aids could support your verbal message. Listeners believe what they see. Appropriate visual aids help you gain and maintain your listeners' attention. Imagine that you are in your audience when you present your message. Visualize how the visual rhetoric as well as the words you speak will have an overall impact on your listeners.

[Photo: Bob Daugherty/AP Images]

make a soufflé or how to build a greenhouse, demonstrating the step-by-step procedures helps your audience understand them.[6] If you wish to explain how hydroelectric power is generated, a series of diagrams can help your listeners understand and visualize the process.

When demonstrating how to make something, such as your prize-winning cinnamon rolls, you can prepare each step of the process ahead of time and show your audience each example as you describe the relevant step; for example, you might have the dough already mixed and ready to demonstrate how you sprinkle on the cinnamon. A climax to your speech could be to unveil a finished pan of rolls still warm from the oven. If time does not permit you to demonstrate how to prepare your rolls, you could have on hand a series of diagrams and photographs to illustrate each step of the procedure.

Today's audiences expect visual support. Contemporary audiences are quite different from those over a century ago when Thomas Edison invented the kinetoscope, a precursor of the movie camera. Edison said, "When we started out it took the average audience a long time to assimilate each image. They weren't trained to visualize more than one thought at a time."[7] Times have changed. The predominance of visual images—on TV, in movies, on the Internet, and even on our phones—attests to how central images are in the communication of information to modern audiences.

Contemporary communicators understand the power of visual rhetoric in informing and persuading others. **Visual rhetoric** is the use of images as an integrated element in the total communication effort a speaker makes to achieve his or her speaking goal.[8] To be a visual rhetorician is to assume the role of an audience member and consider not only what a listener hears but also what a listener sees. A speech should be more than just what a speaker says with a few PowerPoint slides or other visual aids added as an afterthought. Today's listeners are sophisticated and are more likely than listeners of only a few years ago to expect a visually satisfying message to help them make sense out of what you are saying.

Types of Presentation Aids

visual rhetoric

The use of images as an integrated element in the total communication effort a speaker makes to achieve the speaking goal

The first question many students ask when they learn they are required to use presentation aids is "What type of presentation aid should I use?" We will discuss various kinds, grouped into three classes: three-dimensional, two-dimensional, and audiovisual.

Three-Dimensional Presentation Aids

OBJECTS You have played the trombone since you were in fifth grade, so you decide to give an informative speech about the history and function of this instrument. Your trombone is an obvious presentation aid, which you could show to your audience as you talk about how it works. Perhaps you might play a few measures to demonstrate its sound and your talent. Or, you are an art major and have just finished a watercolor painting. Why not bring your picture to class to illustrate your talk about watercolor techniques?

Objects add interest because they are tangible. They can be touched, smelled, heard, and even tasted, as well as seen. Objects are real, and audiences like the real thing.

If you use an object to illustrate an idea, make sure that you can handle the object with ease. If an object is too large, it can be unwieldy and difficult to show to your audience. Tiny objects can only be seen close up. It will be impossible for your listeners to see the detail on your antique thimble, the intricate needlework on your cross-stitch sampler, or the attention to detail in your miniature log cabin. Other objects can be dangerous to handle. One speaker, for example, attempted a demonstration of how to string an archery bow. He made his audience extremely uncomfortable when his almost-strung bow flew over the heads of his listeners. He certainly got their attention, but he lost his credibility.

MODELS If it is not possible to bring the object you would like to show your audience, consider showing them a **model**. You cannot bring a World War II fighter plane to class, so buy or build a scale model instead. To illustrate her lecture about human anatomy, one student brought a plastic model of a skeleton. An actual human skeleton would have been difficult to get and carry to class. Similarly, colleges and universities do not allow firearms on campus. A drawing that shows the features of a gun is much safer than a real gun or even a toy gun as a presentation aid. If you need to show the movable parts of a gun, perhaps a papier-mâché, plastic, or wood model would serve. Make sure, however, that any model you use is large enough to be seen by all members of your audience. When Brad brought his collection of miniature hand-carved guitars to illustrate his talk on rock music, his too-small visuals didn't add to the message; they detracted from it.

PEOPLE At least since Ronald Reagan, U.S. presidents have often used people as visual aids during their State of the Union addresses, relating a poignant story and then asking the protagonist of the story, seated in the balcony, to stand and be recognized. One speechwriter noted that George W. Bush used this strategy to especially good effect, finding it "a way of coming down from the stage, as it were, and mingling with the crowd."[9]

In classroom speeches, too, people can serve as presentation aids. Amelia, a choreographer for the Ballet Folklorico Mexicano, wanted to illustrate an intricate Latin folk dance, so she arranged to have one of the troupe's dancers attend her speech to demonstrate the dance.

Using people to illustrate your message can be tricky, however. It is usually unwise to ask for spur-of-the-moment help from volunteers while you are delivering your speech. Instead, choose a trusted friend or colleague before your presentation so that you can fully inform him or her about what needs to be done. Rehearse your speech using your living presentation aid.

Also, it is distracting to have your support person stand beside you doing nothing. If you don't need the person to demonstrate something during your opening remarks, wait and introduce the person to your audience when needed.

Finally, do not allow your assistants to run away with the show. For example, don't let your dance student perform the *pas de bourré* longer than necessary to illustrate

model
A small object that represents a larger object

Figure 14.1 *If you were to use it for a speech, this remarkable photograph would have to be enlarged so that the back row of your audience could distinguish clearly between the katydid and the rosebud.*

[Photo: Frank Oberle/Stone/Getty Images]

your technique. Nor should you permit your models to prance about too provocatively while displaying your dress designs. And don't allow your buddy to throw you when you demonstrate the wrestling hold that made you the district wrestling champ. Remember, your presentation aids are always subordinate to your speech. You must remain in control.

Generally, *you* can serve as a presentation aid to demonstrate or illustrate major points. If you are talking about tennis, you might bring your racquet to class so that you can illustrate your superb backhand or simply show novices the proper way to hold it. If you are a nurse or an emergency room technician giving a talk about medical procedures, by all means wear your uniform to establish your credibility.

TWO-DIMENSIONAL PRESENTATION AIDS

Although three-dimensional objects, models, and people can be used to illustrate a talk, the most common presentation aids are two-dimensional: drawings, photographs, slides, maps, graphs, charts, flipcharts, chalkboards, and overhead transparencies. Today, you can use computer software to generate many of these forms, as we will discuss a little later in the chapter.

DRAWINGS Drawings are popular and often-used presentation aids because they are easy and inexpensive to make. Drawings can be tailored to your specific needs. To illustrate the functions of the human brain, for example, one student traced an outline of the brain and labeled it to indicate where brain functions are located. Another student wanted to show the different sizes and shapes of leaves of trees in the area, so she drew enlarged pictures of the leaves, using appropriate shades of green.

You don't have to be a master artist to develop effective drawings. As a rule, large and simple line drawings are more effective for stage presentations than are detailed images. If you have absolutely no faith in your artistic skill, you can probably find a friend or relative who can help you prepare a useful drawing, or you may be able to use computer software to generate simple line drawings.

PHOTOGRAPHS Photographs can be used to show objects or places that cannot be illustrated with drawings or that an audience cannot view directly. The problem with photos, however, is that they are usually too small to be seen clearly from a distance. If your listeners occupy only two or three rows, it might be possible to hold a photograph close enough for them to see a key feature of the picture. The details will not be visible, however, beyond the first row. Passing a photograph among your listeners is not a good idea either; it creates competition for your audience's attention.

The only way to be sure that a printed photograph will be effective as a presentation aid for a large audience is to enlarge it (see Figure 14.1). Some photo shops will produce poster-size color laser photocopies at a modest cost. Or, using a scanner or digital camera, you can incorporate your image into a computer program such as PowerPoint and project your image using a TV monitor or video projection system.

SLIDES Slides can help illustrate your talk if you have access to a screen and a slide projector. However, because of the increased use of computer-graphics programs such as PowerPoint, fewer speakers are illustrating their talks with slides. Working with slides can also present problems. Projector bulbs can burn out, and slides can jam in the projector. Moreover, with the lights out, you are less able to receive nonverbal feedback, and you cannot maintain eye contact with your audience.

Giving a slide lecture, therefore, requires considerable preparation. If, after considering all the disadvantages, you believe slides are still a workable option, consider these tips. First, be sure the slides are right side up and in the order in which you want to show them during your speech. Second, know in which direction the slide carousel moves as it feeds the projector so that you will know how to load it. Third, know how to operate the programming feature or the remote-control switch so that you can move back and forth among your slides, if you wish.

MAPS Most maps are designed to be read from a distance of no more than two feet. As with photographs, the details on most maps won't be visible to your audience. You could use a large map, however, to show general features of an area. Or you could use a magnified version of your map. Certain copiers can enlarge images as much as 200 percent. It is possible, using a color copier, to enlarge a standard map of Europe enough for listeners in the last row to see the general features of the continent. Using a dark marker, one speaker highlighted the borders on a map of Europe to indicate the countries she had visited the previous summer (see Figure 14.2). She used a red marker to show the general path of her journey.

GRAPHS A **graph** is a pictorial representation of statistical data in an easy-to-understand format. Because statistics are abstract summaries of many examples, most listeners find that graphs help make the data more concrete. Yet research also suggests that in addition to presenting information in a graph, it's important to narrate the information presented.[10] Don't just show it—talk about it. Graphs are particularly effective in showing overall trends and relationships among data. The four most common types of graphs are bar graphs, pie graphs, line graphs, and picture graphs. Many of today's computer presentation programs can easily convert statistics into visual form.

- **Bar Graphs.** A **bar graph** consists of flat areas—bars—of various lengths to represent information. The bar graph in Figure 14.3 clearly shows the projected growth rates of four different groups. This graph makes the information clear and immediately visible to the listeners. By comparison, words and numbers are more difficult to assimilate, especially in something as ephemeral as a speech.

- **Pie Graphs.** A **pie graph** shows the general distribution of data. The pie graphs in Figure 14.4 show that over a six-year period, there was a shift in where most cosmetic surgeries were performed. Pie graphs are especially useful in helping your listeners to see quickly how data are distributed in a given category or area.

graph
A pictorial representation of statistical data

bar graph
A graph in which bars of various lengths represent information

pie graph
A circular graph divided into wedges that show the distribution of data

Types of Presentation Aids   **313**

Figure 14.3 *Bar graphs can help summarize statistical information clearly so that the information is immediately visible to your audience.*

Source: U.S. Census Bureau

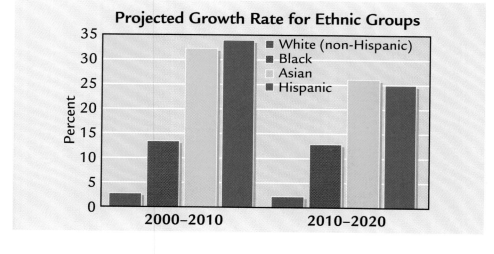

- **Line Graphs. Line graphs** show relationships between two or more variables. Like bar graphs, line graphs organize statistical data to show overall trends (Figure 14.5). A line graph can cover a greater span of time or numbers than a bar graph without looking cluttered or confusing. As with other types of presentation aids, a simple line graph communicates better than a cluttered one.

- **Picture Graphs.** In place of either a line or a bar, you can use pictures to supplement the data you are summarizing (Figure 14.6). **Picture graphs** look somewhat less formal and less intimidating than other kinds of graphs. One of the advantages of picture graphs is that they use few words or labels, which makes them easier for your audience to read.

line graph

A graph that uses lines or curves to show relationships between two or more variables

picture graph

A graph that uses images or pictures to symbolize data

chart

A display that summarizes information by using words, numbers, or images

CHARTS Charts summarize and present a great deal of information in a small amount of space (Figure 14.7, page 316). They have several advantages. They are easy to use, reuse, and enlarge. They can also be displayed in a variety of ways. You can use a flipchart, a poster, or an overhead projector, which can project a giant image of your chart on a screen. As with all other presentation aids, charts must be simple. Do not try to put too much information on one chart.

Figure 14.4 *A pie graph shows general distribution of data.*

Source: Data from the American Society for Aesthetic Plastic Surgery

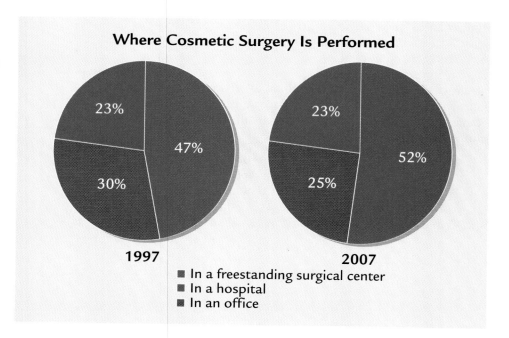

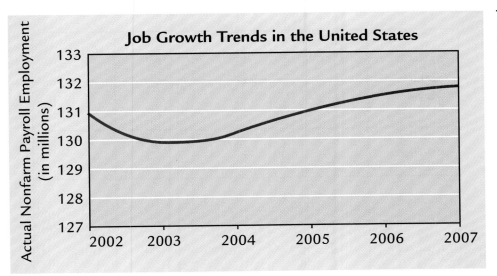

Figure 14.5 *Line graphs show relationships between two or more variables.*

The key to developing effective charts is to prepare the lettering of the words and phrases you use very carefully. If the chart contains too much information, audience members may feel it is too complicated to understand, and ignore it. If your chart looks at all cramped or crowded, divide the information into several charts and display each as needed. Do not handwrite the chart; given the availability of computers, a hand-lettered chart may seem unprofessional. Consider using computer software to prepare large charts or graphs. Make sure your letters are large enough to be seen clearly in the back row. Use simple words or phrases, and eliminate unnecessary words.

FLIPCHARTS A flipchart consists of a large pad of paper resting on an easel. Flipcharts are often used in business presentations and training sessions, although the prevalence of computer graphics software has reduced their use in corporate presentations. You can either prepare your visual aids before your speech or draw on the paper while speaking. Flipcharts are easy to use. During your presentation, you need only flip the page to reveal your next visual. Flipcharts are best used when you have brief information to display or when you want to summarize comments from audience members during a presentation.

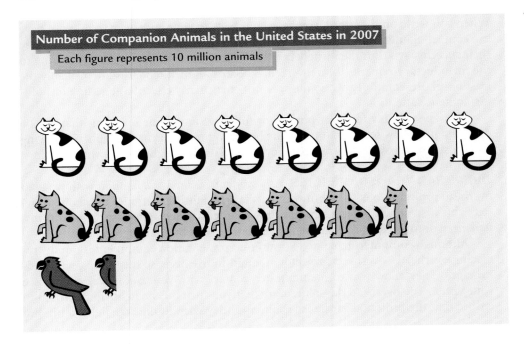

Figure 14.6 *Consider adding visual symbols to enhance your presentation of statistics.*

Source: American Veterinary Medical Association, *2007 U.S. Pet Ownership and Demographic Sourcebook* <www.avma.org>.

Team	W	L	Percent	GB	Streak
Toronto	84	69	.583	—	Won 2
Baltimore	78	64	.549	5	Lost 2
Milwaukee	77	65	.542	6	Won 2
New York	69	74	.483	14	Lost 1

Most experienced flipchart users recommend that you use lined paper to keep your words and drawings neat and well organized. Another suggestion is to pencil in speaking notes on the chart that only you can see. Brief notes on a flipchart are less cumbersome to use than notes on cards or a clipboard. If you do use notes, however, be sure that they are few and brief; using too many notes will tempt you to read rather than have eye contact with your audience.

CHALKBOARDS AND WHITEBOARDS A fixture in classrooms for centuries, chalkboards are often used to offer visual support for spoken words. Whiteboards are replacing chalkboards in both education and business settings; these more contemporary boards serve the same function as chalkboards, but instead of writing on a black or green slate with a piece of chalk, the speaker writes on a whiteboard with a marker. Chalkboards and whiteboards have several advantages: They are inexpensive, simple to use, and low-tech, so you don't need to worry about extension cords or special training.

Although you can find a chalkboard or whiteboard in most classrooms and boardrooms, many public-speaking teachers discourage overuse of them. Why? When you write on the board, you have your back to your audience; you do not have eye contact! Some speakers try to avoid that problem by writing on the board before their speech starts. But then listeners often look at the visual rather than listening to the introductory remarks. Moreover, chalkboards and whiteboards are probably the least novel presentation aids, so they are not particularly effective at getting or holding audience attention.

Use a board only for brief phrases or for very simple line diagrams that can be drawn in just a few seconds. It is usually better to prepare a chart, graph, or drawing on a poster or an overhead transparency than to use a chalkboard or whiteboard.

OVERHEAD TRANSPARENCIES As a student, you may be familiar with what an overhead projector looks like, but you may have had little experience using one yourself. This instrument projects images drawn on clear sheets of plastic, called *transparencies*, onto a screen so that the images can be seen by a large group.

Although computer-generated PowerPoint presentation equipment is rapidly replacing overheads, overhead projectors remain in use because they have several advantages. They allow you to maintain eye contact with your audience, yet still see your visual. The overhead doesn't require that you turn off the lights in the room to ensure that the projected image is visible. You may wish to dim the lights a bit, but most images can be seen clearly in normal room light. Overhead projectors also permit you to prepare your transparency ahead of time and to mark on it during your presentation. If you do write on a transparency during your speech, limit yourself to a few short words or to underlining key phrases. Some speakers use a computer to develop a PowerPoint slide but then make a transparency of the image. Speakers who want to make doubly certain that their PowerPoint images can be projected to their listeners use the transparencies as a backup to using a computer to project the image.

Consider the following suggestions when using an overhead projector.

- **If possible, practice with the overhead projector in the room in which you will be delivering your speech.** That way you can be certain that the projector is the proper distance from the screen and that your image will be large enough to be seen.

- **When you are not showing a visual, turn the overhead projector off so it does not detract from your speech.**

- **Do not put too much information on one transparency.** Use no more than seven lines on one sheet. Do not use a full page of typewritten material in an overhead projection.

- **Align the projector so that the head beams the image directly onto the screen.** If the image is too low, it will get projected up and suffer a distortion called a *keystone effect* (see Figure 14.8), which makes the image seem larger at the top and smaller at the bottom. Besides making sure the projector is properly aligned, you can tilt the projector screen forward if it is mounted high on a wall.

- **When you use an overhead projector, you may need to increase the volume of your voice.** The fan's motor, which keeps the high-intensity projector bulb cool, can be noisy.

- **When developing your transparency, consider using a large type size.** Using 18-point, 24-point, or even larger type will make your words easier to read. Because most students develop written materials using a computer, it is very easy simply to increase the size of the type, even if it means putting your information on more than one transparency. Bigger *is* better.

- **Reveal one line of text at a time by blocking out the text below it with a sheet of paper.** This helps hold the audience's interest.

- **If possible, leave the bottom fourth of your transparency blank.** Images projected low on the screen often are not visible to audience members in the back.

- **Consider using the overhead projector without a transparency as a spotlight to highlight something you have written on a poster or chalkboard.** With a large audience, an accent light can add emphasis to other visuals.

Figure 14.8 *Note the difference between an overhead projector image that produces a keystone effect and an image made by a projector that is properly adjusted.*

- **Consider using color.** Colored acetate sheets are available from most bookstores. You can also use different colors of markers to highlight key points.
- **For ease of handling, place the transparency in a cardboard frame.** These are available wherever acetate sheets are sold. A frame lessens the likelihood that transparencies will stick together or become torn along the edges.

COMPUTER-GENERATED PRESENTATION AIDS

Richard had worked hard on his presentation to the finance committee. He had prepared impressive-looking overhead transparencies, distributed a handout of his key conclusions, and rehearsed his speech so that he had a well-polished delivery. But as he sat down after concluding his speech, certain he had dazzled his listeners, his colleague seated next to him poked him and said, "Why didn't you use PowerPoint slides?"

BASIC PRINCIPLES OF USING COMPUTER-GENERATED PRESENTATION AIDS

Many audiences, especially those in the corporate world, have come to expect to see computer-generated graphics created with such popular software as Power-Point. **Computer-generated graphics** are images, words, charts, and graphs designed and presented with the help of a computer and special computer software. Although computer-generated graphics can be overused and, like any presentation aid, can distract from your message if used improperly, they nonetheless open up professional-looking possibilities for illustrating your speech.

One of the biggest problems with PowerPoint presentations is the fact that a speaker may be tempted to shovel vast amounts of information at listeners without regard for the listeners' attention span. Research supports our now-familiar admonition that the audience should be foremost in your mind as you develop visual images to support your verbal message.[11]

Using a presentation program such as PowerPoint, you can design and create complete presentation aids on your personal computer. You can then use the computer again to display the presentation to your audience by connecting the computer to a special projector. You can run the program manually using a mouse (some computers are even equipped with a wireless mouse) or the keyboard to advance the images as you speak, or you can set the program to run automatically. Even if you don't have access to a computer to use for your in-class presentation, you can create the graphic images you need using a computer at a commercial copy center or campus computer lab and then transfer the images to slides or overhead transparencies. Or you can print the images on paper and develop dazzling posters to display on an easel.

computer-generated graphics
Images, charts, graphs, and words that are created using a computer program

Technology can provide useful tools for speakers. But a glitzy software presentation cannot take the place of a carefully crafted speech.

[Photo: Carl J. Single/The Image Works]

The various presentation software packages are designed to let you easily include a variety of aids in your presentation. For instance, you can develop a key word or phrase outline to emphasize your main points as you speak. You can also incorporate into the presentation computer-generated graphs, charts, or drawings or use presentation software to display statistical information or illustrate particular points. You can also use a scanner to convert any photograph or drawing into digital format, which you can then incorporate as a visual image in your presentation. If you have the necessary equipment, the presentation software can even incorporate video or audio clips. As with any presentation aid, the images or clips that you choose to display must help develop your central idea; otherwise, do not include them.

There is an art to developing effective computer-generated graphics. But you don't have to be a professional artist. That's the advantage of using computer-generated graphics—virtually anyone can use them to craft professional-looking images. In addition to learning the mechanics of the software program, keep the following tips in mind when designing computer graphics.[12]

TIPS FOR USING COMPUTER-GENERATED PRESENTATION AIDS

Keep Sights and Sounds Simple In most aspects of communication, simple is better. Even though you *can* use fancy fonts and add as many images as you like to your visual, we have a suggestion for you: Don't. Keep in mind what we've stressed throughout this chapter: Presentation aids *support* your message; they are not your message. Or, as CEO John W. Roe wisely expressed, "Visual aids should be made to steer, not to row."[13]

What are techniques for keeping your visual message simple? Consider these ideas:

- Use no more than seven lines of text on any single visual.
- Use bullet points.
- Use bullets in parallel structure (such as beginning each bulleted phrase with the same word, as we are doing in this list).
- Use the heading of each slide to summarize the essential point of the visual; if listeners only read the headings of your visuals, they should still be able to follow the key points of the story you're telling.[14]

Most graphics software let you add sound effects to highlight your message. But the sound of a racecar zooming across the computer screen or a typewriter sound as letters pop in place can detract from your speech. Cute sounds often lose their novelty after the first slide or two and can become irritating. We suggest that *you* be the sound track, not your computer.

Control PowerPoint Images When using PowerPoint slides with a computer, there may be times when you want to speak to your audience and not refer to a slide or image. Use a blank PowerPoint slide or, if it's within easy reach, simply cover the projector lens when you don't want the audience to look at a particular slide or image.

Repeat Visual Elements to Unify Your Presentation Use a common visual element, such as a bullet or visual symbol, at the beginning of each word or phrase on a list. Use common color schemes and spacing to give your visuals coherence. Also, avoid mixing and matching different fonts. You get a professional, polished look when you use a similar visual style for each of your images.

Of course, the most significant advantage of computer graphics is the ease with which they allow you to display visual images. Both color and black-and-white images are available as **clip art**. Clip art consists of pictures and images that are either in printed form or stored as electronic images in a computer file. You can incorporate these images into your visuals. Clip art (as shown in Figure 14.9) can give your visuals and graphics a professional touch even if you did not excel in art class.

clip art
Images or pictures stored in a computer file or in printed form that can be used in a presentation aid

Figure 14.9 *Clip art can be used to illustrate visuals.*

Choose a Typeface with Care You'll be able to choose from among dozens of typefaces and **fonts**. Make an informed choice rather than just using a typeface because it strikes your fancy at the moment. Graphic designers divide typefaces into four different types: serif, sans serif, script, and decorative. You'll see each of these illustrated in Figure 14.10. Serif fonts, like the ones you are reading in this book, are easier to read for longer passages because the little lines at the tops and bottoms of the letters (called *serifs*) help guide the eye from one letter to the next. Sans serif fonts (*sans* means "without") do not have the extra lines. Script fonts are designed to look like handwriting; although interesting and dramatic, script fonts should be used sparingly because they are harder to read. And use decorative fonts only when you want to communicate a certain special tone or mood. Regardless of which font style or typeface you use, don't use more than one or two typefaces on a single visual; if you do use two, designers suggest they should be from different font categories.

Make Informed Decisions about Using Color Color communicates. Red and orange are warm colors and communicate excitement and interest (which is why most fast-food restaurant chains use red, yellow, and orange in their color schemes; they literally want to make you hungry and catch your attention). Cooler colors such as green and blue have a more calming effect on viewers. Warm colors tend to come forward and jump out at the viewer, whereas cooler colors recede into the background. What are the implications of the power of color to communicate? Consider using warm colors for positive messages (for example, "Profits are up") and cooler colors for more negative messages ("We're losing money").

Designers caution against using certain color combinations. For example, if some audience members are color-blind, they won't be able to distinguish between red and green. And, don't get carried away using color. To unify your presentation, use the same background color on all visuals and no more than two colors for words.

font

A particular style of typeface

Figure 14.10 *Typefaces grouped by font type*

A dark background with lighter-colored words can have a pleasing effect and can be easy to see.

Allow Plenty of Time to Prepare Your Presentation Aids Prepare your presentation aids well in advance of your speaking date so that you can make them as attractive and polished-looking as possible. Avoid late-night, last-minute construction of your presentation aids. A sloppy, amateurish presentation aid will convey the impression that you are not a credible speaker, even if you have spent many hours preparing the verbal part of your speech. If you haven't used computer-generated graphics before, don't expect to whip out the software manual and produce professional-looking images the night before your presentation. Focus your final hours on rehearsing, not on learning a computer program.

AUDIOVISUAL AIDS

Audiovisual aids combine sound and images to communicate ideas. With audiovisual aids you combine the power of visual rhetoric with a supporting audio rhetoric soundtrack. You are undoubtedly familiar with media that combine images and sound. In addition to using computer software to import sounds and music, you can use DVDs (digital video disks), videotapes, iPods or other MP3 players, as well as more traditional audio aids to help you communicate your ideas.

DVDS A **DVD (digital video disk)** has several advantages over the older technology of videotapes. Not only does it have excellent picture quality (and newer high-definition DVDs have even more dazzling image quality), but it can be started and stopped with precision.

DVD (digital video disk)
An electronic storage mode similar to a CD-ROM, except that it can store much more information and display it with exceptional clarity and fidelity

With the advent of DVD recorders, it's now easy to record video images and audio clips to support speech ideas. But because newer DVD recorders may use a format that is not compatible with DVD players that are even a couple of years old, it would be wise to be certain that your self-recorded DVD will be usable on the equipment that will be available when you deliver your presentation. You may, for example, have recorded something using a DVD-RW format, and the DVD player may only play DVD-R or DVD+RW. It pays to double-check the compatibility of the equipment you use well in advance of your presentation.

VIDEOTAPES Although DVDs are replacing videotapes, there are still some movies and other programs that are only available on videotape. A high-quality VCR allows you to show portions of a videotape using stop-action, freeze-frame, and slow-motion functions.

You can also use a video camera to tape your own images to help you communicate your ideas. (Many video cameras record on DVDs instead of tape.) If, for example, you wanted to illustrate the frustration of not being able to park on your campus, a video of full parking lots and harried commuters hunting for parking spots would help you make your point. Or, to explain how litter and trash are making your downtown area look shabby, a video of the debris blowing across the town square makes your point better than just words alone.

A 25-inch screen is generally visible to an audience of twenty-five or thirty people. For larger audiences, you will need several TV monitors or a large projection TV system. Or, you can use a TV with a large monitor to display your video. Before you decide to use a videotape, however, think about whether it will really enhance your speech. Although movies can dramatically capture and hold your audience's attention, they are not really designed as supporting material for a speech. Usually, they are conceived as self-contained packages, and unless you show only short excerpts, they can quickly overwhelm your speech. Of course, if you are a skilled moviemaker, you will probably have enough control over your medium to tame it and make it serve your purpose. Be sure to rehearse with the equipment until you can handle it smoothly.

AUDIO AIDS CDs (compact disks), tapes, or iPods or other MP3 players can be used to complement visual displays—you might play a few measures of Bach's *Toccata and Fugue in D Minor* on CD or from your iPod or even on a portable electronic

---

SPEAKER'S HOMEPAGE

Using the Internet as a Source for Visuals for Your Speeches

Whether it's Mona Lisa's beguiling smile, Grant Wood's famous "American Gothic" image of the farm couple standing in front of their home, or some other famous painting, you now have the resources of the world's art museums at your fingertips.

Here's a sampling of links from the Allyn and Bacon Web site on public speaking and other sites that you can explore as sources of visuals for your speech.

➤ ART LINKS
www.artcyclopedia.com

➤ TIME & LIFE PHOTO SITE
www.timelifepictures.com/

➤ AMERICAN MEMORY COLLECTION FROM THE LIBRARY OF CONGRESS
www.memory.loc.gov/

➤ YAHOO!
http://www.yahoo.com/

➤ GOOGLE
www.images.google.com/

---

keyboard to illustrate a point. While showing slides of her recent Caribbean vacation, a student used a recording of steel drum music as a soft introductory background for her talk. Another student interviewed frustrated students who had difficulty figuring out the most recent changes in how to apply for financial aid. Rather than reading quotes from irate students who had their financial aid denied, he played a few excerpts of taped interviews.

Today's iPods and MP3 players can be used to play more than just sound. You can store movies and TV programs on them as well. Of course, you'll need external speakers or the proper cables to connect to a TV or video monitor in order to play the sounds and images. But the size and portability of the new digital technology makes it easy to augment your talk with sounds and images.

One last reminder: Don't let your audio soundtrack detract from your speech. Use sound sparingly but effectively to support your points.

Guidelines for Developing Presentation Aids

The following guidelines offer commonsense and research-based strategies that can help you prepare effective presentation aids for your speeches.

MAKE THEM EASY TO SEE

Without a doubt, the most violated principle of using presentation aids in public speaking is "Make it big!" Countless speeches have been accompanied by a chart or graph with writing too small to read, an overhead projector image not large enough to be legible, or a graph on a flipchart that simply can't be deciphered from the back row. If the only principle you carry away from this chapter is to make your presentation aid large enough to be seen by all in your audience, you will have gained more skill than a majority of speakers who use presentation aids in speeches. *Write big!*

KEEP THEM SIMPLE

Simple presentation aids usually communicate best. Some students think that the visuals accompanying a speech must be as complicated as a Broadway production, complete with lights and costumes. Resist trying to make your visuals complicated. Indeed, *any* complexity is too much. Words should be limited to key words or phrases. Lengthy dissertations on poster board or an overhead usually do more harm than good. Don't cram too much information on one chart or overhead. If you have a great deal of information, it is better to use two or three simple charts or overhead transparencies than to attempt to put all your words on one visual.

Here's an outline of an informative speech that uses simple visual aids (which could be displayed on charts or as computer-generated graphics) to clearly communicate the ideas the speaker wishes to convey.[15]

TOPIC:	Standard editorial symbols
GENERAL PURPOSE:	To inform
SPECIFIC PURPOSE:	At the end of my speech, the audience should be able to use and interpret ten standard symbols for editorial changes in written material.

I. The following seven editorial symbols are commonly used to change written text.

A. Use the "pigtail" symbol to delete a letter, a word, or a phrase.

B. Use a caret (it looks like a housetop) to insert a space, a letter, new text, or punctuation.

C. Use what look like two sideways parentheses to remove unwanted space.

D. Use this squiggle line to transpose letters, words, or phrases.

E. Draw three lines under letters to capitalize them.

F. Draw a slash through letters to change them to lowercase.

G. Write the word *stet* to undo previous editing marks.

II. Three editorial symbols are used to rearrange the format of text.

A. Use brackets to add or remove indents or to correct the alignment of text.

B. Use backward bracket marks around text that you want centered on the page.

C. Use a symbol that looks like a backward *p* to mark the beginning of new paragraphs.

After the speech, the speaker could give each audience member a simple one-page handout summarizing these editorial markings.

SELECT THE RIGHT PRESENTATION AIDS

Because there are so many choices, you may wonder, "How do I decide which presentation aid to use?" Here are some suggestions.

- **Consider your audience.** Factors such as audience size dictate the size of the visual you select. If you have a large audience, do not choose a presentation aid unless everyone can see it clearly. The age, interests, and attitudes of your audience also affect your selection of audiovisual support.
- **Think of your speech objective.** Don't select a presentation aid until you have decided on the purpose of your speech.
- **Take into account your own skill and experience.** Use only equipment with which you are comfortable or have had practical experience.
- **Know the room in which you will speak.** If the room has large windows with no shades and no other way to dim the lights, do not consider using visuals that require a darkened room.

DO NOT USE DANGEROUS OR ILLEGAL PRESENTATION AIDS

Earlier, we described a speech in which the speaker accidentally caused an archery bow to fly over the heads of his startled audience. Not only did he lose credibility because he was not able to string the bow successfully, he also endangered his audience by turning his presentation aid into a flying missile. Dangerous or illegal presentation aids may either shock your audience or physically endanger them. These types of aids will also detract from your message. They are never worth the risk of a ruined speech or an injured audience member. If your speech seems to call for a dangerous or illegal object or substance, substitute a picture, chart, or other representational device.

Guidelines for Using Presentation Aids

Now that we have offered strategies for developing effective presentation aids, here are some tips to help you use them for maximum audience impact.

REHEARSE WITH YOUR PRESENTATION AIDS

Jane nervously approached her speech teacher ten minutes before class. She wondered whether class could start immediately, because her presentation aid was melting. She had planned to explain how to get various stains out of clothing, and her first demonstration would show how to remove chewing gum. But she had forgotten the gum, so she had to ask for a volunteer from the audience to spit out his gum so she could use it in her demonstration. The ice she had brought to rub on the sticky gum had by this time melted. All she could do was dribble some lukewarm water on the gummed-up cloth in a valiant but unsuccessful effort to demonstrate her cleaning method. It didn't work. To make matters worse, when she tried to set her poster in the chalkboard tray, it kept falling to the floor. She ended up embarrassed and on the edge of tears. It was obvious that she had not rehearsed with her presentation aids.

Unlike Jane, Marti knew she had an important presentation the next day, and she was well prepared. Because she was going to use PowerPoint computer graphics in her presentation, she carefully developed each visual to coordinate with her talk. She rehearsed her speech in the same room in which she would be speaking; she also practiced her presentation using the same computer that she would use for her speech. She competently sailed through her presentation without a hitch. Although the unexpected can always happen, Marti's thorough preparation and rehearsal boosted both her confidence and her credibility with her listeners.

Your appearance before your audience should not be the first time you deliver your speech while holding up your chart, turning on the overhead projector, operating the slide projector, or using the flipchart. Practice with your presentation aids until you feel at ease with them.

MAKE EYE CONTACT WITH YOUR AUDIENCE, NOT WITH YOUR PRESENTATION AIDS

You may be tempted to talk to your presentation aid rather than to your audience. Your focus, however, should remain on your audience. Of course, you will need to glance at your visual to make sure that it isn't upside down or that it is the proper one. But do not face it while giving your talk. Keep looking your audience in the eye.

EXPLAIN YOUR PRESENTATION AIDS

Some speakers believe that they need not explain a presentation aid. They think it's enough just to show it to their audience. Resist this approach. When you exhibit your chart showing the overall decline in the stock market, tell your audience what point you are trying to make. Visual support performs the same function as verbal support. It helps you communicate an idea. Make sure that your audience knows what that idea is. Don't just unceremoniously announce, "Here are the recent statistics on birth rates in the United States" and hold up your visual without further explanation. Tell the audience how to interpret the data. Always set your visuals in a verbal context.

Do Not Pass Objects among Members of Your Audience

You realize that your marble collection will be too small to see, so you decide to pass some of your most stunning marbles around while you talk. Bad idea. While you are excitedly describing some of your cat's-eye marbles, you have provided a distraction for your audience. People will be more interested in seeing and touching the marbles than in hearing you talk about them.

What can you do if your object is too small to see without passing it around? If no other speaker follows your speech, you can invite audience members to come up and see your object when your speech is over. If your audience is only two or three rows deep, you can even hold up the object and move in close to the audience to show it while you maintain control.

Use Animals with Caution

Most actors are unwilling to work with animals—and for good reason. At best, they may steal the show. And most often, they are unpredictable. You may *think* you have the smartest, best-trained dog in the world, but you really do not know how your dog will react to a strange environment and an unfamiliar audience. The risk of having an animal detract from your speech may be too great to make planning a speech around one worthwhile.

A zealous student at a midwestern university a few years ago decided to give a speech on cattle. What better presentation aid, he thought, than a cow? He brought the cow to campus and led her up several flights of stairs to his classroom. The speech in fact went well. But the student had neglected to consider one significant problem: Cows will go up stairs but not down them.

Another student had a handsome, well-trained German shepherd guard dog. The class was enjoying his speech and his demonstrations of the dog's prowess until the professor from the next classroom poked his head in the door to ask for some chalk. The dog lunged, snarling and with teeth bared, at the unsuspecting professor. Fortunately, he missed—but the speech was concluded prematurely. These and other examples emphasize our point: Use animals with care, if at all.

Use Handouts Effectively

Many speech instructors believe that you should not distribute handouts during a speech. Handing out papers during your presentation will only distract your audience. However, many audiences in business and other types of organizations expect a summary of your key ideas in written form. If you do find it necessary to use written material to reinforce your presentation, keep the following suggestions in mind.

- **Don't distribute your handout during the presentation unless your listeners must refer to the material while you're talking about it.** Do not distribute handouts that have only a marginal relevance to your verbal message. They will defeat your purpose.
- **Control listeners' attention.** If you do distribute a handout and you see that your listeners are giving the written material more attention than

they are giving you, tell them where in the handout you want them to focus. For example, you could say, "I see that many of you are interested in the second and third pages of the report. I'll discuss those items in just a few moments. I'd like to talk about a few examples before we get to page 2."

- ➤ **After distributing your handouts, tell audience members to keep the material face down until you're ready to talk about the material.** This will help listeners not be tempted to peek at your handout instead of keeping their focus on you and your message.

- ➤ **Make sure you clearly number the pages on your handout material.** This will make it easy for you to direct audience members to specific pages in your handouts.

Animals are neither predictable nor dependable as presentation aids.

[Photo: Jason Moore/Zuma/NewsCom]

- ➤ **To make sure your listeners know what page of your handouts you want them to focus on, prepare overhead transparencies of each page of your handout.** You'll be able to display the specific page you're talking about. Even if the words are too small for audience members to read, they will be able to glance up and see what page you're on if they miss your verbal description of where you are in the material. With a transparency, you can also quickly point to the paragraph or chart on the page you want them to focus on. It's not a good idea, however, to economize by *only* displaying material designed to be used as handouts on an overhead projector and not providing handouts. The print will undoubtedly be too small to be seen clearly.

- ➤ **If your listeners do not need the information during your presentation, tell them that you will distribute a summary of the key ideas at the end of your talk.** Your handout might refer to the specific action you want your audience to take, as well as summarize the key information you have discussed.

TIME THE USE OF VISUALS TO CONTROL YOUR AUDIENCE'S ATTENTION

A skillful speaker knows when to show a supporting visual and when to put it away. For example, it's not wise to begin your speech with all your charts, graphs, and drawings in full view unless you are going to refer to them in your opening remarks. Time the display of your visuals to coincide with your discussion of the information contained in them.

Jessica was extremely proud of the huge replica of the human mouth that she had constructed to illustrate her talk on the proper way to brush one's teeth. It stood over two feet tall and was painted pink and white. It was a true work of art. As she began her speech, she set her mouth model in full view of the audience. She opened her speech with a brief history of dentistry in America. But her listeners never heard a word. Instead, they were fascinated by the model. Jessica would have done better to cover her presentation with a cloth and then dramatically reveal it when she wanted to illustrate proper tooth brushing.

Here are a few more suggestions for timing your presentation aids.

➤ **Remove your presentation aid when you move to your next point, unless the information it contains will also help you communicate your next idea.**

➤ **Have your overhead transparency already in place on the projector.** When you are ready to show your visual, simply turn on the projector to reveal your drawing. Change to a new visual as you make your next point. Turn the projector off when you are finished with your visual support.

➤ **Consider asking someone beforehand to help you hold your presentation aid, turn the pages of your flipchart, or change the slides on the projector.** Make sure you rehearse with your assistant so that all goes smoothly during your presentation.

USE TECHNOLOGY EFFECTIVELY

You may be tempted to use some of the new technologies we have described because of their novelty rather than because of their value in helping you communicate your message. Most of them, however, are expensive. And some novice speakers are tempted to overuse presentation aids simply because they can quickly produce eye-catching visuals. Resist this temptation. Also consider that many classrooms and lecture rooms are not equipped with the necessary hardware. And realize that to project images from large-screen projectors or LCD panels, you may have to dim the lights or turn the overhead lights completely off. As we have noted, when you use audiovisual equipment that requires a dark room, you lose vital visual contact with your listeners.

Despite these drawbacks, DVDs and computer-generated graphics are destined to play a growing role in public speaking. If your college or university is equipped for them, be sure to observe the basic cautions we have offered for other, less-glitzy visual aids. Keep your visuals simple. Make sure the words or images are large enough to be seen by your listeners. Integrate the words and images into your talk. Time your visuals to coincide with information you are presenting. And don't forget to rehearse with these visuals. It is especially important to learn in advance of your speech how to operate the hardware efficiently.

REMEMBER MURPHY'S LAW

According to Murphy's Law, if something can go wrong, it will. When you use presentation aids, you increase the chances that problems or snags will develop when you present your speech. The chart may fall off the easel, you may not find any chalk, the bulb in the overhead projector may burn out. We are not saying that you should be a pessimist, just that you should have backup supplies and a backup plan in case your best-laid plans go awry.

If something doesn't go as you planned, do your best to keep your speech on track. If the chart falls over, simply pick it up and keep talking; don't offer lengthy apologies. If you can't find the chalk you will need and it is your turn to speak, quietly ask a friend to go on a chalk hunt in another room. A thorough rehearsal, a double-check of your equipment, and extra supplies such as extension cords, projector bulbs, or masking tape can help repeal Murphy's Law.

SUMMARY

Presentation aids are tools to help you communicate your ideas more dramatically than words alone can. There are different types of presentation aids, and general guidelines can help you use them effectively.

Presentation aids help improve listeners' understanding and recollection of your ideas. They help you communicate the organization of your ideas, gain and maintain the audience's attention, and illustrate a sequence of events or procedures.

Three-dimensional presentation aids include objects, models, and people. Two-dimensional presentation aids include drawings, photographs, slides, maps, graphs, charts, flipcharts, projected transparencies, and chalkboards. Software graphics packages can be used to produce many presentation aids inexpensively and efficiently. Audiovisual aids include DVDs and video-tapes. Audio aids such as tapes and compact disks can also help communicate ideas to your listeners.

When you prepare your presentation aids, make sure your visuals are large enough to be seen clearly by all of your listeners. Adapt your presentation aids to your audience, the speaking environment, and the objectives of your speech. Prepare your visuals well in advance, and make sure they are not illegal or dangerous to use.

As you present your speech, remember to look at your audience, not at your presentation aid; talk about your visual, don't just show it; avoid passing objects among your audience; use handouts to reinforce the main points in your speech; time your visuals carefully; and be sure to have backup supplies and a contingency plan.

BEING AUDIENCE-CENTERED: A SHARPER FOCUS

CONSIDERING YOUR AUDIENCE

- Use presentation aids to support your speech if they will help your listeners understand, remember, or attend to your message. Also use presentation aids if they will help you organize your message or illustrate a sequence of events or procedures for your listeners.

- Revealing one line of text at a time when you are projecting a list of items on an overhead projector helps maintain audience interest.

- When using computer-generated graphics (such as PowerPoint slides), don't let the technology overwhelm your audience: Use simple, brief lines of text and images.

- Maintain eye contact with your audience, not with your presentation aid.

- As a general rule, don't pass objects among your audience while you speak.

CONSIDERING AUDIENCE DIVERSITY

- People from high-context cultures are more likely to focus on the pictures and images in your presentation aids. People from low-context cultures may be especially interested in words and text included on your visuals.

- When you are speaking to an audience whose first language is not the same as your own, consider using images or pictures to help them remember your ideas.

- If you are using an interpreter because of language differences, give a copy of your presentation aids to your interpreter before you speak so that he or she can easily translate your message to your audience.

CRITICAL THINKING QUESTIONS

1. Nikki plans to give a talk to the Rotary Club in an effort to encourage the club members to support a local bond issue for a new library. She wants to make sure they understand how cramped and inadequate the current library is. What type of visual support could she use to make her point?

2. Professor Chou uses only the chalkboard to illustrate her anthropology lectures. Occasionally she writes a word or two on the board. What other types of visual or auditory aids could Professor Chou use in teaching her lessons?

3. Mayor Bryan is going to address the board of directors of a large microchip firm, hoping to lure them to his community. He plans to use handouts, several charts, a short video clip, and an overhead projector to show several transparencies. What advice would you give the mayor to make sure his presentation is effective?

ETHICAL QUESTIONS

1. Masha found the perfect pie chart in *USA Today* to illustrate her talk on U.S. census figures for population trends. If she tells her audience that the source of her visual is *USA Today*, does she also need to cite the U.S. Bureau of the Census?

2. Ceally wants to educate his college classmates about the increased use of profanity in contemporary music. He would like to play sound clips of some of the most offensive lyrics to illustrate his point. Would you advise Ceally to play these songs, even though doing so might offend several members of the audience?

3. Derrick is planning to give a speech about emergency first aid. His brother is a paramedic and licensed nurse. Is it ethical for Derrick to wear his brother's paramedic uniform without telling his listeners that the outfit belongs to his brother?

A Checklist for Using Effective Presentation Aids

Consult the following checklist to ensure that you are using presentation aids appropriately.

WHEN DEVELOPING YOUR PRESENTATION AIDS

➤ Are my presentation aids easy to see? ☐

➤ Are my presentation aids simple and uncluttered? ☐

➤ Do my presentation aids suit my audience, speech objectives, and speech environment? ☐

➤ Are my presentation aids attractive and professional in appearance? ☐

➤ Are my presentation aids legal and nonthreatening to my audience? ☐

➤ Did I rehearse using my presentation aids? ☐

WHEN USING YOUR PRESENTATION AIDS

➤ Do I look at my listeners rather than at my presentation aids while speaking? ☐

➤ Do I explain my presentation aids rather than just showing them? ☐

➤ If I use handouts, do I carefully time when I distribute the handouts? ☐

➤ Do I focus my audience's attention on my presentation aid and then have them focus on what I am saying when I am not referring to the presentation aid? ☐

➤ Can I skillfully operate any computers, video, audio, or other hardware or software needed during my presentation? ☐

Jean-Baptiste Simeon Chardin (1699–1779), *The Young Schoolmistress*. 1740. Art Resource, N.Y.

Not only is there an art in knowing a thing, but also a certain art in teaching it.

—CICERO

Speaking to Inform

outline

objectives

After studying this chapter you should be able to do the following:

1. Identify three goals of speaking to inform.

2. Describe five different types of informative speeches.

3. Effectively and appropriately use four strategies to enhance audience understanding.

4. Effectively and appropriately use three strategies to maintain audience interest.

5. Effectively and appropriately use four strategies to enhance audience recall of information presented in an informative speech.

As you participate in your company's management training class, the group facilitator turns to you and asks you to summarize your team's discussion about the importance of leadership.

Your sociology professor requires each student to give an oral report describing the latest findings from the U.S. census.

At the conclusion of your weekly staff meeting, your boss asks you to give a brief report summarizing the new product you and your team are developing.

In each of these situations, your task is to give information to someone. Whether you are having spontaneous conversation or delivering a rehearsed speech, you will often find that your speaking purpose is to inform, or teach someone something you know. One survey of both speech teachers and students who had taken a speech course found that the single most important skill taught in a public-speaking class is how to give an informative speech.[1]

A **speech to inform** shares information with others to enhance their knowledge or understanding of the information, concepts, and ideas you present. When you inform someone, you assume the role of a teacher by defining, illustrating, clarifying, or elaborating on a topic.

Conveying information to others is a useful skill in most walks of life. You may find that informing others will be an important part of your job. As a regional manager of a national corporation, you may have to report sales figures every fiscal quarter; as an accountant, you may have to teach your administrative assistant how to organize your files. Other activities, such as teaching a Chinese cooking class or chairing monthly meetings of the Baker Street Irregulars, can also require you to provide information.

In this chapter, we will suggest ways to build on your experience and enhance your skill in informing others. We will discuss goals of informative speaking, examine different types of informative tasks, and discuss specific ways to inform others. Finally, we will present some general principles for making your informative presentations memorable.

Goals of Informative Speaking

As a student, you know from experience that you don't always soak up knowledge like a sponge just because a teacher presents information. Informing or teaching others can be a challenge because of a simple fact: Presenting information does not mean that communication has occurred. Communication happens when the listeners make sense of the information.

When trying to help listeners make sense of information, speakers often have one or more of the following goals in mind: to enhance understanding, to gain and maintain interest, or to ensure that listeners can remember what was said. Let's explore each of these three important informative-speaking goals.

SPEAKING TO ENHANCE UNDERSTANDING

Understanding occurs when a listener accurately interprets the intended meaning of a message. Given the fragile nature of meaning, our words and nonverbal expressions

speech to inform
A speech that teaches others new information, ideas, concepts, principles, or processes in order to enhance their knowledge or understanding about something

are often misunderstood by others. Even when your speaking goal is to enhance understanding, the words you select to improve understanding may actually hinder the listener from accurately interpreting your meaning. Someone once noted that the 500 most common words in the English language have over 14,000 different dictionary definitions! And these dictionary definitions do not include the personal or private meanings for words we use. Given the potential for misunderstanding, it's amazing we interpret meaning as well as we do.

When your speaking goal is to enhance understanding, you must first make sure you are using words that your listeners will interpret in the same way as you do. How do you do this? Be audience-centered. If you are using words that require unique background or knowledge your listeners don't have, your meaning will be muddled. The stories you tell, the examples you use, and the statistics you cite will only make sense to listeners if you and they have a common understanding of the words you speak. Otherwise, the job would be like trying to write a term paper on a computer with software designed to keep track of your checkbook rather than to write sentences. Without a common framework, your message won't make sense.

Children's natural affinity for dinosaurs makes it easy for this speaker to maintain their interest in his presentation. What strategies could he use for a different topic?

[Photo: © Arnold Gold/*New Haven Register*/ The Image Works]

Speaking to Maintain Interest

You may have carefully selected words, examples, and illustrations that your listeners understand, but if your listeners are bored and not focusing on your message, you won't achieve your informative-speaking goal.

People may be interested in you and your topic for a variety of reasons. They often listen to what affects them directly, adds to their knowledge, satisfies their curiosity, or entertains them. These reasons are not mutually exclusive. For example, if you were talking to a group of businesspeople about the latest changes in local tax policies, you would be discussing something that directly affects them, adds to their knowledge, and satisfies their curiosity. But your listeners' primary interest would be in how local taxes affect them. By contrast, if you were giving a lecture on fifteenth-century Benin sculpture to a middle-class audience at the YMCA, your listeners would be interested because your talk would add to their knowledge, satisfy their curiosity, and entertain them. Such a talk can also affect your listeners directly by making them more interesting to others. The commonality in both these speaking situations is the focus on listeners' interests and needs. If your audience members feel they will benefit from your speech in some way, your speech will interest them. And an interesting speech commands attention as well as respect.

Speaking to Be Remembered

You may remember from Chapter 4 that one day after hearing a presentation, most audience members will remember only about half of what they were told. And they will recall only about 25 percent two days later. Your job as an informative speaker is to improve on those statistics. Just because listeners do not typically remember what a speaker says, it does not mean that *your* listeners are doomed to a similar fate.

Throughout this book we've offered strategies and suggestions that speakers can use to help listeners remember information. Being organized, being appropriately redundant by using internal summaries and a final summary, and relating the message to listeners' interests are all useful methods of helping your audience increase their retention of the message you've worked so hard to develop. Later in the chapter we'll offer additional suggestions for increasing audience recall of messages.

Types of Informative Speeches

Informative speeches can be classified according to the subject areas they cover. Classifying your speech can help you decide how to organize the information you want to present. As you will see in the following discussion, the demands of your purpose often dictate a structure for your speech. As you look at these suggestions about structure, however, remember that good organization is only one factor in your audience's ability to process your message. In the next section, we will discuss additional strategies for ensuring that your listeners will *understand* and *remember* the information in your speech.

SPEECHES ABOUT OBJECTS

A speech about an object might be about anything tangible—anything you can see or touch. You may or may not show the actual object to your audience while you are talking about it. (Chapter 14 suggests ways to use objects as presentation aids to illustrate your ideas.) Almost any kind of object could form the basis of an interesting speech:

Something from your own collection (rocks, compact disks, antiques, baseball cards, and so on)

Sports cars

Cellos

Personal digital assistants (PDAs)

Digital video cameras

WWII Memorial

Toys

Antique Fiestaware

Staffordshire dogs

The time limit for your speech will determine the amount of detail you can share with your listeners. Even in a 30- to 45-minute presentation, you cannot talk about every aspect of any of the objects listed. So you will need to focus on a specific purpose. Here's a sample outline for a speech about an object:

TOPIC:	Dead Sea Scrolls
GENERAL PURPOSE:	To inform
SPECIFIC PURPOSE:	At the end of my speech, my audience should be able to describe how the Dead Sea Scrolls were found, why they are important to society, and the key content of the ancient manuscripts.

I. The Dead Sea Scrolls were found by accident.

   A. The scrolls were found in caves near the Dead Sea.

   B. The scrolls were first discovered by a shepherd in 1947.

   C. In the late 1940s and early 1950s, archeologists and Bedouins found ten caves that contained Dead Sea Scrolls.

II. The Dead Sea Scrolls are important to society.

   A. The Dead Sea Scrolls are the oldest known manuscripts of any books of the Bible.

   B. The Dead Sea Scrolls give us a look at Jewish life in Palestine over 2000 years ago.

III. The content of the Dead Sea Scrolls gives us a glimpse of the past.
   A. The Dead Sea Scrolls include all the books of the Old Testament except the book of Esther.
   B. The Dead Sea Scrolls include fragments of the Septuagint, the earliest Greek translation of the Old Testament.
   C. The Dead Sea Scrolls include a collection of hymns used by the inhabitants of the Qumran Valley.

Speeches about objects may be organized topically, chronologically, or spatially. The speech about the Dead Sea Scrolls is organized topically. It could, however, be revised chronologically. The first major idea could be Jewish life in Palestine 2000 years ago. The second point could present information about how the scrolls were found in the 1940s and 1950s. The final major idea could be the construction of the museum in Jerusalem that houses the famous scrolls. Or, the speech could be organized spatially, describing the physical layout of the caves in which the scrolls were found.

SPEECHES ABOUT PROCEDURES

A speech about a procedure discusses how something works (for example, the human circulatory system) or describes a process that produces a particular outcome (such as how grapes become wine). At the close of such a speech, your audience should be able to describe, understand, or perform the procedure you have described. Here are some examples of procedures that could be the topics of effective informative presentations:

confidently connecting with your audience

Focus on Your Information Rather Than Your Fear

You nurture your fear when you focus on your anxiety. Consciously keep your mind off of your fear and focused on the message you will present. When you feel your anxiety level rising, do something related to improving your speech rather than letting your anxiety get the best of you. Consider reviewing your introduction, taking another look at your main points, or glancing at your conclusion one more time. By changing your focus from your fear to preparing your talk, you are changing the stimulus that may be triggering additional anxiety.

How state laws are made

How the U.S. patent system works

How an MP3 player works

How to refinish furniture

How to select an inexpensive stereo system

How to plant an organic garden

How to select a graduate school

Notice that all these examples start with the word *how*. A speech about a procedure usually focuses on how a process is completed or how something can be accomplished. Speeches about procedures are often presented in workshops or other training situations in which people learn skills.

Anita, describing how to develop a new training curriculum in teamwork skills, used an organizational strategy that grouped some of her steps together like this:

I. Conduct a needs assessment of your department.
   A. Identify the method of assessing department needs.
      1. Consider using questionnaires.
      2. Consider using interviews.
      3. Consider using focus groups.
   B. Implement the needs assessment.

II. Identify the topics that should be presented in the training.
   A. Specify topics that all members of the department need.
   B. Specify topics that only some members of the department need.

III. Write training objectives.
   A. Write objectives that are measurable.
   B. Write objectives that are specific.
   C. Write objectives that are attainable.

IV. Develop lesson plans for the training.
   A. Identify the training methods you will use.
   B. Identify the materials you will need.

Anita's audience will remember the four general steps much more easily than they would have if each aspect of the curriculum-development process were listed as a separate step.

Many speeches about procedures include visual aids (see Chapter 14). Whether you are teaching people how to hang wallpaper or how to give a speech, showing them how to do something is almost always more effective than just telling them how to do it.

Speeches about People

A biographical speech could be about someone famous or about someone you know personally. Most of us enjoy hearing about the lives of real people, whether famous or not, living or dead, who had some special quality about them. The key to presenting an effective biographical speech is to be selective. Don't try to cover every detail of your subject's life. Relate the key elements in the person's career, personality, or other significant life features so that you are building to a particular point rather than just reciting facts about an individual. Perhaps your grandfather was known for his generosity, for example. Mention some notable examples of his philanthropy. If you are talking about a well-known personality, pick information or a period that is not widely known, such as the person's childhood or private hobby.

One speaker gave a memorable speech about his neighbor:

> To enter Hazel's house is to enter a combination greenhouse and zoo. Plants are everywhere; it looks and feels like a tropical jungle. Her home is always warm and humid. Her dog Peppy, her cat Bones, a bird named Elmer, and a fish called Frank can be seen through the philodendron, ferns, and pansies. While Hazel loves her plants and animals, she loves people even more. Her finest hours are spent serving coffee and homemade chocolate pie to her friends and neighbors, playing Uno with family until late in the evening, and just visiting about the good old days. Hazel is one of a kind.

Note how the speech captures Hazel's personality and charm. Speeches about people should give your listeners the feeling that the person is a unique, authentic individual.

One way to talk about a person's life is in chronological order—birth, school, career, marriage, achievements, death. However, if you are interested in presenting a specific theme, such as "Winston Churchill, master of English prose," you may decide instead to organize those key experiences topically. First you would discuss Churchill's achievements as a brilliant orator whose words defied Germany in 1940, and then trace the origins of his skill to his work as a cub reporter in South Africa during the Boer War of 1899–1902.

Speeches about Events

Where were you on September 11, 2001? Chances are that you clearly remember where you were and what you were doing on that and other similarly fateful days. Major events punctuate our lives and mark the passage of time.

A major event can form the basis of a fascinating informative speech. You can choose to talk about either an event that you have witnessed or one you have researched. Your goal is to describe the event in concrete, tangible terms and to bring the experience to life for your audience. Were you living in New Orleans when Hurricane Katrina struck? Have you witnessed the inauguration of a president, governor, or senator? Have you experienced the ravages of a flood or earthquake? Or you may want to re-create an event that your parents or grandparents lived through. What was it like to be in Pearl Harbor on December 7, 1941?

You may have heard a recording of the famous radio broadcast of the explosion and crash of the dirigible *Hindenburg*. The announcer's ability to describe both the scene and the incredible emotion of the moment has made that broadcast a classic. As that broadcaster was able to do, your purpose as an informative speaker describing an event is to make that event come alive for your listeners and to help them visualize the scene.

Most speeches built around an event follow a chronological arrangement. But a speech about an event might also describe the complex issues or causes behind the event and be organized topically. For example, if you were to talk about the Civil War, you might choose to focus on the three causes of the war:

I. Political
II. Economic
III. Social

Although these main points are topical, specific subpoints may be organized chronologically. However you choose to organize your speech about an event, your audience should be enthralled by your vivid description.

SPEECHES ABOUT IDEAS

Speeches about ideas are usually more abstract than the other types of speeches. The following principles, concepts, and theories might be topics of idea speeches:

Principles of communication

Freedom of speech

Evolution

Theories of aging

Islam

Communal living

Trickle-down theory of economics

Most speeches about ideas are organized topically (by logical subdivisions of the central idea) or according to complexity (from simple ideas to more complex ones). The following example illustrates how one student organized an idea topic into an informative speech:

TOPIC:	Communication theory
GENERAL PURPOSE:	To inform
SPECIFIC PURPOSE:	At the end of my speech, the audience should be able to identify and describe three functions and three types of communication theory.

I. Communication theory has three important functions.

  A. Communication theory helps explain how communication functions.

  B. Communication theory helps us make predictions about how people will communicate with others.

Types of Informative Speeches

SPEECH TYPE	DESCRIPTION	TYPICAL ORGANIZATIONAL PATTERNS	SAMPLE TOPICS
Objects	Presents information about tangible things	Topical Spatial Chronological	The Rosetta Stone Museums International space station Voting machines

Procedures	Reviews how something works or describes a process	Chronological
		Topical
		Complexity
			How to . . .
			    Fix a carburetor
			    Operate a nuclear-power plant
			    Buy a quality used car
			    Trap lobsters

People	Describes either famous people or personal acquaintances	Chronological Topical	Sojourner Truth Nelson Mandela Indira Gandhi Your granddad Your favorite teacher
Events	Describes an event that either has happened or will happen	Chronological Topical Spatial	The 2007 Virginia Tech shooting Inauguration Day Cinco de Mayo
Ideas	Presents abstract information or discusses principles, concepts, theories, or issues	Topical Complexity	Communism Immigration Buddhism Reincarnation

C. Communication theory helps us be more in control of communication situations because we can explain and predict communication behavior.

II. There are several types of communication theory.

A. Communication systems theory helps explain the transactive nature of communication.

B. Rhetorical communication theory helps us explain and predict how public speakers influence others.

C. Functional group communication theory identifies the important group-communication behaviors that can enhance group communication.

Strategies to Enhance Audience Understanding

The skill of teaching and enhancing understanding is obviously important to teachers, but it's also important to virtually any profession. Whether you're a college professor, chief executive officer of a Fortune 500 company, or a parent raising a family, you will be called on to teach and explain. At the heart of creating understanding in someone is the ability to describe both old and new ideas to the person. Just because an idea, term, or concept has been around for centuries doesn't mean that it is easy to understand. A person hearing an old idea for the first time goes through the same process as if he or she were learning about the latest cutting-edge idea. How do you enhance someone's knowledge or understanding? We can suggest several powerful strategies.

SPEAK WITH CLARITY

To speak with clarity is to express ideas so that the listener understands the intended message accurately. Speaking clearly is an obvious goal of an informative speaker. What is not so obvious is *how* to speak clearly. As a speaker you may think you're being clear, but only the listener can tell you whether he or she has received your message. One interesting study made the point that be-cause the information is clear to you, you'll likely think it's also clear to your listener.[2] People were asked to tap the rhythm of well-known songs such as "Happy Birthday to You" or "The Star Spangled Banner" so that another person could guess the song just by hearing the rhythm. About half of the people who tapped the song thought that the listener would easily figure out which song was being tapped. However, less than 2 percent could identify the song. (Try it—see if you can beat the 2 percent average.) The point: When you know something, you're likely to think it's clear to someone else. Whether it's how to drive a car or how to care for an aardvark, if you are already familiar with a topic, you're likely to think your task of communicating an idea to someone is easier than it is. Give careful thought to how you will help listeners understand your message. The most effective speakers (those whose message is both understood and appropriately acted on) build in success by consciously developing and presenting ideas with the listener in mind, rather than flinging information at listeners and hoping some of it sticks.

Communication researcher Joseph Chesebro has summarized several research-based strategies you can use to enhance message clarity.[3]

Some people learn more effectively if they can see as well as hear the message.

[Photo: Gary Walts/Syracuse Newspapers/ The Image Works]

- Preview your main ideas in your introduction.
- Tell your listeners how what you present relates to a previous point.
- Frequently summarize key ideas.
- Provide a visual outline to help listeners follow your ideas.
- Provide a handout prior to your talk with the major points outlined; leave space so that listeners can jot down key ideas.
- Once you announce your topic and outline, stay on message.
- Don't present too much information too quickly.

USE PRINCIPLES AND TECHNIQUES OF ADULT LEARNING

Most public-speaking audiences you face will consist of adults. Perhaps you've heard of **pedagogy**, the art and science of teaching children to learn. The word *pedagogy* is based on the Greek words *paid*, which means "child," and *agogus*, which means "guide." Thus, pedagogy is the art and science of teaching children. Adult learning is called **andragogy**.[4] *Andr* is the Greek word that means "adult." Andragogy is the art and science of teaching adults. Researchers and scholars have found andragogical ap-proaches that are best for adults. (By "adults" we don't just mean people who are over

pedagogy
The art and science of teaching children

andragogy
The art and science of teaching adults

30; if you're a college student over the age of 18, you fit the characteristics of an adult learner.) What are andragogical, or adult-learning, principles? Here are some of the most important ones.

- **Provide information that can be used immediately.** Most people who work in business have an in-basket on their desk to receive letters that must be read and work that must be done. Each of us also has a kind of mental in-basket, an agenda for what we want or need to accomplish. If you present adult listeners with information that they can apply immediately to their "in-basket," they are more likely to focus on and understand your message.

- **Actively involve listeners in the learning process.** Rather than having your listeners sit passively as you speak, consider asking them questions to think about or, in some cases, to respond to on the spot.

- **Connect listeners' life experiences with the new information they learn.** Adult listeners are more likely to understand your message if you help them connect the new information with their past experiences. The primary way to do this is, first, to know the kinds of experiences that your listeners have had, and then refer to those experiences as you present your ideas.

- **Make new information relevant to listeners' needs and their busy lives.** Most adults are busy—probably, if pressed, most will say they are *too* busy for their own good. So when speaking to an adult audience, realize that any information or ideas you share will more likely be heard and understood if you relate what you say to their chock-full-of-activity lives. People working, going to school, raising families, and being involved in their communities need to be shown how the ideas you share relate to their lives.

- **Help listeners solve their problems.** Most people have problems and are looking for solutions to them. People will be more likely to pay attention to information that helps them better understand and solve their problems. Note the cover stories on many magazines; typical stories help people lose weight, avoid stress, enhance their love lives, or be healthy. When presenting information, seek ways to relate the ideas you share to listeners' problems. Doing so will help you solve the problem of how to get people to listen to you.

CLARIFY UNFAMILIAR IDEAS OR COMPLEX PROCESSES

If you are trying to tell your listeners about a complex process, you will need more than definitions to explain what you mean. Research suggests that you can demystify a complex process if you first provide a simple overview of the process with an analogy, vivid description, or word picture.[5]

USE ANALOGIES If a speaker said, "The Milky Way galaxy is big," you'd have a vague idea that the cluster of stars and space material that make up the Milky Way was large. But if the speaker said, "If the Milky Way galaxy were as big as the continent of North America, our solar system would fit inside a coffee cup" you'd have a better idea of just how big the Milky Way is and, by comparison, how small our solar system is.[6] As we discussed in Chapter 8, an analogy is a comparison between two things. It's an especially useful technique to use to describe complex processes because it can help someone understand something difficult to grasp (the size of the Milky Way) by comparing it to something already understood (the size of a coffee cup).[7]

By helping your listeners compare something new to something they already know or can visualize, you are helping to make your message clear. Here's an example of this idea based on what professor of business Chip Heath and communication consultant Dan Heath call the principle of "using what's there—using the information you have (what's there) and relating it to something more familiar."[8] Try this short exercise. Take 15 seconds to memorize the letters below; then close the book and write the letters exactly as they appear in the book.

J FKFB INAT OUP SNA SAI RS

Most people, say these experts, remember about half of the letters. Now, look below to see the same letters organized just a bit differently. The letters haven't changed, but we have regrouped them into acronyms that may make more sense to you. We are more likely to make sense out of something that we already have a mental category for. An analogy works the same way.

JFK FBI NATO UPS NASA IRS

USE VIVID DESCRIPTION When you *describe*, you provide more detail than you do when just defining something. Using descriptive terms that bring a process to life are especially effective when trying to clarify something that is complex. Descriptions answer questions about the who, what, where, why, and when of the process. Who is involved in the process? What is the process, idea, or event that you want to describe? Where and when does the process take place? Why does it occur, or why is it important to the audience? (Of course, not all of these questions apply to every description.)

USE A WORD PICTURE A word picture, a technique introduced in Chapter 8, is a lively description that helps your listeners form a mental image by appealing to their senses of sight, taste, smell, sound, and touch. The following suggestions will help you create effective word pictures.

➤ **Form your own clear mental image of the person, place, or object before you try to describe it.**

➤ **Describe the appearance of the person, place, or object.** What would your listeners see if they were looking at it? Use lively language to describe the flaws and foibles, bumps and beauties of the people, places, and things you want your audience to see. Make your description an invitation to the imagination—a stately pleasure dome into which your listeners can enter and view its treasures with you.

➤ **Describe what your listeners would hear.** Use colorful, onomatopoeic words, such as *buzz, snort, hum, crackle,* or *hiss.* These words are much more descriptive than the more general term *noise.* Imitate the sound you want your listeners to hear mentally. For example, instead of saying, "When I walked in the woods, I heard the sound of twigs breaking beneath my feet and wind moving the leaves above me in the trees," you might say, "As I walked in the woods, I heard the *crackle* of twigs underfoot and the *rustle* of leaves overhead."

➤ **Describe smells, if appropriate.** What fragrance or aroma do you want your audience to recall? Such diverse subjects as Thanksgiving, nighttime in the tropics, and the first day of school all lend themselves to olfactory imagery. No Thanksgiving would be complete without the rich aroma of roast turkey and the pungent, tangy odor of cranberries. A warm, humid evening in Miami smells of salt air and gardenia blossoms. And the first day of school evokes for many the scents of new shoe leather, unused crayons, and freshly painted classrooms. In each case, the associated smells greatly enhance the overall word picture.

➤ **Describe how an object feels.** Use words that are as clear and vivid as possible. Rather than saying that something is rough or smooth, use a simile, such as "the rock was rough as sandpaper" or "the pebble was as smooth as a baby's skin." These descriptions appeal to both the visual and the tactile senses.

➤ **Describe taste, one of the most powerful sensory cues, if appropriate.** Thinking about your grandmother may evoke for you memories of her rich homemade noodles; her sweet, fudgy, nut brownies; and her light, flaky, buttery pie crust. Descriptions of these taste sensations would be welcomed by almost any audience, particularly your fellow college students subsisting mainly on dormitory food or their own cooking! More important, such description can help you paint an accurate, vivid image of your grandmother.

 Describe the emotion that a listener might feel if he or she were to experience the situation you relate. If you experienced the situation, describe your own emotions. Use specific adjectives rather than general terms such as *happy* or *sad*. One speaker, talking about receiving her first speech assignment, described her reaction with these words:

> *My heart stopped. Panic began to rise up inside. Me? . . . For the next five days I lived in dreaded anticipation of the forthcoming event.*[9]

Note how effectively her choices of such words and phrases as "my heart stopped," "panic," and "dreaded anticipation" describe her terror at the prospect of making a speech—much more so than if she had said simply, "I was scared."

The more vividly and accurately you can describe emotion, the more intimately involved in your description the audience will become.

USE EFFECTIVE VISUAL REINFORCEMENT

Research about learning styles suggests that many of your listeners are more likely to remember your ideas if you can reinforce them with presentation aids. As we noted in Chapter 14, pictures, graphs, posters, and computer-generated graphics can help you gain and maintain audience members' attention, as well as increase their retention. Today's audiences are exposed daily to a barrage of messages conveyed through TV and the Internet, both of which are highly visual electronic media. Modern audiences have grown to depend on more than words alone to help them remember ideas and information. When you present summaries of data, a well-crafted line graph or colorful pie chart can quickly and memorably reinforce the words and numbers you cite.

Strategies to Maintain Audience Interest

Before you can inform someone, you must gain and maintain his or her interest. No matter how carefully crafted your definitions, skillfully delivered your description, or visually reinforcing your presentation aid, if your listeners aren't paying attention, you won't achieve your goal of informing them. Strategies for gaining and holding interest are vital in achieving your speaking goal.

In discussing how to develop attention-catching introductions in Chapter 10, we itemized several specific techniques for gaining your listeners' attention. The following strategies build on those techniques.

ESTABLISH A MOTIVE FOR YOUR AUDIENCE TO LISTEN TO YOU

Most audiences will probably not be waiting breathlessly for you to talk to them. You will need to motivate them to listen to you.

Some situations have built-in motivations for listeners. A teacher can say, "There will be a test covering my lecture tomorrow. It will count toward 50 percent of your semester grade." Such methods may not make the teacher popular, but they certainly will motivate the class to listen. Similarly, a boss might say, "Your ability to use these sales principles will determine whether you keep your job." Your boss's statement will probably motivate you to learn the company's sales principles. However, because you will rarely have the power to motivate your listeners with such strong-arm tactics, you will need to find more creative ways to get your audience to listen to you.

Don't assume that your listeners will be automatically interested in what you have to say. Pique their interest with a rhetorical question. Tell them a story. Tell them how the information you present will be of value to them. As the British writer G. K. Chesterton once said, "There is no such thing as an uninteresting topic; there are only uninterested people."[10]

TELL A STORY

Good stories with interesting characters and riveting plots have fascinated listeners for millennia; the words "once upon a time . . ." are usually sure-fire attention-getters. A good story is inherently interesting.

The characteristics of a well-told tale are simple yet powerful. Stories are also a way of connecting your message to people from a variety of cultural backgrounds.[11] Here we elaborate on some of the ideas about storytelling we introduced in Chapter 8. A good story includes conflict, incorporates action, creates suspense, and may also include humor.

◆ **A good story includes conflict.** Stories that pit one side against another, and descriptions of opposing ideas and forces in government, religion, or personal relationships foster attention. The Greeks learned long ago that the essential ingredient for a good play, be it comedy or tragedy, is conflict.

◆ **A good story incorporates action.** An audience is more likely to listen to an action-packed message than to one that listlessly lingers on an idea too long. Good stories have a beginning that sets the stage, a heart that moves to a conclusion, and then an ending that ties up all the loose ends. The key to interest is a plot that moves along to hold interest.

◆ **A good story creates suspense.** TV dramas and soap operas long ago proved that the way to ensure high ratings is to tell a story with the outcome in doubt. Suspense is created when the characters in the story may do one of several things. Keeping people on the edge of their seats because they don't know what will happen next is another element in good story-telling.

- **A good story may incorporate humor.** A fisherman went into a sporting-goods store. The salesperson offered the man a wonderful lure for trout: It had beautiful colors, eight hooks, and looked just like a rare Buckner bug. Finally, the fisherman asked the salesperson, "Do fish really like this thing?"

    "I don't really know," admitted the salesperson, "I don't sell to fish."

    We could have simply said, "It's important to be audience-centered." But using a bit of humor makes the point while holding the listener's attention.

    Not all stories have to be funny. Stories may be sad or dramatic without humor. But adding humor at appropriate times usually helps maintain interest and attention.

PRESENT INFORMATION THAT RELATES TO YOUR LISTENERS

Throughout this book, we have encouraged you to develop an audience-centered approach to public speaking. Being an audience-centered informative speaker means being aware of information that your audience can use. If, for example, you are going to teach your audience pointers about recycling, be sure to talk about specific recycling efforts on your campus or in your own community. Adapt your message to the people who will be in your audience.

LEARNING FROM GREAT SPEAKERS

Oprah Winfrey (1954–)

One of *Time* magazine's 100 Most Influential People of the late 20th and early 21st centuries, Oprah Winfrey is best known as the host of the television talk show that bears her name. Because of her passion, knowledge, and skill in connecting with her listeners, she has a tremendous influence on what people talk about and read. She uses her power as a communicator to inform her listeners about ideas, authors, and causes about which she feels passionate. Her physical immediacy, listening skill, and humor all help to stimulate and reinforce communication among the show's participants and make her messages interesting and memorable.

Oprah Winfrey illustrates how an effective communicator is not afraid to share her natural enthusiasm for a topic with her listeners. When sharing information with your listeners, it's important to let yourself reveal your natural interest in and passion for your subject. Of course, that can only happen if you are talking about ideas and topics that are important to you and about which you have strong feelings. So when you must select a topic for an informative talk, choose one that genuinely interests you.

[Photo: Charles Rex Arbogast/AP Images]

USE THE UNEXPECTED

On a flight from Dallas, Texas to San Diego, California, flight attendant Karen Wood made the following announcement:

> *If I could have your attention for a few moments, we sure would love to point out these safety features. If you haven't been in an automobile since 1965, the proper way to fasten your seat belt is to slide the flat end into the buckle. To unfasten, lift up on the buckle and it will release.*
>
> *As the song goes, there might be fifty ways to leave your lover, but there are only six ways to leave this aircraft: two forward exit doors, two over-wing removable window exits, and two aft exit doors. The location of each exit is clearly marked with signs overhead, as well as red and white disco lights along the floor of the aisle.*
>
> *Made ya look!* [12]

This clever flight attendant took a predictable announcement and added a few surprises and novel interpretations to make a boring but important message interesting. With just a little thought about how to make your message less predictable and unexpected, you can add zest and interest to your talks. Listeners will focus on the unexpected.

Advertisers spend a lot of time trying to get your attention. A young couple is traveling in their car, having a normal, natural conversation and then BAM! CRUNCH!—someone who has run a red light slams into their car. The announcer intones, "Life comes at you fast." You look at the crumpled car and are stunned at how quickly an everyday experience changes in an instant. Like an effective ad, a good speaker knows how to surprise an audience with the same impact as this visual commercial—except that a speaker uses words and stories to metaphorically grab a listener by the shoulders and force him or her to focus on the message.

Besides surprising your listeners, maintain their attention by creating mystery or suspense. Stories are a great way to add drama and interest to a talk—especially a story that moves audience members to try to solve a riddle or problem. One technique to create a "mini mystery" is to ask a rhetorical question. You don't necessary expect an audible answer from audience members, but you do want them to have a mental response. Here's an example: "Would you know what to do if you were stranded, out of gas, at night, without your cell phone?" By getting listeners to ponder your question, you've gotten them actively engaged in your message rather than passively processing your words. [13]

Strategies to Enhance Audience Recall

Think of the best teacher you ever had. He or she was probably a good lecturer with a special talent for being not only clear and interesting but also memorable. The very fact that you can remember your teacher is a testament to his or her talent. Like teachers, some speakers are better than others at presenting information in a memorable way. In this final section, we review strategies that will help your audiences remember you and your message.

BUILD IN REDUNDANCY

It is seldom necessary for writers to repeat themselves. If readers don't quite understand a passage, they can go back and read it again. When you speak, however, it is useful to repeat key points. Audience members generally cannot stop you if a point in your speech is unclear or if their minds wander.

How do you make your message redundant without insulting your listeners' intelligence? We've already mentioned several techniques in this book. Permit us some redundancy here to make our point. A clear preview at the beginning of your talk as well as a summary statement in your conclusion are the most straightforward ways to make sure listeners get your points. Including an internal summary—a short summary after key points during your speech—is another technique to help audiences remember key ideas. Using numeric signposts (numbering key ideas by saying, "My first point is . . . , My second point is . . . , And now here's my third point . . .") is another way of making sure your audience can identify and remember key points. A reinforcing visual aid that displays your key ideas can also enhance recall. If you really want to ensure that listeners come away from your speech with essential information, consider preparing a handout or an outline of key ideas. (But as we noted in the last chapter, when using a handout, make sure the audience is focusing on you, not on your handout.)

MAKE YOUR KEY IDEAS SHORT AND SIMPLE

When we say make your messages simple, we don't mean you need to give 30-second speeches (although we're sure some speakers and listeners would prefer half-minute speeches to longer, more drawn-out versions). Rather, we mean that if you can distill your key ideas down to brief and simple phrases, your audiences will be more likely to remember what you say.[14]

Can you remember more than seven things? One classic research study concluded that people can only hold about seven pieces of information (such as the numbers in a seven-digit phone number) in their short-term memory.[15] If you want your listeners to remember your message, don't bombard them with a lengthy list.

SAMPLE INFORMATIVE SPEECH

CHOOSING A SPEECH TOPIC

by Roger Fringer[17]

Today I'd like to talk to you about [pause] tables. Tables are wood . . . usually . . . and they are . . . . How often do we sit in a class and feel the intelligence draining out of us? In a speech class, we are given the opportunity to add to that feeling or to add to the intelligence. Selecting a meaningful speech topic will make our speeches interesting, important, as well as being informative. As students, we've all been in the situation of being more anxious than necessary because we are talking about an unfamiliar or uninteresting speech topic. In our public speaking class, we spend a number of hours giving speeches and listening to them. If we have four days of speeches, at what—seven speech topics [per day]—that equals 28 hours spent listening to speeches. Let's not forget that we are paying to listen to those speeches. If our tuition is say, $15,000 a year, that's $875 that we have spent listening to those 28 hours of speeches. We work hard for our tuition, so we should spend it wisely. Spending it wisely means we don't waste our time. We don't waste our own time on preparing and giving the speeches, and we don't waste our classmates' time who have to listen to our speeches. The solution is simple if we take choosing our topic seriously.

I recommend that we choose topics following *The Three I's* to guide us. The first I is to make speeches *interesting*. By doing so, we can alleviate the boredom that so often permeates the public speaking classroom. If the topic is interesting to us, we will present it in a manner that shows our interest. We will also keep our audience's attention when we know,

◆ Roger cleverly captures attention by purposefully starting with an unimaginative topic and using halting delivery that makes listeners wonder, "What's this really about?"

◆ Roger establishes a common bond with his listeners by relating to them as fellow students who are often confronted with the same problem: how to select a topic for a speech.

◆ Rather than just saying we waste time and money when listening to speeches, Roger uses statistics specifically adapted to the audience to whom he is speaking; this is a good example of being audience-centered.

◆ He clearly previews his major ideas and links each idea together by beginning each point with a word that begins with *I*.

With the advent of PowerPoint, some speakers may be tempted to spray listeners with a shower of bulleted information. Resist this temptation.

An important speech-preparation technique that we've suggested is to crystallize the central idea of your message into a one-sentence summary of your speech. To help your audience remember your central idea statement, make it short enough to fit on a car bumper sticker. For example, rather than saying, "The specific words people use and the way people express themselves are influenced by culture and other socioeconomic forces," say "Language shapes our culture and culture shapes our language." The message is not only shorter but also uses the technique of antithesis (opposition expressed with a parallel sentence structure) that we discussed in Chapter 12. Perhaps you've heard the same advice we're suggesting here expressed as the KISS principle: Keep It Simple, Stupid. Make your message simple enough for anyone to grasp quickly. Here's the idea we're suggesting, phrased as a bumper sticker: Make it short and simple.

PACE YOUR INFORMATION FLOW

Organize your speech so that you present an even flow of information, rather than bunching up a number of significant details around one point. If you present too much new information too quickly, you may overwhelm your audience. Their ability to understand may falter.[16]

You should be especially sensitive to the flow of information if your topic is new or unfamiliar to your listeners. Make sure that your audience has time to process any new information you present. Use supporting materials both to help clarify new information and to slow down the pace of your presentation.

Again, do not try to see how much detail and content you can cram into a speech. Your job is to present information so that the audience can grasp it, not to show off how much you know.

as students, they can be thinking about a million other things. Choosing an interesting topic will also alleviate some of the angst, anxiety we feel while giving the speech topic.

The second I is to make the speech *important*. The speech should not only be interesting but important to us. It should be relevant to our lives now or in the future.

The third I is to make the speech *informative*. Let's not waste our tuition money by not learning anything new in those 28 hours of class time. This is our opportunity to learn from each other's experiences and expertise.

Now, just picture yourself putting these ideas into practice. Imagine sitting in a classroom, listening to your classmates talk about issues or ideas that are important to them. They are so excited that you can't help but be excited about the topic with them. You're learning from their life experiences, experiences that you would not have had the opportunity to learn about if it had not been for their speech. Then, imagine being able to talk about the experiences and knowledge that are important to you. Sometimes you only have seven minutes to express what is most important to you. Besides that, it's to a captive audience that has no choice but to listen to you. There are few times in our lives when we can have an impact on someone else's life, and we have only a short amount of time to do it. But in our public speaking class, we can have that chance. Let's all think about how we use our time and energy in our public speaking class. I don't want to waste my time or have any unnecessary stress over [pause] tables. I would like all of us to use our opportunities wisely by choosing topics that are interesting, important, and informative.

▶ Here he uses a signpost by clearly noting he's moved to his second point.

▶ Again, he uses a verbal signpost to indicate that this is his third point.

▶ Although Roger's primary purpose is to inform, he uses a hypothetical example to tell the audience how the information he has given them will help them solve a problem—how to find a good speech topic.

▶ Roger provides closure to his message by making a reference to the example he used in his introduction.

REINFORCE KEY IDEAS

This last point is one of the most powerful techniques in the entire chapter: Reinforce key ideas verbally or nonverbally to make your idea memorable.

REINFORCE IDEAS VERBALLY You can reinforce an idea verbally by using such phrases as "This is the most important point" or "Be sure to remember this next point; it's the most compelling one." Suppose you have four suggestions for helping your listeners avoid a serious sunburn, and your last suggestion is the most important. How can you make sure your audience knows that? Just tell them. "Of all the suggestions I've given you, this last tip is the most important one. The higher the SPF level on your sunscreen, the better." Be careful not to overuse this technique. If you claim that every other point is a key point, soon your audience will not believe you.

REINFORCE KEY IDEAS NONVERBALLY How can you draw attention to key ideas nonverbally? Just the way you deliver an idea can give it special emphasis. Gestures serve the purpose of accenting or emphasizing key phrases, as italics do in written messages.

A well-placed pause can provide emphasis and reinforcement to set off a point. Pausing just before or just after making an important point will focus attention on your thought. Raising or lowering your voice can also reinforce a key idea.

Movement can help emphasize major ideas. Moving from behind the lectern to tell a personal anecdote can signal that something special and more intimate is about to be said. As we discussed in Chapter 13, your movement and gestures should be meaningful and natural, rather than seemingly arbitrary or forced. Your need to emphasize an idea can provide the motivation to make a meaningful movement.

SUMMARY

To inform is to teach someone something you know. Public speakers use specific goals, principles, and strategies to inform others. Informative speeches have three goals—to enhance understanding, to maintain interest, and to be remembered. To achieve these goals, you can deliver several different types of informative speeches. Speeches about objects discuss tangible things. Speeches about procedures explain a process or describe how something works. Speeches about people can be about either the famous or the little known. Speeches about events describe major occurrences or personal experiences. Finally, speeches about ideas are often abstract and generally discuss principles, concepts, or theories.

To enhance your listeners' understanding of a message, (1) define ideas clearly, (2) use principles and techniques of adult learning, based on andragogical rather than pedagogical educational assumptions, (3) clarify unfamiliar ideas or complex processes, (4) use descriptions effectively, and (5) use effective visual reinforcement of your ideas when appropriate.

To gain and maintain interest in your informative talk, follow three important principles. First, establish a motive for your audience to listen to you. Next, tell a story; a well-told story almost always works to keep listeners focused on you and your message. Third, present information that relates to your listeners' interests; in essence, be audience-centered. Finally, use the unexpected to surprise your audience.

Help your listeners remember what you told them by being redundant. Redundancy is something that your English teacher told you to avoid; in oral communication, however, it is appropriate to foreshadow or restate the key ideas of your message. Pacing the flow of your information helps listeners recall your ideas. Reinforcing your ideas verbally and nonverbally can also help your audience members remember important points you make.

BEING AUDIENCE-CENTERED: A SHARPER FOCUS

CONSIDERING YOUR AUDIENCE

➤ If you are presenting completely new information to listeners, use simple, familiar examples.

➤ If your audience consists of adult listeners, remember that adults like to hear information that they can use immediately, to be actively involved in the learning process, to connect their life experience with the new information they learn, and to know how the new information is relevant to their needs and busy lives, and they are problem-oriented.

➤ If you're describing a complex process, use more than definitions to explain what you mean. Consider using analogies, word pictures, or visual aids to make your ideas clear.

➤ Most audiences will probably not be waiting breathlessly for you to talk to them. You will need to motivate them to listen to you. Think about what they are interested in and how they can apply the information you share.

➤ Being an audience-centered public speaker means being aware of information that your audience can use.

CONSIDERING AUDIENCE DIVERSITY

➤ A good story is a way to communicate ideas to people from various cultural backgrounds; many cultural groups, such as those from the Middle East, prefer stories and illustrations rather than detailed definitions and data.

➤ When speaking to a group that may have difficulty understanding your message because of language differences, it is important to build redundancy into your message. Use preview statements, internal summaries, and closing summaries to ensure that your audience grasps your major points.

➤ Use visual images to reinforce your verbal message. Visual images can communicate clearly to people from a variety of cultural background, even when they may not clearly understand the words.

CRITICAL THINKING QUESTIONS

1. You have been asked to speak to a kindergarten class about your chosen profession. Identify approaches to this task that would help make your message clear, interesting, and memorable to your audience.

2. Hillary Webster, M.D., will be addressing a medical convention of other physicians to discuss the weight-loss technique she has recently used successfully with her patients. What advice would you give to help her present an effective talk?

3. Ken's boss has given him the task of presenting a report to a group of potential investors about his company's recent productivity trends. The presentation includes many statistics. What suggestions would you offer to help Ken give an interesting and effective informative presentation?

ETHICAL QUESTIONS

1. Before giving a speech to your class in which you share personal information about one of your friends, should you ask permission from your friend?

2. You are a chemistry major, and you are considering whether you should give a speech to your public-speaking class about how pipe bombs are made. Is this an appropriate topic for your audience?

3. In order to give your five-minute speech about nuclear energy, you are going to have to make the presentation very simple, even though the process you describe is complex. How can you avoid misrepresenting your topic? Should you let your audience know that you are oversimplifying the process?

Developing a Vivid Word Picture

A word picture is a lively description of something that helps your listeners form a mental image by appealing to their senses of sight, taste, smell, sound, and touch. Consider the following steps as you develop a vivid word picture for your next speech.

Step One: What is an image that I want my listeners to see or experience in their "mind's eye"? It could be a specific place you describe in your speech, part of a story you tell, or an experience you describe. Indicate what your listeners would see if they were actually in the place or situation you are describing.

They would see . . .

Step Two: Describe what your listeners would hear if they were actually in the place you are describing in your word picture.

They would hear . . .

Step Three: Describe aromas that listeners might smell.

They would smell . . .

Step Four: Describe what listeners might be feeling or touching.

They would touch or feel . . .

Step Five: If appropriate, describe what listeners would taste.

They would taste . . .

Step Six: Describe the emotion listeners might feel if they were actually experiencing the events depicted in your word picture.

They would feel . . .

Sir John Everett Millais (1829–1896), *The Boyhood of Raleigh*. 1870. Oil on canvas, support: 120.6 x 142.2 cm. Tate London/Art Resource, N.Y.

. . . the power of speech, to stir men's blood.

—WILLIAM SHAKESPEARE

Understanding Principles of Persuasive Speaking

outline

objectives

**After studying this chapter you
should be able to do the
following:**

1. Define persuasion.

2. Describe cognitive dissonance.

3. Identify Maslow's five levels of needs, which explain
how behavior is motivated.

4. Select and develop an appropriate topic for a
persuasive speech.

5. Identify three principles of persuasive speaking.

t happens more than 600 times each day. It appears as commercials on TV and radio; as advertisements in magazines and newspapers and on billboards; and as fund-raising letters from politicians and charities. It also occurs when you are asked to give money to a worthy cause or to donate blood. "It" is persuasion. Efforts to persuade you occur at an average rate of once every two and a half minutes each day.[1] Because persuasion is such an ever-present part of your life, it is important for you to understand how it works. What are the principles of an activity that can shape your attitudes and behavior? What do car salespeople, advertising copywriters, and politicians know about how to change your thinking and behavior that you don't?

In this chapter, we are going to discuss how persuasion works. Such information can help you sharpen your own persuasive skills and can also help you become a more informed receiver of the persuasive messages that come your way. We will define persuasion and discuss the psychological principles underlying all or most efforts to persuade others. We will also discuss some tips for choosing a persuasive speech topic and developing arguments for your speeches. In Chapter 17, we will examine some specific strategies for crafting a persuasive speech.

In Chapter 15, we discussed several strategies for informative speaking—the oral presentation of new information to listeners so that they will understand and remember what is communicated. The purposes of informing and persuading are interrelated. Why inform an audience? Why give new information to others? We often provide information to give listeners new insights that may affect their attitudes and behavior. Information alone has the potential to convince others, but if information is coupled with strategies to persuade, the chances of success increase. Persuasive speakers try to influence the listeners' points of view or behavior. If you want your listeners to respond to your persuasive appeal, you will need to think carefully about the way you structure your message to achieve your specific purpose.

In a persuasive speech, the speaker explicitly asks the audience to make a choice, rather than just informing them of the options. As a persuasive speaker, you will do more than teach; you will ask your listeners to respond to the information you share. Audience analysis is crucial to achieving your goal. To advocate a particular view or position successfully, you must understand your listeners' attitudes, beliefs, values, and behavior.

Persuasion Defined

Persuasion is the process of changing or reinforcing attitudes, beliefs, values, or behavior. Although knowing your listeners' attitudes, beliefs, and values can help you craft any message, these three variables—which we introduced in Chapter 5, when discussing psychological audience analysis—are especially important to consider when designing and delivering a persuasive message.

Our attitudes represent our likes and dislikes. Stated more technically, an *attitude* is a learned predisposition to respond favorably or unfavorably toward something.[2]

persuasion
The process of changing or reinforcing a listener's attitudes, beliefs, values, or behavior

In a persuasive speech, you might try to persuade your listeners to favor or oppose a new shopping mall, to like bats because of their ability to eat insects, or to dislike an increase in sales tax.

A persuasive speech could also change or reinforce a belief. A *belief* is what you understand to be true or false. If you believe in something, you are convinced that it exists or is true. You have structured your sense of what is real and what is unreal to account for the existence of whatever you believe. If you believe in God, you have structured your sense of what is real and unreal to recognize the existence of God. Beliefs are typically based on past experiences. If you believe the sun will rise in the east again tomorrow, or that nuclear power is safe, you base these beliefs either on what you've directly experienced or on the experience of someone you find trustworthy. Beliefs are usually based on evidence, but we hold some beliefs based on faith—we haven't directly experienced something, but we believe anyway.

A persuasive speech could also seek to change or reinforce a value. A *value* is an enduring concept of right or wrong, good or bad. If you value something, you classify it as good or desirable, and you tend to think of its opposite or its absence as bad or wrong. If you do not value something, you are indifferent to it. Values form the basis of your life goals and the motivating force behind your behavior. Most Americans value honesty, trustworthiness, freedom, loyalty, marriage, family, and money. Understanding what your listeners value can help you refine your analysis of them and adapt the content of your speech to those values.

Why is it useful to make distinctions among attitudes, beliefs, and values? Since the essence of persuasion is to change or reinforce these three kinds of predispositions, it is very useful to know exactly which one you are targeting. Of the three, audience values are the most stable. Most of us acquired our values when we were very young and have held on to them into adulthood. Our values, therefore, are generally deeply ingrained. It is not impossible to change the values of your listeners, but it is much more difficult than trying to change a belief or an attitude. Political and religious points of view, which are usually based on long-held values, are especially difficult to modify.

A belief is more susceptible to change than a value is, but it is still difficult to alter. Beliefs are changed by evidence. You might have a difficult time, for example, trying to change someone's belief that the world is flat; you would need to show that existing evidence supports a different conclusion. Usually it takes a great deal of evidence to change a belief and alter the way your audience structures reality.

Attitudes (likes and dislikes) are easier to change than either beliefs or values. Today we may approve of the president of the United States; tomorrow we may disapprove of him because of a recent action he has taken. For example, we may still *believe* that the country is financially stable because of the president's programs, and we may still *value* a democratic form of government, but our *attitude* toward the president has changed because of this particular policy decision.

As Figure 16.1 shows, values are the most deeply ingrained; of the three predispositions, they change least frequently. That's why values are in the core of the model. Beliefs change, but not as much as attitudes. Trying to change an audience's attitudes is easier than attempting to change their values. We suggest that you think carefully about your purpose for making a persuasive speech. Know with certainty whether your objective is to change or reinforce an attitude, a belief, or a value. Then decide what you have to do to achieve your objective.

Persuasive messages often attempt to do more than change or reinforce attitudes, beliefs, or values—they may attempt to change behavior. Getting listeners to eat less, to not smoke tobacco, to not consume drugs, to not drink and drive, or to exercise more are typical goals of persuasive messages that we hear. It seems logical that knowing someone's attitudes, beliefs, and values will let us precisely predict how that person will behave. But we are complicated creatures, and human behavior is not always

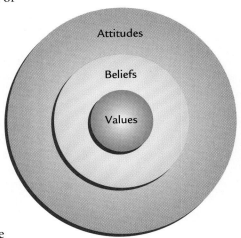

Figure 16.1 *Attitudes—our likes and dislikes—are more likely to change than are our beliefs or values. Our values—our sense of what is right and wrong—are least likely to change over time.*

neatly predictable. Sometimes our attitudes, beliefs, and values may not appear consistent with how we act. For example, you may know that if you're on a low-carb diet, you should avoid that second helping of Dad's homemade chocolate cake; but you cut off a slice and gobble it up anyway.

 ## How Persuasion Works

Now that you know what persuasion is and how attitudes, beliefs, and values influence your behavior, you may still have questions about how persuasion actually works. Knowing how and why listeners change their minds and behaviors can help you construct more effective persuasive messages.

Besides allowing you to persuade others, understanding how persuasion works can also help you analyze why *you* are sometimes persuaded to think or behave in certain ways. Being conscious of why you respond to certain persuasive messages can help you be a better, more discriminating listener to persuasive pitches that come your way.

There are many theories and considerable research that describe how persuasion works. We'll discuss two approaches here: first, a classic approach identified by ancient Greek rhetorician Aristotle, and second, a more contemporary theory that builds on the classic approach.

A CLASSICAL RHETORIC APPROACH TO UNDERSTANDING PERSUASION

Aristotle, a Greek philosopher and rhetorician who lived and wrote in the fourth century B.C.E., was the source of many ideas about communication in general and persuasion in particular. Appendix B provides a closer look at Aristotle and his ideas. As we noted in Chapter 4, he defined *rhetoric* as the process of discovering in any particular case the available means of persuasion. When the goal is to persuade, the communicator selects symbols (words and nonverbal messages, including images and music) to change attitudes, beliefs, values, or behavior. Aristotle identified three general methods (or, using his language, "available means") to persuade. They are ethos, logos, and pathos.

ETHOS To use **ethos** to persuade, an effective communicator presents information that is credible. Aristotle believed that in order to be credible, a public speaker should be ethical, possess good character, have common sense, and be concerned for the well-being of the audience. The more credible and ethical a speaker is perceived to be, the greater the chances are that a listener will believe in, trust, and positively respond to the persuasive message of the speaker. So one of the means or methods of persuasion is for the communicator to present information that can be trusted and to be believable and trustworthy himself or herself. When a friend is trying to convince you to let him borrow your car, he may say, "Trust me. I promise not to do anything whacky with your car. I'm a responsible guy." He's appealing to his credibility as an ethical, trusted friend. We'll discuss specific strategies to enhance your credibility and thus your persuasiveness, in the next chapter.

LOGOS Another means of persuading others is to use **logos**. The word *logos* literally means "the word." Aristotle used this term to refer to the rational, logical arguments that a speaker uses to persuade someone. A skilled persuader not only reaches a logical conclusion but also supports the message with evidence and reasoning. Your friend who is trying to borrow your car may try using a logical, rational argument

ethos
The term Aristotle used to refer to a speaker's credibility

logos
Literally, "the word"; the term Aristotle used to refer to logic—the formal system of using rules to reach a conclusion

supported with evidence to get your car keys. He may say, "I borrowed your car last week and I returned it without a scratch. I also borrowed it the week before that and there were no problems—and I filled the tank with gas. So if you loan me your car today, I'll return it just like I did in the past." Your friend is appealing to your rational side by using evidence to support his conclusion that your car will be returned in good shape. In Chapter 17 we'll provide detailed strategies for developing logical, rational arguments and supporting those arguments with solid evidence.

PATHOS Aristotle used the term **pathos** to refer to the use of appeals to emotion. We sometimes hold attitudes, beliefs, and values that are not logical but that simply make us feel positive. Likewise, we sometimes do things or buy things to make ourselves feel happy, powerful, or energized. Your friend who wants to borrow your wheels may also use pathos—an emotional appeal—to get you to turn over your car keys. He may say, "Look, without transportation I can't get to my doctor's appointment. I'm feeling sick. I need your help. Friends help friends, and I could use a good friend right now." Your buddy is trying to tug on your emotional heartstrings to motivate you to loan him your car. He's hoping to convince you to behave in a way that makes you feel positive about yourself.

What are effective ways to appeal to listeners' emotions? Use emotion-arousing stories and concrete examples, as well as pictures and music. In the next chapter we'll identify ethical strategies to appeal to emotions when persuading others.

All three of these available means of persuasion—ethos (ethical credibility), logos (logic), and pathos (emotion)—are ways of motivating a listener to think or behave in certain ways. **Motivation** is the underlying internal force that drives people to achieve their goals. Our motives explain why we do things.[3] Several factors motivate people to respond to persuasive messages: the need to restore balance to their lives to avoid stress, the need to avoid pain, and the desire to increase pleasure have been documented as influencing attitudes, beliefs, values, and behavior.

ELM: A CONTEMPORARY APPROACH TO UNDERSTANDING PERSUASION

A newer, research-based framework for understanding how persuasion works is called the **elaboration likelihood model (ELM) of persuasion.**[4] This theory has a long name but is actually a simple idea that offers an explanation of how people are persuaded to do something or think about something. Rather than prescribing how to craft a persuasive message from the standpoint of the speaker, as Aristotle does, ELM theory describes how audience members *interpret* persuasive messages. It's an audience-centered theory of how people make sense out of persuasive communication.

The theory suggests that there are two ways you can be persuaded—by a direct, logical route that you follow when you think critically about, or elaborate on, a message, or by an indirect, less rational route whereby you are persuaded based on a general impression of what you're hearing. Which path you follow, direct or indirect, is based on whether you elaborate on the message you hear.

To **elaborate** means to think about the information, ideas, and issues related to the content of the speech you're listening to. When you elaborate on a message, you are critically evaluating what you hear by paying special attention to the arguments and evidence. If you don't elaborate (that is, if you don't think very hard about the information you're listening to), you simply have an overall impression of what the speaker says and how the speaker says it.

THE DIRECT PERSUASION ROUTE If you elaborate on a message, you will likely be directly persuaded by the logic, reasoning, arguments, and evidence presented to you. When you elaborate, you consider what Aristotle would call the underlying logos, or logic, of the message. You carefully and thoughtfully consider the facts and then make a thoughtful decision as to whether to believe or do what the persuader wants.

pathos
The term used by Aristotle to refer to appeals to human emotion

motivation
The internal force that drives people to achieve their goals

elaboration likelihood model (ELM) of persuasion
The theory that people can be persuaded by logic, evidence, and reasoning, or through a more peripheral route that may depend on the credibility of the speaker, the sheer number of arguments presented, or emotional appeals

elaborate
From the standpoint of the elaboration likelihood model (ELM) of persuasion, to think about information, ideas, and issues related to the content of a message

For example, you buy a high-speed Internet connection for your home because you are convinced you will save time downloading information from the Internet; you've read the literature and have made a logical, rational decision. There may be times, however, when you think you are making a decision based on logic, but you're not. Instead, you are being persuaded by less obvious strategies via an indirect path.

THE INDIRECT PERSUASION ROUTE A second way you can be persuaded, according to ELM, is peripheral. When you don't elaborate on a message, you can be persuaded by such indirect factors as catchy music used in an advertisement or your positive reaction to the salesperson who is selling you a product. It's not an evaluation of the logic or content of the advertisement or the salesperson's words that persuades you, it's the overall feeling you have about the product or the salesperson that triggers your purchase. When hearing a speech, you may be persuaded by the appearance of the speaker (he looks nice; I trust him); by the sheer number of research studies in support of the speaker's proposal (there are so many reasons to accept this speaker's proposal; she's convinced me); or by the speaker's use of an emotionally charged story (I can't let that little girl starve; I'll donate 50 cents to save her).

The elaboration likelihood model's concept of an indirect persuasion route for making sense of a message is similar to an idea of Aristotle's, which is that rather than logic, it's the speaker's credibility (ethos) or use of emotional appeal (pathos) that can sometimes become the tipping point in favor of what the persuader wants you to do or think. If, when you are persuaded about something, you can't identify why you are persuaded, you're probably being persuaded by indirect factors.

Like Aristotle's ethos, logos and pathos, the direct and indirect paths to persuasion attempt to influence your motivation so that you will embrace the speaker's position. Sometimes you can identify what motivates you to do something (the direct route to persuasion) and sometimes you can't (the indirect route to persuasion). Both Aristotle's theory (which identifies what a *speaker* does to persuade an audience) and the ELM theory (which stresses how *audience* members may interpret a message) can give you insight into how you are persuaded, as well as help you consider how others may be motivated to change their attitudes, beliefs, values, or behavior. To help you better understand what motivates and subsequently persuades listeners (and what motivates you), we'll examine factors of motivation in greater detail.

How to Motivate Listeners

I t's late at night, and you're watching your favorite talk show before going to bed. The program is interrupted by a commercial extolling the virtues of a well-known brand of ice cream. Suddenly, you remember that you have some of the advertised flavor, Royal Rocky Road. You apparently hadn't realized how hungry you were for ice cream until the ad reminded you of the lip-smacking goodness of the cold, creamy, smooth treat. Before you know it, you are at the freezer, helping yourself to a couple of scoops of ice cream.

If the maker of that commercial knew how effective it had been, he or she would be overjoyed. The ad was persuasive and changed your behavior because the message was tailor-made for you. What principles explain why you were motivated to dig through the freezer at midnight for a carton of ice cream? At the heart of the persuasion process is the audience-centered process of motivating listeners to respond to your message. Persuasion works because listeners are motivated to respond to a message. An audience is more likely to be persuaded if you help members solve their problems or otherwise meet their needs. They can also be motivated if you convince them good things will happen to them if they follow your advice, or bad things will occur if they don't.

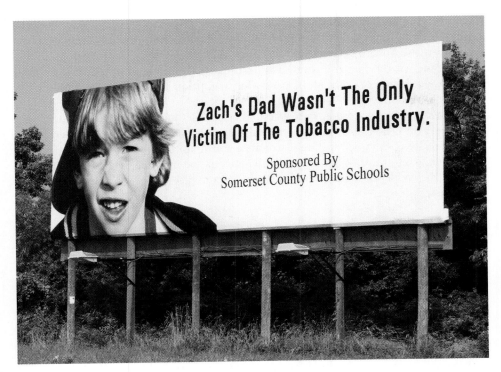

Effective public-service messages often use cognitive dissonance to change people's behaviors. This technique is also often effective for public speakers.

[Photo: Sonda Dawes/The Image Works]

USE DISSONANCE

Dissonance theory is based on the principle that people strive to solve problems and manage stress and tension in a way that is consistent with their attitudes, beliefs, and values.[5] According to the theory, when you are presented with information inconsistent with your current attitudes, beliefs, values, or behavior, you become aware that you have a problem; you experience a kind of discomfort called **cognitive dissonance**. The word *cognitive* has to do with our thoughts. *Dissonance* means "lack of harmony or agreement." When you think of a dissonant chord in music, you probably think of a collection of sounds that are unpleasant or not in tune with the melody or other chords. Most people seek to avoid problems or feelings of dissonance. Cognitive dissonance, then, means that you are experiencing a way of thinking that is inconsistent and uncomfortable. If, for example, you smoke cigarettes and a speaker reminds you that smoking is unhealthy, this reminder creates dissonance. You can restore balance and solve the problem either by no longer smoking or by rejecting the message that smoking is harmful.

Creating dissonance with a persuasive speech can be an effective way to change attitudes and behavior. The first tactic in such a speech is to identify an existing problem or need. For example, a speaker seeking to ban aerosol sprays could begin her speech by focusing on a need we all generally share, such as the need to preserve the environment. The speaker could then point out that the continued use of aerosol sprays depletes the ozone layer, which protects us from the sun's harmful rays. By doing so, the speaker is deliberately creating dissonance. She knows that people in her audience appreciate the convenience of aerosol sprays, so their attitudes about protecting the environment *conflict with* their feelings about getting housework done easily or styling their hair effectively. So next, she would aim at restoring the audience's sense of balance. She could claim that her solution—using nonaerosol sprays—can resolve the conflict. Using this strategy, the speaker may motivate audience members to change their behavior. The change is the speaker's objective.

Political candidates use a similar strategy. A mayoral candidate usually tries first to make his or her audience aware of problems in the community, then may blame

cognitive dissonance

The sense of mental discomfort that prompts a person to change when new information conflicts with previously organized thought patterns

the current mayor for most of the problems. Once dissonance has been created, the candidate then suggests that these problems would be solved, or at least managed better, if he or she were to be elected as the city's next mayor. Using the principles of dissonance theory, the mayoral candidate first upsets the audience, then restores their balance and feeling of comfort by providing a solution to the city's problem: his or her selection as mayor.

In using dissonance theory to persuade, speakers have an ethical responsibility not to rely on false claims just to create dissonance. Claiming that a problem exists when it really doesn't or creating dissonance about a problem that is in fact unlikely to happen is unethical. When listening to a persuasive message, pay particular attention to the evidence that a speaker uses to convince you that a problem really does exist.

HOW LISTENERS COPE WITH DISSONANCE Effective persuasion requires more than simply creating dissonance and then suggesting a solution to the problem. When your listeners confront dissonant information, a number of options are available to them besides following your suggestions. You need to be aware of other ways your audience may react before you can reduce their cognitive dissonance.[6]

◆ **Listeners may discredit the source.** Instead of believing everything you say, your listeners could choose to discredit you. Suppose you drive a Japanese-made car and you hear a speaker whose father owns a Chevrolet dealership advocate that all Americans should drive cars made in the United States. You could agree with him, or you could decide that the speaker is biased because of his father's occupation. Instead of selling your Japanese-made car and buying an American-made car, you could simply suspect the speaker's credibility and ignore the suggestion to buy American automobiles. As a persuasive speaker, you need to ensure that your audience will perceive you as competent and trustworthy so that they will accept your message.

◆ **Listeners may reinterpret the message.** A second way your listeners may overcome cognitive dissonance and restore balance is to hear what they want to hear. They may choose to focus on the parts of your message that are consistent with what they already believe and ignore the unfamiliar or controversial parts. Your job as an effective public speaker is to make your message as clear as possible so that your audience will not reinterpret your message. If you tell a customer looking at a *new* kind of computer software that it takes ten steps to get into the word-processing program, but that the program is easy to use, the customer might focus on those first ten things and decide that the software is too hard to use. Choose your words carefully, and use simple, vivid examples to keep listeners focused on what's most important.

◆ **Listeners may seek new information.** Another way that listeners cope with cognitive dissonance is to seek more information on the subject. Your audience members may look for additional information to negate your position and to refute your well-created arguments. For example, as the owner of a minivan, you would experience dissonance if you heard a speaker describe the recent rash of safety problems with minivans. You might turn to your friend and whisper, "Is this true? Are minivans really dangerous? I've always heard they were safe." You would request new information to validate your ownership of a minivan.

◆ **Listeners may stop listening.** Some messages are so much at odds with listeners' attitudes, beliefs, and values that the audience may decide to stop listening. Most of us do not seek opportunities to hear or read messages that oppose our opinions. It is unlikely that a staunch Democrat would attend a fund-raiser for the state Republican party. The principle of selective exposure suggests that we tend to pay attention to messages that are consistent with our points of view and to avoid those that are not. When we do find ourselves trapped in a situation in which we are forced to hear a message that doesn't support our beliefs, we tend to stop listening. Being aware of the existing attitudes, beliefs, and values of the audience can help you ensure that they won't tune you out.

➤ **Listeners may change their attitudes, beliefs, values, or behavior.** A fifth way an audience may respond to dissonant information is to do as the speaker wishes them to. As we have noted, if listeners change their attitudes, they can reduce the dissonance that they experience. You listen to a life-insurance salesperson tell you that when you die, your family will have no financial support. This creates dissonance; you prefer to think of your family as happy and secure. So you decide to take out a $100,000 policy to protect your family. This action restores your sense of balance. The salesperson has persuaded you successfully. The goals of advertising copywriters, salespeople, and political candidates are similar: They want you to experience dissonance so that you will change your attitudes, beliefs, values, or behavior.

USE LISTENER NEEDS

Need is one of the best motivators. The person who is looking at a new car because he or she needs one right now is more likely to buy one than the person who is just thinking about how nice it would be to drive the latest model. The more you understand what your listeners need, the greater the chances are that you can gain and hold their attention and ultimately get them to do what you want. The classic theory that outlines basic human needs was developed by Abraham Maslow.[7] Maslow suggests that there is a hierarchy of needs that motivate everyone's behavior. Basic physiological needs (such as for food, water, and air) have to be satisfied before we can be motivated to respond to higher-level needs. Figure 16.2 illustrates Maslow's five levels of needs, with the most basic at the bottom. Although the hierarchical nature of Maslow's needs has not been consistently supported by research (we can be motivated by several needs at the same time), Maslow's hierarchy of needs provides a useful checklist of what potentially can motivate a listener. When attempting to persuade an audience, a public speaker tries to stimulate these needs in order to change or reinforce attitudes, beliefs, values, or behavior. Let's examine these needs in some detail.

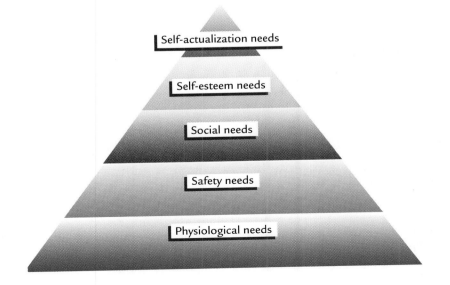

Figure 16.2 *Maslow's hierarchy of needs*

PHYSIOLOGICAL NEEDS The most basic needs for all humans are physiological: We all need air, water, and food. According to Maslow's theory, unless those needs are met, it will be difficult to motivate a listener to satisfy other needs. If your listeners are hot, tired, and thirsty, it will be more difficult to persuade them to vote for your candidate, buy your insurance policy, or sign your petition in support of local pet-leash laws. Be sensitive to the basic physiological needs of your audience so that your appeals to higher-level needs will be heard.

SAFETY NEEDS Listeners are concerned about their safety. We have a need to feel safe, secure, and protected, and we need to be able to predict that our own and our loved ones' needs for safety will be met. The classic sales presentation from insurance salespeople includes appeals to our need for safety and security. Many insurance sales efforts include photos of wrecked cars, anecdotes of people who were in ill health and could not pay their bills, or tales of the head of a household who passed away, leaving the basic needs of his or her family unmet. Appeals to use safety belts, stop smoking, start exercising, and use condoms all play to our need for safety and security.

In a speech titled "Emissions Tampering: Get the Lead Out," John appealed to his listeners' need for safety and security when he began his speech with these observations:

> A major American producer is currently dumping over 8,000 tons of lead into our air each year, which in turn adversely affects human health. The producers of this waste are tampering with pollution control devices in order to cut costs. This tampering escalates the amount of noxious gases you and I inhale by 300 to 800 percent. That producer is the American motorist.[8]

SOCIAL NEEDS We all need to feel loved and valued. We need contact with others and reassurance that they care about us. According to Maslow, these social needs translate into our need for a sense of belonging to a group (fraternity, religious organization, friends). Powerful persuasive appeals are based on our need for social contact. We are encouraged to buy a product or support a particular issue because others are buying the product or supporting the issue. The message is that to be liked and respected by others, we must buy the same things they do or support the same position they support.

SELF-ESTEEM NEEDS The need for self-esteem reflects our desire to think well of ourselves. Jesse Jackson is known for appealing often to the self-worth of his listeners by inviting them to chant, "I am somebody." This is a direct appeal to his listeners' need for self-esteem. Advertisers also appeal to our need for self-esteem when they encourage us to believe that we can be noticed by others or stand out in the crowd if we purchase their product. Commercials promoting luxury cars usually invite you to picture yourself in the driver's seat with a beautiful person next to you while you receive looks of envy from those you pass on the road.

SELF-ACTUALIZATION NEEDS At the top of Maslow's hierarchy is the need for **self-actualization**. This is the need to fully realize one's highest potential. For many years, the U.S. Army used the slogan "Be all that you can be" to tap into the need for self-actualization. Calls to be the best and the brightest are appeals to self-actualization. According to Maslow's assumption that our needs are organized into a hierarchy, needs at the other four levels must be satisfied before we can be motivated to satisfy the highest-level need.

USE POSITIVE MOTIVATION

self-actualization need
The need to achieve one's highest potential

A Depression-era politician claimed that a vote for him would result in a return to prosperity: "A chicken in every pot" was his positive motivational appeal. Positive motivational appeals are statements suggesting that good things will happen if the

speaker's advice is heeded. A key to using positive motivational appeals effectively is to know what your listeners value. Knowing what audience members view as desirable, good, and virtuous can help you select the benefits of your persuasive proposal that best appeal to them.

EMPHASIZE POSITIVE VALUES What do most people value? A comfortable, prosperous life; stimulating, exciting activity; a sense of accomplishment; world, community, and personal peace; and happiness are some of the many things people value. How can you use these values in a persuasive speech? When identifying reasons for your audience to think, feel, or behave as you want them to, review the values just listed to determine what benefits would accrue to your listeners. If, for example, you advocate that your listeners enroll in a sign-language course, what are the benefits to the audience? You could stress the sense of accomplishment, contribution to society, or increased opportunities for friendship that would develop if they learned this new skill. A speech advocating that recording companies print the lyrics of all songs on the label of the recording could appeal to family values.

EMPHASIZE BENEFITS, NOT JUST FEATURES A **benefit** is a good result or something that creates a positive feeling for the listener. A **feature** is simply a characteristic of whatever it is that you're talking about. A benefit creates a positive emotional "sizzle" that appeals to the heart. A feature elicits a rational, cognitive reaction—it appeals to the head. Heart usually trumps head when persuading others.

Most salespeople know that it is not enough just to identify, in general terms, the features of their product. They must translate those features into an obvious benefit that enhances the customer's quality of life. It is not enough for the real-estate salesperson to say, "This floor is the new no-wax vinyl." It is more effective to add, "And this means that you will never have to get down on your hands and knees to scrub another floor." When using positive motivational appeals, be sure your listeners know how the benefits of your proposal can improve their quality of life or the lives of their loved ones.

USE NEGATIVE MOTIVATION

"If you don't stop what you're doing, I'm going to tell Mom!" Whether he or she realizes it or not, the sibling who threatens to tell Mom is using a persuasive technique called *fear appeal*. One of the oldest methods of trying to change someone's attitude or behavior, the use of a threat is also one of the most effective. In essence, the appeal to fear takes the form of an "if–then" statement: If you don't do X, then awful things will happen to you. A persuader builds an argument on the assertion that a need will not be met unless the desired behavior or attitude change occurs. The principal reason that appeals to fear continue to be made in persuasive messages is that they work. A variety of research studies support the following principles for using fear appeals.[9]

- ➤ **A strong threat to a loved one tends to be more successful than a fear appeal directed at the audience members themselves.** A speaker using this principle might say, "Unless you get your children to wear safety belts, they could easily be injured or killed in an auto accident."
- ➤ **The more competent, trustworthy, or respected the speaker, the greater the likelihood that an appeal to fear will be successful.** A speaker with less credibility will be more successful with moderate threats. The U.S. Surgeon General will be more successful in convincing people to use condoms to lessen the risk of AIDS than you will.
- ➤ **Fear appeals are more successful if you can convince your listeners that the threat is real and will probably occur unless they take the action you are advocating.** For example, you could dramatically announce, "Last year, thousands of smokers developed lung cancer and eventually died. Unless

benefit
A good result or something that creates a positive emotional response in the listener.

feature
A characteristic of something you are describing.

you stop smoking, there is a high probability that you could develop lung cancer, too."

◆ **In general, increasing the intensity of a fear appeal increases the chances that the fear appeal will be effective.** This is especially true if the listener can take some action (the action the persuader is suggesting) to reduce the threat.[10] In the past, some researchers and public-speaking textbooks reported that if a speaker creates an excessive amount of fear and anxiety in listeners, the listeners may find the appeal so strong and annoying that they stop listening. More comprehensive research, however, has concluded that there is a direct link between the intensity or strength of the fear appeal and the likelihood that audience members will be persuaded by the message.

LEARNING FROM GREAT SPEAKERS

Elizabeth Cady Stanton (1815–1902)

Elizabeth Cady Stanton began her preparation for persuasive speaking by reading most of her father's law library while she was still a young woman. Incensed by the discrimination she found entrenched in the law, she embarked on a long career of speaking out for women's rights. Stanton gave perhaps her most famous persuasive speech to the first Women's Convention held in 1848 in Seneca Falls, New York. The success of that speech was evident in the results: One hundred men and women signed a Declaration of Sentiments that called for equal rights for women. Throughout the next half-century, Stanton frequently spoke out passionately and forcefully, not only for women's suffrage, but on such related issues as co-education, equal wages, birth control, property rights for women, and reform of divorce laws.[11]

Successful persuaders have strong feelings about their messages. They believe in their cause. But in addition to their strong passion, they also research the issues and are knowledgeable about their messages. So besides having strong convictions about what you are advocating, spend time researching your topic and immersing yourself in the issues you will present to your listeners—both the pros and the cons of what you advocate.

[Photo: The Granger Collection]

Fear appeals work. Strong fear appeals seem to work even better than mild ones, assuming there is evidence to back up the threat made by a credible speaker. The speaker who uses fear appeals has an ethical responsibility to be truthful and not exaggerate when trying to arouse listeners' fear.

➤ **Fear appeals are more successful if you can convince your listeners that they have the power to make a change that will reduce the fear-causing threat.** As a speaker, your goal is not only to arouse their fear, but also to empower them to act. When providing a solution to the fear-inducing problem, make sure that there is something your listeners can do to reduce the threat.[12] If, for example, you tell your listeners that unless they lose weight, they will die prematurely, they may want to shed pounds but think it's just too hard to do. You'll be a more effective persuader if you couple your fear-arousing message (lose weight or die early) with a strategy to make weight loss achievable (here's a diet plan that you can follow; it is simple and it works). The audience-centered principle again applies here. You may think the solution is evident, but will your listeners think the same thing? View the solution from your listeners' point of view.

RECAP

How to Motivate Listeners to Respond to Your Persuasive Message

	DESCRIPTION	EXAMPLE OF MESSAGE
Use cognitive dissonance	Telling listeners about existing problems or information that is inconsistent with their currently held beliefs or known information creates psychological discomfort.	Many high-school students in our district are not computer literate. Without this knowledge, students will not be competitive in today's job market. You should support the local bond proposal that would provide more money for computers in our schools.
Use listeners' needs	People are motivated by unmet needs. The most basic needs are physiological, followed by safety needs, social needs, self-esteem needs, and finally, self-actualization needs.	You could be the envy of people you know if you purchase this sleek new sports car. You will be perceived as a person of high status in your community.
Use positive motivation	People will be more likely to change their thinking or pursue a particular course of action if they are convinced that good things will happen to them if they support what the speaker advocates.	You should take a course in public speaking because it will increase your prospects of getting a good job. Effective communication skills are the most sought-after skills in today's workplace.
Use negative motivation	People seek to avoid pain and discomfort. They will be motivated to support what a speaker advocates if they are convinced that bad things will happen to them unless they do.	If you receive a letter or package that looks suspicious because it is unusually lumpy, has no return address, is marked "personal" or "confidential," or is from someone you do not know, wash your hands after you touch it. Report the suspicious letter or package to the post office immediately. If you do not heed these suggestions, you increase the chances of being contaminated by a biological agent.

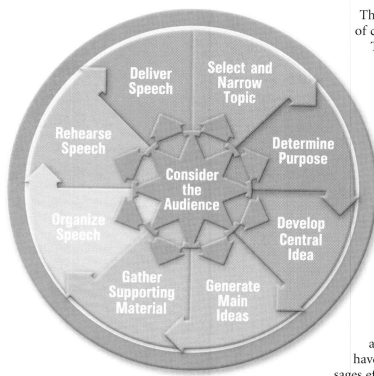

Figure 16.3 *Considering the audience is central to the speech-making process.*

The effectiveness of fear appeals is based on the theories of cognitive dissonance and Maslow's hierarchy of needs. The fear aroused creates dissonance, which can be reduced by following the recommendation of the persuader. Appeals to fear are also based on targeting an unmet need. Fear appeals depend on a convincing insistence that a need will go unmet unless a particular action or attitude change occurs.

Cognitive dissonance, needs, and appeals to the emotions, both positive and negative, can all persuade listeners to change their attitudes, beliefs, values, and behavior. Realize, however, that persuasion is not as simple as these approaches may lead you to believe. There is no precise formula for motivating and convincing an audience. Attitude change occurs differently in each individual; there are no magic words, phrases, or appeals. Persuasion is an art that draws on science. Cultivating a sensitivity to listeners' emotions and needs and ethically using public-speaking strategies you have learned will help you make your persuasive messages effective.

How to Develop Your Persuasive Speech

Now that you understand what persuasion is and how it works, let's turn our attention to the task of preparing a persuasive speech. The process of developing a persuasive speech follows the same audience-centered path you would take to develop any speech.

In the remaining portion of this chapter and in the next, we will amplify our discussion of these essential steps, providing specific examples and strategies to help you prepare a persuasive message. In this chapter, we'll give you some tips for getting started with the speech-construction process. As illustrated by the center of our now-familiar model of the speechmaking process in Figure 16.3, you first consider your audience, especially when attempting to persuade listeners. In the next chapter, we will provide additional practical strategies to help you enhance your credibility, use emotional persuasive appeals, and use evidence and reasoning as supportive material. We'll also present special strategies for organizing persuasive messages.

CONSIDER THE AUDIENCE

Although being audience-centered is important in every speaking situation, it is vital when your objective is to persuade. It would be a challenge to persuade someone without knowing something about his or her interests, attitudes, beliefs, values, and behaviors.

Remember that while you're speaking, audience members have a variety of thoughts running through their heads. Your job as a persuader is to develop a message that anticipates, as best you can, what your audience may be thinking and feeling when they listen to you. You may want to review the elements of audience analysis and adaptation that we presented in Chapter 5 to help you think more concretely about who your listeners are and why they should listen to you.

CONSIDER AUDIENCE DIVERSITY One essential aspect of being audience-centered that we've emphasized throughout the book is being sensitive to the culturally diverse nature of most contemporary audiences. In our multicultural society, how persuasion works for one cultural group is different from how it works for others. Researchers have discovered no universal, cross-cultural approach to persuasion that is effective in each culture. North Americans, for example, tend to place considerable importance on direct observations and verifiable facts. Our court system places great stock in eyewitness testimony. People in some Chinese cultures, however, consider such evidence unreliable because they believe that what people observe is always influenced by personal motives. In some African cultures, personal testimony is also often suspect; it is reasoned that if you speak up to defend someone, for example, you have an ulterior motive, and therefore the observation is discounted.[13] Although your audience may not include listeners from Africa or China, given the growing diversity of Americans, that possibility is increasing. Or you may have listeners from other cultures with different perspectives. Our point: Don't design a persuasive message using strategies that would be effective only for you or those from your cultural background. An effective communicator is especially sensitive to cultural differences between himself or herself and the audience, while at the same time being cautious not to make stereotypical assumptions about an audience based only on cultural factors.

REMEMBER YOUR ETHICAL RESPONSIBILITIES AS A PERSUADER As you think about your audience and how to adapt your message to them, we remind you of your ethical responsibilities when persuading others. Fabricating evidence or trying to frighten your listeners with bogus information is not ethical. Creating dissonance in the minds of your listeners based on information that you know is not true is also not ethical. Adapting to your listeners does not mean that you only tell people what they want to hear. It means developing an ethical message that your listeners will listen to thoughtfully.

SELECT AND NARROW YOUR PERSUASIVE TOPIC

In your public-speaking class you may be given considerable latitude in selecting a topic. Deciding on a persuasive speech topic sometimes stumps beginning speakers. But rather than just picking the first idea that pops into your mind, select a topic that is important to you. What are you passionate about? What issues stir your heart and mind? You'll present a better speech if you've selected a topic you can speak about with sincere conviction. In addition to your interests, always reflect on your audience's passions and convictions. The ideal topic speaks to a need, concern, or issue of the audience as well as to your interests and zeal.

Controversial issues make excellent sources for persuasive topics. A controversial issue is a question about which people disagree. Here are several: Should the university increase tuition so that faculty members can have a salary increase? Should public schools distribute condoms to students? Should the government provide health insurance to all citizens? In choosing a controversial topic, you need to be audience-centered—to know the local, state, national, or international issues that interest your listeners. In addition, the best persuasive speech topics focus on important rather than frivolous issues.

Pay attention to the media and the Internet to stay current on the important issues of the day. If you're not already doing so, you should read at least one newspaper every day, especially the editorial page. Also take a look at a national news magazine such as *Time*, *Newsweek*, or *U.S. News and World Report* to keep in touch with issues and topics of interest. Another interesting source of controversial issues is talk radio programs. Both national and local radio call-in programs may give you ideas that are appropriate for a persuasive speech. You might also monitor chat rooms on the Internet or peruse the homepages of print and broadcast media Web sites for ideas. Even if you already have a clear idea of your speech topic, keeping up with the media and the

If you want to be effectively persuasive, it's important to know where your audience stands on the issue you're speaking about.

[Photo: Duane A. Laverty/*Waco Tribune-Herald*/AP Images]

Internet can give you additional ideas to help narrow your topic or find interesting and appropriate supporting material.

DETERMINE YOUR PERSUASIVE PURPOSE

When your goal is to persuade, you've already decided on your general purpose: You want the members of your audience to change or reinforce their attitudes, beliefs, values, or behavior. But you still must develop your specific purpose.

When you persuade others, you don't always have to strive for dramatic changes in the attitudes, beliefs, values, and behavior of your audience. People rarely make major life changes after hearing just one persuasive message. Your persuasive speaking goal may be to move listeners *a bit closer* to your ultimate persuasive objective. **Social judgment theory** suggests that when listeners are confronted with a persuasive message, their responses can be classified into one of three categories: latitude of acceptance (they generally agree with the speaker), latitude of rejection (they disagree), or latitude of noncommitment (they're not sure how to respond).[14] If most of your listeners' attitudes and beliefs are in the latitude of rejection with regard to your position (for example, you're in favor of gay marriage and they are against it), it's going to be difficult to move them to a latitude of acceptance in one ten-minute speech. If you can get them to be less rejecting of the message and at least move toward being noncommitted, you've made progress toward your goal. It's important to know where they stand on an issue (their latitude of acceptance, rejection, or noncommitment) before you craft your message so that you can ethically adapt to them.

DEVELOP YOUR CENTRAL IDEA AND MAIN IDEAS

The overall structure of your speech flows from your central idea and the main ideas that support your central idea. Your central idea, as you recall, is a one-sentence summary of your speech. When persuading others, most speakers find it useful to state their central idea in the form of a proposition. A **proposition** is a statement with which you want your audience to agree. In the following list, note how each proposition is actually the central idea of the speech:

> All students should be required to take a foreign language.
>
> Organic gardening is better for the environment than gardening with chemicals.
>
> The United States should not provide economic aid to other countries.

There are three categories of propositions: propositions of fact, propositions of value, and propositions of policy. Determining which category your persuasive proposition fits into not only can help you clarify your central idea, but can also give you an idea of how to select specific persuasive strategies that will help you achieve your specific purpose. Let's examine each type of proposition in more detail.

PROPOSITION OF FACT A **proposition of fact** focuses on whether something is true or false or on whether it did or did not happen. Al Gore received more votes nationwide than George W. Bush in the 2000 presidential election. The Boston Red Sox won the 2007 World Series. Texas is bigger than Poland. Each of these statements is a proposition of fact that can be verified simply by consulting an appropriate source. Other propositions of fact will take more time and skill—perhaps an entire persua-

social judgment theory
Theory that categorizes listener responses to a persuasive message as in the latitude of acceptance, the latitude of rejection, or the latitude of noncommitment

proposition
A statement that summarizes the ideas with which a speaker wants an audience to agree

proposition of fact
A proposition that focuses on whether something is true or false or whether it did or did not happen

sive speech—to prove. Here are examples of more controversial propositions of fact:

> When women joined the military, the quality of the military improved.
>
> Children who were abused by their parents are more likely to abuse their own children.
>
> U.S. foreign policy has increased the chance that the United States will experience more terrorist attacks.
>
> The gasoline engine is the prime culprit in the deterioration of the ozone layer.
>
> Global warming is not occurring in our atmosphere.

To prove each of these propositions, a speaker would need to provide specific supporting evidence. To persuade listeners to agree with a proposition of fact, the speaker must focus on changing or reinforcing their beliefs. Most persuasive speeches that focus on propositions of fact begin by identifying one or more reasons that the proposition is true.

The following persuasive speech outline on the topic of low-carb diets is based on a proposition of fact:

TOPIC:	Low-carbohydrate diets
GENERAL PURPOSE:	To persuade
PROPOSITION:	Low-carbohydrate diets are safe and effective.
SPECIFIC PURPOSE:	At the end of my speech, audience members will agree that low-carb diets are safe and effective.

MAIN IDEAS:

I. Carbohydrates are a significant part of our diets.
   A. Many people eat a significant amount of fast food that is laden with carbohydrates.
   B. Lunches provided by the cafeterias in elementary schools include significant amounts of carbohydrates.
   C. Many people eat a significant amount of highly processed, carb-rich foods.

II. Carbohydrates are making people fat and unhealthy.
   A. A diet rich in carbohydrates leads to obesity.
   B. A diet rich in carbohydrates leads to Type II diabetes.

III. Low-carb diets are a safe and effective way to lose weight and maintain your health.
   A. The safety of such low-carb diets as the South Beach diet or the Atkins diet is documented by research.
   B. The effectiveness of such low-carb diets is documented by research.

confidently connecting with your audience

Breathe to Relax

When you feel your body start to tense, take a deep, relaxing breath to help quiet your fears. It's normal to experience a quickened heartbeat and a change in your breathing patterns as physiological responses to increased anxiety. To signal to your brain that *you* are in charge, consciously take several slow breaths. As you breathe, make your breaths unobtrusive; no one need know to that you are using a deep breathing technique to manage your fear. Whether you are at your seat in your classroom getting ready to be the next speaker or sitting on a platform in front of an audience, a few slow, calming breaths will help you relax and calm your spirit.

PROPOSITION OF VALUE A **proposition of value** is a statement that calls for the listener to judge the worth or importance of something. Values, as you recall, are enduring concepts of good and bad, right and wrong. Value propositions are statements

proposition of value

A proposition that calls for the listener to judge the worth or importance of something that something is either good or bad, or that one thing or course of action is better than another. Note these examples:

It is wrong to turn away immigrants who want to come to the United States.

Communication is a better major than home economics.

A private-school education is more valuable than a public-school education.

It is better for citizens to carry concealed weapons than to let criminals rule society.

Each of these propositions either directly states or implies that something is better than something else. Value propositions often directly compare two things and suggest that one of the options is better than the other.

Manny's speech was designed to convince his audience that reggae music is better than rock music.

TOPIC:	Reggae music
GENERAL PURPOSE:	To persuade
PROPOSITION:	Reggae music is better than rock music for three reasons.
SPECIFIC PURPOSE:	After listening to my speech, the audience should listen to reggae music more often than they listen to rock music.
MAIN IDEAS:	I. Reggae music communicates a message of equality for all people.
	II. Reggae music and its rhythms evoke a positive, uplifting mood.
	III. Reggae music draws on a variety of cultural and ethnic traditions.

PROPOSITION OF POLICY The third type of proposition, a **proposition of policy**, advocates a specific action—changing a policy, procedure, or behavior. Note how all the following propositions of policy include the word *should*; this is a tip-off that the speaker is advocating a change in policy or procedure.

The Gifted and Talented Program in our school district should have a full-time coordinator.

Our community should set aside one day each month as "Community Cleanup Day."

Senior citizens should pay for more of their medical costs.

In a speech based on a proposition of policy, Paul aimed to convince his audience that academic tenure for college professors should be abolished. He organized his speech topically, identifying reasons academic tenure is no longer a sound policy for most colleges and universities. To support his proposition of policy, he used several propositions of fact. Note, too, that Paul's specific purpose involved specific action on the part of his audience.

TOPIC:	Academic tenure
GENERAL PURPOSE:	To persuade
PROPOSITION:	Our college, along with other colleges and universities, should abolish academic tenure.
SPECIFIC PURPOSE:	After listening to my speech, audience members should sign a petition calling for the abolition of academic tenure.

proposition of policy
A proposition that advocates a change in a policy, procedure, or behavior

MAIN IDEAS:	I. Academic tenure is outdated.
	II. Academic tenure is abused.
	III. Academic tenure contributes to ineffective education.

Here's another outline for a persuasive speech based on a proposition of policy. Again, note how the major ideas are propositions of fact used to support the proposition of policy.

TOPIC:	Computer education
GENERAL PURPOSE:	To persuade
PROPOSITION:	Every person in our society should know how to use a personal computer.
SPECIFIC PURPOSE:	After listening to my speech, all audience members who have not had a computer course should sign up for one.
MAIN IDEAS:	I. Most people who own a personal computer do not know how to use most of its features.
	II. Computer skills will help you with your academic studies.
	III. Computer skills will help you get a good job, regardless of your major or profession.

Putting Persuasive Principles into Practice

We have identified some of the factors that can motivate an audience and have provided some clues for formulating a proposition for your speech. We conclude this chapter by discussing three general principles to help you link the theory of persuasion with the practice of persuasion.

Principle: *Audience members' attitudes, beliefs, and values help predict how they will respond to a persuasive message.*

Practice: When persuading an audience, it is important to have an accurate understanding of listeners' likes and dislikes, beliefs about what is true or false, and perceptions of good or bad. You can do a better job of finding out what motivates an audience if you know their attitudes, beliefs, and values.

Principle: *Audience members are motivated to avoid dissonance, to make sure their needs are met, to do things that give them pleasure, and to avoid things that create pain.*

Practice: Develop persuasive messages that help listeners avoid inconsistent or dissonant feelings. Or tell listeners how your proposal will help solve a problem that is creating dissonance for them. Show how your ideas will address their needs or result in positive, pleasurable outcomes or help them to avoid negative consequences.

Principle: *Fear appeals, ethically used, can motivate your listeners to take action.*

Practice: When using fear appeals, you have an ethical responsibility to make sure that the threat to listeners' well-being is an actual one.

Persuasive Propositions: Developing Your Central Idea

TYPE	DEFINITION	EXAMPLES
Proposition of fact	A statement that focuses on whether something is true or false.	The state legislature has raised tuition 10 percent during the last three years. There are more terrorist attacks in the world today than at any previous time in human history.
Proposition of value	A statement that either asserts that something is better than something else or presumes what is right and wrong or good and bad.	The electoral college is a better way to elect presidents than is direct popular vote. It is better to keep your financial records on a personal computer than to make the calculations by hand.
Proposition of policy	A statement that advocates a change in policy or procedures.	Our community should adopt a curfew for all citizens under eighteen. All handguns should be abolished.

Your use of fear appeals will be more successful if (1) the threat is directed toward a loved one, (2) the source of the fear appeal is credible, (3) the threat is real and will actually occur, (4) there is action that listeners can take, and (5) listeners have the power to put a plan into action to reduce the threat to them or their loved ones.

The principles described in this chapter should give you some insight into the way persuasion works. Our overview of the approaches to persuasion should help you choose a persuasive topic and formulate a specific speech purpose. In Chapter 17, we will build on the principles reviewed here and suggest specific strategies for developing your persuasive message.

SPEAKER'S HOMEPAGE

Finding Out about Congressional Legislation for Persuasive Speeches

You may find yourself giving a persuasive speech about issues pertaining to public policy and issues about which there is pertinent legislation pending in Congress. If so, the Internet can be a useful resource for finding out the latest information about pending legislation.

➤ U.S. CONGRESS
www.gpoaccess.gov/crecord/index.html

➤ YAHOO! DIRECTORY OF STATE GOVERNMENT
http://dir.yahoo.com/Government/
U_S_Government/State_Government/

➤ WORLD WIDE WEB VIRTUAL LIBRARY OF THE U.S. GOVERNMENT INFORMATION SOURCES
www.lib.isu.edu/gov/fedgov.html

➤ STATE AND LOCAL GOVERNMENTS ON THE NET
www.statelocalgov.net/index.cfm

SUMMARY

Various theories explain how persuasion works to change or reinforce attitudes, beliefs, and values, which are the determinants of behavior. You can incorporate this theoretical knowledge into your speech preparation to deliver a persuasive message.

Persuasion is the process of changing or reinforcing attitudes, beliefs, values, or behavior. Attitudes are learned predispositions to respond favorably or unfavorably toward something. A belief is a person's understanding of what is true and what is false. A value is a conception of right and wrong.

There are several ways to motivate listeners. One approach is based on the theory of cognitive dissonance, the human tendency to strive for balance or consistency in our thoughts. When a persuasive message invites us to change our attitudes, beliefs, values, or behavior, we respond by trying to maintain intellectual balance, or cognitive consistency.

A second theory explains why we are motivated to respond to persuasion by proposing that we wish to satisfy our needs. Abraham Maslow identified a five-level hierarchy of physiological, safety, social, self-esteem, and self-actualization needs.

Third, positive motivational appeals can help you develop a persuasive message by encouraging listeners to respond favorably to your message.

A fourth approach to persuasion is the use of negative motivational appeals—notably, appeals to fear. Fear can motivate us to respond favorably to a persuasive suggestion. To avoid pain or discomfort, we may follow the recommendation of a persuasive speaker.

Preparing and presenting a persuasive speech require the same approach as preparing any other kind of speech. A key first concern is to consider the audience. The next concern is choosing an appropriate topic.

Speakers can apply broad principles of persuasion to prepare a persuasive speech.

BEING AUDIENCE-CENTERED: A SHARPER FOCUS

CONSIDERING YOUR AUDIENCE

➤ When persuading others, it is important that you understand your listeners' attitudes, beliefs, values, and behavior.

➤ To motivate listeners to respond to your message, consider using one or more of the following strategies: Ethically use cognitive dissonance to your advantage, speak to listeners' needs, use positive motivational appeals, or use negative motivational appeals (such as fear appeals).

➤ Consider the interests and backgrounds of your listeners when selecting and narrowing your persuasive speech topic.

➤ When crafting your central idea for your persuasive speech, develop a proposition of fact, value, or policy that is reasonable based on your audience's background and expectations.

CONSIDERING AUDIENCE DIVERSITY

➤ Persuasion is an art rather than an exact science; your audience's cultural background and expectations play a significant role in determining which persuasive strategies are effective and appropriate.

➤ Researchers have discovered no universal, cross-cultural approach to persuasion that is effective in every culture.

➤ If you are speaking to a culturally diverse audience, don't design a persuasive message using strategies that would be effective only for you or those from your cultural background.

CRITICAL THINKING QUESTIONS

1. Your local chamber of commerce has asked for your advice in developing a speakers' bureau that would address public-safety issues in your community. What suggestions would you offer to motivate citizens to behave in ways that would protect them from AIDS, traffic, and severe weather?

2. Martha has been asked to speak to the Association for the Preservation of the Environment. What are possible persuasive topics and propositions that would be appropriate for her audience?

3. If you were attempting to sell a new computer system to the administration of your school, what persuasive principles would you draw on to develop your message?

ETHICAL QUESTIONS

1. Zeta plans to give a persuasive speech to convince her classmates that term limits should be imposed for senators and members of Congress—even though she is personally against term limits. Is it ethical to develop a persuasive message based on a proposition with which you personally disagree?

2. Tom plans to begin his speech on driver safety using a graphic photo of traffic-accident victims who were maimed or killed because they did not use safety belts. Is such graphic use of fear appeals ethical?

Developing a Persuasive Speech

On a separate sheet of paper, answer the following questions, which will help you develop a persuasive speech topic, specific purpose, and persuasive strategy.

1. What is my persuasive speech topic? (Note: Use the topic selection workshop on pages 144–145 to help you develop a persuasive speech topic.)

2. **a.** What are key audience attitudes toward your speech topic? That is, what are their likes and dislikes?
   b. What are audience beliefs (what they perceive as true or false) about your topic and the issues?
   c. What are the audience's core values (what they perceive as right or wrong, good or bad)?

3. State the specific purpose of your persuasive speech: At the end of my speech, the audience should be able to . . . .

4. State the central idea of your speech, a one-sentence summary of your message.

5. Determine if your central idea is a proposition of fact, value, or policy.
   - It's a statement of fact if you are trying to prove that something is true or false or that something did or did not happen. (Hint: A proposition of fact is supported with evidence that something did or did not occur.)
   - It's a statement of value if you want the audience to judge the worth or importance of something (Hint: A proposition of value seeks to convince a listener that something is good, bad, better, or worse than something else.)
   - It's a statement of policy if you are suggesting that the audience should take some action such as change a policy, procedure, behavior, attitude, or belief. (Hint: A proposition of policy usually includes the word *should*.)

6. How can you motivate your listeners to change or reinforce their attitudes, beliefs, values, or behavior?
   - Can you create dissonance?
   - What specific audience needs can you address?
   - How can you use positive motivation?
   - How can you ethically use fear appeals or negative motivation?

Henri Matisse (1869–1954). *Jazz* (1947). Portfolio of twenty pochoirs. Composition: various; sheet: 16 ³/₄ × 25 ¹¹/₁₆″. Publisher: Tériade Éditeur, Paris. Printer: Edmond Vairel and Draeger Frères, Paris. Edition: 250. The Museum of Modern Art, Gift of the artist, 1948. (291. 1948.13) © Succession H. Matisse, Paris/ARS, NY. Erich Lessing/Art Resource, N.Y.

Speech is power: Speech is to persuade, to convert, to compel.

—RALPH WALDO EMERSON

Using Persuasive Strategies

outline

objectives

After studying this chapter you should be able to do the following:

1. Identify strategies to improve your initial, derived, and terminal credibility.

2. Use principles of effective reasoning to develop a persuasive message.

3. Employ effective techniques of using emotional appeal in a persuasive speech.

4. Adapt your persuasive message to receptive, neutral, and unreceptive audiences.

5. Identify strategies for effectively organizing a persuasive speech.

"Persuasion," said rhetoric scholar Donald C. Bryant, "is the process of adjusting ideas to people and people to ideas."[1] To be an audience-centered persuasive speaker is to use ethical and effective strategies to adjust your message so that listeners will thoughtfully respond to your presentation. But precisely what are the strategies that can enhance your credibility, help you develop logical arguments, and use emotional appeals to speak to the hearts of your listeners? In the last chapter we noted that Aristotle defined rhetoric as the process of discovering the available means of persuasion. In this chapter we provide more detailed strategies to help you prepare your persuasive speech. Specifically, we will suggest how to gain credibility, develop well-reasoned arguments, and move your audience with emotion. We will also discuss how to adapt your specific message to your audience, and we will end with some suggestions for organizing your persuasive message.

Establishing Credibility

If you were going to buy a new car, to whom would you turn for advice? Perhaps you would ask a trusted family member, or you might seek advice from *Consumer Reports*, a monthly publication that reports studies of various products on the market, among them automobiles. In other words, you would probably turn to a source that you consider knowledgeable, competent, and trustworthy—a source you think is credible.

You'll recall from Chapter 10 that *credibility* is the audience's perception of a speaker's competence, trustworthiness, and dynamism. As a public speaker, especially one who wishes to persuade an audience, you hope that your listeners will have a favorable attitude toward you. Current research points clearly to a relationship between credibility and speech effectiveness: The more believable you are to your listener, the more effective you will be as a persuasive communicator.

As we noted in Chapter 16, Aristotle used the term *ethos* to refer to a speaker's credibility. He thought that to be credible, a public speaker should be ethical, possess good character, have common sense, and be concerned for the well-being of the audience. Quintilian, a Roman teacher of public speaking, believed that an effective public speaker also should be a person of good character. Quintilian's advice was that a speaker should be "a good person speaking well." The importance to a speaker of a positive public image has been recognized for centuries. But don't get the idea that credibility is something that a speaker literally possesses or lacks. Credibility is based on the listeners' mindset regarding the speaker. Your listeners, not you, determine whether you have credibility or lack it.

Credibility is not just a single factor or a single view of you on the part of your audience. It encompasses many factors and many views. Aristotle's speculations as to the factors that influence a speaker's credibility have been generally supported by modern experimental studies.

One clear factor in credibility is *competence*—to be credible, a speaker should be considered informed, skilled, or knowledgeable about the subject he or she is talking about. If a used-car salesman sings the virtues of a car on his lot, you want to know what qualifies him to give believable information about the car.

Do competent speakers always get positive results? Although there are no absolutes, one comprehensive study found that the candidates for U.S. president who emphasized policy proposals more than their own character in their campaign speeches were more likely to win elections.[2] Although audiences are certainly swayed by a variety of issues, they seem to highly value solid ideas that enhance competence.

When you give a speech, you will be more persuasive if you convince your listeners that you are knowledgeable about your topic. If, for example, you say it would be a good idea for everyone to have a medical checkup each year, your listeners might mentally ask, "Why? What are your qualifications to make such a proposal?" But if you support your conclusion with medical statistics showing how having a physical exam each year leads to a dramatically prolonged life, you enhance the credibility of your suggestion. Thus, one way to enhance your competence is to cite credible evidence to support your point.

A second major factor that influences your audience's response to you is **trustworthiness**. You trust people whom you believe to be honest. While delivering your speech, you have to convey honesty and sincerity. Your audience will be looking for evidence that they can trust you, that you are believable.

Earning an audience's trust is not something that you can do simply by saying, "Trust me." You earn trust by demonstrating that you have had experience dealing with the issues you talk about. Your listeners would be more likely to trust your advice about how to travel around Europe on $50 a day if you had been there than they would if you took your information from a tour book you bought from the bargain table at the bookstore. Your trustworthiness may be suspect if you advocate something that will result in a direct benefit to you. That's why salespersons and politicians are often stereotyped as being untrustworthy; if you do what they say, they will clearly benefit from a sales commission if you buy a product, or gain power and position if you give your vote.

A third factor in credibility is the speaker's **dynamism**, or energy. Dynamism is often projected through delivery. **Charisma** is a form of dynamism. A charismatic person possesses charm, talent, magnetism, and other qualities that make the person attractive and energetic. Many people considered Presidents Franklin Roosevelt and Ronald Reagan charismatic speakers.

Enhancing Your Credibility

Speakers establish their credibility in three phases, the first of which is **initial credibility**. This is the impression of your credibility your listeners have even before you speak. Giving careful thought to your appearance and establishing eye contact before you begin your talk will enhance both your confidence and your credibility. It is also wise to prepare a brief description of your credentials and accomplishments so that the person who introduces you can use it in his or her introductory remarks. Even if you are not asked for a statement beforehand, be prepared with one.

Derived credibility is the perception of your credibility your audience forms as you present yourself and your message. Most of this book presents principles and skills that help establish your credibility as a speaker. Several specific research-supported skills for enhancing your credibility as you speak include establishing common ground with your audience, supporting your key arguments with evidence, and presenting a well-organized and well-delivered message.

You establish common ground by indicating in your opening remarks that you share the values and concerns of your audience. To begin to persuade an audience that she understands why budget cuts upset parents, a politician might speak of her own children. If you are a student persuading classmates to enroll in an economics class, you could stress that understanding economic issues will be useful as they face the process of interviewing for a job. Of course, you have an ethical responsibility to be truthful when outlining the common goals you and your audience share.

trustworthiness
An aspect of a speaker's credibility that reflects whether the speaker is perceived as believable and honest

dynamism
An aspect of a speaker's credibility that reflects whether the speaker is perceived as energetic

charisma
Characteristic of a talented, charming, attractive speaker

initial credibility
The impression of a speaker's credibility that listeners have before the speaker starts a speech

derived credibility
The perception of a speaker's credibility that is formed during a speech

Having evidence to support your persuasive conclusions strengthens your credibility.[3] Margo was baffled as to why her plea for donations for the homeless fell flat. No one offered any financial support for her cause when she concluded her speech. Why? She offered no proof that there really were any homeless people in the community. If she had provided well-documented evidence that there was a problem and that the organization she supported could effectively solve the problem, she would have been more likely to gain support for her position.

Presenting a well-organized message also enhances your credibility as a competent and rational advocate.[4] Rambling, emotional requests rarely change or reinforce listeners' opinions or behavior. Regardless of the organizational pattern you use, it is crucial to ensure that your message is logically structured and uses appropriate internal summaries, signposts, and enumeration of key ideas.

Your delivery also affects your derived credibility. For most North Americans, regular eye contact, varied vocal inflection, and appropriate attire have positive influences on your ability to persuade listeners to respond to your message.[5] Why does delivery affect how persuasive you are? Researchers suggest that if your listeners expect you to be a good speaker and you aren't, they are less likely to do what you ask them to do.[6] So don't violate their expectations by presenting a poorly delivered speech. Effective delivery also enhances your ability to persuade, because it helps gain and maintain listener attention and affects whether listeners will like you.[7] If you can arouse listeners' attention and if they like you, you'll be more persuasive than if you don't gain their attention and they don't like you. Do speakers who use humor enhance their credibility? There is some evidence that although using humor may contribute to making listeners like you, humor does not have a major impact on ultimately persuading listeners to support your message.[8]

The last phase of credibility, called **terminal credibility**, or final credibility, is the perception of your credibility your listeners have when you finish your speech. Again we emphasize the value of eye contact. Also, don't start leaving the lectern or the speaking area until you have finished your closing sentence. Even if there is no planned question-and-answer period following your speech, be ready to respond to questions from interested listeners.

Using Logic and Evidence to Persuade

"The reason we need to cut taxes is to improve the economy," claimed the politician on a Sunday-morning talk show. "The stock market has lost 300 points this month. People aren't buying things. A tax cut will put money in their pockets and give the economy a boost." In an effort to persuade reluctant members of her political party to support a tax cut, this politician was using a logical argument supported with evidence that stock prices were dropping. As we noted in Chapter 4 when we discussed how to be a critical listener, logic is a formal system of rules for making inferences. Because wise audience members will be listening, persuasive speakers need to give careful attention to the way they use logic to reach a conclusion. Aristotle called logic *logos*, which literally means "the word." Using words as well as statistical information to develop logical arguments can make your persuasive efforts more convincing. It can also clarify your own thinking and help make your points clear to your listeners. Logic is central to all persuasive speeches. In Chapter 4, we introduced a discussion of logic and evidence to help you become a critical listener or consumer of messages. Here, we'll amplify that discussion to help you use logical arguments and evidence to persuade others.

Aristotle said that any persuasive speech has two parts: First, you state your case. Second, you prove your case. In essence, he was saying that you must present evidence and then use appropriate reasoning to lead your listeners to the conclusion you advocate. Reasoning is the process of drawing a conclusion from evidence. The Sunday-

terminal credibility

The final impression listeners have of a speaker's credibility, after a speech concludes

morning talk-show politician reached the conclusion that a tax cut was necessary because stock prices had tumbled and people weren't buying things. Evidence consists of the facts, examples, statistics, and expert opinions that you use to support the points you wish to make. When advancing an argument, it is your task to prove your point. Proof consists of the evidence you offer plus the conclusion you draw from it. The evidence in the claim made by the politician was lower stock-market values and fewer people buying things. The conclusion: We need a tax cut to stimulate the economy. Let's consider the two key elements of proof in greater detail. Specifically, we will look more closely at types of reasoning and provide ways to test the quality of evidence.

UNDERSTANDING TYPES OF REASONING

Developing well-reasoned arguments for persuasive messages has been important since antiquity. If your arguments are structured in a rational way, you have a greater chance of persuading your listeners. There are three major ways to structure an argument to reach a logical conclusion: inductively (including reasoning by analogy), deductively, and causally.

INDUCTIVE REASONING Reasoning that arrives at a general conclusion from specific instances or examples is known as **inductive reasoning**. Using this classical approach, you reach a general conclusion based on specific examples, facts, statistics, and opinions. You may not know for a certainty that the specific instances prove that the conclusion is true, but you decide that, in all *probability*, the specific instances support the general conclusion. According to contemporary logicians, you reason inductively when you claim that an outcome is probably true because of specific evidence.

For example, if you were giving a speech attempting to convince your audience that foreign cars are unreliable, you might use inductive reasoning to make your point. You could announce that you recently bought a foreign car that gave you trouble. Your cousin also bought a foreign car that kept stalling on the freeway. Finally, your English professor told you her foreign car has broken down several times in the

inductive reasoning
Reasoning that uses specific instances or examples to reach a general, probable conclusion

past few weeks. Based on these specific examples, you ask your audience to agree with your general conclusion: Foreign cars are unreliable.

TESTING THE VALIDITY OF INDUCTIVE REASONING As a persuasive speaker, your job is to construct a sound argument. That means basing your generalization on evidence. When you listen to a persuasive message, notice how the speaker tries to support his or her conclusion. To judge the validity of a **generalization** arrived at inductively, keep the following questions in mind.

- **Are there enough specific instances to support the conclusion?** Are three examples of problems with foreign cars enough to prove your point that all foreign cars are unreliable? Of the several million foreign cars manufactured, three cars, especially if they are of different makes, are not a large sample. If those examples were supported by additional statistical evidence that more than 50 percent of foreign-car owners complained of serious engine malfunctions, the evidence would be more convincing.

- **Are the specific instances typical?** Are the three examples you cite representative of all foreign cars manufactured? How do you know? What are the data on the performance of foreign cars? Also, are you, your cousin, and your professor typical of most car owners? The three of you may be careless about routine maintenance of your autos.

- **Are the instances recent?** If the foreign cars you are using as examples of poor reliability are more than three years old, you cannot reasonably conclude that today's foreign cars are unreliable products. Age alone may explain the poor performance of your sample.

The logic in the example of the problematic foreign cars, therefore, is not particularly sound. The speaker would need considerably more evidence to prove his or her point.

REASONING BY ANALOGY Reasoning by analogy is a special type of inductive reasoning. An *analogy* is a comparison. This form of inductive reasoning compares one thing, person, or process with another, to predict how something will perform and respond. In previous chapters we've suggested that using an analogy is an effective way to clarify ideas and enhance message interest. When you observe that two things have a number of characteristics in common and that a certain fact about one is likely to be true of the other, you have drawn an analogy, reasoning from one example to reach a conclusion about the other. If you try to convince an audience that mandatory safety-belt laws in Texas and Florida have reduced highway deaths and therefore should be instituted in Kansas, you are reasoning by analogy. You would also be reasoning by analogy if you claimed that capital punishment reduced crime in Brazil and therefore should be used in the United States as well. But as with reasoning by generalization, there are questions that you should ask to check the validity of your conclusions.

- **Do the ways in which the two things are alike outweigh the ways they are different?** Can you compare the crime statistics of Brazil to those of the United States and claim to make a valid comparison? Are the data collected in the same way in both countries? Could other factors besides the safety-belt laws in Texas and Florida account for the lower automobile accident death rate? Maybe differences in the speed limit or the types of roads in those states can account for the difference.

- **Is the assertion true?** Is it really true that capital punishment has deterred crime in Brazil? You will need to give reasons the comparison you are making is valid and evidence that will prove your conclusion true.

DEDUCTIVE REASONING According to a centuries-old perspective, reasoning from a general statement or principle to reach a specific conclusion is called **deductive reasoning**. This is just the opposite of inductive reasoning. Contemporary logic specialists add that when the conclusion is *certain* rather than probable, you are rea-

generalization
An all-encompassing statement

deductive reasoning
Reasoning that moves from a general statement of principle to a specific, certain conclusion

soning deductively. The certainty of your conclusion is based on the validity or truth in the general statement that forms the basis of your argument.

Deductive reasoning can be structured in the form of a syllogism. A **syllogism** is a way of organizing an argument into three elements: a major premise, a minor premise, and a conclusion. To reach a conclusion deductively, you start with a general statement that serves as the **major premise**. In a speech attempting to convince your audience that the communication professor teaching your public-speaking class is a top-notch teacher, you might use a deductive reasoning process. Your major premise is "All communication professors have excellent teaching skills." The certainty of your conclusion hinges on the soundness of your major premise. The **minor premise** is a more specific statement about an example that is linked to the major premise. The minor premise in the argument you are advancing is "John Smith, our teacher, is a communication professor." The **conclusion** is based on the major premise and the more specific minor premise. In reasoning deductively, you need to ensure that both the major premise and the minor premise are true and can be supported with evidence. The conclusion to our syllogism is "John Smith has excellent teaching skills." The persuasive power of deductive reasoning derives from the fact that the conclusion cannot be questioned if the premises are accepted as true.

Here's another example you might hear in a speech. Ann was trying to convince the city council not to approve a building permit for Mega-Low-Mart, a large chain discount store that wants to move into her town. She believes the new store would threaten her downtown clothing boutique. Here's the deductive structure of the argument she advanced:

Major premise:	Every time a large discount store moves into a small community, the merchants in the downtown area lose business and the town loses tax revenue from downtown merchants.
Minor premise:	Mega-Low-Mart is a large discount store that wants to build a store in our town.
Conclusion:	If Mega-Low-Mart is permitted to open a store in our town, the merchants in the downtown area will lose business and the city will lose tax revenue.

The strength of Ann's argument rests on the validity of her major premise. Her argument is sound if she can prove that the presence of large chain discount stores does, in fact, result in a loss of business and tax revenue for merchants in nearby towns. (Also note Ann's efforts to be audience-centered; addressing the city council, she argues that not only will she lose money but the city will lose tax revenue as well—something in which city council members are deeply interested.) In constructing arguments for your persuasive messages, assess the soundness of the major premise on which you build your argument. Likewise, when listening to a persuasive pitch from someone using a deductive argument, critically evaluate the accuracy of the major premise.

To test the truth of an argument organized deductively, consider the following questions.

➤ **Is the major premise (general statement) true?** In our example about communication professors, is it really true that *all* communication professors have excellent teaching skills? What evidence do you have to support this statement? The power of deductive reasoning hinges in part on whether your generalization is true.

➤ **Is the minor premise (the particular statement) also true?** If your minor premise is false, your syllogism can collapse right there. In our example, it is easy enough to verify that John Smith is a communication professor. But not all minor premises can be verified as easily. For example, it would be difficult to prove the minor premise in this example:

syllogism
A three-part way of developing an argument, using a major premise, a minor premise, and a conclusion

major premise
A general statement that is the first element of a syllogism

minor premise
A specific statement about an example that is linked to the major premise; the second element of a syllogism

conclusion
The logical outcome of a deductive argument, which stems from the major premise and the minor premise

Comparing Types of Reasoning

	INDUCTIVE REASONING	DEDUCTIVE REASONING	CAUSAL REASONING
Reasoning begins with . . .	Specific examples	A general statement	Something known
Reasoning ends with . . .	A general conclusion	A specific conclusion	A speculation about something unknown occurring, based on what is known
Reasoning conclusion is that something is . . .	Probable or improbable	True or false	Likely or not likely
Goal of reasoning is . . .	To reach a general conclusion or discover something new	To reach a specific conclusion by applying what is known	To link something known with something unknown
Example	When tougher drug laws went into effect in Kansas City and St. Louis, drug traffic was reduced. The United States should therefore institute tougher drug laws, because these will decrease drug use nationwide.	Instituting tough drug laws in medium-sized communities results in diminished drug-related crime. San Marcos, Texas, is a medium-sized community. San Marcos should institute tough drug laws in order to reduce drug-related crimes.	Since the 70-mile-per-hour speed limit was reinstated, traffic deaths have increased. The increased highway speed has caused an increase in highway deaths.

All gods are immortal.

Zeus is a god.

Therefore, Zeus is immortal.

We can accept the major premise as true because immortality is part of the definition of *god*. But proving that Zeus is a god would be very difficult. In this case, the truth of the conclusion hinges on the truth of the minor premise.

CAUSAL REASONING A third type of reasoning is called **causal reasoning**. When you reason by cause, you relate two or more events in such a way as to conclude that one or more of the events caused the others. For example, you might argue that having unprotected sex causes the spread of AIDS.

There are two ways to structure a causal argument. First, you can reason from cause to effect, moving from a known fact to a predicted result. You know, for example, that interest rates have increased in the past week. Therefore, you might argue that *because* the rates are increasing, the Dow Jones Industrial Average will decrease. In this case, you move from something that has occurred (rising interest rates) to something that has not yet occurred (decrease in the Dow). Weather forecasters use the same method of reasoning when they predict the weather. They base a conclusion about tomorrow's weather on what they know about today's meteorological conditions.

A second way to frame a causal argument is to reason backward, from known effect to unknown cause. You know, for example, that a major earthquake has oc-

causal reasoning

Reasoning in which the relationship between two or more events leads you to conclude that one or more of the events caused the others

curred (known effect). To explain this event, you propose that the cause of the earthquake was a shift in a fault line (unknown cause). You cannot be sure of the cause, but you are certain of the effect. A candidate for president of the United States may claim that the cause of current high unemployment (known effect) is mismanagement by the present administration (unknown cause). He then constructs an argument to prove that his assertion is accurate. To prove his case, he needs to have evidence that the present administration mismanaged the economy. The key to developing strong causal arguments is in the use of evidence to link something known with something unknown. An understanding of the appropriate use of evidence can enhance inductive, deductive, and causal reasoning.

A gathering of representatives from different nations is perhaps an extreme example of diversity in an audience, but every audience has its own level of diversity, which you will do well to take into consideration.

[Photo: David Karp/AP Images]

Persuading the Diverse Audience

Effective strategies for developing your persuasive objective will vary depending on the background and cultural expectations of your listeners. If a good portion of your audience has a cultural background different from your own, it's wise not to assume that they will have the same assumptions about what is logical and reasonable that you have. In addition to reasoning and evidence, cultural differences may suggest you modify how you appeal to your listeners to take a specific action (whether you should make direct or indirect appeals), your overall message structure, or the general style you assume when persuading.

REASONING Most of the logical, rational methods of reasoning discussed in this chapter evolved from Greek and Roman traditions of argument (see Appendix B). Rhetoricians from the United States typically use a straightforward, factual-inductive method of supporting ideas and reaching conclusions.[9] First, they identify facts and link them to support a specific proposition or conclusion. For example, in a speech to prove that the government spends more money than it receives, a speaker could cite year-by-year statistics on income and expenditures to document the point. North Americans also like debates involving a direct clash of ideas and opinions. Our low-context culture encourages people to be more direct and forthright in dealing with issues and disagreement than do high-context cultures.

Not all cultures assume a direct, linear, methodical approach to supporting ideas and proving a point.[10] People from high-context cultures, for example, may expect that participants will establish a personal relationship before debating issues. Some cultures use a deductive pattern of reasoning, rather than an inductive pattern. They begin with a general premise and then link it to a specific situation when they attempt to persuade listeners. During several recent trips to Russia, your authors have noticed that to argue that Communism was ineffective, many Russians start with a general assumption: Communism didn't work. Then they use this assumption to explain specific current problems in areas such as transportation and education.

Middle Eastern cultures usually do not use standard inductive or deductive structures. They are more likely to use narrative methods to persuade an audience. They tell stories that evoke feelings and emotions and use extended analogies, examples, and illustrations, allowing their listeners to draw their own conclusions by inductive association.[11]

Although this book stresses the kind of inductive reasoning that will be persuasive to most North Americans, you may need to use alternative strategies if your audience is from another cultural tradition. Consider the following general principles to help you construct arguments that a culturally diverse audience will find persuasive.

USE APPROPRIATE EVIDENCE According to intercultural communication scholars Myron Lustig and Jolene Koester, "There are no universally accepted standards about what constitutes evidence."[12] They suggest that for some Muslim and Christian audiences, parables or stories are a dramatically effective way to make a point. A story is told and a principle is derived from the lesson of the story. For most North Americans and Europeans, a superior form of evidence is an observed fact. A study by two communication scholars reported that both African Americans and Hispanic Americans found statistical evidence more persuasive than stories alone.[13] Statistics, said the respondents, are more believable and verifiable; stories can more easily be modified. In some African cultures, eyewitness testimony is often not perceived as credible; it's believed that if you speak up to report what you saw, you may have a particular slant on the event, and therefore what you have to say may not be believable.[14] What may be convincing evidence to you may not be such an obvious piece of evidence for others. If you are uncertain whether your listeners will perceive your evidence as valid and reliable, you could test your evidence on a small group of people who will be in your audience before you address the entire group.

USE APPROPRIATE APPEALS TO ACTION In some high-context cultures, such as in Japan and China, the conclusion to your message can be stated indirectly. Rather than spell out the precise action explicitly, you can imply what you'd like your listeners to do. In a low-context culture such as the United States, listeners may generally expect you to more directly state the action you'd like your audience members to take.

USE APPROPRIATE MESSAGE STRUCTURE Most North Americans tend to like a well-organized message with a clear, explicit link between the evidence used and the conclusion drawn. North Americans also are comfortable with a structure that focuses on a problem and then offers a solution, or a message in which causes are identified and the effects are specified. Audiences in the Middle East, however, would expect less formal structure and greater use of a narrative style of message development. The audience either infers the point or the speaker may conclude by making the point clear. Being indirect or implicit may sometimes be the best persuasive strategy.

Not all audiences expect a speech to sound like the summation of an attorney making a legal case loaded with evidence. In fact, some lawyers decide, after "reading" their jury, that the best way to conclude their case is to tell a story rather than to present a litany of the facts and evidence.

USE AN APPROPRIATE DELIVERY STYLE We've placed a considerable emphasis on logos by appropriately emphasizing logical structure and the use of evidence. But another cultural factor that influences how receptive listeners are to a message is the presentation style of the speaker. A speaker's overall style includes the use of emotional appeals, delivery style, language choice, and rhythmic quality of the words and gestures used. Some Latin American listeners, for example, expect speakers to express more emotion and passion when speaking than North American listeners are accustomed to. If you focus only on analyzing and adapting to the audience's expectations about logic and reasoning, without also considering the overall impression you make on your audience, you may present compelling arguments but still not achieve your overall goal. The best way to assess the preferred speaking style of an audience with which you're not familiar is to observe other successful speakers addressing the audience you will face. Or talk with audience members before you speak to identify expectations and communication-style preferences.

SUPPORTING YOUR REASONING WITH EVIDENCE

You cannot simply state a conclusion without proving it with evidence. Evidence in persuasive speeches consists of facts, examples, statistics, and expert opinions.

In Chapter 8, we discussed the essential details of using these types of supporting material in speeches. When attempting to persuade listeners, it is useful to make sure that your evidence logically supports the inductive, deductive, or causal reasoning you are using to reach your conclusion.

FACTS When using facts to support your conclusion, make sure your fact is really a fact. A *fact* is something that has been directly observed to be true or can be proved to be true. The shape of the earth, the number of women university presidents, the winner of the 2008 Super Bowl have all been directly observed or counted. Without direct observation or measurement, we can only make an inference. An *inference* is a conclusion based on available evidence, or partial information. It's a fact that the sale of foreign-made cars are increasing in the United States; it's an inference that foreign-made cars are always the highest-quality cars.

EXAMPLES **Examples** are illustrations that are used to dramatize or clarify a fact. Only valid, true examples can be used to help prove a point. For example, one speaker, in an effort to document the increased violence in children's television programs, told her audience, "Last Saturday morning as I watched cartoons with my daughter, I was shocked by the countless times we saw examples of beatings and even the death of the cartoon characters in one half-hour program." The conclusion she wanted her audience to reach: Put an end to senseless violence in children's television programs.

A hypothetical example, one that is fabricated to illustrate a point, should not be used to reach a conclusion. It should be used only to clarify. David encouraged his listeners to join him in an effort to clean up the San Marcos River. He wanted to motivate his audience to help by asking them to "imagine bringing your children to the river ten years from now. You see the river bottom littered with cans and bottles." His example, while effective in helping the audience to visualize what might happen in the future, does not prove that the river ecosystem will deteriorate. It only illustrates what might happen if action isn't taken.

OPINIONS *Opinions* can serve as evidence if they are expressed by an expert, someone who can add credibility to your conclusion. The best opinions to use in support of a persuasive argument are those expressed by someone known to be unbiased, fair, and accurate. If the U.S. Surgeon General has expressed an opinion regarding drug testing, his or her opinion would be helpful evidence. Even so, opinions are usually most persuasive if they are combined with other evidence, such as facts or statistics, that support the expert's position.

STATISTICS A *statistic* is a number used to summarize several facts or samples. In an award-winning speech, Jeffrey Jamison used statistics effectively to document the serious problem of alkali batteries polluting the environment. He cited evidence from the *New York Times* that documents ". . . each year we are adding 150 tons of mercury, 130 tons of lead, and 170 tons of cadmium to the environment."[15] Without these statistics, Jeffrey's claim that alkali batteries are detrimental to the environment would not have been as potent. Again, you may want to review the discussion on the appropriate use of statistics in Chapter 8.

example
An illustration used to dramatize or clarify a fact

Does the type of evidence you use make a difference in whether your listeners will support your ideas? One research study found that examples and illustrations go a long way in helping to persuade listeners.[16] Additional research documents the clear power of statistical evidence to persuade.[17] And yet another research study concluded that using *both* statistics and specific examples is especially effective in persuading listeners.[18] Poignant examples may touch listeners' hearts, but statistical evidence appeals to their intellect. Because we believe that messages should be audience-centered rather than source-centered, we suggest that you consider your listeners to determine the kind of evidence that will be the most convincing to them.

If you are using an inductive-reasoning strategy (reasoning from specific examples to a general conclusion), you need to make sure you have enough facts, examples, statistics, and credible opinions to support your conclusion. If you reason deductively (from a generalization to a specific conclusion), you need evidence to document the truth of your initial generalization. When developing an argument using causal reasoning, evidence is also vital as you attempt to establish that one or more events caused something to happen.

USING EVIDENCE EFFECTIVELY

We've identified what evidence is and why it's important to use evidence to support your conclusions. But what are strategies for using evidence effectively? Here are a few suggestions.[19]

USE CREDIBLE EVIDENCE Your listeners are more likely to respond to your arguments if they believe the evidence you use is credible—from a trustworthy, knowledgeable and unbiased source. Remember, it's the listener, not you, who determines whether the evidence is credible.

One type of evidence that is especially powerful is reluctant testimony. **Reluctant testimony** is a statement by someone who has reversed his or her position on a given issue, or a statement that is not in the speaker's best interest. For example, at one point the owner of a large construction company, who wanted the contract to build a new dam being considered, was in favor of building the new dam to create a water reservoir. But after further thought the construction company owner changed his mind and now is against building the dam. The reluctant testimony of the construction company owner would bolster your argument that the dam is a financial boondoggle. Reluctant testimony is especially effective when speaking to a skeptical audience; it demonstrates how another person has changed his or her mind and implicitly suggests that listeners should do the same.[20]

USE NEW EVIDENCE By "new" we don't just mean recent, although contemporary evidence is often perceived to be more credible than evidence that's out of date. But besides seeking up-to-date evidence, try to find evidence to support your point that the listener hasn't heard before—evidence that's new to the listener. You don't want the listener to think, "Oh, I've heard all of that before." Audience members are more likely to keep focusing on your message if they learn something new rather than hearing a rehash of what they already know.

USE SPECIFIC EVIDENCE "Many people will be hurt if we don't do something now to stop global warming," said Julia. How many people will be hurt? What precisely will happen? Julia would make her point more effectively if she had specific evidence that, for example, identified how many homes would be lost as a result of rising ocean levels rather than just saying "many people" or "a lot of people."

USE EVIDENCE TO TELL A STORY Facts, examples, statistics, and opinions may be credible, new, and specific—but your evidence will be even more powerful if it fits together to tell a story to make your point. Besides listing a litany of the problems that

reluctant testimony
A statement by someone who has reversed his or her position on a given issue

will occur because of global warming, Julia could personalize the evidence by telling a story about how the rising ocean levels will hurt individual families. Using evidence to support a story adds emotional power to your message and makes your evidence seem less abstract.[21]

AVOIDING FAULTY REASONING

We have emphasized the importance of developing sound, logical arguments supported with appropriate evidence. You have an ethical responsibility to use your skill to construct arguments that are well supported with logical reasoning and sound evidence. Not all people who try to persuade you will use sound arguments to get you to vote for them, buy their product, or donate money to their cause. Many persuaders use inappropriate techniques called fallacies. A **fallacy** is false reasoning that occurs when someone attempts to persuade without adequate evidence or with arguments that are irrelevant or inappropriate. You will be both a better and more ethical speaker and a better listener if you are aware of the following fallacies.

CAUSAL FALLACY The Latin term for the causal fallacy is *post hoc, ergo propter hoc*, which translates as "after this, therefore, because of this." The **causal fallacy** is making a faulty causal connection. Simply because one event follows another does not mean that the two are related. If you declared that your school's football team won this time because you sang your school song before the game, you would be guilty of a causal fallacy. There are undoubtedly other factors that explain why your team won, such as good preparation or facing a weaker opposing team. For something to be a cause, it has to have the power to bring about a result. "That howling storm last night knocked down the tree in our backyard" is a logical causal explanation.

Here are more examples of causal fallacies:

The increased earthquake and hurricane activity is caused by the increase in violence and war in our society.

As long as you wear this lucky rabbit's foot, you will never have an automobile accident.

In each instance, there is not enough evidence to support the cause-effect conclusion.

BANDWAGON FALLACY Someone who argues that "everybody thinks it's a good idea, so you should too" is using the **bandwagon fallacy**. Simply because "everyone" is "jumping on the bandwagon," or supporting a particular point of view, does not make the point of view correct. Sometimes speakers use the bandwagon fallacy in more subtle ways in their efforts to persuade:

Everybody knows that talk radio is our primary link to a free and democratic society.

Most people agree that we spend too much time worrying about the future of Medicare.

Beware of sweeping statements that include you and others without offering any evidence that the speaker has solicited opinions.

EITHER/OR FALLACY Someone who argues that there are only two approaches to a problem is trying to oversimplify the issue by using the **either/or fallacy**. "It's either vote for higher property taxes or close the library," asserts Daryl at a public hearing on tax increases. Such a statement ignores a variety of other solutions to a complex problem. When you hear someone simplifying the available options by saying it's either this or that, you should be on guard for the either/or fallacy. Rarely is any issue as simple as a choice between only two alternatives. The following are examples of inappropriate either/or simplistic reasoning:

fallacy
False reasoning that occurs when someone attempts to persuade without adequate evidence or with arguments that are irrelevant or inappropriate

causal fallacy
A faulty cause-and-effect connection between two things or events

bandwagon fallacy
Reasoning that suggests that because everyone else believes something or is doing something, then it must be valid or correct

either/or fallacy
The oversimplification of an issue into a choice between only two outcomes or possibilities

Either television violence is reduced, or we have an increase in child and spouse abuse.

Either more people start volunteering their time to work for their community, or your taxes increase.

HASTY GENERALIZATION A person who reaches a conclusion from too little evidence or nonexistent evidence is making a **hasty generalization**. For example, simply because one person became ill after eating the meat loaf in the cafeteria does not mean that everyone eating in the cafeteria will develop food poisoning. Here are some additional hasty generalizations:

It's clear that our schools can't educate children well, because my niece went to school for six years and she still can't read at her grade level.

The city does a terrible job of taking care of the elderly—my grandmother lives in a city-owned nursing home, and the floors there are always filthy.

AD HOMINEM Also known as attacking the person, an **ad hominem** (Latin for "to the man") approach involves attacking irrelevant personal characteristics about the person who is proposing an idea rather than attacking the idea itself. A statement such as "We know Janice's idea won't work because she has never had a good idea yet" does not really deal with the idea, which may be perfectly valid. Don't dismiss an idea solely because you have been turned against the person who presented it. Here are some more examples of ad hominem attacks:

She was educated in a foreign country and could not possibly have good ideas for improving education in our community.

Tony is an awful musician and is not sensitive enough to chair the parking committee.

RED HERRING The **red herring** fallacy is used when someone attacks an issue by using irrelevant facts or arguments as distractions. This fallacy gets its name from an old trick of dragging a red herring across a trail to divert the dogs that may be following. Speakers use a red herring when they want to distract an audience from the real issues. For example, a politician who had been accused of taking bribes while in office calls a press conference. During the press conference, he talks about the evils of child pornography, rather than addressing the charge against him. He is using the red herring technique to divert attention from the real issue—did he or did he not take the bribe? Or, consider another example of a fallacious argument using the red herring method, from a speech against gun control: The real problem is not eliminating handguns; the real problem is that pawnshops that sell guns are controlled by the Mafia.

APPEAL TO MISPLACED AUTHORITY When ads use baseball catchers to endorse automobiles and TV heroes to sell political candidates or an airline or hotel, we are faced with the fallacious **appeal to misplaced authority**. Although we have great respect for these people in their own fields, they are no more expert than we are in the areas they are advertising. As both a public speaker and a listener, you must recognize what is valid expert testimony and what is not. For example, a physicist who speaks on the laws of nature or the structure of matter could reasonably be accepted as an expert. But if the physicist speaks on politics, the opinion expressed is not that of an expert and is no more significant than your own. The following examples are appeals to misplaced authority:

Former Congressman Smith endorses the new art museum, so every business should get behind it, too.

Katie Couric thinks this cookie recipe is the best, so you should try it too.

NON SEQUITUR If you argue that a new parking garage should not be built on campus because the grass has not been mowed on the football field for three weeks, you are guilty of a **non sequitur** (Latin for "it does not follow"). Grass growing on

hasty generalization
A conclusion reached without adequate evidence

ad hominem
An attack on irrelevant personal characteristics of the person who is proposing an idea, rather than on the idea itself

red herring
Irrelevant facts or information used to distract someone from the issue under discussion

appeal to misplaced authority
Use of the testimony of an expert in a given field to endorse an idea or product for which the expert does not have the appropriate credentials or expertise

non sequitur
Latin for "it does not follow"; an idea or conclusion that does not logically relate to or follow from the previous idea or conclusion

the football field has nothing to do with the parking problem. Your conclusion simply does not follow from your statement. The following are examples of non sequitur conclusions:

> We should not give students condoms, because TV has such a pervasive influence on our youth today.

> You should endorse me for Congress, because I have three children.

> We need more parking on our campus, because we are the national football champions.

Using Emotion to Persuade

R oger Ailes, a political communication consultant, has nominated several memorable moments as outstanding illustrations of speakers using emotional messages powerfully and effectively.[22]

Martin Luther King, announcing his vision of brotherhood and equality at the Lincoln Memorial in 1963, extolled, "I have a dream!"

General Douglas MacArthur, in announcing his retirement before a joint session of Congress, April 19, 1951, closed his speech with "Old soldiers never die; they just fade away. And like the old soldier of that ballad, I now close my military career and just fade away."

President Ronald Reagan, in his 1986 speech to help a grieving nation cope with the death of the space shuttle Challenger *crew, said, "The crew of the space shuttle* Challenger *honored us by the manner in which they lived their lives. We will never forget them, nor the last time we saw them, this morning as they prepared for their journey and waved goodbye and slipped the surly bonds of earth to touch the face of God."*

Emotion is a powerful way to move an audience and support your persuasive purpose. An appeal to emotion (or what Aristotle called *pathos*) can be an effective way to achieve a desired response from an audience. Whereas logical arguments may appeal to our reason, emotional arguments generally appeal to nonrational sentiments. Often we make decisions based not on logic, but on emotion.

One theory suggests that emotional responses can be classified along three dimensions—pleasure, arousal, and dominance.[23] First, you respond with varying degrees of *pleasure* or *displeasure*. Pleasurable stimuli consist of such things as images of smiling, healthy babies or daydreams about winning millions in a sweepstakes. Stimuli causing displeasure may be TV news stories of child abuse or dreadful images of terrorism.

A second dimension of emotional responses exists on a continuum of *arousal–nonarousal*. You become aroused emotionally, for example, by seeing a snake in your driveway, or you may be lulled into a state of nonarousal by a boring lecture.

The third dimension of emotional responses is one's feeling of *dominance* or *powerlessness* when confronted with some stimulus. When thinking about the destructive force of nuclear weapons or the omnipotence of God, you may feel insignificant and powerless. Or perhaps you feel a sense of power when you imagine yourself conducting a symphony or winning an election.

These three dimensions—pleasure, arousal, and dominance—are believed to form the bases of all emotional responses. Theory predicts that if listeners feel pleasure and are also aroused by something, such as a political candidate or a product, they will tend to form a favorable view of the candidate or product. A listener's feeling of being dominant has to do with being in control and having permission to behave as he or she wishes. A listener who feels dominant is more likely to respond to the message.

As a public speaker trying to sway your listeners to your viewpoint, your job is to use emotional appeals to achieve your goal. If you wanted to persuade your listeners that capital punishment should be banned, you would try to arouse feelings of displeasure and turn them against capital punishment. Advertisers selling soft drinks typically strive to arouse feelings of pleasure in those who think of their product. Smiling people, upbeat music, and good times are usually part of the formula for selling soda pop.

TIPS FOR USING EMOTION TO PERSUADE

Although the underlying theory of emotions may help you understand how emotions work, as a public speaker your key concern is "How can I ethically use emotional appeals to achieve my persuasive purpose?" Let's consider several methods.

USE CONCRETE EXAMPLES THAT HELP YOUR LISTENERS VISUALIZE WHAT YOU DESCRIBE Describing what the town of Saragosa, Texas, was like after a tornado destroyed it can evoke strong emotions. The images used to evoke the emotions can also help communicate the power of nature and the value of taking proper precautions when a storm warning is sounded.

> *The town is no more. No homes in the western Texas town remain standing. The church where twenty-one people perished looks like a heap of twisted metal and mortar. A child's doll can be seen in the street. The owner, four-year-old Maria, will no longer play with her favorite toy; she was killed along with five of her playmates when the twister roared through the elementary school.*

USE EMOTION-AROUSING WORDS Words and phrases can trigger emotional responses in your listeners. *Mother, flag, freedom,* and *slavery* are among a large number of emotionally loaded words. Patriotic slogans, such as "Remember Pearl Harbor" or "Remember 9/11," can produce strong emotional responses.[24]

USE NONVERBAL BEHAVIOR TO COMMUNICATE YOUR EMOTIONAL RESPONSE The great Roman orator Cicero believed that if you want your listeners to experience a certain emotion, you should first model that emotion for them. If you want an audience to feel anger at a particular law or event, you must display anger and indignation in your voice, movement, and gesture. As we have already noted, delivery plays the key role in communicating your emotional responses. If you want your audience to become excited about and interested in your message, you must communicate that excitement and interest through your delivery.

USE VISUAL IMAGES TO EVOKE EMOTIONS In addition to nonverbal expressions, pictures or images of emotion-arousing scenes can amplify your speech. An image of a lonely homeowner looking out over his waterlogged house following a ravaging flood in Houston, Texas, can communicate his sense of despair. A picture of children in war-torn Macedonia can communicate the devastating effects of violence with greater impact than mere words can. In contrast, a photo of a refugee mother and child reunited after an enforced separation can communicate the true meaning of joy. You can use similar images as visual aids to evoke your audience's emotions, both positive and negative. Remember, however, that when you use visual images, you have the same ethical responsibilities as you do when you use verbal forms of support: Make sure your image is from a credible source and that it has not been altered or taken out of context.

USE APPROPRIATE METAPHORS AND SIMILES As we noted in Chapter 12, a metaphor is an implied comparison between two things. The person who says, "Our lives are quilts upon which we stitch the patterns of our character. If you don't pay attention to the ethical dimension of the decisions you make, you will be more likely to make a hideous pattern in your life quilt," is using a metaphor. A simile makes a

LEARNING FROM GREAT SPEAKERS

Franklin Delano Roosevelt
(1882–1945)

The 32nd president of the United States, Franklin D. Roosevelt, is remembered as a great speaker, one who rekindled hope in the American people when he took office during the Great Depression. Roosevelt played an active role in crafting his first inaugural address, editing verb tenses to heighten immediacy and substituting strong verbs for weak ones. Roosevelt delivered the speech emphatically and used pauses strategically to ensure applause. He succeeded in persuading the American people that "the only thing we have to fear is fear itself," and he rallied the nation behind his New Deal for economic recovery.[25]

Roosevelt was a master in knowing his audience and skillfully using rhetorical strategies to move his audience with both logic and emotion. When presenting your persuasive messages, it's vital to consider the logical arguments that will resonate with your listener's minds as well as the emotional messages that will speak to their hearts.

[Photo: AP Images]

direct comparison between two things using the word *like* or *as*. Here's an example of a simile: "Not visiting your academic counselor regularly is like being a gambler in a high-stakes poker game; you're taking a big chance that you're taking the right courses." Several research studies have found that speakers who use appropriate and interesting metaphors and similes are more persuasive than those who don't use such stylistic devices.[26] Using metaphors and similes can create a fresh, emotional perspective on a persuasive point; they can both enhance your credibility and develop an emotional image in a way that nonmetaphorical language can't.[27]

USE APPROPRIATE FEAR APPEALS The threat that harm will come to your listeners unless they follow your advice is an appeal to fear. As discussed in Chapter 16, listeners can be motivated to change their behavior if appeals to fear are used appropriately. Research suggests that high fear arousal ("You will be killed in an auto accident unless you wear a safety belt") is more effective than moderate or low appeals, if you are a highly credible speaker.[28]

CONSIDER USING APPEALS TO SEVERAL EMOTIONS Appealing to the fears and anxieties of your listeners is one of the most common types of emotional appeals used to persuade, but you could also elicit several other emotions to help achieve your persuasive goal.

- **Hope.** Listeners could be motivated to respond to the prospect of a brighter tomorrow. When Franklin Roosevelt said, "The only thing we have to fear is fear itself," he was invoking hope for the future.

- **Pride.** When a politician says, "It's time to restore our nation's legacy as a beacon of freedom for all people" she is appealing to national pride. To appeal to pride is to invoke feelings of pleasure and satisfaction based on accomplishing something important. A persuasive appeal to achieve a goal based on pride in oneself or one's country, state, or community can be very powerful.

- **Courage.** Challenging your audience to take a bold stand or to step away from the crowd can emotionally charge your listeners to take action. Referring to courageous men and women as role models can help motivate your listeners to take similar actions. Patrick Henry's famous "Give me liberty, or give me death!" speech appealed to his audience to take a courageous stand on the issues before them.

- **Reverence.** The appeal to the sacred and the revered can be an effective way to motivate. Sacred traditions, revered institutions, or cherished and celebrated individuals can inspire your audience to change or reinforce attitudes, beliefs, values, or behavior. The late Mother Teresa, holy writings, and the Congress of the United States are examples of people, things, or institutions that your listeners may perceive as sacred. As an audience-centered speaker, however, you need to remember that what may be sacred to one individual or audience may not be sacred to another.

TAP AUDIENCE MEMBERS' BELIEFS IN SHARED MYTHS Often people talk about a "myth" as something that is factually untrue. The Easter Bunny, the Tooth Fairy, and Santa Claus are often labeled myths. But in a rhetorical sense, a **myth** is a belief held in common by a group of people and based on their values, cultural heritage, and faith. A myth may, in fact, be factual—or it may be based on a partial truth that a group of people believes to be true. Myths are the "big stories" that give meaning and coherence to a group of people or culture. The myth of the "Old West" is that the pioneers of yesteryear were strong, adventurous people who sacrificed their lives in search of a better tomorrow. Similarly, our parents, grandparents, and great-grandparents belonged to "the greatest generation" because they overcame a devastating

myth
A shared belief based on the underlying values, cultural heritage, and faith of a group of people

economic depression and were triumphant in two world wars. The myth of the 1950s was that U.S. families were prosperous and lived like Ward and June Cleaver and their sons, Wally and "The Beaver," in the TV program *Leave It to Beaver*. Religious myths are beliefs shared by a group of faithful disciples. So, a myth is not necessarily "false" — it is a belief that a group of people share and that provides emotional support for the way they view the world.

As a public speaker, you can draw on the myths you and your audience members share to provide emotional and motivational support for your message. Referring to a shared myth is a way to identify with your listeners and help them see how your ideas support their ideas; it can help you develop a common bond with audience members. In trying to convince his listeners to vote, Ron argued, "We can't let down those who fought for our freedom. We must vote to honor those who died for the privilege of voting that we enjoy today." He was drawing on the powerful myth that people have died for our freedoms. To gain parent support for a new high school, Cynthia said, "Our parents and grandparents lived through the Great Depression and the world wars of the past century so that we can send our children to the best public schools in the world. Vote for the new high school." She was appealing to the myth that the previous generation sacrificed, so we also have a responsibility to sacrifice for our children. Again we reemphasize that *myth* does not mean "false" or "made up." People really *did* die for our freedom, and our parents and grandparents *did* live through the Depression and tragic world wars; a myth is powerful because the audience knows that those events occurred. Myth becomes a powerful underlying story that evokes an emotional response to the message.

Politicians use myth when they show pictures of themselves surrounded by their families. The underlying myth is "I cherish what you cherish—to live in a country that supports and nurtures the family values we hold dear." Appealing directly or indirectly to the commonly held myths of an audience is a powerful way to evoke emotional support for your message. But as with any form of support, especially emotional support, you have an ethical responsibility to use this strategy wisely and not to exploit your listeners.

USING EMOTIONAL APPEALS: ETHICAL ISSUES

Regardless of which emotions you use to motivate your audience, you have an obligation to be ethical and forthright. Making false claims, misusing evidence to arouse emotions, or relying only on emotions without any evidence to support a conclusion violates ethical standards of effective public speaking.

A **demagogue** is a speaker who attempts to gain power or control over others by using impassioned emotional pleas and appealing to listeners' prejudices. The word *demagogue* comes from the Greek word *demagogos*, meaning "popular leader." Speakers who become popular by substituting emotion and fallacies in place of well-supported reasoning are guilty of demagoguery. During the early 1950s, Wisconsin Senator Joseph McCarthy sought to convince the nation that Communists had infiltrated government, education, and the entertainment industry. This was at the height of the Cold War, and anything or anyone remotely connected to Communism elicited an immediate negative emotional response. For a time, McCarthy was successful in his effort to expose the unpatriotic Communists among us. His evidence, however, was scanty, and he relied primarily on scaring his listeners about the potential evil of alleged Communists. His trumped-up evidence and unethical use of fear appeals eventually undermined his credibility and earned him a reputation as a demagogue. You have an ethical responsibility not to misuse emotional appeals when persuading others.

Your credibility, reasoning, and emotional appeals are the chief ways to persuade an audience. Your use of these persuasive strategies depends on the composition of your audience. As we have observed several times before, an early task in the

demagogue
A speaker who gains control over others by using unethical emotional pleas and appeals to listeners' prejudices

Tips for Using Emotion to Persuade

Use concrete examples.

Use emotion-arousing words.

Use nonverbal behavior to communicate your emotional response.

Use visual images.

Use appropriate metaphors and similes.

Use appropriate fear appeals.

Use appeals to a variety of emotions such as hope, pride, courage, and reverence.

Tap audience members' beliefs in shared myths.

public-speaking process is to analyze your audience. This is particularly important in persuasion. Audience members are not just sitting there waiting to respond to every suggestion a speaker makes.

Strategies for Adapting Ideas to People and People to Ideas

We opened this chapter with Donald C. Bryant's pithy definition of persuasion as ". . . the process of adjusting ideas to people and people to ideas."[29] His description of the rhetorical process gets at the heart of what an effective persuader does—he or she ethically adapts the message and delivery to create agreement.

Audience members may hold differing views of you and your subject. Your task is to find out whether there is a prevailing viewpoint held by a majority of your listeners. If they are generally friendly toward you and your ideas, you need to design your speech differently from the way you would if your listeners were neutral, apathetic, or hostile. Research studies as well as seasoned public speakers can offer some useful suggestions to help you adapt your approach to your audience. We will discuss three general responses your audience may have to you: receptive, neutral, and unreceptive.

PERSUADING THE RECEPTIVE AUDIENCE

It is always a pleasure to face an audience that already supports you and your message. In speaking to a receptive group, you can explore your ideas in greater depth than otherwise. Here are some suggestions that may help you make the most of your speaking opportunity.

IDENTIFY WITH YOUR AUDIENCE To establish common ground with her audience of fellow students, Rita told them, "Just like most of you, I struggle to pay my way through college. That's why I support expanding the campus work-study program." Like Rita, if you are a college student speaking to other college students with similar backgrounds and pressures, point to your similar backgrounds and struggles.

Emphasize the similarities between you and your audience. What other common interests do you have? The introductory portion of your speech is a good place to mention your common interests and background.

CLEARLY STATE YOUR SPEAKING OBJECTIVE When speaking to a group of her campaign workers, mayoral candidate Maria Hernandez stated early in her speech, "My reason for coming here today is to ask each of you to volunteer three hours a week to help me become the next mayor of our city." We have stressed several times how important it is to provide an overview of your major point or purpose. This is particularly so when speaking to a group who will support your point of view.[30]

TELL YOUR AUDIENCE EXACTLY WHAT YOU WANT THEM TO DO Besides telling your listeners what your speaking objective is, you can also tell them how you expect them to respond to your message. Be explicit in directing your listeners' behavior.

ASK LISTENERS FOR AN IMMEDIATE SHOW OF SUPPORT Asking for an immediate show of support helps to cement the positive response you have developed during your speech. For example, Christian evangelists usually speak to favorable audiences. Evangelist Billy Graham, who has spoken to more people in live public-speaking situations than anyone else in the twentieth century, always asks those who support his Christian message to come forward at the end of his sermon.

USE EMOTIONAL APPEALS EFFECTIVELY You are more likely to move a favorable audience to action with strong emotional appeals while also reminding them of the evidence that supports your conclusion. If the audience already supports your position, you need not spend a great deal of time on lengthy, detailed explanations or factual information. You can usually assume that your listeners already know much of that material.

MAKE IT EASY FOR YOUR LISTENERS TO ACT It is a good idea not only to tell your listeners precisely what you want them to do and ask for an immediate response, but also to make sure that what you're asking them to do is clear and easy. If you're asking them to write or e-mail someone, hand out postcards already addressed to the recipient, or distribute an e-mail address printed on a card for handy reference. If you want listeners to call someone, make sure each person has the phone number—it's even better if you can give a toll-free number.

Persuading the Neutral Audience

Think how many lectures you go to with an attitude of indifference. Probably quite a few. Many audiences will fall somewhere between wildly enthusiastic and unreceptive; they will simply be neutral or indifferent. They may be neutral because they don't know much about your topic or because they just can't make up their minds whether to support your point of view. They may also be indifferent because they don't see how the topic or issue affects them. Regardless of the reason for your listeners' indifference, your challenge is to make them interested in your message. Let's look at some approaches to gaining their attention and keeping their interest.

CAPTURE YOUR LISTENERS' ATTENTION EARLY IN YOUR SPEECH "Bill Farmer died last year, but he's about to fulfill his lifelong dream of going into space."[31] In a speech about the high cost of funerals, Karmen's provocative opening statement effectively captures the attention of her listeners.

REFER TO BELIEFS THAT MANY LISTENERS SHARE When speaking to a neutral audience, identify common concerns and values that you plan to address. Martin Luther King's "I Have a Dream" speech (Appendix C) includes references to his listeners' common beliefs.

RELATE YOUR TOPIC NOT ONLY TO YOUR LISTENERS BUT ALSO TO THEIR FAMILIES, FRIENDS, AND LOVED ONES You can capture the interest of your listeners by appealing to the needs of people they care about. Parents will be interested in ideas and policies that affect their children. People are generally interested in matters that may affect their friends, neighbors, and others with whom they identify, such as members of their own religion or economic or social class.

BE REALISTIC ABOUT WHAT YOU CAN ACCOMPLISH Don't overestimate the response you may receive from a neutral audience. People who start with an attitude of indifference are probably not going to become as enthusiastic as you are after hearing just one speech. Persuasion does not occur all at once or at a first hearing of arguments.

PERSUADING THE UNRECEPTIVE AUDIENCE

One of the biggest challenges in public speaking is to persuade audience members who are against you or your message. If they are hostile toward you personally, your job is to seek ways to enhance your credibility and persuade them to listen to you. If they are unreceptive to your point of view, there are several approaches that you can use to encourage them to listen to you.

DON'T IMMEDIATELY ANNOUNCE THAT YOU PLAN TO CHANGE THEIR MINDS Paul wondered why his opening sales pitch ("Good morning. I plan to convince you to purchase this fine set of knives at a cost to you of only $250") was not greeted enthusiastically. If you immediately and bluntly tell your listeners that you plan to change their opinions, it can make them defensive. It is usually better to take a more subtle approach when announcing your persuasive intent.[32]

BEGIN YOUR SPEECH BY NOTING AREAS OF AGREEMENT BEFORE YOU DISCUSS AREAS OF DISAGREEMENT In addressing the school board, one community member began his persuasive effort to convince board members they should not raise taxes by stating, "I think each of us here can agree with one common goal: We want the best education for our children." Once you help your audience understand that there are issues on which you agree (such as agreeing that the topic you will discuss is controversial), your listeners may be more attentive when you explain your position.

DON'T EXPECT A MAJOR SHIFT IN ATTITUDE FROM A HOSTILE AUDIENCE Set a realistic limit on what you can achieve. A realistic goal might be to have your listeners hear you out and at least consider some of your points.

ACKNOWLEDGE THE OPPOSING POINTS OF VIEW THAT MEMBERS OF YOUR AUDIENCE MAY HOLD Summarize the reasons individuals may oppose your point of view. Doing this communicates that you at least understand the issues.[33] Your listeners will be more likely to listen to you if they know that you understand their viewpoint. Of course, after you acknowledge the opposing point of view, you will need to cite evidence and use arguments to refute the opposition and support your conclusion. Early in his speech to a neighborhood group about the possibility of building a new airport near their homes, City Manager Anderson acknowledged, "I am aware that a new airport brings unwanted changes to a neighborhood. Noise and increased traffic are not the type of challenges you want near your homes." He went on to identify the actions the city would take to minimize the problems a new airport would cause.

ESTABLISH YOUR CREDIBILITY Being thought credible is always an important goal of a public speaker, and it is especially important when talking to an unreceptive audience. Let your audience know about the experience, interest, knowledge, and skill that give you special insight into the issues at hand.

CONSIDER MAKING UNDERSTANDING RATHER THAN ADVOCACY YOUR GOAL Sometimes your audience disagrees with you because its members just don't understand your point. Or they may harbor a misconception about you and your message. For example, if your listeners think that AIDS is transferred though kissing or other casual contact rather than through unprotected sexual contact, you'll first have to acknowledge their beliefs and then construct a sound argument to show how inaccurate their assumptions are. To change such a misconception and enhance accurate understanding, experienced speakers use a four-part strategy.[34]

- **Summarize the common misconceptions about the issue or idea you are discussing.** "Many people think that AIDS can be transmitted through casual contact such as kissing or that it can easily be transmitted by your dentist or physician."

- **State why these misconceptions may seem reasonable.** Tell your listeners why it is logical for them to hold that view or identify "facts" they may have heard that would lead them to their current conclusion. "Since AIDS is such a highly contagious disease, it may seem reasonable to think it can be transmitted through such casual contact."

- **Dismiss the misconceptions and provide evidence to support your point.** Here you need sound and credible data to be persuasive. "In fact, countless medical studies have shown that it is virtually impossible to be infected with the AIDS virus unless you have unprotected sexual contact or use unsterilized hypodermic needles that have also been used by someone who has AIDS." In this instance, you would probably cite specific results from two or three studies to lend credibility to your claim.

- **State the accurate information that you want your audience to remember.** Reinforce the conclusion you want your listeners to draw from the information you presented with a clear summary statement, such as "According to recent research, the most common factor contributing to the spread of AIDS is unprotected sex. This is true for individuals of both sexes and all sexual orientations."

Strategies for Organizing Persuasive Messages

I s there one best way to organize a persuasive speech? The answer is no. Specific approaches to organizing speeches depend on audience, message, and desired objective. But how you organize your speech does have a major effect on your listeners' response to your message.

Research suggests that there are some general principles to keep in mind when preparing your persuasive message.[35]

- **If you feel that your audience may be hostile to your point of view, advance your strongest arguments first.** If you save your best argument for last, your audience may have already stopped listening.

- **Do not bury key arguments and evidence in the middle of your message.** Your listeners are more likely to remember information presented first and last.[36] In speaking to his fraternity about the evils of drunk driving, Frank wisely began his speech with his most powerful evidence: The leading cause

A persuasive speaker who wants to motivate her audience to take action should place her call for action near the end of the speech.

[Photo: Kayte Deioma/PhotoEdit]

of death among college-age males is alcohol-related automobile accidents. He got their attention with his sobering fact.

◆ **If you want your listeners to take some action, it is best to tell them what you want them to do at the end of your speech.** If you call for action in the middle of your speech, it won't have the same power as including it in your conclusion.

◆ **When you think your listeners are well informed and are familiar with the disadvantages of your proposal, it is usually better to present both sides of an issue, rather than just the advantages of the position you advocate.** If you don't acknowledge arguments your listeners have heard, they will probably think about them anyway.

◆ **Make some reference to the counterarguments, and then refute them with evidence and logic.** It may be wise to compare the proposal you are making with an alternative proposal, perhaps one offered by someone else. By comparing and contrasting your solution with another recommendation, you can show how your proposal is better.[37]

We discussed ways of organizing speeches in Chapter 9, but there are special ways to organize persuasive speeches. Here we will present four organizational patterns: problem–solution, refutation, cause and effect, and the motivated sequence.

PROBLEM–SOLUTION

The most basic organizational pattern for a persuasive speech is to make the audience aware of a problem, then present a solution that clearly solves it. Almost any problem can be phrased in terms of something you want more of or less of. The problem–solution pattern works best when a clearly evident problem can be documented and a solution can be proposed to deal with the evils of the well-documented problem.

If you are speaking to an apathetic audience, or if listeners are not aware that a problem exists, a problem–solution pattern works nicely. Your challenge will be to provide ample evidence to document that your perception of the problem is accurate. You'll also need to convince your listeners that the solution you advocate is the most appropriate one to resolve the problem.

Many political candidates use a problem–solution approach. *Problem:* The government wastes your tax dollars. *Solution:* Vote for me and I'll see to it that government waste is eliminated. *Problem:* We need more and better jobs. *Solution:* Vote for me and I'll institute a program to put people back to work.

Note in the following outline of Jason Fruit's speech, "The Dangers of Electromagnetic Fields," how he plans to first document a clear problem and then recommend strategies for managing the problem.

PROBLEM:

I. Power lines and power stations around the country emit radiation and are now being shown to increase the risk of cancer.
  A. Childhood leukemia rates are higher in children who live near large power lines.
  B. The International Cancer Research Institute in Lyon, France, published a report linking electromagnetic fields and childhood cancer.

SOLUTION:

II. Steps can be taken to minimize our risk of health hazards caused by electromagnetic energy.
  A. The federal government should establish enforceable safety standards for exposure to electromagnetic energy.
  B. Contact your local power company to make sure its lines are operated safely.
  C. Stop using electric blankets.
  D. Use protective screens for computer-display terminals.

The problem–solution arrangement of ideas applies what you learned about cognitive dissonance in Chapter 16. Identify and document a concern that calls for change, and then suggest specific behaviors that can restore cognitive balance.

REFUTATION

Another way to persuade an audience to support your point of view is to prove that the arguments against your position are false—that is, to refute them. To use refutation as a strategy for persuasion, you first identify objections to your position that your listeners might raise and then refute or overcome those objections with arguments and evidence. You would be most likely to use refutation as your organizational strategy when your position was being attacked. Or, if you know what your listeners' chief objections are to your persuasive proposal, you could organize your speech around the arguments your listeners hold.

As we noted earlier, research suggests that in most cases it is better to present both sides of an issue rather than just the advantages of the position you advocate. Even if you don't acknowledge arguments your listeners have heard, they will probably think about them anyway.

Suppose, for example, you plan to speak to a group of real-estate developers and advocate a new zoning ordinance that would reduce the number of building permits granted in your community. Your listeners will undoubtedly have some concerns over how the ordinance will affect new housing starts and the overall economic forecast. You could organize your presentation to this group using those two obvious concerns as major issues to refute. Your major points could be as follows:

I. The new zoning ordinance will not cause an overall decrease in the number of new homes built in our community.
II. The new zoning ordinance will have a positive effect on economic growth in our community.

If, after making a persuasive presentation using a refutation strategy, there is a question-and-answer forum, you should be prepared to answer questions. Credible evidence, facts, and data will be more effective than emotional arguments alone when you are attempting to persuade an audience that you know is not in favor of your persuasive objective. In your postspeech session, you can use your refutation skills to maintain a favorable audience response to your message in the face of criticism or attacks on the soundness of your logic.

CAUSE AND EFFECT

Like the problem–solution pattern to which it is closely related, the cause-and-effect approach was introduced in Chapter 9 as a useful organizational strategy. One way to use the cause–effect method is to begin with an effect, or problem, and then identify the causes of the problem in an effort to convince your listeners that the problem is significant. A speech on the growing problem of gangs might focus on poverty, drugs, and a financially crippled school system.

You could also organize a message by noting the problem and then spelling out the effects of the problem. If you identify the problem as too many unsupervised teenagers roaming your community's streets after 11 P.M., you could organize a speech noting the effects this problem is having on your fellow citizens.

The goal of using cause-and-effect organization for a persuasive speech is to convince your listeners that one event caused another. As we noted earlier, you argue that something known caused something else to happen. For example, you may try to reason that students in your state have low standardized test scores because they had poor teachers. Of course, you must prove that there are no other factors responsible for the low test scores. It may not be the teachers who caused the low test scores; perhaps it was the lack of parent involvement, or one of a number of other factors.

The challenge in using a cause-and-effect organizational strategy is to *prove* that one event *caused* something else to occur. Simply because two events occurred at the same time or in close succession does not prove that there is a cause-and-effect relationship. Earlier we noted the causal fallacy ("after this, therefore because of this" or *post hoc, ergo propter hoc*). As an example of the challenge in documenting a cause-and-effect relationship, consider a study that found that people who spend several hours daily on the Internet are also psychologically depressed. This finding does not necessarily *prove* that Internet use causes depression—other factors could cause the depression. Perhaps people who are depressed are more likely to use the Internet, or psychologically depressed people may find general comfort and security in using technology.

Here's an example of how a persuasive speech could be organized using a cause-and-effect strategy:

I. There is high uncertainty about whether interest rates will increase or decrease. *(cause)*

II. Money markets are unstable in Asia, Eastern Europe, and Latin America. *(cause)*

III. There has been a rise in unemployment. *(cause)*

IV. In the late 1920s in the United States, these three conditions were followed by a stock-market crash. Thus, because of today's similar economic uncertainty, you should decrease the amount of money you have invested in stocks; if you don't, you will lose money. *(effect)*

THE MOTIVATED SEQUENCE

The motivated sequence is a five-step organizational plan that has proved successful for several decades. Developed by Alan Monroe, this simple yet effective strategy for organizing speeches incorporates principles that have been confirmed by research and practical experience.[38] Based on the problem–solution pattern, it also uses the cognitive-dissonance approach, which we discussed in Chapter 16: First, disturb your listeners, and then point them toward the specific change you want them to adopt. The five steps are attention, need, satisfaction, visualization, and action.

Using Persuasive Strategies

1. Attention. Your first goal is to get your listeners' attention. In Chapter 10, we discussed specific attention-catching methods of beginning a speech. Remember the particular benefits of using a personal or hypothetical example, a startling statement, an unusual statistic, a rhetorical question, or a well-worded analogy. The attention step is, in essence, the introduction to your speech.

James Chang began his prize-winning speech titled "Sustainable Giving" with this riveting, attention-catching introduction:

> Beatrice Biira, a nine-year-old girl in Uganda, lives in abject poverty. Living in a shanty home where the rain seeps through the roof every night, neither she nor any of her siblings has ever stepped foot in a school. Her story, sadly, is not unique. The World Bank in 2001 concluded that nearly 3 billion people live on less than two dollars a day.[39]

2. Need. After getting the attention of your audience, establish why your topic, problem, or issue should concern your listeners. Arouse dissonance. Tell your audience why the current program, politician, or whatever you're attempting to change is not working. Convince them there is a need for a change. You must also convince your listeners that this need for a change affects them directly. During the need step, you should develop logical arguments backed by ample evidence to support your position.

To document the need for increased charitable giving to support the world's most impoverished people, James provided specific evidence to describe the problem.

> The UN Food and Agricultural Organization reports in the 2002 assessment of the state of food insecurity in the world that more than 840 million people in the world are malnourished and more than 150 million of them are under the age of five. Six million children die every year as a result of hunger.[40]

3. Satisfaction. After you present the problem or need for concern, you next briefly identify how your plan will satisfy the need. What is your solution to the problem? At this point in the speech, you need not go into great detail. Present enough information so that your listeners have a general understanding of how the problem may be solved.

James suggests that the solution to the problem of world hunger is to donate money to the Heifer Project—an organization that helps the world's poor by teaching them how to use contemporary farming techniques. Here's how he introduced the satisfaction step:

> The old adage goes, "give a man a fish, and you feed him for a day; teach a man to fish, and you feed him for a lifetime." It was the belief of the founders in the simple premise that people should have the ability to feed themselves that was the foundation for the Heifer Project. Heifer International operates Animals to Families as sustainable gifts. The families raise the animals, benefiting from the products of those animals and selling them as a source of revenue.[41]

4. Visualization. Now you need to give your audience a sense of what it would be like if your solution were or were not adopted. You could take a *positive-visualization* approach: Paint a picture with words to communicate how wonderful the future will be if your solution is adopted. You could take a *negative-visualization* approach: Tell your listeners how awful things will be if your solution is not adopted. If they think things are bad now, just wait; things will get worse. Or, you could present both a positive and a negative visualization of the future: The problem will be solved if your solution is adopted, and the world will be a much worse place if your solution is not adopted.

To encourage his audience to visualize the benefits of providing sustainable resources to help families climb out of poverty, James describes how one family was able to take out a small loan in order to start a small business.

> Irma Hernandez, a woman from Honduras, joined with four other women in taking out a loan for $120 from the Adelante Foundation. . . . Her husband

worked full-time as a farm laborer, but because work was not always available, the income was simply too low and too unstable to support the five children that they had. With the money that Irma borrowed, she was able to buy the necessary tools to start a clothes-making business that brought a steady second income to the family.[42]

James could have made his visualization step even stronger by noting not only what happens when people benefit from the proposal he advocates, but also what happens when people do not receive help. Using both a positive and a negative visualization approach demonstrates how your solution (satisfaction step) directly addresses the problem you have described (need step).

Martin Luther King Jr. drew on visualization as a rhetorical strategy in his moving "I Have a Dream" speech (Appendix C). Note how King powerfully and poetically paints a picture with words that continue to provide hope and inspiration today.

I have a dream that one day this nation will rise up and live out the true meaning of its creed, "We hold these truths to be self-evident, that all men are created equal."

I have a dream that one day on the red hills of Georgia the sons of former slaves and the sons of former slaveowners will be able to sit down together at the table of brotherhood.

I have a dream that one day even the state of Mississippi, a state sweltering with the heat of injustice, sweltering with the heat of oppression, will be transformed into an oasis of freedom and justice.

I have a dream that my four little children will one day live in a nation where they will be judged not by the color of their skin but by the content of their character. I have a dream today.

I have a dream that one day, down in Alabama, with its vicious racists, with its governor having his lips dripping with the words of interposition and nullification, one day right there in Alabama little black boys and black girls will be able to join hands with little white boys and white girls as sisters and brothers. I have a dream today.

I have a dream that one day every valley shall be exalted, every hill and mountain shall be made low, the rough places will be made plain and the crooked places will be made straight, and the glory of the Lord shall be revealed, and all flesh shall see it together.[43]

5. Action. This last step forms the basis of your conclusion. You tell your audience the specific action they can take to implement your solution. Identify exactly what you want your listeners to do. Give them simple, clear, easy-to-follow steps to achieve your goal. For example, you could give them a phone number to call for more information, provide an address so that they can write a letter of support, hand them a petition to sign at the end of your speech, or tell them for whom to vote. Outline the specific action you want them to take.

In his "Sustainable Giving" speech, James describes a specific action for his listeners to take to help solve the problem he has described:

The most important question that should then remain is how you personally can help out. On an institutional level, the United States Agency for International Development, USAID, is one of the leaders in fighting global poverty and should be encouraged to strengthen and increase its sustainable programs. Information about USAID and the ability to contact the agency can be found on its Web site at usaid.org.[44]

James concluded by making a specific appeal to his listeners to donate money to USAID, the Heifer Project, or other organizations dedicated to eradicating world hunger. Note that he directed his listeners to a specific Web address; the best action step precisely spells out the next step your audience should take.

You can modify the motivated sequence to suit the needs of your topic and audience. If, for example, you are speaking to a receptive audience, you do not have to spend a great deal of time on the need step. They already agree that the need is serious. They may, however, want to learn about some specific actions that they can take to implement a solution to the problem. Therefore, you would be wise to emphasize the satisfaction and action steps.

Conversely, if you are speaking to a hostile audience, you should spend considerable time on the need step. Convince your audience that the problem is significant and that they should be concerned about the problem. You would probably not propose a lengthy, detailed action.

If your audience is neutral or indifferent, spend time getting their attention and inviting their interest in the problem. The attention and need steps should be emphasized.

The motivated sequence is a guide, not an absolute formula. Use it and the other suggestions about speech organization to help you achieve your specific objective. Be audience-centered; adapt your message to your listeners.

RECAP

Organizational Patterns for Persuasive Messages

TYPE	DEFINITION	EXAMPLE
Problem–solution	Present the problem; then present the solution	I. The national debt is too high. II. We need to raise taxes to lower the debt.
Refutation	Anticipate your listeners' key objections to your proposal and then address them.	I. Even though you may think we pay too much tax, we are really undertaxed. II. Even though you may think the national debt will not go down, tax revenue will lower the deficit.
Cause-and-effect	First present the cause of the problem; then note how the problem affects the listeners. Or identify a known effect; then document what causes the effect.	I. The high national debt is caused by too little tax revenue and too much government spending. II. The high national debt will increase both inflation and unemployment.
Motivated sequence	A five-step pattern of organizing a speech, whose steps include attention, need, satisfaction, visualization, and action.	I. *Attention:* Imagine a pile of $1000 bills 67 miles high. That's our national debt. II. *Need:* The increasing national debt will cause hardships for our children and grandchildren. III. *Satisfaction:* We need higher taxes to reduce our debt. IV. *Visualization:* Imagine our country in the year 2050; it could have low inflation and full employment or be stuck with a debt ten times our debt today. V. *Action:* If you want to lower the debt by increasing tax revenue, sign my petition that I will send to our senators.

TOMATO TALK

Megan Loden, West Texas A&M University

Children's book author Barry Sims released a socially driven book in 2005 that quickly took fifth grade classrooms in Seattle, Washington, by storm. The book, *A Tale of Two Tomatoes*, chronicles the journey of Local Lucy and Traveling Tom—two tomatoes, one from Tallahassee, FL, the other from a local farm in Seattle, who ended up on the exact same dinner plate. Sims's tale is an extension of the "Eat Local" movement in Seattle, and although the images and rhetoric of his story are quite amusing, the problems behind long-distance food transportation are no laughing matter. On February 19, 2007, the Global Food and Drink Federation, or GFDF, released a statement reporting that "global food miles (or the distance food is transported) have increased by 15 percent in the last five years." Consequently, the January 3, 2007 *Journal of Sustainable Agriculture* reports, "Long-distance transported foods are wasting our planet's energy, contributing to world pollution, and causing human health problems faster than we realize." Therefore, we must first examine the problems with long-distance food transportation; second, investigate the causes of this inedible epidemic; and finally, explore some solutions that make eating locally—and making a difference—easier.

Initially, the problems of long-distance food transportation are three-fold: First, there is a consolidation of the U.S. food industry; second, the transported foods contain unhealthy substances; and finally, long-distance food transportation is an environmental hazard. First, the food industry is consolidating at an alarming rate due to the fact that most of our food supply comes from a handful of mass-production giants. The February 2007 *World Watch* magazine reports that "three produce distributors (Dole, Chiquita, and Sunkist) [are responsible for] 86.3 percent of all of the fruits and vegetables consumed in the U.S." These large companies are taking over the global food system, demanding long-distance transport, and making it virtually impossible for smaller, local farms to sustain themselves due to their control over the markets for the same products.

Second, not only are production giants mass-producing foods, but they are producing chemically altered foods. As the March 12, 2007 *Time* magazine clarifies, "what happens after harvest—how food is shipped and handled—is even more important than how it was grown." In order to better survive the long journey to market, many fruits and vegetables are picked while hard and then gassed with a hormone to help them artificially ripen along their journey. Sadly, our own health is sacrificed for convenience and profit. For example, the November *Journal of Agriculture and Food Chemistry* warns that "the treatment chemicals used to artificially ripen fruits and vegetables contain certain carcinogens that increase our risks for cancer and everyday viral and bacterial diseases."

Finally, the environment is extensively harmed by the transport of these goods. The November 4, 2006 *Journal of Geophysical Research* found that "the number-one source of human-induced greenhouse gases is food production and transportation." And in an *Economist* article from March 3, 2007, it was emphasized that "9 percent of America's energy consumption is used to produce, process, and transport our foods." Consequently, large-scale environmental problems such as global warming, renewable energy depletion, and poor air quality can all be traced back to long-distance food transportation.

Next, the causes for this inedible epidemic are two-fold: a decrease in farmers' profit, and produce supply and demand. Initially, farmers are barely holding on, due to their lack of profit from the local foods they are trying to produce. An *Ecotrust* article from January 11, 2007 estimates that "In 2007, farmers will only receive close to 7 cents of every dollar of profit they receive as opposed to in 1997 when they received nearly 41 cents to every dollar." At this rate it should come as no surprise that the January 2007 *Farmers' Almanac* reports

Megan begins her speech in an interesting way by referring to characters from a children's story to introduce the main idea of her message.

Because her audience is likely not hostile to her message, she explicitly provides an overview of her major ideas and her persuasive purpose.

Here Megan uses signposts to identify three key elements of the problem she is describing.

Her clear oral citation indicates the source of the evidence to support her point.

Here Megan cites evidence that directly supports her key conclusion.

that the number of local farms has decreased by nearly 40 percent in the last ten years. High risks for failure and minimal financial return create a vicious cycle that not only forces long-distance food transportation, but feeds (all puns intended) the mass-production giants even more. Next, as Jessica Williams informs us in her 2001 book *50 Facts That Should Change the World,* "even when it's snowing outside [people want to eat strawberries] or cook with peas." In other words, long-distance transported fruits and vegetables suffer from the simple concept of supply and demand. Most households and companies are not willing to change their menu based on what is in season. Furthermore, as a *Miami Herald* article from March 2, 2007 points out, in order to make sure that their products can reach long distances quickly, "food producers are turning to machine packaging to speed up the transportation process." And although this makes the supply end move faster, it often threatens the quality of the product. On March 16, 2007, the *Wall Street Journal* asserted that of the "over one hundred food contamination scares in the last ten years, 98 percent were traced back to large production companies that use machine packaging." Indisputably, there must be a better option.

> Megan provides evidence that clearly communicates the essence of her persuasive objective.

Luckily, there are *many* options on both a governmental and a personal level. First, the United States needs to introduce ETDs, or Ecological Tax Deductions, to ensure that food prices accurately reflect the full environmental and social costs of food production. The September 2006 *Journal of Sustainable Agriculture* explains that ETDs "would directly address the problematic situation where a locally grown apple is more expensive than a mass-produced apple that has traveled thousands of miles." ETDs have already been in place in several countries within the European Union since the late '70s, and have drastically lowered the price of small-scale produce, thankfully to the benefit of local farmers. Most importantly, though, there are ways we can make a difference. Clearly, we can grow our own food and eat seasonally. *Eatlocal.com,* an organization sponsoring the Eat Local movement, expresses on their Web site, last updated March 1, 2007, that in addition to growing our own food, we can ask our local grocery store which seasonal fruits and vegetables are locally grown, support restaurants and venders that buy locally produced foods, or, simply pull over when we see a roadside produce stand. But finally, there is a solution that literally requires no more than lifting a finger. The system is called CSA, or Community Supported Agriculture. Just log on to *eatwellguide.org,* type in your zip code, and "subscribe" to a CSA near you. A crate of seasonal fresh fruits and vegetables will be delivered right to your doorstep for five to twenty dollars a week. CSAs ensure that their fruits and vegetables are picked once they are ripe, have no added growth hormones, and only deliver within a fifty-mile radius surrounding their farm. With minor mindset and lifestyle adjustments, eating locally is affordable, convenient, and smart.

> After clearly enumerating the problems she has documented, she turns to clearly identifying solutions to the problem.

> Megan's use of reasoning by analogy helps to document that her proposed solution has a good possibility of addressing the problems she cites.

> She provides a clear, simple action step that listeners could take to solve the problem.

After reviewing the problems and causes surrounding long-distance food transportation and exploring some simple solutions to make eating locally easier, we simply must be willing to take action. As Barry Sims's *Tale of Two Tomatoes* quickly inspired fifth graders, his message has the potential to inspire the world. Education is great, but action is better, and we can make a difference. The problems with long-distance food transportation are complex, but the solutions are simple. Although it might seem like a step back into primitive times for society to advocate a practice of food supply that doesn't require traveling, rest assured that choosing Local Lucy over Traveling Tom will always be a step in the right direction.

> In her conclusion, Megan cogently summarizes the essential ideas she has shared in her message.

> She ends her speech by making a reference to her introduction, which is an effective way to provide closure to her message.

From *Winning Orations, 2007* (Mankato, MN: Interstate Oratorical Association, Larry Schnoor, Ex. Sec. 2007)

SUMMARY

Means of persuasion are techniques that can help you convince your listeners to follow your recommendations. You can persuade with credibility, logic, and emotion.

Credibility is a listener's view of a speaker. The three factors contributing to credibility are competence, trustworthiness, and dynamism. Specific strategies can enhance your credibility before, while, and after you speak.

The effectiveness of logical arguments hinges on the proof you employ. Proof consists of evidence plus the reasoning that you use to draw conclusions from the evidence. Three types of reasoning are inductive reasoning, which moves from specific instances or examples to reach a general, probable conclusion; deductive reasoning, which moves from a general statement to reach a specific, more certain conclusion; and causal reasoning, relating two or more events so as to be able to conclude that one or more of the events caused the others. You can use four types of evidence: facts, examples, opinions, and statistics. Avoid using fallacious arguments.

Emotion theory has identified three dimensions of emotional response to a message: pleasure–displeasure, arousal–nonarousal, and dominance–powerlessness. Specific suggestions for appealing to audience emotions include using examples; emotion-arousing words; nonverbal behavior; selected appeals to fear; and appeals to such emotions as hope, pride, courage, or the revered.

To persuade skillfully, you need to adapt your message to receptive, neutral, and unreceptive audiences.

Four patterns for organizing a persuasive speech are problem–solution, refutation, cause-and-effect, and the motivated sequence. The five steps of the motivated sequence are attention, need, satisfaction, visualization, and action. Adapt the motivated sequence to your specific audience and persuasive objective.

 BEING AUDIENCE-CENTERED: A SHARPER FOCUS

CONSIDERING YOUR AUDIENCE

▶ To persuade the receptive audience, consider the following strategies: Identify with the audience. State your speaking objective. Tell the audience members what you want them to do. Ask for an immediate show of support. Use emotional appeals effectively. Make it easy for your listeners to act.

▶ To persuade the neutral audience, draw on these persuasive approaches: Capture your listeners' attention early in your speech by referring to beliefs that many listeners share. Relate your topic not only to your listeners but also to their families, friends, and loved ones. Be realistic in what you expect to accomplish.

▶ For an unreceptive audience, consider these persuasive strategies: Don't immediately announce that you plan to change your listeners'

minds. Begin your speech by noting areas of agreement before you discuss areas of disagreement. Don't expect a major shift in attitude from a hostile audience. Acknowledge the opposing points of view that members of your audience may hold. Establish your credibility early in your message. Consider making understanding rather than advocacy your goal. Advance your strongest argument first.

▶ If you want your listeners to take some action following your speech, it is best to tell them what you want them to do during the conclusion of your speech.

▶ Refer to counterarguments your audience may already know, and then refute these counterarguments with evidence and logic.

CONSIDERING AUDIENCE DIVERSITY

➤ Keep the cultural expectations of your listeners in mind when using strategies to establish or maintain your credibility; credibility is in the mind of the beholder.

➤ Before debating issues, people from high-context cultures often prefer to establish a personal relationship between speaker and listener.

➤ Middle Eastern cultures usually do not use standard inductive- or deductive-reasoning structures; they are more likely to use narrative (story telling) strategies to evoke feelings and emotions, allowing their listeners to draw their own conclusions by inductive associations. In some high-context cultures such as Japan and China, the conclusion to a message is stated more indirectly. In a low-context culture such as the United States, listeners may generally expect you to make a more direct statement of the action you'd like your audience members to take.

CRITICAL THINKING QUESTIONS

1. Imagine that you are delivering your final speech of the semester in your public-speaking class. What specific strategies can you implement to enhance your initial, derived, and final credibility as a public speaker in the minds of your classmates?

2. Josh is speaking to his neighborhood homeowners' association, attempting to persuade his neighbors that a crime-watch program should be organized. What logical arguments and emotional strategies would help him ethically achieve his persuasive objective?

3. Janice is pondering options for organizing her persuasive speech, which has the following purpose: "The audience should be able to support the establishment of a wellness program for our company." Using this purpose, draft the main ideas for a speech organized according to each of the following organizational patterns: problem–solution, refutation, cause-and-effect, the motivated sequence.

ETHICAL QUESTIONS

1. Karl believes strongly that the tragedy of the Holocaust could occur again. He plans to show exceptionally graphic photographs of Holocaust victims during his speech to his public-speaking class. Is it ethical to show graphic, emotion-arousing photos to a captive audience?

2. Tony was surfing the Internet and found just the statistics he needs for his persuasive speech. Yet he does not know the original source of the statistics—just the Internet address. Is that sufficient documentation for the statistics?

3. Martika wants to convince her classmates, a captive audience, that they should join her in a twenty-four-hour sit-in at the university president's office to protest the recent increase in tuition and fees. The president has made it clear that any attempt to occupy his office after normal office hours will result in arrests. Is it appropriate for Martika to use a classroom speech to encourage her classmates to participate in the sit-in?

Adapting Ideas to People and People to Ideas

Step One: Based on your analysis of your audience, indicate on the following 10-point scale whether they are receptive, neutral, or unreceptive to your persuasive message:

Generally receptive   Generally neutral   Generally unreceptive
1   2   3   4   5   6   7   8   9   10

Note below how you will adapt your message to your audience, given their disposition toward your topic.

If my audience is receptive:

◀ How will I identify with them?

◀ How will I clearly state my objective?

◀ How will I phrase my request for an immediate show of support?

◀ What emotional appeals will be ethical and appropriate?

◀ How will I make it easy for my listeners to respond?

If my audience is neutral:

➤ How will I capture and maintain my listeners' attention?

➤ What common beliefs of my audience should I refer to?

➤ How will I relate my topic and the issues to audience members' friends, family, and loved ones?

➤ What can I realistically expect to accomplish in one speech?

If my audience is unreceptive:

➤ How will I ensure that I refrain from telling them I plan to change their minds?

➤ What areas of agreement with my audience will I stress?

➤ How can I acknowledge opposing points of view my audience holds?

➤ How will I establish my credibility?

➤ How will I try to help my audience better understand my ideas and change any misconceptions they might hold?

➤ What can I realistically expect to accomplish in one speech?

Jacques Louis David (1748–1825), *The Death of Socrates*. 1787. Oil on canvas, 51 x 77 $\frac{1}{4}$ in. (129.5 x 196.2 cm). Catharine Lorillard Wolfe Collection, Wolfe Fund, 1931 (31.45). The Metropolitan Museum of Art/Art Resource, N.Y.

Historians agree that the greatest banquet speech in history was the one by the ancient Greek philosopher Socrates moments after he drank hemlock. "Gack," he said, falling face-first into his chicken. The other Greeks applauded like crazy.

—DAVE BARRY

Speaking for Special Occasions and Purposes

outline

objectives

After studying this chapter you should be able to do the following:

1. Identify and explain the requirements for two types of speaking situations likely to arise in the workplace.

2. List and describe nine types of ceremonial speeches.

3. Explain the purpose and characteristics of an after-dinner speech.

4. List and explain strategies for creating humor in a speech.

here is money in public speaking. Many of the politicians, athletes, management gurus, and entertainment personalities who speak professionally earn six- or even seven-figure fees for a single talk.

- Former New York Mayor Rudi Giuliani commands $100,000 for a speech, not including such expenses as a private Gulfstream jet and as many as five hotel rooms for him and his entourage.[1]
- Former Vice President Al Gore's fee for speaking on global warming, the subject of his film *An Inconvenient Truth*, is $125,000.[2]
- Seven-time Tour de France champion and cancer survivor Lance Armstrong reportedly asks $200,000 and above.[3]
- Actress Nicole Kidman was recently paid $435,000 for a 25-minute speech to the Forbes Global CEO Conference in Australia.[4]
- And Bill Clinton made nearly $40 million in speaking fees in the six years after leaving the White House.[5]

But the record speaking fee may still be the $2 million for two 20-minute speeches given by former President Ronald Reagan to a Japanese company in 1989.[6]

Although most of us will never be rewarded so lavishly for our public-speaking efforts, it *is* likely that we will at some time be asked to make a business or professional presentation or to speak on some occasion that calls for celebration, commemoration, inspiration, or entertainment. Special occasions are important enough and frequent enough to merit study, regardless of the likelihood of resulting wealth or fame for the speaker.

In this chapter, we will discuss the various types of speeches that may be called for on special occasions, and we will examine the specific and unique audience expectations for each. First, we will discuss two speaking situations that are likely to occur in the workplace. We will then turn our attention to several types of ceremonial speeches and the after-dinner speech.

Public Speaking in the Workplace

Nearly every job requires some public-speaking skills. In many careers and professions, public speaking is a daily part of the job. Workplace audiences may range from a group of three managers to a huge auditorium filled with company employees. Presentations may take the form of routine meeting management, reports to company executives, training seminars within the company, or public-relations speeches to people outside the company. The occasions and opportunities are many, and chances are good that you will be asked or expected to do some on-the-job public speaking in the course of your career.

GROUP PRESENTATIONS

After a group has reached a decision, solved a problem, or uncovered new information, group members often present their findings to others. The audience-centered principles of preparing an effective speech apply to group members designing a group oral presentation, as well as to individual speakers.

As our now-familiar model in Figure 18.1 suggests, the first and most important step is to analyze the audience who will listen to the presentation. Who are these listeners? What are their interests and backgrounds? And what do they need to know? One business consultant suggests,

Tune your audience in to radio station WIIFM—What's In It For Me. Tell your listeners where the benefits are for them, and they'll listen to everything you have to say.[7]

As when developing an individual speech, make sure you have a clear purpose and central idea, divided into logical main ideas. This is a group effort, so you need to make sure *each* group member can articulate the purpose, the central idea, main ideas, key supporting material, and the overall outline for the presentation.

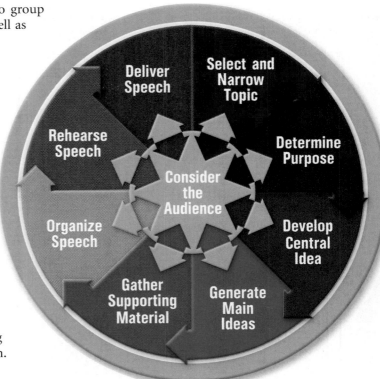

Figure 18.1 *Use the audience-centered model of public speaking as an agenda to help your group plan a group presentation.*

SELECTING A PRESENTATION FORMAT Unless a format for your group presentation has been specified, your group will need to determine how to deliver the presentation. Three primary formats for sharing reports and recommendations with an audience are the symposium presentation, the forum presentation, and the panel discussion.

- A **symposium** is a public discussion during which the members of a group share responsibility for presenting information to an audience. Usually a moderator and the group members are seated in front of the audience, and each group member is prepared to deliver a brief report. Each speaker should know what the others will present so the same ground is not covered twice. At the end of the speeches, the moderator may summarize the key points. The audience can then participate in a question-and-answer session or a forum presentation.

- In a **forum** presentation, audience members direct questions and comments to a group, and group members respond with short impromptu speeches. In ancient Rome, the *forum* was a marketplace where citizens went to shop and discuss the hot issues of the day. It later became a public meeting place where political speeches were often delivered.

  A forum often follows a more structured presentation, such as a symposium or a prepared speech by one group member. Forum presentations work best when all group members know the issues and are prepared to respond unhesitatingly to questioners.

- A **panel discussion** is an informative group presentation. Individuals on the panel may use notes on key facts or statistics, but they do not present formal speeches. Usually a panel discussion is organized and led by an appointed chairperson or moderator.

  An effective moderator gets all the panelists to participate, summarizes their statements, and serves as a gatekeeper to make sure that no member of the panel dominates the discussion. Panel discussions are often followed by a question-and-answer period, or forum.

symposium
A public discussion in which a series of short speeches is presented to an audience

forum
A question-and-answer session that usually follows a public discussion or symposium

panel discussion
A group discussion designed to inform an audience about issues or a problem or to make recommendations

Planning a group presentation involves not only making sure that all members of the group understand the general task but also assigning specific tasks to individual group members.

[Photo: SuperStock]

PLANNING A GROUP PRESENTATION Working in groups requires a coordinated team effort. If you are used to developing reports and speeches on your own, it may be a challenge to work with others on a group assignment. Consider these suggestions to enhance teamwork:

- **Make sure group members understand the task or assignment and work together to identify a topic.** Take a few moments to verbalize the goals and objectives of the assignment. Don't immediately plunge in and try to start dividing up the work just so you can hurry off to your next class or responsibility.

- **If your group assignment is to solve a problem or to inform the audience about a specific issue, try brainstorming to develop a topic or question** (see Chapter 6). Then assess your audience's interests as well as group members' interests and talents to help you choose among your ideas.

- **Give group members individual assignments.** After you decide on your group's presentation topic, divide up the tasks involved in investigating the issues. Also, devise a plan for keeping in touch with one another frequently to share information and ideas.

- **Develop a group outline and decide on an approach.** After group members have researched key issues, begin drafting an outline of your group presentation.

- **Decide on your presentation approach.** Determine whether you will use a symposium, a forum, a panel presentation, or some combination of these approaches. Make decisions about who will present which portions of your outline. Your presentation should have an introduction and a definite ending that reflect your group's work as an integrated problem-solving team.

- **Rehearse the presentation.** Just as you would for an individual speech, rehearse the presentation. If you are using visual aids, be sure to incorporate them in your rehearsal. Also, be sure to time your presentation when you rehearse.

- **Incorporate principles and skills of effective audience-centered public speaking when giving the group presentation.** Adapt to your listeners. Your delivery and comments should be well organized and fluent. Your visual aids should enhance your presentation by being clear and attractive.

MAKING A GROUP PRESENTATION By now it is probably clear that the skills needed for giving a group presentation mirror those we've presented throughout the book. But because a group presentation creates the additional challenge of coordinating your communication efforts with other group or team members, keep the following tips in mind as you offer your conclusions or recommendations.

- **Clarify your purpose.** Just as with an individual speech, it's important for listeners to know what your group's speaking goal is and to understand why you are presenting the information to them; it's also important for each group member to be reminded of the overarching goal of the presentation. It would be useful if the first speaker could ensure that the audience has a good understanding of the group's purpose. If your group is responding to a specific discussion question, it may be useful to write the question or purpose of the presentation on a chalkboard, whiteboard, flipchart, or overhead transparency.

- **Use presentation aids effectively.** You can use presentation aids not only to clarify your purpose, but also to summarize key findings and recommendations. Visual aids can serve the important function of unifying your group presentation. If your group is using PowerPoint visuals, consider having each group member use the same template and font style to add to the coordinated look and feel of your presentation.

- **Choose someone to serve as coordinator or moderator.** Groups need a balance between structure and interaction. Without adequate structure, conversation can bounce from person to person and the presentation will lack a clear focus. A moderator can help provide needed structure to a group presentation by introducing both the topic and the group members. A moderator can also help keep track of time and ensure that people neither dominate the discussion nor speak too little.

- **Be ready to answer questions.** Communication, as we've emphasized, is more than just giving people information; it also includes responding to feedback and questions from listeners. Group presentations often include a question-and-answer session (forum) following the presentation. Besides being informed about your topic, it's a wise idea to have thoroughly read any written report the group has distributed.

In Chapter 13 we presented several strategies for responding to questions, including tips for responding to hostile questions. If someone asks a question that has just been asked and answered, or asks an irrelevant or poorly worded question, don't criticize the questioner. Be polite, tactful, and gracious. Rather than self-righteously saying, "That's a dumb question" or "Someone just asked that," calmly provide an answer and move on. If you don't understand a question, just ask for more clarification. Also, don't let a questioner start making a speech. If it looks like a questioner is using the question-and-answer period to give an oration, gently ask, "And what is your question?" or "How can we help you?" This approach should elicit a question that you can then address and return the communication process back to the control of the group.

Public-Relations Speeches

People who work for professional associations, blood banks, utility companies, government agencies, universities, churches, or charitable institutions, as well as those employed by commercial enterprises, are often called on to speak to an audience about what their organization does or about a special project the organization has taken on. These speeches are **public-relations speeches**. They are designed to inform the public and improve relations with them—either in general, or because a particular program or situation has raised some questions.

A public-relations speaker first discusses the need or problem that has prompted the speech. Then he or she goes on to explain how the company or organization is working to meet the need or solve the problem, or why it believes there is no problem.

It is important in public-relations speaking to anticipate criticism. The speaker may acknowledge and counter potential problems or objections, especially if past presenters have encountered some opposition to the policy or program. The speaker should emphasize the positive aspects of the policy or program and take care not to become defensive. He or she wants to leave the impression that the company or organization has carefully worked through potential pitfalls and drawbacks. It should be noted that not all public-relations speeches make policy recommendations. Many

public-relations speech
A speech designed to inform the public, to strengthen alliances with them, and in some cases to recommend policy

confidently connecting with your audience

Seek a Variety of Speaking Opportunities

The more positive experiences you have when speaking publicly, the more likely you are to grow more confident when you speak.[8] Look at new speaking situations as opportunities to increase your confidence so that communication apprehension becomes less of an obstacle when you speak to others.

simply summarize information for those who need to know. For example, local developer Jack Brooks is very aware that many of those present at the city council meeting are opposed to his developing an area of land within the popular Smythson Creek greenbelt. Rather than ignore the objections, he deliberately and carefully addresses them:

> Many of you here tonight played in the Smythson Creek greenbelt as children. It was there that you learned to swim and that you hiked with your friends. I, too, share memories of those experiences.
>
> I want to assure you that my proposed development will actually help to preserve the greenbelt. We will dedicate in perpetuity an acre of unspoiled greenbelt for each acre we develop. Further, we will actively seek to preserve that unspoiled land by hiring an environmental specialist to oversee its protection.
>
> As things stand now, we risk losing the entire greenbelt to pollution and unmanaged use. I can promise a desirable residential development, plus the preservation of at least half the natural environment.

Ceremonial Speaking

Kairos is the Greek term rhetoricians use to describe the circumstances surrounding or the occasion for a speech. If the occasion is one that brings people together to celebrate, thank, or praise someone else, or mourn, a speech given on that occasion is known as a **ceremonial**, or **epideictic, speech**. We will explore nine types of ceremonial speeches: introductions, toasts, award presentations, nominations, acceptances, keynote addresses, commencement addresses, commemorative addresses and tributes, and eulogies.

INTRODUCTIONS

Most of us have heard poor introductions. A nervous speaker making a **speech of introduction** stands up and mispronounces the main speaker's name. Or the introducer speaks for five or ten minutes before yielding to the main speaker. An introductory speech is much like an informative speech. The speaker delivering the introduction provides information to the audience about the main speaker. The ultimate purpose of an introduction, however, is to arouse interest in the speaker and his or her topic. When you are asked to give a speech of introduction for a featured speaker or an honored guest, your purposes are similar to those of a good opening to a speech: You need to get the attention of the audience, build the speaker's credibility, and introduce the speaker's general subject. You also need to make the speaker feel welcome while revealing some of the speaker's personal qualities so that the audience can feel they know the speaker more intimately. There are two cardinal rules for giving introductory speeches: be brief and be accurate.

 Be brief. The audience has come to hear the main speaker or honor the guest, not to listen to you.

 Be accurate. Nothing so disturbs a speaker as having to begin by correcting the introducer. If you are going to introduce someone at a meeting or dinner, ask that person to supply you with biographical data beforehand. If someone else provides you with the speaker's background, make sure the information is accurate. Be certain that you know how to pronounce the speaker's name and any other names or terms you will need to use.

kairos
The circumstances surrounding or the occasion for a speech

ceremonial (epideictic) speech
A speech delivered on a special occasion for celebration, thanksgiving, praise, or mourning

speech of introduction
A speech that provides information about another speaker

The following short speech of introduction adheres to the two criteria we have just suggested: It's brief and it's accurate.

> *This evening, friends, we have the opportunity to hear one of the most innovative mayors in the history of our community. Mary Norris's experience in running her own real-estate business gave her an opportunity to pilot a new approach to attracting new businesses to our community, even before she was elected mayor in last year's landslide victory. She was recently recognized as the most successful mayor in our state by the Good Government League. Not only is she a skilled manager and spokesperson for our city, but she is also a warm and caring person. I am pleased to introduce my friend Mary Norris.*

Finally, keep the needs of your audience in mind at all times. If the person you are introducing truly needs no introduction to the group, do not give one! Just welcome the speaker and step aside. (Note that the President of the United States is always introduced simply: "Ladies and gentlemen, the President of the United States.")

TOASTS

Most people are asked at some time or another to provide a **toast** for some momentous occasion—a wedding, a celebration of the birth of a new baby, a reunion of friends, or a successful business venture. A toast is a brief salute to such an occasion, usually accompanied by a round of drinks and immediately followed by the raising or clinking together of glasses or goblets. The custom is said to have taken its name from the old custom of tossing a bit of bread or a crouton into a beverage for flavoring.[9] "Drinking the toast" was somewhat like enjoying a dunked doughnut.

The modern toast is usually quite short—only a few sentences at most. Some toasts are very personal, as, for example, one given by a wedding guest who is a close friend of both the bride and the groom:

> *I would like to say a few words about this couple. You see, I knew Rachel and Ben before they were a couple—when they were friends. I first met Rachel when we were freshmen in high school. Her sarcastic sense of humor has kept me laughing ever since.*[10]

In contrast, a toast made by someone who does not know the primary celebrants as intimately may be more generic. Here is an example of such a generic wedding toast:

> *When the roaring flames of your love have burned down to embers, may you find that you've married your best friend.*[11]

If you are asked to make an impromptu toast, let your audience and the occasion dictate what you say. Sincerity is more important than wit. At a dinner your authors attended in Moscow a few years ago, all the guests were asked to stand at some point during the meal and offer a toast. Although this Russian custom took us by surprise, one of our friends gave a heartfelt and well-received toast that went something like this:

> *We have spent the past week enjoying both the natural beauty and the man-made marvels of your country. We have visited the exquisite palaces of the czars and stood in amazement before some of the world's great art treasures. But we have also discovered that the most important national resource of Russia is the warmth of her people. Here's to new and lasting friendships.*

Our Russian hosts were most appreciative. The rest of us were impressed. Mary's toast was a resounding success because she spoke sincerely about her audience and the occasion.

toast
A brief salute to a momentous occasion

AWARD PRESENTATIONS

Presenting an award is somewhat like introducing a speaker or a guest: Remember that the audience did not come to hear you, but to see and hear the winner of the award. Nevertheless, delivering a **presentation speech** is an important responsibility, one that has several distinct components.

First, when presenting an award, you should refer to the occasion of the presentation. Awards are often given to mark the anniversary of a special event, the completion of a long-range task, the accomplishments of a lifetime, or high achievement in some field.

Next, you should talk about the history and significance of the award. This section of the speech may be fairly long if the audience knows little about the award; it will be brief if the audience is already familiar with the history and purpose of the award. Whatever the award, a discussion of its significance will add to its meaning for the person who receives it.

The final section of an award presentation will be naming the person to whom the award has been given. The longest part of this segment is the description of the achievements that elicited the award. That description should be given in glowing terms. Hyperbole is appropriate here. If the name of the person getting the award has already been made public, you may refer to him or her by name throughout your description. If you are going to announce the individual's name for the first time, you will probably want to recite the achievements first and leave the person's name for last. Even though some members of the audience may recognize the recipient from your description, you should still save the drama of the actual announcement until the last moment.

NOMINATIONS

presentation speech
A speech that accompanies the presentation of an award

nomination speech
A speech that officially recommends someone as a candidate for an office or position

Nomination speeches are similar to award presentations. They too involve noting the occasion and describing the purpose and significance of, in this case, the office to be filled. The person making the nomination should explain clearly why the nominee's skills, talents, and past achievements serve as qualifications for the position. And the actual nomination should come at the end of the speech. When Senate minority leader Everett Dirksen nominated Barry Goldwater for the Republican presidential candidacy in 1964, he emphasized those personal qualities of the admittedly controversial candidate that he thought would appeal to the audience:

> Whether in commerce or finance, in business or industry, in private or public service, there is such a thing as Competence. What is it but the right vision, the right touch, in the right way, at the right time? What man could be a jet pilot without this touch? But Barry Goldwater has demonstrated it over and over in his every activity. As Chief of Staff of his state National Guard, he brought about its desegregation shortly after World War II and long before Civil Rights became a burning issue. He brought integration to his own retail enterprises. For his own employees he established the five-day week and a health and life insurance plan. All this was done without fanfare or the marching of bands.[12]

And Dirksen ended his speech with the nomination itself:

> I nominate my friend and colleague Barry Goldwater of Arizona to be the Republican candidate for President of the United States.

ACCEPTANCES

Anyone who receives an award or nomination usually responds with a brief **acceptance speech**. Acceptance speeches have received something of a bad name because of the lengthy, emotional, rambling, and generally boring speeches delivered annually on prime-time TV by the winners of the film industry's Oscars. As the late humorist Erma Bombeck once wryly noted,

> People exchange wedding vows in under thirty seconds. . . . You only get thirty seconds to come up with the final "Jeopardy" answer. My kids can demolish a pizza in thirty seconds.
> So how long does it take to say, "Thank you?"[13]

The same audience who may resent a lengthy oration will readily appreciate a brief, heartfelt expression of thanks. In fact, brief acceptance speeches can actually be quite insightful, even inspiring, and can leave the audience feeling no doubt that the right person won the award. Two months before he died in 1979, John Wayne accepted an honorary Oscar with these touching words:

> Thank you, ladies and gentlemen. Your applause is just about the only medicine a fella would ever need. I'm mighty pleased I can amble here tonight. Oscar and I have something in common. Oscar first came on the Hollywood scene in 1928. So did I. We're both a little weatherbeaten, but we're still here and plan to be around a whole lot longer.[14]

If you ever have to give an acceptance speech, it may be impromptu, because you may not know that you have won until the award is presented. A fairly simple formula should help you compose a good acceptance speech on the spur of the moment.

First, you should thank the person making the presentation and the organization that he or she represents. It is also gracious to thank a few people who have contributed greatly to your success—but resist thanking a long list of everyone you have ever known, down to the family dog.

The best acceptance speeches are brief but gracious.

[Photo: Kevin Winter/Getty Images]

acceptance speech
A speech of thanks for an award, nomination, or other honor

Next, you should comment on the meaning or significance of the award to you. You may also wish to reflect on the larger significance of the award to the people and ideals it honors. Elie Wiesel, Holocaust survivor, author, and lifelong advocate of human rights, began his eloquent acceptance speech for the 1986 Nobel Peace Prize with these words:

> It is with a profound sense of humility that I accept the honor you have chosen to bestow upon me. I know your choice transcends me. This both frightens and pleases me.
>
> It frightens me because I wonder: Do I have the right to represent the multitudes who have perished? Do I have the right to accept this great honor on their behalf? I do not. That would be presumptuous. No one may speak for the dead, no one may interpret their mutilated dreams and visions.
>
> It pleases me because I may say that this honor belongs to all the survivors and their children, and through us, to the Jewish people with whose destiny I have always been identified.[15]

Finally, try to find some meaning the award may have for your audience—people who respect your accomplishments and who may themselves aspire to similar achievements. In what has become one of the most often quoted acceptance speeches ever made, novelist William Faulkner dedicated his 1950 Nobel Prize for Literature to

> the young men and women already dedicated to the same anguish and travail, among whom is already that one who will some day stand here where I am standing.[16]

KEYNOTE ADDRESSES

A **keynote address** is usually presented at or near the beginning of a meeting or conference. The keynote emphasizes the importance of the topic or the purpose of the meeting, motivates the audience to learn more or work harder, and sets the theme and tone for other speakers and events.

The hardest task the keynote speaker faces is being specific enough to arouse interest and inspire the audience. One way a keynote speaker can interest and inspire is to incorporate examples and illustrations to which the audience can relate. The late Texas congresswoman Barbara Jordan delivered keynote addresses at two Democratic National Conventions, one in 1976 and the other in 1992. Note how she used specific examples in this excerpt from the 1992 keynote:

> The American dream . . . is slipping away from too many. It is slipping away from too many black and brown mothers and their children; from the homeless of every color and sex; from the immigrants living in communities without water and sewer systems. The American dream is slipping away from the workers whose jobs are no longer there because we are better at building war equipment that sits in warehouses than we are at building decent housing.[17]

COMMENCEMENT ADDRESSES

Cartoonist Garry Trudeau has said that **commencement addresses** "were invented largely in the belief that outgoing college students should never be released into the world until they have been properly sedated."[18] Unfortunately, most commencement speeches deserve Trudeau's assessment. Commencement speakers are often oblivious to the audience on an occasion that demands and deserves audience-centeredness. To be audience-centered, a commencement speaker must fulfill two important functions.

First, the commencement speaker should praise the graduating class. Because the audience includes the families and friends of the graduates, the commencement speaker can gain their goodwill (as well as that of the graduates themselves) by pointing out the significance of the graduates' accomplishments. Texas State Repre-

keynote address
A speech that sets the theme and tone for a meeting or conference

commencement address
A speech delivered at a graduation or commencement ceremony

sentative Patrick Rose congratulated 2006 graduates of Texas State University–San Marcos with these words:

> Texas State excels today because its students—each of you who graduate today— you are among the best in Texas and among the best in America.[19]

A second function of an audience-centered commencement speaker is to turn graduates toward the future. A commencement address is not the proper forum in which to bemoan the world's inevitable destruction or the certain gloomy economic future of today's graduates. Rather, commencement speakers should suggest bright new goals and try to inspire the graduates to reach for them, as U.S. Ambassador to Mexico Antonio Garza told 2006 University of Texas graduates:

> Life will test you in ways you cannot imagine. And one of the ways it will test you— over and over—is how you treat others who don't look like you, talk like you or earn like you.[20]

Commencement speakers who want to be audience-centered can learn from Hewlett Packard CEO Carly S. Fiorina, who consulted by e-mail with the graduating class of the Massachusetts Institute of Technology, whom she was scheduled to address. She discovered that students wanted a speech based on life experience, not theory, and advice on how to make the decisions needed to live life. And, Fiorina adds, "On one point there was complete unanimity: Please don't run over your time."[21]

COMMEMORATIVE ADDRESSES AND TRIBUTES

Commemorative addresses—those delivered during ceremonies held to celebrate some past event—are often combined with tributes to the person or persons involved. For example, a speech given on the Fourth of July both commemorates the signing of the Declaration of Independence and pays tribute to those who signed it. Your town's sesquicentennial celebrates both the founding and the founders of the town. And if you were asked to speak at the reception for your grandparents' fiftieth wedding anniversary, you would probably relate the stories they've told you of their wedding day and then go on to praise their accomplishments during their fifty years together.

The speaker who commemorates or pays tribute is, in part, an informative speaker. He or she needs to present some facts about the event and/or the people being celebrated. Then the speaker builds on those facts, urging the audience to let past accomplishments inspire them to achieve new goals. Speaking at Pointe du Hoc, France, during June 1994 ceremonies to commemorate the fifty-year anniversary of D-Day, President Bill Clinton paid tribute to the assembled veterans:

> We are the children of your sacrifice. We are the sons and daughters you saved from tyranny's reach. We grew up behind the shield of the strong alliances you forged in blood upon these beaches, on the shores of the Pacific and in the skies above us. We flourished in the nation you came home to build. The most difficult days of your lives bought us fifty years of freedom.[22]

His tribute completed, Clinton added this challenge:

> Let us carry on the work you began here. You completed your mission here, but the mission of freedom goes on; the battle continues.

EULOGIES

A **eulogy**—a speech of tribute delivered when someone has died—can be one of the most significant and memorable and also one of the most challenging forms of commemorative address. As the editor of a recent collection of eulogies notes,

commemorative address
A speech delivered during ceremonies held in memory of some past event and/or the person or persons involved

eulogy
A speech of tribute delivered when someone has died

A good eulogy can be . . . a bridge between the living and the dead, between us and them, memory and eternity. The more specific and real the remembrances spoken, the stronger the bridge.[23]

When you deliver a eulogy, you should mention—indeed, linger on—the unique achievements of the person to whom you are paying tribute, and, of course, express a sense of loss. It is also proper in a eulogy to include personal and even humorous recollections of the person who has died. In his eulogy for his beloved Aunt Betty, Texas Lutheran University Provost John T. Masterson, Jr., related this humorous story:

Whereas other relatives sent books, clothing, or sensible toys for Christmas and birthdays, Aunt Betty tended toward the offbeat. . . . There was the year she (or the mail order house) got the order number wrong and sent me reflective driveway markers for Christmas. The thing about Aunt Betty was that if you received a gift like that, you didn't recognize it as a mistake; instead, my family and I sat around the Christmas tree trying to figure out the joke![24]

Finally, turn to the living, and encourage them to transcend their sorrow and sense of loss and feel instead gratitude that the dead person was once alive among them. In his eulogy for Gerald Ford, former Secretary of State Henry Kissinger told Ford's grieving friends and family,

Having lived with him will be a badge of honour for the rest of our lives.[25]

After-Dinner Speaking: Using Humor Effectively

If you are a human being or even a reasonably alert shrub, chances are that sooner or later a club or organization will ask you to give a speech. The United States is infested with clubs and organizations, constantly engaging in a variety of worthwhile group activities such as (1) eating lunch; (2) eating dinner; (3) eating breakfast; and of course (4) holding banquets. The result is that there is a constant demand for post-meal speakers, because otherwise all you'd hear would be the sounds of digestion.[26]

With typically irreverent wit, columnist Dave Barry thus begins his observations of the activity known as after-dinner speaking. Certainly he is right about one thing: the popularity of mealtime meetings and banquets with business and professional organizations and service clubs. And such meetings inevitably require an **after-dinner speech**.

Interestingly, not only is the after-dinner speech not always after *dinner* (as Barry points out, the meal is just as likely to be breakfast or lunch), but it is also not always *after* anything. The after-dinner speech may also be delivered before the meal or even between courses. Former First Lady Barbara Bush preferred to schedule speeches first and dinner later during state dinners. In another variation, Librarian of Congress James Billington, at a dinner in honor of philosopher Alexis de Tocqueville, served up one speech between each course, "so that one had to earn the next course by listening to the speech preceding it."[27] Regardless of the variation, the after-dinner speech is something of an institution, and one with which a public speaker should be prepared to cope.

After-dinner speeches may present information or persuade, but their primary purpose is to entertain—arguably the most inherently audience-centered of the three general purposes for speaking discussed in Chapter 6.

after-dinner speech
An entertaining speech, usually delivered in conjunction with a mealtime meeting or banquet

HUMOROUS TOPICS

Because humor is listener-centered, the central question for the after-dinner speaker seeking a topic must be this: What do audiences find funny?

The Comedy Gym in Austin, Texas, a school for aspiring stand-up comedians, advocates that speakers start with "themselves, their lives, what makes them laugh."[28] Audiences almost always enjoy hearing a speaker poke fun at himself or herself. Comedy writer John Macks points out that self-deprecating humor is "an instant way to establish a rapport with an audience."[29]

Even serious subjects can lend themselves to humorous presentations. One speechwriter notes that humor can help a speaker achieve rapport with the audience and can help the audience remember the speaker's message:

> If you can find a way to make a point with humor, you've improved the odds of making your message stick. For example, say you're expecting a tax increase, and you want to let your audience know. You might say, "Well, Congress has finally decided how to divide up the pie; trouble is, we're *the pie*."[30]

Increased taxes, not an inherently humorous topic, can still be treated humorously. So can other serious topics. Earlier in this chapter we discussed the use of humor in eulogies. Gun control and the U.S. health care industry, two subjects tackled by Michael Moore in the films *Bowling for Columbine* and *Sicko*, respectively, are additional examples of serious topics made more palatable to listeners by the use of humor. For example, in *Sicko*,

> a scrolling text of the pre-existing medical conditions that insurance companies use to reject prospective applicants is set to the Star Wars *theme against an outer-space backdrop*.[31]

Although Moore's medium is film, rather than speech, the same principle applies: Many serious subjects can be treated with humor.

Are any subjects *in*appropriate for an after-dinner speech? In June 2007, comedian Robin Williams appeared on *The Tonight Show with Jay Leno* to talk about his film *License to Wed*, in which Williams plays a Protestant minister. Spinning off from that character, Williams launched into a comic treatment of pedophilia among Catholic priests, provoking outrage from Catholic organizations.

While Williams's comic routines often push boundaries of propriety and taste, audience-centered public speakers should exercise greater restraint. Because it is the audience that "gives attempts at humor their success or failure,"[32] topics that might create a great deal of emotional noise (such as grief or anger) for particular audiences would not be good topics for humorous speeches to those groups. A humorous treatment of childhood cancer would most likely only distress an audience of parents who had lost children to that disease.

HUMOROUS STORIES

Humorous stories should be simple. Complicated stories and jokes are rarely perceived by audiences as funny. Jay Leno claims that "Jokes work best when they're easy to understand."[33]

Successful after-dinner speakers also need a broad repertoire. The austere, even dour reputation of British Prime Minister Gordon Brown, can be blamed at least in part on lines intended to be funny but that suffer from "the absence of new [humorous] material."[34] One successful after-dinner speaker says that she tries

> to get about 25 to 30 jokes, anecdotes or one-liners before I write the speech. This will be reduced to the best and most appropriate 6 or 7, but one needs as much material as possible to begin with.[35]

Finally, it is important to know your anecdotes very well. Nothing deflates a humorous story more than getting halfway through and then saying, "Oh, and I forgot to tell you. . . ." Rehearse your jokes. Only if you know the material can you hope to deliver it with the intonation and timing that will make it funny.

HUMOROUS VERBAL STRATEGIES

Either a humorous anecdote or a shorter "one-liner" may rely on one of the following verbal strategies for humorous effect.

PLAYS ON WORDS Most of us are familiar with the use of such verbal devices as **puns**, which rely on double meanings, to create humor. For example, the old joke in which an exasperated speaker tries to explain the meaning of "hide" by shouting, "Hide! Hide! A cow's outside!" provokes the response, "I'm not afraid of cows." The joke relies on the pun on the words *hide* and *outside*.

Another play on words is the **spoonerism**, named for William Spooner, a professor at Oxford University in the 1930s, who frequently used it (inadvertently, in his case). A spoonerism occurs when someone switches the initial sounds of words in a single phrase: "sublic peaking" instead of "public speaking," for example. In one joke that relies on a spoonerism, the Chatanooga Choo-choo becomes the "cat who chewed the new shoes." Many parodies and satires employ spoonerisms to avoid charges of libel or copyright infringement; a spoonerism might be employed to name a boy wizard "Perry Hotter."

A third play on words is the **malapropism**, named for the unfortunate Mrs. Malaprop in Richard Brinsley Sheridan's eighteenth-century play *The School for Scandal*. A malapropism is the mistaken use of a word that sounds much like the intended word: "destruction" for "instruction," for example. Archie Bunker, on the 1970s TV series *All in the Family*, achieved much of his humor through malapropisms.

HYPERBOLE **Hyperbole**, or exaggeration, is often funny. In an after-dinner speech on "The Alphabet and Simplified Spelling," Mark Twain claimed,

> *Simplified spelling brought about sun-spots, the San Francisco earthquake, and the recent business depression, which we would never have had if spelling had been left all alone.*[36]

Of course, spelling could not have caused such catastrophes, but by using hyperbole, Twain makes his point in a humorous way.

UNDERSTATEMENT The opposite of hyperbole, **understatement** involves downplaying a fact or event. Microsoft founder and Harvard dropout Bill Gates downplayed his meteoric success by telling the Harvard class of 2007,

> *I did the best of everyone who failed.*[37]

VERBAL IRONY A speaker who employs **verbal irony** says just the opposite of what he or she really means. Student Chris O'Keefe opens his speech on reading Shakespeare with the following statement:

> *At a certain point in my life, I came to the realization that I wanted to spend my life's effort to become a great playwright.*[38]

Chris reveals the verbal irony of the statement when he continues,

> *It has been about an hour and a half now and the feeling is still going strong.*

WIT One of the most frequently used verbal strategies for achieving humor is the use of **wit**: relating an incident that takes an unexpected turn at the end. Research suggests that witty humor may enhance a speaker's credibility.[39] Accepting the 2007 Oscar for Best Actress, Helen Mirren paid tribute to the monarch she had portrayed on screen:

pun
The use of double meanings to create humor

spoonerism
A phrase in which the initial sounds of words are switched

malapropism
The mistaken use of a word that sounds much like the intended word

hyperbole
Exaggeration

understatement
Downplaying a fact or event

verbal irony
Saying the opposite of what one means

wit
Relating an incident that takes an unexpected turn at the end

Strategies for Achieving Humor in After-Dinner Speeches

Humorous Topics	Inherently funny subjects or humorous treatments of more serious subjects
Humorous Stories	Funny anecdotes
Humorous Verbal Strategies	
Plays on words	Intentional errors such as puns, spoonerisms, and malapropisms
Hyperbole	Exaggeration
Understatement	Downplaying a fact or event
Verbal irony	Saying just the opposite of what one means
Wit	An unexpected turn at the end of a fact or incident
Humorous Nonverbal Strategies	Physical or vocal elements such as posture, gesture, pauses, and intonation

For 50 years and more, Elizabeth Windsor has maintained her dignity, her sense of duty and her hairstyle.[40]

The wit occurs in the final phrase "her hairstyle," which catches off-guard the audience anticipating another majestic attribute.

HUMOROUS NONVERBAL STRATEGIES

After-dinner speakers often create humor through such nonverbal cues as posture, gesture, and voice. Well-timed pauses are especially crucial delivery cues for after-dinner speakers to master. One experienced after-dinner speaker advocates "a slight pause before the punch line, then pause while the audience is laughing."[41]

It is true that some people seem to be "naturally" funny. If you are not one of them—if, for example, you struggle to get a laugh from even the funniest joke—you may still be able to use the strategies outlined above to prepare and deliver an after-dinner speech that is lighthearted and clever, if not uproariously funny. Such a speech can still be a success.

LEARNING FROM GREAT SPEAKERS

Dave Barry (1947–)

Syndicated columnist and Pulitzer Prize–winning commentator Dave Barry is much in demand as a special-occasion speaker at conferences, corporate meetings, writers' and speakers' group, and great speakers series. A recent review of a speech Barry presented at the New York State Writer's Institute credits his success as a humorous speaker to his wit, sense of timing, and ability to tell a story well.[42]

Much of Dave Barry's humor comes from seeing everyday events in a new light. As you consider adding humor to your talks, look for the humor in your own life and the lives of your listeners. Poking fun at yourself can especially help you score points with your audience.

[Photo: Jason Connel/Getty Images]

SUMMARY

Chances are that at some time you will be called on to speak in a business or professional setting or on some occasion that calls for celebration, commemoration, inspiration, or entertainment. These special-occasion speeches require the speaker to use critical thinking to apply his or her speaking skills to unique situations.

Public-speaking skills are used frequently in the workplace when making group presentations or representing your company or profession before the public.

These two professional speaking challenges each have unique requirements.

Ceremonial speeches include introductions, toasts, award presentations, nominations, acceptances, keynote addresses, commencement addresses, commemorative addresses and tributes, and eulogies.

Finally, after-dinner speaking is an established institution in which speakers entertain through the use of humorous topics and stories, humorous verbal strategies, and humorous nonverbal strategies.

BEING AUDIENCE-CENTERED: A SHARPER FOCUS

CONSIDERING YOUR AUDIENCE

- When you make a business presentation, tell the members of your audience what benefits will accrue to them directly as a result of your proposal.

- It is important in public-relations speaking to anticipate criticism.

- As when you introduce a speaker, when you present an award, remember that the audience did not come to hear you. Be brief.

- A commencement is an occasion that demands and deserves audience-centeredness.

- When called on to deliver a eulogy, encourage your audience to transcend their sorrow and sense of loss and instead feel gratitude that the dead person was once alive among them.

CONSIDERING AUDIENCE DIVERSITY

- Workplace audiences may range from a group of three managers to a huge auditorium filled with company employees.

CRITICAL THINKING QUESTIONS

1. Maya has to present her first report to her colleagues at work. You and she became friends when you took public speaking as college sophomores, and she has called to ask your advice in preparing for this oral presentation. Explain to Maya how she can apply some of the principles and skills the two of you learned in public-speaking class as she presents her report.

2. Pulitzer Prize–winning poet Rita Dove is coming to campus for a series of readings and lectures. Because you are president of the English Club, you have been asked to introduce Dove at her opening reading. What will you do to ensure that you follow the two cardinal rules of introductory speeches?

ETHICAL QUESTIONS

1. On the Web site <www.customeulogies.com>, you can purchase a library of 50 "fill-in-the-blank" eulogies for $19.95, or get a custom eulogy in 12 hours or less for $49.95. If you were asked to deliver a eulogy, would it be ethical to buy such a speech?

2. You have been a member of the jury during a highly publicized and controversial murder trial in your community. After the verdict is delivered, you find yourself in great demand as a keynote speaker for meetings of local organizations. Several offer to pay you well. Is it ethical to "cash in" on your experiences in this way?

SPEECH WORKSHOP

Introducing a Speaker

Use the following worksheet to help you prepare a brief, accurate introduction of another speaker.

Person's name:

Educational background:

Experience related to the topic he/she will discuss:

Awards and recognition received:

Personal characteristics (e.g., hard working, caring, selfless volunteer):

Epilogue

Your completion of this course is the commencement of your continuing development as a public speaker.

[Photo: © Bill Aron/PhotoEdit]

Now that you are about to complete your public-speaking course, you may barely be able to resist the temptation to pat yourself on the back. Before taking this course, you, like the survey population we mentioned in Chapter 1, may have feared public speaking more than death! But you have survived and perhaps even excelled. Now you can file away your notes and will never have to give another speech, right? Wrong!

There is indeed life after public-speaking class—a life that will demand frequent practice and sharpening of the skills to which you have been introduced in this course. Your classroom experience has taught you how to become a better public speaker. We hope that it has also taught you to become your own best critic—able to say, "I need to make more eye contact," or "I need a statistic to prove this point," or "I need a transition here." But one course cannot make you a polished speaker. Learning to speak in public is an ongoing process rather than a static goal.

In the years to come, both in college and beyond, you will use and continue to develop your public-speaking skills in many areas of your professional and personal life. In Chapter 2, we discussed some of the skills you would learn and practice as a public speaker: organization, audience analysis and adaptation, research, effective presentation, and critical listening. Certainly you will find yourself applying these skills to numerous situations—to speaking opportunities, of course, but also to other situations that require critical listening and analytic thinking. As you take other courses, apply for a job, prepare a report for your company, attend city council meetings, and go about your day-to-day personal business, you will find yourself using the skills you learned in your public-speaking class.

Of course, chances are that you will also find yourself in a number of actual public-speaking situations. Perhaps you will give few "laboratory" speeches like those you have given in your speech class. But you will undoubtedly deliver one or more of the

types of special-occasion speeches that we discussed in Chapter 18. You will make a business presentation, introduce a speaker, present or receive an award, deliver a speech to commemorate a person or an occasion, give a book review, make a sales pitch. And you will look back to this course for guidance.

Realistically, you will not remember every detail of the course or of this book. But we hope that you will remember the bottom line: that to be effective, public speaking must be *audience-centered*. Every step of the public-speaking process, from selecting and narrowing the topic, to preparing the speech, to final delivery, must be approached with the audience in mind. If the audience does not understand your message or does not respond as you had hoped, your speech cannot be a success, regardless of the hours of research or rehearsal you may have dedicated to the task.

One final note about the audience-centered approach is in order here: Being audience-centered is not the same as being manipulative. As we discussed in Chapter 2, if you adapt to your audience to the extent that you abandon your own values and sense of truth, you have become an unethical speaker rather than an audience-centered one. An audience-centered speaker does not tell an audience only what its members want to hear.

One type of special-occasion speech discussed in Chapter 18 was the commencement address. Your completion of this course is also the commencement—the beginning—of your continuing development as a public speaker. The traditional theme of the commencement speaker is "Go forth. You have been prepared for the future." We leave you with that thought: Go forth. You have been prepared for the future.

Speaking in Small Groups

Groups are an integral part of our lives. Work groups, family groups, therapy groups, committees, and class-project groups are just a few of the groups in which we may participate at one time or another. Chances are that you have had considerable experience in communicating in small groups.

Why learn about group communication in a public-speaking class? Aristotle identified the link between public speaking and group discussion over two thousand years ago when he wrote "Rhetoric is the counterpart of dialectic." He meant that our efforts to persuade are closely linked to our group efforts to search for truth.

In Aristotle's time, people gathered to discuss and decide public issues in a democratic manner. Today we still turn to a committee, jury, or task force to get facts and make recommendations. We still "search for truth" in groups. And, as in ancient Athens, once we believe we have found the truth, we present the message to others in speeches and lectures.

In this Appendix, you will learn some key communication principles and skills to help you work as a productive member of a small group. Specifically, you will discover what small group communication is, learn ways to improve group problem solving, enhance your leadership skills, and become an effective group participant or group leader.[1]

What is **small group communication**? It is interaction among from three to a dozen people who share a common purpose, feel a sense of belonging to the group, and influence one another. Communication in groups larger than twelve people usually resembles public speaking more than small group communication.

Working in groups has several advantages compared to working on projects alone. Groups typically make better-quality decisions than do individuals for several reasons:[2]

- Groups usually have more information available.
- Groups are often more creative; the very presence of others can spark innovation.

small group communication
Interaction among from three to twelve people who share a common purpose, feel a sense of belonging to the group, and influence one another

- When you work in groups, you're more likely to remember what you discussed, because you're actively involved in processing information.
- Group participation usually results in group members being more satisfied with their results than if someone just told them what to do.

Although we've characterized working in groups as a positive experience, you also know that working in groups can be challenging. Here are some of the potential disadvantages of working in groups:[3]

- Group members may use excessive pressure to get others to conform to their point of view.
- One person may dominate the discussion.
- Group members may rely too much on others and may not do their part.
- Group work is more time-consuming; many people consider this the biggest disadvantage.

The goal of this chapter is to help decrease the disadvantages and increase the advantages of working with others.

Is there a difference between a group and a team? Yes. A **team** is a coordinated small group of people organized to work together, with clearly defined roles and responsibilities, explicitly stated rules for operation, and well-defined goals.[4] A team is a special kind of group that, as our definition suggests, coordinates its efforts through a clearly defined structure of who does what. All teams are groups, but not all groups are teams. Think of a sports team in which members play by rules, have assigned roles, and have a clear objective—to win the game. Work teams too have well-defined procedures for accomplishing tasks. Teams are formed for a variety of reasons, such as to sell products, get a political candidate elected, or build an international space station.

Solving Problems in Groups and Teams

central purpose of many groups and teams is solving problems. Problem solving is a means of finding ways of overcoming obstacles to achieve a desired goal: How can we raise money for the new library? What should be done to improve the local economy? How can we make higher education affordable for everyone in our state? Each of these questions implies that there is an obstacle (lack of money) blocking the achievement of a desired goal (new library, stronger local economy, affordable education).

Imagine that you have been asked to suggest ways to make a college education more affordable. The problem: The high cost of higher education keeps many people from their goal of attending college. How would you begin to organize a group to solve this problem? In 1910, John Dewey, a philosopher and educator, identified the way most individuals tackle a problem.[5] He called his method of problem solving **reflective thinking**. His multistep method has been adapted by many groups as a way to organize the process of solving problems. Here are his suggestions: (1) Identify and define the problem, (2) analyze the problem, (3) generate possible solutions, (4)

team

A coordinated small group of people organized to work together, with clearly defined roles and responsibilities, explicit rules, and well-defined goals

reflective thinking

A method of structuring a problem-solving discussion that involves (1) identifying and defining the problem, (2) analyzing the problem, (3) generating possible solutions, (4) selecting the best solution, and (5) testing and implementing the solution

select the best solution, and (5) test and implement the solution. Although not every problem-solving discussion has to follow these steps, reflective thinking does provide a helpful blueprint that can relieve some of the uncertainty that exists when groups try to solve problems.

1. IDENTIFY AND DEFINE THE PROBLEM

Groups work best when they define their problem clearly and early in their problem-solving process. To reach a clear definition, the group should consider the following questions:

- What is the specific problem that concerns us?
- What terms, concepts, or ideas do we need to understand in order to solve the problem?
- Who is harmed by the problem?
- When do the harmful effects occur?

Policy questions can help define a problem and also identify the course of action that should be taken to solve it. As you recall from Chapter 16, policy questions often begin with phrases such as "What should be done about" or "What could be done to improve." Here are some examples:

- What should be done to improve security at U.S. airports?
- What should be done to increase employment in our state?
- What steps could be taken to improve the U.S. trade balance with other countries?

If your group were investigating the high cost of pursuing a college education, for example, after defining such key terms as "higher education" and "college" and gathering statistics about the magnitude of the problem, you could phrase your policy question this way: "What could be done to reduce the high cost of attending college?"

2. ANALYZE THE PROBLEM

Ray Kroc, founder of McDonald's, said, "Nothing is particularly hard if you divide it into small jobs." Once the group understands the problem and has a well-worded question, the next step is to analyze the problem. **Analysis** is a process of examining the causes, effects, symptoms, history, and other background information that will help a group eventually reach a solution. When analyzing a problem, a group should consider the following questions:

- What is the history of the problem?
- How extensive is the problem?
- What are the causes, effects, and symptoms of the problem?
- Can the problem be subdivided for further definition and analysis?
- What methods do we already have for solving the problem, and what are their limitations?
- What obstacles might keep us from reaching a solution?

To analyze the problem of the high cost of attending college, your discussion group will have to use a library or the Internet to research the history of the problem and existing methods of solving it (see Chapter 7).

Included in the process of analyzing the problem is identifying criteria. **Criteria** are standards for identifying an acceptable solution. They help you recognize a good solution when you discover one; criteria also help the group stay focused on its goal. Typical criteria for an acceptable solution specify that the solution should be imple-

analysis
Examination of the causes, effects, and history of a problem to understand it better

criteria
Standards for identifying an acceptable solution to a problem

mented on schedule, should be agreed to by all group members, should be achieved within a given budget, and should remove the obstacles causing the problem.

3. GENERATE POSSIBLE SOLUTIONS

When your discussion group has identified, defined, and analyzed the problem, you will be ready to generate possible solutions using group brainstorming (see Chapter 6). Use the following guidelines:

- **Set aside judgment and criticism.** Criticism and faultfinding stifle creativity. If group members find withholding judgment difficult, have the individual members write suggestions on paper first and then share the ideas with the group.

- **Think of as many possible solutions to the problem as you can.** All ideas are acceptable, even wild and crazy ones. Piggyback off one another's ideas. All members must come up with at least one idea.

- **Have a member of the group record all the ideas that are mentioned.** Use a flipchart or chalkboard, if possible, so that all group members can see and respond to the ideas.

- **After a set time has elapsed, evaluate the ideas, using criteria the group has established.** Approach the solutions positively. Do not be quick to dismiss an idea, but do voice any concerns or questions you might have. The group can brainstorm again later if it needs more creative ideas.

Some groups have found it useful to use technology to help them generate options and possible solutions.[6] For example, group members can brainstorm possible solutions to a problem individually, then e-mail their list of ideas to each other. Or the group's leader could collect all of the ideas, eliminate duplicate suggestions, and then share them with the group. Research suggests that groups can generate more ideas if group members first generate ideas individually and then collaborate.[7]

4. SELECT THE BEST SOLUTION

Next, the group needs to select the solution that best meets the criteria and solves the problem. At this point, the group may need to modify its criteria or even its definition of the problem.

Research suggests that after narrowing the list of possible solutions, the most effective groups carefully consider the pros and the cons of each proposed solution.[8] Groups that don't do this often make poor decisions because they haven't carefully evaluated the implications of their solution; they haven't looked before they leaped.

To help in evaluating the solution, consider the following questions:

- Which of the suggested solutions deals best with the obstacles?
- Does the suggestion solve the problem in both the short term and the long term?
- What are the advantages and disadvantages of the suggested solution?
- Does the solution meet the established criteria?
- Should the group revise its criteria?
- What is required to implement the solution?
- When can the group implement the solution?
- What result will indicate success?

If the group is to reach agreement on a solution, some group members will need to abandon their attachment to their individual ideas for the overall good of the group. Experts who have studied how to achieve **consensus**—support for the final

consensus
The support and commitment of all group members to the decision of the group

Steps in Problem Solving

1. Identify and clearly define the problem.
2. Analyze the problem and identify criteria.
3. Generate possible solutions.
4. Select the best solution.
5. Test and implement the solution.

decision by all members—suggest that summarizing frequently and keeping the group oriented toward its goal are helpful. Emphasizing where group members agree, clarifying misunderstandings, writing down known facts for all members to see, and keeping the discussion focused on issues rather than on emotions are also strategies that facilitate group consensus.[9]

5. TEST AND IMPLEMENT THE SOLUTION

The group's work is not finished when it has identified a solution. "How can we put the solution into practice?" and "How can we evaluate the quality of the solution?" have yet to be addressed. The group may want to develop a step-by-step plan that describes the process for implementing the solution, a time frame for implementation, and a list of individuals who will be responsible for carrying out specific tasks.

 Participating in Small Groups

To be an effective group participant, you have to understand how to manage the problem-solving process. But knowing the steps is not enough; you also need to prepare for meetings, evaluate evidence, effectively summarize the group's progress, listen courteously, and be sensitive to conflict.

COME PREPARED FOR GROUP DISCUSSIONS

To contribute to group meetings, you need to be informed about the issues. Prepare for group discussions by researching the issues. If the issue before your group is the use of asbestos in school buildings, for example, research the most recent scientific findings about the risks of this hazardous material. Chapter 7 described how to use the library and the Internet to gather information for your speeches. Use those research techniques to prepare for group deliberations as well. Bring your research notes to the group; don't just rely on your memory or your personal opinion to carry you through the discussion. Without research, you will not be able to analyze the problem adequately.

DO NOT SUGGEST SOLUTIONS BEFORE ANALYZING THE PROBLEM

Research suggests that you should analyze a problem thoroughly before trying to zero in on a solution.[10] Resist the temptation to settle quickly on one solution until your group has systematically examined the causes, effects, history, and symptoms of a problem.

EVALUATE EVIDENCE

One study found that a key difference between groups that make successful decisions and those that don't is group members' ability to examine and evaluate evidence.[11] Ineffective groups are more likely to reach decisions quickly without considering the validity of evidence (or sometimes without any evidence at all). Such groups usually reach flawed conclusions.

HELP SUMMARIZE THE GROUP'S PROGRESS

Because it is easy for groups to get off the subject, group members need to summarize frequently what has been achieved and to point the group toward the goal or task at hand. One research study suggests that periodic overviews of the discussion's progress can help the group stay on target.[12] Ask questions about the discussion process rather than about the topic under consideration: "Where are we now?" "Could someone summarize what we have accomplished?" and "Aren't we getting off the subject?"

LISTEN AND RESPOND COURTEOUSLY TO OTHERS

Chapter 4's suggestions for improving listening skills are useful when you work in groups, but understanding what others say is not enough. You also need to respect their points of view. Even if you disagree with someone's ideas, keep your emotions in check and respond courteously. Being closed-minded and defensive usually breeds group conflict.

HELP MANAGE CONFLICT

In the course of exchanging ideas and opinions about controversial issues, disagreements are bound to occur.[13] You can help prevent conflicts from derailing the problem-solving process by doing the following:

- Keep the discussion focused on issues, not on personalities.
- Rely on facts rather than on personal opinions for evidence.
- Seek ways to compromise; don't assume that there must be a winner and a loser.
- Try to clarify misunderstandings in meaning.
- Be descriptive rather than evaluative and judgmental.
- Keep emotions in check.

If you can apply these basic principles, you can help make your group an effective problem-solving team.

Leading Small Groups

Rudyard Kipling wrote, "For the strength of the pack is the wolf, and the strength of the wolf is the pack." Group members typically need a leader to help the group collaborate effectively and efficiently, and a leader needs followers in order to lead. In essence, **leadership** is the process of influencing others through communication. Some see a leader as one individual empowered to delegate work and direct the group. In reality, however, group leadership is often shared.

leadership
The process of influencing others through communication

Leadership Responsibilities

Leaders are needed to help get tasks accomplished and maintain a healthy social climate for the group. Rarely does one person perform all these leadership responsibilities, even if a leader is formally appointed or elected. Most often a number of individual group members assume some specific leadership task, based on their personalities, skills, sensitivity, and the group's needs. If you determine that the group needs a clearer focus on the task or that maintenance roles are needed, be ready to influence the group appropriately to help get the job done in a positive, productive way. Table AA.1 lists specific roles for both *task* leaders and *maintenance* leaders.

Leadership Styles

Leaders can be described by the types of behavior, or leadership styles, that they exhibit as they influence the group to help achieve its goal. When you are called on to

Table AA.1 Leadership Roles in Groups and Teams

	Leadership Role	Description
Task leaders	Agenda setter	Helps establish the group's agenda
Help get tasks accomplished	Secretary	Takes notes during meetings and distributes handouts before and during the meeting
	Initiator	Proposes new ideas or approaches to group problem solving
	Information seeker	Asks for facts or other information that helps the group deal with the issues and may also ask for clarification of ideas or obscure facts
	Opinion seeker	Asks for clarification of the values and opinions expressed by group members
	Information giver	Provides facts, examples, statistics, and other evidence that helps the group achieve its task
	Opinion giver	Offers opinions about the ideas under discussion
	Elaborator	Provides examples to show how ideas or suggestions would work
	Evaluator	Makes an effort to judge the evidence and the conclusion the group reaches
	Energizer	Tries to spur the group to further action and productivity
Group maintenance leaders	Encourager	Offers praise, understanding, and acceptance of others' ideas
Help maintain a healthy social climate	Harmonizer	Mediates disagreements that occur between group members
	Compromiser	Attempts to resolve conflicts by trying to find an acceptable middle ground between disagreeing group members
	Gatekeeper	Encourages the participation of less talkative group members and tries to limit lengthy contributions of other group members

Source: Adapted from Kenneth D. Benne and Paul Sheats, "Functional Roles of Group Members," *Journal of Social Issues* 4 (Spring 1948): 41–49.

lead, do you give orders and expect others to follow you? Or do you ask the group to vote on the course of action to follow? Or maybe you don't try to influence the group at all. Perhaps you prefer to hang back and let the group work out its own problems.

These strategies describe three general leadership styles: *authoritarian, democratic,* and *laissez-faire.*[14] Authoritarian leaders assume positions of superiority, giving orders and assuming control of the group's activity. Although authoritarian leaders can usually organize group activities with a high degree of efficiency and virtually eliminate uncertainty about who should do what, most problem-solving groups prefer democratic leaders.

Having more faith in their groups than do authoritarian leaders, democratic leaders involve group members in the decision-making process rather than dictating what should be done. Democratic leaders focus more on guiding discussion than on issuing commands.

Laissez-faire leaders allow group members complete freedom in all aspects of the decision-making process. They do little to help the group achieve its goal. This style of leadership (or nonleadership) often leaves a group frustrated because it lacks guidance and has to struggle with organizing the work. Table AA.2 compares the three styles.

What is the most effective leadership style? Research suggests that no single style is effective in every group situation. Sometimes a group needs a strong authoritarian leader to make decisions quickly so that the group can achieve its goal. Although most groups prefer a democratic leadership style, leaders sometimes need to assert their authority to get the job done. The best leadership style depends on the nature of the group task, the power of the leader, and the relationship between the leader and his or her followers.

One contemporary approach to leadership is transformational leadership. Transformational leadership is not so much a particular style of leadership as it is a quality

Table AA.2 Leadership Styles

	Authoritarian Leaders	Democratic Leaders	Laissez-Faire Leaders
Group Policy Formation	All determinations of policy are made by the leader.	All policies are a matter of group discussion and decision; leader assigns and encourages group discussion and decision making.	Complete freedom for individual or group decisions; minimal leader participation
Group Activity Development	Group techniques and activities are dictated by the leader, one at a time; future steps are always largely unknown to group members.	Discussion yields broad perspectives and general steps to the group goal; when technical advice is needed, leader suggests alternative procedures.	Leader supplies various materials, making it clear that he or she can supply information when asked, but takes no other part in the discussion.
Source of Work Assignments	Leader dictates specific work tasks and teams; leader tends to remain aloof from active group participation except when directing activities.	Members are free to work with anyone; group decides on division of tasks.	Complete non-participation by leader
Praise/ Criticism	Leader tends to be personal in praise or criticism of each member.	Leader is objective and fact-oriented in praise and criticism, trying to be a regular group member in spirit without doing too much of the work.	Leader offers infrequent spontaneous comments on member activities and makes no attempt to appraise or control the course of events.

Using Parliamentary Procedure to Give Structure to Large Groups

Some say that chairing a large group meeting is like herding cats. It's difficult. We have noted that effective meetings need a balance of two things: structure and interaction. When you try to lead a very large group, you need to impose considerable structure to help you keep the group focused on its goals.

Parliamentary procedure is a system of rules and formal procedures to help keep a very large group organized. We emphasize that a small group does not need to use parliamentary procedure—it would be overkill. But if you are faced with the opportunity and challenge of chairing a large group or a formal meeting, knowing what motions need a two-thirds majority to be approved and what "call the question" means can be very valuable. The basic parliamentary procedure information that you need in order to organize a group may be found at

➤ ROBERT'S RULES OF ORDER
www.robertsrules.com

transformational leadership

The process of influencing others by building a shared vision of the future, inspiring others to achieve, developing high-quality individual relationships with others, and helping people see how what they do is related to a larger framework or system

or characteristic of relating to others.[15] **Transformational leadership** is the process of influencing others by building a shared vision of the future, inspiring others to achieve, developing high-quality individual relationships with others, and helping people see how what they do is related to a larger framework or system. To be a transformational leader is not just to perform specific tasks or skills, but to have a philosophy of helping others see "the big picture" and inspiring them to make the vision of the future reality.[16] Transformational leaders are good communicators who support and encourage rather than demean or demand.

The Classical Tradition of Rhetoric*

by Thomas R. Burkholder

Preparing and delivering a speech always seems to be a very personal task. You must research your own topic. You must analyze and attempt to adapt to the particular audience you will face. You must find a way to cope with your own nervousness. When you confront those problems, it is sometimes helpful to remember that countless others have done so before you. And for as long as people have been giving speeches, they have been looking for ways to make them better. In fact, the study of speeches and speechmaking, or the study of rhetoric, dates back to the earliest years of Western civilization, hundreds of years before the birth of Christ. So in a way, your own efforts are a continuation of that classical tradition.

Speechmaking is probably as old as language itself. And speech criticism is probably as old as listening! But perhaps the earliest recorded evidence of "rhetorical consciousness," the awareness of excellence in speechmaking, appears in the epic poetry of Homer, the ancient Greek poet. His *Iliad*, composed before 700 B.C., contains numerous well-organized speeches or orations. They appear in scenes depicting debates between humans and gods, in councils of military leaders, and so forth. And they demonstrate that the ancient Greeks had a clear sense of rhetorical excellence.

The Earliest Teachers of Rhetoric

We will probably never know who first offered advice to another person who was preparing to deliver an oration. But many ancient writers credit a teacher named Corax with the "invention" of rhetoric sometime around 476 B.C. Corax was a resident of the city of Syracuse on the island of Sicily. He developed a "doctrine of general probability," to be used by speakers in the courts. Imagine a small man being brought into court and accused of beating a much larger, stronger man. According to the doctrine of general probability, the small man should defend himself by saying something like "It is surely unlikely (not probable) that I would beat this man. After all, he is much larger and stronger than I. I would be crazy to risk making him angry by hitting him." But the larger man could resort to the same doctrine in response: "Of course people would think it unlikely that he would hit me. That is exactly why he felt safe in doing it!"

*Reprinted by Permission of Thomas R. Burkholder

Another similar exchange was the basis of the most famous story about Corax and his student Tisias. Tisias refused to pay Corax for his lessons in rhetoric, so Corax sued him in court. Corax addressed the judges: "Tisias must pay me regardless of your decision. If he wins the case, that proves the lessons I taught him were valuable and I deserve payment. And if he loses, the court will force him to pay. So either way, he must pay." But Tisias responded, "I shall pay nothing. If I lose the case, that will prove the training I received from Corax was worthless and he does not deserve payment. But if I win the case, the court will decree that I owe him nothing. So either way, I shall not pay." The judges quickly tired of such banter and threw the case out of court with the admonition "Mali corvi malum ovum," or "A bad egg from a bad crow!" Legend has it that Tisias promptly left Syracuse and opened his own school of rhetoric in Greece.

Beginning of the Greek Tradition: The Sophists

Whether Tisias actually went to Greece is unknown. But by the middle of the fifth century B.C., schools of rhetoric flourished in the Greek city states. Citizens often spoke in the assemblies or legislatures, and because there were no lawyers, they presented their own cases in the courts. It was soon apparent that the most skilled speakers prevailed in the assembly and won in court. Speech teachers were in great demand. The Greeks called these teachers "Sophists," a term that literally means "wisdom bearer." The rhetorical training offered by these teachers varied greatly. Some, such as Antiphon (480–411 B.C.) and Lysias (459–380 B.C.), were actually logographers. They merely wrote speeches to be delivered by their clients and made no effort to provide training in rhetoric. Others, like Protagoras (481–411 B.C.) and Gorgias (485–380 B.C.), advertised themselves as teachers of eloquence, or the art of effective speaking.

Protagoras is often considered to be the originator of academic debating, because he required his students to argue opposing sides of issues. He believed that each side of important questions had merit, and that humans could never be certain of the "truth." Thus, he encouraged his students to build the strongest possible case for the side of the issue they were assigned to debate. Such training, he felt, would best prepare his students to conduct their affairs in the assembly and the courts. Gorgias was perhaps the first teacher of rhetoric to encourage careful use of language. He believed that speakers would be more persuasive if their speaking style was embellished. He encouraged the use of stylistic devices familiar to modern writers, such as assonance, alliteration, antithesis, and parallelism.

One of the most famous Sophists was Isocrates (436–338 B.C.). Unlike Protagoras and Gorgias, who taught only rhetoric, Isocrates claimed to train citizens to be statesmen. He made rhetoric the center of a more fully developed course of study designed to make his students wise as well as eloquent. Isocrates believed that three qualities were necessary for a person to be a great orator and statesman. First, that person must possess natural ability. Second, that ability must be developed and refined through practice and experience. Finally, to be a great orator and statesman, a person must be well educated, not just in rhetoric, but in philosophy as well. While no one can teach natural ability, Isocrates endeavored to provide his students with practice, experience, and philosophical education.

Although the Sophists attracted many students, and many Sophists became wealthy from their teaching efforts, they were not without their critics. Many felt that the training provided by the Sophists was worthless, if not dangerous. Teachers like Gorgias were accused of providing worthless training by emphasizing florid language with no regard for substance. Teachers like Protagoras were accused of training speakers to "make the worse case appear the better" by urging speakers to develop strong speeches on both sides of any issue. And Sophists in general were often criticized for failing to make their students better, more virtuous people. Without question, the most severe critic of the Sophists was the great Greek philosopher Plato (427–347 B.C.).

Plato

Plato was the student of Socrates (469–399 B.C.), and he went on to become one of the most profound and influential thinkers in history. In 385 B.C., Plato founded the famous Academy in Athens. The Academy attracted the best and brightest students and teachers in all of Greece and remained in operation for almost nine hundred years. Plato's writings were a major influence in the development of Western philosophy and culture. His *Republic* was a blueprint for the ideal political state ruled over by a philosopher-king. His other writings covered a wide variety of subjects, including psychology, logic, and rhetoric. Most of his writings were "dialogues," which resembled plays in which the characters discussed important issues. In many of Plato's dialogues, Socrates was the chief character.

In a typical dialogue, Plato had Socrates attempt to determine the truth relevant to the issue at hand by engaging other characters in a series of questions and answers. That approach is now frequently called the "Socratic method" or the "Platonic method." It illustrated the process of "dialectic," which Plato believed was the means of discovering truth. The dialogues were often named after the characters who opposed Socrates in the discussion. Two of the dialogues, *Gorgias* and *Phaedrus*, named after those Sophists, dealt explicitly with rhetoric.

Plato's dialogues are complicated and often difficult to understand fully. Scholars have debated their meaning for centuries. Some have argued that *Gorgias* and *Phaedrus* presented inconsistent and conflicting views of rhetoric; that Plato condemned rhetoric in *Gorgias* and then praised it in *Phaedrus*. In fact, when taken together, the two dialogues presented Plato's clear and coherent view of the nature and function of rhetoric.

In *Gorgias*, Plato, through the character of Socrates, condemned rhetoric *as practiced* by many Sophists of his day. He said that the rhetoric of the Sophists was merely a "knack," or a form of flattery, intended only to please the ears of listeners much like cookery pleases the palate. He condemned the Sophists for using florid language, pleasant to the ear, to "make the worse case appear the better." And he accused them of first claiming to impart wisdom and thus to make their students more just and virtuous, and then of failing to do so. But these charges were leveled at rhetoric as the Sophists practiced it, not at rhetoric itself.

In *Phaedrus*, once again through the character of Socrates, Plato praised rhetoric as it *ought to be practiced*. The Sophists focused their attention on speaking in assemblies and courts. But Plato saw the true rhetoric as a means of using language to influence the minds of listeners, wherever they might be. Going further, he saw rhetoric as a means of influencing the very souls of listeners, thus making them more virtuous. The difference between the Sophistic and Platonic ideas of rhetoric grew from Plato's understanding of "truth."

In Plato's view, truth, or knowledge, existed on several levels. The lowest, least reliable, yet most common level was called *doxa*. This sort of knowledge was the product of the human senses, of what people observed. It was least reliable because it was so easily corrupted; the senses were easily misled. Thus, Plato's condemnation of the rhetoric of the Sophists *grew* from its aim of pleasing (and often, he felt, misleading) the senses of listeners. On the other end of Plato's scale was *episteme*, or true knowledge. It was the product not of sensory observation, but rather of philosophical inquiry. For Plato, rhetoric as it ought to be practiced was grounded in *episteme*. Only this "true" rhetoric could be trusted to influence the souls of listeners.

The idea of rhetoric based on truth is appealing. But before we award too much praise to Plato, we must know also that he thought most people were not capable of achieving true knowledge. Only philosophers could attain true knowledge, and thus, in the ideal political state described in his *Republic*, only the philosopher-king was allowed to use rhetoric, for the good of the state. Such uses of rhetoric are frightening. Seen in that light, the Sophists' idea that both sides of important issues should be debated in public seems preferable indeed.

Aristotle

Plato's most famous student was Aristotle (384–322 B.C.). Of all ancient scholars, including Plato, no other was more influential than Aristotle. He wrote extensively on subjects as diverse as philosophy, drama, natural science, and rhetoric. Like his teacher, Aristotle had a profound effect on the development of Western culture.

Throughout his life, Aristotle was directly associated with the most brilliant and important people of his time. His father, Nicomachus, was physician in the court of Amyntas II, king of Macedon and father of Philip the Great. When Aristotle was seventeen, he was sent to Athens to study in the Academy. There he remained until Plato's death. In 343 B.C., he was summoned back to Macedon to become tutor to Philip's son, Alexander the Great. Aristotle returned to Athens in 335 B.C. and eventually founded his own school, the Lyceum. After the death of Alexander in 323 B.C., he came under suspicion in Athens because of his prior close association with Macedon. Aristotle fled to the city of Chalcis where he died the next year.

Aristotle's *Rhetoric* is the earliest systematic discussion of speechmaking of which we have record. It probably existed first as his own notes for lectures he gave to students in the Lyceum. Legend has it that his students edited and published those notes after Aristotle's death. His approach to rhetoric was influenced by the philosophy of Plato. But his practical suggestions for speakers demonstrate that Aristotle was influenced by the Sophists as well. In effect, he was able to transcend both Plato and the Sophists and form a distinctive theory of rhetoric. The impact of his work continues today. Indeed, much of what appears earlier in this textbook originated with Aristotle.

Like Plato, Aristotle believed in true or ultimate knowledge. Also like Plato, he believed that only through philosophical inquiry, which was beyond the ability of most people, could true knowledge be attained. But Plato viewed rhetoric as a means through which, for the good of the state, philosopher-kings might manipulate those incapable of gaining true knowledge. Aristotle took a very different position. He believed that even those who could not attain true knowledge could, nevertheless, be persuaded to the good. Thus, persuasion was an acceptable, although inferior, substitute for true knowledge. In Plato's ideal state, only the philosopher-king could employ rhetoric because in the hands of the unenlightened, rhetoric could do great harm. In contrast, Aristotle believed that rhetoric was a morally neutral art. He did not restrict the use of rhetoric to rulers alone because he believed that, in any dispute, good would prevail provided both sides were equally well prepared; that is, provided both sides were equally well trained in rhetoric.

Aristotle envisioned rhetoric as an art, as a system that could be taught. He defined rhetoric as "the faculty of discovering, in any given case, the available means of persuasion." These means of persuasion he classified into three types: *ethos*, or ethical appeals, based on the degree of credibility awarded to a speaker by listeners; *logos*, or logical appeals; and *pathos*, or appeals to listeners' emotions. The *Rhetoric* offered speakers extremely detailed suggestions for discovering, understanding, and implementing each means of persuasion.

Aristotle also classified the different situations, or "given cases," in which speeches might be given. Those were deliberative, or legislative speaking; forensic, or speaking in the courts; and epideictic, or what he called the "ceremonial oratory of display." Today, we would call that last type "special-occasion" speaking. According to Aristotle, those types were determined by the role listeners must play in each case; by the sort of "decision" they must make after hearing a particular speech. In that regard, Aristotle took an "audience-centered approach" to speechmaking.

In Aristotle's system of classification, those who heard deliberative speeches were asked to render a decision regarding the most expedient course for future action. Those who heard forensic speeches were asked to judge the justice or injustice of a person's past action. And those who heard epideictic speeches were asked to award either praise or blame to the subject (usually a person) of the speech, and to judge the orator's skill as well. The *Rhetoric* offered speakers detailed suggestions for demonstrating the expedience or inexpediency of proposed courses of action, the justice or injustice of a person's deeds, and those qualities worthy of praise or blame. Aristotle also allowed for considerable overlap between the three types, indicating that although one type would predominate, elements of all three might appear in a single speech.

His discussions of expediency, justice, and qualities worthy of praise or blame made Aristotle's *Rhetoric* more than a simple "handbook" for speakers. Those discussions provided a philosophical or ethical foundation for speechmaking. But its practical suggestions made the *Rhetoric* an extremely useful manual for public speaking as well.

The Roman Tradition

The Greek tradition of rhetoric had its most immediate, and perhaps its greatest, influence in the Roman educational system. In the second century B.C., Rome's military might extended the Republic to the east. There, Romans became familiar with Greek culture and the Greek educational system. Much of what they discovered was incorporated into Roman society, and that included training in rhetoric. In fact, rhetorical training eventually became the center of Roman education.

The Roman education system was designed to prepare citizens to participate in the affairs of the state. Primarily, that meant citizens must be prepared to speak in the legislatures and the courts. Rhetorical instruction began in the Roman grammar schools. There, students engaged in a progressive series of written and spoken exercises called the *Progymnasmata*. The lessons built on each other, with each more difficult than the one that preceded it. Near the end of the program of instruction, students were assigned a thesis which required them to develop arguments on a given theme, such as whether it was more noble to be a soldier or a lawyer. The series of lessons culminated in exercises in which students were required to speak for and against an existing law.

With grammar-school instruction completed, most students moved on to schools of rhetoric. Instruction there was more broad in scope, but it continued to focus on preparing students to be productive citizens of Rome; that is, to be effective speakers. Students were required to learn a vast body of rhetorical theories and concepts based on centuries of oratorical study. They were taught that the art of rhetoric consisted of five separate arts: *invention*, which involved gathering and analyzing facts and physical evidence; *arrangement*, or organization; *style*, or the eloquent and effective use of language; *memory*, or recollection of the speech for presentation; and *delivery*. These five classical "canons" of rhetoric are familiar to today's students of public speaking. The exercises in which students in Roman times participated were of two types, *suasoria* and *controversia*. *Suasoria* were exercises in legislative speaking. Students debated hypothetical questions of public policy, laws, and so forth. *Controversia* were exercises in forensic or legal speaking. Students argued opposing sides of hypothetical court cases, much as present-day law students do in "moot court" contests.

Following their training in schools of rhetoric, Roman students were often apprenticed to practicing rhetoricians, such as legislators or lawyers. There the students were given opportunities to learn by observing other speakers in legislative and judicial situations. Thus, the entire Roman educational system was designed to prepare citizens to assume roles as orators in the society. Rome produced many scholars who contributed to the rhetorical tradition. Two of the most important were Cicero (106–43 B.C.) and Quintilian (A.D. 35–95).

Marcus Tullius Cicero was the child of an upper-middle-class family from central Italy. Social custom dictated that he pursue his education in Rome, where he studied with the leading rhetoricians of his day. According to many, he became the greatest orator in all Rome. His most famous works on the theory and practice of rhetoric were *De Inventione*, written when he was approximately twenty years old; *De Oratore*, published in 55 B.C.; and *Brutus* and *Orator*, both written in approximately 46 B.C. Cicero's aim in these works was to gather, synthesize, and expand on the greatest teachings of previous Greek and Roman rhetoricians. He was appalled by the emphasis given to style and delivery in some schools of rhetoric and felt the true orator should be a fully educated person. Cicero saw rhetoric as far more than courtroom pleading. Rather, he believed that the ideal orator was the learned philosopher-statesman, who used his talent for the good of the state. In his view, the true orator should be able to speak with eloquence and wisdom on any important subject.

Marcus Fabius Quintilianus was born in the part of the Roman Empire that is now Spain. Like Cicero, he was the product of a traditional Roman education. But unlike Cicero, Quintilian lived in a time when oratory began to be repressed. Tyrants ruled the Roman Empire; the legislative speaking and even the legal speaking that had characterized Cicero's time were greatly restricted. Despite that fact, or perhaps because of it, Quintilian's aim as a teacher of rhetoric was to educate the perfect orator. His most famous rhetorical treatise was *Institutio Oratoria*, which emphasized the moral and ethical uses of rhetoric. For Quintilian, the ideal orator was "a good man speaking well." Unfortunately, that dictum has been much abused by many modern rhetorical scholars, often to justify the study of the speaking and speeches of only highly successful political figures who were usually white and male. In fact, Quintilian urged those who would become great orators to pursue not only eloquence, but excellence in morality and ethical character as well—qualities that are certainly not limited to, or perhaps even characteristic of, successful politicians!

 ## Conclusion

The rhetorical tradition that began with the ancient Greeks and Romans has been a significant influence in Western civilization. Their theories and guidelines for successful rhetorical practice have been analyzed, refined, and extended by countless scholars for thousands of years. This book is a part of that tradition. Many of the rhetorical principles and suggestions for effective speechmaking that appear in this book can be traced through the ages back to such classical rhetoricians as Isocrates, Plato, Aristotle, Cicero, and Quintilian. Throughout history, other rhetorical scholars have made important contributions as well. As you work to prepare your own speeches, to be delivered in class or in other settings, it is interesting and perhaps even comforting to know that your efforts are a continuation of a classical tradition of rhetoric as old as Western culture.

REFERENCES

Aristotle. *Rhetoric and Poetics.* Translated by W. Rhys Roberts and Ingram Bywater. New York: Modern Library, 1954.

Black, Edwin. "Plato's View of Rhetoric." *Quarterly Journal of Speech* 44 (Dec. 1958): 361–74.

Clark, Donald Lemen. *Rhetoric in Greco–Roman Education.* New York: Columbia UP, 1957.

Guthrie, W. K. C. *The Sophists.* Cambridge, England: Cambridge UP, 1971.

Hamilton, Edith, and Huntington Cairns, eds. *The Collected Dialogues of Plato.* Princeton: Princeton UP, 1961.

Kauffman, Charles. "The Axiological Foundations of Plato's Theory of Rhetoric." *Central States Speech Journal* 33 (Summer 1982): 353–66.

Kennedy, George. *The Art of Persuasion in Greece.* Princeton: Princeton UP, 1963.

Murphy, James J., ed. *A Synoptic History of Classical Rhetoric.* Davis, CA: Hermagoras, 1983.

Murphy, James J., ed. *Quintilian on the Teaching of Speaking and Writing.* Translations from Books 1, 2, and 10 of *Institutio Oratoria.* Carbondale: Southern Illinois UP, 1987.

Watson, J. S., trans. *Cicero on Oratory and Orators.* Carbondale: Southern Illinois UP, 1970.

RECAP

The Classical Tradition of Rhetoric

RHETORICIANS	DATES	CONTRIBUTIONS
The First Teachers		
Corax and Tisias	476 B.C.	Doctrine of general probability
The Greek Tradition		
The Sophists		
Protagoras	481–411 B.C.	Originator of academic debate
Gorgias	485–380 B.C.	Effective language use
Isocrates	436–338 B.C.	The orator-statesman
Plato	427–347 B.C.	*Gorgias* and *Phaedrus*; philosopher-king as orator
Aristotle	384–322 B.C.	*Rhetoric*; philosophical and practical guide for orators; rhetoric as a teachable art
The Roman Tradition		
Cicero	106–43 B.C.	*De Inventione, De Oratore, Brutus,* and *Orator*; Rome's greatest orator; philosopher-statesman as the ideal orator
Quintilian	A.D. 35–95	*Institutio Oratoria*; eloquence combined with moral and ethical excellence; the good man speaking well

Speeches for Analysis and Discussion

I Have a Dream*

by Martin Luther King Jr., Washington, D.C., August 28, 1963

I am happy to join with you today in what will go down in history as the greatest demonstration for freedom in the history of our nation.

Five score years ago, a great American, in whose symbolic shadow we stand today, signed the Emancipation Proclamation. This momentous decree came as a great beacon light of hope to millions of Negro slaves, who had been seared in the flames of withering injustice. It came as a joyous daybreak to end the long night of their captivity.

But one hundred years later, the Negro is still not free. One hundred years later, the life of the Negro is still sadly crippled by the manacles of segregation and the chains of discrimination. One hundred years later, the Negro lives on a lonely island of poverty in the midst of a vast ocean of material prosperity. One hundred years later, the Negro is still languished in the corners of American society and finds himself an exile in his own land. And so we've come here today to dramatize a shameful condition.

In a sense we've come to our nation's Capitol to cash a check. When the architects of our republic wrote the magnificent words of the Constitution and the Declaration of Independence, they were signing a promissory note to which every American was to fall heir. This note was a promise that all men—yes, black men as well as white men—would be guaranteed the inalienable rights of life, liberty, and the pursuit of happiness.

It is obvious today that America has defaulted on this promissory note insofar as her citizens of color are concerned. Instead of honoring this sacred obligation, America has given the Negro people a bad check—a check which has come back marked "insufficient funds."

But we refuse to believe that the bank of justice is bankrupt. We refuse to believe that there are insufficient funds in the great vaults of opportunity of this nation. And so we've come to cash this check—a check that will give us upon demand the riches of freedom and the security of justice.

We have also come to this hallowed spot to remind America of the fierce urgency of now. This is no time to engage in the luxury of cooling off or to take the tranquilizing drug of gradualism. Now is the time to make the real promises of democracy. Now is the time to rise from the dark and desolate valley of segregation to the sunlit path of racial justice. Now is the time to lift our nation from the quicksands of racial injustice to the solid rock of brotherhood. Now is the time to make justice a reality for all of God's children.

It would be fatal for the nation to overlook the urgency of the moment. This sweltering summer of the Negro's legitimate discontent will not pass until there is an invigorating autumn of freedom and equality. Nineteen sixty-three is not an end, but a beginning. Those who hope that the Negro needed to blow off steam and will now be content will have a rude awakening if the nation returns to business as usual. There will be neither rest nor tranquility in America until the Negro is granted his citizenship rights. The whirlwinds of revolt will continue to shake the foundations of our nation until the bright day of justice emerges.

But there is something that I must say to my people, who stand on the warm threshold which leads into the palace of justice. In the process of gaining our rightful place, we must not be guilty of wrongful deeds. Let us not seek to satisfy our thirst for freedom by drinking from the cup of bitterness and hatred.

We must forever conduct our struggle on the high plane of dignity and discipline. We must not allow our creative protest to degenerate into physical violence. Again and again we must rise to the majestic heights of meeting physical force with soul force.

The marvelous new militance which has engulfed the Negro community must not lead us to a distrust of all white people. For many of our white brothers, as evidenced by their presence here today, have come to realize that their destiny is tied up with our destiny. They have come to realize that their freedom is inextricably bound to our freedom. We cannot walk alone.

As we walk, we must make the pledge that we shall always march ahead. We cannot turn back. There are those who are asking the devotees of civil rights, "When will you be satisfied?" We can never be satisfied as long as the Negro is the victim of the unspeakable horrors of police brutality. We can never be satisfied as long as our bodies, heavy with the fatigue of travel, cannot gain lodging in the motels of the highways and hotels of the cities. We cannot be satisfied as long as the Negro's basic mobility is from a smaller ghetto to a larger one. We can never be satisfied as long as our children are stripped of their selfhood and robbed of their dignity by signs stating "For Whites Only." We cannot be satisfied as long as a Negro in Mississippi cannot vote and a Negro in New York believes he has nothing for which to vote. No, no, we are not satisfied, and we will not be satisfied until justice rolls down like waters, and righteousness like a mighty stream.

I am not unmindful that some of you have come here out of great trials and tribulations. Some of you have come fresh from narrow jail cells. Some of you have come from areas where your quest for freedom left you battered by the storms of persecution and staggered by the winds of police brutality. You have been the veterans of creative suffering. Continue to work with the faith that unearned suffering is redemptive.

Go back to Mississippi, go back to Alabama, go back to South Carolina, go back to Georgia, go back to Louisiana, go back to the slums and ghettos of our Northern cities, knowing that somehow this situation can and will be changed. Let us not wallow in the valley of despair.

I say to you today, my friends, so even though we face the difficulties of today and tomorrow, I still have a dream. It is a dream deeply rooted in the American dream.

I have a dream that one day this nation will rise up and live out the true meaning of its creed, "We hold these truths to be self-evident, that all men are created equal."

I have a dream that one day on the red hills of Georgia the sons of former slaves and the sons of former slaveowners will be able to sit down together at the table of brotherhood.

I have a dream that one day even the state of Mississippi, a state sweltering with the heat of injustice, sweltering with the heat of oppression, will be transformed into an oasis of freedom and justice.

I have a dream that my four little children will one day live in a nation where they will not be judged by the color of their skin but by the content of their character. I have a dream today.

I have a dream that one day, down in Alabama, with its vicious racists, with its governor having his lips dripping with the words of interposition and nullification, one day right there in Alabama little black boys and black girls will be able to join hands with little white boys and white girls as sisters and brothers. I have a dream today.

I have a dream that one day every valley shall be exalted, every hill and mountain shall be made low, the rough places will be made plain and the crooked places will be made straight, and the glory of the Lord shall be revealed, and all flesh shall see it together.

This is our hope. This is the faith that I go back to the South with. With this faith we will be able to hew out of the mountain of despair a stone of hope. With this faith we will be able to transform the jangling discords of our nation into a beautiful symphony of brotherhood. With this faith we will be able to work together, to pray together, to struggle together, to go to jail together, to stand up for freedom together knowing that we will be free one day.

This will be the day—this will be the day when all of God's children will be able to sing with new meaning, "My country 'tis of thee, sweet land of liberty, of thee I sing. Land where my fathers died, land of the Pilgrims' pride, from every mountainside, let freedom ring." And if America is to be a great nation, this must become true.

So let freedom ring from the prodigious hilltops of New Hampshire. Let freedom ring from the mighty mountains of New York. Let freedom ring from the heightening Alleghenies of Pennsylvania!

Let freedom ring from the snowcapped Rockies of Colorado! Let freedom ring from the curvaceous slopes of California!

But not only that. Let freedom ring from Stone Mountain of Georgia!

Let freedom ring from Lookout Mountain of Tennessee!

Let freedom ring from every hill and molehill of Mississippi. From every mountainside, let freedom ring.

And when this happens, when we allow freedom to ring—when we let it ring from every village and every hamlet, from every state and every city—we will be able to speed up that day when all of God's children, black men and white men, Jews and Gentiles, Protestants and Catholics, will be able to join hands and sing, in the words of the old Negro spiritual, "Free at last! Free at last! Thank God almighty, we are free at last!"

Van Gogh's Incredible Life

by Kristy Shaw

When you hear the name Vincent Van Gogh, does the picture of an insane artist who cut off his ear come to mind? That's what I first thought about him until I learned more about his life. And now I feel to remember him that way is to deny him the genius of his work and the fascinating details of his life.

Though Van Gogh's life was short—he was only 37 when he killed himself—his life was marked by depression, madness, loneliness, and lost love. According to the 1992 Carol Strickland's book, *The Annotated Mona Lisa*, Van Gogh once said, "I'd rather die of passion instead of boredom." Van Gogh's certainly was a life of passion. He experienced outbursts of intense joy, brotherly love, and creative spurts that produced brilliant artwork that we still admire to this day. During this speech, I will walk you through this fascinating man's life. I will tell you about his beginnings; the troubled teen years where he bounced around trying to find his niche in the world; and the creative middle years where he decided to be an artist and [threw] himself into the field; and finally, the last two years of his life that marked his rapid demise into madness and eventually drove him to commit suicide.

According to the Van Gogh Museum Web site entitled "Van Gogh's Life and Times," Van Gogh was born in 1853 on March 30th in the Netherlands. He was the eldest of six children, and his favorite brother, Theo, was born four years later. Theo would be his financial and emotional supporter throughout his life. Van Gogh attempted two careers in his lifetime. The first was an apprenticeship at Goupil & Cie, an international art dealership with which he joined after he dropped out of school at the age of 16. He worked at a branch office there for seven years until, at the age of 23, he was fired. After becoming disillusioned with the art trade, he reportedly told customers they were buying junk. Between the ages of 23 and 27, Van Gogh attempted to be a minister. He was driven by a desire to help the common man, and he wanted to be a clergyman. Soon, he became obsessed with evangelical Christianity, and he even tried to enroll in the Amsterdam Theology School, but he failed the entrance exam. Therefore, he became a lay minister. He worked among impoverished miners. He slept on the floor, gave away all his possessions, and preached to them. Finally, the church ended up dismissing him due to his overzealous commitments.

After two failed careers, at the age of 27, Van Gogh's mental health is suffering. He's in acute poverty. He's in the middle of a spiritual crisis. He's a failure in the eyes of his family. He has no job, no income, and he's searching for something to dedicate his life to. It is in 1880 that Van Gogh discovers art. He feels it's a way to express himself and God and to also get income from his work. Between the years 1880 and 1887, Van Gogh funnels his time and enthusiasm into being an artist. At the age of 27, Van Gogh begins to study watercolor and oils. In 1883, he begins to paint bleak landscapes and peasant worker pictures. He completes 40 painted studies of peasants and gives them to Theo to sell. An example is the 1885 piece, *Potato Eaters*. As you can see, he begins to use dark colors in his painting. However, at this time, Van Gogh and Theo have personal tensions between them. Van Gogh accuses Theo of not selling his work. And Theo explains that Van Gogh's style, which is dark colors, does not meet the current style, which is bright, lively colors. And therefore, his painting won't sell.

During this time, Van Gogh also hits a series of love disasters in his lifetime. First, he falls in love with his cousin, Kee Vos-Stricker. Van Gogh disgraces his family with this unacceptable affair. And to top it all off, Vos-Stricker rejects him. Two years later in 1882, Van Gogh again scandalizes his family by bringing a pregnant prostitute named Sien Hoornik and her 11-year-old daughter into his household. Now, initially, Van Gogh wanted Hoornik to pose for his art, but she refuses. Eventually, she is thrown out of the household for causing too much trouble. But Van Gogh contracts gonorrhea during this time.

Between the age of 32 and 34, Van Gogh begins to blend his creativity and vision to form his own unique style. While visiting Theo in Paris, he is introduced to impressionistic style of painting. He likes the light colors and the short brush strokes. And he begins to use colors to symbolize emotions. He also experiments with many different types of hues and changes to the lighter palette. According to the Think Quest Web site entitled "Van Gogh in Essence," Van Gogh said, "Instead of trying to reproduce exactly what's before my eyes I use color more arbitrarily to express myself more forcibly."

Lawrence and Elizabeth Hanson's 1955 book, *Passionate Pilgrim*, states that Van Gogh becomes unlucky in love once again. This time he falls in love with his neighbor, Margot Begemann. Begemann is a spinster who is 10 years older than he. And even though his feelings are reciprocated at this time and they plan to marry, his parents don't approve of the marriage, and they won't let them. Begemann poisons herself in protest. And even though she survives, her parents take her away. And she and Van Gogh never see each other again. Van Gogh slips into depression over another lost love.

The last few years of Van Gogh's life are marked by creative brilliance, but also by mental instability that eventually leads him to commit suicide. When Van Gogh is 35 years old he is worn down by his activities in Paris. He retreats to a province in France; [he] rents a studio with little distractions; he begins to paint. As far as art goes, he enters a period of sustained creativity where he paints more than 200 canvases, including *Sunflowers in the Vase*. As you can see, this painting features light colors as opposed to the dark colors of *Potato Eaters*. Van Gogh, however, cannot sell any of his paintings, and he lives in poverty, relying solely on Theo for money and support. Soon, he begins to suffer from fits of madness, depression, and hallucinations. But one good thing in Van Gogh's life is that he is eagerly awaiting his friend and mentor, Paul Gauguin. Gauguin visits him in the fall, and for nine months, they paint side by side and have wonderful art discussions. But soon, personal tensions grow between the two men, and Van Gogh threatens Gauguin with a razor blade. Now Gauguin is unharmed, but this is the infamous incident where Van Gogh cuts off his left earlobe. He wraps the earlobe in paper and gives it to a prostitute as a present, as recorded in Hansons' book.

At the age of 36, the Van Gogh Museum Web site states that Van Gogh is admitted into a psychiatric hospital. He's subject to attacks ranging from depression to frantic bursts of energy. But he is able to find some solace in the asylum's structured days. But there is one episode where he eats paint in a failed attempt to commit suicide. While at the asylum, Van Gogh finds inspiration in its long gardens, and he paints more than 150 paintings while there, including *Starry Night*, for which he receives favorable reviews. The Van Gogh Museum Web site records Van Gogh as saying, "I feel happier here with my work than I could be on the outside. By staying here a good, long time I shall have learned regular habits. And in the long run there will be more order in my life."

Van Gogh [is] released from the hospital under a physician's care and moves near Paris to be closer to Theo. When Van Gogh is 37 years old, he begins to feverishly paint, producing a painting a day for the next two months. His paintings focus on portraits and nearby landscapes. But mentally, Van Gogh's passion for art begins to fade. He feels like a failure. And when informed that Theo is beginning to start his own business, and therefore, money will be short, he becomes concerned about his financial situation and worries about becoming a greater burden. According to Think Quest Web site, Van Gogh states, "I feel a failure. That's it as far as I'm concerned. I feel that this is the destiny that I must accept. And that will never change." On July 27th, 1890, Van Gogh walks into a field and shoots himself in the stomach with a pistol. He stumbles back to the house and dies two days later with Theo at his side. Van Gogh's dying words were "Who would believe their life could be so sad?"

Van Gogh's life was not an easy one. He experienced troubled teen years where he struggled to find what he wanted to do with his life; middle years that were full of creativity; and finally, the last years of his life where mental illness took over and eventually drove him to commit suicide. Despite an unhappy life marked by turmoil, depression, and loneliness, Van Gogh managed to leave a lasting impression on the world by expressing himself the only way he knew how—through his paintings. According to Strickland, Van Gogh once said, "I have risked my life for my work. And my mind has half floundered." It is these paintings that are the legacy of Van Gogh. Though marked by personal tragedy and despair, Van Gogh was always driven to paint. It was the only thing he knew how to do. Hansons' book cites a passage from a letter Van Gogh wrote to his brother; in it, Van Gogh writes, "A white worm must eat salad roots to attain its transformation. And I think that a painter must paint. Perhaps there'll be something after that."

REFERENCES

Hanson, L. & Hanson, E. (1995). *Passionate pilgrim: The life of Vincent van Gogh.* New York: Random House.

Strickland, C. (1992). *The annotated Mona Lisa.* Kansas City, MO: Universal Press Syndicate Company.

Van Gogh at Etten–sketches and billboards. (n.d.). *Think Quest,* http://library.thinkquest.org/C001734/eng/textonly.html.

Van Gogh's life and times. (n.d.). *Van Gogh Museum, Amsterdam,* http://www.vangoghmuseum.nl/bisrd/top-1-2-2-4-1.html.

Harvard Commencement Speech*

by Bill Gates, June 7, 2007

President Bok, former President Rudenstine, incoming President Faust, members of the Harvard Corporation and the Board of Overseers, members of the faculty, parents, and especially, the graduates: I've been waiting more than 30 years to say this: "Dad, I always told you I'd come back and get my degree." I want to thank Harvard for this timely honor. I'll be changing my job next year . . . and it will be nice to finally have a college degree on my resume.

I applaud the graduates today for taking a much more direct route to your degrees. For my part, I'm just happy that the *Crimson* has called me "Harvard's most successful dropout." I guess that makes me valedictorian of my own special class . . . I did the best of everyone who failed. But I also want to be recognized as the guy who got Steve Ballmer to drop out of business school. I'm a bad influence. That's why I was invited to speak at your graduation. If I had spoken at your orientation, fewer of you might be here today.

Harvard was just a phenomenal experience for me. Academic life was fascinating. I used to sit in on lots of classes I hadn't even signed up for. And dorm life was terrific. I lived up at Radcliffe, in Currier House. There were always lots of people in my dorm room late at night discussing things, because everyone knew I didn't worry about getting up in the morning. That's how I came to be the leader of the anti-social group. We clung to each other as a way of validating our rejection of all those social people.

Radcliffe was a great place to live. There were more women up there, and most of the guys were science-math types. That combination offered me the best odds, if you know what I mean. This is where I learned the sad lesson that improving your odds doesn't guarantee success.

One of my biggest memories of Harvard came in January 1975, when I made a call from Currier House to a company in Albuquerque that had begun making the world's first personal computers. I offered to sell them software. I worried that they would realize I was just a student in a dorm and hang up on me. Instead they said, "We're not quite ready, come see us in a month," which was a good thing, because we hadn't written the software yet. From that moment, I worked day and night on this little extra credit project that marked the end of my college education and the beginning of a remarkable journey with Microsoft.

---

*Remarks by Bill Gates at the Harvard University commencement on June 7, 2007. Reprinted with the permission of the Bill & Melinda Gates Foundation.

What I remember above all about Harvard was being in the midst of so much energy and intelligence. It could be exhilarating, intimidating, sometimes even discouraging, but always challenging. It was an amazing privilege—and though I left early, I was transformed by my years at Harvard, the friendships I made, and the ideas I worked on.

But taking a serious look back . . . I do have one big regret. I left Harvard with no real awareness of the awful inequities in the world—the appalling disparities of health, and wealth, and opportunity that condemn millions of people to lives of despair. I learned a lot here at Harvard about new ideas in economics and politics. I got great exposure to the advances being made in the sciences. But humanity's greatest advances are not in its discoveries—but in how those discoveries are applied to reduce inequity. Whether through democracy, strong public education, quality health care, or broad economic opportunity—reducing inequity is the highest human achievement.

I left campus knowing little about the millions of young people cheated out of educational opportunities here in this country. And I knew nothing about the millions of people living in unspeakable poverty and disease in developing countries. It took me decades to find out.

You graduates came to Harvard at a different time. You know more about the world's inequities than the classes that came before. In your years here, I hope you've had a chance to think about how—in this age of accelerating technology—we can finally take on these inequities, and we can solve them.

Imagine, just for the sake of discussion, that you had a few hours a week and a few dollars a month to donate to a cause—and you wanted to spend that time and money where it would have the greatest impact in saving and improving lives. Where would you spend it?

For Melinda and for me, the challenge is the same: How can we do the most good for the greatest number with the resources we have? During our discussions on this question, Melinda and I read an article about the millions of children who were dying every year in poor countries from diseases that we had long ago made harmless in this country. Measles, malaria, pneumonia, hepatitis B, yellow fever. One disease I had never even heard of, rotavirus, was killing half a million kids each year—none of them in the United States. We were shocked. We had just assumed that if millions of children were dying and they could be saved, the world would make it a priority to discover and deliver the medicines to save them. But it did not. For under a dollar, there were interventions that could save lives that just weren't being delivered.

If you believe that every life has equal value, it's revolting to learn that some lives are seen as worth saving and others are not. We said to ourselves: "This can't be true. But if it is true, it deserves to be the priority of our giving." So we began our work in the same way anyone here would begin it. We asked, "How could the world let these children die?" The answer is simple, and harsh. The market did not reward saving the lives of these children, and governments did not subsidize it. So the children died because their mothers and their fathers had no power in the market and no voice in the system. But you and I have both.

We can make market forces work better for the poor if we can develop a more creative capitalism—if we can stretch the reach of market forces so that more people can make a profit, or at least make a living, serving people who are suffering from the worst inequities. We also can press governments around the world to spend taxpayer money in ways that better reflect the values of the people who pay the taxes. If we can find approaches that meet the needs of the poor in ways that generate profits for business and votes for politicians, we will have found a sustainable way to reduce inequity in the world.

This task is open-ended. It can never be finished. But a conscious effort to answer this challenge will change the world. I am optimistic that we can do this, but I talk to skeptics who claim there is no hope. They say, "Inequity has been with us since the beginning, and will be with us till the end—because people just . . . don't . . . care."

I completely disagree. I believe we have more caring than we know what to do with.

All of us here in this Yard, at one time or another, have seen human tragedies that broke our hearts, and yet we did nothing—not because we didn't care, but because we didn't know what to do. If we had known how to help, we would have acted. The barrier to change is not too little caring; it is too much complexity. To turn caring into action, we need to see a problem, see a solution, and see the impact. But complexity blocks all three steps.

Even with the advent of the Internet and 24-hour news, it is still a complex enterprise to get people to truly see the problems. When an airplane crashes, officials immediately call a press conference. They promise to investigate, determine the cause, and prevent similar crashes in the future. But if the officials were brutally honest, they would say, "Of all the people in the world who died today from preventable causes, one half of one percent of them were on this plane. We're determined to do everything possible to solve the problem that took the lives of the one half of one percent."

The bigger problem is not the plane crash, but the millions of preventable deaths. We don't read much about these deaths. The media covers what's new—and millions of people dying is nothing new. So it stays in the background, where it's easier to ignore. But even when we do see it or read about it, it's difficult to keep our eyes on the problem. It's hard to look at suffering if the situation is so complex that we don't know how to help. And so we look away. If we can really see a problem, which is the first step, we come to the second step: cutting through the complexity to find a solution.

Finding solutions is essential if we want to make the most of our caring. If we have clear and proven answers any time an organization or individual asks "How can I help?," then we can get action—and we can make sure that none of the caring in the world is wasted. But complexity makes it hard to mark a path of action for everyone who cares—and that makes it hard for their caring to matter.

Cutting through complexity to find a solution runs through four predictable stages: determine a goal, find the highest-leverage approach, discover the ideal technology for that approach, and, in the meantime, make the smartest application of the technology that you already have—whether it's something sophisticated, like a drug, or something simpler, like a bednet. The AIDS epidemic offers an example. The broad goal, of course, is to end the disease. The highest-leverage approach is prevention. The ideal technology would be a vaccine that gives lifetime immunity with a single dose. So governments, drug companies, and foundations fund vaccine research. But their work is likely to take more than a decade, so in the meantime, we have to work with what we have in hand—and the best prevention approach we have now is getting people to avoid risky behavior. Pursuing that goal starts the four-step cycle again. This is the pattern. The crucial thing is to never stop thinking and working—and never do what we did with malaria and tuberculosis in the 20th century—which is to surrender to complexity and quit.

The final step—after seeing the problem and finding an approach—is to measure the impact of your work and share your successes and failures so that others learn from your efforts. You have to have the statistics, of course. You have to be able to show that a program is vaccinating millions more children. You have to be able to show a decline in the number of children dying from these diseases. This is essential not just to improve the program, but also to help draw more investment from business and government. But if you want to inspire people to participate, you have to show more than numbers; you have to convey the human impact of the work—so people can feel what saving a life means to the families affected.

I remember going to Davos some years back and sitting on a global health panel that was discussing ways to save millions of lives. Millions! Think of the thrill of saving just one person's life—then multiply that by millions. . . . Yet this was the most boring panel I've ever been on—ever. So boring even I couldn't bear it. What made that experience especially striking was that I had just come from an event where we were introducing version 13 of some piece of software, and we had people jumping and shouting with excitement. I love getting people excited about software—but why can't we generate even more excitement for saving lives? You can't get people excited unless you can help them see and feel the impact. And how you do that is a complex question.

Still, I'm optimistic. Yes, inequity has been with us forever, but the new tools we have to cut through complexity have not been with us forever. They are new—they can help us make the most of our caring—and that's why the future can be different from the past.

The defining and ongoing innovations of this age—biotechnology, the computer, the Internet—give us a chance we've never had before to end extreme poverty and end death from preventable disease.

Sixty years ago, George Marshall came to this commencement and announced a plan to assist the nations of post-war Europe. He said, "I think one difficulty is that the problem is one of such enormous complexity that the very mass of facts presented to the public by press and radio make it exceedingly difficult for the man in the street to reach a clear appraisement of the situation. It is virtually impossible at this distance to grasp at all the real significance of the situation." Thirty years after Marshall made his address, as my class graduated without me, technology was emerging that would make the world smaller, more open, more visible, less distant.

The emergence of low-cost personal computers gave rise to a powerful network that has transformed opportunities for learning and communicating. The magical thing about this network is not just that it collapses distance and makes everyone your neighbor. It also dramatically increases the number of brilliant minds we can have working together on the same problem—and that scales up the rate of innovation to a staggering degree. At the same time, for every person in the world who has access to this technology, five people don't. That means many creative minds are left out of this discussion—smart people with practical intelligence and relevant experience who don't have the technology to hone their talents or contribute their ideas to the world.

We need as many people as possible to have access to this technology, because these advances are triggering a revolution in what human beings can do for one another. They are making it possible not just for national governments, but for universities, corporations, smaller organizations, and even individuals to see problems, see approaches, and measure the impact of their efforts to address the hunger, poverty, and desperation George Marshall spoke of 60 years ago.

Members of the Harvard Family: Here in the Yard is one of the great collections of intellectual talent in the world. What for? There is no question that the faculty, the alumni, the students, and the benefactors of Harvard have used their power to improve the lives of people here and around the world. But can we do more? Can Harvard dedicate its intellect to improving the lives of people who will never even hear its name?

Let me make a request of the deans and the professors—the intellectual leaders here at Harvard: As you hire new faculty, award tenure, review curriculum, and determine degree requirements, please ask yourselves: Should our best minds be dedicated to solving our biggest problems? Should Harvard encourage its faculty to take on the world's worst inequities? Should Harvard students learn about the depth of global poverty . . . the prevalence of world hunger . . . the scarcity of clean water . . . the girls kept out of school . . . the children who die from diseases we can cure? Should the world's most privileged people learn about the lives of the world's least privileged? These are not rhetorical questions—you will answer with your policies.

My mother, who was filled with pride the day I was admitted here, never stopped pressing me to do more for others. A few days before my wedding, she hosted a bridal event, at which she read aloud a letter about marriage that she had written to Melinda. My mother was very ill with cancer at the time, but she saw one more opportunity to deliver her message, and at the close of the letter she said, "From those to whom much is given, much is expected." When you consider what those of us here in this Yard have been given—in talent, privilege, and opportunity—there is almost no limit to what the world has a right to expect from us. In line with the promise of this age, I want to exhort each of the graduates here to take on an issue—a complex problem, a deep inequity—and become a specialist on it. If you make it the focus of your career, that would be phenomenal. But you don't have to do that to make an impact. For a few hours every week, you can use the growing power of the Internet to get informed, find others with the same interests, see the barriers, and find ways to cut through them.

Don't let complexity stop you. Be activists. Take on the big inequities. It will be one of the great experiences of your lives. You graduates are coming of age in an amazing time. As you leave Harvard, you have technology that members of my class never had. You have awareness of global inequity, which we did not have. And with that awareness, you likely also have an informed conscience that will torment you if you abandon these people whose lives you could change with very little effort. You have more than we had; you must start sooner, and carry on longer. Knowing what you know, how could you not?

And I hope you will come back here to Harvard 30 years from now and reflect on what you have done with your talent and your energy. I hope you will judge yourselves not on your professional accomplishments alone, but also on how well you have addressed the world's deepest inequities . . . on how well you treated people a world away who have nothing in common with you but their humanity. Good luck.

Tissue Trade Reform*

by Christina Costanzo

For nearly three generations, Alistair Cooke brought culture and a little bit of comedy to TV audiences around the world through the program *Masterpiece Theatre*. He shared with us the finest classic and contemporary works for over 21 years, but Alistair Cooke has switched genres. For his death, and the subsequent handling of his remains, is bringing a horror show to light that is scarier and more disturbing than anything you'll see on television. Following his death from cancer, Cooke's 95-year-old body was processed by a tissue trader who fraudulently sold bits and pieces of his body to hospitals and clinics around the country, possibly endangering the lives of hundreds of people. According to the World Health Organization's Web site, last accessed April 25, 2007, more than 70,000 organ and tissue transplants are done each year, and with the scope of the problem being so large, it must be dealt with quickly. In order to do this, we'll first discuss exactly what the problems in the tissue trade are, then, we'll explore its underlying causes before finally reviewing a few potential solutions to ensure that we are safe from fraud and danger, whether we're dead or alive.

The tissue trade began in the 1800s as a way for new doctors to obtain bodies to dissect and study. At that time, however, only the bodies of murderers could be traded, creating greater demand than supply and spawning a black market industry of body-snatching grave robbers. While body snatching is no longer a pressing issue, the tissue trade is facing new issues, including supersaturated demand, personal harm, and a severe lack of testing. Just like the 1800s, the demand for cadavers is once again high. According to the *San Diego Tribune* of March 30, 2007, the recent increase in demand is due to the immediate lack of organ donors around the world. There are currently 96,000 people in the U.S. alone waiting for an organ transplant and it is approximated that, due to the shortage in supply, only a third will receive the transplants they need.

The lack of a sufficient tissue supply has already put many in danger. The *Associated Press* of June 10, 2006 tells the sad fates of many victims of the tissue trade. For

*From *Winning Orations, 2007* (Mankato, MN: Interstate Oratorical Association, Larry Schnoor, Ex. Sec., 2007).

example, Bryan Lykins was an otherwise healthy 23-year-old who went into the hospital for a routine knee surgery, during which a cadaver was used. Four days after the surgery, he died from a raging infection because the cartilage he was given came from a cadaver that sat unrefrigerated for over 19 hours and bacteria had built up on the tissue. In similar cases, Ken Alesescu died from a fungus-infested heart valve after a transplant, and Alan Minvielle lost his job and his leg to gangrene from a bad tendon.

Two recent cases shed light on the severe lack of testing within the tissue trade. According to the *Lexington Herald-Leader* on August 31, 2006, Donor Referral Services of North Carolina did not properly test for diseases such as HIV, hepatitis, and syphilis before distributing tissues to hospitals. Some of these tissue samples had the potential to fully regenerate these dangerous and deadly diseases in recipient's bodies. In addition, the *New Zealand Herald* reported on July 5, 2006 that Biomedical Tissue Services of Fort Lee, New Jersey was shut down only after complaints led investigators to discover that they were taking organs and tissue from bodies without the proper consent from the deceased's families. For example, Alistair Cooke's body parts were sold without consent from his daughter. In addition, as *MSNBC* reported on September 18, 2006, the medical information that accompanied Cooke's body lowered his age by 10 years and altered his cause of death; both acts of fraud which made his cadaver much more desirable and valuable.

These problems are due, in part, to the fact that the FDA has no industry standards for the tissue trade. Underlying causes such as a lack of regulation, a lack of consumer awareness, and greed driven motivations on behalf of some involved in the industry are, slowly but surely, stripping the tissue trade of any credibility it had. But, first—the lack of regulation. Neither the Food and Drug Administration nor any other federal entity maintains specific regulations or codes that govern individuals or corporations involved in the tissue trade. Because of this lack of regulation, the industry has spun out of control. The American Association of Tissue Banks maintains guidelines over issues such as record keeping, quality control, donor selection criteria, patient history, and safety. According to their Web site, last accessed April 25, 2007, however, they are merely an accreditation institution. In other words, those involved in the tissue trade do not have to belong to this association, and there is no state or federal oversight to ensure that these standards are being met. Other than an initial corporate registration, the FDA is kept completely out of the loop. As the *News & Observer* of August 28, 2006 points out, however, this registration process is little more than bureaucratic fluff. You see, obtaining a license to legally participate in the tissue trade requires filling out an online form, which takes five minutes, then waiting eight weeks for the license to be mailed out. Once this is done, one is able to trade in human remains, free of any formal inspection for years.

The lack of regulation is only matched by a lack of awareness on behalf of medical consumers. Recipients of donated tissue and organs may be completely unaware of the circumstances that surround the donor, harvesting, storage, and transportation of the tissues that will go into their bodies. In fact, according to the *Contra Costa Times* of September 2, 2006, some surgical procedures, such as dental implants and joint reconstruction, may involve the use of cadaver tissue without the knowledge of the patient at all.

While doctors may not disclose all the details of a procedure to their patients because of complacency, ignorance, or poor communication skills, those involved in the tissue trade are motivated to engage in misinformation and shortcuts because of the potential monetary gain. The previously mentioned lack of a sufficient tissue supply has led to a spike in the value of a cadaver, and an increase in the number of fraudulent cases. The April 28, 2006 *USA Today* points out that a healthy cadaver is worth between $200,000 and $250,000 for all its parts. Because of the high level of motivation, people are continually committing atrocities very similar to the case of Alistair Cooke.

With such a large problem only now coming to the forefront, many steps need to be taken if the tissue trade is to recover from its giant wounds. Changes must be made on governmental, institutional, and personal levels. As far as the government is concerned, stricter regulations on the trade are beyond necessary. According to the Food and Drug Administration Web site, last accessed April 25, 2007, they are currently forming the Human Tissue Task Force, whose goal is to identify additional steps needed to further protect public health while assuring the availability of safe tissue products. But this is not enough. The FDA needs to start now by closely monitoring this industry and begin by tightening the paperwork requirements for licensure, including background checks, thorough inspections before approval, and random monitoring to make sure procedures are being carried out properly.

In the meantime, as the *States News Service* of August 30, 2006, points out, at an institutional level, doctors should disclose all aspects of a tissue-oriented procedure and contact all patients who received tissues in the past, to urge them to get tested for HIV, hepatitis, syphilis, and a number of other conditions. While this measure is not necessarily preventative, it will ensure that such diseases are detected and treated to the best of modern science's ability. In addition, in order to ensure that tissues are properly harvested and treated, those companies that participate in the tissue trade must be required to maintain membership in the American Association of Tissue Banks.

On a personal level, we need to become more informed. As patients, we should discuss all the details of procedures with our doctors. We should also talk to family and friends and ensure that they are informed of these problems as well. As a result of a better informed public, we'll all remain safe from the dangers of the tissue trade. Just as fresh tissue and organs can restore the human body, more regulation and better attention to detail can revive the tissue trade that reeks of debilitation, disease, and even death.

And now that we've explored the problems within the tissue trade, its impact on society, and what we can do on governmental, institutional, and personal levels to solve this problem, we are better prepared to protect our society, our families, and even ourselves. Alistair Cooke's television career brought the prestige of the arts into our living rooms for generations. And now that Cooke's death has come to the forefront of controversy in the tissue trade, he is, once again, shedding light on new topics. This one, however, may do more than just engage our minds; it may indeed save lives.

Ovarian Cancer: Breaking the Silence*

by Viqar Mohammad

Johanna Silver Gordon was a healthy and active woman. She ate a heart-healthy diet, exercised regularly, but above all else she was diligent in receiving an annual Pap smear and mammogram. To everyone she appeared to be in the best of health. Naturally she was alarmed after a few weeks of minor gastrointestinal upset—and made an appointment with her doctor. There, she was informed that she had Stage four ovarian cancer. At age 55, this mother of two was told that she had less than three years to live.

According to the National Ovarian Cancer Coalition, every 9 minutes in the United States a woman is diagnosed with ovarian cancer. Each year 15,000 women die from the insidious and deadly disease. Simply put, ovarian cancer is the deadliest of all gynecological cancers. However, it is crucial for us to realize that this is not just a speech about women. Just as speeches about prostrate or testicular cancers are not just about men. I can speak from experience while working as a student nurse on an oncology floor that gender-specific cancer does not only affect that gender. Therefore it is imperative that we first, examine this most deadly—yet when detected early, most preventable—cancer, second, discuss the lack of information and awareness

*From *Winning Orations, 2007* (Mankato, MN: Interstate Oratorical Association, Larry Schnoor, Ex. Sec., 2007).

surrounding this silent killer, and finally, offer some practical steps that we can take to save the lives of our nation's women.

According to *Mosby's Medical Dictionary*, ovarian cancer is traditionally a carcinoma: a type of cancer that infests the lining of organs and rapidly spreads to other parts of the body. Typically this kind of cancer effects women in their 40s or 50s, but is capable of affecting just about anyone. Take, for example, Jacqui Lowe, who was diagnosed with Stage 4 ovarian cancer at the age of 23. Similar to many other kinds of cancer, ovarian cancer has a genetic predisposition. According to the National Cancer Institute's Web site, updated daily, for every first-degree relative that has ovarian cancer, your risk increases three times. Now, during the initial tumor growth, the cancer is said to be in Stage 1 and is generally contained to the ovaries themselves. During this time, the survival rate is above 90 percent. However, treatment does require a total hysterectomy. Tragically, Stage 4 cancer spreads into another organ system entirely— leaving the patient with a terminal prognosis. Clearly it is evident that the early detection is crucial, but according to the American Cancer Society, only 19 percent of cases are detected during this time when survival rates are as high as 90 percent.

So, why are 81 percent of cases going undetected? To put it simply, the misinformation and myths surrounding ovarian cancer are deadly. The confusion stems from two levels—a gross misunderstanding of early warning signs and the misinformation surrounding available diagnostic testing.

You see, the symptoms of ovarian cancer are anything but overt—as one woman describes it, "Ovarian cancer whispers; the warnings are ever so subtle and the result so deadly." A study published by the National Ovarian Cancer Association on September 7, 2006 reports that 96 percent of women incorrectly identified typical ovarian cancer symptoms. Unlike other cancers where symptoms are much more pronounced, the typical early warning signs of ovarian cancer are extremely elusive. Innocuous signs such as gastrointestinal upset, feeling bloated, or abdominal cramping are too often dismissed entirely or attributed to stress or the menstrual cycle and subsequently ignored. The inherent danger of these subtle warning sounds is compounded by the confusion over diagnostic testing.

In a similar study conducted by the National Ovarian Cancer Coalition in April of 2006, two in three women stated that they believed their annual pap smear detected ovarian cancer. In actuality, the Pap smear screening only detects precursors for cervical or uterine cancer. This "one size fits all" mentality of cancer screening is incredibly dangerous. Take, for example, 30-year-old Katherine Nazar who responded to her diagnosis of Stage 3 ovarian cancer with "I was shocked . . . just 6 weeks earlier I had a pelvic exam and a pap test. I just assumed this would certainly catch any gynecological problem." However, perhaps this confusion is at least understandable when one realizes that there are simply no early diagnostic methods available. A recent study published April 17, 2006 by the Society of Gynecologic Oncologists established a method of combining traditional ultrasounds with the new CA125 antigen test. This blood test detects serum tumor markers found in ovarian cancer. Admittedly, the combination of screening techniques promotes the correct detection of ovarian cancer in 93 percent of patients. However neither of these diagnostic examinations detects ovarian cancer in early stage, when the prognosis is optimistic. This lack of awareness, misunderstanding of early symptoms, and the confusion over diagnostic testing all contribute to this silent disease.

Now that we know exactly what ovarian cancer is and why so many women needlessly succumb to it, we need to examine solutions that will help us protect the lives of our nation's women. First, we need to increase the awareness about ovarian cancer and exactly what resources are available. On the national level, the Ovarian Cancer Coalition has spearheaded this fight by launching their "Break the Silence" campaign. The program provides free educational materials at their Web site ovarian.org in addition to a 24-hour-a-day hotline at 1-888-OVARIAN. Increased awareness and education will only improve earlier diagnosis [and] treatment and help save lives. This is a great start, but as Elizabeth Ross, executive director of the National Ovarian Cancer

Alliance, warns, "We've got a lot to do, in terms of awareness. Ovarian cancer is where breast cancer was 20 years ago today."

Work is already being done at the legislative level with the introduction of Johanna's Law, named for Johanna Silver Gordon. This provides funding for such public services as the "Break the Silence" campaign, along with important research funding to discover new early screening methods. The CA125 test shows promise, but research must continue until we have a tool as reliable for ovarian cancer as the colonoscopy is for colon cancers.

Until then, the most important weapon—the only weapon—against ovarian cancer is awareness and education. As Barbara O'Brien, president of the Massachusetts Ovarian Cancer Coalition states, "Education can save your life and ignorance can kill you. This is no truer than with ovarian cancer." Finally, we need a behavioral change in how we view disease and healthcare. We need to take the responsibility to inform our doctors when we feel something isn't right. As obstetrician Dr. Craig Hinkle, an expert in ovarian cancer, stresses to his patients, "Pay attention. No one knows your body the way you do."

According to the CDC, twenty years ago the mortality rate of prostate cancer was 30 percent. Three out of ten men died due to a lack of awareness, improper diagnostic testing, and the overarching assumption that it "couldn't happen to me." Over two decades of increased funding, increased awareness, and improvements in treatment, now the mortality rate is just 3 percent. Today, we are at the same turning point with ovarian cancer. Currently, the mortality rate of ovarian cancer is above 90 percent. Just imagine how much lower that number could be.

In the last 9 minutes, we've explored ovarian cancer, the deadly problems associated with the disease, and analyzed solutions to break the silence. In the last 9 minutes, a woman has been diagnosed with ovarian cancer. Women like the mother of Rene Rossi, who in the last months of her life told her daughter, "You must do something about this disease." In the past 9 minutes you have been given the power to do just that. Do it for the women in our lives—our mothers, our daughters, our loved ones. Shout out this silent killer.

The Hillbilly Girl*

by Bridget Traut

"Sallie Mae sounds like a naïve and barefoot hillbilly girl, but in fact they are a ruthless and aggressive conglomeration of bullies located in a tall brick building somewhere in Kansas. I picture it to be the tallest building in that state and I have decided they hire their employees straight out of prison. It scares me." Author David Sedaris presents his image of the student loan company Sallie Mae in "The Santaland Diaries." Sedaris hit the nail on the head when he referred to the company's ruthless and aggressive approach to student loans. The April 17, 2007 *Boston Globe* reports that Sallie Mae earned $3.6 billion last year, making it one of the most profitable companies in the world. Additionally the April 2, 2007 *Washington Post* reveals that Sallie Mae manages $142 billion in student loans, making it by far the largest student lender in the country. And the April 16, 2007 *New York Times* explains that the recent $25 billion deal to sell the company to equity buyers will ultimately increase Sallie Mae's profits and give it even more of an advantage over smaller rivals.

Sallie Mae has gotten rich by taking no risks and taking advantage of the students who are most desperately in need of college loans. We live in a society where a college education is becoming crucial to one's success and students are encouraged to go into

*From *Winning Orations, 2007* (Mankato, MN: Interstate Oratorical Association, Larry Schnoor, Ex. Sec., 2007).

debt to obtain that education, yet giant corporations such as Sallie Mae are allowed to prey on students, who the January 6, 2005 *Wall Street Journal* identifies as financially unsophisticated borrowers. Therefore, it is imperative that we put a stop to Sallie Mae's predatory lending practices by first, examining the problems students encounter when dealing with Sallie Mae, second, investigating the causes of Sallie Mae's disturbing success, before finally exploring some practical solutions to ensure that obtaining a higher education does not turn into a greater financial burden than it already is.

Behind the barefeet and hillbilly wholesomeness of Sallie Mae lies a ruthless criminal. Yet the name alone conjures connotations of innocence and honesty, thus making Sallie Mae appear to be approachable and trustworthy. But once she lures her victims in, there's no escape. Sallie Mae's most lucrative business comes from its private loan market. The previously cited *New York Times* explains these private loans help close the gap between tuition costs and federal aid, such as Direct Loans and Pell Grants from the U.S. Department of Education. The problem is, according to *Fortune* magazine of December 14, 2005, these private loans can have astronomical interest rates, some as high as 28 percent. Compare that to the current interest rate of 6.8 percent on Direct Loans from the Department of Education. What's worse, these private loans from Sallie Mae are targeted at low-income students who have already exhausted federal funds and have no other means of affording college. And these low-income students are precisely the students who need a college education. In a cruel twist of fate, today's students are encouraged to go into debt to pursue a higher education and, according December 12, 2005 *New York Times*, nearly half of those who start college never graduate, in part because of the financial burden.

Moreover, Sallie Mae has no incentive to be nice, because the company makes money no matter what happens to us students. If you pay back on time, Sallie Mae makes money from the interest. If you default on a loan, the federal government pays Sallie Mae the principle and interest because it has guaranteed the loan. And it gets even better for Sallie Mae. The company has the opportunity to hunt you down to try and collect on the loan. According to the May 7, 2006 *60 Minutes*, Sallie Mae owns some of the biggest collection agencies in the country and gets to keep up to 25 percent of any amount recovered. Furthermore, StudentLoanJustice.org, a grassroots organization devoted to bringing about student lending reform, last updated April 23, 2007, notes that if you do default on a loan, your wages can be garnished, income tax returns can be seized, public employment can be terminated, and social security and disability payments can be confiscated, effectively leaving you with virtually no hope of ever repaying the mounting fees and interest. Moreover, the January 11, 2007 *Denver Post* reports that most student loans are exempt from bankruptcy laws.

Ultimately, Sallie Mae's legally underhanded practices leave students with little hope. StudentLoanJustice.org offers hundreds of testimonials from student borrowers of all ages about their negative experiences with student lenders, in particular Sallie Mae. Erica, a woman making monthly payments of over $1,000, remarked, "Makes you wonder why you tried to better yourself in the first place." David, a graduate from chiropractic school who started with about $40,000 in loans, now owes over $300,000, can't renew his license in order to generate income to make payments, and has contemplated suicide. Brit Napoli asks, "How does the American middle class dream of an affordable higher education become a nightmare? Default on a student loan."

Sallie Mae may have initially started out as a barefoot hillbilly girl, but she certainly grew up fast and, in the process, caused a lot of problems for students. The May 17, 2006 *Free-Market News* explains that Sallie Mae was created with good intentions as a governmental agency, but the government never completely severed its ties when the company became private in 2004. The article further reports that Sallie Mae's stock price has risen 2,000 percent, more than Microsoft. According to CNNMoney.com of March 30, 2007, from 1995 to 2005, Sallie Mae had a 26 percent annual rate of total return to investors compared to Microsoft's 18.5 percent. In the

April 16, 2007 *Washington Post*, Colin Blaydon, a professor at Dartmouth's Tuck School of Business, suggests that the $25 billion deal to sell Sallie Mae could ultimately make the company more profitable. The April 17, 2007 *Washington Post* further explains that Sallie Mae, Bank of America, and J.P. Morgan Chase will have combined resources, thus helping them withstand threats from Congress and move from restrictive federal loans into the lucrative private loan market, debt collection, and marketing of college savings plans.

Perhaps the biggest problem with Sallie Mae is that the government virtually guarantees that the company will make money. Basically, Congress wanted to help students who otherwise would not qualify for a loan, and so created "the guaranteed loan program" for private lenders, also known as the Federal Family Education Loan Program, or the FFELP. Under this program, the government promises to repay virtually all the losses that Sallie Mae and other private lenders incur when students default on loans. In other words, Sallie Mae has virtually no risk when making private loans to students and thus can target anyone, particularly low-income students.

Furthermore, it would appear that Sallie Mae has a partner in crime. The recent investigation by the New York Attorney General into how private lenders secure spots on what are known as schools' preferred lender lists reveals a shady partnership between universities and lenders such as Sallie Mae. Sallie Mae dominates the competition by offering kickbacks to colleges who steer their students toward the company. It's called the school-as-lender. Basically, Sallie Mae pays universities to help administer Sallie Mae loans, and, to return the favor, universities push their students to Sallie Mae. In a May 8, 2006 response to *60 Minutes*, Sallie Mae claims that schools have benefited from competition and having the option of choosing among lenders instead of only dealing with the federal government. Ironic that a corporation that, according to the aforementioned April 2, 2007 *Washington Post*, is clearly the unchallenged giant of the student loan industry is attempting to create the façade that there is a competition.

Basically, the cunning criminal Sallie Mae has ripped off her hillbilly mask, backed us into a corner, and attempted to rob us blind. Luckily, there is hope for escape with some simple, practical solutions at the governmental and individual level. First, the government should completely switch to the Direct Loan Program to ensure that the people benefiting from student loan programs are, in fact, students. According to a September 29, 2006 report from the *Congressional Research Service*, the nonpartisan research arm of Congress, the Direct Loan Program was originally introduced to expand and replace the FFELP. But 1998 amendments to the Higher Education Act stopped the Direct Loan phase-in. According to the December 12, 2005 *New York Times*, a recent Government Accountability Office report revealed that direct loans cost the government one-fifth as much as subsidized loans over the past 10 years. Furthermore, Representative George Miller, chairman of the House Education and Labor Committee, estimates that the government could save $60 billion over the next decade by completely switching to the Direct Loan Program. Those savings could then transform into a 50 percent increase in Pell Grant money. These grants would increase the amount of free money available to low-income students while simultaneously decreasing the amount of private loans they would need.

Secondly, although it is difficult to force the federal government to stop subsidizing Sallie Mae's loans, the solution to this problem really relies on us. As college students, graduate students, parents and parents-to-be of college students, the chances are good that we are at least somewhat familiar with loans. But, if we do have loans, we need to become sophisticated borrowers and, as *Newsweek* of April 16, 2007 suggests, read the fine print about our loans. I urge you to check with your school's financial aid office because, according to Sallie Mae's Web site on March 30, 2007, schools can recommend lenders to borrow from, but, ultimately, the choice is up to us. Avoid borrowing from Sallie Mae if at all possible. Instead, if you are eligible, make sure your college loans are from the government through the Direct Loan Program. If, however, you already have loans from Sallie Mae, make sure you make your payments on time and, if you are able, pay more than the minimum. Furthermore, you might consider consolidating your loans at a lower interest rate to get away from Sallie Mae. Finally, if you know of someone thinking about taking out loans to pay for college, encourage them to borrow from a lender other than Sallie Mae.

Ultimately, if we, as Americans, continue to place a significant value on a college education, we must be willing to help students find a way to afford that education. We first examined the problems Sallie Mae creates for students, investigated the causes, and explored some practical solutions. Sallie Mae, with our help, has graduated from bare feet and overalls to Prada shoes and Versace dresses. Now, it's up to us to send her back to the cornfields where she belongs.

 ## A Jury Not of Her Peers*

by Colston Reid

Manny Babbitt, a diagnosed paranoid schizophrenic, returned from the conflict in Vietnam a broken man. His brother, Bill Babbitt, explained to an audience at John Jay College of Criminal Justice on Nov. 2, 2006 that due to his illness, Manny spent most of his adult life between mental hospitals and the streets until the day he unknowingly killed an elderly California woman without understanding his motivations. The prosecutor vowed before the trial not to seek the death penalty, but the Babbitt family became concerned when prospective jurors were asked a simple question: Could you follow the law and sentence a man to death? Those who would not were dismissed, resulting in a jury who—to no one's surprise—voted to convict and execute Manny.

Our justice system promises that the accused are innocent until proven guilty; however, a procedure employed in capital trials, which forces jurors to consider punishment before conviction, has become the accepted norm in our justice system. Death Qualification, according to the March 2007 *Journal of Applied Social Psychology*, is a questioning process employed during voir dire, or jury selection, which eliminates all potential jurors who voice opposition to the death penalty. Because *Amnesty International* of December 12, 2006 reports that death-qualified juries decided the fate of nearly 3,400 death penalty cases within the last year, we must first examine the prejudice of jury death qualification; next, identify its roots, so that finally, we can explore solutions with the power to save our trial by jury system, an institution that the Fall 2006 edition of *Policy and Politics* claims is the last bastion of direct democracy in our country.

The 2006 *Buffalo Public Interest Law Journal* argues that we would never exclude anyone who opposes the death penalty from voting in an election, so why do we exclude them in the courtroom? Doing so creates two problems: First, the jury does not represent a fair cross-section of the community, and next, the jury is biased toward the prosecution. First, the constitution requires all criminal proceedings have a fair and impartial jury. The *Washington Post* of February 11, 2007 reports that 48 percent of Americans favor life imprisonment over the death penalty. In order to ensure a fair cross-section of the community, some death penalty objectors would have to be on the jury; guaranteeing a group that the 2006 *Journal of Personality and Social Psychology* claims is less biased and subject to group think. The January 2007 *Journal of Applied Social Psychology* argues that once death penalty objectors are removed, the resulting jury pool is likely to be male, Caucasian, financially secure, politically conservative, and Protestant Christian; leaving nearly half of the American public unrepresented.

*From *Winning Orations, 2007* (Mankato, MN: Interstate Oratorical Association, Larry Schnoor, Ex. Sec., 2007).

Next, death qualification biases jurors toward conviction. The 2007 edition of *Behavioral Sciences and the Law* explains that death-qualified juries are more likely to have a pessimistic world outlook, believe in the infallibility of the criminal justice system, and exhibit an unwillingness to impartially consider the evidence before them. Harold Wilson understands this all too well. He tells the *Philadelphia Bulletin* of April 16, 2007, that, had it been up to the state of Pennsylvania, he would be dead right now. Wilson spent 17 years on Pennsylvania's death row, all because Assistant District Attorney Jack McMahon was able to utilize death qualification to assure that his jury was not only racially prejudiced but unwilling to consider evidence that would have exonerated him. Sadly, Wilson's case is the norm in capital trials and not the exception. The Fall 2006 *Arizona State Law Review* explains that the effect of watching jurors who cannot impose the death penalty be replaced by someone who can biases the remaining panel towards conviction. Why else would jurors be willing to consider punishment before the trial has even begun? Once this process is complete, the result is a jury that is pro-prosecution, pro-conviction, and pro-death.

If justice is supposed to be blind, then why do those who oppose the death penalty never serve on capital trials? First, because the Supreme Court affirmed the death-qualification process, and next, because our legal system fears nullifying the death penalty. First, the 1986 *Lockhart v. McCree* Supreme Court ruling upheld the constitutionality of death-qualified juries. In their published opinion, released in 1986, the Supreme Court conceded that death qualification produces more conviction-prone juries, but claimed that there was nothing in the Constitution that prohibits their use. The 2007 *Indiana Law Review* explains that death penalty objectors do not represent a distinctive segment of society, such as a racial or gender group, so excluding them isn't technically discrimination. In making this ruling, the Supreme Court made a bold statement: that the 6th Amendment's promise of a fair and impartial jury, put in place to assure the due process for the accused, does not exist when deciding issues of death.

Next, the primary purpose of death qualification is to ensure the death penalty remains a viable punishment. The April 2006 *Journal of Law and Human Behavior* explains some death penalty objectors will attempt to get on capital juries precisely for the opportunity to vote for innocence. Because the *Atlanta Journal Constitution* of February 11, 2007 explains that the death penalty requires unanimous approval from all jurors, avoiding these potential nullifiers is the primary intent behind voir dire questions such as Are you able to follow the law? Or, would you allow your morals to get in the way? John Clark, the Arkansas attorney general, explained in his opening remarks during the *Lockhart v. McCree* hearing that had the court overturned death qualification, 90 percent of death row inmates would have to be retried and 30 of the 37 states who have legalized the death penalty would have to change their laws.

Regardless of our opinions surrounding the death penalty, it is our responsibility to ensure that when the law requires its use, the sentencing jury makes their decision with as little bias or predisposition as possible. However, only if action is taken on a federal, judicial, and personal level can we begin to level the scales of justice in our legal system. First, the Federal Jury Selection and Service Act of 1968 mandates that no jury show bias towards any particular race, gender, religion, or economic stature. However, this law does not apply to death qualification. The Judicial Committee of Congress must revisit this act and amend it to ensure that prosecutors are no longer allowed to discriminate against death penalty ideology, just as they would not discriminate against race or religion. Next, the *Arizona Republic* of February 7, 2007 explains that it is difficult to find public defenders trained to handle death penalty cases and the death qualification process. When a prosecutor asks, "Are you willing to sentence a man to die?" the defense must be prepared to balance it with a question of their own, such as, "Will the defendant's background or mental capacity play a role in your verdict?" or "Could you follow the law and sentence a man to life in prison with or without parole?" These two sample questions remind the jury not only that the defendant has not been convicted, but that there are alternatives to the death penalty.

Finally, as citizens we must recognize that death qualification exists, and keep that in mind if you are ever called to serve as a juror on a capital trial. When asked if you have the capacity to impose the death penalty, it is your responsibility to acknowledge the motivations behind the question. Answer the question honestly, but understand that your response could dictate the outcome of the trial. Jury death qualification poses a grave threat, not only to the rights of the accused, but also to the fair and impartial administration of justice.

After examining the injustices of jury death qualification, uncovering their roots, and finally exploring some solutions, one thing is clear. Manny Babbitt never had a chance. From the moment his jury was impaneled, they were predisposed towards death. Only by reforming the death qualification process can we ensure that others do not share a similar fate.

Endnotes

CHAPTER 1

1. Louis Nizer, *Reflections Without Mirrors*, quoted in Jack Valenti, *Speak Up with Confidence: How to Prepare, Learn, and Deliver Effective Speeches* (New York: Morrow, 1982) 34.

2. Judy C. Pearson, Jeffrey T. Child, and David H. Kahl, Jr., "Preparation Meeting Opportunity: How Do College Students Prepare for Public Speeches?" *Communication Quarterly* 54.3 (Aug. 2006): 351.

3. Pearson, Child, and Kahl, "Preparation Meeting Opportunity": 355.

4. James C. Humes, *The Sir Winston Method: Five Secrets of Speaking the Language of Leadership* (New York: Morrow, 1991) 13–14.

5. Charles Schwab, as quoted in Brent Filson, *Executive Speeches: Tips on How to Write and Deliver Speeches from 51 CEOs* (New York: Wiley, 1994) 45.

6. Dee-Ann Durbin, "Study: Plenty of Jobs for Graduates in 2000," *Austin American-Statesman* 5 Dec. 1999: A28.

7. Dan B. Curtis, Jerry L. Winsor, and Ronald D. Stephens, "National Preferences in Business and Communication Education," *Communication Education* 38 (Jan. 1989): 6–14. See also Iain Hay, "Justifying and Applying Oral Presentations in Geographical Education," *Journal of Geography in Higher Education* 18.1 (1994): 44–45.

8. Jerry L. Winsor, Dan B. Curtis, and Ronald D. Stephens, "National Preferences in Business and Communication Education: A Survey Update," *Journal of the Association for Communication Administration* (3 Sept. 1997): 174.

9. University of Wisconsin–River Falls, Career Services, "What Skills and Attributes Employers Seek When Hiring Students." June 4, 2007 <http://www.uwrf.edu/ccs/skills/htm>.

10. Camille Luckenbaugh and Kevin Gray, "Employers Describe Perfect Job Candidate," National Association of Colleges and Employers Survey. June 4, 2007 <http://www.naceweb.org/press/display.asp?year=2003&prid=169>.

11. Randall S. Hansen and Katharine Handson, "What Do Employers Really Want? Top Skills and Values Employers Seek from Job-Seekers." June 4, 2007 <http://www.quintcareers.com/job_skills_values.html>.

12. Melinda Henneberger, "In Speech Process Reversal, Gore Wrote, Aides Whittled," *The New York Times* 18 Aug. 2000: A1.

13. PBS, "The March on Washington." 6 June 2004 <www.pbs.org/greatspeeches/timeline/m_king_b1.html>.

14. L. M. Boyd, syndicated column, *Austin American-Statesman* 8 Aug. 2000: E3.

15. Herman Cohen, *The History of Speech Communication: The Emergence of a Discipline: 1914–1945* (Annandale, VA: Speech Communication Association, 1994) 2.

16. Mark Twain, *The Adventures of Tom Sawyer*, 1876, ed. Stephen Railton and the U of Virginia Library. 2000. 4 July 2001 <http://etext.virginia.edu/railton/about/srchmtf.html>.

17. George W. Bush, Address to the nation on 11 Sept. 2001, *The New York Times* 22 Sept. 2001: A4.

18. Adetokunbo F. Knowles-Borishade, "Paradigm for Classical African Orature," Christine Kelly et al., eds., *Diversity in Public Communication: A Reader*, (Dubuque, IA: Kendall-Hunt, 1994) 100.

19. Patricia A. Sullivan, "Signification and African-American Rhetoric: A Case Study of Jesse Jackson's 'Common Ground and Common Sense' Speech," *Communication Quarterly* 41.1 (1993): 1–15.

20. Gadi Dechter, "Trudeau Advises Grads Their Time Will Come," *BaltimoreSun.com*. 26 May 2007. 8 June 2007 <http://www.baltimoresun.com/news/education/balmd.goucher26may26,0,4799301.story?track=rss>.

21. Survey conducted by R. H. Bruskin and Associates, *Spectra* 9 (Dec. 1973): 4; D. Wallechinsky, Irving Wallace, and Amy Wallace, *The People's Almanac Presents the Book of Lists* (New York: Morrow, 1977).

22. Steven Booth Butterfield, "Instructional Interventions for Reducing Situational Anxiety and Avoidance," *Communication Education* 37 (1988): 214–23; also see Michael Motley, *Overcoming Your Fear of Public Speaking: A Proven Method* (New York: McGraw-Hill, 1995).

23. Joe Ayres and Theodore S. Hopf, "The Long-Term Effect of Visualization in the Classroom: A Brief Research Report," *Communication Education* 39 (1990): 75–78.

24. John Burk, "Communication Apprehension among Master's of Business Administration Students: Investigating a Gap in Communication Education," *Communication Education* 50 (Jan. 2001): 51–58; Lynne Kelly and James A. Keaten, "Treating Communication Anxiety: Implications of the Communibiological Paradigm," *Communication Education* 49 (Jan. 2000): 45–57; Amber N. Finn, Chris R. Sawyer, and Ralph R. Behnke, "Audience-Perceived Anxiety Patterns of Public Speakers," *Communication Education* 51 (Fall 2003): 470–81.

25. Maili Porhola, "Orientation Styles in a Public-Speaking Context," paper presented at the National Communication Association convention, Seattle, Washington, Nov. 2000; Ralph R. Behnke and Michael J. Beatty, "A Cognitive-Physiological

Model of Speech Anxiety," *Communication Monographs* 48 (1981): 158–63.

26. Ralph R. Behnke and Chris R. Sawyer, "Public Speaking Anxiety as a Function of Sensitization and Habituation Processes," *Communication Research Reports* 53 (Apr. 2004): 164–73.

27. Amy M. Bippus and John A. Daly, "What Do People Think Causes Stage Fright? Naïve Attributions About the Reasons for Public-Speaking Anxiety," *Communication Education* 48 (1999): 63–72.

28. Yang Lin and Andrew S. Rancer, "Sex Differences in Intercultural Communication Apprehension, Ethnocentrism, and Intercultural Willingness to Communicate," *Psychological Reports* 92 (2003): 195–200.

29. Michael J. Beatty, James C. McCroskey, and A. D. Heisel, "Communication Apprehension as Temperamental Expression: A Communibiological Paradigm," *Communication Monographs* 65 (1998): 197–219; Michael J. Beatty and Kristin Marie Valencic, "Context-Based Apprehension Versus Planning Demands: A Communibiological Analysis of Anticipatory Public Speaking Anxiety," *Communication Education* 49 (Jan. 2000): 58–71.

30. Kay B. Harris, Chris R. Sawyer, and Ralph R. Behnke, "Predicting Speech State Anxiety from Trait Anxiety, Reactivity, and Situational Influences," *Communication Quarterly* 54 (May 2006): 213–26.

31. Kelly and Keaten, "Treating Communication Anxiety."

32. Maili Porhola, "Arousal Styles during Public Speaking," *Communication Education* 51 (Oct. 2002): 420–38.

33. Kelly and Keaten, "Treating Communication Anxiety."

34. Leon Fletcher, *How to Design & Deliver Speeches* (New York: Longman, 2001) 3.

35. Ralph R. Behnke and Chris R. Sawyer, "Public-Speaking Procrastination as a Correlate of Public-Speaking Communication Apprehension and Self-Perceived Public-Speaking Competence," *Communication Research Reports* 16 (1999): 40–47.

36. Peter D. MacIntyre and J. Renee MacDonald, "Public-Speaking Anxiety: Perceived Competence and Audience Congeniality," *Communication Education* 47 (Oct. 1998): 359–65.

37. Joe Ayres, Terry Schliesman, and Debbie Ayres Sonandre, "Practice Makes Perfect but Does It Help Reduce Communication Apprehension?" *Communication Research Reports* 15 (Spring 1998): 170–79.

38. Melanie Booth-Butterfield, "Stifle or Stimulate? The Effects of Communication Task Structure on Apprehensive and Non-Apprehensive Students," *Communication Education* 35 (1986): 337–48; Charles R. Berger, "Speechlessness: Causal Attributions, Emotional Features, and Social Consequences," *Journal of Language & Social Psychology* 23 (June 2004): 147–79.

39. Joe Ayres, Tim Hopf, and Elizabeth Peterson, "A Test of Communication-Orientation Motivation (COM) Therapy," *Communication Reports* 13 (Winter 2000): 35–44; Joe Ayres and Tanichya K. Wongprasert, "Measuring the Impact of Visualization on Mental Imagery: Comparing Prepared Versus Original Drawings," *Communication Research Reports* 20 (Winter 2003): 45–53.

40. Joe Ayers and Theodore S. Hopf, "Visualization: A Means of Reducing Speech Anxiety," *Communication Education* 34 (1985): 318–23. Although researchers have found evidence that visualization is helpful, some question whether visualization techniques work better than just gaining experience in public speaking. Critics of systematic desensitization argue that there

may be a placebo effect: Just thinking that a treatment will reduce apprehension may contribute to reduced apprehension. See Desiree C. Duff, Timothy R. Levine, Michael J. Beatty, Jessica Woolbright, and Hee Sun Park, "Testing Public Anxiety Treatments Against a Credible Placebo Control," *Communication Education* 56 (Jan. 2007): 72–88.

41. Ayres and Wongprasert, "Measuring the Impact of Visualization on Mental Imagery."

42. Ayres and Wongprasert, "Measuring the Impact of Visualization on Mental Imagery."

43. Joe Ayres and Debbie M. Ayres Sonandre, "Performance Visualization: Does the Nature of the Speech Model Matter?" *Communication Research Reports* 20 (Summer 2003): 260–68.

44. Duff, Levine, Beatty, Woolbright, and Park, "Testing Public Anxiety Treatments Against a Credible Placebo Control."

45. Joe Ayres and Brian L. Heuett, "An Examination of the Impact of Performance Visualization," *Communication Research Reports* 16 (1999): 29–39.

46. Penny Addison, Ele Clay, Shuang Xie, Chris R. Sawyer, and Ralph R. Behnke, "Worry as a Function of Public Speaking State Anxiety Type," *Communication Reports* 16 (Summer 2003): 125–31.

47. MacIntyre and MacDonald, "Public-Speaking Anxiety"; Peter D. MacIntyre and K. A. Thivierge, "The Effects of Audience Pleasantness, Audience Familiarity, and Speaking Contexts on Public-Speaking Anxiety and Willingness to Speak," *Communication Quarterly* 43 (1995): 456–66; Peter D. MacIntyre, K. A. Thivierge, and J. Renee MacDonald, "The Effects of Audience Interest, Responsiveness, and Evaluation on Public-Speaking Anxiety and Related Variables," *Communication Research Reports* 14 (1997): 157–68.

48. MacIntyre and MacDonald, "Public-Speaking Anxiety"; R. B. Rubin, A. M. Rubin, and F. F. Jordan, "Effects of Instruction on Communication Apprehension and Communication Competence," *Communication Education* 46 (1997): 104–14.

49. Lisa M. Schroeder, "The Effects of Skills Training on Communication Satisfaction and Communication Anxiety in the Basic Speech Course," *Communication Research Reports* 19 (2002): 380–88; Alain Morin, "History of Exposure to Audiences as a Developmental Antecedent of Public Self-Consciousness," *Current Research in Social Psychology* 5 (Mar. 2000): 33–46.

50. Stephen R. Covey, *The 7 Habits of Highly Successful People* (New York: Simon and Schuster, 1989).

CHAPTER 2

1. The late Waldo Braden, long-time professor of speech communication at Louisiana State University, presented a memorable speech at the 1982 meeting of the Florida Speech Communication Association in which he emphasized "The audience writes the speech" to indicate the importance and centrality of being an audience-centered speaker.

2. J. C. Pearson, J. T. Child, and D. H. Kahl, Jr., "Preparation Meeting Opportunity: How Do College Students Prepare for Public Speeches?" *Communication Quarterly*, 54(3) (Aug. 2006): 351–66.

3. William Herndon, "Lecture on January 24, 1866," quoted in "Abraham Lincoln as a Speaker." 2004. 7 June 2004 <showcase .netins.net/web/creative/Lincoln/speeches/speaker.htm>.

4. Dover, New Hampshire *Inquirer,* March 8, 1860, quoted in

"Abraham Lincoln as a Speaker." 2004. 7 June 2004 <showcase .netins.net/web/creative/Lincoln/speeches/speaker.htm>.

5. Clifford Stoll, as cited by Kevin A. Miller, "Capture: The Essential Survival Skill for Leaders Buckling Under Information Overload," *Leadership* (Spring 1992): 85.

6. Greg Winter, "The Chips Are Down: Frito-Lay Cuts Costs with Smaller Servings," *Austin American-Statesman* 2 Jan. 2001: A6.

7. We thank Barbara Patton of Texas State University for sharing her speech outline with us.

8. Pearson, Child, and Kahl, Jr., "Preparation Meeting Opportunity."

9. Sample speech written by Pao Yang Lee, "Our Immigration Story," in Tasha Van Horn, Lori Charron, and Michael Charron, *Allyn & Bacon Video II User's Guide*, 2002.

CHAPTER 3

1. Liz Rhoades, "Author Isaacs Calls on Graduates to Speak Up." *Queens Chronicle*. 7 June 2007. 10 June 2007 <http:www .zwire.com/site/news.cfm?newsid=18450494&BRD= 2731&PAG=461&dept_id=574902&rfi=6">.

2. See Wayne Ham, *Man's Living Religions* (Independence, MO: Herald Publishing House, 1966) 39–40; Huston Smith, *The World's Religions* (San Francisco: HarperSanFrancisco, 1991).

3. National Communication Association. "NCA Credo for Communication Ethics." 1999. 27 June 2001 <http://www.natcom .org/conferences/Ethics/ethicsconfcredo99.htm>.

4. Samuel Walker, *Hate Speech* (Lincoln: U of Nebraska P, 1994) 162.

5. "Libel and Slander." *The Ethical Spectacle*. 1 June 1997 <http://www.spectacle.org/freespch/musm/libel.html>.

6. "Three Decades Later, Free Speech Vets Return to UC Berkeley," *Sacramento Bee* 3 Dec. 1994: A1.

7. James S. Tyre, "Legal Definition of Obscenity, Pornography." 1 June 1997 <http://internet.ggu.edu/university_library/reg/ _legal_obscene.html>.

8. "Supreme Court Rules: Cyberspace Will Be Free! ACLU Hails Victory in Internet Censorship Challenge." *American Civil Liberties Union Freedom Network*. 26 June 1997. 1 June 1998 <http://www.aclu.org/news/no62697a.html>.

9. Sue Anne Pressley, "Oprah Winfrey Wins Case Filed by Cattlemen." *Washington Post* 27 Feb. 1998. 1 June 1998 <http:// www.washingtonpost.com/wp-srv/WPlate/ 1998-02/27/1001-022798-idx.html>.

10. Associated Press, "Free-Speech, Other Groups File Briefs Opposing Patriot Act." 4 Nov. 2003. 13 June 2004 <http://www .firstamendmentcenter.org/news.aspx?id=12174>.

11. Brian Schweitzer, "Proclamation of Clemency for Montanans Convicted under the Montana Sedition Act in 1918–1919." 3 May 2006. (Thanks to George Moss, Vaughn College, Flushing, NY, for providing the authors with a copy of this document.)

12. Bill Carter and Felicity Barringer, "Patriotic Time, Dissent Muted," *The New York Times* 28 Sept. 2001: A1.

13. Walker, *Hate Speech*, 2.

14. Christopher N. Osher, "Churchill Part of Bigger Fight." *denverpost.com*. 30 May 2007. 11 June 2007 <http:www .denverpost.com/ci_6015760?source=rss>.

15. Edwin R. Bayley, *Joe McCarthy and the Press* (Madison: Wisconsin U P, 1981) 29.

16. Chidsey Dickson, "Re: question." Online posting. 27 October 2005. WPA Listserv. 27 October 2005 <http://lists.asu.edu/ cgi-bin/wa?A2=ind0510&L=WPA-L&P=R117883&I=-3>.

17. "Spurlock Sorry for Speech," *Austin American-Statesman* 29 March 2006: A2.

18. Kathy Fitzpatrick, "U.S. Public Diplomacy," *Vital Speeches of the Day* (15 April 2004): 412–17.

19. Peg Tyre, "Improving on History," *Newsweek* 2 July 2001: 34.

20. The History Channel, "Mohandas Gandhi, Indian Independence Leader, Speaks to Press Upon Arrival in London." *Great Speeches* 2004. 7 June 2004 <www.historychannel.com/ speeches/archive/speech_107.html>.

21. *Publication Manual of the American Psychological Association*, 4th ed. (Washington, DC: American Psychological Association, 1994) 294.

22. *The Fundamental Values of Academic Integrity* (Duke University: Center for Academic Integrity, October 1999) 1–2.

23. Todd Holm, "Public Speaking Students' Perceptions of Cheating," *Communication Research Reports* (Winter 2002): 70.

24. CNN, "Analysts: Biden's Performance Strongest." CNN.com. 4 June 2007. 10 June 2007 <http:www.cnn.com/2007/POLITICS/ 06/04/debate.analysis/index.html?section=cnn_latest>.

25. Harold Barrett, *Rhetoric and Civility: Human Development, Narcissism, and the Good Audience* (Albany: SUNY, 1991) 154.

26. Kenneth L. Woodward, "Heard Any Good Sermons Lately?" *Newsweek* 4 Mar. 1996: 51.

27. Patricia Sullivan, "Signification and African-American Rhetoric: A Case Study of Jesse Jackson's 'Common Ground and Common Sense' Speech," *Communication Quarterly* 41.1 (1993): 11.

28. Richard M. Weaver, "A Responsible Rhetoric," speech delivered at Purdue University, 29 Mar. 1955, ed. Thomas Clark and Richard Johannesen for *The Intercollegiate Review* (Winter 1976–77): 82.

29. Waldo W. Braden, *Abraham Lincoln, Public Speaker* (Baton Rouge: Louisiana State U P, 1988) 90.

30. Gail Shister, "CBS Evening Blues." *philly.com*. 22 April 2007. 11 June 2007 <http://www.philly.com/inquirer/entertainment/ 20070422_Gail_Shister_CBS_evening-blues.html>.

CHAPTER 4

1. Study conducted by Paul Cameron, as cited in Ronald B. Adler and Neil Town, *Looking Out/Looking In: Interpersonal Communications* (New York: Holt, Rinehart and Winston, 1981) 218.

2. L. Boyd, syndicated column, *Austin American-Statesman* 7 Dec. 1995: E7.

3. John T. Masterson, Steven A. Beebe, and Norman H. Watson, *Invitation to Effective Speech Communication* (Glenview, IL: Scott, Foresman, 1989) 4.

4. Frank E. X. Dance, *Speaking Your Mind: Private Thinking and Public Speaking* (Dubuque, IA: Kendall/Hunt Publishing Company, 1994).

5. Ralph G. Nichols and Leonard A. Stevens, "Six Bad Listening Habits," in *Are You Listening?* (New York: McGraw-Hill, 1957).

6. M. Fitch-Hauser, D. A. Barker, and A. Hughes, "Receiver Apprehension and Listening Comprehension: A Linear or Curvilinear Relationship?" *Southern Communication Journal* (1988): 62–71.

7. Joseph L. Chesebro, "Effects of Teacher Clarity and Nonverbal Immediacy on Student Learning, Receiver Apprehension, and Affect," *Communication Education* 52 (Apr. 2003): 135–47.

8. Fitch-Hauser, Barker, and Hughes, "Receiver Apprehension and Listening Comprehension."
9. Albert Mehrabian, *Nonverbal Communication* (Hawthorne, NY: Aldine, 1972).
10. Paul Ekman and Wallace Friesen, "Head and Body Cues in the Judgement of Emotion: A Reformulation," *Perceptual and Motor Skills* 25 (1967): 711–24.
11. Paul Rankin, "Listening Ability: Its Importance, Measurement and Development," *Chicago Schools Journal* 12 (Jan. 1930): 177–79.
12. Nichols and Stevens, "Six Bad Listening Habits."
13. Kitty W. Watson, Larry L. Barker, and James B. Weaver, *The Listener Style Inventory* (New Orleans: LA SPECTRA, 1995).
14. S. L. Sargent and James B. Weaver, "Correlates Between Communication Apprehension and Listening Style Preferences," *Communication Research Reports* 14 (1997): 74–78.
15. M. D. Kirtley and J. M. Honeycutt, "Listening Styles and Their Correspondence with Second Guessing," *Communication Research Reports* 13 (1996): 174–82.
16. California Curriculum Project, "Cesar Chavez Biography." Hispanic Biographies, 1994. 8 June 2004 <http://www.sfsu.edu/~cecipp/cesar_chavez/cesarbio5-12.htm>.
17. John N. Gardner and A. Jerome Jewler, *Your College Experiences: Strategies for Success*, 2nd ed. (Belmont, CA: Wadsworth, 1995) 104.
18. Mike Allen, Sandra Berkowitz, Steve Hunt, and Allan Louden, "A Meta-Analysis of the Impact of Forensics and Communication Education on Critical Thinking," *Communication Education* 48 (Jan. 1999): 18–30.
19. For a comprehensive list of definitions of rhetoric, see Patricia Bizzell and Bruce Herzberg (Eds.), *The Rhetorical Tradition: Readings from Classical Times to the Present* (Boston: Bedford, 1990).
20. Aristotle, *On Rhetoric*. Translated by George A. Kennedy (New York: Oxford University Press, 1991) 14.
21. Isocrates, *Isocrates*, Vol. II. Translated by George Norlin (Cambridge, MA: Harvard University Press, 1929). Also see "Isocrates," in Bizzell and Herzberg, *The Rhetorical Tradition*.
22. Kenneth Burke, *A Rhetoric of Motives* (Berkeley: University of California Press, 1950). Also see Barry Brummett, *Reading Rhetorical Theory* (Fort Worth, TX: Harcourt College Publishers, 2000) 741.
23. Cited by Marie Hochmuth, ed., A *History and Criticism of American Public Address*, Vol. 3 (New York: Longmans, Green, 1955) 4; and by James R. Andrews, *The Practice of Rhetorical Criticism* (New York: Macmillan, 1983) 3–4.
24. Andrews, *The Practice of Rhetorical Criticism*.
25. Masterson, Beebe, and Watson, *Invitation to Effective Speech Communication*.
26. Robert Rowland, *Analyzing Rhetoric: A Handbook for the Informed Citizen in a New Millennium* (Dubuque, IA: Kendall/Hunt Publishing Company, 2002).
27. Rowland, *Analyzing Rhetoric*, 17–28.

CHAPTER 5

1. "The Nobel Prize in Literature, 1953." 16 June 2000. 8 June 2004 <www.nobel.se/literature/laureates/1953/index.html>.
2. Robert H. Farrell, ed. *Off the Record: The Private Papers of Harry S Truman* (New York: Harper & Row, 1980) 310.
3. N. Howe and W. Strauss, *Millennials Rising: The Next Great Generation* (New York: Vintage Books. 2000). Also see Hank Karp, Connie Fuller, and Danilo Sirias, *Bridging the Boomer–Xer Gap: Creating Authentic Teams for High Performance at Work* (Palo Alto, California: Davies-Black, 2002).
4. For an excellent review of gender and persuasibility research see Daniel J. O'Keefe, *Persuasion: Theory and Research* (Newbury Park, CA: Sage, 1990) 176–77. Also see James B. Stiff, *Persuasive Communication* (New York: The Guilford Press, 1994) 133–36.
5. O'Keefe, *Persuasion*.
6. O'Keefe, *Persuasion*.
7. Gregory Herek, "Study Offers 'Snapshot' of Sacramento-Area Lesbian, Gay, and Bisexual Community." 23 July 2001 <http://psyweb.ucdavis.edu/rainbow/html/sacramento_study.html>. For an excellent literature review about sexual orientation and communication, see T. P. Mottet, "The Role of Sexual Orientation in Predicting Outcome Value and Anticipated Communication Behaviors," *Communication Quarterly* 48 (2000): 233–39.
8. The research summarized here is based on pioneering work by Geert Hofstede, *Culture's Consequences: International Differences in Work-Related Values* (Beverly Hills, CA: Sage, 1984). Also see Edward T. Hall, *Beyond Culture* (New York: Doubleday, 1976).
9. M. E. Ryan, "Another Way to Teach Migrant Students," *Los Angeles Times* March 31, 1991: B20, as cited by M. W. Lustig and J. Koester, *Intercultural Competence: Interpersonal Communication Across Cultures* (Boston: Allyn & Bacon, 2003) 11.
10. G. Chen and W. J. Starosta, "A Review of the Concept of Intercultural Sensitivity," *Human Communication* 1 (1997): 7.
11. Eric Schmitt, "Whites in Minority in Largest Cities, the Census Shows," *The New York Times* 30 Apr. 2001: A1.
12. Sam Roberts, "New Demographic Racial Gap Emerges," *The New York Times* 17 May 2007: A19.
13. David W. Kale, "Ethics in Intercultural Communication," *Intercultural Communication: A Reader*, 6th ed., eds. Larry A. Samovar and Richard E. Porter (Belmont, CA: Wadsworth, 1991) 423; also see discussion in Lustig and Koester, *Intercultural Competence*.
14. Donald E. Brown, "Human Universals and Their Implications," in *Being Humans: Anthropological Universality and Particularity in Transdisciplinary Perspectives*, ed. N. Roughley (New York: Walter de Gruyter, 2000). For an applied discussion of these universals, see Steven Pinker, *The Blank Slate: The Modern Denial of Human Nature* (London: Penguin Books, 2002).
15. Larry A. Samovar and Richard E. Porter, *Communication Between Cultures* (Stamford, CT: Wadsworth and Thomson Learning, 2006) 29.
16. Henry Sweets, "Mark Twain in India," *The Fence Painter: Bulletin of the Mark Twain Boyhood Home Associates* 26 (Winter 1996): 1.
17. Ashley Tinnell, "Recipe for Disaster," prepared for Individual Events/Persuasive Speaking Competition, The University of Texas, Spring 2007.
18. For an excellent discussion of how to adapt to specific audience situations, see Jo Sprague and Douglas Stuart, *The Speaker's Handbook* (Belmont, CA: Wadsworth and Thompson, 2005) 345.
19. For example, see Leonard Spinrad and Thelma Spinrad, *Speaker's Lifetime Library* (West Nyack, New York: Parker Publishing Company, 1979).

20. Devorah Lieberman, *Public Speaking in the Multicultural Environment* (Boston: Allyn and Bacon, 2000). Also see Edward T. Hall, *The Silent Language* (Greenwich, CT: Fawcett, 1959); and Edward T. Hall, *The Hidden Dimension* (Garden City, NY: Doubleday, 1966).

CHAPTER 6

1. Andrew Mytelka, "This Just In: Tim Russert's Crimson Face." *The Chronicle of Higher Education.* 10 June 2005. 12 June 2007 <http://chronicle.com/prm/daily/2005/06/2005061006n.htm>.

2. Roger Fringer, "Choosing a Speech Topic," in Tasha Van Horn, Lori Charron, and Michael Charron, *Allyn & Bacon Video II User's Guide*, 2002.

3. Bruce Gronbeck, from his presidential address, delivered at the annual conference of the Speech Communication Association, ts., November 1994.

4. Henry H. Sweets III, "Mark Twain's Lecturing Career Continuation—Part II," *The Fence Painter* (Winter 2000–2001).

5. Alex F. Osborn, *Applied Imagination* (New York: Scribner's, 1962).

6. Monique Russo, "The 'Starving Disease' or Anorexia Nervosa," student speech, University of Miami, 1984.

7. Brian Sosnowchik, "The Cries of American Ailments," *Winning Orations 2000* (Mankato, MN: Interstate Oratorical Association, 2000) 114.

8. Judith Humphrey, "Taking the Stage: How Women Can Achieve a Leadership Presence," *Vital Speeches of the Day* 1 May 2001: 437.

9. Charles W. Chesnutt, *Frederick Douglass*. Electronic edition published by Academic Affairs Library, University of North Carolina at Chapel Hill. 2001. 8 June 2004 <docsouth.unc.edu/neh/chesnutt/chesnutt.html>.

10. Adapted from Erin Gallagher, "Upholstered Furniture Fires: Sitting in the Uneasy Chair," *Winning Orations 2000* (Mankato, MN: Interstate Oratorical Association, 2000) 99–101.

11. NASA, "Past Shuttle Missions." 2 February 2004. 14 June 2004 <www.spaceflight.nasa.gov/shuttle/archives/>.

12. Adapted from Nicole Tremel, "The New Wasteland: Computers," *Winning Orations 2000* (Mankato, MN: Interstate Oratorical Association, 2000) 37–40.

13. Erin Kane, "Alternative Defense," *Winning Orations 1995* (Mankato, MN: Interstate Oratorical Association, 1995) 82.

CHAPTER 7

1. Danny Sullivan, "Google 2.0: Google Universal Search." *Search Engine Land* 16 May 2007 <http://searchengineland.com/070516-143312.php>.

2. The actual number of sites yielded by each step of this sample search will vary, depending on the date on which the search is conducted.

3. Elizabeth Kirk, "Practical Steps in Evaluating Internet Resources." 7 May 2001. 22 May 2001 <http://milton.mse.jhu.edu:8001/research/education/practical.html>.

4. James A. W. Heffernan et al., *Writing: A College Handbook*, 5th ed. (New York: Norton, 2001) 53–54.

5. Paul Gorski, "A Multicultural Model for Evaluating Educational Web Sites." Dec. 1999. 22 May 2001 <http://curry.edschool.virginia.edu/go/multicultural/net/comps/model.html>.

6. Matthew Mirapaul, "Making Federal Web Sites Friendly to Disabled Users," *The New York Times* 11 June 2001: B2.

7. Gould Library, Carleton College, "Using Wikipedia." 26 January 2007. 13 June 2007 <http://apps.carleton.edu/campus/library/for_faculty/faculty_find/wikipedia/>.

8. U.S. Government Printing Office, "National Bibliography Program." GPO Access. 8 May 2007. 13 June 2007 <http://www.access.gpo.gov/su_docs/fdlp/cip/index.html>.

9. Eleanor Roosevelt National Historic Site, Hyde Park, New York, "Eleanor Roosevelt and Civil Rights." 9 June 2004 <www.nps.gov/elro/teach-er-vk/lesson-plans/notes-er-and-civil-rights.htm>.

10. Ralph R. Behnke and Chris R. Sawyer, "Public-Speaking Procrastination as a Correlate of Public-Speaking Communication Apprehension and Self-Perceived Public-Speaking Competence," *Communication Research Reports* 16 (1999): 40–47; J. C. Pearson, J. T. Child, and D. H. Kahl, Jr., "Preparation Meeting Opportunity: How Do College Students Prepare for Public Speeches?" *Communication Quarterly* 54.3 (August 2006): 351–66.

CHAPTER 8

1. Bettijane Levine, "Fighting the Giant," *Los Angeles Times* 10 Aug. 1994: E-1.

2. Suzanne Alexander, Testimonial. TobaccoFree.org. April 2003. 19 June 2007 <www.tobaccofree.org/clients.htm#colleges>.

3. Michael Cunningham, quoted in Dinitia Smith, "In the Age of the Overamplified, a Resurgence for the Humble Lecture," *The New York Times* 17 March 2006: B1–B5.

4. Sandra Zimmer, quoted in Vickie K. Sullivan, "Public Speaking: The Secret Weapon in Career Development," *USA Today* 24–25 May 2005: 133. WilsonWeb. Texas State U-San Marcos Lib., San Marcos, TX. 19 June 2007 <hwwilsonweb.com>.

5. John McCain, Address on immigration, June 4, 2007. 19 June 2007 <www.johnmccain.com/Informing/News/Speeches>.

6. Andrew B. Wilson, "How to Craft a Winning Speech," *Vital Speeches of the Day* (1 September 2005): 685–89. ProQuest. Texas State U-San Marcos Lib., San Marcos, TX. 19 June 2007 <proquest.umi.com>.

7. Mike Eskew, "We All Need Access to the Global Community: Encouraging Diversity," *Vital Speeches of the Day* (1 September 2006): 623–26. ProQuest. Texas State U-San Marcos Lib., San Marcos, TX. 19 June 2007 <proquest.umi.com>.

8. Professor Frazer White, University of Miami.

9. Wilson, "How to Craft a Winning Speech."

10. George W. Bush, "Speech at the 60th Anniversary D-Day ceremony, 6 June 2004." *The Tocqueville Connection* 6 June 2004. 6 June 2004 <www.ttc.org/200406061205.i56c5hp2962.1.htm>.

11. Edwin Pittock, "America's Crisis in Aging: Is Living Longer More Than We Bargained For?" *Vital Speeches of the Day* (1 February 2004): 249–53. ProQuest. Texas State U-San Marcos Lib., San Marcos, TX. 20 June 2007 <proquest.umi.com>.

12. Shana Dale, "Mars Is Our Ultimate Goal," *Vital Speeches of the Day* (1 January 2007): 12–16. ProQuest. Texas State U-San Marcos Lib., San Marcos, TX. 19 June 2007 <proquest.umi.com>.

13. Shannon Burger, "Will It Hurt?" *Winning Orations 1994* (Mankato, MN: Interstate Oratorical Association, 1994) 89.

14. Sidney Taurel, "An Update on the Biomedical Revolution," *Vital Speeches of the Day* (1 February 2007): 69–72. ProQuest.

Texas State U-San Marcos Lib., San Marcos, TX. 19 June 2007 <proquest.umi.com>.

15. Barbara Bush, "Choices and Change," *Contemporary American Public Discourse*, ed. Halford Ross Ryan (Prospect Heights, IL: Waveland Press, 1992) 382.

16. Stephen Dannhauser, "Enlarged European Union," *Vital Speeches of the Day* (15 April 2004): 409–12. ProQuest. Texas State U-San Marcos Lib., San Marcos, TX. 20 June 2007 <proquest.umi.com>.

17. Elizabeth Cady Stanton, "Address to the First Women's Rights Convention (1848)," *A Treasury of the World's Great Speeches*, ed. Houston Peterson (New York: Simon & Schuster, 1965) 388–92.

18. Ralph Shrader, "Solid Connections in a Liquid World," *Vital Speeches of the Day* (1 May 2007): 201–03. ProQuest. Texas State U-San Marcos Lib., San Marcos, TX. 19 June 2007 <proquest.umi.com>.

19. Cal Darden, "The Sustainable Promise of Globalization," *Vital Speeches of the Day* (15 April 2004): 405–09. ProQuest. Texas State U-San Marcos Lib., San Marcos, TX. 19 June 2007 <proquest.umi.com>.

20. Ajay Krishnan, "Is Mr. Goodwrench Really Mr. Rip Off?" *Winning Orations 1998* (Mankato, MN: Interstate Oratorical Association, 1998) 120.

21. "Sorry, You've Got the Wrong Number," *The New York Times* 26 May 2001: A17.

22. "The Texas Miracle," *CBSnews.com*. 7 January 2004. 7 January 2004 <www.cbsnews.com/stories/2004/01/06/60II/main591676.shtml>.

23. Hillary Clinton, "Civil Rights: On the 42nd Anniversary of Bloody Sunday in Selma," March 4, 2007. 19 June 2007 <www.hillaryclinton.com>.

24. Data available from U.S. Census Bureau, "Current Population Survey: 2006 Annual Social and Economic Supplement." 20 June 2007 <http://pubdb3.census.gov/macro/032006/health/h01_001.htm>.

25. J. Edward Hill, "Pandemic Flu," *Vital Speeches of the Day* (1 October 2006): 687–89. ProQuest. Texas State U-San Marcos Lib., San Marcos, TX. 19 June 2007 <proquest.umi.com>.

26. Arnold Schwarzenegger, State of the State address, January 9, 2007, *Vital Speeches of the Day* (1 February 2007): 66–69. ProQuest. Texas State U-San Marcos Lib., San Marcos, TX. 19 June 2007 <proquest.umi.com>.

27. Dena Craig, "Clearing the Air about Cigars," *Winning Orations 1998* (Mankato, MN: Interstate Oratorical Association, 1998) 13.

28. Walter Harrison, "Race, College Admissions," *Vital Speeches of the Day* (1 April 2004): 374–76. ProQuest. Texas State U-San Marcos Lib., San Marcos, TX. 19 June 2007 <proquest.umi.com>.

29. Julia Debes, "Keeping Our Promise," *Winning Orations 2007* (Mankato, MN: Interstate Oratorical Association, 2007) 28.

30. Hope Stallings, "Safe Seats," *Winning Orations 2007* (Mankato, MN: Interstate Oratorical Association, 2007) 14.

31. Robert Rager, "Amusement Park Safety," *Winning Orations 1985* (Mankato, MN: Interstate Oratorical Association, 1985) 38.

32. Ali Heidarpour, "Binge Drinking on College Campuses," *Winning Orations 2003* (Mankato, MN: Interstate Oratorical Association, 2003) 59.

33. Rager, "Amusement Park Safety."

34. Rager, "Amusement Park Safety."

35. Joseph K. Ott, "America's Internal Cold War," *Winning Orations 1985* (Mankato, MN: Interstate Oratorical Association, 1985) 45.

36. Ott, "America's Internal Cold War."

37. Nichole Olson, "Flying the Safer Skies," *Winning Orations 2000* (Mankato, MN: Interstate Oratorical Association, 2000) 122.

CHAPTER 9

1. Joel Ayres, "The Impact of Time, Complexity, and Organization on Self-Reports of Speech Anxiety," *Communication Research Reports* 5.1 (June 1988): 58–63. Ebsco, Texas State U-San Marcos Lib., San Marcos, TX. 21 June 2007 <web.ebscohost.com>.

2. Information in this example comes from National Institutes of Health, "Stem Cells: A Primer," May 2000. 19 July 2001 <http://www.nih.gov/news/stemcell/primer.htm>.

3. Adapted from John Kuehn, untitled speech, *Winning Orations 1994* (Mankato, MN: Interstate Oratorical Association, 1994) 83–85.

4. Dennis Lloyd, "Instant Expert: A Brief History of iPod," *iLounge* (26 June 2004). 20 June 2007 <www.ilounge.com/index.php/articles/comments/instant-expert-a-brief-history-of-ipod/>; "Apple iPod, History of an Icon," *ipod games* 20 June 2007 <www.ipodgames.com/other/ipod.php>.

5. Fact Sheet. *YouTube.com*. 2007. 20 June 2007 <www.youtube.com/t/fact_sheet>.

6. Philip Shenon, "A Showcase for Indian Artifacts," *The New York Times* 29 August 2004: TR 3.

7. Adapted from Vonda Ramey, "Can You Read This?" *Winning Orations 1985* (Mankato, MN: Interstate Oratorical Association, 1985) 32–35.

8. Adapted from Laurel Johnson, "Where There's a Will There's a Way," *Winning Orations 1986* (Mankato, MN: Interstate Oratorical Association, 1986) 59–62.

9. Adapted from Amy Stewart, untitled speech, *Winning Orations 1994* (Mankato, MN: Interstate Oratorical Association, 1994) 47–49.

10. The following information is adapted from Devorah A. Lieberman, *Public Speaking in the Multicultural Environment* (Englewood Cliffs, NJ: Prentice Hall, 1994).

11. Desmond Tutu, "Nobel Lecture, December 11, 1984." 6 April 2004. 10 June 2004 <http://www.nobel.se/peace/laureates/1984/tutu-lecture.html>.

12. "Passenger: Washington Teen Was Texting at Time of Accident in Idaho," *The Olympian* 19 June 2007. 21 June 2007 <www.theolympian.com>.

13. Risa Lavizzo-Mourey, "Childhood Obesity," *Vital Speeches of the Day* 15 April 2004.

14. John Seffrin, "The Worst Pandemic in the History of the World," *Vital Speeches of the Day* 1 April 2004.

15. Kristin Rose Cipolla, "Unnecessary Prescription Drugs: A Real Medical Emergency," *Winning Orations 2003* (Mankato, MN: Interstate Oratorical Association, 2003) 10.

16. Nichole Olson, "Flying the Safer Skies," *Winning Orations 2000* (Mankato, MN: Interstate Oratorical Association, 2000) 122.

17. Adapted from Mike Stobbe, "Beachgoers Often Overlook Sand as Danger," *Corpus Christi Caller-Times* 21 June 2007: 12A.

18. Melody Hopkins, "Collegiate Athletes: A Contradiction in Terms," *Winning Orations 1986* (Mankato, MN: Interstate Oratorical Association, 1986) 111.

19. Linh Thu Q. Do, "Children of the Diet Culture," *Winning Orations 1999* (Mankato, MN: Interstate Oratorical Association, 1999) 122.

20. Arwen Williams, "Organic Farming: Why Our Pesticide Paranoia Is Starving the World," *Winning Orations 2000* (Mankato, MN: Interstate Oratorical Association, 2000) 145.

21. Molly A. Lovell, "Hotel Security: The Hidden Crisis," *Winning Orations 1994* (Mankato, MN: Interstate Oratorical Association, 1994) 18.

22. Neela Latey, "U.S. Customs Procedures: Danger to Americans' Health and Society," *Winning Orations 1986* (Mankato, MN: Interstate Oratorical Association, 1986) 22.

23. Susan Stevens, "Teacher Shortage," *Winning Orations 1986* (Mankato, MN: Interstate Oratorical Association, 1986) 27.

24. Heather Green, "Radon in Our Homes," *Winning Orations 1986* (Mankato, MN: Interstate Oratorical Association, 1986) 5.

25. Ben Crosby, "The New College Disease," *Winning Orations 2000* (Mankato, MN: Interstate Oratorical Association, 2000) 133.

26. Lori Van Overbeke, "NutraSweet," *Winning Orations 1986* (Mankato, MN: Interstate Oratorical Association, 1986) 58.

27. Adapted from Heath Honaker, "A New Brand of Homeless," *Winning Orations 1986* (Mankato, MN: Interstate Oratorical Association, 1986) 108–11.

CHAPTER 10

1. K. Phillip Taylor, "Speech Teachers' Pet Peeves: Student Behaviors That Public Instructors Find Annoying, Irritating, and Unwanted in Student Speeches," *The Florida Communication Journal* 33.2 (2005): 56.

2. Chandra Palubiak, "To Tattoo or Not to Tattoo," *Winning Orations 2002* (Mankato, MN: Interstate Oratorical Association, 2002) 11.

3. Sheena Holliday, "Uninvited Visitor," *Winning Orations 2003* (Mankato, MN: Interstate Oratorical Association, 2003) 84.

4. Edwin Pittock, "America's Crisis in Aging," *Vital Speeches of the Day* 1 February 2004.

5. Darnetta Clinkscale, "The Other Crisis in Our Schools," *Vital Speeches of the Day* 1 April 2004.

6. Jennifer Sweeney, "Racial Profiling," *Winning Orations 2000* (Mankato, MN: Interstate Oratorical Association, 2000) 1.

7. Barack Obama, "Cutting Costs and Covering America: A 21st Century Health Care System," speech delivered at the University of Iowa, May 29, 2007. 22 June 2007 <www.barackobama .com/2007/05/29/cutting_costs_and_covering_ame.php>.

8. Kristin Rose Cipolla, "Unnecessary Prescription Drugs: A Real Medical Emergency," *Winning Orations 2003* (Mankato, MN: Interstate Oratorical Association, 2003) 9.

9. Terrika Scott, "Curing Crisis with Community," *Winning Orations 1995* (Mankato, MN: Interstate Oratorical Association, 1995) 11.

10. Theresa Clinkenbeard, "The Loss of Childhood," *Winning Orations 1984* (Mankato, MN: Interstate Oratorical Association, 1984) 4.

11. Thad Noyes, "Dishonest Death Care," *Winning Orations 1999* (Mankato, MN: Interstate Oratorical Association, 1999) 73.

12. Marvin Olasky, "Responding to Disaster," *Vital Speeches of the Day* (1 November 2006): 744. ProQuest. Texas State U-San Marcos Lib., San Marcos, TX. 22 June 2007 <proquest.umi .com>.

13. Joe Griffith, *Speaker's Library of Business Stories, Anecdotes, and Humor* (Englewood Cliffs, NJ: Prentice Hall, 1990) 335.

14. Douglas MacArthur, "Farewell to the Cadets," address delivered at West Point, 12 May 1962. Reprinted in Richard L. Johannesen, R. R. Allen, and Wil A. Linkugel, eds., *Contemporary American Speeches*, 7th ed. (Dubuque, IA: Kendall/Hunt, 1992) 393.

15. "Insert Funny Story Here," *Austin American-Statesman* 7 Apr. 2001: A14.

16. Lisa M. Kralik, "Geographical Illiteracy," *Winning Orations 1987* (Mankato, MN: Interstate Oratorical Association, 1987) 76.

17. Richard Propes, "Alone in the Dark," *Winning Orations 1985* (Mankato, MN: Interstate Oratorical Association, 1985) 22.

18. Beth Moberg, "Licensed to Kill," *Winning Orations 1985* (Mankato, MN: Interstate Oratorical Association, 1985) 89.

19. Dick Cheney, "Remembering 9/11," *Vital Speeches of the Day* (1 October 2006): 661–62. ProQuest. Texas State U-San Marcos Lib., San Marcos, TX. 22 June 2007 <proquest.umi.com>.

20. Adam Winegarden, "The After-Dinner Speech," in Tasha Van Horn, Lori Charron, and Michael Charron, eds., *Allyn & Bacon Video II User's Guide*, 2002.

21. Larry Cox, "A Vision of a World Made New," *Vital Speeches of the Day* 1 February 2004.

22. Glenn Schaffer, "Philanthropy," *Vital Speeches of the Day* 15 February 2004.

23. Laura Bush, remarks at Harlem Renaissance event. *The White House Web site.* 13 March 2002. 11 March 2004 <www .whitehouse.gov/news/releases/2002/03/20020313-11.html>.

24. Student speech, University of Miami, 1981.

25. MacArthur, "Farewell to the Cadets" 396.

26. Lou Gehrig, "Farewell Speech," *Lou Gehrig: The Official Web Site* 23 June 2007 <www.lougehrig.com/about/speech.htm>.

27. Noelle Stephens, "The WWW.CON of Higher Education," *Winning Orations 1999* (Mankato, MN: Interstate Oratorical Association, 1999) 12.

28. John Ryan, "Emissions Tampering: Get the Lead Out," *Winning Orations 1985* (Mankato, MN: Interstate Oratorical Association, 1985) 63.

29. Melanie Loehwing, untitled speech, *Winning Orations 2003* (Mankato, MN: Interstate Oratorical Association, 2003) 23–24.

30. Richard Kelley, "Ready, Aim, Thrive: Strategies for 2007," *Vital Speeches of the Day* (1 December 2006): 763–67. ProQuest. Texas State U-San Marcos Lib., San Marcos, TX. 22 June 2007 <proquest.umi.com>.

31. N. Joyce Payne, "A Family Member Needs Long-Term Care," *Vital Speeches of the Day* (1 Oct 2006): 692–94. ProQuest. Texas State U-San Marcos Lib., San Marcos, TX. 23 June 2007 <proquest.umi.com>.

32. Sonja Ralston, "Medical Reprocessing," *Winning Orations 2000* (Mankato, MN: Interstate Oratorical Association, 2000) 131.

33. Robert Browning, "Rabbi Ben Ezra," *Dramatis Personae* (1864), quoted by John Mietus, Jr., "The Best Is Yet to Be," *Winning Orations 1987* (Mankato, MN: Interstate Oratorical Association, 1987) 54.

34. Mietus, "The Best Is Yet to Be" 57.

35. Benjamin P. Berlinger, "Health and the Hubris of Human Nature: The Tragic Myth of Antibiotics," *Winning Orations 1987* (Mankato, MN: Interstate Oratorical Association, 1987) 35.

36. James W. Robinson, "Create a Fireworks Finale," *Executive Speeches* (April 1989): 41–44. ProQuest. Texas States U-San Marcos Lib., San Marcos, TX. 26 June 2007 <proquest.umi .com>.

37. Martin Luther King Jr., "I Have a Dream," in Richard L. Johannesen, R. R. Allen, and Wil A. Linkugel, eds., *Contemporary American Speeches*, 7th ed. (Dubuque, IA: Kendall/Hunt, 1992) 369.

38. Jake B. Schrum, investiture speech as President of Southwestern University, Georgetown, Texas, 4 April 2001.

CHAPTER 11

1. Judy C. Pearson, Jeffrey T. Child, and David H. Kahl, Jr., "Preparation Meeting Opportunity: How Do College Students Prepare for Public Speeches?" *Communication Quarterly* 54.3 (Aug. 2006): 351–66.

2. John O'Brien, quoted in Brent Filson, *Executive Speeches* (New York: Wiley, 1994) 144–45.

3. Charles Parnell, "Speechwriting: The Profession and the Practice," *Vital Speeches of the Day* 15 January 1990: 56.

4. The sample outlines in this chapter are adapted from Ashley Tinnell, "Recipe for Disaster," prepared for Individual Events/Persuasive Speaking Competition, The University of Texas, Spring 2007.

5. Our discussion of how to edit speeches relies heavily on information in Brent Filson, *Executive Speeches: Tips on How to Write and Deliver Speeches from 51 CEOs* (New York: John Wiley & Sons, 1994) 150–53.

6. William Saletan. "Kerryism of the Day," *Slate* 18 May 2004. 19 May 2004 <slate.msn.com/toolbar.asapx?action=print&id= 2100720>.

7. Clive Thompson, "PowerPoint Makes You Dumb," *The New York Times Magazine* 14 December 2003: 88.

CHAPTER 12

1. Advertisements and headlines compiled by Jay Leno, *Headlines* (New York: Wing Books, 1992).

2. Ken Herman, "Bush Tosses Out a Heck of a Lot of Hecks," *Austin American-Statesman* 15 Jan. 2006: A1.

3. George W. Bush, Presidential victory speech, delivered at Austin, Texas. 13 Dec. 2000. 14 Dec. 2000 <http://dailynews. yahoo.com/h/ap/20001214/el/recount_bush_text_1.html>.

4. Al Gore, "The Common Good of All Americans" (presidential election concession speech), *Vital Speeches of the Day* 1 January 2001: 163.

5. Nemanja Savic, "Hope—in the Voices of Africa," speech delivered at Wake Forest University May 14, 2006. *Window on Wake Forest*. 15 May 2006. 25 June 2007 <www.wfu.edu/wowf/ 2006/2006.05.15/orations.html>.

6. Max Woodfin, "Three Among Many Lives Jordan Touched," *Austin American-Statesman* 20 Jan. 1996: A13.

7. John Lister, quoted in "At the End of the Day, It Annoys." The Associated Press. 24 March 2004. 24 March 2004 <www. cbsnews.com/stories/2004/03/24/world/printable608391. shtml>.

8. Paul Roberts, "How to Say Nothing in Five Hundred Words," in William H. Roberts and Gregoire Turgeson, eds., *About Language* (Boston: Houghton Mifflin, 1986) 28.

9. George Orwell, "Politics and the English Language," in William H. Roberts and Gregoire Turgeson, eds., *About Language* (Boston: Houghton Mifflin, 1986) 282.

10. Erma Bombeck, "Missing Grammar Genes Is, Like, the Problem," *Austin American-Statesman* 3 Mar. 1992.

11. Robin Tolmach Lakoff, "From Ancient Greece to Iraq, the Power of Words in Wartime." *The New York Times Online*. 18 May 2004. 21 May 2004 <www.nytimes.com/2004/05/18/ science/18LANG.html>.

12. Martin Carcasson, "Herbert Hoover and the Presidential Campaign of 1932: The Failure of Apologia," *Presidential Studies Quarterly* (Spring 1998).

13. William Safire, "Words at War," *The New York Times Magazine* 30 Sept. 2001: Section 6.

14. John S. Seiter, Jarrod Larsen, and Jacey Skinner, " 'Handicapped' or 'Handicapable?': The Effects of Language About Persons with Disabilities on Perceptions of Source Credibility and Persuasiveness," *Communication Reports* 11:1 (1998): 21–31.

15. Edward Rothstein, "Is a Word's Definition in the Mind of the User?" *The New York Times* 25 Nov. 2000: A21.

16. Peggy Noonan, *What I Saw at the Revolution* (New York: Random House, 1990) 71.

17. Michael M. Klepper, *I'd Rather Die Than Give a Speech* (New York: Carol Publishing Group, 1994) 45.

18. We acknowledge the following source for several examples used in our discussion of language style: William Jordan, "Rhetorical Style," *Oral Communication Handbook* (Warrensburg, MO: Central Missouri State U, 1971–1972) 32–34.

19. Nelson Mandela, speech delivered at Live 8 concert, July 2, 2005. *ONE: The Campaign to Make Poverty History*. 25 June 2007 <www.one.org>.

20. Barack Obama, speech delivered on March 4, 2007, in Selma, AL, in commemoration of the Selma Voting Rights March. *Barack Obama.com* 4 March 2007. 26 June 2007 <www.barackobama .com/2007/03/04/selma_voting_rights_march_comm.php>.

21. Samuel Hazo, "Poetry and Public Speech," *Vital Speeches of the Day* (1 April 2007): 685–89. ProQuest. Texas State U-San Marcos Lib., San Marcos, TX. 25 June 2007 <proquest.umi.com>.

22. Michiko Kakutani, "Struggling to Find Words for a Horror Beyond Words," *The New York Times* 13 Sept. 2001: E1.

23. Franklin Roosevelt, Inaugural address of 1933 (Washington, DC: National Archives and Records Administration, 1988) 22.

24. George F. Will, " 'Let Us . . .'? No, Give It a Rest," *Newsweek* 22 Jan. 2001: 64.

25. John F. Kennedy, Inaugural address (20 Jan. 1961), in Bower Aly and Lucille F. Aly, eds., *Speeches in English* (New York: Random House, 1968) 272.

26. George W. Bush, "Bush's Speech at the Houston Memorial Service for Shuttle's Crew," *The New York Times* 5 Feb. 2003: A17.

27. Gordon Brown, leadership acceptance speech, June 24, 2007. 25 June 2007 <uk.news.yahoo.com>.

28. Rudy deLeon, "The Tuskegee Airmen," *Vital Speeches of the Day* 1 November 2000: 43.

29. Nikki Giovanni, convocation address at Virginia Tech, April 17, 2007. 25 June 2007 <www.vt.edu/remember/archive/ giovanni_transcript.php>.

30. Ralph Waldo Emerson, "The American Scholar," speech delivered 31 Aug. 1837, in Glenn R. Capp., ed., *Famous Speeches in American History* (Indianapolis: Bobbs-Merrill, 1963) 84.

31. George W. Bush, State of the Union Address. *The White House*

Web site. 20 January 2004. 21 January 2004 <www.whitehouse.gov/news/releases/2004/01/print/20040120-7.html>.

32. Roosevelt, Inaugural address of 1933.

33. Kennedy, Inaugural address 275.

34. William Faulkner, speech in acceptance of the Nobel prize for literature, delivered 10 Dec. 1950, in Houston Peterson, ed., *A Treasury of the World's Great Speeches* (New York: Simon & Schuster, 1965) 814–15.

35. Roosevelt, Inaugural address of 1933.

36. Franklin D. Roosevelt, first fireside chat on 12 Mar. 1933, in Peterson, *Treasury* 751–54.

37. Winston Churchill, "finest hour" address, delivered 18 June 1940, in Peterson, *Treasury* 754–60.

38. Winston Churchill, address to the Congress of the United States, delivered on 26 Dec. 1941, in Bower Aly and Lucille F. Aly, eds., *Speeches in English* (New York: Random House, 1968) 233.

39. Dick Cheney, acceptance speech for the Republican vice-presidential nomination, delivered 2 Aug. 2000, *The New York Times* 3 Aug. 2000: A24.

40. "JFK's Trumpet Call." 6 June 2004 <www.pbs.org/greatspeeches/timeline/j_kennedy_b1.html>.

41. Adapted from Jordan, *Oral Communication Handbook* 34.

42. "Dear Abby," *San Marcos Daily Record* 5 Jan. 1993: 7.

43. Activity developed by Loren Reid, *Speaking Well* (New York: McGraw-Hill, 1982) 96.

44. "Reference to Rape Edited from Graduation Speech," *The Kansas City Star* 5 June 1995: B3.

CHAPTER 13

1. For an excellent discussion of the importance of speaker delivery as discussed by both classical and contemporary rhetoricians, see J. Fredal, "The Language of Delivery and the Presentation of Character: Rhetorical Action in Demosthenes 'Against Meidias,'" *Rhetoric Review* 20 (2001): 251–67.

2. James W. Gibson, John A. Kline, and Charles R. Gruner, "A Re-examination of the First Course in Speech at U.S. Colleges and Universities," *Speech Teacher* 23 (Sept. 1974): 206–14.

3. Ray Birdwhistle, *Kinesics and Context* (Philadelphia: U of Pennsylvania, 1970).

4. Judee K. Burgoon and Beth A. Le Poire, "Nonverbal Cues and Interpersonal Judgments: Participant and Observer Perceptions of Intimacy, Dominance, Composure, and Formality," *Communication Monographs* 66 (1999): 105–24; Beth A. Le Poire and Stephen M. Yoshimura, "The Effects of Expectancies and Actual Communication on Nonverbal Adaptation and Communication Outcomes: A Test of Interaction Adaptation Theory," *Communication Monographs* 66 (1999): 1–30.

5. Albert Mehrabian, *Nonverbal Communication* (Hawthorne, NY: Aldine, 1972).

6. D. Lapakko, "Three Cheers for Language: A Closer Examination of a Widely Cited Study of Nonverbal Communication," *Communication Education* 46 (1997): 63–67.

7. Elaine Hatfield, J. T. Cacioppo, and R. L. Rapson, *Emotional Contagion* (New York: Cambridge University Press, 1994); also see John T. Cacioppo, Gary G. Berntson, Jeff T. Larsen, Kirsten M. Poehlmann, and Tiffany A. Ito, "The Psychophysiology of Emotion," in Michael Lewis and Jeannette M. Haviland-Jones, eds., *Handbook of Emotions*, 2nd ed. (New York: Guilford Press, 2004), 173–91.

8. Steven A. Beebe and Thompson Biggers, "The Effect of Speaker Delivery upon Listener Emotional Response," paper presented at the International Communication Association meeting, May 1989.

9. Paul Ekman, Wallace V. Friesen, and K. R. Schere, "Body Movement and Voice Pitch in Deception Interaction," *Semiotica* 16 (1976): 23–27; Mark Knapp, R. P. Hart, and H. S. Dennis, "An Exploration of Deception as a Communication Construct," *Human Communication Research* 1 (1974): 15–29.

10. Roger Ailes, *You Are the Message* (New York: Doubleday, 1989) 37–38.

11. David Gates, "Prince of the Podium," *Newsweek* June 14, 1996: 82.

12. *Austin-American Statesman*, 15 Jan. 2007: A11

13. Cicero, *De Oratore*. Vol. 4. Translated by E. W. Sutton (Cambridge: Harvard University Press, 1988).

14. Steven A. Beebe, "Eye Contact: A Nonverbal Determinant of Speaker Credibility," *Speech Teacher* 23 (Jan. 1974): 21–25; Steven A. Beebe, "Effects of Eye Contact, Posture and Vocal Inflection upon Credibility and Comprehension," *Australian Scan Journal of Nonverbal Communication* 7–8 (1979–1980): 57–70; Martin Cobin, "Response to Eye Contact," *Quarterly Journal of Speech* 48 (1963): 415–19.

15. Beebe, "Eye Contact" 21–25.

16. Khera Communications, Inc., "Business Tips for India." *More Business*. 2001. 8 June 2004 <www.morebusiness.com/running_your_business/management/d930585271.brc?highlightstring=Business+Tips+for+India>.

17. Brent Filson, *Executive Speeches: Tips on How to Write and Deliver Speeches from 51 CEOs* (New York: John Wiley & Sons, Inc., 1994).

18. Albert Mehrabian, *Silent Messages* (Belmont, CA: Wadsworth, 1971).

19. For a comprehensive review of immediacy in an instructional context, see Virginia P. Richmond, Derek R. Lange, and James C. McCroskey, "Teacher Immediacy and the Teacher-Student Relationship," in Timothy P. Mottet, Virginia P. Richmond, and James C. McCroskey, *Handbook of Instructional Communication: Rhetorical and Relational Perspectives.* (Boston: Allyn and Bacon, 2006) 167–93.

20. See Virginia P. Richmond, Joan Gorham, and James C. McCroskey, "The Relationship Between Selected Immediacy Behaviors and Cognitive Learning," in M. McLaughlin, ed., *Communication Yearbook* 10 (Beverly Hills, CA: Sage, 1987), 574–90; Joan Gorham, "The Relationship Between Verbal Teacher Immediacy Behaviors and Student Learning," *Communication Education* 37 (1988): 40–53; Diane M. Christophel, "The Relationship Among Teacher Immediacy Behaviors, Student Motivation, and Learning," *Communication Education* 39 (1990): 323–40; James C. McCroskey, Virginia P. Richmond, Aino Sallinen, Joan M. Fayer, and Robert A. Barraclough, "A Cross-Cultural and Multi-Behavioral Analysis of the Relationship Between Nonverbal Immediacy and Teacher Evaluation," *Communication Education* 44 (1995): 281–90; Timothy P. Mottet and Steven A. Beebe, "Relationships Between Teacher Nonverbal Immediacy, Student Emotional Response, and Perceived Student Learning," *Communication Research Reports* (Jan. 2002).

21. Michael J. Beatty, "Some Effects of Posture on Speaker Credibility," library paper, University of Central Missouri, 1973.

22. Albert Mehrabian and M. Williams, "Nonverbal Concomitants

of Perceived and Intended Persuasiveness," *Journal of Personality and Social Psychology* 13 (1969): 37–58.

23. Paul Ekman, Wallace V. Friesen, and S. S. Tomkins, "Facial Affect Scoring Technique: A First Validity Study," *Semiotica* 3 (1971).

24. Paul Ekman and Wallace Friesen, *Unmasking the Face* (Englewood Cliffs, NJ: Prentice Hall, Inc. 1975); D. Keltner and P. Ekman, "Facial Expression of Emotion," in M. Lewis and J. M. Haviland-Jones, eds., *Handbook of Emotions* (New York: Gilford, 2000) 236–49; D. Keltner, P. Ekman, G. S. Gonzaga, and J. Beer, "Facial Expression of Emotion," in R. J. Davidson, K. R. Scherer, and H. H. Goldsmith eds., *Handbook of Affective Sciences* (New York: Oxford University Press, 2003) 415–32.

25. Adapted from Lester Schilling, *Voice and Diction for the Speech Arts* (San Marcos: Southwest Texas State U, 1979).

26. Mary M. Gill, "Accent and Stereotypes: Their Effect on Perceptions of Teachers and Lecture Comprehension," *Journal of Applied Communication* 22 (1994): 348–61.

27. Kenneth K. Sereno and G. J. Hawkins, "The Effects of Variations in Speakers' Nonfluency upon Audience Ratings of Attitude toward the Speech Topic and Speakers' Credibility," *Speech Monographs* 34 (1967): 58–74; Gerald R. Miller and M. A. Hewgill, "The Effect of Variations in Nonfluency on Audience Ratings of Source Credibility," *Quarterly Journal of Speech* 50 (1964): 36–44; Mehrabian and Williams, "Nonverbal Concomitants of Perceived and Intended Persuasiveness."

28. These suggestions were made by Jo Sprague and Douglas Stuart, *The Speaker's Handbook* (Fort Worth, TX: Harcourt Brace Jovanovich, 1992) 331, and were based on research by Patricia A. Porter, Margaret Grant, and Mary Draper, *Communicating Effectively in English: Oral Communication for Non-Native Speakers* (Belmont, CA: Wadsworth, 1985).

29. James W. Neuliep, *Intercultural Communication: A Contextual Approach* (Boston: Houghton Mifflin, 2000) 247.

30. Stephen Lucas, *The Art of Public Speaking* (New York: Random House, 1986) 231.

31. Research cited by Leo Fletcher, *How to Design & Deliver Speeches* (New York: Addison Wesley Longman, 2001) 73.

32. "Comment," *The New Yorker* 1 Mar. 1993.

33. John S. Seiter and Andrea Sandry, "Pierced for Success? The Effects of Ear and Nose Piercing on Perceptions of Job Candidates' Credibility, Attractiveness, and Hirability," *Communication Research Reports* 20(4) (2003): 287–98.

34. For an excellent review of the effects of immediacy in the classroom, see Mehrabian, *Silent Messages*; also see James C. McCroskey, Aino Sallinen, Joan M. Fayer, Virginia P. Richmond, and Robert A. Barraclough, "Nonverbal Immediacy and Cognitive Learning: A Cross-Cultural Investigation," *Communication Education* 45 (1996): 200–11.

35. Larry A. Samovar and Richard E. Porter, *Communication Between Cultures* (Stamford, CT: Thomson Learning, 2001) 166.

36. William B. Gudykunst, *Bridging Differences: Effective Intergroup Communication* (Thousand Oaks, CA: Sage, 1998) 12.

37. Kent E. Menzel and Lori J. Carrell, "The Relationship Between Preparation and Performance in Public Speaking," *Communication Education* 43 (1994): 17–26; Tony E. Smith and Ann Bainbridge Frymier, "Get 'Real': Does Practicing Speeches Before an Audience Improve Performance?" *Communication Quarterly* 54(1) (Feb. 2006): 111–25; Judy C. Pearson, Jeffrey T. Child, and David H. Kahl, Jr., "Preparation Meeting Opportunity: How Do College Students Prepare for Pubic Speeches?" *Communication Quarterly* 54(3) (Aug. 2006): 351–66.

38. Patricia Wilson, "Dean Jokes About 'Screeching' in Iowa." *Reuters News Service.* 22 Jan. 2004. 22 Jan. 2004 <news.yahoo.com/news?tmpl=story2+cid=564&u=/nm/20040 122/ts_nm/campaign_dean_dc_4&printer=1>.

39. Filson, *Executive Speeches*.

40. Filson, *Executive Speeches*.

CHAPTER 14

1. Emil Bohn and David Jabusch, "The Effect of Four Methods of Instruction on the Use of Visual Aids in Speeches," *The Western Journal of Speech Communication* 46 (Summer 1982): 253–65.

2. J. S. Wilentz. *The Senses of Man* (New York: Crowell, 1968).

3. Michael E. Patterson, Donald F. Dansereau, and Dianna Newbern, "Effects of Communication Aids and Strategies on Cooperative Teaching," *Journal of Educational Psychology* 84 (1992): 453–61.

4. Louise Rehling, "Teaching in a High-Tech Conference Room: Academic Adaptations and Workplace Simulations," *Journal of Business and Technical Communication*, 19(1) (Jan. 2005): 98–113.

5. PBS, "Ethos." 6 June 2004 <www.pbs.org/greatspeeches/ timeline/r_Reagan_b2.html>.

6. Richard E. Mayer and Valerie K. Sims, "For Whom Is a Picture Worth a Thousand Words? Extensions of a Dual-Coding Theory of Multimedia Learning," *Journal of Educational Psychology* 86 (1994): 389–401.

7. Brent Filson, *Executive Speeches: Tips on How to Write and Deliver Speeches from 51 CEOs* (New York: John Wiley & Sons, Inc., 1994) 212.

8. Dale Cyphert, "The Problem of PowerPoint: Visual Aid or Visual Rhetoric?" *Business Communication Quarterly* (March 2004): 80–84.

9. Andrew Wilson, "In Defense of Rhetoric," *The Toastmaster* 70.2 (Feb. 2004): 8–11.

10. Roxanne Parrott, Kami Sikl, Kelly Dorgan, Celeste Condit, and Tina Harris, "Risk Comprehension and Judgments of Statistical Evidentiary Appeals: When a Picture Is Not Worth a Thousand Words," *Human Communication Research* 31 (July 2005): 423–52.

11. Rebecca B. Worley and Marilyn A. Dyrud, "Presentations and the PowerPoint Problem," *Business Communication Quarterly*, 67 (Mar. 2004): 78–80.

12. We acknowledge Dan Cavanaugh's excellent supplement *Preparing Visual Aids for Presentation* (Boston: Allyn and Bacon/Longman, 2001) as a source for many of our tips and suggestions.

13. Brent Filson, *Executive Speeches*.

14. For a good discussion of how to develop and use PowerPoint visuals, see Jerry Weissman, *Presenting to Win: The Art of Telling Your Story* (Upper Saddle River, NJ: Financial Times/Prentice Hall, 2003).

15. We thank Stan Crowley, a student at Texas State U, for his permission to use his speech outline.

CHAPTER 15

1. John R. Johnson and Nancy Szczupakiewicz, "The Public Speaking Course: Is It Preparing Students with Work-Related

Public Speaking Skills?" *Communication Education* 36 (Apr. 1987): 131–37.

2. Pamela J. Hinds, "The Curse of Expertise: The Effects of Expertise and Debiasing Methods on Predicting Novice Performance," *Journal of Experimental Psychology: Applied* 5 (1999): 205–21. Research summarized in Chip Heath and Dan Heath, *Made to Stick: Why Some Ideas Survive and Others Die* (New York: Random House, 2007) 19–21.

3. Joseph L. Chesebro, "Effects of Teacher Clarity and Nonverbal Immediacy on Student Learning, Receiver Apprehension, and Affect," *Communication Education* 52 (Apr. 2003): 135–47.

4. Malcolm Knowles, *The Adult Learner: A Neglected Species*, 3rd ed. (Houston: Gulf Publishing Company, 1990).

5. Katherine E. Rowan, "A New Pedagogy for Explanatory Public Speaking: Why Arrangement Should Not Substitute for Invention," *Communication Education* 44 (1995): 236–50.

6. Philip Yancy, *Prayer: Does It Make Any Difference?* (Grand Rapids, MI: Zondervan, 2006) 20.

7. Michael A. Boerger and Tracy B. Henley, "The Use of Analogy in Giving Instructions," *Psychological Record* 49 (1999): 193–209.

8. Heath and Heath, *Made to Stick* 63–64.

9. Marcie Groover, "Learning to Communicate: The Importance of Speech Education in Public Schools," *Winning Orations 1984* (Mankato, MN: Interstate Oratorical Association, 1984) 7.

10. As cited by Eleanor Doan, *The New Speaker's Sourcebook* (Grand Rapids, MI: Zondervan, 1968).

11. C. S. Lewis, "On Stories," *Essays Presented to Charles Williams*, C. S. Lewis, ed. (Oxford: Oxford University Press, 1947); also see Walter R. Fisher, *Communication as Narration: Toward a Philosophy of Reason, Value, and Action* (Columbia: University of South Carolina Press, 1987).

12. Heath and Heath, *Made to Stick*.

13. See Bruce W. A. Whittlesea and Lisa D. Williams, "The Discrepancy-Attribution Hypothesis II: Expectation, Uncertainty, Surprise, and Feelings of Familiarity," *Journal of Experimental Psychology: Learning, Memory, and Cognition* 2 (2001): 14–33; also see Suzanne Hidi, "Interest and Its Contribution as a Mental Resource for Learning," *Review of Educational Research* 60 (1990): 549–71; Mark Sadoski, Ernest T. Goetz, and Maximo Rodriguez, "Engaging Texts: Effects of Concreteness of Comprehensibility, Interest, and Recall in Four Text Types," *Journal of Educational Psychology* 92 (2000): 85–95.

14. Heath and Heath, *Made to Stick* 51–52.

15. George Miller, "The Magical Number Seven, Plus or Minus Two," *Psychological Review* 63 (1956): 81–97.

16. D. K. Cruickshank and J. J. Kennedy, "Teacher Clarity," *Teaching & Teacher Education* 2 (1986): 43–67.

17. Roger Fringer, "Choosing a Speech Topic," in Tasha Van Horn, Lori Charron, and Michael Charron, *Allyn & Bacon Video II User's Suide,* 2002.

CHAPTER 16

1. Alvin Toffler, *Future Shock* (New York: Bantam Books, 1970) 3.

2. Martin Fishbein and I. Ajzen, *Belief, Attitude, Intention, and Behavior: An Introduction to Theory and Research* (Reading, MA: Addison-Wesley, 1975).

3. For a discussion of motivation in social settings, see Douglas T. Kenrick, Steven L. Neuberg, and Robert B. Cialdini, *Social Psychology: Unraveling the Mystery* (Boston, MA: Allyn & Bacon, 2002).

4. For a discussion of the elaboration likelihood model, see R. Petty and D. Wegener, "The Elaboration Likelihood Model: Current Status and Controversies," in S. Chaiken and Y. Trope, eds., *Dual Process Theories in Social Psychology* (New York: Guilford, 1999) 41–72; also see R. Petty and J. T. Cacioppo, *Communication and Persuasion: Central and Peripheral Routes to Attitude Change* (New York: Springer-Verlag, 1986).

5. Leon Festinger, *A Theory of Cognitive Dissonance* (Evanston, IL: Row, Peterson, 1957).

6. For additional discussion, see Wayne C. Minnick, *The Art of Persuasion* (Boston: Houghton Mifflin, 1967).

7. Abraham H. Maslow, "A Theory of Human Motivation," in *Motivation and Personality* (New York: Harper & Row, 1954) chap. 5.

8. John Ryan, "Emissions Tampering: Get the Lead Out," *Winning Orations 1985* (Mankato, MN: Interstate Oratorical Association, 1985) 50.

9. For a discussion of fear appeal research, see Irving L. Janis and Seymour Feshback, "Effects of Fear Arousing Communications," *Journal of Abnormal and Social Psychology* 48 (Jan. 1953): 78–92; Frederick A. Powell and Gerald R. Miller, "Social Approval and Disapproval Cues in Anxiety-Arousing Situations," *Speech Monographs* 34 (June 1967): 152–59; Kenneth L. Higbee, "Fifteen Years of Fear Arousal: Research on Threat Appeals, 1953–68," *Psychological Bulletin* 72 (Dec. 1969): 426–44.

10. Paul A. Mongeau, "Another Look at Fear-Arousing Persuasive Appeals," in Mike Allen and Raymond W. Preiss, eds., *Persuasion: Advances Through Meta-Analysis* (Cresskill, NJ: Hampton Press, 1998) 65.

11. Diane Boerner, "Elizabeth Cady Stanton of Johnstown, New York," speech presented at the dedication of the plaque to Elizabeth Cady Stanton in the City Park of Johnstown, New York, on October 21, 1989. 11 June 2004 <www.rootsweb.com/~nyfulton/ecadystan.html>.

12. K. Witte, "Putting the Fear Back into Fear Appeals: The Extended Parallel Process Model," *Communication Monographs* 59 (1992): 329–47.

13. See discussions in Myron W. Lustig and Jolene Koester, *Intercultural Competence: Interpersonal Communication Across Cultures* (Boston, MA: Allyn & Bacon, 2006) 347; Larry A. Samovar and Richard E. Porter, *Communication Between Cultures* (Stamford, CT: Wadsworth and Thomson Learning, 2004) 29.

14. C. W. Sherif, M. Sherif, and R. E. Nebergall, *Attitudes and Attitude Change: The Social Judgment-Involvement Approach* (Philadelphia: Saunders, 1965).

CHAPTER 17

1. Donald C. Bryant, "Rhetoric: Its Functions and Its Scope," *Quarterly Journal of Speech* 39 (Dec. 1953): 26.

2. William L. Benoit, "Topic of Presidential Campaign Discourse and Election Outcome," *Western Journal of Communication* 67 (Winter 2003): 97–112.

3. J. C. Reinard, "The Empirical Study of the Persuasive Effects of Evidence: The Status after Fifty Years of Research," *Human Communication Research* 15 (1988): 3–59.

4. James C. McCroskey and R. S. Rehrley, "The Effects of Disorganization and Nonfluency on Attitude Change and Source Credibility," *Speech Monographs* 36 (1969): 13–21.

5. For an excellent meta-analysis of forty-nine studies examining the influence of delivery variables and persuasion, see Chris Segrin, "The Effects of Nonverbal Behavior on Outcomes of Compliance Gaining Attempts," *Communication Studies* 44 (1993): 169–87.

6. Judee K. Burgoon, T. Birk, and M. Pfau, "Nonverbal Behaviors, Persuasion, and Credibility," *Human Communication Research* 17 (1990): 140–69.

7. Segrin, "The Effects of Nonverbal Behavior on Outcomes of Compliance Gaining Attempts."

8. Robin L. Nabi, Emily Moyer-Guse, & Sahara Byrne, "All Joking Aside: A Serious Investigation into the Persuasive Effect of Funny Social Issue Messages," *Communication Monographs* 74 (Mar. 2007): 29–54.

9. For an excellent discussion of the influence of culture on public speaking, see Devorah A. Lieberman, *Public Speaking in the Multicultural Environment* (Englewood Cliffs, NJ: Prentice Hall, 1994) 10.

10. Devorah Lieberman and G. Fisher, "International Negotiation," in Larry A. Samovar and Richard E. Porter, eds., *Intercultural Communication: A Reader* (Belmont, CA: Wadsworth, 1991) 193–200.

11. Lieberman and Fisher, "International Negotiation."

12. Myron W. Lustig and Jolene Koester, *Intercultural Competence: Interpersonal Communication Across Cultures* (Boston: Allyn & Bacon, 2006).

13. K. Ah Yun and L. L. Massi, "The Differential Impact of Race on the Effectiveness of Narrative versus Statistical Appeals to Persuade Individuals to Sign an Organ Donor Card," paper presented at the meeting of the Western States Communication Association, Sacramento, CA; cited by Lisa L. Massi-Lindsey and Kimo Ah Yun, "Examining the Persuasive Effect of Statistical Messages: A Test of Mediating Relationships," *Communication Studies* 54 (Fall 2003): 306–21.

14. Lustig and Koester, *Intercultural Competence* 241.

15. Jeffrey E. Jamison, "Alkali Batteries: Powering Electronics and Polluting the Environment," *Winning Orations 1991* (Mankato, MN: Interstate Oratorical Association, 1991) 43.

16. H. B. Brosius and A. Bathelt, "The Utility of Exemplars in Persuasive Communications," *Communication Research* 21 (1994): 48–78.

17. Massi-Lindsey and Ah Yun, "Examining the Persuasive Effect of Statistical Messages"; D. C. Kazoleas, "A Comparison of the Persuasive Effectiveness of Qualitative versus Quantitative Evidence: A Test of Explanatory Hypotheses," *Communication Quarterly* 41 (1993): 40–50; also see M. Allen and R. W. Preiss, "Comparing the Persuasiveness of Narrative and Statistical Evidence Using Meta-Analysis," *Communication Research Reports* (1997): 125–31.

18. Franklin J. Boster, Kenzie A. Cameron, Shelly Campo, Wen-Ying Liu, Janet K. Lillie, Esther M. Baker, and Kimo Ah Yun, "The Persuasive Effects of Statistical Evidence in the Presence of Exemplars," *Communication Studies* 51 (Fall 2000): 296–306; also see E. J. Baesler and Judee K. Burgoon, "The Temporal Effects of Story and Statistical Evidence on Belief Change." *Communication Research* 21 (1994): 582–602.

19. Reinard, "The Empirical Study of the Persuasive Effects of Evidence 37–38.

20. William L. Benoit and I. A. Kennedy, "On Reluctant Testimony," *Communication Quarterly* 47 (1999): 376–87. Although this study raises questions about whether reluctant testimony is persuasive, reluctant testimony as well as neutral testimony is better than testimony perceived to be obviously biased.

21. E. J. Baesler, "Persuasive Effects of Story and Statistical Evidence," *Argumentation and Advocacy* 33 (1997): 170–75.

22. Roger Ailes, *You Are the Message* (New York: Doubleday, 1989).

23. Albert Mehrabian and J. A. Russell, *An Approach to Environmental Psychology* (Cambridge: MIT Press, 1974); T. Biggers and B. Pryor, "Attitude Change as a Function of Emotion-Eliciting Qualities," *Personality and Social Psychology Bulletin* 8 (1982): 94–99; Steven A. Beebe and T. Biggers, "Emotion-Eliciting Qualities of Speech Delivery and Their Effect on Credibility and Comprehension," paper presented at the annual meeting of the International Communication Association, New Orleans, May 1989.

24. Donald Dean Morely and Kim B. Walker, "The Role of Importance, Novelty, and Plausibility in Producing Belief Change," *Communication Monographs* 54 (1987): 436–42; also see Chip Heath and Dan Heath, *Made to Stick: Why Some Ideas Survive and Others Die* (New York: Random House, 2007), 63–97.

25. "Franklin Delano Roosevelt: The Great Depression." 6 June 2004 <www.pbs.org/greatspeeches/timeline/f_roosevelt_b.html>.

26. John W. Bowers and Michael M. Osborn, "Attitudinal Effects of Selected Types of Concluding Metaphors in Persuasive Speeches," *Speech Monographs* 33 (1966): 147–55; James C. McCroskey and W. H. Combs, "The Effects of the Use of Analogy on Attitude Change and Source Credibility," *Journal of Communication* 19 (1969): 333–39; N. L. Reinsch, "An Investigation of the Effects of the Metaphor and Simile in Persuasive Discourse," *Speech Monographs* 38 (1971): 142–45.

27. Pradeep Sopory and James Price Dillard, "The Persuasive Effects of Metaphor: A Meta-Analysis," *Human Communication Research* 28 (July 2002): 382–419.

28. See Irving Janis and S. Feshback, "Effects of Fear-Arousing Communication," *Journal of Abnormal and Social Psychology* 48 (1953): 78–92; Fredric A. Powell, "The Effects of Anxiety-Arousing Message When Related to Personal, Familial, and Impersonal Referents," *Speech Monographs* 32 (1965): 102–6.

29. Donald C. Bryant, "Rhetoric: Its Functions and Its Scope," *Quarterly Journal of Speech* 39 (Dec. 1953): 26.

30. William L. Benoit, "Forewarning and Persuasion," in Mike Allen and Raymond W. Preiss, eds., *Persuasion: Advances Through Meta-Analysis* (Cresskill, NJ: Hampton Press, 1998) 139–54.

31. Karmen Kirtley, "Grave Matter: The High Cost of Living," *Winning Orations* 1997 (Mankato, MN: Interstate Oratorial Association, 1997).

32. Benoit, "Forewarning and Persuasion."

33. Mike Allen, "Comparing the Persuasive Effectiveness of One- and Two-Sided Messages," in Mike Allen and Raymond W. Preiss, eds., *Persuasion: Advances Through Meta-Analysis* (Cresskill, NJ: Hampton Press, 1998) 87–98.

34. Katherine E. Rowan, "A New Pedagogy for Explanatory Public Speaking: Why Arrangement Should Not Substitute for Invention," *Communication Education* 44 (1995): 236–50.

35. Carl I. Hovland, Arthur A. Lunsdaine, and Fred D. Sheffield, "The Effects of Presenting 'One Side' versus 'Both Sides' in

Changing Opinions on a Controversial Subject," in *Experiments on Mass Communication* (Princeton: Princeton U, 1949). Also see Arthur Lunsdaine and Irving Janis, "Resistance to 'Counter-Propaganda' Produced by a One-Sided versus a Two-Sided 'Propaganda' Presentation," *Public Opinion Quarterly* (1953): 311–18.

36. N. Miller and Donald T. Campbell, "Recency and Primacy in Persuasion as a Function of the Timing of Speeches and Measurements," *Journal of Abnormal and Social Psychology* 59 (1959): 1–9; Adrian Furnham, "The Robustness of the Recency Effect: Studies Using Legal Evidence," *The Journal of General Psychology* 113 (1986): 351–57; R. Rosnow, "Whatever Happened to the 'Law of Primacy'?" *Journal of Communication* 16 (1966): 10–31.

37. Robert B. Ricco, "Analyzing the Roles of Challenge and Defense in Argumentation," *Argumentation and Advocacy* 39 (Summer 2002): 1–22.

38. Douglas Ehninger, Bruce E. Gronbeck, Ray E. McKerrow, and Alan H. Monroe, *Principles and Types of Speech Communication* (Glenview, IL: Scott, Foresman 1986) 15.

39. James Chang, "Sustainable Giving," *Winning Orations 2003* (Mankato, MN: Interstate Oratorical Association, 2003) 3.

40. Chang, "Sustainable Giving" 3.

41. Chang, "Sustainable Giving" 3.

42. Chang, "Sustainable Giving" 3.

43. Martin Luther King Jr., "I Have a Dream" (28 Aug. 1963), in Houston Peterson, ed., *A Treasury of the World's Great Speeches* (New York: Simon & Schuster, 1965) 835–39.

44. Chang, "Sustainable Giving" 3.

CHAPTER 18

1. Andrew Zajac, "Giuliani Speaking Fees Draw Scrutiny," *Chicago Tribune* 7 February 2007. 27 June 2007 <www.chicagotribune.com/news>.

2. "Al Gore Coming to Saskatchewan," *CBC News* 5 April 2007. 27 June 2007 <www.cbc.ca/canada/saskatchewan/story>.

3. "Culp and Cosby on The Tonight Show," *I Spy: the Definitive Site* 3 February 2007. 27 June 2007 <www.network54.com>.

4. "Nicole Kidman Gets Paid," *ABC7.com* 27 June 2007. 27 June 2007 <abclocal.go.com>.

5. "Clinton's Speaking Fees Nearly Total $40 Million," *The Huffington Post* 23 February 2007. 27 June 2007 <www.huffingtonpost.com>.

6. Leslie Wayne, "In World Where Talk Doesn't Come Cheap, Former Officials Are Finding Lucrative Careers," *The New York Times* 10 March 2004: A14.

7. Roger E. Flax, "A Manner of Speaking," *Ambassador* (May–June 1991): 37.

8. Peter D. MacIntyre and K. A. Thivierge, "The Effects of Audience Pleasantness, Audience Familiarity, and Speaking Contexts on Public-Speaking Anxiety and Willingness to Speak," *Communication Quarterly* 43 (1995): 456–66.

9. *Slainte! Toasts, Blessings, and Sayings.* March 1998. 28 June 1998 <http://zinnia.umfacad.maine.edu/~donaghue/toasts.html>.

10. Sarah Husberg, "A Wedding Toast," in Tasha Van Horn, Lori Charron, and Michael Charron, eds., *Allyn & Bacon Video II User's Guide*, 2002.

11. Jeff Brooks, *Wedding Toasts.* March 1998. 29 June 1998 <http://zinnia.umfacad.maine.edu/~donaghue/toasts07.html>.

12. Everett M. Dirksen, "Nominating Speech for Barry Goldwater" (15 July 1964), in James R. Andrews and David Zarefsky, eds., *Contemporary American Voices* (New York: Simon & Schuster, 1965) 815.

13. Erma Bombeck, "Abbreviated Thank-you's Allow Us More Time to Study Danson's Head," *Austin American-Statesman* 22 June 1993: F3.

14. Cindy Pearlman, "Oscar Speeches: Statues in Their Hands, Feet in Their Mouths," *Austin American-Statesman* 24 Mar. 1997: E8.

15. Elie Wiesel, "Acceptance of the 1986 Nobel Peace Prize," *The New York Times* 11 Dec. 1986: A8.

16. William Faulkner, acceptance of the Nobel prize for literature (10 Dec. 1950), in Houston Peterson, ed., *A Treasury of the World's Great Speeches* (New York: Simon & Schuster, 1965) 815.

17. Barbara Jordan, "Change: From What to What?" *Vital Speeches of the Day* 15 Aug. 1992: 651.

18. David Abel, "Commencement Addresses Leave Audiences Lost," *The Boston Globe* 5 June 2000: B4.

19. Patrick Rose, 2006 Texas State University–San Marcos commencement address, *Currents* 26 January 2007. 27 January 2007 <Talbot.mrp.txstate.edu/currents>.

20. Antonio O. Garza, Jr., University of Texas commencement address, excerpted in Sam Dillon, "Graduates Get an Earful, from Left, Right and Center," *The New York Times* 11 June 2006: A28.

21. Abel, "Commencement Addresses Leave Audiences Lost," B4.

22. Bill Clinton, speech at Pointe du Hoc, France (June 1994), as quoted in David Shribman, "President, a Child of World War II, Thanks a Generation," *Boston Globe* 7 June 1994: 1.

23. Cyrus Copeland, "Death, Be Not Ponderous," *The New York Times* 31 Oct. 2004.

24. John T. Masterson, Jr., eulogy for Betty Stalvey, 26 March 2005.

25. Henry Kissinger, eulogy for Gerald Ford, quoted in " 'America Needed Him,' Bush Says in Ford Eulogy," *CBC News* 2 Jan. 2007. 27 June 2007 <www.cbc.ca/world/story/2007/01/02/ford-funeral.html>.

26. Dave Barry, "Speak! Speak!" *Austin American-Statesman* 2 June 1991: C4.

27. Sarah Booth Conroy, "State Dinners Offer Speech as First Course," *Austin American-Statesman* 10 Nov. 1989.

28. Debi Martin, "Laugh Lines," *Austin American-Statesman* 20 May 1988: D1.

29. Jon Macks, *How to Be Funny* (New York: Simon & Schuster, 2003).

30. Matt Hughes, "Tricks of the Speechwriter's Trade," *Management Review* 79 (November 1990): 56–58. ABI/INFORM Global, Texas State U–San Marcos Lib., San Marcos, TX. 27 June 2007 <ABI/INFORMGlobal>.

31. Michael Koresky, "Prognosis: Dire, Michael Moore's 'Sicko,' " *indieWIRE* 22 June 2007. 27 June 2007 <www.indiewire.com/movies>.

32. John C. Meyer, "Humor as a Double-Edged Sword: Four Functions of Humor in Communication," *Communication Theory* 10 (Aug. 2000): 311.

33. Joe Queenan, "How to Tell a Joke," *Reader's Digest* Sept. 2003: 73.

34. Quoted in Maurice Chittenden, "Brown Seeks Comic Prop," *The Sunday Times* (7 July 2005): 1:4.

35. Alison White, "Writing a Humorous Speech." 3 June 2004 <www.bizinternet.com.au/StGeorges/humour.html>.

36. Mark Twain, "The Alphabet and Simplified Spelling," address at the dedication of the New York Engineers' Club, 9 Dec. 1907. *Mark Twain's Speeches; with an Introduction by William Dean Howells*, Electronic Text Center, University of Virginia Library. 4 June 2004 <etext.lib.Virginia.edu>.

37. Bill Gates, 2007 Harvard commencement address, *Harvard University Gazette Online* 7 June 2007. 27 June 2007 <www.news.harvard.edu/gazette>.

38. Chris O'Keefe, untitled speech, in John K. Boaz and James Brey, eds., *1987 Championship Debates and Speeches* (Speech Communication Association and American Forensic Association, 1987) 99.

39. Owen H. Lynch, "Humorous Communication: Finding a Place for Humor in Communication Research," *Communication Theory* 12.4 (Nov. 2002): 423–45.

40. "Mirren 'Too Busy' to Meet Queen," *BBC News* 10 May 2007. 13 June 2007 <newsvote.bbc.co.uk>.

41. Susan Wallace, "Seriously, How Do I Write a Humorous Speech?" as reported by Mike Dicerbo, Leadership in Action 1 Nov. 2000. 2 June 2004 <www.angelfire.com/az2/D3tmLeadership3/NewsNovSusanWallace.html>.

42. Michael Eck, "Barry Keeps the Crowd Laughing." *Times Union* (Albany, New York), 5 May 2004. 11 June 2004 <www.albany.edu/writers-inst/tu_barry_dave_page-hall.html>.

APPENDIX A

1. Group communication principles presented in this chapter are adapted from Steven A. Beebe and John T. Masterson, *Communicating in Small Groups. Principles and Practices*, 9th ed. (Boston: Allyn and Bacon, 2009).

2. For a discussion of the advantages and disadvantages of working in small groups, see Norman R. F. Maier, "Assets and Liabilities in Group Problem Solving: The Need for an Integrative Function," *Psychological Review* 74 (1967): 239–49; Michael Argyle, *Cooperation: The Basis of Sociability* (London: Routledge, 1991).

3. Maier, "Assets and Liabilities in Group Problem Solving;" Argyle, *Cooperation*.

4. Our definition of a team is based on a discussion in Beebe and Masterson, *Communicating in Small Groups*; and in Steven A. Beebe, Susan J. Beebe, and Diana K. Ivy, *Communication Principles for a Lifetime* (Boston: Allyn and Bacon, 2007) 240–41.

5. John Dewey, *How We Think* (Boston: Heath, 1910).

6. H. Barki, "Small Group Brainstorming and Idea Quality: Is Electronic Brainstorming the Most Effective Approach?" *Small Group Research* 32 (2001): 158–205; B. A. Nijstad, W. Stroebe, and H. F. M. Lodewijkx, "Cognitive Stimulation and Interference in Groups: Exposure Effects in an Idea Generation Task," *Journal of Experimental Social Psychology* 38 (2002): 535–44.

7. K. L. Dugosh, P. B. Paulus, E. J. Roand, and H. C. Yang, "Cognitive Stimulation in Brainstorming," *Journal of Personality and Social Psychology* 79 (2000): 722–35.

8. R. Y. Hirokawa and A. J. Salazar, "Task-Group Communication and Decision-Making Performance," in L. Frey, ed., *The Handbook of Group Communication Theory and Research* (Thousand Oaks, CA: Sage, 1999) 167–91; D. Gouran and R. Y. Hirokawa, "Functional Theory and Communication in Decision-Making and Problem-Solving Groups: An Expanded View," in R. Y. Hirokawa and M. S. Poole, eds., *Communication and Group Decision Making* (Thousand Oaks, CA: Sage, 1996) 55–80.

9. C. A. VanLear and E. A. Mabry, "Testing Contrasting Interaction Models for Discriminating Between Consensual and Dissentient Decision-Making Groups," *Small Group Research* 30 (1999): 29–58; also see T. J. Saine and D. G. Bock, "A Comparison of the Distributional and Sequential Structures of Interaction in High and Low Consensus Groups," *Central States Speech Journal* 24 (1973): 125–39.

10. Randy Y. Hirokawa and Roger Pace, "A Descriptive Investigation of the Possible Communication-Based Reasons for Effective and Ineffective Group Decision Making," *Communication Monographs* 50 (Dec. 1983): 363–79.

11. Randy Y. Hirokawa, "Group Communication and Problem-Solving Effectiveness: An Investigation of Group Phases," *Human Communication Research* 9 (Summer 1983): 291–305.

12. Dennis S. Gouran, "Variables Related to Consensus in Group Discussion of Question of Policy," *Speech Monographs* 36 (Aug. 1969): 385–91.

13. For a summary of research about conflict management in small groups, see S. M. Farmer and J. Roth, "Conflict-Handling Behavior in Work Groups: Effects of Group Structure, Decision Processes, and Time," *Small Group Research* 29 (1998): 669–713; also see Beebe and Masterson, *Communicating in Small Groups*.

14. Ralph White and Ronald Lippitt, "Leader Behavior and Member Reaction in Three 'Social Climates,' " in Darwin Cartwright and Alvin Zander, eds., *Group Dynamics*, 3rd ed. (New York: Harper & Row, 1968) 319.

15. Peter M. Senge, "Leading Learning Organizations," in Richard Beckhard et al., eds., *The Leader of the Future* (San Francisco: Jossey-Bass, 1996); Bernard M. Bass and M. J. Avolio, "Transformational Leadership and Organizational Culture," *International Journal of Public Administration* 17 (1994): 541–54; Lynn Little, "Transformational Leadership," *Academic Leadership* 15 (Nov. 1999): 4–5.

16. Francis J. Yammarino and Alan J. Dubinsky, "Transformational Leadership Theory: Using Levels of Analysis to Determine Boundary Conditions," *Personnel Psychology* 47 (1994): 787–809.

Index

ABC News, 345
ABI/Inform, 156
Abstraction, ladder of, 261
Academic Search Complete, 156
Academy, in Athens, 445
Acceptance
    latitude of, 370
    speeches of, 423–424
Accommodation, 50–51, 55–56
Action
    in motivated sequence, 406
    model of communication as, 7–8
Action-oriented listener, 71
Active listening, 72–74
Ad hominem fallacy, 392
Adaptation, audience. *See* Audience
    adaptation
Advanced Public Speaking Institute, 204
Adventures of Tom Sawyer, The (Twain),
    11
African American audiences, 55, 118
After-dinner speeches, 426–429
Age, of audience, 96–97
Ailes, Roger, 393
All in the Family, 428
Alliteration, 269
Allyn & Bacon Public Speaking Web site,
    204
Almanacs, 157
American Civil Liberties Union, 47, 56
*American Heritage Dictionary of the English
    Language, The*, 264, 268
American Psychological Association (APA),
    53, 162
American Rhetoric Web site, 82
Analogies, 181–182
    in informative speeches, 342–343
    in persuasive speeches, 384
Analysis
    audience. *See* Audience analysis
    personal, 28–29
    problem, 436–437
Anderson, Timothy, 233
Andragogy, 341–342
Anecdotes, 224

Animals, as presentation aids, 326
Anthropology, cultural, 105–106
Antiphon, 444
Antithesis, 268–269
Anxiety, 13–20, 23, 37, 265
APA, 53, 162
Appeal. *See also* Ethos; Logos; Pathos;
    Persuasion; Persuasive speeches
    to action, 388
    fear, 365–368, 373–374, 396
    inspirational, 234–235
    to misplaced authority, 392
Appearance, personal, 294–295, 299
Applause, 118
Apprehension, communication, 13–20, 23,
    37, 66–67, 265
Arab culture, 99. *See also* High-context
    cultures
Aristotle, 9, 12, 54, 77, 88, 97, 276, 358,
    359, 360, 380, 382, 393, 434, 446–447
Armstrong, Lance, 416
Arousal–nonarousal dimension, 394
Arrangement, Roman art of, 447
Articulation, 289–290
Atlases, 157
Attention, of listeners, 62–63, 405
Attitude, 106–109, 356–357, 373
Audience. *See also* Audience adaptation;
    Audience analysis
    appeals/challenges to, 234–235, 358–360,
        380, 382, 388, 393–398, 399, 446
    attention of, 62–63, 405
    central idea and, 137–138
    conclusion and, 231–235
    delivery and, 276–278, 295–296, 388
    demographics of, 91, 92, 96–100,
        102–106
    diversity of, 12–13, 27–28, 99–100,
        103–106, 295–296, 369, 387–388. *See
        also* Cultures
    editing for, 246
    as ethical listeners, 54–57
    ethical speech and, 49–54
    informative speeches and, 340–350
    introduction and, 220–224

motivated sequence and, 404–407
needs of, 363–364, 368
persuasive speeches and, 359, 360–369
rapport with, 37–38
role of, 6, 19–20
size of, 109–110
target, 104–105
topic and, 125–126
support from, 84. *See also* Nonverbal
    cues
understanding of, 63, 334–335, 340–344
Audience adaptation, 95–96, 103–106,
    112–117, 263–265, 398–401, 412–413
Audience analysis, 16, 27, 28, 91–94,
    96–112, 117–119, 120–121, 417
Audience-centered model of public speak-
    ing, 26, 27, 91, 125, 135, 149, 197, 297,
    299, 368, 417
Audiovisual aids, 321–323
Auditory channel, 8
Authoritarian leaders, 441
Authority, appeal to misplaced, 392
Autoformat feature, 242
Average style of communication apprehen-
    sion, 14, 15
Award presentations, 422

Bandwagon fallacy, 391
Bar graphs, 313, 314
Barker, Larry, 71
Barrett, Harold, 55
Barry, Dave, 414, 426, 429
Bartlett's Familiar Quotations, 33, 157
BBC, 228
Behavioral objective, 132–135
Behavioral responses, 118–119, 287,
    357–358
Beliefs, 106–107, 357, 373, 400
Benefit, 365
Berkeley Free Speech Movement, 48
Best, Joel, 184
Biased language, 264–265
Bibliography, 53–54
    preliminary, 162–164
Biden, Joseph, 52